A bioarchaeological study of medieval burials on the site of St Mary Spital

Excavations at Spitalfields Market, London E1, 1991–2007

MOLA Monograph Series

For more information about these titles and other MOLA publications visit the publications page at www.mola.org.uk

1 Excavations at the priory and hospital of St Mary Spital, London

2 The National Roman Fabric Reference Collection: a handbook

3 The Cross Bones burial ground, Redcross Way, Southwark, London: archaeological excavations (1991–8) for the London Underground Limited Jubilee Line Extension Project

4 The eastern cemetery of Roman London: excavations 1983–90

5 The Holocene evolution of the London Thames: archaeological excavations (1991–8) for the London Underground Limited Jubilee Line Extension Project

6 The Limehouse porcelain manufactory: excavations at 108–116 Narrow Street, London, 1990

7 Roman defences and medieval industry: excavations at Baltic House, City of London

8 London bridge: 2000 years of a river crossing

9 Roman and medieval townhouses on the London waterfront: excavations at Governor's House, City of London

10 The London Charterhouse

11 Medieval 'Westminster' floor tiles

12 Settlement in Roman Southwark: archaeological excavations (1991–8) for the London Underground Limited Jubilee Line Extension Project

13 Aspects of medieval and later Southwark: archaeological excavations (1991–8) for the London Underground Limited Jubilee Line Extension Project

14 The prehistory and topography of Southwark and Lambeth

15 Middle Saxon London: excavations at the Royal Opera House 1989–99

16 Urban development in north-west Roman Southwark: excavations 1974–90

17 Industry in north-west Roman Southwark: excavations 1984–8

18 The Cistercian abbey of St Mary Stratford Langthorne, Essex: archaeological excavations for the London Underground Limited Jubilee Line Extension Project

19 Material culture in London in an age of transition: Tudor and Stuart period finds c 1450–c 1700 from excavations at riverside sites in Southwark

20 Excavations at the priory of the Order of the Hospital of St John of Jerusalem, Clerkenwell, London

21 Roman and medieval Cripplegate, City of London: archaeological excavations 1992–8

22 The royal palace, abbey and town of Westminster on Thorney Island: archaeological excavations (1991–8) for the London Underground Limited Jubilee Line Extension Project

23 A prestigious Roman building complex on the Southwark waterfront: excavations at Winchester Palace, London, 1983–90

24 Holy Trinity Priory, Aldgate, City of London: an archaeological reconstruction and history

25 Roman pottery production in the Walbrook valley: excavations at 20–28 Moorgate, City of London, 1998–2000

26 Prehistoric landscape to Roman villa: excavations at Beddington, Surrey, 1981–7

27 Saxon, medieval and post-medieval settlement at Sol Central, Marefair, Northampton: archaeological excavations, 1998–2002

28 John Baker's late 17th-century glasshouse at Vauxhall

29 The medieval postern gate by the Tower of London

30 Roman and later development east of the forum and Cornhill: excavations at Lloyd's Register, 71 Fenchurch Street, City of London

31 Winchester Palace: excavations at the Southwark residence of the bishops of Winchester

32 Development on Roman London's western hill: excavations at Paternoster Square, City of London

33 Within these walls: Roman and medieval defences north of Newgate at the Merrill Lynch Financial Centre, City of London

34 The Augustinian priory of St Mary Merton, Surrey: excavations 1976–90

35 London's Roman amphitheatre: excavations at the Guildhall

36 The London Guildhall: an archaeological history of a neighbourhood from early medieval to modern times

37 Roman London and the Walbrook stream crossing: excavations at 1 Poultry and vicinity, City of London

38 The development of early medieval and later Poultry and Cheapside: excavations at 1 Poultry and vicinity, City of London

39 Burial at the site of the parish church of St Benet Sherehog before and after the Great Fire: excavations at 1 Poultry, City of London

40 London's delftware industry: the tin-glazed pottery industries of Southwark and Lambeth

41 Early and Middle Saxon rural settlement in the London region

42 Roman Southwark settlement and economy: excavations in Southwark 1973–91

43 The Black Death cemetery, East Smithfield, London

44 The Cistercian abbey of St Mary Graces, East Smithfield, London

45 The Royal Navy victualling yard, East Smithfield, London

46 St Marylebone church and burial ground in the 18th to 19th centuries: excavations at St Marylebone school, 1992 and 2004–6

47 Great houses, moats and mills on the south bank of the Thames: medieval and Tudor Southwark and Rotherhithe

48 The Rose and the Globe – playhouses of Shakespeare's Bankside, Southwark: excavations 1988–91

49 A dated type series of London medieval pottery: Part 5, Shelly-sandy ware and the greyware industries

50 The Cluniac priory and abbey of St Saviour Bermondsey, Surrey: excavations 1984–95

51 Three Ways Wharf, Uxbridge: a Lateglacial and Early Holocene hunter-gatherer site in the Colne valley

52 The impact of the railways in the East End 1830–2010: historical archaeology from the London Overground East London line

53 Holywell Priory and the development of Shoreditch up to 1600: archaeology from the London Overground East London line

54 Archaeological landscapes of east London: six multi-period sites excavated in advance of gravel quarrying in the London Borough of Havering

55 Mapping past landscapes in the lower Lea valley: a geoarchaeological study of the Quaternary sequence

56 Disease in London, 1st–19th centuries: an illustrated guide to diagnosis

57 The Augustinian nunnery of St Mary Clerkenwell, London: excavations 1974–96

58 The northern cemetery of Roman London: excavations at Spitalfields Market, London E1, 1991–2007

59 The medieval priory and hospital of St Mary Spital and the Bishopsgate suburb: excavations at Spitalfields Market, London E1, 1991–2007

60 A bioarchaeological study of medieval burials on the site of St Mary Spital: excavations at Spitalfields Market, London E1, 1991–2007

A bioarchaeological study of medieval burials on the site of St Mary Spital

Excavations at Spitalfields Market, London E1, 1991–2007

Brian Connell, Amy Gray Jones, Rebecca Redfern and Don Walker

MOLA MONOGRAPH 60

MUSEUM OF LONDON ARCHAEOLOGY

Published by Museum of London Archaeology
Copyright © Museum of London Archaeology 2012

All rights reserved. No part of this publication may be reproduced, stored in a retrieval system or transmitted, in any form or by any means, electronic, mechanical, photocopying, recording or otherwise, without prior permission of the copyright owner.

The Ordnance Survey mapping included in this publication is provided by the City of London under licence from the Ordnance Survey © Crown copyright. Unauthorised reproduction infringes Crown copyright and may lead to prosecution or civil proceedings.
City of London 100023243-2012

A CIP catalogue record for this book is available from the British Library

Production and series design by Tracy Wellman
Typesetting and design by Sue Cawood
Reprographics by Andy Chopping
Copy editing by Katy Carter
Series editing by Sue Hirst/Susan M Wright

Printed by the Lavenham Press

Front cover: skull of a 12–17-year-old adolescent [21037] showing a depressed crush fracture, a type of injury caused by a blunt weapon or falling on to a sharp edge (Fig 204, p 181)

CONTRIBUTORS

Principal authors (human bone) — Brian Connell, Amy Gray Jones, Rebecca Redfern, Don Walker

Stratigraphy — Christopher Thomas

Graphics — Carlos Lemos, Judit Peresztegi

Photography — Andy Chopping, Maggie Cox

Project managers — Paul Falcini, Christopher Thomas

Editor — Natasha Powers

CONTENTS

List of figures xi
List of tables xvi
Summary xix
Acknowledgements xx

Introduction   **1**   1.1   Background to the project 1
                               The circumstances of excavation 1
                               Summary of the archaeological context 3
                               Aims and objectives of the monograph 5
                   1.2   The hospital in an urban context 8
                               Health, urban environments and the environment
                               of medieval London 10
                               Socio-cultural change during the medieval period . . 12
                               Intra-cemetery variation 13
                               St Mary Spital and other cemeteries in the London
                               region 14
                               The health status of Londoners in bioarchaeological
                               perspective 15
                   1.3   Framework for analysis and discussion: a
                               bioarchaeological approach 16

Materials and methods   **2**   2.1   Materials 19
                               Sample design 19
                               Sub-sampling the cemetery 19
                               Criteria for inclusion in the study sample 20
                   2.2   Recording methods 20
                               Determination of age at death 20
                               Determination of biological sex 21
                               Metric data 21
                               Non-metric data 21
                               Recording and diagnosing pathology 21
                   2.3   Repeatability of results 22
                   2.4   Taphonomy and preservation 22
                   2.5   Levels of bone recovery 23

Results   **3**   3.1   Number of individuals studied by sex, age and period . 25
                   3.2   Demography 25
                               Burials *c* 1120–*c* 1200 (period 14) (512 individuals) . . . 25
                               Burials *c* 1200–50 (period 15) (1390 individuals) 30
                               Burials *c* 1250–*c* 1400 (period 16) (2835 individuals) . . 32
                               Burials *c* 1400–1539 (period 17) (650 individuals) . . . 33
                               Overall observations 35
                   3.3   Adult stature 36

	Adult stature *c* 1120–*c* 1200 (period 14)	36
	Adult stature *c* 1200–50 (period 15)	36
	Adult stature *c* 1250–*c* 1400 (period 16)	36
	Adult stature *c* 1400–1539 (period 17)	36
	Overall observations	37
3.4	Subadult growth	37
	Subadult growth *c* 1120–*c* 1200 (period 14)	37
	Subadult growth *c* 1200–50 (period 15)	38
	Subadult growth *c* 1250–*c* 1400 (period 16)	38
	Subadult growth *c* 1400–1539 (period 17)	38
	Overall observations	38
3.5	Metric analyses	39
	Cranial indices	39
	Post-cranial indices	39
3.6	Dental disease	40
	Caries	41
	Enamel hypoplasia	49
	Periapical lesions	55
	Calculus	56
	Ante-mortem tooth loss	58
	Periodontal disease	58
3.7	Joint disease	60
	Extra-spinal osteoarthritis	60
	Charcot joint	71
	Ochronotic osteoarthropathy	71
	Ankylosis	72
	Rotator cuff injuries	72
	Diffuse idiopathic skeletal hyperostosis (DISH)	72
	Erosive osteoarthropathies	73
	Seronegative osteoarthropathies	75
	Other osteoarthropathies	76
	Spinal joint disease	76
3.8	Trauma	88
	All fractures	88
	Skull fractures	91
	Long bone fractures	95
	Joint fractures	98
	Vertebral fractures	98
	Subadult fractures	100
	Injury recidivism	101
	Zonal fracture distribution	102
	Injury mechanism	103
	Fracture healing and treatment	105

			Soft tissue injuries	108
	3.9		Infectious disease	109
			Non-specific infection	109
			Specific infection	112
	3.10		Nutritional and metabolic disease	118
			Scurvy	118
			Rickets	118
			Osteomalacia	120
			Cribra orbitalia	120
			Porotic hyperostosis of the cranial vault	123
			Indicators of stress in subadults	124
			Osteoporosis	127
	3.11		Neoplastic disease	127
	3.12		Circulatory disorders	130
			Osteonecroses	130
			Osteochondroses	130
			Osteochondritis dissecans	131
			Hypertrophic osteoarthropathy	132
	3.13		Congenital and developmental abnormalities	132
			Cranial anomalies	132
			Bathrocrania	132
			Craniofacial anomalies	133
			Spinal anomalies	133
			Limb and joint anomalies	143
	3.14		Miscellaneous pathological conditions	146
			Hyperostosis frontalis interna (HFI)	146
			Paget's disease of bone	146
			Endocranial lesions	147
			Diaphyseal aclasia	148

St Mary Spital in context   4

	4.1	Medieval London	149
		Housing	149
		Health risks and exposure to pollutants	152
		Health risks in the domestic environment	156
		Industry and occupation	157
		Diet and economy	161
		A subadult perspective on medieval London	168
		Violence and the risk of injury or death	181
		Impairment and disability	187
	4.2	Hospitals, well-being and treatment	194
		Healing and treatment	201
		Surgery	212
	4.3	Defining catastrophe: mass burial at St Mary Spital	217

		Comparison of burial types *c* 1120–*c* 1200 (period 14)	218
		Comparison of burial types *c* 1200–50 (period 15)	222
		Comparison of burial types *c* 1250–*c* 1400 (period 16)	224
		Comparison of burial types *c* 1400–1539 (period 17)	226
		Volcanoes and vicissitudes	228
	4.4	Comparison between St Mary Spital and other London cemeteries	232
		Prevalence of specific infectious diseases	232
		Prevalence of non-specific infection	233
		Dental disease	234
		Joint disease	236
		Diffuse idiopathic skeletal hyperostosis (DISH)	237
		Trauma: evidence of injury or violence	238
		Metabolic disease	239
		Neoplastic disease	240
		Other pathological conditions	241
		Paget's disease of bone	241
		Patterns and trends in population structure	241
		Comparison of the mass burials with a catastrophe cemetery from London	243
	4.5	St Mary Spital in a national and European perspective	245
		Dental health	247
		Joint disease	248
		Trauma	249
		Infectious disease	253
		Nutritional and metabolic disease	254
		Neoplastic disease	254
		Circulatory disease	255
		Congenital and developmental anomalies	256
		Miscellaneous pathological conditions	257
		Stature	258
		Growth	259
		Living environment and health	259
		Summary	270

Conclusions   **5**

	5.1	An overview of the data set	271
	5.2	Relationship between St Mary Spital and London	272
	5.3	Health status of medieval Londoners	272
	5.4	Value of a bioarchaeological approach	273
	5.5	Achievement of the project aims	274
	5.6	Future research potential of the St Mary Spital skeletal sample	275
		Demography	275

Non-metric traits	275
Tuberculosis	275
Trauma	275
Markers of stress	276
Diet	276
Stable isotopes	276
Other work	276

French and German summaries 278

Bibliography 280

Index 298

FIGURES

Fig 1	Location of the Spitalfields Market study area	1
Fig 2	Location of archaeological investigations	4
Fig 3	Cemetery plans for each period, showing the location of the medieval burials	6
Fig 4	The 14th-century cemetery chapel under excavation	8
Fig 5	Detail from a copperplate map of *c* 1559, showing Bishopsgate and the area of the former precinct of St Mary Spital	9
Fig 6	Examples of typical burial types	13
Fig 7	Comparison of the levels of bone recovery in single and multiple burials	23
Fig 8	Age at death by burial type, *c* 1120–*c* 1200 (period 14)	29
Fig 9	Female age at death, *c* 1120–*c* 1200 (period 14)	30
Fig 10	Male age at death, *c* 1120–*c* 1200 (period 14)	30
Fig 11	Age at death by burial type, *c* 1200–50 (period 15)	30
Fig 12	Female age at death, *c* 1200–50 (period 15)	31
Fig 13	Male age at death, *c* 1200–50 (period 15)	31
Fig 14	Age at death by burial type, *c* 1250–*c* 1400 (period 16)	32
Fig 15	Female age at death, *c* 1250–*c* 1400 (period 16)	33
Fig 16	Male age at death, *c* 1250–*c* 1400 (period 16)	33
Fig 17	Age at death by burial type, *c* 1400–1539 (period 17)	34
Fig 18	Female age at death, *c* 1400–1539 (period 17)	35
Fig 19	Male age at death, *c* 1400–1539 (period 17)	35
Fig 20	Females as a percentage of sexed adults	35
Fig 21	Percentage of sexed adults in burial type ABC	35
Fig 22	Percentage of sexed adults in burial type D	35
Fig 23	Graph showing stature by period, burial type and sex	37
Fig 24	Mean male stature	37
Fig 25	Mean female stature	37
Fig 26	Subadult growth measured by mean femoral length	37
Fig 27	Comparison between periods of subadult growth in burial type ABC	38
Fig 28	Comparison between periods of subadult growth in burial type D	38
Fig 29	Frequency of distribution of caries, ante-mortem tooth loss and periapical lesions by tooth position	46
Fig 30	Comparison of caries frequency in males and females	46
Fig 31	Distribution of carious cavities in burial type ABC	47
Fig 32	Distribution of carious cavities in burial type D	47
Fig 33	True prevalence rate of female caries by burial type and period	48
Fig 34	True prevalence rate of male caries by burial type and period	48
Fig 35	Distribution by period of carious lesions on surfaces of permanent teeth in adults	49
Fig 36	Percentage frequency distribution of teeth showing enamel hypoplastic defects	51
Fig 37	Enamel hypoplastic defects in the mandibular and maxillary dentition of 18–25-year-old female [12886]	51
Fig 38	Distribution of teeth with enamel hypoplastic defects in burial type ABC	54
Fig 39	Distribution of teeth with enamel hypoplastic defects in burial type D	55
Fig 40	Caries and associated periapical lesions in 18–25-year-old male [1055]	55
Fig 41	True prevalence rate of adult supra-gingival calculus	58
Fig 42	True prevalence rate of adult sub-gingival calculus	58
Fig 43	Comparison of the position of calculus deposits by tooth position in males and females	59
Fig 44	True prevalence rate of adult periodontal disease by period	60
Fig 45	Distribution of periodontal disease	60
Fig 46	Crude prevalence rate of extra-spinal osteoarthritis by period	60
Fig 47	Crude prevalence rate of extra-spinal osteoarthritis by burial type	61
Fig 48	Crude prevalence rate of extra-spinal osteoarthritis by sex	61
Fig 49	Crude prevalence rate of extra-spinal osteoarthritis in burial type ABC	61
Fig 50	Crude prevalence rate of extra-spinal osteoarthritis in burial type D	61
Fig 51	Crude prevalence rate of male extra-spinal osteoarthritis by burial type	62
Fig 52	Crude prevalence rate of female extra-spinal osteoarthritis by burial type	62
Fig 53	Crude prevalence rate of extra-spinal osteoarthritis by age	63
Fig 54	Crude prevalence rate of male extra-spinal osteoarthritis by age	63
Fig 55	Crude prevalence rate of female extra-spinal osteoarthritis by age	63
Fig 56	Crude prevalence rate of male extra-spinal osteoarthritis by age in burial type ABC	64
Fig 57	Crude prevalence rate of female extra-spinal osteoarthritis by age in burial type ABC	64
Fig 58	Crude prevalence rate of male extra-spinal osteoarthritis by age in burial type D	65
Fig 59	Crude prevalence rate of female extra-spinal osteoarthritis by age in burial type D	65
Fig 60	Ochronotic osteoarthropathy in 36–45-year-old female [10095]	72
Fig 61	DISH in the thoracolumbar spine of 36–45-year-old male [12498]	73
Fig 62	Distal articular surfaces of the radii with evidence for rheumatoid osteoarthritis in 18–25-year-old male [11371]	73

Fig 63	Erosive changes suggestive of gout in the foot elements of 18–25-year-old female [21193]	74
Fig 64	A seronegative spondyloarthropathy in the thoracolumbar spine of ≥46-year-old adult male [8962]	75
Fig 65	Crude prevalence rate of spinal joint disease in 12–17-year-olds by period and burial type	76
Fig 66	Crude prevalence rate of vertebral joint disease by age	77
Fig 67	Crude prevalence rate of vertebral joint disease by period in 18–25-year-olds	77
Fig 68	Crude prevalence rate of male vertebral joint disease by burial type and period	77
Fig 69	Crude prevalence rate of vertebral joint disease by sex in burial type ABC	78
Fig 70	Crude prevalence rate of vertebral joint disease by sex in burial type D	78
Fig 71	Crude prevalence rate of male intervertebral osteophytosis by burial type and period	79
Fig 72	Crude prevalence rate of male intervertebral disc disease by burial type and period	79
Fig 73	Crude prevalence rate of male apophyseal joint osteoarthritis by burial type and period	79
Fig 74	Crude prevalence rate of female intervertebral disc disease by burial type and period	80
Fig 75	Crude prevalence rate of female apophyseal joint osteoarthritis by burial type and period	80
Fig 76	Crude prevalence rate of vertebral joint disease in males and females by lesion type	80
Fig 77	Crude prevalence rate of male joint disease by spinal segment in burial type ABC	81
Fig 78	Crude prevalence rate of male joint disease by spinal segment in burial type D	81
Fig 79	Crude prevalence rate of female joint disease by spinal segment in burial type ABC	81
Fig 80	Crude prevalence rate of female joint disease by spinal segment in burial type D	81
Fig 81	Crude prevalence rate of joint disease by cervical spine segment, sex and period in burial type ABC	82
Fig 82	Crude prevalence rate of joint disease by cervical spine segment, sex and period in burial type D	82
Fig 83	Crude prevalence rate of fracture by age group	88
Fig 84	Crude prevalence rate of adult fracture by age and sex	88
Fig 85	Crude prevalence rate of fracture by period	89
Fig 86	Crude prevalence rate of fracture by sex	89
Fig 87	Crude prevalence rate of fracture by period and burial type	90
Fig 88	Crude prevalence rate of female fracture by period and burial type	90
Fig 89	Crude prevalence rate of male fracture by period and burial type	90
Fig 90	Crude prevalence rate of male and female fracture in burial type ABC	91
Fig 91	Crude prevalence rate of male and female fracture in burial type D	91
Fig 92	Crude prevalence rate of types and locations of skull fracture by sex	91
Fig 93	Cranial vault fracture distribution	92
Fig 94	True prevalence rate of cranial vault fracture by period	92
Fig 95	True prevalence rate of female cranial vault fracture by burial type and period	92
Fig 96	True prevalence rate of male cranial vault fracture by burial type and period	92
Fig 97	True prevalence rate of cranial vault fracture in period 16 by sex and burial type	93
Fig 98	True prevalence rate of frontal bone fracture in period 16 by sex and burial type	90
Fig 99	True prevalence rate of parietal bone fracture in period 16 by sex and burial type	93
Fig 100	Sharp force injury to the cranium of 26–35-year-old male [9488]	93
Fig 101	True prevalence rate of cranial vault sharp force fracture	94
Fig 102	Peri-mortem blunt force cranial injury in 36–45-year-old female [3243]	94
Fig 103	True prevalence rate of cranial vault blunt force fracture by sex and period	95
Fig 104	True prevalence rates of male frontal and parietal blunt force fracture in period 16 by burial type	95
Fig 105	True prevalence rates of long bone fractures by sex	96
Fig 106	Healed radial and ulna fractures in 36–45-year-old male [23722]	96
Fig 107	True prevalence rates of female ulna fractures by period and burial type	97
Fig 108	True prevalence rates of male ulna fractures by period and burial type	97
Fig 109	True prevalence rates of long bone fractures by side	97
Fig 110	Long bone shaft fracture distribution in female upper limbs	97
Fig 111	Long bone shaft fracture distribution in male upper limbs	97
Fig 112	Long bone shaft fracture distribution in female lower limbs	98
Fig 113	Long bone shaft fracture distribution in male lower limbs	98
Fig 114	True prevalence rates of joint fractures	98
Fig 115	True prevalence rates of vertebral body fracture	99
Fig 116	True prevalence rates of vertebral body fractures by sex	99
Fig 117	True prevalence rates of vertebral body fractures by period	99
Fig 118	Frequency of fractures in subadults	100
Fig 119	Frequency of subadult fractures in adults	101
Fig 120	Subadult humeral fracture in 18–25-year-old male [14945], showing disruption of proximal growth plate	101

Fig 121	Adults with multiple injuries by period and burial type 102	Fig 153	Evidence for brucellosis in the third and fourth lumbar vertebrae of 18–25-year-old male [11849] . 117
Fig 122	Proportion of individuals with multiple injuries including long bone involvement 102	Fig 154	Scurvy in 6–11-year-old [3933], showing porosity on the greater wings of sphenoid and palate 119
Fig 123	Proportion of individuals with multiple injuries including spinal involvement 102	Fig 155	Rickets in 1–5-year-old [18339] 119
Fig 124	Distribution of adult fractures by zone 103	Fig 156	Changes to the axial and appendicular skeleton of ≥46-year-old adult female [3699] due to osteomalacia 120
Fig 125	Distribution of adult fractures by period 103		
Fig 126	Distribution of adult fractures by sex 103	Fig 157	True prevalence rate of male cribra orbitalia by period 122
Fig 127	Female fracture distribution by burial type in period 15 104		
Fig 128	Female fracture distribution by burial type in period 16 104	Fig 158	True prevalence rate of female cribra orbitalia by period 122
Fig 129	Distribution of adult and subadult fractures 104	Fig 159	Temporal comparison of indicators of stress in subadults 127
Fig 130	Long bone shaft fracture type 104	Fig 160	Crude prevalence rate of neoplastic disease by age 128
Fig 131	Distribution of identified injury mechanism 104		
Fig 132	Distribution of direct force injuries 105	Fig 161	Crude prevalence rate of neoplastic disease in adults by sex 128
Fig 133	Frequency of direct ulna shaft fractures as a percentage of bone fractures 105		
Fig 134	Frequency of female direct ulna shaft fractures by period and burial type 105	Fig 162	Crude prevalence rate of neoplastic disease by period 128
Fig 135	Crude prevalence of soft tissue injury by sex and age group 108	Fig 163	Distribution of types of bone tissue neoplasia by individual 129
Fig 136	Frequency of dislocation by element or joint . . . 108	Fig 164	Distribution of types of cartilage tissue neoplasia in affected individuals 129
Fig 137	Comparison of frequency distribution of periostitis between burial types 110	Fig 165	Distribution of osteochondromas in parts of the body 129
Fig 138	Comparison of frequency distribution of sinusitis between burial types 111	Fig 166	Osteochondroma in the left mandible of 36–45-year-old male [13279] 129
Fig 139	Septic arthropathy in the right sacroiliac joint of 26–35-year-old probable male [3645] 111	Fig 167	Osteochondroma with possible secondary malignancy (chondrosarcoma) of the right scapula of 26–35-year-old female [11661] 129
Fig 140	Left second to fifth metatarsals of 26–35-year-old female [2487], with evidence for tuberculoid leprosy 112		
		Fig 168	Multiple changes to the thoracic vertebrae in 26–35-year-old male [22764] 131
Fig 141	Number of treponemal infections by sex and period 113	Fig 169	Right second metatarsal with Freiberg's disease in 36–45-year-old female [3860] 131
Fig 142	Caries sicca and rhinomaxillary destruction in the skull of 10–11-year-old [6974] 113	Fig 170	Unilateral cleft palate in 12–17-year-old [2480] . . 133
Fig 143	Gummatous lesions in the right tibia and left humerus of 10–11-year-old [6974] 113	Fig 171	Kyphoscoliosis of the second to sixth thoracic vertebrae in 18–25-year-old female [20488] . . . 135
Fig 144	Crude prevalence rate of tuberculosis by sex and period 114	Fig 172	Kyphoscoliosis and limb atrophy in 18–25-year-old female [20488] 135
Fig 145	Healed tuberculous lesions in the lumbar vertebrae of 36–45-year-old male [22806] 114	Fig 173	18–25-year-old female [20488] as excavated, showing the unusual burial position 135
Fig 146	Crude prevalence rate of tuberculosis by period . . 114	Fig 174	Scoliosis in the thoracic vertebrae of 36–45-year-old male [6413] 136
Fig 147	Crude prevalence rate of tuberculosis by age and sex 115		
Fig 148	Crude prevalence rates of tuberculosis by sex, period and burial type 115	Fig 175	26–35-year-old female [11230] with scoliosis, as excavated 136
Fig 149	Tubercular infection of the left elbow of 26–35-year-old male [17273] 116	Fig 176	18–25-year-old male [6571] with scoliosis and lower limb atrophy, burial reconstruction 136
Fig 150	Tubercular infection of the left wrist of 36–45-year-old male [17394] 116	Fig 177	Spondylolisthesis affecting the fourth and fifth lumbar vertebrae of ≥46-year-old female [3790] . . 138
Fig 151	Active rib lesions in 12–17-year-old [22829] with Pott's disease of the thoracolumbar spine . . . 116	Fig 178	Proximal left radius and ulna of 36–45-year-old female [16964], showing congenital synostosis . . . 144
Fig 152	Healed cranial lesion to the left parietal bone of 6–11-year-old [31901] 117	Fig 179	Ilia and femora of 26–35-year-old female [12726], illustrating bilateral hip anomaly 145
		Fig 180	Dislocation of the left hip in ≥46-year-old male [5970] 145

xiii

Fig 181	Congenital talipes equinovarus: left calcaneus and talus of 18–25-year-old male [20417]	146
Fig 182	Paget's disease of bone in the right tibia of 36–45-year-old male [14106]	147
Fig 183	Diaphyseal aclasia in the right humerus, right tibia and fibulae of 36–45-year-old male [19378]	148
Fig 184	Plan of the medieval city of London	150
Fig 185	Diagram of a medieval jettied building from Canterbury	150
Fig 186	A chalk cellar from a medieval house at St Mary Spital	151
Fig 187	A large back garden cesspit from a medieval house at St Mary Spital	152
Fig 188	St Mary Spital infirmary latrines	153
Fig 189	Rib lesions in 18–25-year-old male [31293]	154
Fig 190	Osteomyelitis in the frontal sinuses of 12–17-year-old [3263]	155
Fig 191	Example of Pott's disease in 36–45-year-old male [19599]	155
Fig 192	Healed greenstick fracture in the sternal end of the right clavicle of 18–25-year-old female [9626]	157
Fig 193	Epiphyseal plate injury in the right tibia of *c* 17-year-old [29075]	157
Fig 194	A 15th-century illustration of a trader selling eggs	158
Fig 195	Women spinning and carding wool, from an English text dating from *c* 1325–35	159
Fig 196	Detail from the bell founders' window at York Minster, depicting women casting a bell	160
Fig 197	Two men with clubs knocking down acorns for their pigs, depicted in the Queen Mary psalter, *c* 1310–20	161
Fig 198	Harvesting a cereal crop, depicted in the Luttrell psalter, *c* 1325–35	162
Fig 199	Medieval market traders selling meat	163
Fig 200	Butchery of pigs, from the Queen Mary psalter, *c* 1310–20	163
Fig 201	A medieval illustration of fish and imaginary aquatic creatures, *c* 1230–40	164
Fig 202	Spine of individual [12498] with evidence of DISH	168
Fig 203	'Little leaguer's elbow' in 18–25-year-old male [12190]	179
Fig 204	Healed blunt force injury to the skull of 12–17-year-old [21037]	181
Fig 205	True prevalence rates of upper limb fractures	182
Fig 206	True prevalence rates of lower limb fractures	182
Fig 207	Crude prevalence rate of adults with multiple injuries by age and sex	184
Fig 208	Age-related percentage increase in number of individuals with multiple injuries	184
Fig 209	Age-related percentage increase in number of individuals with fractures	184
Fig 210	Detail from the early 15th-century St William window at York Minster, showing the use of crutches	189
Fig 211	Ankylosis of the left knee of 26–35-year-old female [21769]	191
Fig 212	Scoliosis in the thoracic vertebrae of 18–25-year-old male [6571]	194
Fig 213	Detail from Wyngaerde's panorama of the city *c* 1540, showing St Mary Spital	195
Fig 214	Plan of the infirmary block after the refoundation of St Mary Spital in 1235	196
Fig 215	Suggested appearance of the infirmary and chapel at St Mary Spital *c* 1250	196
Fig 216	The 15th-century infirmary hall at the hospital at Beaune, France	197
Fig 217	Group of small keys discarded *c* 1280 and thought to open infirmary lockers	197
Fig 218	Excavation of the north arm of the church with the infirmary hall and its extension	198
Fig 219	Plan of the church, infirmary and adjacent buildings at St Mary Spital	199
Fig 220	Individual [7652], found with chalice and paten, as excavated	201
Fig 221	Proportion of long bone fractures with deformities in the attritional cemetery	202
Fig 222	Proportion of long bone fractures with deformities in the catastrophic cemetery	202
Fig 223	Rates of unsuccessful healing of united fractures in long bones	203
Fig 224	Rates of unsuccessful healing of united long bone fractures by sex	203
Fig 225	Types of deformity resulting from unsuccessful healing	203
Fig 226	Successful healing of united long bone fractures by period	204
Fig 227	Successful healing of united long bone fractures by sex and period	204
Fig 228	Fractured tibia of ≥46-year-old male [22429] with secondary osteomyelitis	205
Fig 229	Non-union of left ulna fracture of 36–45-year-old male [23722]	206
Fig 230	Sharp force injury to the cranial vault of 26–35-year-old male [29693]	207
Fig 231	Copper-alloy plate found between the knees of 36–45-year-old male [12441]	208
Fig 232	Lead sheeting around the right shin of 26–35-year-old female [7186]	209
Fig 233	A white (opium) poppy from Culpeper's *Herbal* (1653)	210
Fig 234	14th-century distillation vessel from St Mary Spital	210
Fig 235	Proportion of perinatal individuals by period and burial type	212
Fig 236	A surgeon treating a head wound, depicted in an early 14th-century copy of the *Chirurgia*	213
Fig 237	Cranium of 36–45-year-old male [1934]	213
Fig 238	Cranium of 36–45-year-old male [19893], showing the alignment of a nasal fracture and sharp force (weapon) injury	214

Fig 239 Cranium of 36–45-year-old male [19893] 214
Fig 240 Left parietal of the cranium of 36–45-year-old male [26580], showing an oval lesion perforating the skull 215
Fig 241 Remodelling following amputation of the right leg of 26–35-year-old male [32152] 216
Fig 242 Individual [32152] with amputated right lower leg, as excavated 217
Fig 243 The top layer of a mid 13th-century mass burial pit under excavation in the hospital cemetery. . . . 218
Fig 244 Comparison of subadult growth between the attritional and catastrophic burials, c 1120–c 1200 (period 14) 219
Fig 245 Comparison of subadult growth between the attritional and catastrophic burials, c 1200–50 (period 15) 222
Fig 246 Comparison of subadult growth between the attritional and catastrophic burials, c 1250–c 1400 (period 16) 224
Fig 247 Comparison of subadult growth between the attritional and catastrophic burials, c 1400–1539 (period 17) 226
Fig 248 Frequency distribution of subadults in larger medieval cemetery samples 242
Fig 249 Average (mean) stature for all comparative sites . . 259
Fig 250 Inter-site analysis of growth profiles 259

TABLES

Table 1	Archaeological fieldwork in the Spitalfields Market study area	2
Table 2	Disease stressors present in rural and urban environments	10
Table 3	Comparative medieval cemeteries in the London area and their relevance to periods at St Mary Spital	14
Table 4	Age groups	21
Table 5	Summary of demographic data by burial type, c 1120–c 1200 (period 14)	26
Table 6	Summary of demographic data by burial type, c 1200–50 (period 15)	26
Table 7	Summary of demographic data by burial type, c 1250–c 1400 (period 16)	26
Table 8	Summary of demographic data by burial type, c 1400–1539 (period 17)	28
Table 9	Summary of demographic data for all burials, c 1120–1539	28
Table 10	Demographic data for burial type ABC, c 1120–c 1200 (period 14)	28
Table 11	Demographic data for burial type D, c 1120–c 1200 (period 14)	29
Table 12	Demographic data for burial type ABC, c 1200–50 (period 15)	31
Table 13	Demographic data for burial type D, c 1200–50 (period 15)	31
Table 14	Demographic data for burial type ABC, c 1250–c 1400 (period 16)	32
Table 15	Demographic data for burial type D, c 1250–c 1400 (period 16)	32
Table 16	Demographic data for burial type ABC, c 1400–1539 (period 17)	34
Table 17	Demographic data for burial type D, c 1400–1539 (period 17)	34
Table 18	Summary of adult stature by range, mean and standard deviation	36
Table 19	Summary data for cranial indices by mean, standard deviation, coefficient of variation, range, and standard error	39
Table 20	Femoral and tibial indices by range and mean, by period, burial type and sex	39
Table 21	Frequency of adult tooth positions and teeth, and distribution of dental pathology in period 14	40
Table 22	Frequency of adult tooth positions and teeth, and distribution of dental pathology in period 15	40
Table 23	Frequency of adult tooth positions and teeth, and distribution of dental pathology in period 16	42
Table 24	Frequency of adult tooth positions and teeth, and distribution of dental pathology in period 17	42
Table 25	Frequency of deciduous tooth positions and teeth, with caries distribution	44
Table 26	Subadult dental health by period and burial type	44
Table 27	Distribution of carious lesions on surfaces of adult permanent teeth by period and sex	48
Table 28	Distribution of adult caries by period, burial type, sex and tooth type	50
Table 29	Distribution of adult enamel hypoplastic defects by burial type and sex	52
Table 30	Distribution and severity of enamel hypoplastic defects in period 14	53
Table 31	Distribution and severity of enamel hypoplastic defects in period 15	53
Table 32	Distribution and severity of enamel hypoplastic defects in period 16	53
Table 33	Distribution and severity of enamel hypoplastic defects in period 17	54
Table 34	Number of periapical lesions in adult dentitions by period	56
Table 35	Frequency and location of calculus deposits in period 14 adults by sex	56
Table 36	Frequency and location of calculus deposits in period 15 adults by sex	57
Table 37	Frequency and location of calculus deposits in period 16 adults by sex	57
Table 38	Frequency and location of calculus deposits in period 17 adults by sex	57
Table 39	Distribution of periodontitis by period	60
Table 40	Crude prevalence rate of extra-spinal osteoarthritis by age and sex	64
Table 41	True prevalence rate of extra-spinal osteoarthritis for affected joints in period 14	65
Table 42	True prevalence rate of extra-spinal osteoarthritis for affected joints in period 15	66
Table 43	True prevalence rate of extra-spinal osteoarthritis for affected joints in period 16	67
Table 44	True prevalence rate of extra-spinal osteoarthritis for affected joints in period 17	68
Table 45	Total true prevalence rate of extra-spinal osteoarthritis for affected joints	69
Table 46	Crude prevalence rates of specific osteoarthropathies by period, sex and burial type	71
Table 47	Crude prevalence rate of rotator cuff disease by period, sex and burial type	72
Table 48	Crude prevalence rate of DISH by period, sex and burial type	73
Table 49	Crude prevalence rate of erosive osteoarthropathies by period, sex and burial type	74
Table 50	Crude prevalence rate of seronegative osteoarthropathies by period, sex and burial type	75
Table 51	Crude prevalence rate of non-specific osteoarthropathies by period, sex and burial type	76
Table 52	Crude prevalence rate of vertebral joint disease by sex and burial type	77

Table 53	Crude prevalence rate of male vertebral joint disease by burial type and period	77
Table 54	Crude prevalence rate of female vertebral joint disease by burial type and period	78
Table 55	Crude prevalence rate of male vertebral lesions by period	78
Table 56	Crude prevalence rate of female vertebral lesions by period	79
Table 57	Crude prevalence rate of male joint disease by spinal segment	80
Table 58	Crude prevalence rate of female joint disease by spinal segment	81
Table 59	True prevalence rates of Schmorl's nodes	82
Table 60	Summary of prevalence of Schmorl's nodes by vertebral joint in period 14	87
Table 61	Summary of prevalence of Schmorl's nodes by vertebral joint in period 15	87
Table 62	Summary of prevalence of Schmorl's nodes by vertebral joint in period 16	87
Table 63	Summary of prevalence of Schmorl's nodes by vertebral joint in period 17	87
Table 64	Trauma crude prevalence summary	88
Table 65	Fracture crude prevalence summary	88
Table 66	Crude prevalence rate of fracture by age and sex	88
Table 67	Statistical testing of fracture crude prevalence rate by age and sex	89
Table 68	Crude prevalence rate of fracture by period and burial type	89
Table 69	Crude prevalence rate of female fracture by period and burial type	90
Table 70	Crude prevalence rate of male fracture by period and burial type	90
Table 71	Fracture true prevalence summary	91
Table 72	True prevalence of fracture by period	91
Table 73	Skull fracture crude prevalence summary	91
Table 74	Crude prevalence rate of skull fracture by location and sex	91
Table 75	Cranial vault fracture true prevalence summary	92
Table 76	True prevalence rate of male cranial vault fracture by period	92
Table 77	True prevalence summary of cranial vault sharp force fracture	93
Table 78	True prevalence summary of cranial vault blunt force fracture	94
Table 79	True prevalence summary of facial blunt force fracture	95
Table 80	Dental fracture true prevalence summary	95
Table 81	True prevalence rates of long bone fractures	95
Table 82	Ulna shaft fractures by side	97
Table 83	True prevalence rate of vertebral body fractures by spinal segment	98
Table 84	True prevalence rates of vertebral body fractures by period	99
Table 85	True prevalence rate of clay shoveller's fractures	100
Table 86	Crude prevalence rate of clay shoveller's fractures by sex	100
Table 87	Crude prevalence of subadult fracture by period	100
Table 88	Crude prevalence of subadult fracture in period 16 by burial type	100
Table 89	Injuries in sexed adults by age	101
Table 90	Crude prevalence rate of multiple injury by age and sex	102
Table 91	Individuals with unhealed fractures	105
Table 92	Individuals with unhealed fractures as a proportion of those with fractures	105
Table 93	Long bone fractures with complications	106
Table 94	Complications as a percentage of all fractured bones	106
Table 95	Complications as a percentage of all fractured bones by sex	106
Table 96	Radiographic analysis of fractured long bones	107
Table 97	Long bone fracture healing	107
Table 98	Female long bone fracture healing	108
Table 99	Male long bone fracture healing	108
Table 100	Crude prevalence of soft tissue injury by sex	108
Table 101	Crude prevalence of dislocation by sex	108
Table 102	Crude prevalence rate of sinusitis by sex	110
Table 103	Distribution of sinusitis by period and burial type	110
Table 104	Crude prevalence rate of leprosy by period, sex and burial type	112
Table 105	Distribution of treponemal infections by period	112
Table 106	Overall crude prevalence rate of tuberculosis by sex or age	114
Table 107	Crude prevalence rate of tuberculosis in subadults by period and burial type	117
Table 108	Crude prevalence rate of tuberculosis or brucellosis cases by period, burial type and sex or age	118
Table 109	Crude prevalence rate of scurvy in subadults	118
Table 110	Crude prevalence rate of rickets by age, sex and period	119
Table 111	True prevalence of cribra orbitalia in period 14	121
Table 112	True prevalence of cribra orbitalia in period 15	121
Table 113	True prevalence of cribra orbitalia in period 16	122
Table 114	True prevalence of cribra orbitalia in period 17	122
Table 115	True prevalence rate of porotic hyperostosis in period 14	123
Table 116	True prevalence rate of porotic hyperostosis in period 15	124
Table 117	True prevalence rate of porotic hyperostosis in period 16	125
Table 118	True prevalence rate of porotic hyperostosis in period 17	125
Table 119	Crude prevalence of stress indicators in subadults by period and burial type	126
Table 120	Crude prevalence of neoplastic disease by age	128
Table 121	Crude prevalence of neoplastic disease in adults by sex	128
Table 122	Distribution of different types of neoplasia	129
Table 123	Crude prevalence of osteonecroses by period	130

Table 124 Crude prevalence of osteochondroses by period and burial type 130	
Table 125 Crude prevalence of osteochondritis dissecans by period and burial type 131	
Table 126 Crude prevalence of hypertrophic osteoarthropathy by period and burial type . . . 132	
Table 127 Crude prevalence of cranial anomalies by period and burial type 132	
Table 128 Crude prevalence of bathrocrania by period . . . 133	
Table 129 Crude prevalence of spinal anomalies by period and burial type 134	
Table 130 Crude prevalence of spondylolysis by period and burial type 137	
Table 131 Crude prevalence rate of spondylolisthesis by period and burial type 138	
Table 132 True prevalence rate of segmentation failure in period 14 139	
Table 133 True prevalence rate of segmentation failure in period 15 140	
Table 134 True prevalence rate of segmentation failure in period 16 140	
Table 135 True prevalence rate of segmentation failure in period 17 141	
Table 136 True prevalence rate of border shifts 141	
Table 137 Crude prevalence rate of limb anomalies by period and burial type 143	
Table 138 Crude prevalence rate of joint anomalies by period and burial type 143	
Table 139 Crude prevalence rate of hand and foot anomalies by period and burial type 145	
Table 140 Crude prevalence rate of HFI by period and burial type 146	
Table 141 Crude prevalence rate of Paget's disease of bone by period and burial type 147	
Table 142 Crude prevalence rate of endocranial lesions by period and burial type 147	
Table 143 Multiple injuries in adults of known age and sex 183	
Table 144 Crude prevalence rate of conditions indicative of impairment 191	
Table 145 Long bone deformity type 202	
Table 146 Crude prevalence rate of dental enamel hypoplasia in subadults by period and burial type 219	
Table 147 Crude prevalence rate of porotic hyperostosis by period and burial type 220	
Table 148 Crude prevalence rate of tuberculosis by period and burial type 221	
Table 149 Comparison of crude prevalence of specific infectious disease in London medieval cemetery samples 232	
Table 150 Comparison of non-specific infectious disease rates in London medieval cemetery samples . . . 234	
Table 151 Comparison of crude prevalence of osteoarthritis and DISH in London medieval cemetery samples 237	
Table 152 Comparison of crude prevalence of trauma in London medieval cemetery samples 238	
Table 153 Comparison of crude prevalence of vitamin deficiency diseases in London medieval cemetery samples 239	
Table 154 Comparison of crude prevalence of cribra orbitalia in London medieval cemetery samples . 240	
Table 155 Comparison of crude prevalence of HFI in London medieval cemetery samples 241	
Table 156 Comparison of crude prevalence of Paget's disease of bone in London medieval cemetery samples 241	
Table 157 Summary of sites used for comparative purposes . 245	
Table 158 Inter-site comparison of adult dental health . . . 247	
Table 159 Inter-site comparison of subadult dental health . 248	
Table 160 Inter-site crude prevalence rate of joint disease . 248	
Table 161 Inter-site true prevalence rates of fracture by site and long bone 250	
Table 162 Fracture distribution in the comparative sample	
Table 163 Inter-site crude prevalence rate of infectious disease 251, 255	
Table 164 Inter-site crude prevalence rate of metabolic disease 255	
Table 165 Inter-site crude prevalence rate of neoplastic disease 255	
Table 166 Inter-site crude prevalence rate of circulatory disease 256	
Table 167 Inter-site crude prevalence rate of congenital skull anomalies 256	
Table 168 Inter-site crude prevalence rate of congenital spinal anomalies 257	
Table 169 Inter-site crude prevalence rate of congenital and developmental joint anomalies 257	
Table 170 Inter-site crude prevalence rate of Paget's disease of bone 258	
Table 171 Inter-site crude prevalence rate of endocranial lesions 258	
Table 172 Summary of inter-site stature data 258	

SUMMARY

The Augustinian priory and hospital of St Mary without Bishopsgate (later known as St Mary Spital), east London, was one of about 200 hospitals founded in 12th-century England. It became one of the largest hospitals in the country in the medieval period, providing shelter for the sick, the poor, the elderly and the homeless.

In advance of a proposal to redevelop the area of the former Spitalfields Market, a series of archaeological investigations was carried out between 1992 and 2007. During the main phase of excavation from 1999 to 2002, the remains of over 10,500 individuals were recovered. This medieval cemetery sat within a complex archaeological site, but unprecedented accuracy of dating and phasing was achieved using a targeted programme combining relative (stratigraphic) and absolute (radiocarbon) dating techniques. Burials were divided into four chronological periods: period 14, c 1120–c 1200; period 15, c 1200–50; period 16, c 1250–c 1400; and period 17, c 1400–1539.

In 2003, four osteologists began the colossal task of studying the burials from St Mary Spital. This volume presents the results, interpretation and discussion of osteological analysis of a sample of 5387 individuals from the cemetery. Among the significant discoveries are some of the earliest cases of syphilis in Europe. The results provide a unique insight into the lives of medieval Londoners from the 12th to the early 16th centuries and have enabled discussion of the effects of urban living on child health, the role and influence of the hospital, and the reasons behind the mass burial of almost 4000 people.

The majority of mass burials pre-date the plague epidemic known as the Black Death (1348–9), but historical sources reveal a series of recurrent famines and epidemics with closely corresponding dates. The largest phases of mass burials, in the mid 13th century, correspond with a period of famine thought to have been caused by climatic fluctuations resulting from a massive volcanic eruption in the tropics. Osteological analysis also revealed that the population interred in the cemetery underwent a period of prolonged stress, probably reflecting repeated incidences of famine.

The analysis of this group indicates that living in London promoted the transmission of communicable diseases and increased the risk of injury compared with living in other towns and cities or in the countryside.

ACKNOWLEDGEMENTS

The archaeological excavations at Spitalfields Market in 1991–2007 were generously funded by a number of developers and Museum of London Archaeology (MOLA) is very grateful for their support. The lead developer was the Spitalfields Development Group and we would like to thank, in particular, Mike Bear, Toby Brown and Steve Wood. The various stages of the redevelopment of Spitalfields Market and the surrounding area were funded by individual developers, principally ABN AMRO, Ballymore Properties, City (formerly Corporation) of London, Hammerson UK Properties plc, Mercury Asset Management Ltd, Royal London Asset Management Ltd, St George plc and the London International Finance Futures and Options Exchange. Thanks are also due to Second London Wall Project Management Ltd, in particular Mike Blinco, Max Highfield, Shane Lincoln and Lee Sims. Several main contractors and subcontractors provided invaluable support during the excavations, including Balfour Beatty, Costain, Keltbray, L & B and Sir Robert McAlpine. Thanks are also due to all the members of the design teams, particularly Foster and associates Foggo and Arup.

English Heritage supported the excavations and provided extremely helpful guidance and advice throughout the project: we thank especially Ellen Barnes, Steven Brindle, David Divers, Jane Sidell and Nick Truckle.

Over 150 archaeological staff worked on the Spitalfields sites and our first debt is to the hard work and dedication of these archaeologists. The authors of the MOLA monographs which report the results of these excavations and subsequent post-excavation analyses would very much like to thank the supervisors who ran the excavations, in particular Rosalind Aitken, David Bowsher, Mark Burch, Jessica Cowley, Andy Daykin, Charles Harward, Nick Holder, Isca Howell, Malcolm McKenzie, Adrian Miles, Ken Pitt, Lucy Thompson and Paul Thrale.

The authors of this publication on the medieval burials would, in addition, like to express their gratitude to Ethne Barnes, Alex Bayliss, Megan Brickley, Jane Buikstra, Della Collins Cook, Roberta Gilchrist, Rebecca Gowland, Charles Harward, Simon Hillson, Malin Holst, Rachel Ives, Louise Loe, Simon Mays and the radiography staff at English Heritage, Malcolm McKenzie, Irina Metzler, Piers Mitchell, MOLA IT staff, Don Ortner, Peter Rauxloh, Charlotte Roberts, Judith Sture, Sarah Tatham, the late William (Bill) White and other colleagues at MOLA and the Museum of London, and all the volunteers and field staff at Spitalfields Market, especially Alan Aris.

1

Introduction

Brian Connell, Rebecca Redfern and Christopher Thomas

1.1 Background to the project

The medieval priory and hospital of St Mary Spital was originally founded in about 1197 by a group of wealthy London merchants. The foundation arose as a result of an expanding population and an increased need to provide care for the elderly, sick and infirm. The charity given at St Mary Spital also extended to the poor or wayfarers, such as pilgrims, and women in childbirth (Thomas et al 1997, 104). The initial precinct in the priory was relatively small but was enlarged in 1235 when the establishment was re-founded. The founders issued a new charter which showed that they had acquired new lands for the hospital. Thomas (2004, 43) notes that 'writing some 60 years after the hospital [St Mary Spital] closed John Stow had said that the hospital had 180 beds in its infirmary, making it the largest hospital in London'. Following the dissolution of the priory by Henry VIII in 1539 the area was gradually developed for housing and inhabited by minor members of the aristocracy, while the southern parts of the precinct were used as an artillery ground.

An early cemetery lay to the south of the 12th-century infirmary and a second one, associated with the 1235 rebuilding, lay to the west of the 13th-century infirmary. This part of the site (including the excavated human bones) was the subject of MoLAS monograph 1, by Thomas et al (1997; sites A–F, Table 1). The osteological data from these sites are not included in the present study, but the main findings of the analysis by Conheeney (1997) are brought into the wider discussion.

The main (largest) part of the medieval cemetery occupied areas to the south and east of the church. This was excavated between November 1998 and August 2001 by Museum of London Archaeology (MOLA), formerly the Museum of London Archaeology Service (MoLAS), under the direction of Christopher Thomas. Small-scale archaeological investigations at St Mary Spital had been carried out since 1976, and part of the main cemetery was investigated in 1982 and 1985; in the late 1990s, however, an ambitious programme of urban regeneration meant that further large-scale archaeological investigations were necessary. These investigations resulted in the largest cemetery excavation ever undertaken in Britain to date. For a full account of the history and archaeology of St Mary Spital see Thomas et al (1997), Thomas (2004) and Harward et al (in prep).

This volume provides an analysis of the medieval skeletal assemblage, while there are also three companion volumes, on Roman Spitalfields (McKenzie and Thomas in prep), medieval Spitalfields (Harward et al in prep) and 16th- to 19th-century Spitalfields (Daykin et al in prep). A substantial part of the site lies within a Scheduled Ancient Monument (GL 162), the priory and hospital of St Mary Spital.

The circumstances of excavation

Spitalfields Market covered a total area of approximately 4ha to the east of Bishopsgate, immediately outside the boundaries of the City of London in the London Borough of Tower Hamlets, and about 400m north of the Roman and medieval city walls.

Introduction

The site included the 19th-century market buildings (constructed on the site of the original 17th-century market); the 1928 extension to these; Eden House and the Flower Market, built in the mid 1930s; St Botolph's Hall and the former Central Foundation School for Girls; lorry parks for the use of market suppliers and traders; an office building on Bishopsgate (formerly used by Norwich Union); derelict sites formerly occupied by a post office and a cafe; and both public and private roads.

In 1987, a proposal was agreed to move Spitalfields Market to an out-of-town location, in line with other markets such as Covent Garden and Billingsgate, and to redevelop the site of the existing market. To this end, a new market was opened in Leyton in 1991 and a master plan for development of the existing market was agreed with the local authority in 1994. This plan allowed for wholesale redevelopment of the site but with the preservation of the listed 19th-century market buildings and St Botolph's Hall.

The main archaeological campaign began with a desk-based assessment of the archaeological resource (Thomas 1990) and was followed by an evaluation in 1991 of the redevelopment site within the Scheduled Ancient Monument (Thomas 1992) (Fig 1; site H, Table 1). Previous investigations were carried out by the Department of Greater London Archaeology in 1982 and 1985 on the site of the Central Foundation School for Girls (sites J and K, Table 1), and by the Department of Urban Archaeology on Stothard Place (site M) in 1986; 282–294 Bishopsgate (site N) in 1987; 298–306 Bishopsgate (site G) in 1989; and 274–280 Bishopsgate (site O) in 1990 (Table 1).

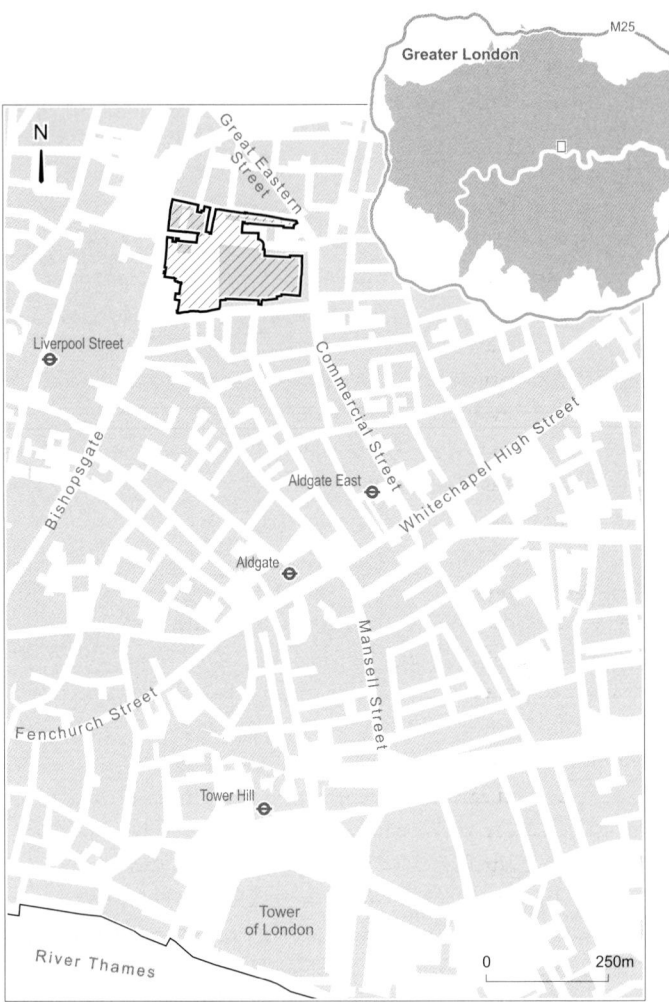

Fig 1 Location of the Spitalfields Market study area, superimposed on the modern Ordnance Survey streetplan (scale 1:15,000)

Table 1 Archaeological fieldwork in the Spitalfields Market study area

Prefix	Address	Site code	Type of fieldwork
A	12–14 Folgate St	FLG82	watching brief
B	1–3 Norton Folgate	NRT85	excavation
C	4–12 Norton Folgate	NRF88	excavation
D	15 Spital Square	SIN88	excavation
E	4 Spital Square	SPQ88	excavation
F	38 Spital Square	SSQ88	excavation
G	298–306 Bishopsgate	BOG89	excavation
H	Spitalfields Scheduled Monument	SPI91	evaluation
I	28–36 Brushfield Street	BFL97	watching brief
J	Central Foundation School for Girls	SPT85	excavation
K	Central Foundation School for Girls	SPT82	evaluation
L	The Curate's House	GBP93	evaluation
M	Stothard Place	STO86	excavation
N	282–294 Bishopsgate	BOS87	excavation
O	274–280 Bishopsgate	PSO90	excavation
P	Spitalfields Residential	SQU94	evaluation, excavation and watching brief
Q	250 Bishopsgate	STE95	evaluation and excavation
R	Spitalfields Market	SPM96	evaluation
S	Old Spitalfields Market	BHF97	watching brief
T	288 Bishopsgate	BGE98	excavation
U	280 Bishopsgate and the Spitalfields Ramp	SRP98	excavation
V	St Botoloph's Hall	BPH87	evaluation
W	St Botoloph's Hall	SSA01	evaluation
X	Eden House	SQR00	evaluation
Y	18 Folgate Street	FOG01	excavation

The northern part of the site was evaluated in 1994 (Thomas 1994) and was developed for residential properties by St George plc between that year and 1998 (site P). It was developed (and therefore investigated) in four phases: phases 1 and 3 as a watching brief; phase 2 as a watching brief and excavation of new pile locations; and phase 4 as a full-scale excavation. This was necessitated by the greater depth of the basement car park, so that the ground floor could be at ground level rather than raised to facilitate access. No archaeological remains survived beneath the former Flower Market. A further phase of works included the evaluation and subsequent watching brief and excavation of a new route for a 33,000 volt cable which was moved, in advance of the main development, from Lamb Street and Spital Square to a route along Folgate Street.

The south-western part of the site, known as 250 Bishopsgate (site Q), was evaluated in 1995 (Dunwoodie 1995) and excavated in 1996 before its redevelopment as the headquarters of ABN AMRO, although no archaeological remains survived under the area, formerly occupied by the Norwich Union offices. The north-western part of the development involved the excavation of previously uninvestigated areas of the former 282–300 Bishopsgate in 1998 in advance of the construction of a new office building, 288 Bishopsgate (site T).

The largest phase of works involved the complete excavation of the northern part of the former lorry park and sites formerly excavated in the 1980s (280 Bishopsgate), and the excavation of the northern part of Steward Street, together with Spital Square and Lamb Street, for the construction of an underground ramp to service 250 and 280 Bishopsgate and the proposed new buildings of Bishop Square (site U). This work included uncovering the east wall of the medieval priory church in order to place protection works around it to preserve it during development. Investigations to the west of this wall were confined to achieving this objective and so the full archaeological sequence was not excavated, except in two small areas where the realignment of a deep-level sewer was required. During this phase of works a well-preserved medieval cemetery chapel was uncovered. It was agreed to preserve this building within the new development, and together with a surrounding berm it was not fully excavated.

The basement of the extension to Spitalfields Market was evaluated in 1996 (site R; Thomas 1996). The north-western part was excavated in 2000, while the building was still standing, as there were substantial numbers of medieval burials there (site U).

The southern part of Steward Street (site U) was excavated in 2001. The berm to the south of the cemetery chapel was excavated in 2002 so that piles could be constructed to transfer the weight of the new building over the chapel, and at the same time the north-eastern part of the site was excavated in Lamb Street. The remaining areas beneath the market basement, and an additional area immediately to its east, were recorded during an archaeological watching brief in 2002. This entire area was then redeveloped as 1 and 10 Bishop Square. Service trenches to those buildings were monitored in 2002 and 2003. This work included evaluation of an electricity cable route, which uncovered the south wall of the medieval church.

These main phases formed the majority of the excavation of the medieval cemetery and provide the skeletal data analysed for this volume.

Trial pits in the 19th-century Spitalfields Market were observed in 1995 and 2000 (Thomas 2000) and a watching brief was carried out in advance of the construction of new pavilions in 2005 (site S).

The former curate's house next to St Botolph's Hall was evaluated in 1993 (site L; Thomas 1993) and the hall and surrounding areas were evaluated in 2001–2 and 2005 (site W; Harward 2002; Daykin 2005). A watching brief on service trenches and limited excavation were carried out on the site in 2007 before the refurbishment of the hall and the construction of a restaurant and residential properties.

Eden House was primarily evaluated in 1991 (Thomas 1992) but additional structural investigations were monitored in 2000 (Thomas 2001), and the main phase of works was undertaken in 2006 (site X). This involved the excavation of post-medieval deposits on the western side of the site and the preservation of earlier material beneath; the total excavation of the few remaining deep archaeological features beneath the basement; and limited excavation for new services and structural support works on the northern part of the site where there was no basement. Additional service trenches in Spital Square were monitored and a new shaft for a tunnel to the main deep-level sewer was excavated in Spital Square.

Summary of the archaeological context

The medieval cemetery sits within a complex archaeological site, the primary component of which was the priory and hospital of St Mary Spital. The non-cemetery aspects of the site were assigned to seven periods of activity (periods 4 to 10), based upon stratigraphic evidence and dating evidence such as ceramics and coins. The skeletal remains were assigned to four phases, based primarily on stratigraphic grounds and the interpretation of the cemetery layout. This phasing was tested by Alex Bayliss and Jane Sidell through a programme of radiocarbon dating and Bayesian modelling. The final estimation of the accuracy of the skeletal phasing was 84% (Harward et al in prep). The radiocarbon dates provided the following chronological framework for the cemetery. Burial on the site (period 14) started between 1040 and 1155, most probably 1090–1145; period 15 is estimated to have commenced between 1170 and 1210, most probably 1180–1205; period 16 between 1230 and 1260, most probably 1235–55; and period 17 between 1365 and 1410, most probably 1380–1400. Burial is likely to have ceased between 1485 and 1525, most probably (68% probability) between 1485 and 1510, but possibly when the priory closed in 1539.

Sidell et al (2007) outline how the phasing results were achieved using Bayesian modelling. Three alternative models were tested in order to address the issue of the marine reservoir effect, the first based on terrestrial calibration, the

Introduction

second on an offset of 10±5% marine carbon and the third an offset of 20±5% marine carbon. The conclusion was that the difference between the results of the three models did not significantly alter the date ranges. In addition, the average $\delta^{13}C$ value for the individuals tested was 19.6‰, suggesting that marine resources did not form a significant part of their diet, which is consistent with the low quantities of fish bone recovered from the site, and historical sources which indicate that trade in marine fish was significant in London only in the later medieval period.

To summarise, the four principal period designations used throughout this report are: period 14, c 1120–c 1200; period 15, c 1200–50; period 16, c 1250–c 1400; and period 17, c 1400–1539 (assuming use continued up until the closure of the monastery) (Fig 2). Full details of all the radiocarbon dates, with a discussion of the phasing, can be found in Harward et al (in prep). Individuals and accessioned finds from site U, the subject of this report, are referred to, respectively, by context number (eg [12441]) and accession number (eg <2678>), omitting the site prefix letter.

The cemetery seems to have been in use before the founding of the hospital c 1197. The land on which it stood seems to have lain behind a developing extramural settlement lining Bishopsgate. There is no documentation relating to this early cemetery, so its origins and location remain unexplained: but extramural medieval cemeteries not associated with a religious foundation are sufficiently rare that some form of interpretation is required. The cemetery may have been associated with another religious establishment but physically distant from it. The later associations between St Mary Spital and St Paul's are sufficiently strong that it could be argued that the cemetery was in some way associated with St Paul's: the land itself was certainly in the ownership of the Bishop of London. This early phase of the cemetery also included a significant number of burials in large pits, which were originally excavated as quarry pits, probably in the first half of the 12th century, and subsequently reused for burial. It is possible that one of the initial reasons for the foundation of this cemetery was to provide an emergency burial ground to deal with periods of unusually high mortality.

The priory and hospital of St Mary Spital had been founded by the beginning of the 13th century, but analysis of the documentation indicates that it lay on a plot adjacent to the

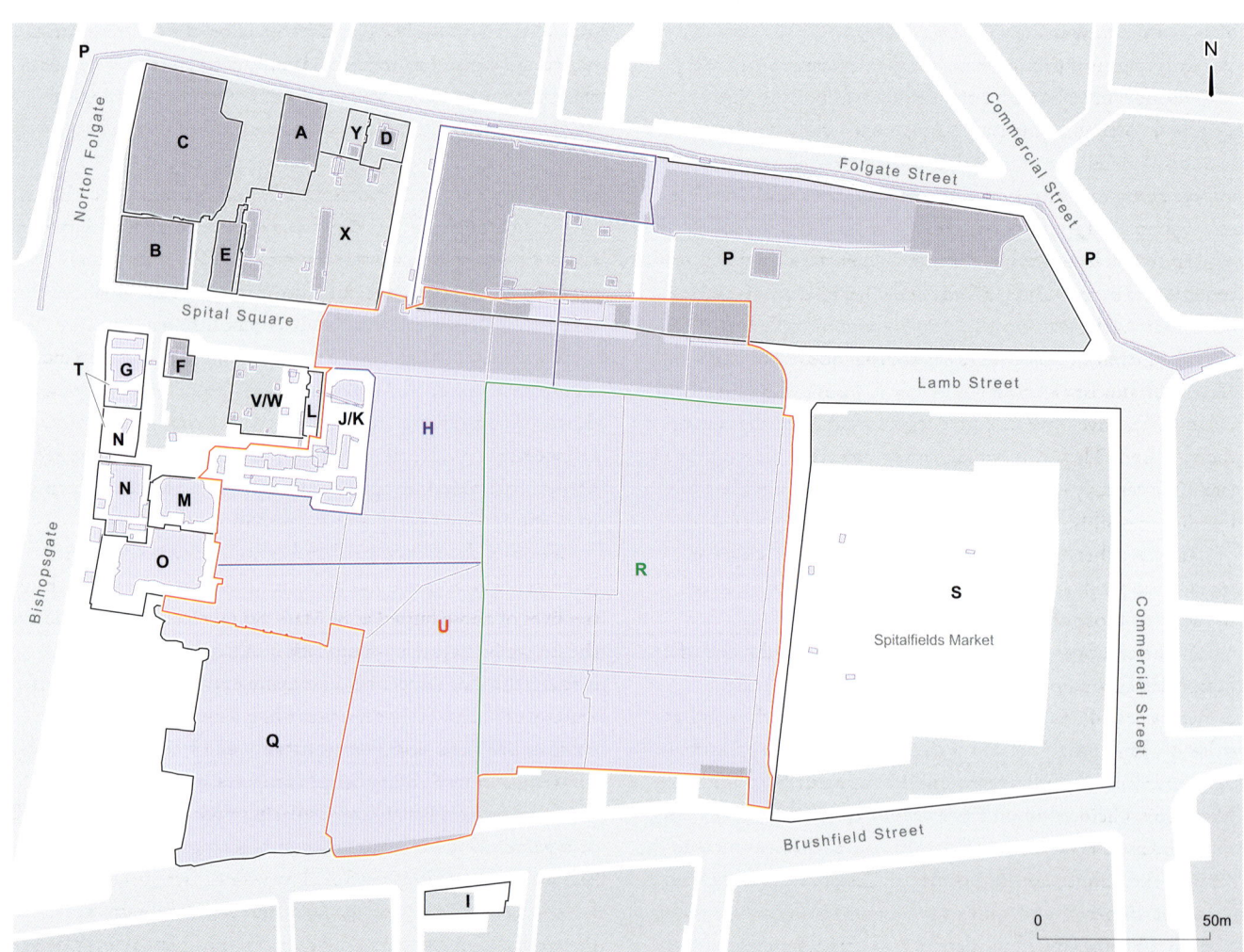

Fig 2 Location within the Spitalfields study area of the archaeological investigations listed in Table 1 (scale 1:2000)

cemetery and had its own burial ground (Thomas et al 1997, 19–23). The hospital was subsequently re-founded in 1235 on a much larger plot of land that included the main cemetery. Until about 1280, the infirmary used a separate cemetery, which has been fully excavated (Thomas et al 1997, 37–40); its continued use suggests that the main cemetery was not used for hospital burials until after this date, although it may have been used for burials of the canons, lay staff, residents or benefactors from 1235.

In the mid 13th century, large, purpose-dug pits were dug in two broad phases, and together contained many thousands of interments. The period 15 pits (ie those dating from before *c* 1250) had commonly between 10 and 20 individuals in each; those dating from period 16 (after *c* 1250) each contained 20–40 individuals. The period 15 pits were dug on a WNW–ESE alignment while the period 16 pits were dug east–west. In many cases the period 16 pits, though designed to lie between the rows of period 15 pits, actually cut through their ends, truncating many of the burials. A significant number of complete limbs in the period 16 pits did not originate from the individuals within them, indicating that the bodies in the period 15 pits had not completely decomposed by the time the period 16 pits were dug, which would have allowed individual bones to become disarticulated. This suggests that the period 16 pits must date to no more than a few years after the period 15 pits, perhaps as little as a single year.

Early in the 14th century, a chapel dedicated to St Mary Magdalene and St Edmund the Bishop was built in the cemetery. Although the chapel had been totally destroyed towards the end of the 17th century, its charnel house survived mostly complete. The lower storey was partly subterranean, and was entered by a door in the east wall. The base of a flight of stone stairs leading to the upper chapel was discovered in the west wall. There were originally six slit windows, splayed on the inside, in the south wall. Originally used to store bones disturbed from the cemetery, the charnel house had been cleared of almost all human remains at around the time of the Dissolution, save for a pile near the stairs and another group at the west end. The central vault of the cemetery chapel reused a late 12th-century chevron moulded arch from an earlier building, possibly an earlier chapel in the cemetery (Fig 3).

Various other burial pits in the cemetery were dug and filled, possibly in the early part of the 14th century, but not on the scale of those of the mid 13th century.

At the end of the 14th century, and marking the end of period 16, a stone pulpit was built in the centre of the cemetery (Fig 4). Sermons were held here on Sundays and a cycle of sermons at Easter was shared with St Paul's; St Paul's held sermons on Good Friday and Easter Saturday while St Mary Spital held them on Easter Monday, Tuesday and Wednesday. It is possible that large parts of the cemetery to the west of the pulpit went out of use at this point, although a group of 15th-century tombs were constructed in this area. Significant numbers of children were buried immediately north of the pulpit and to the east of the cemetery chapel, suggesting that these areas were specifically chosen for the burial of children.

The cemetery continued in use throughout the 15th century and presumably up until the Dissolution (1539), although the radiocarbon dating suggests that it may have ceased to be used in the early 16th century (*c* 1500).

Aims and objectives of the monograph

In Britain, and indeed in Europe as a whole, an archaeological cemetery excavation that produces an extremely large sample of skeletons (more than 1000) is rarely encountered. The total number of individuals excavated from St Mary Spital stands at a staggering 10,516 skeletons. The scale of this sample is both unprecedented and unparalleled, but the Herculean task of examining the material was simplified with the help of research aims developed following the MAP2 assessment (Connell 2002).

The principal aim of the monograph is to examine demographic and palaeopathological trends from the 12th to 16th centuries, as revealed by the excavated human remains and with specific references to the cause of death among those buried in the numerous burial pits. To achieve this aim, patterns are discussed within a chronological narrative, charting changes in population structure and disease frequency.

To provide the reader with an understanding of the nature of the skeletal assemblage, and knowledge of how the team of bioarchaeologists recorded the data, a materials and methods chapter sets out the techniques used during the osteological project and the criteria used in the creation of a sampling strategy. The information gained from the osteological analysis is then analysed and discussed in relation to a number of broad themes, including the local and wider environment of London. An attempt is also made to integrate skeletal, cultural and contextual data in order to explore the impact of work, housing, diet, migration and status on health.

To chronicle intra-site variation, differences between men and women, adults and children and different burial types are discussed in relation to funerary treatment and health status. It is important to remember that St Mary Spital functioned as a hospital: the role of hospitals in this period is therefore discussed in relation to well-being and the provision of treatment.

The burials are compared and contrasted with those from other cemeteries in the London area in order to document how the lives of those buried at St Mary Spital changed in relation to the dynamic, expanding population of London itself. We are fortunate in this respect because many excavations have taken place over the past 20 years, providing a broad base of comparative data. Another important aim of the monograph is to examine how St Mary Spital compares with other medieval cemeteries across Britain, particularly in relation to urban–rural differences, in order to place the cemetery population in a national context. St Mary Spital provides a firm foundation from which to investigate patterns and trends in human biocultural adaptation in a large urban centre from north-west Europe; accordingly the health status of Londoners is also explored from an international perspective.

Introduction

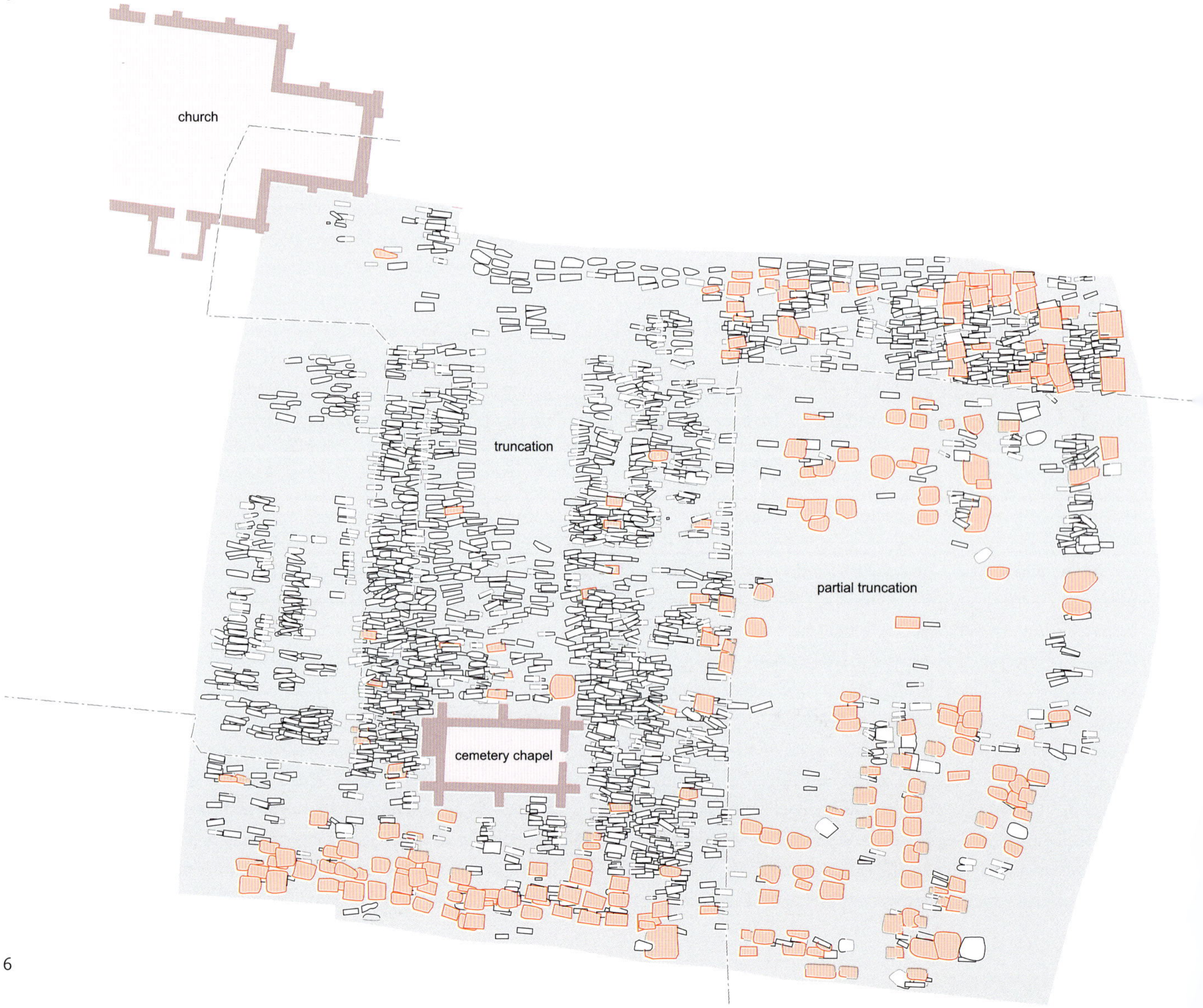

a

N

c

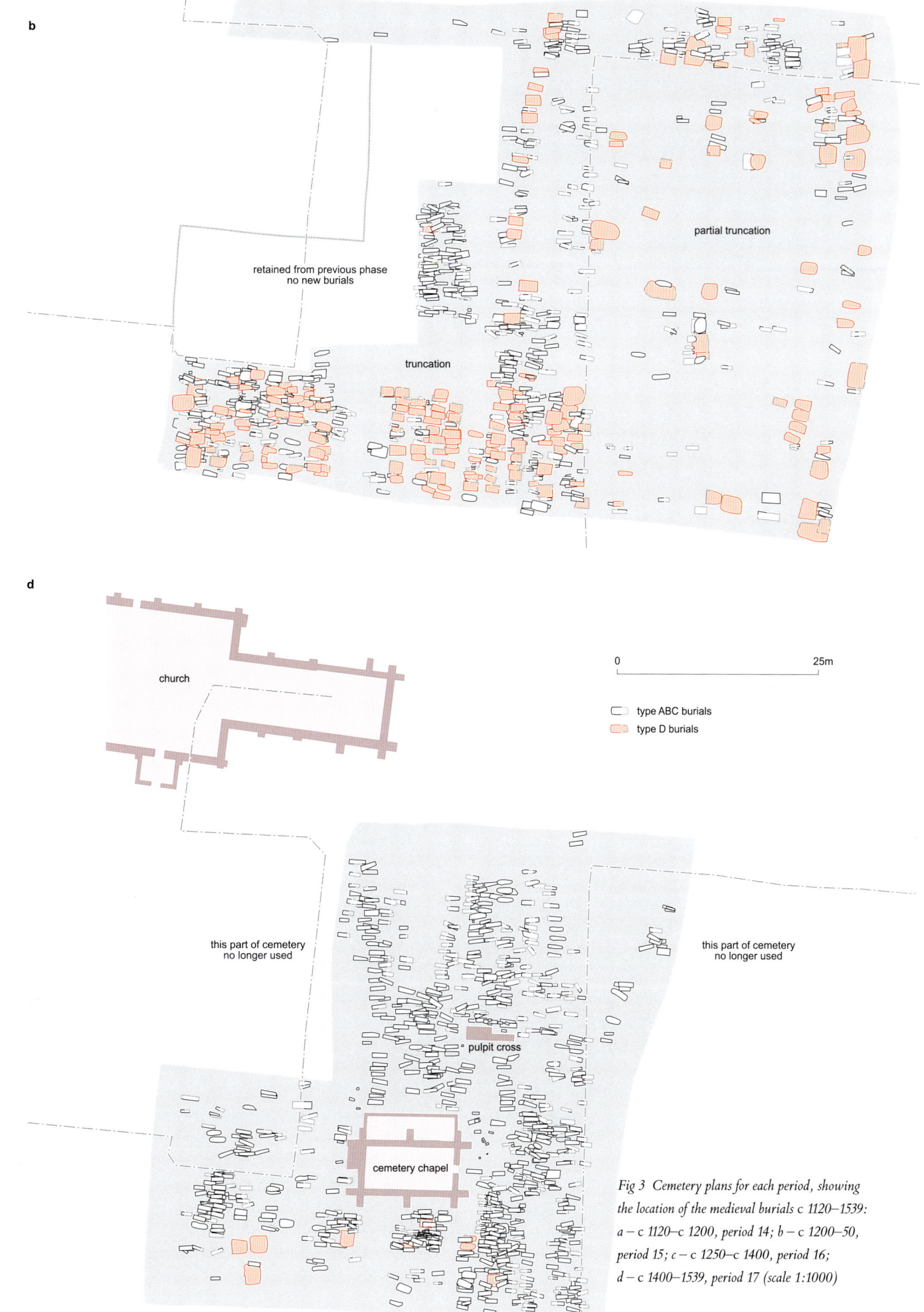

Fig 3 Cemetery plans for each period, showing the location of the medieval burials c 1120–1539: a – c 1120–c 1200, period 14; b – c 1200–50, period 15; c – c 1250–c 1400, period 16; d – c 1400–1539, period 17 (scale 1:1000)

Introduction

Fig 4 The 14th-century cemetery chapel under excavation, looking east

1.2 The hospital in an urban context

Many hospitals were built in Britain during the medieval period. Thomas et al (1997, 2) note that at least 200 hospitals were founded as charitable institutions in the 12th century, and perhaps as many as 300 in the 13th century. In London, hospitals tended to be located on major routes, and St Mary Spital was situated on the northern road out of the city (Fig 5), a location which was crucial to its development: it has been noted that towns tended to expand along major routes to and from city centres (Roberts and Cox 2003, 229), and most of the principal routes into and out of the City of London had a hospital located nearby (Thomas et al 1997, 125). The locations of these hospitals were well known, and there would have been a steady flow of travellers, pilgrims, the disabled and sick.

As well as topographic considerations, the social function of the hospital of St Mary Spital must be borne in mind when discussing the nature of the cemetery population. In a hospital-derived sample we might expect an exaggerated prevalence of disease and treatment relative to the overall population (Waldron 1994). Skeletal assemblages from cemeteries associated with infirmaries might also be strongly biased in terms of selective mortality. Hospitals had a variety of roles in society, and here demographic factors come into play. Gilchrist and Sloane (2005) conducted a large-scale study of monastic cemeteries in Britain which included an examination of the social function of hospitals. They pointed to demographic specialisations and suggested that suburban infirmaries catered for younger males, perhaps rural migrants (ibid, 206).

In a medieval hospital, care would be provided more on a religious basis than on a medical one as we might understand it today. For many minor ailments the provision of good, regular meals, shelter and rest might have been all that was required for a sick individual to recover or heal sufficiently to return to his or her previous life. Obviously, this would not apply to more serious, life-threatening or debilitating conditions, but under these circumstances St Mary Spital could provide care for the dying. Following a death in the infirmary, some individuals might be buried in the cemetery, with attendant religious ceremony, and perhaps extension of the hospital's spiritual care to the friends or family of the deceased. The role of the hospital is discussed in detail in Chapter 4.2.

The hospital in an urban context

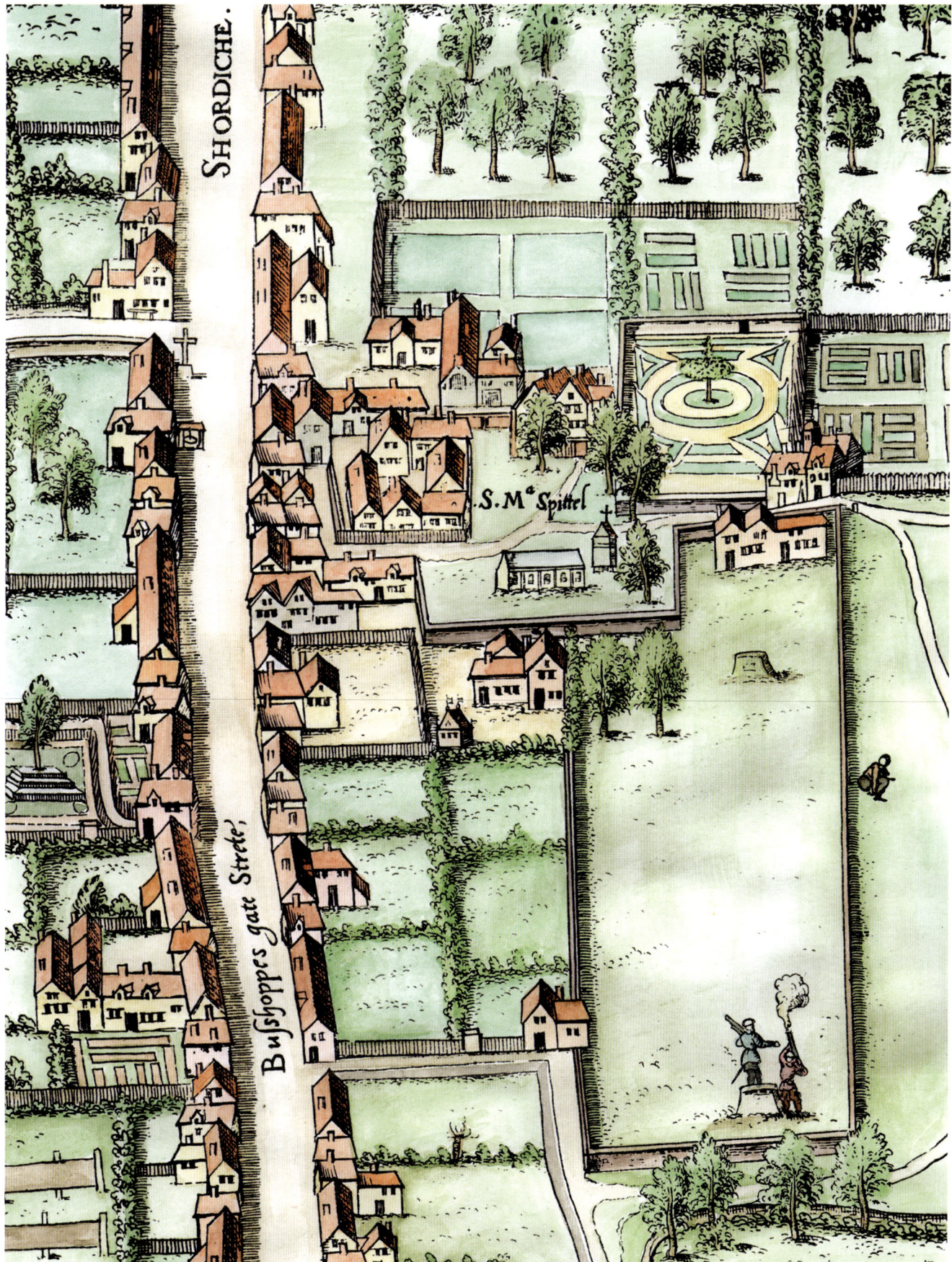

Fig 5 Detail from a copperplate map of c 1559, showing Bishopsgate and the area of the former precinct of St Mary Spital; the artillery ground to the right lies over the former cemetery (Guildhall Library; Saunders and Schofield 2001)

Introduction

Health, urban environments and the environment of medieval London

Health in urban environments

The relationship between an individual and the urban environment has been shown directly to affect health and well-being. Multi- and inter-disciplinary research has demonstrated that the urban environment influences (among other things) growth, diet and the diseases suffered, with individuals experiencing social and environmental buffers or stressors mediated by their genetic predisposition, social status and access to socio-economic resources (McElroy and Townsend 1996, 25). Schell and Ulijaszek (1999, 6) note that a biocultural approach is needed to understand these links. The analysis of the biological response to urban environments enables us to assess the influence of culture on health (Schell 1992, 139).

Saunders (2002, 1) states that our search to create an 'ideal' environment is expressed in the creation of towns and cities. Urban environments are not homogeneous but are made up of numerous micro-environments shaped by urban planning, building construction and individual dwellings, all of which have a direct impact on daily life (Fitzpatrick and LaGory 2000, 61). Each city has its own distinctive character and culture, being made up of different ethnic and cultural groups, causing differences in daily life, disease and local environment (Tuan 1978; Schell and Ulijaszek 1999, 9). These stressors often differ between urban and rural environments (Schell 1997, 68; Schell and Ulijaszek 1999, 3, 11).

Towns and cities differ from rural centres in a number of important ways. They rely on safe and adequate foodstuffs being brought in from the surrounding areas. Urban dwellers have different levels of physical activity mediated by age, gender, occupation and lifestyle. Cities and towns need migrants to sustain their population, which dictates their demography, and also to support specialist professions, which have their own risks of disease and mortality. Population densities are higher, while air quality, waste disposal and hygiene practices are generally worse (Ulijaszek 1999, 254; Coleman 1999, 119; Bogin 2001, 191; Cohen and Crane-Kramer 2003, 90). Bioarchaeological research has demonstrated the differences between rural and urban populations, including disparities in health status. For example, Brothwell's (1994) analysis of urban–rural differences in Yorkshire concluded that the urban dead had suffered higher rates of trauma, indicators of stress (in the form of Harris lines) and infection. Table 2 shows that while both urban and rural communities were exposed to the same stressors (eg zoonoses), urban dwellers had a higher risk because the population was larger, there was greater population movement, and the living environment was more crowded.

The range of cultural buffers will be more diverse in an urban area, because ethnic and cultural distinctions influence behaviour, local environment, diet, activity pattern and exposure to risk (Schell and Ulijaszek 1999, 3, 9). Consequently, comparisons between urban and rural populations 'can only detect the sum result of all such factors acting on any biological outcome of difference' (ibid, 7).

Palaeopathological analysis of subadult health in pre-industrial societies suggests that archaeologically derived subadults from urban centres had sustained greater levels of biological stress and that this had resulted in higher mortality rates than those seen among their rural counterparts (Storey 1992, 40–1). This is supported by Lewis's (2003) study of urban–rural differences in medieval England.

Migration and urban centres

Migration is central to the understanding of urban health: it can result in the reduction of a population's well-being, demonstrated by poor growth, greater mortality at all ages and compromised health. Rural-to-urban migrants have higher rates of disease and are susceptible to diseases from both their new environment and their place of origin, although their initial health status is better than those who did not migrate. Children born to settled urban migrants have a greater chance of survival compared to their rural counterparts, and in contrast to children born before their families migrate, have a lower mortality risk (Harrison et al 1988, 520; Bogin 2001, 192–219).

In the late medieval period, the majority of the British population lived in nucleated rural settlements and engaged in mixed agriculture (Dyer 1998). Settlements were usually located near sources of water, with homes arranged around a road or a green, and had a population of less than 200, although communities of 500 people were not unknown. These

Table 2 Disease stressors present in rural and urban environments (Lewis 2003; Roberts and Cox 2003, 229)

Stressor	Rural environment	Urban environment
Zoonoses (from livestock and secondary products, ie skins)	yes	yes
Contaminated water supply due to waste disposal practices	no	yes
Crowded living conditions	no	yes
High population movement	no	yes
Food contamination	yes	yes
Poor air quality (burning of coal/wood)	yes	yes
Occupation (exposure to heavy metals etc)	yes	yes
Poor waste disposal practices	no	yes
Reliance upon food imports	no	yes

communities were predominantly comprised of peasant farmers, whose lives were governed by the controlling laws of the feudal system. This dictated land tenure and the giving of service to the manor lord. Many social aspects of medieval life, such as permission to marry or migrate, were subject to feudal control. Rural communities consisted of small nuclear families who often shared their living space with livestock in the winter. Rural communities did not remain static, as settlements, livelihoods and population size were directly affected by famines, plagues and warfare. These catastrophic events could devastate the rural economy, causing a dramatic decrease in the size of the rural population and desertion of many settlements. They could also instigate population movement, particularly to towns (Singman 1999, 67, 83; Dyer 1998, 109–87).

Although the reasons for urban migration would have been complex, the rural economy would not have been able to provide everyone with an adequate living, and many were thus faced with long-term impoverishment: economic deprivation was probably the biggest motivating factor for migration to urban centres (Dyer 2002, 187). Specialised crafts undertaken by both sexes, including spinning, metalworking, leather working, textile production and brewing, provided many individuals with skills that enabled them to find employment in towns, as discussed in Chapter 4.1. The migration of predominantly children and young adults from rural areas and smaller towns ensured that larger settlements continued to thrive, despite the fluctuations in population size which occurred throughout the medieval period in response to catastrophic events. Consequentially, urban populations developed a different demographic profile from that of rural settlements. This in turn influenced the disease patterns observed in urban cemeteries (Brothwell 1994, 129, 134; Dyer 1998, 188–93).

An overview of the environment of medieval London

During the 11th and 14th centuries, urban areas expanded and developed rapidly. This development halted in the mid to late 14th century and 15th century due to a series of catastrophic events, which resulted in an international decrease in population (Singman 1999, xi). In the period under study, London was the only urban centre in England that was comparable to cities on the Continent (Nicholas 1997a; 1997b). It was surrounded by suburbs, drawing on the surrounding rural areas for food, people and natural resources (McDonnell 1978; Thomas 2002, 66). When examining health in medieval London we are therefore seeing the biological consequences of urban, suburban and rural ways of life. The environment of medieval London is discussed in detail in Chapter 4.1.

CLIMATE AND WEATHER

At the macro-scale of environmental conditions, the period between the late 12th and mid 15th centuries was one of climatic change, with the ending of the medieval warm epoch and the beginning of the little ice age. During the little ice age, cooling temperatures caused shorter growing seasons, longer winters and wetter weather, which affected food production, reducing the amount of viable agricultural land and causing a decrease in cod fishing (Brimblecombe 1982, 11; Fagan 2000; Howe 1997, 32; Lamb 1995). The rapid deterioration in London's climate and its consequences for food and wine production were noted in William Gregory's chronicle for the period 1189–1249, in which he recorded that 'yere were grete tempestys of wedyr ande raynes … ande hyale stonys the grettenys of eggys fylle downe a monge the rayne, where of treys and vynys … ande alle maner of frute were gretely dystryde' (Gregory 1876). As today, medieval London acted as a 'heat island', being significantly warmer than surrounding areas, and would have experienced markedly different wind and rainfall patterns from the surrounding suburbs and rural areas.

PUBLIC SERVICES AND WASTE DISPOSAL

London, although undoubtedly unpleasant by modern Western standards, was considered to be more sanitary than cities on the Continent as it had introduced city ordinances and employed street cleaners. From 1303 onwards, city streets began to be paved, with each ward electing a street inspector (Nicholas 1997b, 333–4; Dyer 1998, 191). Rolls of the City of London in 1343 record that on 18 July, Simon de Warfeld was prosecuted for 'throwing stinking trade-refuse into the street … notwithstanding frequent warnings, and also calling John Causton, Alderman, opprobrious names' (Thomas 1926, roll A4, m 9). Waste disposal was taken seriously, even though the link between contagions and health was not known at this time (Nutton 1983, 14), and by the 13th century piped water was provided from a public building, adding to the numerous public wells, fountains and washing-places (Thomas 2002, 73–4). The primary pollutant was organic waste from industries and private housing (Nicholas 1997b, 331).

HOUSING

Most housing, both within and outside the city, was constructed from timber and wattle and daub. Only rich citizens had stone houses (Schofield and Vince 2003, 85). Plot size varied throughout the city, and space was also dependent upon individual socio-economic status. Plots could contain many buildings: for example, small, two-cell strip dwellings were often built in front of larger buildings (ibid, 80–8). Excavations at the waterfront have shown that in the 14th century housing density was very high (Grenville 1997, 190). Building construction within the City of London was subject to legislation, with the assize of buildings regulating wall thickness, roof design and building materials (organic material was banned) (Schofield and Vince 2003, 108). Many urban properties were multistorey and had internal chimneys and staircases or ladders (Dyer 1998, 203).

Living conditions were influenced by the method of construction, location and size of the housing, with the occupier determining levels of cleanliness. Many homes were poorly ventilated and had particulate-laden atmospheres from the burning of coal or wood fires and oil or fat lamps. Floors were made from cobbles or flagstones, or comprised organic matter laid on a packed earth floor, which would have been infrequently changed. Archaeological evidence from the deserted medieval village of Wharram Percy in North Yorkshire suggests that the chalk floors there were regularly swept, although floors would have been damp, whatever flooring material was used (Dyer 1998, 168; Thomas 2002, 72).

ECONOMY AND TRADE

The suburbs of London consisted of open spaces, woodlands, meadows and fields. These extramural areas were exploited by many industries and workers, such as millers, bakers, fisheries, brick and tile makers, and the more polluting trades, such as fulling and tanning, which were not allowed to operate within the City of London (McDonnell 1978, 23, 57; Nicholas 1997b, 331). Agriculture was also important, with dairy and sheep farms and crops of cereals and legumes. Farming would have employed people living in suburban areas, as well as city dwellers and migrants from rural areas (McDonnell 1978, 54, 58–9; Keene 1990, 99, 114–17). However, over time, many of the open spaces and areas of agricultural land were taken over by industry and housing, for example in Thameside and Whitechapel during the 15th century. Development was particularly focused along the important roads running north and east: Ermine Street left Bishopsgate leading north, and another ran from Aldgate to Essex and East Anglia (McDonnell 1978, 67).

London, the most prominent trading centre in England at this time, imported considerable quantities of exotic fruit, cereals, nuts, vegetables and spices from the Continent and Far East (Hammond 1998, 60–1). For meat, the city relied on the surrounding suburbs and hinterland. As London was a trading centre for fish, it is more likely that if people were constrained from eating fish, it was for economic reasons (Dyer 2000, 102–9). People obtained fish from local and national sources: the salting of fish enabled it to be transported great distances, and many estates (including St Mary Spital) kept large fishponds to provide a ready supply of freshwater fish (Barrett et al 2004; Barrett et al 2008; Dyer 2000, 101; Schofield and Vince 2003, 227). Throughout most of the medieval period, diet was dominated by cereals, supplemented by meat and fish (Dyer 2000, 98). Fresh vegetables and fruit were sourced from the suburbs, whereas cereals and grain were brought in from counties such as Berkshire, Oxfordshire and Surrey by boat (Galloway 2000; Thomas et al 1997, 127).

The medieval city and suburbs of London were mutually dependent environments, which relied upon the movement of people, animals and goods. These interactions formed the pathways of disease and influenced patterns of health. By analysing this evidence using a bioarchaeological approach it is possible to assess how people adapted to living in the dynamic environment of London.

Socio-cultural change during the medieval period

To fully understand how the patterns identified from the human remains relate to a socio-cultural context it is important to acquire an overview of the events that affected the population of London during the 12th to 16th centuries. Many factors would have influenced how London's population grew and developed, and the rate of that growth. There have been massive shifts in population structure as London's population rapidly expanded and was then affected by a series of catastrophic events. The population of London grew steadily as the result of intrinsic expansion and migration from the rural areas around it. During the 12th to 16th centuries migration would have played a key role in sustaining the economic expansion of the city as young workers moved into large towns and cities seeking employment. Medieval migrants would have journeyed to London from all parts of England, but until the mid 13th century most came from the Home Counties (those bordering London) and the south-east (Sheppard 1998, 115).

In addition to the intrinsic health issues of migration, increased settlement density resulting from the influx of migrant workers has implications for sanitation, hygiene and the spread of communicable disease. Rapid population expansion and increased settlement density meant a transition from a rural to an urban lifestyle for these migrant workers. Increased trade also provided the opportunity for the introduction of new diseases into the community (Lewis 2002, 5).

Throughout the medieval period London was populated principally by immigrants, drawn from every social class. During the 13th century, London witnessed a period of particularly rapid growth, during which the population may have doubled. This led to an increase in the density of the street grid as the construction of new lanes subdivided existing plots, in response to the need for more housing (Thomas 2002, 66).

This expansion was soon checked by one of the first major crises to face London's unsuspecting residents: the Great Famine of 1315–18, which began with a poor harvest in 1314, and was succeeded by two years of wet weather and disastrous harvests (Dyer 2002, 229). This was followed by an event of national significance. The Black Death of 1348–9 is thought to have wiped out up to one-third of London's population (Thomas 2002, 113). Its effects were devastating: all the available evidence indicates that the population of London did not reach pre-plague levels again until the early 16th century (Bailey 1996, 2; Sheppard 1998, 92). The Black Death not only killed thousands but also had a serious economic impact; no other event in London's history has been quite so disastrous (Thomas 2002, 169). A measure of its scale is provided by Dyer (2002, 233) who notes that its effects were universal – no village, town or region for which records exist escaped.

Frequent epidemics during the medieval period not only killed many but would have left in their wake distorted demographic structures that would have severely inhibited the reproductive ability of the population (Hatcher 1996, 68). The disruption to social and economic life would have been compounded by massively increased mortality levels and the loss of social cohesion. People would have also fled from London during the Black Death. Despite the catastrophic nature of events like famine and plague, there is no evidence to suggest that the government of London took any initiative in coping with the crisis (Barron 2004, 239), probably because they could not have been expected to anticipate mortality on such a scale (ibid). Despite the ability of London to attract immigrants from other parts of England, there can be little doubt that the city in the later medieval period suffered from substantial and long-term population decline (ibid). Fortunately, the decline in the size of the population did not result in London's economic disintegration.

Hatcher (1996, 63) suggests that it is mistaken to assume that demographic decline could only be affected by national epidemics of spectacular proportions, and points to the fact that there is every reason to believe that the cumulative impact of lesser and local epidemics could be equally serious. This effect could be increased if the young were afflicted in disproportionately higher numbers (ibid). In terms of the living population of London at the time, Barron (2004, 239) makes the interesting point that it is not certain when the Black Death outbreak occurred in 1348, and whether the population was static or rising at this time. This has important demographic implications for St Mary Spital in terms of the 'non-stationarity' of the contributing population (see Wood et al 1992). The lack of statistics means that any analysis of late medieval demography has to content itself with broad speculation about basic changes in overall birth and death rates (Bailey 1996, 2).

Intra-cemetery variation

Layout of the cemetery

The medieval skeletons from St Mary Spital form the largest collection of human skeletons from a documented archaeological context in Europe. The cemetery is not only very large, but also very complex. This complexity arises from the number of different burial practices used and the fact that the assemblage can be subdivided into temporally distinct phases. Both these factors have important implications for the investigation of those buried at St Mary Spital, as they allow us to break down the skeletal sample into smaller groups which can be used to compare and contrast patterns in the data, spatially and over time, charting changes in the population as a whole.

Burial practices

About half the bodies were buried in single graves, classified as burial type A, and half in multiple graves (Fig 6). Using the stratigraphic data it was possible to create a series of further subdivisions of burial type based on two factors: the number of bodies per grave and the arrangement of those bodies within the grave. Where more than one corpse had been placed in a grave, they could be arranged in horizontal groups, vertical stacks, or both. A single horizontal layer of bodies, often two or three in a row, is classified as burial type B (typically consisting of two to seven bodies); where bodies were stacked directly on top of one another (typically two to 11 bodies deep) this is classified as a stacked multiple burial, or burial type C (Fig 6).

For analytical purposes, all skeletons from burial types A, B and C were pooled and are referred to as burial type ABC. These burials reflect the general level of mortality in the living population during the 350-year use of the cemetery; thus burial type ABC is referred to as the attritional cemetery in Chapter 4.

Multi-layered burials, with bodies buried in a number of horizontal rows stacked on top of each other within a single grave cut, are classified as burial type D (typically eight to 45 bodies) (Fig 6).

The multiple and multi-layered burial pits tended to be furthest away from the church, and were divided into two broad phases (Thomas et al 1997, 119). An initial phase, containing 10 to 20 bodies per grave, had been cut through by a second phase of larger pits. There were many such burials which varied in size, ranging from double and triple inhumations to burial pits containing up to 45 people. These reflect burials that took place within a narrow timescale (within days or a week) and, because there were so many corpses to dispose of, they are considered to be the result of a catastrophe. This is discussed further in Chapter 4, where burial type D is referred to as the catastrophic group.

In some cases it was not possible to classify whether a multiple burial was of type B, C or D, and so these were classified as burial type E. Type E only applied to a handful of individuals and these were not included in the study sample.

Source population

Burial first began in the cemetery associated with St Mary Spital, Open Area 2 (OA2), between 1197 and 1235 (Thomas et al 1997). Within the cemetery, which forms the focus of this study, burials were made in four principal periods as outlined in Chapter 1.1.

Earlier excavations at St Mary Spital revealed skeletons buried within the church (Building 100). Some documentary evidence exists for these burials (Thomas et al 1997, 120) but

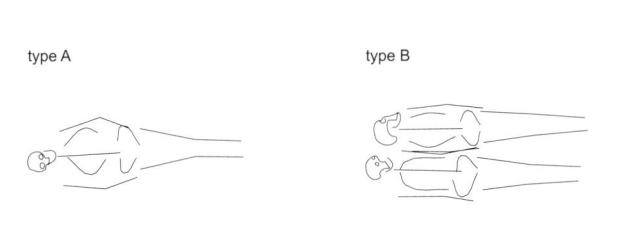

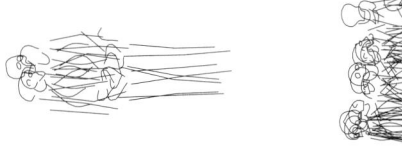

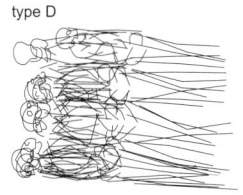

Fig 6 Examples of typical burial types

Introduction

they are the exception, as generally there are no surviving records or accounts of those buried in the main cemetery. Nevertheless, it is important briefly to consider the types of people buried in the cemetery at St Mary Spital. Since the priory had a hospital function, and indeed was one of London's largest hospitals, it is reasonable to expect that many inmates from the infirmary were buried here. The cemetery would also have catered for the religious community, including monks and lay sisters – whose function was equivalent to that of modern-day nurses (Thomas et al 1997, 119) – and to their wealthy benefactors.

Those of higher social status are most likely to have been afforded a 'high-status burial', for example one close to or within the church buildings. Archaeological evidence of priestly burials was seen, with seven burials accompanied by a symbolic pewter chalice and paten (Thomas et al 1997, 119). Mays highlights a lack of skeletal assemblages from monastic sites which can be identified confidently as monastic brethren, rather than lay benefactors or patrons (Mays 2006a, 179). Other spatial foci for specific burial types include the pulpit cross, where high-status tombs and a preponderance of infant burials were found; the western entrance to the cemetery from Bishopsgate, where again tombs and grave goods suggesting high-status individuals were seen; and the cemetery chapel, which had a concentration of infant burials on its east side and high-status burials to its west.

Those individuals classified as burial type A are most likely to be a mix of hospital inmates, officials and benefactors, and Thomas et al (1997, 120) suggest that the smaller multiple burials (burial types B and C, containing the bodies of two or more people) might represent people who died on the same day. Questions arise as to whether or not St Mary Spital was acting as an overflow cemetery, since the larger burial pits (burial type D) were used in response to a catastrophic emergency. It is also clear that the cemetery pre-dates the foundation of the hospital and that the buried population exceeds the numbers that might conceivably have been generated by the hospital. It is thus clear that the buried population here was drawn from across London and the wider region. Consequently, although St Mary Spital was a religious foundation, this cemetery population must be considered principally a secular one.

St Mary Spital and other cemeteries in the London region

The excavation of the priory and hospital of St Mary Spital follows a long line of cemetery excavations that have taken place in London. The extensive archaeological work in the post-war period has resulted in the accumulation of an impressive archive of over 17,000 skeletons (including those from St Mary Spital) covering all periods of London's development (White 2006). This massive collection of skeletal material from a single city (held at the London Archaeological Archive and Research Centre) allows the study of cultural, environmental and genetic continuity. The direct comparison of skeletal populations across wider geographic areas, such as between differing countries or climatic zones, can be problematic because of the environmental, social and economic differences that exist between different human groups. However, this problem can effectively be bypassed in London, allowing the city to be viewed as a single economic unit. Pfeiffer (1991) has even suggested that the study of palaeopathology can be relevant from the past to the present in that there is genetic, behavioural and environmental continuity.

During the medieval period, London underwent unrivalled economic growth as a pivotal city in an international system of trade and communications (Keene 1989). Although there are difficulties in estimating the overall size of the living population at any given time, Keene (1989) has suggested that by about 1300 London's population had reached a peak of 80,000–100,000 people. It is the medieval period that dominates London's skeletal archive, represented by over 12,700 skeletons, with the greater bulk of this made up of the 10,516 skeletons from St Mary Spital.

Much of the comparative medieval skeletal material derives from a series of cemeteries attached to monastic houses (Table 3). These include the Augustinian priories of St Mary Merton and Holy Trinity Aldgate, the Cistercian abbeys of St Mary Graces and St Mary Stratford Langthorne, and the Cluniac priory and (later) abbey of St Saviour Bermondsey. Mays (2006a) has noted that it should be possible to investigate differences between monastic orders using dietary indicators or differences in physical activity patterns using skeletal remains.

Table 3 Comparative medieval cemeteries in the London area and their relevance to periods at St Mary Spital

Institution/location	Description	No. of analysed individuals	Date range of burials	Relevant to periods	Reference
St Mary Merton	Augustinian priory	664	c 1117–1538	14–17	Conheeney 2007
Holy Trinity Aldgate	pre-priory cemetery and Augustinian priory (founded 1107 x 1108)	58	c 1040–c 1250	14–15	Conheeney 2005
East Smithfield	Black Death cemetery	634	1348–50	16	Cowal et al 2008
St Mary Graces	Cistercian abbey	378	1350–1539	16–17	Bekvalac and Kausmally 2011
St Mary Stratford Langthorne	Cistercian abbey (Savigniac to 1147)	647	c 1135–1538	14–17	White 2004
St Saviour Bermondsey	Cluniac priory and (later) abbey	193	c 1100–c 1430	14–17	Connell and White 2011
St Nicholas Shambles	parish cemetery	234	c 1000/1050–c 1300	14–16	White 1988; Schofield 1997

However, such an analysis lies outside the scope of this project and monastic cemeteries are used here to provide general comparative data, alongside data from some of the London parish cemeteries. These are discussed below.

London cemeteries attached to Augustinian houses

The Augustinian rule was the most common form of regulation used to govern the lives of hospital inmates (Thomas et al 1997, 3). Excavated material from the cemetery of the Augustinian priory of St Mary Merton (664 individuals) was extensively studied by Conheeney (2007). This sample was subdivided into four major periods. The earliest phase of burials was made in *c* 1117–1222 and is similar in date range to St Mary Spital period 14; this is followed by a phase dated 1222–*c* 1300 which is similar in range to period 15. Later phases of burial at St Mary Merton were made *c* 1300–90 and *c* 1390–1538, both of which are broadly contemporaneous with periods 16 and 17 at St Mary Spital. This makes the sites especially suitable for comparison, being both contemporaneous and of the same religious order.

The site of Holy Trinity Priory, at Aldgate in the City of London, contained burials dated *c* 1040–*c* 1250. The excavated burials (n = 58) were recovered from two separate areas, and were part of a pre-priory cemetery or lay outside the priory church. Although the sample size is smaller than either St Mary Spital or St Mary Merton, it remains appropriate for comparison. Holy Trinity Aldgate was the earliest established Augustinian house in the London area, founded in 1107 or 1108 (Schofield and Lea 2005, 13).

London cemeteries on the site of or attached to Cistercian houses

The two large cemetery samples on the site of or associated with houses of the Cistercian order, St Mary Graces and St Mary Stratford Langthorne, together comprise some 1659 individuals. The first consists of two adjacent samples from the former site of the Royal Mint and is probably the cemetery sample that is most directly suited to comparison with St Mary Spital. It consists of two groups: East Smithfield, a catastrophic cemetery associated with the Black Death of 1348–9, and a later burial ground associated with the abbey of St Mary Graces and dated to 1350–1539 (White 2006, 108). There are further subdivisions within these groups, based on stratigraphically distinct burial types or locations. This site provides the only other catastrophic cemetery sample in Britain which is not associated with warfare and is therefore useful for comparison to St Mary Spital burial type D.

The St Mary Graces sample (378 individuals; Grainger and Phillpotts 2011) can itself be subdivided into three subgroups. The first, containing 199 burials and dated 1350–*c* 1400, is thought to include some of the dead from a further outbreak of plague in 1361–2. It is broadly contemporaneous with St Mary Spital period 16. The second subgroup comes from the abbey churchyard (78 individuals) and the third consists of 101 skeletons from areas distributed throughout the nave, chapels and cloisters of St Mary Graces church.

The East Smithfield group (634 individuals; Cowal et al 2008) can be subdivided into individual burials placed in rows (248 individuals), skeletons from trenches containing multiple burials associated with the Black Death (328 individuals) and a further 11 adult burials, and a smaller number (47 individuals) from an eastern cemetery group.

Together, East Smithfield and St Mary Graces comprise the only other medieval sample from London to produce over 1000 skeletons (1012 individuals) and this has important implications for the statistical validity of patterns found in the data.

St Mary Stratford Langthorne was founded by William de Montfichet in 1135, and transferred to the Cistercians in 1147 (White 2004). This is also a large sample (647 individuals) and therefore can be readily used for comparative purposes. At Stratford Langthorne the skeletons are phased into three periods, *c* 1135–*c* 1230, *c* 1230–*c* 1350 and *c* 1350–1538, the first of which is roughly contemporaneous with St Mary Spital period 14 (*c* 1120–*c* 1200). However, later periods of cemetery use overlap with St Mary Spital, for example falling within both periods 15 and 16 (*c* 1200–*c* 1400) (ibid). Nevertheless, St Mary Stratford Langthorne can still be used for comparative purposes when data sets are pooled.

London cemeteries attached to Cluniac houses

The Cluniac order is represented by a single site, the priory and (later) abbey of St Saviour Bermondsey. Founded in the 1080s, this was the only Cluniac house in Surrey (Dyson et al 2011). This sample of skeletons (193 individuals) dates from *c* 1100 to *c* 1430, which is roughly contemporaneous with St Mary Spital periods 14–16 and extends into period 17 (*c* 1400–1539). The skeletal sample was phased but is treated here as one homogeneous group (Connell and White 2011).

London parish cemeteries

St Nicholas Shambles is a medium-sized sample (234 individuals) from the City of London. The skeletons from this site, an 11th- to 13th-century parish cemetery, were extensively studied by White (1988). This material offers a useful comparison because it is not directly associated with a major religious order. The dating of the cemetery (Schofield 1997) makes it comparable to periods 14–15, overlapping with 16, at St Mary Spital. Another smaller sample, but equally useful for comparison, is that of St Lawrence Jewry churchyard, adjacent to the Guildhall (64 individuals). These burials are dated to between the 11th and mid 13th centuries (*c* 1050–*c* 1270) (White 2007).

The health status of Londoners in bioarchaeological perspective

The need to understand the health of past populations within their bioarchaeological context was recognised from the earliest days of human palaeopathology (Buikstra and Beck 2006), and

Introduction

has been the priority of this monograph, because St Mary Spital represents the largest sample of human remains excavated from an urban context. London was unique in medieval Britain and comparable in size, wealth and economic activity to cities in France, Italy and Germany. Its mercantile and political activity connected it to Europe and beyond through exploration, trade and military activity (Nicholas 1997a, 238; Thomas 2002).

Comparison between medieval cities usually focuses on temporal and spatial changes, with the emphasis on the built environment and trade. In Britain, the majority of bioarchaeological work is directed towards palaeopathology, with publications dominated by case studies (Mays 1997b, 601, 604). This bias limits our ability to characterise patterns of health and disease between populations, and between and within regions, from a temporal perspective (Larsen 1999, 3). This has particular relevance for St Mary Spital due to disparities in sample size between other sites from London and beyond. The dominance within the available literature of case studies focusing on particular categories of disease or rare examples of disease or trauma means that it is difficult to compare like with like, and has led to a paucity of studies directed towards frequently occurring lesions, such as periosteal new bone formation (see Weston 2004; 2008). One factor encountered during analysis of St Mary Spital was the small number of late medieval cemetery publications containing a sufficiently detailed human bone report; many site reports remain unpublished or receive limited distribution as so-called 'grey' literature, making it difficult to access raw data. This situation was further compounded by the considerable variation in data quality and quantity, and the frequent lack of disease prevalence calculated using true prevalence rates. Roberts (2003) and Roberts and Cox (2003, 22–30, 397–401) have outlined and discussed these problems, and conclude that standard methods of recording would minimise such difficulties, as demonstrated in the comparison of St Mary Spital to other London sites (Chapter 4.4).

British studies of human remains rarely place their findings in context by examining similar sites from other countries within Europe. This is due to differences in publication style, methods of recording and the availability of data. As in Britain, many data are published in the form of case studies or disseminated through publications (or conference papers) on specific aspects of health. The issue is further complicated by difficulties in translating specialist reports. Although it has not been possible systematically to compare St Mary Spital with a large city or hospital cemetery from medieval Europe, a range of palaeopathological data from (predominantly) northern Europe has been used (Chapter 4.5). Only two studies (in English) have investigated health in both British and European samples using a standard method of recording. Jakob's (2004) research on early medieval populations (5th–8th centuries AD) from England and south-west Germany has demonstrated that such research can achieve new insights into health, and show how different communities responded to environmental and social change. Tatham's (2004) analysis of 10th- and 12th-century samples from Sweden, France and England has shown that health did vary between populations, and urban dwellers (particularly in France) had higher rates of specific infectious diseases. Unfortunately, only the data provided by Tatham were presented in a manner which allowed them to be systematically compared to those from St Mary Spital.

1.3 Framework for analysis and discussion: a bioarchaeological approach

The structure of this monograph differs from most of those previously published by MOLA as it focuses in detail on a single specialism. Results are presented and tabulated in Chapter 3 and are followed in subsequent chapters by detailed discussion of and conclusions on different aspects of medieval life. The final sections outline the potential to enhance the published analysis with future research.

In order to provide such a synthesised understanding of the human remains from St Mary Spital, a bioarchaeological framework of analysis and discussion has been employed. Ortner (2006, xiv) states that this interpretative tool is the most important development in the study of past human societies. This framework was generated by the field of physical anthropology in the United States, where it is directly associated with the study of human remains. Buikstra and Beck's review of bioarchaeological studies (2006) has shown that the framework can contribute to palaeodemography, biodistance analyses, palaeopathology and funerary research. However, in Britain the term bioarchaeology is not synonymous with human remains, and is most frequently used to refer to all archaeologically derived biological material (Roberts 2006, 418; see for example Hall and Kenward 2006). This cemetery report follows the North American approach, with bioarchaeology defined as 'the contextual analysis of human populations from archaeological sites … focusing on the osteobiography of individuals and the biocultural adaptations of populations as viewed through the lens of archaeological context' (Beck 2006, 83). Within British literature, this type of analysis is frequently termed 'biocultural' as it also connects osteological data with evidence for culture, environment and society (Roberts and Cox 2003, 13); its aims are '(1) to assess the biological condition of human populations and its consequences for the biological and cultural reproduction of the society and (2) to consider the selective effects of culture on the population under study and its survival … the biocultural approach places emphasis on the integration and inter-relatedness of biological and cultural systems' (Bush and Zvelebil 1991, 5).

In the medieval period, individuals were aware of social and economic inequalities based upon differences in status, age and gender, in addition to other determining factors such as ethnicity and religion (Farmer and Pasternak 2003). In recent years, research interests have expanded to include hitherto neglected social groups, such as children, through the use of gender and age theory (Moore and Scott 1997; Crawford 1999; Derevenski 2000; Gilchrist 2000; 2002; Stafford and Mulder-Bakker 2000; Horrox and Ormrod 2006; Youngs 2006). The study of impairment and of other socially excluded groups (eg the elderly) has also received greater attention (Díaz-Andreu et al 2005; Fay 2006; Metzler 2006). Such interests also existed within human bioarchaeology, and were developed by many osteoarchaeologists working on medieval samples who promoted the use of human remains to explore these areas in cemetery reports and specialist articles (eg Fiorato et al 2000; Weis-Krejci 2005; Buckberry and Hadley 2008).

The data generated from the study of human remains affect the interpretation of past societies. One of the basic divisions of these data sets is by biological sex, which has proven to act as a determining factor in health and longevity. Its influence upon the observed data is briefly discussed. The cultural construction of assigning biological sex to an individual based upon his or her skeletal remains, particularly the binary division of osteological data, has been critiqued by many (eg Claassen 1992). Sofaer's discussion of this paradox (2006b, 157–8) concludes that the osteological identification of sex does not have to result in gender becoming a void concept, as it enables a skeleton to be interpreted as a 'product of social action and of biology together'. Sex differences in immune status have been explored by Ortner, who has suggested, based upon clinical findings, that because females have an enhanced immune status, they will have a lower prevalence of specific infectious disease than males and are more likely to display chronic long-term infections (Ortner 1998, 88–9; 2003, 117). However, this suggestion is accepted with caution, as medical research acknowledges that the more complex interactions of the immune system, such as population and individual variation in immune development and function, are not entirely understood (McDade 2003, 121). This situation is made more complex by an individual's susceptibility and response to infectious disease being genetically determined, and by age-related changes in immune response; and these factors are compounded by our incomplete understanding of the influence of the environment, socio-cultural factors and ageing on immune status (Effros 2001; Han et al 2001). A commonly observed trend within palaeodemography is a sex difference in longevity (Chamberlain 2006, 18–19). Throughout life, males have a decreased lifespan, which is considered to reflect multiple factors. From birth females are more able to cope with environmental stress and are better at enduring diseases; even when socio-cultural frameworks disadvantage females, they still achieve a greater life expectancy and lifespan (cf MacIntyre et al 1996, who note that greater female longevity is based upon inconsistent findings). Increased male sensitivity to environmental factors is exacerbated by their involvement in high-risk behaviour or activities, creating a high mortality risk during young adulthood (Stillion 1995, 47–59; Stinson 1985, 123–8; Hazzard 2001). The relationship between sex and frailty in medieval London has recently been explored at St Mary Graces (DeWitte and Bekvalac 2010) and East Smithfield (DeWitte 2009; 2010).

The social sciences have demonstrated that there are three distinct categories of ageing – biological, chronological, and social – which are determined and defined by socio-cultural associations (Binstock and George 2001). Within human osteology we are able to identify biological age (particularly in subadults) but understanding that an individual's health status is influenced by his or her chronological and social ages is crucial. Social anthropology has shown that by the age of ten, children can be heads of households, prinicipal wage earners, and soldiers, or remain as dependants (James 1998, 62), with each role having its own risk of mortality and disease. Gowland's (2006) work showed that a 'life-course' perspective can be effectively employed to understand past communities. This emphasises the role of gender in the timing of age transitions and the accumulative impact of earlier life events as shaped by historical circumstances (Arber and Ginn 1995; Hagestad and Dannefer 2001; Hareven 2001), and enables the bioarchaeologist to challenge the 'unspoken hegemony' of viewing the past through a purely adult perspective (Gowland 2006, 145).

In the medieval period, the relationship between environment, culture and health was recognised by medical thought, based upon the teaching of Graeco-Roman authors (Porter 1997, 107). These relationships are also important factors in the buffers and stressors associated with health and disease (Goodman et al 1988). The environment includes both the landscape and local environment, which contains constructed and defined areas that are lived in and used according to socio-cultural conventions (McElroy and Townsend 1996, 26); and the wider environment, which determines health with regard to weather and climate, chemical concentrations in water (eg iodine and fluorine) and trace elements in the soil (Howe 1976, 1–15). The local environment is influenced by technology as well as cultural factors, such as sharing dwellings with animals and methods of sanitation (ibid, 4–6). The importance of the relationship between health status and social status has been exemplified by many palaeopathological studies, and socio-cultural factors have been shown to influence health and well-being (Steckel and Rose 2002). Society and culture influence health, because they frequently determine the entire life course (Rousham and Humphrey 2002, 127); people who are disadvantaged both socially and economically can have a shorter life expectancy and an increased risk of developing a serious illness. They are also more likely to experience a higher burden of disease and suffer more illnesses throughout life, due to the cumulative effects of inadequate diet, limited access to treatment and poor local environmental conditions. If such conditions are experienced during childhood, an individual's well-being during adulthood will be directly affected. Poor diet and social conditions allow infectious and metabolic diseases to flourish, and can result in failure to achieve growth potential (McElroy and Townsend 1996, 100–5, 111–17; Courtenay 2003, 12–13; Roberts and Cox 2003, 7; Wilkinson and Marmot 2006, 7–15).

In conclusion, a bioarchaeological approach enables us to have a greater appreciation of the underlying differences which influence the health patterns we observe. The importance of such an approach is demonstrated by its inclusiveness and ability to be applied to any set of skeletal data. Social archaeology enables the health of individuals to be understood in relation to both socio-cultural concepts and archaeological paradigms.

2

Materials and methods

Brian Connell

2.1 Materials

The material that forms the basis of this study is derived from a total of 10,516 skeletons excavated from the cemetery of St Mary Spital, London. All the skeletons were excavated by hand by MOLA archaeologists. The skeletons of infants and small children were block-lifted wherever possible, to ensure complete recovery. Following excavation, the bone was washed over a 1mm nylon mesh to ensure that loose teeth and the smaller bones such as hyoids or sesamoids were retained. The bones were then air-dried at room temperature and packed for archive deposition. The skeletal material was assessed by MOLA osteologists to quantify the assemblage and inform the post-excavation project design (Connell 2002; assessed individuals n = 10,417).

The assemblage is archived at the Centre for Human Bioarchaeology within the London Archaeological Archive and Research Centre, Museum of London, 150 London Wall, London EC2Y 5HN. All data recorded during analysis are available for direct consultation via the database and the further potential of those data sets which were not fully explored during the publication project is discussed in Chapter 5.6 (www.museumoflondon.org.uk/Collections-Research/LAARC/Centre-for-Human-Bioarchaeology).

Sample design

The systematic analysis and investigation of a human skeletal assemblage as large as St Mary Spital has not been attempted before. In order accurately to determine the significance of the remains and design an effective research and sampling strategy, it was considered crucial to gather a series of small quantitative data sets to act as a predictive resource for the project design and enable pre-testing of the recording methodology. Orton (2000) and Robb (2000) had already highlighted the importance of pilot studies for discovering potential errors in data recording or inappropriate sample design. To address these concerns a small-scale pilot study was carried out in advance of the main analytical phase of the project (Connell 2002). The combination of data from the pilot study and the assessment enabled the project team to design an effective sampling strategy.

Sub-sampling the cemetery

Despite the extremely large size of this cemetery population it must be remembered that not all the interments made in the cemetery have been recovered. Many hundreds, perhaps thousands, of burials were disturbed by the digging of new graves during the cemetery's use, and then by later construction activities. The westward extension of the Spitalfields Market building in September 1926 truncated a large portion of the cemetery and burials in the upper levels of this area were destroyed. We can glean some idea of the number of burials disturbed during this work from a sample of skulls kept and studied by Morant (1931), who indicated that a minimum of 950 individuals were represented. Thomas (2004, 47) analysed the density of burials across the undisturbed areas of the cemetery and estimated that at least 18,000 people were originally buried at St Mary Spital. The present archaeologically documented cemetery sample is, therefore, an incomplete representation of all of the interments originally made, and incomplete cemetery samples have been known to bias mortality profiles (Saunders et al 1995a; 1995b; Waldron 1994).

The St Mary Spital skeletal sample is static, whereas the living population from which it is derived would have been dynamic and steadily changing over the period that the cemetery was in use. The conversion of static data to dynamic models involves a degree of assumption which is not straightforward (Boddington 1987, 193). Chief among these assumptions is that skeletal samples directly reflect patterns in demography and health in the contributing population. Skeletons are derived from mortality samples and thus can be considered biased samples of the living (Milner et al 2000, 473). The selective mortality bias inherent in skeletal samples relative to their living contributing population is well recognised (Wood et al 1992; Waldron 1994; Larsen 1999; Chamberlain 2000; 2006; Hoppa and Vaupel 2002). In addition to this, there are many factors that affect how a skeletal sample is composed and these factors have a direct impact on sample representivity. This reinforces the notion that a cemetery is an entirely artificial biological sample and that further, structured sub-sampling should not have any direct effect on sample representivity.

Criteria for inclusion in the study sample

The question of sample representivity not only applies to cemetery populations, but also applies at the level of the individual. The post-excavation assessment indicated that the remains of some 2996 individuals consist of less than a quarter of the skeleton (Connell 2002). The completeness of a skeleton has implications for the availability of osteological features used in the determination of age at death and biological sex. It is these parameters that, at a population level, provide an interpretative framework for palaeodemographic and palaeoepidemiological analyses and, in the case of St Mary Spital, form the basis for analysing intraspecific variation as well as comparing with skeletal data from other populations. Skeletal completeness also has implications for the accuracy of classification of disease. It has been noted that 'when classifying the pathological changes in a skeleton into their most probable cause (or causes), it is often of great help to be able accurately to establish their distribution around the skeleton' (Waldron 1987, 63).

A series of selection criteria were developed during the pilot project and these are based principally on skeletal completeness. This sampling strategy was applied to the entire cemetery. On this basis, the minimum level of skeletal completeness was set at equal to or greater than 35%, and only the more complete skeletons were selected for detailed study. Skeletons at or above this threshold consisting of the following were also excluded from further study: neurocranial fragments only (no teeth or tooth positions); upper limb elements only (from the pectoral girdle to the hand phalanges of one or both limbs); upper limb elements (from pectoral girdle to hand phalanges <20%) with a portion of torso not containing zones diagnostic of age or sex, ie pubis, auricular surface or greater sciatic notch; lower limb elements (from femoral head to foot phalanges or any portion thereof of one or both limbs); and portion of torso (vertebrae, ribs, sternum, pelvis) represented by <30% with no pelvic age/sex diagnostic zones (pubic symphysis/auricular surface/ greater sciatic notch).

Specifically targeting the more complete skeletons ensured that maximum resources were focused on skeletons that would ultimately provide the most comprehensive and accurate data. The more intact skeletons (greater than 35% complete) number in their thousands and provided a more than adequate platform from which to launch population-based skeletal research. The severely truncated skeletons consisting of fragments of limb bones would have, at best, produced low-grade data, limited in their capacity for correlation with other morphological or metric observations.

The application of the above criteria resulted in the selection of a total of 6950 skeletons suitable for detailed analysis (66.1% of the total excavated sample) of which 5387 could be recorded within the project timeframe. The analysed assemblage amounts to 77.5% of the skeletons suitable for recording, or 51.2% of the entire excavated sample.

The truncation and disturbance of a large number of burials from the cemetery also meant that there was a large quantity of disarticulated bone in the general cemetery soil. All disarticulated bone was reburied during excavation and was not subject to analysis.

2.2 Recording methods

The project team was able to benefit from recently updated and revised recording guidelines (Mays et al 2002a; Brickley and McKinley 2004), together with the pre-tested data-recording protocol derived from the sample-specific pilot project (Connell 2002). Following this, a relational database was designed to enable direct entry of bone data (Connell and Rauxloh 2003). The principal aim of the computer-based recording was to standardise the recording of all metric and morphological variability expressed in the human skeleton. The system was designed to be applicable to any skeleton regardless of age at death (ie both adults and subadults). To enable recording of data, each skeleton was unpacked and laid out in anatomical position. A full account of the methods employed can be found in Connell and Rauxloh (2003) and Powers (2008); these methods are briefly summarised below.

Determination of age at death

Age determination of subadults was estimated using a range of dental and skeletal methods: long bone diaphyses, following

Maresh (1970) and Scheuer et al (1980); stage of dental development (Moorrees et al 1963a; 1963b; Smith 1991); overall state of epiphyseal fusion (Scheuer and Black 2000); and the general stage of tooth eruption (Gustafson and Koch 1974). The determination of age at death in adults was based on morphological changes to the pubic symphysis (Brooks and Suchey 1990), the auricular surface (Lovejoy et al 1985) and changes at the costo-chondral junction (Iscan et al 1984; 1985). The amount of wear on the molar teeth was also used as a broad guide to age at death (Brothwell 1981).

It is recognised that difficulties exist in ascribing age estimates to adult remains, particularly for older adults; broad age groups are therefore used for analysis. The age categories used for both adults and subadults are outlined in Table 4.

Table 4 Age groups (following Connell and Rauxloh 2003)

Description	Age range
Intrauterine/neonate	up to 4 weeks
Early postnatal infant	1–6 months
Later postnatal infant	7–11 months
Early childhood	1–5 years
Later childhood	6–11 years
Adolescent	12–17 years
Subadult	<18 years
Young adult	18–25 years
Early middle adult	26–35 years
Later middle adult	36–45 years
Mature adult	≥46 years
Adult	≥18 years

Determination of biological sex

The sex of adult skeletons was based on visual observation of pelvic and skull characters following Phenice (1969) and Ferembach et al (1980). A total of seven pelvic features and seven skull characteristics were scored on a five-point scale following Buikstra and Ubelaker (1994), ie male, probable male, intermediate, probable female and female. Where poor preservation, truncation, or the absence of sexually dimorphic elements prevented observations, adult remains were classified as of undetermined sex. For analysis, data for males and probable males and for females and probable females were pooled to produce overall statistics for each biological sex, unless otherwise stated. Sex determination in subadult individuals is problematic because the secondary sexual characteristics are not usually manifest until puberty, and was not therefore attempted for individuals under 18 years old.

Metric data

A series of measurements was recorded from each skeleton in order to evaluate adult stature. Measurements (in mm) were taken with digital and spreading callipers, osteometric boards and tape measures (stature is expressed in cm in Chapters 3 and 4).

Three comparative skeletal indices were calculated (cranial, platymeric and platycnemic). In addition to the particular measurements required for these evaluations, an extended series was taken for a general quantification of size, following Buikstra and Ubelaker (1994) and Brothwell (1981). Nineteen skull measurements and 14 post-cranial measurements on the left and right limb bones (28 measurements) were recorded, giving a total of 47 measurements on each adult skeleton (see Powers 2008).

Canines and first molars were measured following Buikstra and Ubelaker (1994) and Hillson (1996, 70–1) (buccolingual and mesiodistal crown diameters). Measurements of permanent teeth were taken to establish an adult baseline and deciduous teeth were recorded in all subadults.

The calculation of adult stature was based on the formulae devised by Trotter (1970) and expressed in centimetres. The calculated height of an individual skeleton will vary depending on which bone is used: Waldron (1998) demonstrated that statistically significant differences could be generated if different bones were used within the same sample. For the purposes of consistency in this project the femur was selected for stature estimates, as this was the most frequently occurring, intact long bone.

Subadult growth curves were calculated following the methods of Lewis (2002).

All measurements and statistical calculations are expressed to one decimal place. Calculations resulting in rates of less than 0.1% have been expressed as such (ie <0.1%).

All metric data have been archived.

Non-metric data

Non-metric variation was recorded following the definitions of Berry and Berry (1967) and Buikstra and Ubelaker (1994) for the skull, Finnegan (1978) for the post-cranial skeleton, and Buikstra and Ubelaker (1994) and Hillson (1996) for dental non-metric variants (see Powers 2008). Non-metric data were recorded for a suite of 24 cranial traits, 24 post-cranial traits and 11 dental traits in over 2000 individuals, to provide a statistically valid sample.

Multiple genes determine the presence or absence of these traits and the genetic and environmental factors that govern their expression are still poorly understood; the main areas of controversy relating to the use of non-metric traits have still to be resolved (Tyrrell 2000, 293). Following a review of the recorded data, the decision was taken to focus this volume on aspects of the osteological record that could provide clear interpretative results within the project constraints. All non-metric data are available in the project archive through the London Archaeological Archive and Research Centre, and the opportunity remains for future research in this contentious area (Chapter 5.6).

Recording and diagnosing pathology

All pathological alteration was described following Roberts and Connell (2004). General classifications of disease processes follow Aufderheide and Rodríguez-Martín (1998) and Ortner (2003), supported with comparisons with clinical data from

Resnick (2002). References to more specific diagnostic criteria are also provided within the monograph when discussing individual cases. The Museum of London method statement provides further detail concerning the diagnosis of osteological change (Powers 2008).

Scurvy was diagnosed following the criteria developed by Ortner and Eriksen (1997), and the diagnosis of osteomalacia was based on the criteria given by Brickley et al (2005).

Periodontal disease was recorded by observation of the severity of resorption of the alveolar margin and was recorded in three grades (1 = 2–3mm, 2 = 3–5mm and 3 = ≥5mm) following Brothwell (1981, fig 6.14c). The distance between the cemento-enamel junction and the alveolar crest is considered to be 2mm in a healthy young adult.

The size of any calculus deposit was graded following Brothwell (1981, fig 6.14b) and the position of the deposit on the tooth surface was also noted, ie supra-gingival or sub-gingival, measured in relation to the cemento-enamel junction.

Further analyses of pathological data were supported by radiography and digital photography. In some cases the pathological changes in the skeleton were extensive or represented a challenge in terms of differential diagnosis. In these cases it was beneficial to produce a detailed written (paper-based) account of the differential diagnosis and the diagnostic options. This facilitated the full description of the locations and types of lesions, as recommended by Roberts and Connell (2004). These records are located in the project archive.

Fractured bones were recorded following the recommended procedures of Roberts (2000c, 346–9). However, due to the large size of the skeletal sample, provision was made for the taking of radiographs only when they might specifically aid diagnosis of injury. Radiography of other pathological bones was carried out in support of the differential diagnosis of pathology.

Spinal and extra-spinal joint disease prevalence was recorded by joint. The joint was considered present if one or both of the adjacent elements was observable. Crude prevalence rates were also calculated by individual and, for certain conditions, by spinal segment (cervical, thoracic, lumbar or sacral). Prevalence of spinal anomalies which presented at the junction between different spinal segments was calculated as a percentage of the number of junctions represented, ie where the vertebrae above and/or below the junction were observable.

Crude (individuals affected) and true (elements affected) prevalence rates for all categories of disease are presented as percentages, with the sample number for each data set given, often in parenthesis, to aid the reader when considering the wealth of data presented here.

2.3 Repeatability of results

The project team comprised four bioarchaeologists. For any project with more than one observer undertaking analysis and recording, the potential problem of inter-observer error is introduced. Given the scale of the project it was recognised that, left unchecked, such error had the potential to affect some data sets. To investigate this problem, the pilot study contained an exercise to examine repeatability across a broad suite of categorical (eg bone identification, age and sex indicator data) and continuous (eg bone and tooth measurements) data from both adult and subadult individuals. Twenty skeletons were randomly selected and re-recorded, providing a measure of intra-observer error. The same 20 skeletons were then independently recorded by another team member, providing a measure of inter-observer error. The first recording undertaken in the main pilot study represented the baseline to which the other two data sets were then compared. Results demonstrated good concordance both within and between observers (Connell 2002).

At the beginning of the analytical phase, care was taken to train the team of qualified bioarchaeologists to the same standard in the quantitative methods set out in Connell and Rauxloh (2003). At regular intervals through the project, a skeleton was selected for recording by all four team members and the results from each observer were compared. This showed good agreement between observers in categorical and continuous data. Particular attention was paid to the classification of pathological lesions. Many studies in palaeopathology have stressed the need to control for these potential sources of error (see for example Jacobi and Danforth 2002; Macchiarelli et al 1994; Waldron and Rogers 1991). To ensure maximum consistency in the identification and scoring of pathological lesions there was regular consultation and discussion within the project team.

2.4 Taphonomy and preservation

The quality of bone preservation within each skeleton was visually graded on a three-point scale (good, moderate or poor) following Connell and Rauxloh (2003):

1) bone surface in **good** condition with no erosion: fine surface detail such as coarse woven bone deposition would be clearly visible (if present)
2) bone surface in **moderate** condition with some post-mortem erosion on long bone shafts, but the margins of articular surfaces are eroded and some prominences are eroded
3) bone surface in **poor** condition with extensive post-mortem erosion resulting in pitted and eroded cortical surfaces and long bones with articular surfaces missing or severely eroded.

As these are broad-based categories, in cases where the degree of preservation was variable within the same skeleton, the predominant grade was assigned.

The overwhelming majority of skeletons (65.3–78.3%) were very well preserved, with no major differences in the distribution of bone preservation scores between periods 14 and 17. The excellent state of preservation meant that of all the skeletons studied, only a very small percentage (2.1–7.1%) were poorly preserved. Identical patterns in preservation were seen in both burial type ABC and burial type D. A comparison of preservation was also made between adults and subadults and male and female skeletons. No significant differences were observed, suggesting that neither biological sex nor age affected bone survivability. These results suggest that overall, taphonomic factors were uniform across the cemetery.

A series of soil samples were taken from ten graves during excavation, to investigate the possibility that parasitc ova might be preserved (following Reinhard et al 1992). These soil samples were screened for the eggs of intestinal parasitic nematodes: two of them contained the remains of possible *Trichuris* sp eggs. However, Carrott (1999) considered these to be too poorly preserved to be of any interpretative value and, based on these results, no further sampling was carried out.

2.5 Levels of bone recovery

The cemetery at St Mary Spital was used extensively over a period of approximately 350 years from the 12th to 16th centuries. Digging new graves inevitably resulted in the disturbance of previous interments, and large numbers of skeletons had therefore been truncated by later burials. The severely truncated skeletons would not have satisfied the sample selection criteria and therefore were not studied. It has already been noted that the levels of recovery have important implications for the identification of disease, and so it is important to assess how this might affect the sample in terms of skeletal representation. To examine the levels of bone recovery across the cemetery, two small samples from different burial types were taken and used to compare the recovery rates of individual skeletal elements. Two samples, each consisting of 100 skeletons, randomly selected and including all demographic groups, were taken, one from burial type A (single inhumations), and the other from burial type D (multiple burials). The relative representation of individual skeletal elements is shown in Fig 7. For both types of burial the recovery of smaller bones, such as the carpals, tarsals, phalanges and coccyx, was relatively low. This is to be expected as the reliance on hand retrieval is known to favour the recovery of larger bones (Payne 1975; Waldron 1987). Bones in the digits are the most seriously under-represented and foot phalanges appear to show lower recovery rates than hand phalanges; again this is most probably due to their size. Waldron (1987) noted an underrepresentation of anterior skeletal elements such as the sternum, coracoid and acromion of the scapula, the pubis and the patellae. This is reflected at St Mary Spital: for example, the number of patellae recovered is much lower than expected given the level of recovery of lower limb long bones. Again, this is most probably a reflection of the size of the elements.

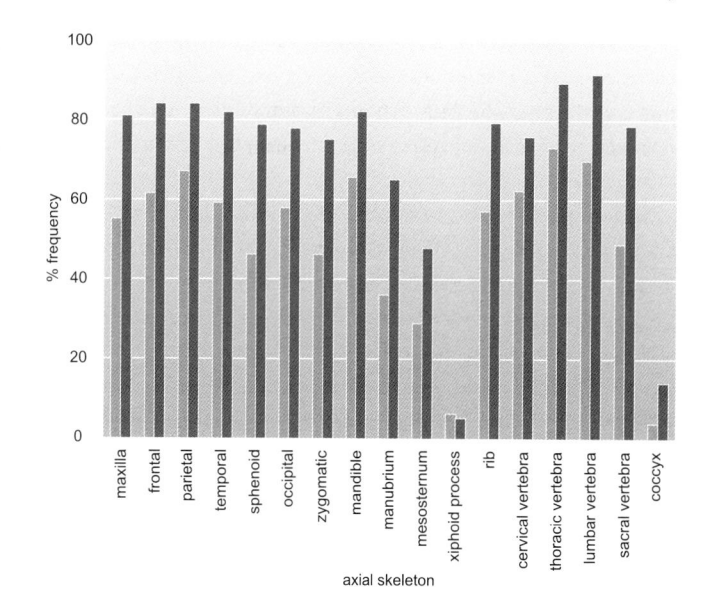

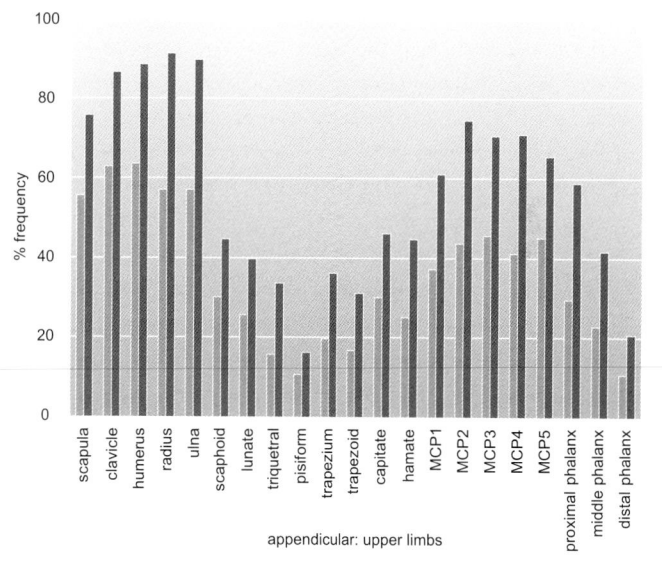

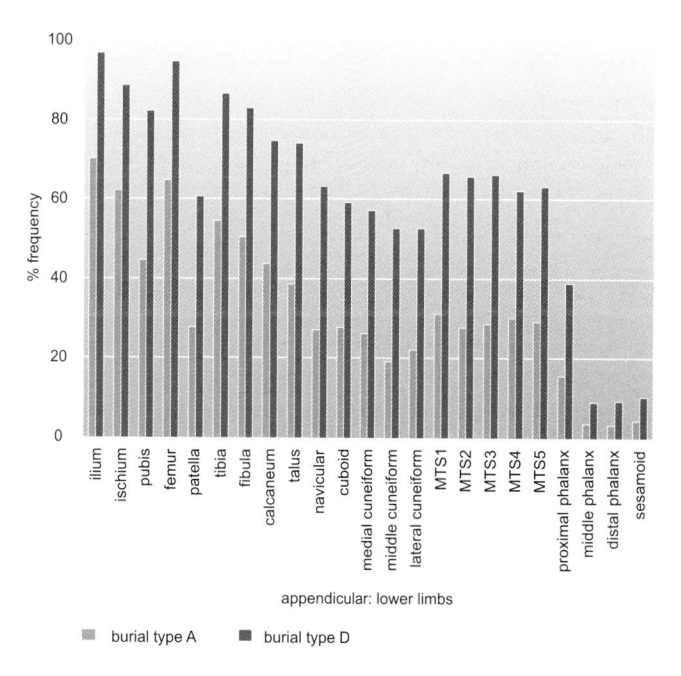

Fig 7 Comparison of the levels of bone recovery in single (A) and multiple (D) burials (MCP = metacarpal, MTS = metatarsal)

Overall, there was a lower relative frequency of all skeletal elements in single inhumations (burial type A), which is a product of the truncation of earlier burials by later ones: there was extensive intercutting of graves, particularly for burial type ABC. Fig 7 also shows that, despite the fact that single burials were more frequently truncated, the overall pattern was roughly the same in both groups. This suggests that truncation does not affect the sample in terms of the relative recovery of skeletal elements. This agrees with work by Mays (1992), who found that burials showed similar patterns of relative representation of skeletal elements whether or not they had been cut by later features.

The skeletons in burial type A (single inhumations) were generally less complete than those from burial type D (multiple burials). The pits containing multiple burials had a lower level of truncation than the rest of the cemetery and hence those skeletons interred within them were much more complete.

3

Results

Brian Connell, Amy Gray Jones, Rebecca Redfern and Don Walker

This chapter presents the product of the analysis of osteological data from the cemetery. Interpretation and discussion are reserved for later chapters, with text in this section kept to a minimum. For the purposes of the project, burials were divided into four chronological periods to allow comparisons over time and within the cemetery population: period 14 – *c* 1120–*c* 1200; period 15 – *c* 1200– 50; period 16 – *c* 1250– *c* 1400; and period 17 – *c* 1400–1539 (Chapter 1.1). Within these periods, the burials were placed into one of two separate groups of burial types, ABC or D (Chapter 1.2). The results from these two groups were compared and contrasted, permitting further characterisation of the sample in the interpretative and discursive sections.

The terms attritional and catastrophic are considered interpretative and thus have not been used in this chapter. Where appropriate, observations from later chapters are accompanied by cross references to the results section.

The number of individuals within the study sample was 5387.

3.1 Number of individuals studied by sex, age and period

The basic demographic data for the medieval cemetery, outlining the sample studied within each period and burial type, can be seen in Tables 5–8. Although the tables display data for each burial type separately, the results sections that follow combine burial types A, B and C into a single burial type (ABC).

3.2 Demography

Amy Gray Jones and Don Walker

This section provides a summary of the demographic results for each of the four periods used in the cemetery analysis (periods 14–17), divided into two groups: burial type ABC and burial type D (Table 9).

Burials *c* 1120–*c* 1200 (period 14) (512 individuals)

The numbers of individuals in burial types ABC and D in period 14 are shown in Table 10 and Table 11.

In period 14 the two groups had a similar adult age-at-death profile; the number of burials increased with age, and then decreased in the two older age categories (Fig 8). Both burial type ABC and burial type D groups contained few subadults below the age of 6–11 years. As a proportion of individuals for whom age at death could be assigned, there were few perinatal individuals (burial type ABC 4/335: 1.2%; burial type D 2/163: 1.2%), and neither burial type contained individuals who had

Results

Table 5 Summary of demographic data by burial type, c 1120–c 1200 (period 14)

	Burial type A						Burial type B				
Age	Female	Male	Intermediate	Undetermined	Subadult	Total	Female	Male	Intermediate	Subadult	Total
Perinatal	0	0	0	0	0	0	0	0	0	3	3
1–5 years	0	0	0	0	3	3	0	0	0	2	2
6–11 years	0	0	0	0	5	5	0	0	0	3	3
12–17 years	0	0	0	0	21	21	0	0	0	12	12
Subadult	0	0	0	0	1	1	0	0	0	0	0
18–25 years	14	18	5	3	0	40	2	3	1	0	6
26–35 years	35	32	5	1	0	73	10	11	0	0	21
36–45 years	24	41	4	0	0	69	10	10	0	0	20
≥46 years	11	17	1	0	0	29	1	0	0	0	1
Adult	1	8	0	0	0	9	0	2	0	0	2
Total	85	116	15	4	30	250	23	26	1	20	70

Table 6 Summary of demographic data by burial type, c 1200–50 (period 15)

	Burial type A						Burial type B					
Age	Female	Male	Intermediate	Undetermined	Subadult	Total	Female	Male	Intermediate	Undetermined	Subadult	Total
Perinatal	0	0	0	0	3	3	0	0	0	0	1	1
1–6 months	0	0	0	0	0	0	0	0	0	0	0	0
1–5 years	0	0	0	0	3	3	0	0	0	0	0	0
6–11 years	0	0	0	0	12	12	0	0	0	0	10	10
12–17 years	0	0	0	0	36	36	0	0	0	0	17	17
Subadult	0	0	0	0	3	3	0	0	0	0	0	0
18–25 years	24	28	4	2	0	58	9	17	2	0	0	28
26–35 years	36	39	8	2	0	85	18	19	0	0	0	37
36–45 years	24	38	1	1	0	64	13	14	0	1	0	28
≥46 years	10	10	1	0	0	21	5	3	0	0	0	8
Adult	0	6	0	0	0	6	0	1	0	1	0	2
Total	94	121	14	5	57	291	45	54	2	2	28	131

Table 7 Summary of demographic data by burial type, c 1250–c 1400 (period 16)

	Burial type A						Burial type B					
Age	Female	Male	Indeterminate	Undetermined	Subadult	Total	Female	Male	Indeterminate	Undetermined	Subadult	Total
Perinatal	0	0	0	0	8	8	0	0	0	0	3	3
1–6 months	0	0	0	0	0	0	0	0	0	0	0	0
7–11 months	0	0	0	0	0	0	0	0	0	0	0	0
1–5 years	0	0	0	0	13	13	0	0	0	0	2	2
6–11 years	0	0	0	0	48	48	0	0	0	0	30	30
12–17 years	0	0	0	0	57	57	0	0	0	0	17	17
Subadult	0	0	0	0	0	0	0	0	0	0	1	1
18–25 years	67	91	12	1	0	171	26	14	4	0	0	44
26–35 years	134	149	18	0	0	301	29	31	4	0	0	64
36–45 years	77	157	12	1	0	247	28	28	3	0	0	59
≥46 years	35	50	3	1	0	89	11	9	0	0	0	20
Adult	16	26	7	3	0	52	4	3	1	2	0	10
Total	329	473	52	6	126	986	98	85	12	2	53	250

Demography

		Burial type C					Burial type D				Grand total
Female	Male	Subadult	Total		Female	Male	Intermediate	Subadult	Total		
0	0	1	1		0	0	0	2	2		6
0	0	0	0		0	0	0	0	0		5
0	0	0	0		0	0	0	13	13		21
0	0	1	1		0	0	0	27	27		61
0	0	0	0		0	0	0	0	0		1
1	4	0	5		14	12	4	0	30		81
5	5	0	10		23	23	0	0	46		150
1	7	0	8		14	22	1	0	37		134
0	2	0	2		3	5	0	0	8		40
0	0	0	0		1	1	0	0	2		13
7	18	2	27		55	63	5	42	165		512

		Burial type C					Burial type D					Grand total
Female	Male	Intermediate	Subadult	Total		Female	Male	Intermediate	Undetermined	Subadult	Total	
0	0	0	2	2		0	0	0	0	8	8	14
0	0	0	0	0		0	0	0	0	1	1	1
0	0	0	0	0		0	0	0	0	8	8	11
0	0	0	6	6		0	0	0	0	75	75	103
0	0	0	7	7		0	0	0	0	109	109	169
0	0	0	0	0		0	0	0	0	0	0	3
6	8	0	0	14		81	76	6	0	0	163	263
12	17	0	0	29		130	109	7	2	0	248	399
7	16	0	0	23		77	97	12	0	0	186	301
1	3	0	0	4		36	25	1	0	0	62	95
2	0	1	0	3		10	6	3	1	0	20	31
28	44	1	15	88		334	313	29	3	201	880	1390

		Burial type C						Burial type D					Grand total
Female	Male	Intermediate	Undetermined	Subadult	Total		Female	Male	Intermediate	Undetermined	Subadult	Total	
0	0	0	0	1	1		0	0	0	0	10	10	22
0	0	0	0	1	1		0	0	0	0	0	0	1
0	0	0	0	0	0		0	0	0	0	1	1	1
0	0	0	0	2	2		0	0	0	0	14	14	31
0	0	0	0	9	9		0	0	0	0	100	100	187
0	0	0	0	17	17		0	0	0	0	174	174	265
0	0	0	0	0	0		0	0	0	0	0	0	1
12	13	4	0	0	29		115	135	12	2	0	264	508
14	33	2	0	0	49		201	184	13	2	0	400	814
16	20	1	1	0	38		130	163	8	0	0	301	645
4	4	0	0	0	8		65	61	0	1	0	127	244
1	0	0	1	0	2		24	21	6	1	0	52	116
47	70	7	2	30	156		535	564	39	6	299	1443	2835

27

Results

Table 8 Summary of demographic data by burial type, c 1400–1539 (period 17)

Age	Burial type A Female	Male	Intermediate	Undetermined	Subadult	Total	Burial type B Female	Male	Intermediate	Subadult	Total
Perinatal	0	0	0	0	19	19	0	0	0	5	5
7–11 months	0	0	0	0	1	1	0	0	0	0	0
1–5 years	0	0	0	0	7	7	0	0	0	2	2
6–11 years	0	0	0	0	14	14	0	0	0	8	8
12–17 years	0	0	0	0	31	31	0	0	0	4	4
18–25 years	43	46	4	0	0	93	5	3	2	0	10
26–35 years	46	71	10	2	0	129	9	11	0	0	20
36–45 years	26	59	5	0	0	90	6	4	0	0	10
≥46 years	14	24	0	0	0	38	5	2	0	0	7
Adult	2	5	1	2	0	10	0	1	0	0	1
Total	131	205	20	4	72	432	25	21	2	19	67

Table 9 Summary of demographic data for all burials, c 1120–1539

Age	Female	Male	Intermediate	Undetermined	Subadult	Total
Perinatal	0	0	0	0	68	68
1–6 months	0	0	0	0	2	2
7–11 months	0	0	0	0	2	2
1–5 years	0	0	0	0	58	58
6–11 years	0	0	0	0	348	348
12–17 years	0	0	0	0	544	544
Subadult	0	0	0	0	5	5
18–25 years	428	481	62	8	0	979
26–35 years	716	752	69	9	0	1546
36–45 years	467	700	48	4	0	1219
≥46 years	211	222	7	2	0	442
Adult	61	82	19	12	0	174
Total	1883	2237	205	35	1027	5387

Table 10 Demographic data for burial type ABC, c 1120–c 1200 (period 14)

Age	Female	Male	Intermediate	Undetermined	Subadult	Total
Perinatal	0	0	0	0	4	4
1–5 years	0	0	0	0	5	5
6–11 years	0	0	0	0	8	8
12–17 years	0	0	0	0	34	34
Subadult	0	0	0	0	1	1
18–25 years	17	25	6	3	0	51
26–35 years	50	48	5	1	0	104
36–45 years	35	58	4	0	0	97
≥46 years	12	19	1	0	0	32
Adult	1	10	0	0	0	11
Total	115	160	16	4	52	347

| | Burial type C | | | | | Burial type D | | | | | Grand total |
Female	Male	Intermediate	Subadult	Total	Female	Male	Intermediate	Undetermined	Subadult	Total	
0	0	0	0	0	0	0	0	0	2	2	26
0	0	0	0	0	0	0	0	0	0	0	1
0	0	0	1	1	0	0	0	0	1	1	11
0	0	0	2	2	0	0	0	0	13	13	37
0	0	0	1	1	0	0	0	0	13	13	49
1	2	1	0	4	8	11	1	0	0	20	127
4	4	0	0	8	10	14	2	0	0	26	183
3	4	0	0	7	11	20	1	0	0	32	139
0	2	1	0	3	10	5	0	0	0	15	63
0	1	0	0	1	0	1	0	1	0	2	14
8	13	2	4	27	39	51	4	1	29	124	650

Table 11 Demographic data for burial type D, c 1120–c 1200 (period 14)

Age	Female	Male	Intermediate	Subadult	Total
Perinatal	0	0	0	2	2
6–11 years	0	0	0	13	13
12–17 years	0	0	0	27	27
18–25 years	14	12	4	0	30
26–35 years	23	23	0	0	46
36–45 years	14	22	1	0	37
≥46 years	3	5	0	0	8
Adult	1	1	0	0	2
Total	55	63	5	42	165

died in the first year of life. Only burial type ABC contained any subadults who had died aged 1–5 years (5/335: 1.5%).

There was a significantly higher proportion of subadults in burial type D (42/165: 25.5%) than in type ABC (52/347: 15%) (χ^2 = 8.18, df = 1, p ≤ 0.01); and, of those for whom age at death could be assigned, there were significantly more subadults in burial type D who were aged 6–11 years at death (burial type D 13/163: 8%; burial type ABC 8/335: 2.4%; χ^2 = 8.47, df = 1, p ≤ 0.01) and 12–17 years (burial type D 27/163: 16.6%; burial type ABC 34/335: 10.1%; χ^2 = 4.20, df = 1, p ≤ 0.05).

While there was a higher proportion of young adults in burial type D than in type ABC, this was not statistically significant. In each age group above 26 years of age, there were slightly fewer adults in burial type D than in burial type ABC. The adult individuals in burial type D were, in general, younger than those in type ABC, although none of the age categories presented statistically different results.

Of the total sample from burial type ABC, 33.1% of individuals were female (115/347) and 46.1% were male (160/347), a ratio of 1.4:1 males to females (χ^2 = 12.20, df = 1, p ≤ 0.001). In burial type D there was no statistical difference between the numbers of females and males within the sample: 33.3% were female (55/165) and 38.2% were male (63/165), a ratio of males to females of 1.15:1.

In burial type ABC, the majority of males and females died aged 26–45 years. Female age at death peaked at 26–35 years, while male age at death peaked at 36–45 years. Of those individuals for whom age at death could be assigned, there were

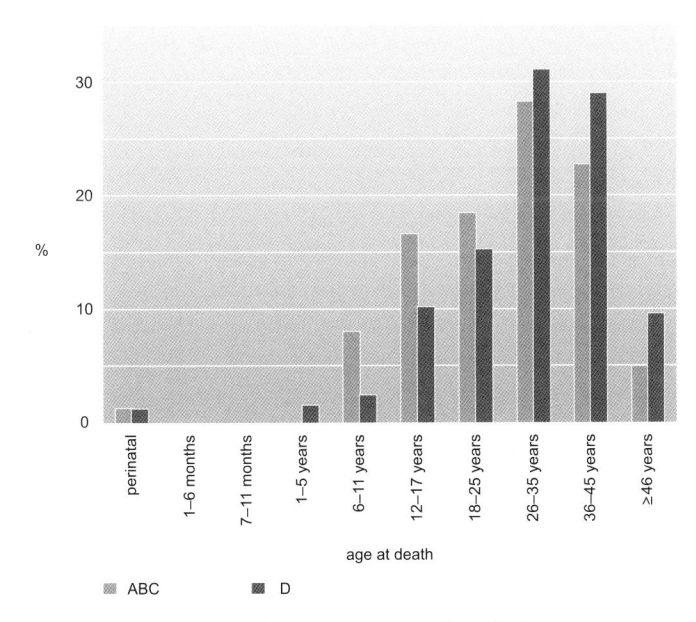

Fig 8 Age at death by burial type, c 1120–c 1200 (period 14)

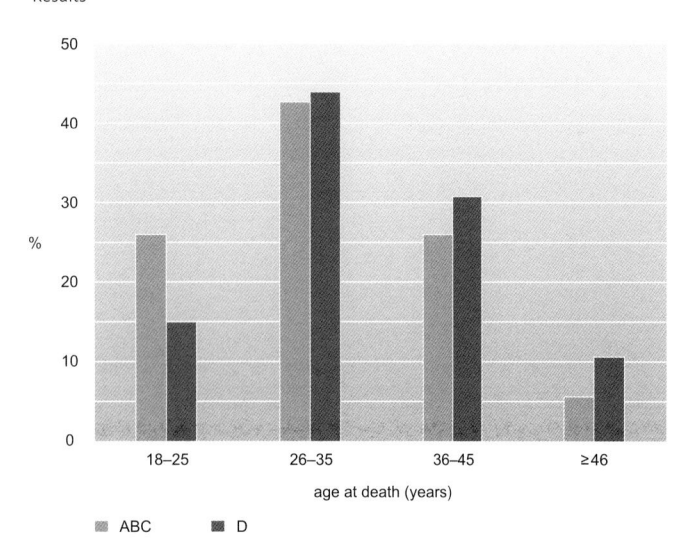

Fig 9 Female age at death, c 1120–c 1200 (period 14)

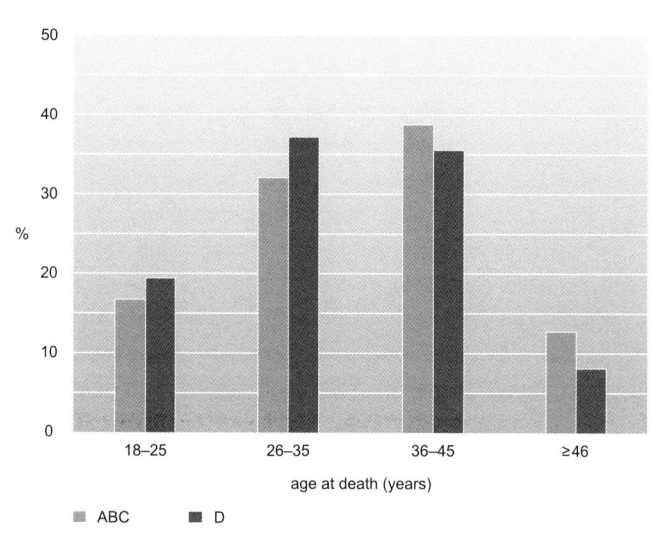

Fig 10 Male age at death, c 1120–c 1200 (period 14)

similar proportions of 18–25-year-old adult males (25/150: 16.7% of total aged males) and females (17/114: 14.9% of total aged females), but there were significantly more 26–35-year-old females (50/114: 43.9%) than males (48/150: 32%) (χ^2 = 3.90, df = 1, p ≤ 0.05). The differences in the 36–45 year age group were not statistically significant, while there were similar proportions of older adult (≥46 years) females (12/114: 10.5%) and males (19/150: 12.7%) (Fig 9; Fig 10).

The majority of males and females in burial type D died in middle age (26–45 years). Female age at death peaked at 26–35 years, whereas for males the proportions of individuals dying in early and later middle age were similar. Of those individuals for whom age at death could be assigned, there were slightly more 18–25-year-old and 26–35-year-old females than males (18–25 years – 14/54: 25.9% of females; 12/62: 19.4% of males; 26–35 years – 23/54: 42.6% of females; 23/62: 37.1% of males), fewer 36–45-year-old females (14/54: 25.9%; males 22/62: 35.5%) and fewer females ≥46 years (3/54: 5.6%; males 5/62: 8.1%). There was no statistically significant variation in these results. Although there was a higher proportion of 18–25-year-olds in burial type D than type ABC, these were not statistically significant differences.

Burials c 1200–50 (period 15) (1390 individuals)

The numbers of individuals in burial types ABC and D in period 15 are shown in Table 12 and Table 13.

The age-at-death profile in period 15 was similar to that in period 14 and the results from burial types ABC and burial type D again followed the same trend (Fig 11).

Unlike in period 14 there was no significant difference between the proportions of subadults in the two groups (burial type ABC 100/510: 19.6%; burial type D 201/880: 22.8%). Of those individuals for whom age at death could be assigned, there were few subadults below the age of 6–11 years, and a low proportion of perinatal individuals (burial type ABC 6/496: 1.2%; burial type D 8/860: 0.9%). As in period 14, there were no individuals who died in the first year of life and there were few subadults aged 1–5 years, though they were present in both burial types. There was a significantly higher proportion of 6–11-year-olds in burial type D (75/860: 8.7%) than burial type ABC (28/496: 5.6%) (χ^2 = 4.24, df = 1, p ≤ 0.05).

Adult age at death again peaked at 26–35 years and although there was a slightly higher percentage of adults in burial type ABC in each age category, there were no significant differences between the burial types.

In burial type ABC, 219/510 (42.9%) of individuals were male and 167/510 (32.7%) were female, a statistically significant difference (χ^2 = 11.27, df = 1, p ≤ 0.001) and a ratio of 1.31:1. In burial type D, 35.6% (313/880) of individuals were male and 38% (334/880) were female, a ratio of 1.07:1. The lower proportion of males in burial type D than in burial type ABC was statistically significant (χ^2 = 7.43, df = 1, p ≤ 0.01): the difference in females between burial types was not.

In burial type ABC there were similar proportions of 18–25-year-old females (as a percentage of total aged females)

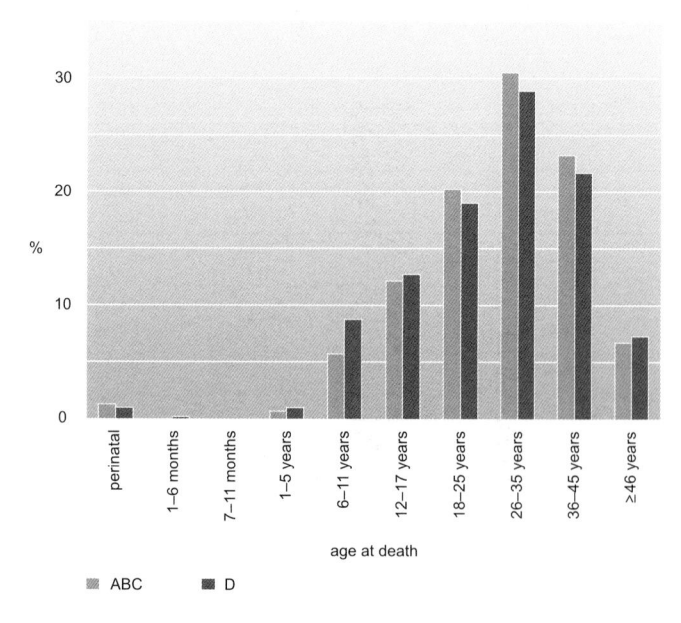

Fig 11 Age at death by burial type, c 1200–50 (period 15)

Table 12 Demographic data for burial type ABC, c 1200–50 (period 15)

Age	Female	Male	Intermediate	Undetermined	Subadult	Total
Perinatal	0	0	0	0	6	6
1–5 years	0	0	0	0	3	3
6–11 years	0	0	0	0	28	28
12–17 years	0	0	0	0	60	60
Subadult	0	0	0	0	3	3
18–25 years	39	53	6	2	0	100
26–35 years	66	75	8	2	0	151
36–45 years	44	68	1	2	0	115
≥46 years	16	16	1	0	0	33
Adult	2	7	1	1	0	11
Total	167	219	17	7	100	510

Table 13 Demographic data for burial type D, c 1200–50 (period 15)

Age	Female	Male	Intermediate	Undetermined	Subadult	Total
Perinatal	0	0	0	0	8	8
1–6 months	0	0	0	0	1	1
1–5 years	0	0	0	0	8	8
6–11 years	0	0	0	0	75	75
12–17 years	0	0	0	0	109	109
18–25 years	81	76	6	0	0	163
26–35 years	130	109	7	2	0	248
36–45 years	77	97	12	0	0	186
≥46 years	36	25	1	0	0	62
Adult	10	6	3	1	0	20
Total	334	313	29	3	201	880

and males (as a percentage of total aged males): 23.6% (39/165) and 25.0% (53/212) respectively. Both male and female age at death peaked at 26–35 years, although in females this peak was greater (Fig 12; Fig 13).

As a proportion of individuals for whom age at death could be assigned, there were similar proportions of 18–25-year-old males (76/307: 24.8%) and females (81/324: 25%) in burial type D. Again, female age at death peaked at 26–35 years, with 40.1% (130/324) of aged females in this category. Male age at death also peaked at 26–35 years (109/307: 35.5% of aged males). The number of 36–45-year-old males as a proportion of aged males (97/307: 31.6%) was significantly higher than the

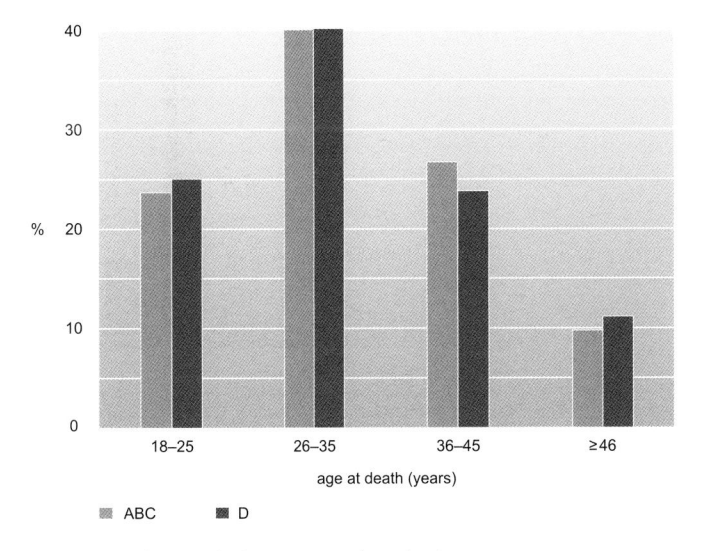

Fig 12 Female age at death, c 1200–50 (period 15)

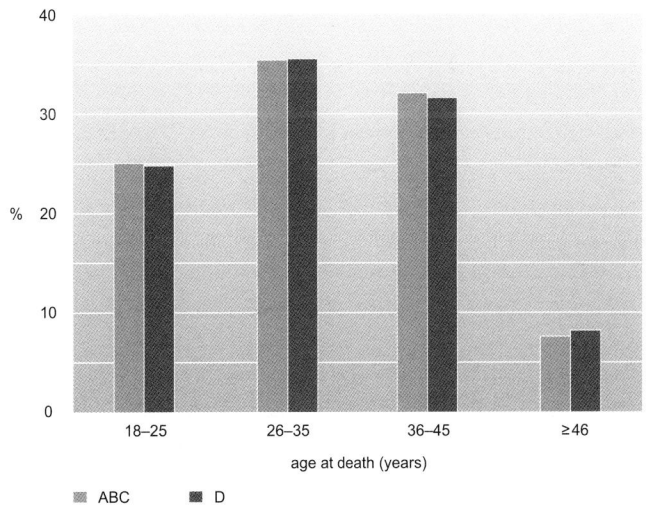

Fig 13 Male age at death, c 1200–50 (period 15)

female equivalent (77/324: 23.8%) (χ^2 = 4.84, df = 1, p ≤ 0.05). However, there was no such difference when 36–45-year and ≥46-year categories were combined. It is possible that this variation resulted from the problems of accurately ageing older adults by macroscopic means. Trial studies of samples of known age have revealed that older individuals tend to be underaged, while those between 30 and 40 years can be overaged (Cox 2000, 75). Thus the analysis of results based on middle and older adult age categories should be interpreted with care.

In males there was little difference in the pattern of age at death between burial types, and the same was true for females. Overall there were similar rates of 18–25-year-old males and females but more females than males appear to have died aged 26–35 years when compared to males. Male age at death was highest at 26–35 and 36–45 years.

Burials c 1250–c 1400 (period 16) (2835 individuals)

The numbers of individuals in burial types ABC and D in period 16 are shown below (Table 14; Table 15).

In period 16, burials from both groups again had similar overall age-at-death patterns, with very few subadults below the age of 6 years (Fig 14).

There was a significantly higher proportion of subadults in burial type D (299/1443: 20.7%) than in burial type ABC (209/1392: 15%: χ^2 = 15.69, df = 1, p ≤ 0.001). Of those individuals for whom age at death could be assigned, there were

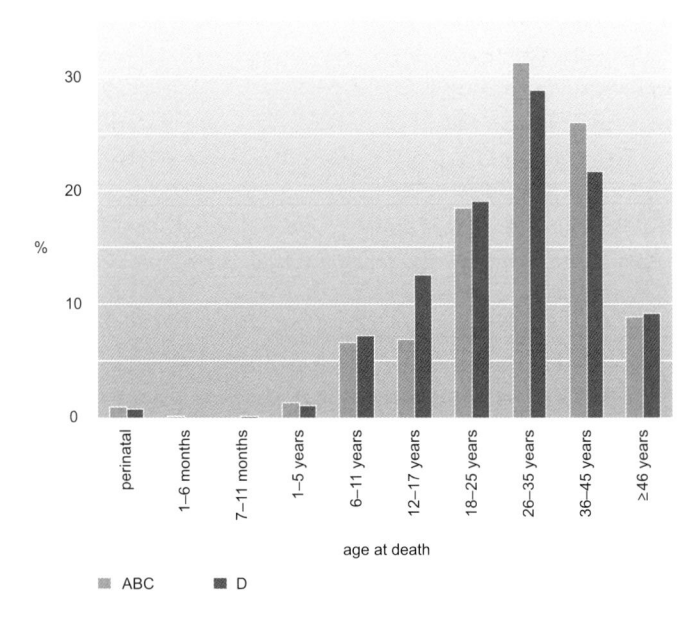

Fig 14 Age at death by burial type, c 1250–c 1400 (period 16)

Table 14 Demographic data for burial type ABC, c 1250–c 1400 (period 16)

Age	Female	Male	Intermediate	Undetermined	Subadult	Total
Perinatal	0	0	0	0	12	12
1–6 months	0	0	0	0	1	1
1–5 years	0	0	0	0	17	17
6–11 years	0	0	0	0	87	87
12–17 years	0	0	0	0	91	91
Subadult	0	0	0	0	1	1
18–25 years	105	118	20	1	0	244
26–35 years	177	213	24	0	0	414
36–45 years	121	205	16	2	0	344
≥46 years	50	63	3	1	0	117
Adult	21	29	8	6	0	64
Total	474	628	71	10	209	1392

Table 15 Demographic data for burial type D, c 1250–c 1400 (period 16)

Age	Female	Male	Intermediate	Undetermined	Subadult	Total
Perinatal	0	0	0	0	10	10
7–11 months	0	0	0	0	1	1
1–5 years	0	0	0	0	14	14
6–11 years	0	0	0	0	100	100
12–17 years	0	0	0	0	174	174
18–25 years	115	135	12	2	0	264
26–35 years	201	184	13	2	0	400
36–45 years	130	163	8	0	0	301
≥46 years	65	61	0	1	0	127
Adult	24	21	6	1	0	52
Total	535	564	39	6	299	1443

few perinatal individuals (less than 1% in both burial types) and no individuals died in the first year of life. There were also few 1–5-year-olds (burial type ABC 17/1327: 1.3%; burial type D 14/1391: 1%). A larger proportion of subadults were aged 6–11 years at death, with little difference between the burial types (burial type ABC 87/1327: 6.6%; burial type D 100/1391: 7.2%), but a significantly higher proportion of 12–17-year-olds were found in burial type D (174/1391: 12.5%) than in burial type ABC (91/1327: 6.9%) (χ^2 = 24.65, df = 1, p ≤ 0.001).

There were similar proportions of 18–25-year-old adults in burial type ABC (244/1327: 18.4%) to burial type D (264/1391: 19%) and for both groups adult age at death peaked at 26–35 years (burial type ABC 414/1327: 31.2%; burial type D 400/1391: 28.8%).

In burial type ABC, 45.1% (628/1392) of individuals were male and 34.1% (474/1392) were female, a ratio of 1.3:1 (χ^2 = 35.62, df = 1, p ≤ 0.001), in contrast to burial type D, where 39.1% (564/1443) of individuals were male and 37.1% (535/1443) were female, a ratio of 1.05:1. The higher proportion of males in burial type ABC when compared to burial type D was statistically significant (χ^2 = 10.57, df = 1, p ≤ 0.001).

In burial type ABC there were similar proportions of 18–25-year-olds, with slightly fewer males (as a percentage of total aged males) (118/599: 19.7%) than females (as a percentage of total aged females) (105/453: 23.2%). The greatest proportion died aged 26–35 years, again with slightly fewer males (213/599: 35.6%) than females (177/453: 39.1%). At 36–45 years, the proportion of females decreased to 26.7% (121/453) and the number of males remained approximately the same at 34.2% (205/599). Significantly more males than females were found to be aged 36–45 years (χ^2 = 6.81, df = 1, p ≤ 0.01) (Fig 15; Fig 16).

In the mass burials there were similar proportions of males and females within the 18–25-year category: 22.5% (115/511) of females (as a percentage of aged females), compared to 24.9% (135/543) of males (as a percentage of aged males). For males, this was a significantly higher proportion than was found in burial type ABC (χ^2 = 4.40, df = 1, p ≤ 0.05). Again the largest group was aged 26–35 years, the proportion of females increasing to 39.3% (201/511) and males to 33.9% (184/543). There was a lower proportion of females (130/511: 25.4%) aged 36–45 years when compared to males (163/543: 30%).

Burials *c* 1400–1539 (period 17) (650 individuals)

The numbers of individuals in burial types ABC and D for period 17 are shown in Table 16 and Table 17.

In period 17 there was more variation in age at death between the burial types, although there were still few subadults aged 6–11 years. Far fewer individuals from burial type D were found in period 17 when compared to the preceding periods.

In burial type ABC there was a mortality peak at 26–35 years. In burial type D this peak was later, at 36–45 years. There was a higher proportion of subadults in burial type D (29/124: 23.4%) when compared to burial type ABC (95/526: 18.1%), although this difference was not significant. Period 17 contained the highest proportion of perinatal individuals, particularly in burial type ABC (24/514: 4.7% of individuals; burial type D 2/122: 1.6%). Few individuals died between 1 and 5 years of age (burial type ABC 10/514: 1.9%, burial type D 1/122: 0.8%). There was a sharp increase in the number of 6–11-year-olds compared with those aged 1–5 years, which was most obvious in burial type D where 10.7% (13/122) of individuals were aged 6–11 years at death compared to 0.8% (1/122) in the 1–5-year category.

Of those in burial type ABC, 20.8% (107/514) were 18–25 years at death compared to 16.4% (20/122) in burial type D. There was a higher proportion of individuals aged 26–35 years in burial type ABC (157/514: 30.5%) than in burial type D (26/122: 21.3%) (χ^2 = 4.10, df = 1, p ≤ 0.05).

Of the individuals in burial type ABC, 45.4% (239/526) were male and 31.2% (164/526) were female (χ^2 = 22.60, df = 1, p ≤ 0.001), a ratio 1.5:1. In burial type D, 41.1% (51/124) were male and 31.5% (39/124) were female, a ratio of 1.3:1.

In burial type ABC, the main differences between males and females were observed in the 18–25-year and 36–45-year age

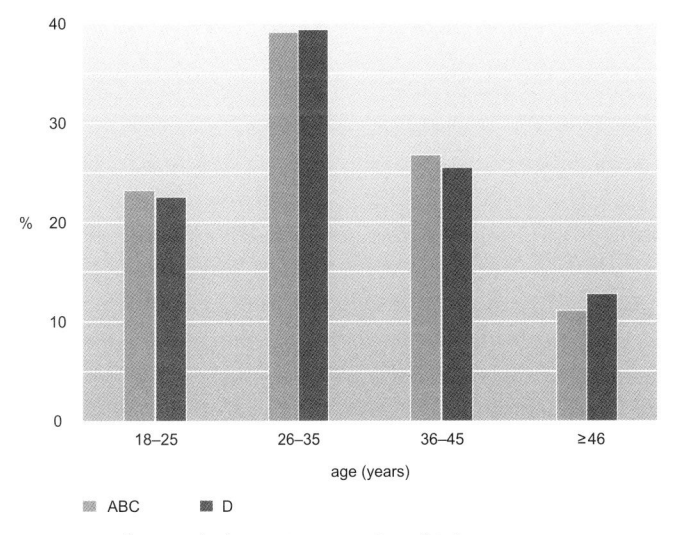

Fig 15 Female age at death, c 1250–c 1400 (period 16)

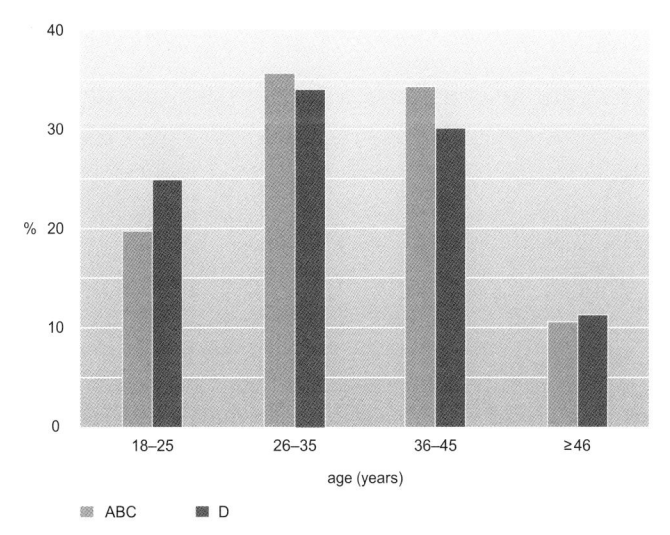

Fig 16 Male age at death, c 1250–c 1400 (period 16)

Results

Table 16 Demographic data for burial type ABC, c 1400–1539 (period 17)

Age	Female	Male	Intermediate	Undetermined	Subadult	Total
Perinatal	0	0	0	0	24	24
7–11 months	0	0	0	0	1	1
1–5 years	0	0	0	0	10	10
6–11 years	0	0	0	0	24	24
12–17 years	0	0	0	0	36	36
18–25 years	49	51	7	0	0	107
26–35 years	59	86	10	2	0	157
36–45 years	35	67	5	0	0	107
≥46 years	19	28	1	0	0	48
Adult	2	7	1	2	0	12
Total	164	239	24	4	95	526

Table 17 Demographic data for burial type D, c 1400–1539 (period 17)

Age	Female	Male	Intermediate	Undetermined	Subadult	Total
Perinatal	0	0	0	0	2	2
1–5 years	0	0	0	0	1	1
6–11 years	0	0	0	0	13	13
12–17 years	0	0	0	0	13	13
18–25 years	8	11	1	0	0	20
26–35 years	10	14	2	0	0	26
36–45 years	11	20	1	0	0	32
≥46 years	10	5	0	0	0	15
Adult	0	1	0	1	0	2
Total	39	51	4	1	29	124

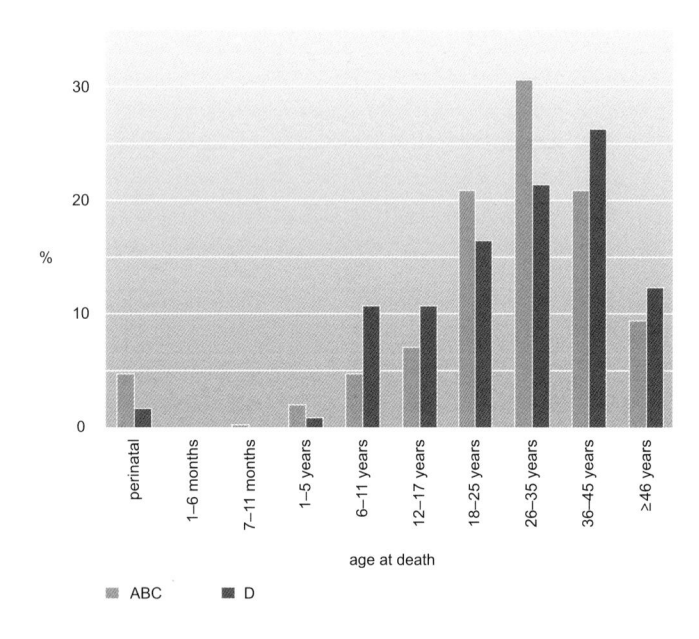

Fig 17 Age at death by burial type, c 1400–1539 (period 17)

groups. There were more 18–25-year-old females as a proportion of total aged females (49/162: 30.2%) when compared to the male equivalent (51/232: 22%). There was also a higher proportion of 36–45-year-old males (67/232: 28.9%) compared to females (35/162: 21.6%). Neither of these differences was statistically significant. The greatest percentage of aged males in burial type ABC was found in the 26–35 year group: 86/232: 37.1%. As in other periods, the smallest proportion of adults was those aged ≥46 years (Fig 18; Fig 19).

Within burial type D, there were similar proportions of males (11/50: 22%) and females (8/39: 20.5%) aged 18–25 years. This was also true of those aged 26–35 years (males 14/50: 28%; females 10/39: 25.6%). At 36–45 years there was a higher proportion of males (20/50: 40%) than females (11/39: 28.2%), although this difference was not significant. There was a lower proportion of males aged ≥46 years (5/50: 10%) than females (10/39: 25.6%) ($\chi^2 = 3.82$, df = 1, $p \leq 0.05$).

There was a higher proportion of 26–35-year-old males within burial type ABC (86/232: 37.1%) than burial type D (14/50: 28%). However, there were fewer 36–45-year-old males in burial type ABC (67/232: 28.9%) compared to burial type D (20/50: 40%). Neither of these results was statistically significant.

Female age at death varied between the burial types. There was a higher proportion of 18–25-year-old and 26–35-year-old females in burial type ABC (49/162: 30.2% and 59/162: 36.4% respectively) compared to burial type D (8/39: 20.5% and 10/39: 25.6%), but this was not statistically significant. Conversely, in burial type D there was a statistically higher proportion of 36–45-year-old females (burial type ABC 35/162:

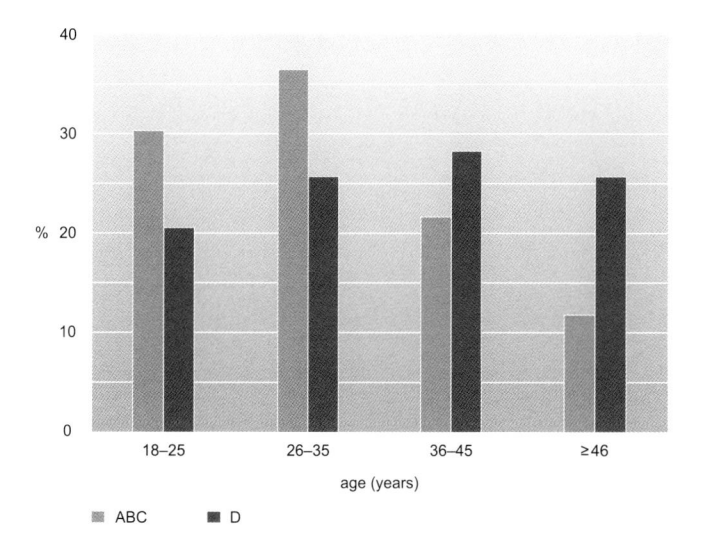

Fig 18 Female age at death, c 1400–1539 (period 17)

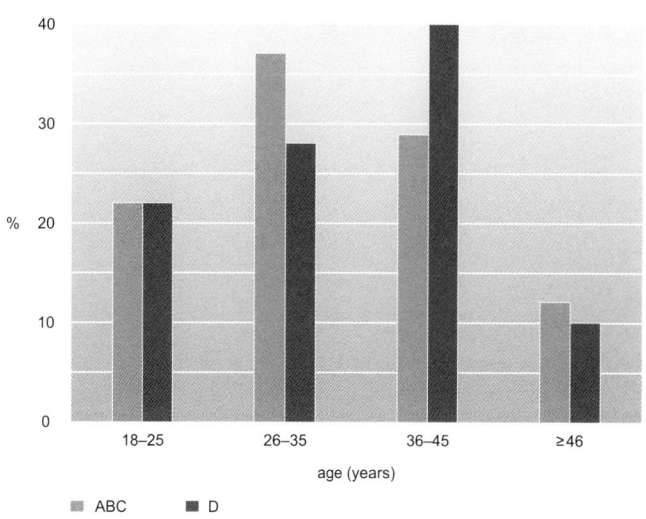

Fig 19 Male age at death, c 1400–1539 (period 17)

21.6%, burial type D 11/39: 28.2%) and females aged ≥46 years (burial type ABC 19/162: 11.7%, burial type D 10/39: 25.6%; χ^2 = 4.93, df = 1, p ≤ 0.05). In this period the age-at-death pattern suggests that the females in burial type ABC died younger than those in burial type D.

Overall observations

In each period there was a higher proportion of females (as a percentage of sexed adults) in burial type D than in burial type ABC. For periods 15 and 16 these results were significant (period 15: burial type ABC 167/386: 43.3%; burial type D 334/647: 51.6% (χ^2 = 3.82, df = 1, p ≤ 0.05); period 16: burial type ABC 474/1102: 43.0%, burial type D 535/1099: 48.7% (χ^2 = 7.12, df = 1, p ≤ 0.01)) (Fig 20).

The male and female percentages of sexed adults remain relatively constant over time in burial type ABC (Fig 21). This contrasts with burial type D, where male and female percentages are closely similar in periods 15 and 16 (Fig 22).

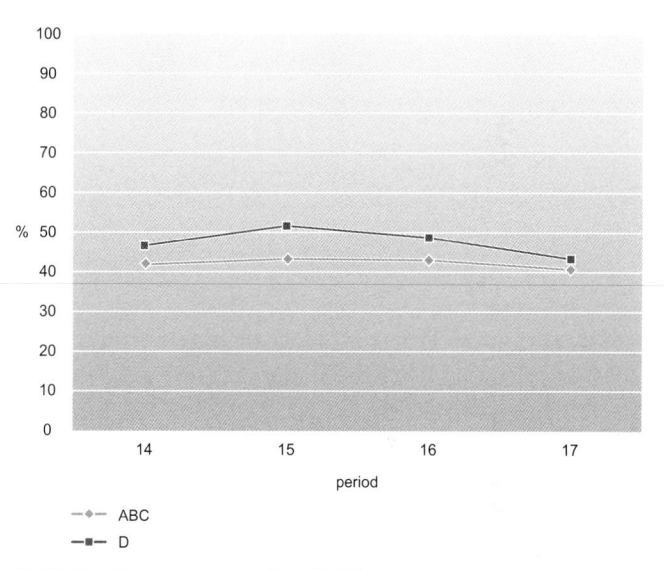

Fig 20 Females as a percentage of sexed adults

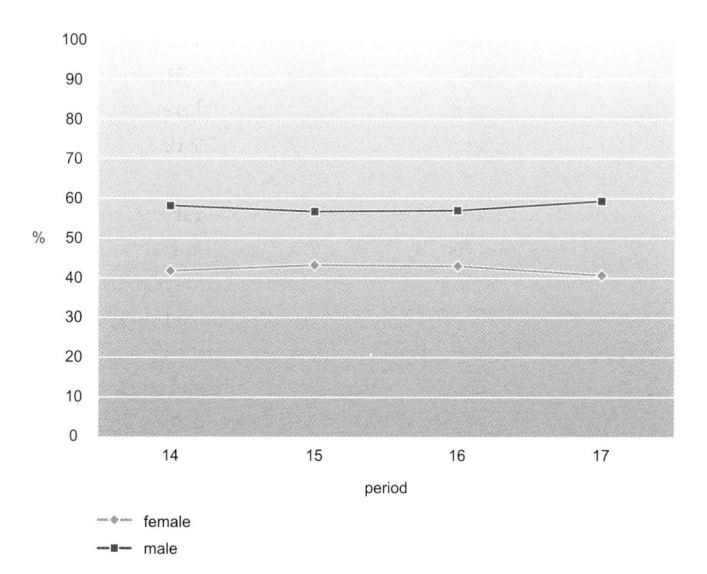

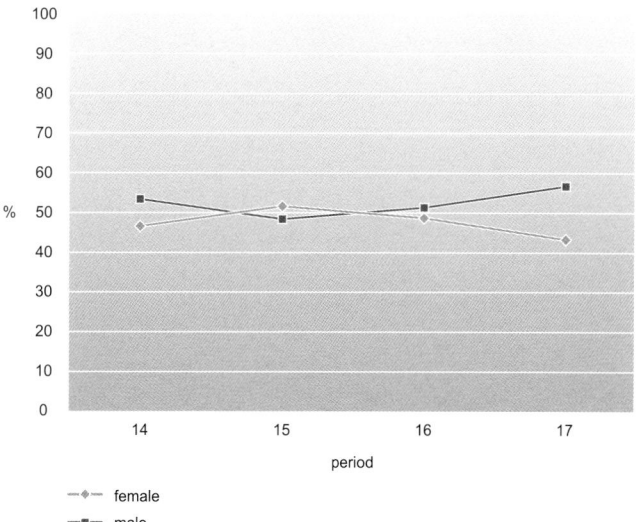

Fig 21 Percentage of sexed adults in burial type ABC

Fig 22 Percentage of sexed adults in burial type D

3.3 Adult stature

Rebecca Redfern

Stature could be calculated for 1635 adults and is summarised in Table 18.

Adult stature *c* 1120–*c* 1200 (period 14)

The mean stature for males was 169.4cm in burial type ABC and 167.0cm in type D. Female mean stature was 162.2cm in burial type ABC and 162.1cm in type D. Stature differences were observed between the burial types for both sexes, but females showed the smallest difference. The greatest differences were observed between the sexes for burial type ABC (7.2cm), and between males from burial types ABC and D (2.4cm). The difference in the overall male and female means was found to be statistically significant (df = 164, p ≤ 0.001), as was the difference for burial types ABC (df = 112, p ≤ 0.001) and D (df = 50, p ≤ 0.001). Male mean stature also differed significantly between burial types (df = 93, p ≤ 0.03).

Adult stature *c* 1200–50 (period 15)

A decrease in mean stature was observed for both sexes and burial types from period 14, apart from for males from burial type D, where a small rise (0.7cm) was found. The mean stature for males was 168.5cm in burial type ABC and 167.7cm in type D. Female mean stature was 159.7cm in burial type ABC and 161.4cm in type D. The largest difference observed between the sexes was seen in burial type D. The overall difference between male and female means was found to be statistically significant (df = 389, p ≤ 0.001), as was the difference between the sexes for burial types ABC (df = 149, p ≤ 0.001) and D (df = 238, p ≤ 0.001). No differences were found between burial types for each sex.

Adult stature *c* 1250–*c* 1400 (period 16)

In this period, a small difference in mean attained stature by burial type was observed in both sexes. The mean stature for males was 168.4cm in burial type ABC and 167.2cm in burial type D, the latter remaining virtually static from period 15 (167.7cm). In females, the mean stature was 161.3cm in burial type ABC and 161.1cm in burial type D. The same pattern was seen in the female data, with a mean of 161.3cm in burial type ABC and 161.1cm in burial type D. Regardless of burial type, the mean was 167.0cm in males and 161.0cm in females. The overall difference in male and female means was found to be statistically significant (df = 833, p ≤ 0.001). As in period 14, the difference in mean male stature between burial types was found to be statistically significant (df = 458, p ≤ 0.017), as were differences between the sexes in burial types ABC (df = 436, p ≤ 0.001) and D (df = 395, p ≤ 0.001).

Adult stature *c* 1400–1539 (period 17)

Mean male stature of 169.6.cm was seen for burial type ABC and 165.7cm for burial type D. In females, the mean stature for burial type ABC was 161.5cm and 160.4cm in burial type D. The largest difference between the sexes in each burial type was observed in this period, a difference of 8.1cm for burial type ABC and 5.3cm for burial type D. The greatest difference between the burial types for males was also found in this period (3.9cm). For both sexes in burial type ABC, there is an increase in attained stature from period 16. In burial type D, attained male stature decreased by 1.5cm and for females by 0.7cm from period 16. The difference in male and female means was found to be statistically significant for both groups (df = 241, p ≤ 0.001), as was the difference in mean male stature between burial types (df = 140, p ≤ 0.001), and between the sexes in burial types ABC (df = 189, p ≤ 0.001) and D (df = 50, p ≤ 0.004).

Table 18 Summary of adult stature by range, mean and standard deviation (SD)

Period	Burial type	Sex	Min	Max	Mean	SD	No. individuals
14	ABC	male	157.1	183.5	169.4	5.3	63
		female	154.5	173.7	162.2	5.1	51
	D	male	156.8	176.6	167.0	5.0	32
		female	149.5	168.0	162.1	4.4	20
15	ABC	male	155.4	182.8	168.5	6.0	86
		female	148.0	175.9	159.7	5.8	65
	D	male	151.8	182.8	167.7	6.0	122
		female	145.2	175.9	161.4	5.7	118
16	ABC	male	153.5	183.5	168.4	5.2	242
		female	145.9	176.8	161.3	5.4	196
	D	male	149.7	180.6	167.2	5.2	218
		female	147.1	175.6	161.1	5.6	179
17	ABC	male	160.1	184.1	169.6	5.1	113
		female	151.4	178.3	161.5	5.6	78
	D	male	152.8	181.4	165.7	6.6	29
		female	150.7	178.0	160.4	6.1	23

Overall observations

The greatest difference between male and female attained stature was observed in period 15 for burial type ABC (8.8cm). For burial type D, the greatest difference was observed in periods 15 and 16 (6.3 and 6.1cm respectively). Differences in female attained stature by burial type were greatest in period 17 (1.1cm) and smallest in period 14 (0.1cm). Male differences in attained stature by burial type were greatest in period 17 and in period 14 (3.9 and 2.4cm respectively), and smallest for period 15 (0.8cm). These results indicate that the St Mary Spital population shows marked sexual dimorphism (Fig 23). Variations in mean stature throughout the period when the cemetery was in use are displayed in Fig 24 and Fig 25.

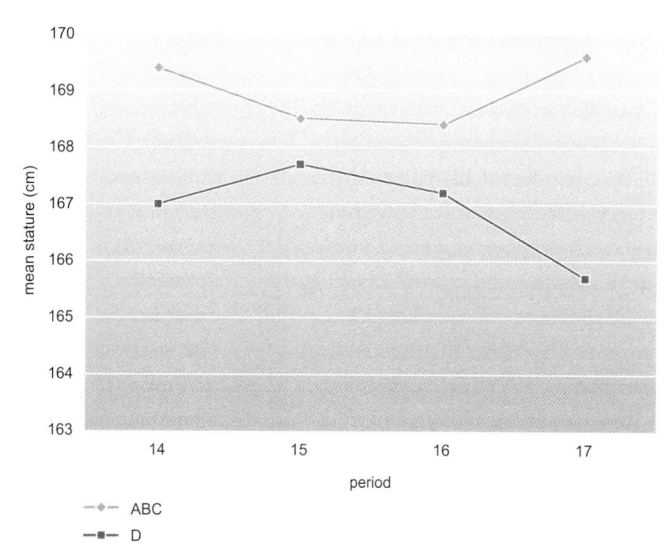

Fig 24 Mean male stature

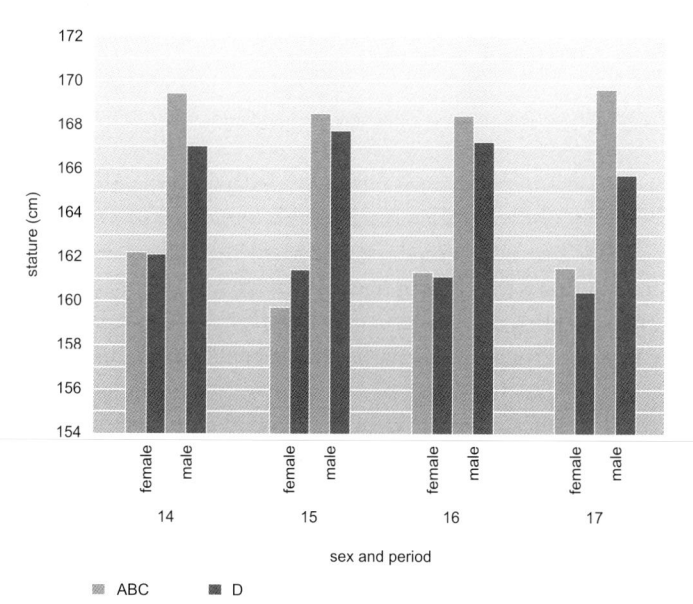

Fig 23 Graph showing stature by period, burial type and sex

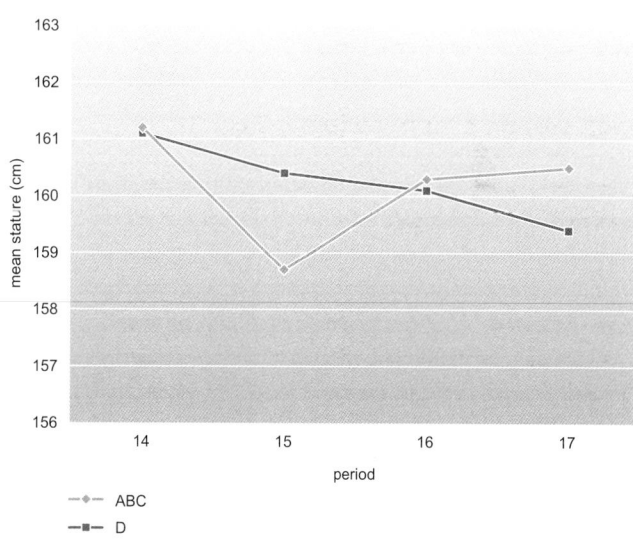

Fig 25 Mean female stature

3.4 Subadult growth

Rebecca Redfern

Femoral length-for-age was calculated for 142 individuals aged between 3 and 17 years (Fig 26). The mean could not be provided for all ages or burial types and, where data were missing for an age group, the average was calculated using data from the age groups above and below it (see Lewis 2002, 35–6). The differences observed between the burial types are discussed further in Chapter 4.3.

Subadult growth *c* 1120–*c* 1200 (period 14)

The greatest disparities in height-for-age between individuals from the different burial types were observed at 9 and 13 years, where burial type D subadults were 49mm and 71mm shorter respectively than their ABC counterparts. This contrasts with those aged 6 years, where those from burial type D were on average 17mm taller than those from type ABC.

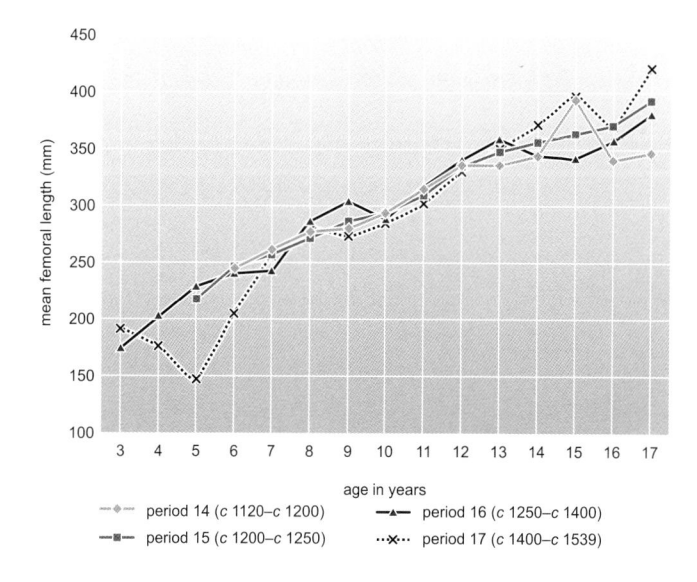

Fig 26 Subadult growth measured by mean femoral length

Results

Subadult growth *c* 1200–50 (period 15)

A comparison of subadult growth profile for ages 5–17 years showed that subadults in burial type D were, until the age of 14, smaller than those in type ABC. After 14 years of age, growth in both burial types followed the same trend. Burial type D displayed an outlier at the age of 13 years (379mm) whose femoral length was greater than others from the same burial type aged 14–17 years.

Subadult growth *c* 1250–*c* 1400 (period 16)

A comparison of subadult growth profiles, based on those aged 3–17 years, showed that there was very little divergence between the trends for the two burial types.

Subadult growth *c* 1400–1539 (period 17)

A comparison of subadult growth profiles, based on those aged 3–17 years, showed that there was very little difference between the trends for the two burial types; for example at 8 years old, only 8mm difference was observed. Subadults in this period achieved the highest final growth compared with the preceding periods.

Overall observations

When data from both burial types were pooled and compared across time, at 17 years old period 17 individuals were found to have the longest femora (420mm) and period 14 the shortest (347mm), despite different growth trajectories during development. Those from period 15 had the most linear growth trajectory, particularly when compared to those from period 17, where large decreases occurred at the ages of 5 and 16 years.

When growth was examined for individuals between the ages of 3 and 17 years, considerable differences were observed between periods. At 3 years old, the longest femora were observed in period 17 (192mm); at 4 years old, in period 16 (202mm); and at 5 years, in periods 15 (217mm) and 16 (230mm). At age 5, the shortest femoral lengths were observed in period 17 (149mm).

At 6 years old individuals from periods 14 to 16 displayed similar growth trajectories, with femoral lengths of 245mm, 247mm and 241mm respectively, whereas individuals in period 17 only attained 204mm, 36mm less than their earlier counterparts. At 7 years old, individuals in periods 14, 15 and 17 had similar femoral lengths (261mm, 257mm and 257mm), and period 16 individuals had the shortest (242mm). Between the ages of 8 and 9 years, individuals in periods 14, 15 and 17 were most similar, and those in period 16 had the longest femora (304mm). At the age of 9 years, individuals in periods 14 and 15 were most similar (280mm and 287mm); the longest femora were observed in period 16 (304mm) and the shortest in period 17 (273mm). Between 10 and 12 years, femoral length was similar in all periods, although period 17 individuals had the shortest femora. At the age of 13, femoral lengths in periods 15 and 17 were most similar (348mm and 350mm); period 16 individuals had the longest femora (359mm) and those in period 14 the shortest (336mm). From the ages of 14 to 17 years, periods 15 and 16 have the most similar trajectories: period 17 individuals had the longest femora and period 14 the shortest, apart from at age 15 where an outlier in the data (394mm) lies closest to period 17 (399mm).

Temporal comparison of the two burial types demonstrates that both follow the same trajectory, although burial type ABC individuals usually had longer femora, except at the age of 3. In burial type ABC, the widest disparities were at the ages of 5, 12 and 13 years, particularly between periods 16 and 17 (Fig 27). In burial type D, the widest disparities were at the ages of 6, 8, 13 and 15 (Fig 28). These data show that differences in growth in burial type ABC occurred a year earlier than in burial type D.

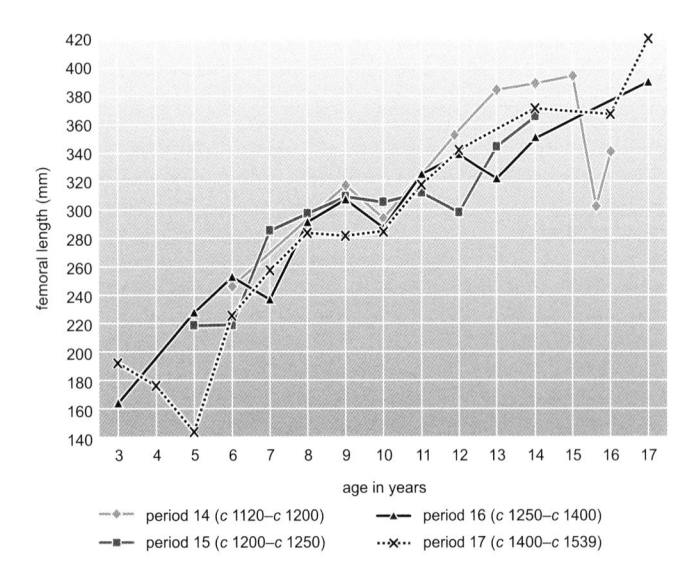

Fig 27 Comparison between periods of subadult growth in burial type ABC

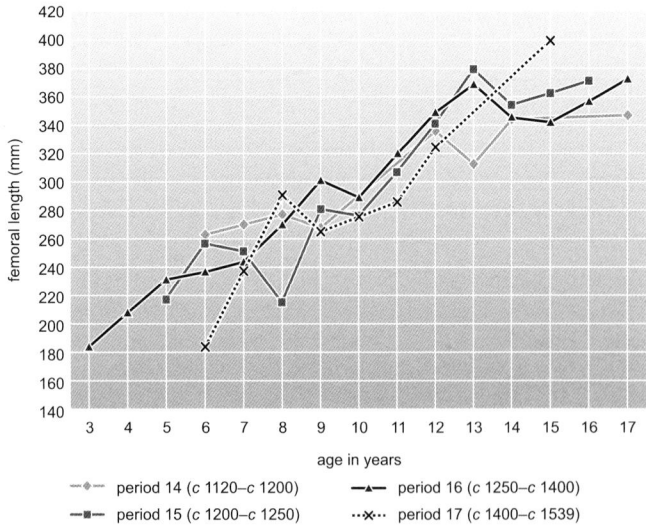

Fig 28 Comparison between periods of subadult growth in burial type D

3.5 Metric analyses

Brian Connell

Cranial indices

One of the most frequently used methods of investigating biological relationships in past populations is the cranial index: the breadth of a skull expressed as a percentage of its length, ie (B × 100)/L. Most values typically lie in the range 70–90%. The cranial index can be classified into one of four major groups: dolichocrany (≤74.9), mesocrany (75.0–79.9), brachycrany (80.0–84.9) and hyperbrachycrany (≥85.0). However, these subdivisions of cranial form are essentially arbitrary and we may fall into the trap of typing individuals based on a single quantitative characteristic. The ability of the cranial index to discriminate between populations is also questionable (Pietrusewsky 2000, 376).

Indices could be calculated for 1379 sexed adults. A summary of the descriptive statistics is provided in Table 19.

An overall mean value of 80.2 placed males at the bottom end of the brachycranic (broad or round headed) category. The overall range for males was 67.6–95.1 and there was no discernable variation between periods. A similar picture was seen in females, with an overall mean value of 80.5 and a range of 68.3–94.5. Hypsicrany (a cranial index greater than 75) was observed in a female from period 16 (1/1009 females: 0.1%).

Post-cranial indices

The post-cranial indices calculated for the lower limbs are used to investigate external diaphyseal morphology, particularly the degree of flattening, which many authors have linked to mechanical stresses (Larsen 1999, 222). Femoral and tibial indices by period, sex and burial type are shown in Table 20.

For period 14, no differences between the burial types were observed for male femoral and tibial indices. No side or sex differences were found, an unexpected result according to Brothwell (1981, 89). Only the left tibial index for the combined data for males from both burial groups varied, being platycnemic. Mesocnemic tibial indices were observed in females from burial type ABC and when the data for both burial groups were collated.

For periods 15 and 16, the femora of both sexes were platymeric and the tibiae were eurycnemic. There were no differences between sides or burial types in these periods. However, in period 17 femoral indices for both sexes showed a temporal change: right femora in burial type D (and for males

Table 19 Summary data for cranial indices by mean, standard deviation (SD), coefficient of variation (V), range, and standard error (SE)

Period	Sex	No.	Mean	SD	V	Min	Max	SE
14	male	77	80.3	4.8	5.98	67.6	90.2	0.545
	female	49	80.6	4.6	5.71	72.6	94.5	0.658
15	male	160	80.5	4.4	5.47	71.3	94.7	0.347
	female	160	80.8	4.4	5.45	68.3	93.2	0.351
16	male	411	80.2	4.5	5.61	67.7	95.1	0.223
	female	370	80.5	3.9	4.84	69.5	90.2	0.203
17	male	94	79.6	3.9	4.90	70.8	89.2	0.403
	female	58	79.4	4.5	5.67	70.4	88.8	0.591
Total	male	742	80.2	4.4	5.49	67.6	95.1	0.163
Total	female	637	80.5	4.2	5.22	68.3	94.5	0.165

Table 20 Femoral and tibial indices by range and mean, by period, burial type and sex (platymeric ≤84.9, eurymeric 85.0–99.9; platycnemic 55.0–62.9, mesocnemic 63.0–69.9, eurycnemic ≥70.0)

Period	Burial type	Sex	Right femoral index No.	Mean	Min	Max	Left femoral index No.	Mean	Min	Max	Right tibial index No.	Mean	Min	Max	Left tibial index No.	Mean	Min	Max
14	ABC	male	102	71.0	64.7	105.7	102	72.9	64.1	106.8	125	80.0	55.2	91.6	68	82.8	59.4	92.8
		female	79	79.5	62.3	96.7	77	79.1	60.5	91.0	60	79.8	63.5	84.9	87	68.3	62.2	87.4
	D	male	51	81.6	68.3	109.1	48	80.1	69.7	96.7	46	74.4	55.2	85.6	46	72.8	59.0	86.1
		female	36	82.4	70.9	109.3	39	80.2	70.6	96.5	24	72.7	60.9	86.7	30	71.9	62.7	81.4
15	ABC	male	358	84.4	64.9	103.7	141	83.2	62.6	107.2	116	73.5	53.0	93.1	109	71.6	57.3	100.3
		female	109	85.0	65.2	109.8	115	84.9	64.9	98.7	92	74.0	53.3	86.4	91	70.2	56.5	90.4
	D	male	220	81.4	62.9	111.3	224	80.0	64.6	107.8	186	72.5	58.8	94.8	194	71.0	55.2	92.8
		female	208	83.4	65.5	104.0	204	67.8	64.8	98.0	184	73.0	56.7	90.9	181	71.6	58.2	130.0
16	ABC	male	422	83.7	64.3	105.9	432	80.0	63.9	100.9	365	79.5	56.5	99.0	359	80.0	54.7	95.9
		female	339	82.9	65.6	110.2	332	83.3	64.1	104.0	282	73.2	54.1	91.3	283	73.6	53.5	89.4
	D	male	402	81.3	63.4	111.1	409	79.5	62.5	124.1	326	73.6	52.9	97.3	326	71.5	53.4	89.9
		female	381	84.0	64.2	106.6	384	82.3	64.4	106.8	323	73.1	57.4	92.9	304	71.8	57.9	123.4
17	ABC	male	168	72.0	69.9	110.5	163	77.6	66.1	114.8	142	74.8	58.9	89.2	135	69.5	59.4	92.7
		female	122	83.3	69.4	102.5	120	83.1	65.1	103.5	98	73.0	59.8	84.5	96	71.1	62.1	110.9
	D	male	46	87.3	72.7	109.5	46	77.4	71.3	111.4	37	75.2	58.1	89.5	39	74.8	59.4	84.9
		female	35	86.7	71.3	96.1	35	81.5	70.3	108.1	31	75.3	63.2	84.5	35	73.6	62.5	85.6

Results

from burial types ABC and D) were eurymeric whereas left femora continued to be platymeric. According to Brothwell (1981, 89), this is a typical result.

Overall, the results show little temporal change. Brothwell (1981, 89) notes that many authors expect platymeria to be more common in females and in the left femur. However, in period 14 the left female tibial indices were mesocnemic in burial type ABC, and in period 17 burial type D males and females had eurymeric right femora.

3.6 Dental disease

Brian Connell

Dental disease is one of the most frequently encountered types of pathology in archaeological human remains. The term covers a range of lesions, from tooth decay (caries), periodontal disease and dental abscesses through to enamel hypoplasia and calculus (tartar) deposits.

Table 21 Frequency of adult tooth positions and teeth, and distribution of dental pathology in period 14 (FDI = Fédération Dentaire Internationale; FDI 1971)

Tooth/tooth position (FDI)	11	12	13	14	15	16	17	18	21	22	23	24	25	26	27
Tooth positions present	241	243	241	242	240	238	232	225	242	245	250	248	243	240	231
Teeth lost post-mortem	38	38	19	15	13	12	11	11	34	31	21	15	10	10	6
% lost post-mortem	15.8	15.6	7.9	6.2	5.4	5.0	4.7	4.9	14.0	12.7	8.4	6.0	4.1	4.2	2.6
Teeth lost ante-mortem	17	9	8	17	29	54	44	34	15	13	10	19	19	59	50
% lost ante-mortem	7.1	3.7	3.3	7.0	12.1	22.7	19.0	15.1	6.2	5.3	4.0	7.7	7.8	24.6	21.6
Tooth unerupted	1	2	0	0	3	0	0	33	0	5	1	0	2	0	0
% unerupted	0.4	0.8	-	-	1.3	-	-	14.7	-	2.0	0.4	-	0.8	-	-
Periapical lesions	5	5	5	11	7	20	15	5	5	4	2	13	11	19	21
% periapical lesions	2.1	2.1	2.1	4.5	2.9	8.4	6.5	2.2	2.1	1.6	0.8	5.2	4.5	7.9	9.1
Teeth present	185	194	214	210	195	172	177	147	193	196	218	214	212	171	175
Carious lesion(s)	5	4	11	19	22	32	36	24	1	4	11	14	23	38	43
% carious teeth	2.7	2.1	5.1	9.0	11.3	18.6	20.3	16.3	0.5	2.0	5.0	6.5	10.8	22.2	24.6
Calculus deposits	148	161	179	164	146	146	139	119	158	163	185	172	159	141	138
% calculus deposits	80.0	83.0	83.6	78.1	74.9	84.9	78.5	81.0	81.9	83.2	84.9	80.4	75.0	82.5	78.9
Enamel hypoplasia	33	34	62	42	24	13	14	9	33	31	65	43	32	17	14
% hypoplastic defects	17.8	17.5	29.0	20.0	12.3	7.6	7.9	6.1	17.1	15.8	29.8	20.1	15.1	9.9	8.0

Table 22 Frequency of adult tooth positions and teeth, and distribution of dental pathology in period 15

Tooth/tooth position (FDI)	11	12	13	14	15	16	17	18	21	22	23	24	25	26	27
Tooth positions present	635	648	648	649	642	619	607	543	649	652	664	660	651	634	600
Teeth lost post-mortem	103	98	49	54	43	27	19	38	116	87	35	40	32	31	33
% lost post-mortem	16.2	15.1	7.6	8.3	6.7	4.4	3.1	7.0	17.9	13.3	5.3	6.1	4.9	4.9	5.5
Teeth lost ante-mortem	22	25	17	36	54	121	99	69	21	19	20	39	53	135	95
% lost ante-mortem	3.5	3.9	2.6	5.5	8.4	19.5	16.3	12.7	3.2	2.9	3.0	5.9	8.1	21.3	15.8
Tooth unerupted	0	6	3	2	0	0	0	98	0	6	3	0	1	0	0
% unerupted	-	0.9	0.5	0.3	-	-	-	18.0	-	0.9	0.5	-	0.2	-	-
Periapical lesions	3	9	17	31	23	41	32	13	3	8	10	37	26	49	36
% periapical lesions	0.5	1.4	2.6	4.8	3.6	6.6	5.3	2.4	0.5	1.2	1.5	5.6	4.0	7.7	6.0
Teeth present	510	519	579	557	545	471	489	338	512	540	606	581	565	468	472
Carious lesion(s)	14	23	27	47	76	89	87	56	17	27	22	55	67	88	102
% carious teeth	2.7	4.4	4.7	8.4	13.9	18.9	17.8	16.6	3.3	5.0	3.6	9.5	11.9	18.8	21.6
Calculus deposit	447	432	485	442	406	415	392	246	439	452	513	461	433	399	374
% calculus deposit	87.6	83.2	83.8	79.4	74.5	88.1	80.2	72.8	85.7	83.7	84.7	79.3	76.6	85.3	79.2
Enamel hypoplasia	91	85	164	83	63	39	38	17	87	93	158	96	62	32	36
% hypoplastic defects	17.8	16.4	28.3	14.9	11.6	8.3	7.8	5.0	17.0	17.2	26.1	16.5	11.0	6.8	7.6

A general summary of dental disease encountered in each period is given by tooth position for adult permanent teeth. These data are calculated true prevalence rates based on the availability of each tooth or tooth position for individuals 18 years and over (Tables 21–4).

For deciduous dentition, tooth positions, ante-mortem tooth loss and caries frequency are given in Table 25.

Subadult dental health by burial type is summarised in Table 26 and discussed further in Chapter 4.3.

Caries

A carious cavity arises as a result of oral bacteria which ferment sugars found in the diet. A by-product of this process is the production of acid from plaque, which in turn demineralises the surface of the tooth (Hillson 1996, 269). In time this causes a cavity to develop on the enamel surface which grows until it penetrates through dentine into the pulp cavity. This process can result in the entire crown of the tooth being destroyed.

28	31	32	33	34	35	36	37	38	41	42	43	44	45	46	47	48	Total
219	271	269	270	269	269	275	275	270	268	270	273	273	272	276	275	265	8160
20	39	27	16	17	14	7	11	10	34	25	19	13	11	12	6	6	571
9.1	14.4	10.0	5.9	6.3	5.2	2.5	4.0	3.7	12.7	9.3	7.0	4.8	4.0	4.3	2.2	2.3	7.0
39	19	5	6	8	24	73	49	48	17	5	3	9	33	76	53	43	907
17.8	7.0	1.9	2.2	3.0	8.9	26.5	17.8	17.8	6.3	1.9	1.1	3.3	12.1	27.5	19.3	16.2	11.1
33	0	0	0	0	3	1	0	43	0	0	0	0	1	0	0	39	167
15.1	-	-	-	-	1.1	0.4	-	15.9	-	-	-	-	0.4	-	-	14.7	2.0
13	6	14	3	3	2	21	7	6	9	4	1	1	2	16	7	3	266
5.9	2.2	5.2	1.1	1.1	0.7	7.6	2.5	2.2	3.4	1.5	0.4	0.4	0.7	5.8	2.5	1.1	3.3
127	213	237	248	244	228	194	215	169	217	240	251	251	227	188	216	177	6515
20	2	4	8	10	22	36	28	14	2	4	8	13	16	29	28	27	558
15.7	0.9	1.7	3.2	4.1	9.6	18.6	13.0	8.3	0.9	1.7	3.2	5.2	7.0	15.4	13.0	15.3	8.6
101	202	221	232	214	182	157	179	142	206	225	222	200	184	154	181	140	5460
79.5	94.8	93.2	93.5	87.7	79.8	80.9	83.3	84.0	94.9	93.8	88.4	79.7	81.1	81.9	83.8	79.1	83.8
7	25	28	80	40	25	10	10	8	27	32	82	47	31	11	10	6	945
5.5	11.7	11.8	32.3	16.4	11.0	5.2	4.7	4.7	12.4	13.3	32.7	18.7	13.7	5.9	4.6	3.4	14.5

28	31	32	33	34	35	36	37	38	41	42	43	44	45	46	47	48	Total
548	701	712	720	723	726	728	727	702	711	714	725	725	732	732	732	704	21,563
29	123	83	72	52	40	31	25	20	148	95	60	42	37	16	24	32	1734
5.3	17.5	11.7	10.0	7.2	5.5	4.3	3.4	2.8	20.8	13.3	8.3	5.8	5.1	2.2	3.3	4.5	8.0
75	33	17	12	25	66	202	119	112	27	17	13	29	71	217	126	102	2088
13.7	4.7	2.4	1.7	3.5	9.1	27.7	16.4	16.0	3.8	2.4	1.8	4.0	9.7	29.6	17.2	14.5	9.7
101	1	0	2	1	2	0	0	163	1	0	1	0	3	2	3	146	545
18.4	0.1	-	0.3	0.1	0.3	-	-	23.2	0.1	-	0.1	-	0.4	0.3	0.4	20.7	2.5
9	5	2	0	3	6	37	21	7	5	6	6	7	11	50	17	4	534
1.6	0.7	0.3	-	0.4	0.8	5.1	2.9	1.0	0.7	0.8	0.8	1.0	1.5	6.8	2.3	0.6	2.5
343	544	612	634	645	618	495	583	407	535	602	651	654	621	497	579	424	17,196
59	3	12	18	25	51	90	104	54	5	5	16	23	69	109	101	60	1601
17.2	0.6	2.0	2.8	3.9	8.3	18.2	17.8	13.3	0.9	0.8	2.5	3.5	11.1	21.9	17.4	14.2	9.3
231	528	585	573	563	510	411	465	305	519	573	568	551	503	404	474	320	14,419
17.3	97.1	95.6	90.4	87.3	82.5	83.0	79.8	74.9	97.0	95.2	87.3	84.3	81.0	81.3	81.9	75.5	83.9
12	71	101	188	115	82	30	46	14	76	107	214	94	77	35	38	18	2462
3.5	13.1	16.5	29.7	17.8	13.3	6.1	7.9	3.4	14.2	17.8	32.9	14.4	12.4	7.0	6.6	4.2	14.3

Results

Table 23 Frequency of adult tooth positions and teeth, and distribution of dental pathology in period 16

Tooth/tooth position (FDI)	11	12	13	14	15	16	17	18	21	22	23	24	25	26	27
Tooth positions present	1489	1503	1514	1497	1481	1453	1394	1251	1474	1501	1517	1507	1485	1445	1387
Teeth lost post-mortem	272	231	137	95	95	66	56	80	248	205	110	88	76	51	56
% lost post-mortem	18.3	15.4	9.0	6.3	6.4	4.5	4.0	6.4	16.8	13.7	7.3	5.8	5.1	3.5	4.0
Lost ante-mortem	73	78	62	139	173	344	267	194	74	81	63	130	172	364	295
% lost ante-mortem	4.9	5.2	4.1	9.3	11.7	23.7	19.2	15.5	5.0	5.4	4.2	8.6	11.6	25.2	21.3
Tooth unerupted	0	14	0	3	2	0	0	224	2	11	0	1	3	0	0
% unerupted	-	0.9	-	0.2	0.1	-	-	17.9	0.1	0.7	-	0.1	0.2	-	-
Periapical lesion	17	32	36	65	47	114	74	37	20	18	32	75	44	127	68
% periapical lesion	1.1	2.1	2.4	4.3	3.2	7.8	5.3	3.0	1.4	1.2	2.1	5.0	3.0	8.8	4.9
Teeth present	1144	1180	1315	1260	1211	1043	1071	753	1150	1204	1344	1288	1234	1030	1036
Carious lesion(s)	40	48	89	139	182	214	236	139	37	52	99	165	191	237	212
% carious teeth	3.5	4.1	6.8	11.0	15.0	20.5	22.0	18.5	3.2	4.3	7.4	12.8	15.5	23.0	20.5
Calculus deposits	971	997	1116	959	908	874	872	556	984	1013	1143	1056	943	880	870
% calculus deposits	84.9	84.5	84.9	76.1	75.0	83.8	81.4	73.8	85.6	84.1	85.0	82.0	76.4	85.4	84.0
Enamel hypoplasia	202	196	321	183	133	79	86	40	201	168	324	187	128	94	81
% hypoplastic defects	17.7	16.6	24.4	14.5	11.0	7.6	8.0	5.3	17.5	14.0	24.1	14.5	10.4	9.1	7.8

Table 24 Frequency of adult tooth positions and teeth, and distribution of dental pathology in period 17

Tooth/tooth position (FDI)	11	12	13	14	15	16	17	18	21	22	23	24	25	26	27
Tooth positions present	348	348	355	357	357	355	338	300	343	341	346	347	347	344	326
Teeth lost post-mortem	58	37	25	16	19	18	14	17	62	47	27	20	24	15	11
% lost post-mortem	16.7	10.6	7.0	4.5	5.3	5.1	4.1	5.7	18.1	13.8	7.8	5.8	6.9	4.4	3.4
Lost ante-mortem	20	23	19	36	45	96	68	52	23	18	18	43	49	97	65
% lost ante-mortem	5.7	6.6	5.4	10.1	12.6	27.0	20.1	17.3	6.7	5.3	5.2	12.4	14.1	28.2	19.9
Tooth unerupted	0	5	0	1	0	0	0	54	0	4	0	0	0	0	0
% unerupted	-	1.4	-	0.3	-	-	-	18.0	-	1.2	-	-	-	-	-
Periapical lesion	3	3	11	18	12	32	23	9	6	6	14	18	16	26	18
% periapical lesion	0.9	0.9	3.1	5.0	3.4	9.0	6.8	3.0	1.7	1.8	4.0	5.2	4.6	7.6	5.5
Teeth present	270	283	311	304	293	241	256	177	258	272	301	284	274	232	250
Carious lesion(s)	21	18	27	44	50	60	55	36	21	17	22	38	45	49	57
% carious teeth	7.8	6.4	8.7	14.5	17.1	24.9	21.5	20.3	8.1	6.3	7.3	13.4	16.4	21.1	22.8
Calculus deposits	229	241	255	227	218	199	197	121	214	218	251	205	202	202	194
% calculus deposits	84.8	85.2	82.0	74.7	74.4	82.6	77.0	68.4	82.9	80.1	83.4	72.2	73.7	87.1	77.6
Enamel hypoplasia	44	33	71	33	24	16	15	6	47	32	65	31	26	21	23
% hypoplastic defects	16.3	11.7	22.8	10.9	8.2	6.6	5.9	3.4	18.2	11.8	21.6	10.9	9.5	9.1	9.2

28	31	32	33	34	35	36	37	38	41	42	43	44	45	46	47	48	Total
80	1698	1714	1727	1715	1724	1737	1731	1656	1692	1714	1739	1727	1731	1745	1748	1673	50,649
82	287	214	152	122	101	68	55	53	262	192	143	100	94	57	59	61	3968
6.4	16.9	12.5	8.8	7.1	5.9	3.9	3.2	3.2	15.5	11.2	8.2	5.8	5.4	3.3	3.4	3.6	7.8
10	125	81	52	87	195	556	383	297	129	83	51	88	219	576	367	301	6309
6.4	7.4	4.7	3.0	5.1	11.3	32.0	22.1	17.9	7.6	4.8	2.9	5.1	12.7	33.0	21.0	18.0	12.5
14	4	1	2	2	4	1	4	371	4	1	0	1	5	2	4	349	1229
6.7	0.2	0.1	0.1	0.1	0.2	0.1	0.2	22.4	0.2	0.1	-	0.1	0.3	0.1	0.2	20.9	2.4
29	21	16	16	17	17	85	39	19	22	18	16	20	18	88	36	14	1297
2.3	1.2	0.9	0.9	1.0	1.0	4.9	2.3	1.1	1.3	1.1	0.9	1.2	1.0	5.0	2.1	0.8	2.6
74	1282	1418	1521	1504	1424	1112	1289	935	1297	1438	1545	1538	1413	1110	1318	962	39,143
43	19	29	41	74	129	219	247	143	19	29	52	70	156	198	247	152	4047
8.5	1.5	2.0	2.7	4.9	9.1	19.7	19.2	15.3	1.5	2.0	3.4	4.6	11.0	17.8	18.7	15.8	10.3
87	1243	1337	1348	1262	1136	924	1055	700	1264	1359	1357	1293	1131	894	1063	741	32,836
5.8	97.0	94.3	88.6	83.9	79.8	83.1	81.8	74.9	97.5	94.5	87.8	84.1	80.0	80.5	80.7	77.0	83.9
40	163	206	433	236	155	76	70	19	166	198	469	246	175	60	58	13	5206
5.2	12.7	14.5	28.5	15.7	10.9	6.8	5.4	2.0	12.8	13.8	30.4	16.0	12.4	5.4	4.4	1.4	13.3

28	31	32	33	34	35	36	37	38	41	42	43	44	45	46	47	48	Total
97	400	400	403	405	403	407	410	391	396	401	403	403	403	407	411	395	11,887
18	67	49	32	25	22	14	16	13	71	45	37	28	21	11	12	10	901
6.1	16.8	12.3	7.9	6.2	5.5	3.4	3.9	3.3	17.9	11.2	9.2	6.9	5.2	2.7	2.9	2.5	7.6
61	29	19	17	23	49	142	107	91	28	17	11	22	52	156	105	80	1681
0.5	7.3	4.8	4.2	5.7	12.2	34.9	26.1	23.3	7.1	4.2	2.7	5.5	12.9	38.3	25.5	20.3	14.1
45	0	0	0	0	0	0	0	84	0	0	1	0	0	1	1	80	276
5.2	-	-	-	-	-	-	-	21.5	-	-	0.2	-	-	0.2	0.2	20.3	2.3
7	5	4	4	9	10	28	9	7	7	7	7	2	5	13	19	11	7	369
2.4	1.3	1.0	1.0	2.2	2.5	6.9	2.2	1.8	1.8	1.7	0.5	1.2	3.2	4.7	2.7	1.8	3.1
73	304	332	354	357	332	251	287	203	297	339	354	353	330	239	293	225	9029
33	8	11	22	34	43	67	60	35	8	13	26	30	61	67	71	49	1198
9.1	2.6	3.3	6.2	9.5	13.0	26.7	20.9	17.2	2.7	3.8	7.3	8.5	18.5	28.0	24.2	21.8	13.3
26	285	310	308	284	264	193	229	138	281	317	316	284	249	186	238	176	7357
2.8	93.8	93.4	87.0	79.6	79.5	76.9	79.8	68.0	94.6	93.5	89.3	80.5	75.5	77.8	81.2	78.2	81.5
4	35	49	96	56	18	16	15	7	33	49	104	57	30	12	8	10	1086
2.3	11.5	14.8	27.1	15.7	5.4	6.4	5.2	3.4	11.1	14.5	29.4	16.1	9.1	5.0	2.7	4.4	12.0

Results

Table 25 Frequency of deciduous tooth positions and teeth, with caries distribution

Tooth/tooth position (FDI)	51	52	53	54	55	61	62	63	64	65	71	72	73	74	75	81	82	83	84	85	Total
Tooth positions present																					
Period 14	3	5	13	11	14	2	5	14	8	14	3	4	10	13	22	4	5	8	13	18	189
Period 15	8	14	43	32	54	8	15	41	41	58	7	17	42	51	75	8	16	38	53	76	697
Period 16	24	35	79	75	95	23	33	69	67	96	20	33	83	109	136	25	38	89	107	131	1367
Period 17	8	9	23	18	25	7	9	22	16	21	10	12	19	27	30	11	12	19	31	31	360
Total	43	63	158	136	188	40	62	146	132	189	40	66	154	200	263	48	71	154	204	256	2613
Teeth lost post-mortem																					
Period 14	3	2	2	1	2	1	2	2	0	1	1	1	4	1	2	2	3	5	1	1	37
Period 15	1	4	1	0	1	0	0	2	3	0	4	5	2	1	1	4	5	4	2	3	43
Period 16	6	7	9	2	1	8	6	9	5	0	7	6	14	6	1	11	7	13	3	2	123
Period 17	3	2	5	0	0	2	2	6	1	1	6	5	9	3	2	2	6	7	4	2	68
Total	13	15	17	3	4	11	10	19	9	2	18	17	29	11	6	19	21	29	10	8	271
Teeth lost ante-mortem																					
Period 14	0	0	0	0	0	0	0	1	0	0	0	0	0	0	0	0	0	0	0	0	1
Period 15	1	1	0	0	0	1	1	0	0	0	0	0	1	0	0	0	0	0	0	0	5
Period 16	0	1	0	0	0	1	1	0	0	0	1	0	0	0	0	0	0	0	0	0	4
Period 17	0	0	0	0	1	0	0	0	0	1	0	0	0	0	1	0	0	0	1	1	5
Total	1	2	0	0	1	2	2	1	0	1	1	0	1	0	1	0	0	0	1	1	15
Teeth present																					
Period 14	0	3	11	10	12	1	3	11	8	13	2	3	6	12	20	2	2	3	12	17	151
Period 15	6	9	42	32	53	7	14	39	38	58	3	12	39	50	74	4	11	34	51	73	649
Period 16	18	27	70	73	94	14	26	60	62	96	12	27	69	103	135	14	31	76	104	129	1240
Period 17	5	7	18	18	24	5	7	16	15	19	4	7	10	24	27	9	6	12	26	28	287
Total	29	46	141	133	183	27	50	126	123	186	21	49	124	189	256	29	50	125	193	247	2327
Teeth with caries																					
Period 14	0	0	3	3	4	0	0	4	5	7	0	0	0	1	4	0	0	0	2	2	35
Period 15	0	0	5	3	4	0	0	4	14	22	0	0	1	3	4	0	0	1	2	7	70
Period 16	1	0	3	13	22	1	0	3	22	23	0	0	2	10	7	0	0	3	10	6	126
Period 17	1	0	1	2	5	0	0	2	4	2	0	1	0	1	2	0	0	1	2	4	28
Total	2	0	12	21	35	1	0	13	45	54	0	1	3	15	17	0	0	5	16	19	259
Carious teeth (%)	6.9	-	8.5	15.8	19.1	3.7	-	10.3	36.6	29.0	-	2.0	2.4	7.9	6.6	-	-	4.0	8.3	7.7	11.1

Table 26 Subadult dental health by period and burial type

Period	Age (years)	Burial type	Dentition	Teeth present	Pathology	No. affected	%
14	1–5	ABC	deciduous	28	calculus	18	64.3
					caries	2	7.1
					periodontitis	1	3.6
	6–11	ABC	deciduous	32	calculus	18	56.3
					caries	2	6.3
					hypoplasia	17	53.1
					periodontitis	1	3.1
			permanent	42	calculus	18	42.9
					caries	2	4.8
					hypoplasia	17	40.5
					periodontitis	1	2.4
		D	deciduous	80	calculus	47	58.8
					caries	15	18.8
					periodontitis	6	7.5
			permanent	130	calculus	51	39.2
					caries	7	5.4
					hypoplasia	22	16.9
					periapical lesion	1	0.8
					periodontitis	7	5.4
	12–17	ABC	permanent	682	calculus	448	65.7
					caries	14	2.1

Period	Age (years)	Burial type	Dentition	Teeth present	Pathology	No. affected	%
14 (cont)					hypoplasia	122	17.9
					periapical lesion	4	0.6
					periodontitis	61	8.9
		D	deciduous	8	calculus	4	50.0
					periodontitis	1	12.5
	subadult	ABC	deciduous	3	calculus	3	100.0
					caries	1	33.3
					periodontitis	1	33.3
			permanent	26	calculus	25	96.2
15	1–5	ABC	deciduous	42	calculus	12	28.6
					caries	4	9.5
					periapical lesion	1	2.4
					periodontitis	1	2.4
			permanent	12	calculus	2	16.7
					caries	1	8.3
					hypoplasia	6	50.0
		D	deciduous	95	calculus	22	23.2
					caries	7	7.4
			permanent	4	hypoplasia	1	25.0
	6–11	ABC	deciduous	115	calculus	61	53.0

Table 26 (cont)

Period	Age (years)	Burial type	Dentition	Teeth present	Pathology	No. affected	%
15 (cont)					caries	12	10.4
					periodontitis	13	11.3
			permanent	279	calculus	123	44.1
					hypoplasia	46	16.5
					periodontitis	1	0.4
		D	deciduous	385	calculus	231	60.0
					caries	57	14.8
					hypoplasia	1	0.3
					periapical lesion	8	2.1
					periodontitis	30	7.8
			permanent	804	calculus	313	38.9
					caries	18	2.2
					hypoplasia	233	29.0
					periodontitis	6	0.7
	12–17	ABC	deciduous	6	calculus	4	66.7
					caries	1	16.7
			permanent	1240	calculus	752	60.6
					caries	48	3.9
					hypoplasia	305	24.6
					periapical lesion	3	0.2
					periodontitis	47	3.8
		D	deciduous	33	calculus	24	72.7
					caries	6	18.2
					periapical lesion	1	3.0
					periodontitis	9	27.3
			permanent	2275	calculus	1385	60.9
					caries	47	2.1
					hypoplasia	546	24.0
					periapical lesion	3	0.1
					periodontitis	155	6.8
	subadult	ABC	permanent	27	calculus	14	51.9
					caries	1	3.7
					periodontitis	16	59.3
16	1–5	ABC	deciduous	182	calculus	21	11.5
					caries	2	1.1
		D	deciduous	88	calculus	10	11.4
					caries	3	3.4
					hypoplasia	42	47.7
					periapical lesion	2	2.3
	6–11	ABC	deciduous	453	calculus	239	52.8
					caries	55	12.1
					hypoplasia	9	2.0
					periapical lesion	1	0.2
					periodontitis	13	2.9
			permanent	869	calculus	393	45.2
					caries	16	1.8
					hypoplasia	228	26.2
					periodontitis	16	1.8
		D	deciduous	543	calculus	287	52.9
					caries	56	10.3
					hypoplasia	3	0.6
					periapical lesion	4	0.7
					periodontitis	16	2.9

Period	Age (years)	Burial type	Dentition	Teeth present	Pathology	No. affected	%
16 (cont)			permanent	1033	calculus	432	41.8
					caries	14	1.4
					hypoplasia	255	24.7
					periapical lesion	1	0.1
					periodontitis	22	2.1
	12–17	ABC	deciduous	8	calculus	7	87.5
					caries	1	12.5
					periodontitis	4	50.0
			permanent	1767	calculus	1182	66.9
					caries	64	3.6
					hypoplasia	316	17.9
					periapical lesion	3	0.2
					periodontitis	135	7.6
		D	deciduous	26	calculus	17	65.4
					caries	4	15.4
			permanent	3839	calculus	2340	61.0
					caries	82	2.1
					hypoplasia	870	22.7
					periapical lesion	11	0.3
					periodontitis	357	9.3
	subadult	ABC	permanent	3	calculus	2	66.7
17	1–5	ABC	deciduous	103	caries	1	1.0
					calculus	47	45.6
		D	deciduous	5	caries	3	60.0
					periapical lesion	1	20.0
			permanent	4	calculus	3	75.0
	6–11	ABC	deciduous	120	calculus	54	45.0
					caries	17	14.2
					periodontitis	5	4.2
			permanent	203	calculus	111	54.7
					caries	6	3.0
					hypoplasia	74	36.5
					periodontitis	10	4.9
		D	deciduous	69	calculus	30	43.5
					caries	5	7.2
					hypoplasia	3	4.3
			permanent	203	calculus	88	43.3
					caries	1	0.5
					hypoplasia	35	17.2
					periodontitis	1	0.5
	12–17	ABC	deciduous	1	calculus	1	100.0
			permanent	846	calculus	538	63.6
					caries	32	3.8
					hypoplasia	190	22.5
					periapical lesion	4	0.5
					periodontitis	90	10.6
		D	deciduous	1	calculus	1	100.0
			permanent	309	calculus	175	56.6
					caries	4	1.3
					hypoplasia	73	23.6
					periapical lesion	1	0.3
					periodontitis	11	3.6

Results

In this population caries was very common, with the frequencies in all teeth from periods 14–17 ranging from 8.6% to 13.3%. The true prevalence rate of caries was 9.2% (8040/87,315 teeth), with 10.3% (7604/71,883) of adult teeth and 4.1% (636/15,432) of all subadult teeth, including 11.1% (259/2327) of deciduous teeth, affected. Female teeth (3399/32,227: 10.5%) displayed a slightly higher rate of caries than male teeth (3663/36,471: 10.0%). The highest frequencies occurred in the cheek-teeth, with caries most common of all in the first molars, followed by second and third molars respectively. Canine teeth showed the lowest frequencies of carious lesions (Fig 29).

The adult caries prevalence increased over the period of use of the cemetery, from 8.6% (558/6515) in period 14 to 13.3% (1198/9029) in period 17. The increase from period 16 (4047/39,143: 10.3%) to period 17 (1198/9029: 13.3%) was statistically significant ($\chi^2 = 64.89$, df = 1, $p \leq 0.001$) (Fig 30). Females also show higher frequencies of caries than males in period 15 and period 17, but both sexes show a gradual increase in caries frequency from the earliest phases of cemetery use.

At St Mary Spital, females were more strongly affected than males by tooth decay in both burial types in periods 14–17 (Fig 31; Fig 32) and the application of a Kolmogorov–Smirnov test indicated that this was highly significant (K = 0.032, $p \leq 0.01$). This is unlikely, however, to represent major dietary differences between males and females and can most likely be attributed to variations in the age-at-death profiles of each period, ie young males with low caries experience and older females with high caries experience.

Teeth from burial type ABC (4038/35,830: 11.3%) were more often affected than teeth from burial type D (3364/35,960: 9.4%) ($\chi^2 = 71.18$, df = 1, $p \leq 0.001$). However, in period 14 the caries rate in burial type D was higher than in burial type ABC, and to a statistically significant level when data for both sexes were combined (burial type ABC 324/3957: 8.2%; burial type D 217/2216: 9.8%; $\chi^2 = 4.57$, df = 1, $p \leq 0.05$).

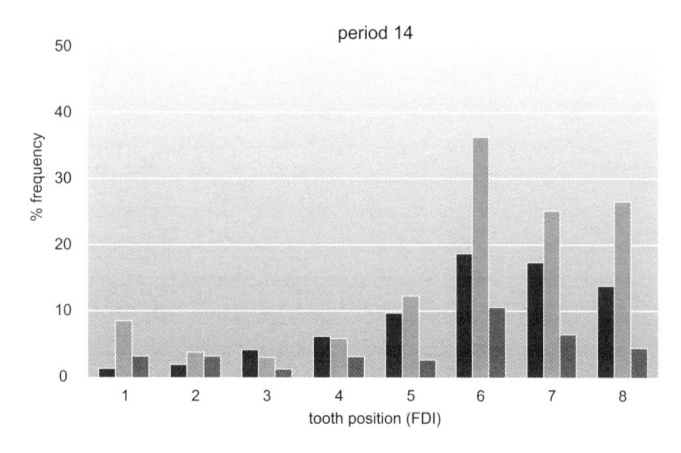

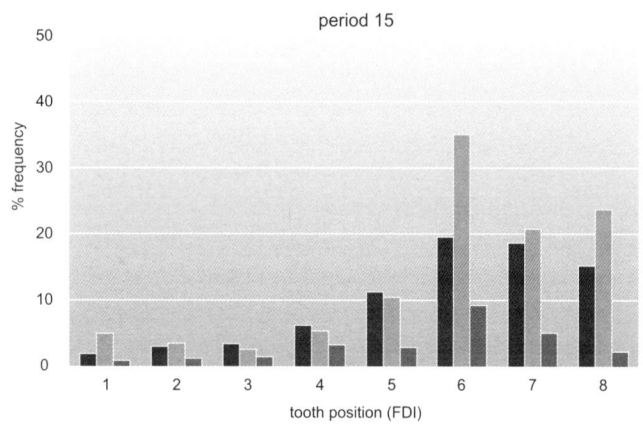

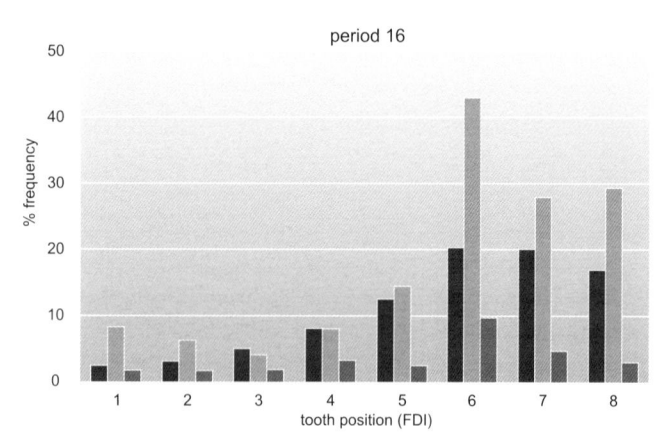

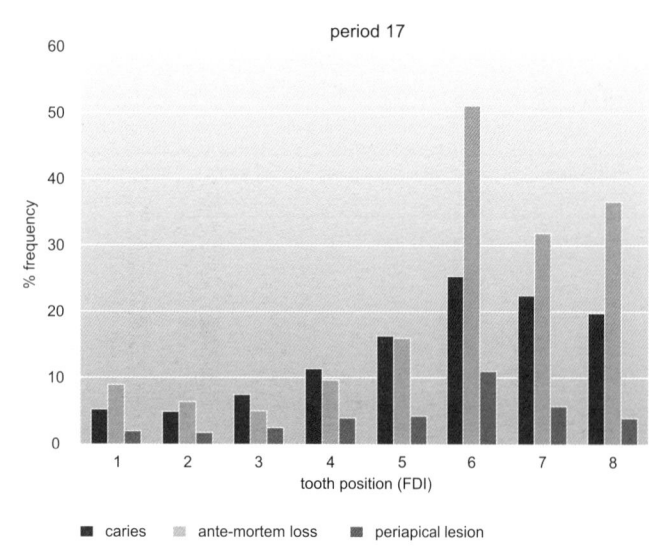

Fig 29 Frequency of distribution of caries, ante-mortem tooth loss and periapical lesions by tooth position

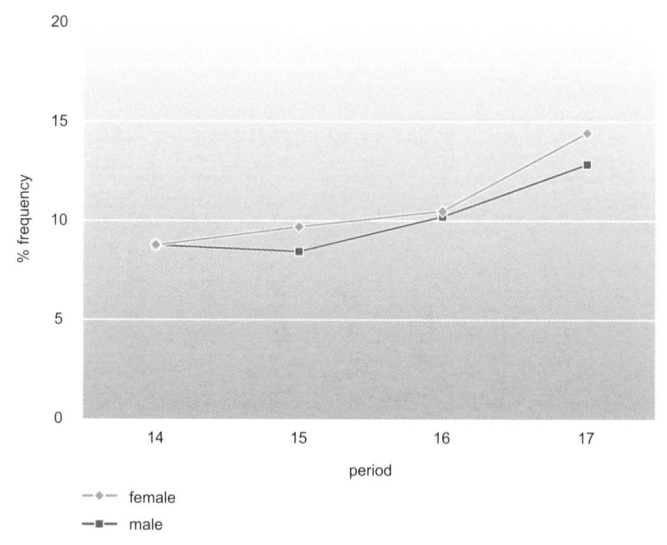

Fig 30 Comparison of caries frequency in males and females

Dental disease

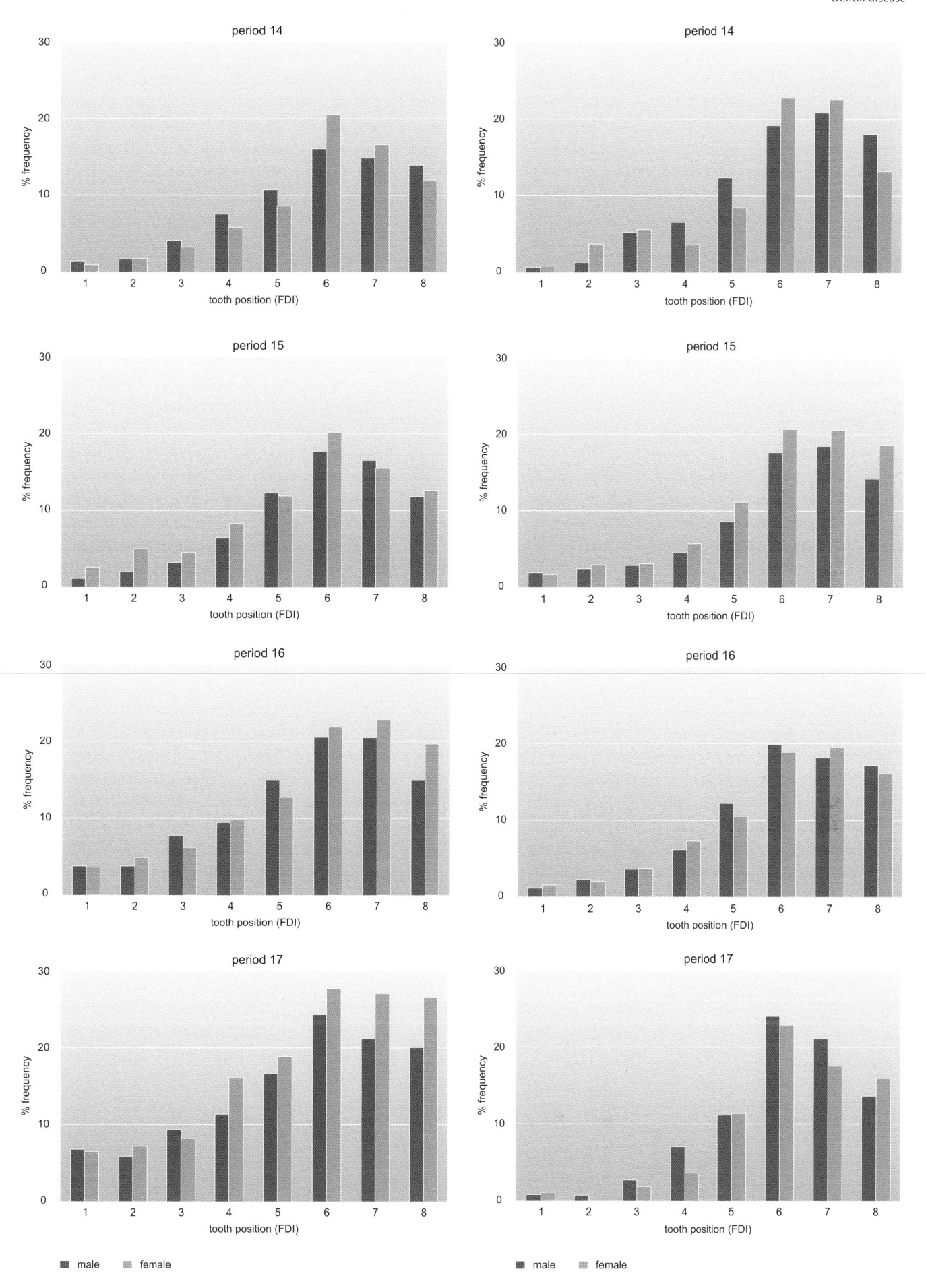

Fig 31 Distribution of carious cavities in burial type ABC

Fig 32 Distribution of carious cavities in burial type D

Results

Over time, males and female caries rates followed similar patterns. The graphs for each sex show that the true prevalence rates for caries remained stable in burial type D throughout the use of the cemetery, but gradually rose in burial type ABC (Fig 33; Fig 34).

A useful dietary indicator is provided by examining the site of origin of a carious lesion. Lesions were classified according to the surface of the crown in which they appeared. Where advanced destruction of the crown made the exact origin of the lesion difficult to identify, caries was classified as 'gross'. Gross caries occurred in high frequencies, varying from 22.7% to 27.2% in periods 14–17. The examination of the distribution of caries in the teeth showed that the most frequent sites are on mesial (25.3%) and distal (24.8%) surfaces (Table 27). This distribution holds true for all periods (14–17) and all burial types (Fig 35). The lingual tooth surfaces have little caries, most probably because of wash from the salivary glands situated in the area.

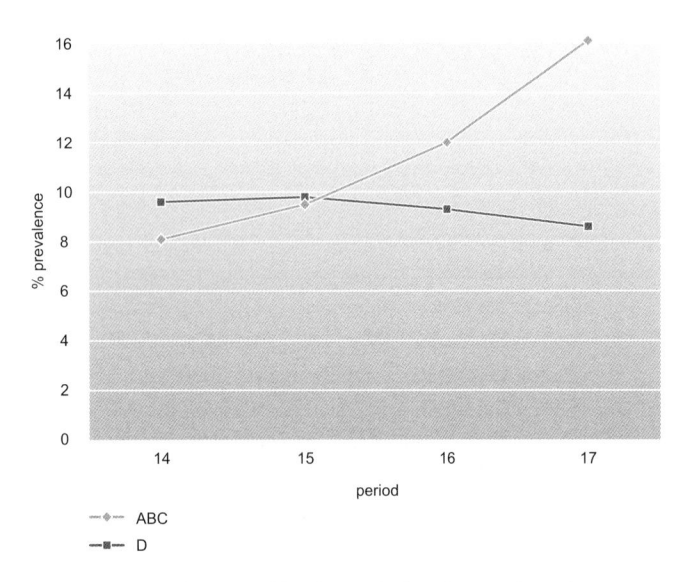

Fig 33 True prevalence rate of female caries by burial type and period

Fig 34 True prevalence rate of male caries by burial type and period

Table 27 Distribution of carious lesions on surfaces of adult permanent teeth by period and sex

Period	Sex	Occlusal No.	%	Lingual No.	%	Buccal No.	%	Mesial No.	%	Distal No.	%	Gross No.	%	Root No.	%	All locations Carious teeth	Teeth present	%
14	male	21	7.0	4	1.3	12	4.0	86	28.5	66	21.9	92	30.5	21	7.0	302	3443	8.8
	female	21	8.8	1	0.4	11	4.6	69	28.8	56	23.3	57	23.8	25	10.4	240	2741	8.8
	not sexed	1	6.3	0	-	1	6.3	6	37.5	4	25.0	3	18.8	1	6.3	16	331	4.8
	total	43	7.7	5	0.9	24	4.3	161	28.9	126	22.6	152	27.2	47	8.4	558	6515	8.6
15	male	42	6.2	5	0.7	58	8.5	162	23.8	170	25.0	170	25.0	73	10.7	680	8046	8.5
	female	50	6.2	7	0.9	60	7.4	231	28.6	212	26.2	179	22.1	70	8.7	809	8348	9.7
	not sexed	4	3.6	1	0.9	12	10.7	36	32.1	25	22.3	33	29.5	1	0.9	112	802	14.0
	total	96	6.0	13	0.8	130	8.1	429	26.8	407	25.4	382	23.9	144	9.0	1601	17,196	9.3
16	male	160	7.9	10	0.5	149	7.3	533	26.2	495	24.3	466	22.9	223	11.0	2036	19955	10.2
	female	132	7.1	30	1.6	165	8.9	426	23.0	481	25.9	422	22.7	199	10.7	1855	17705	10.5
	not sexed	15	9.6	4	2.6	21	13.5	33	21.2	38	24.4	29	18.6	16	10.3	156	1483	10.5
	total	307	7.6	44	1.1	335	8.3	992	24.5	1014	25.1	917	22.7	438	10.8	4047	39,143	10.3
17	male	37	5.7	5	0.8	72	11.2	154	23.9	146	22.6	171	26.5	60	9.3	645	5027	12.8
	female	28	5.7	4	0.8	61	12.3	120	24.2	128	25.9	114	23.0	40	8.1	495	3433	14.4
	not sexed	1	1.7	1	1.7	10	17.2	20	34.5	13	22.4	9	15.5	4	6.9	58	569	10.2
	total	66	5.5	10	0.8	143	11.9	294	24.5	287	24.0	294	24.5	104	8.7	1198	9029	13.3
Total	male	260	7.1	24	0.7	291	7.9	935	25.5	877	23.9	899	24.5	377	10.3	3663	36471	10.0
	female	231	6.8	42	1.2	297	8.7	846	24.9	877	25.8	772	22.7	334	9.8	3399	32227	10.5
	not sexed	21	6.1	6	1.8	44	12.9	95	27.8	80	23.4	74	21.6	22	6.4	342	3185	10.7
	total	512	6.9	72	1.0	632	8.5	1876	25.3	1834	24.8	1745	23.6	733	9.9	7404	71,883	10.3

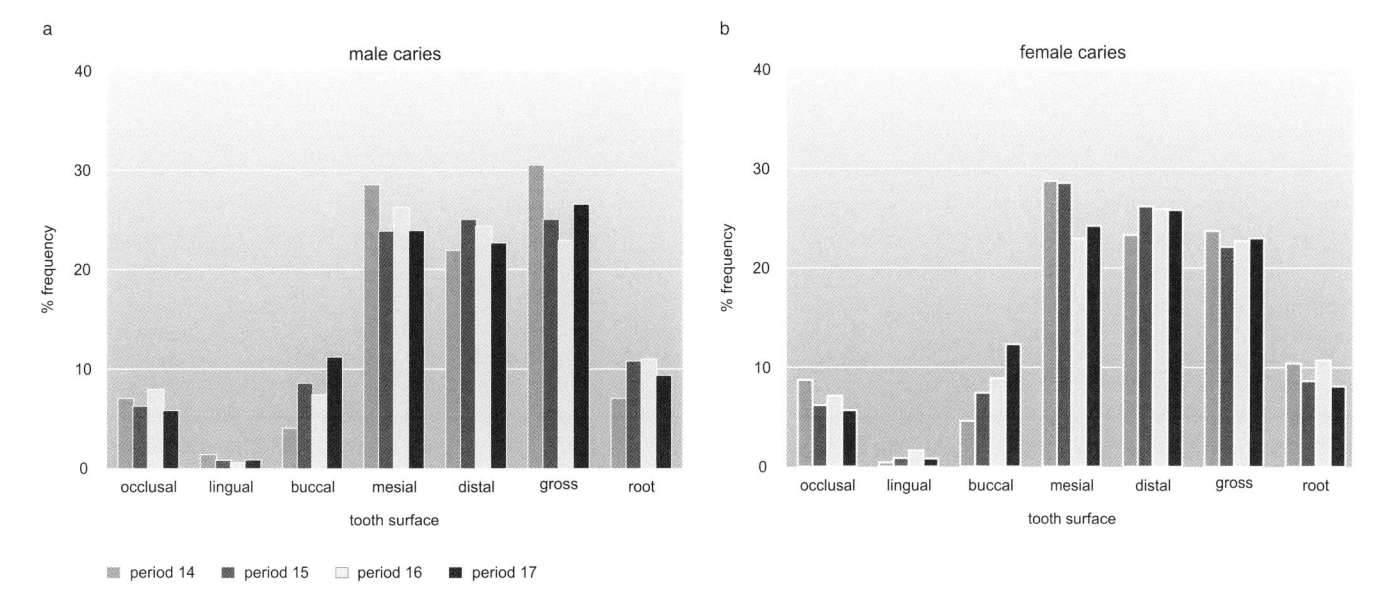

Fig 35 Distribution by period of carious lesions on surfaces of permanent teeth: a – adult males; b – adult females

Carious lesion distribution was identical in both males and females (Table 28). A high frequency of lesions classified as gross presumably represents the end stage of caries initiated from inter-proximal sites. A large number of teeth also had carious lesions on the roots: 10.3% of cavities in males and 9.8% of cavities in females were on root surfaces, indicating that other oral pathology such as periodontal disease exposed the roots to cariogenic processes.

The caries frequency in deciduous teeth (Table 25) shows that the most frequently affected teeth were the deciduous first molars. No significant differences between the burial types emerged. When all deciduous teeth were pooled, 11.1% (259/2327) showed at least one cavity. In period 14 the highest caries frequency was seen at 23.2% (35/151) and following that the frequency remains fairly constant at *c* 10.0%. A similar picture emerges in the teeth of older children if the first permanent molar in an individual aged up to 17 years is taken as an indicator. In period 14 there was a high frequency of caries (12.4%), and in periods 15–17 the rate remained fairly constant at 7–8%.

Enamel hypoplasia

Dental enamel hypoplasia can be recognised as pits or grooves on the enamel surfaces of the teeth which represent temporary interruptions in amelogenesis (enamel formation). Hillson (1996, 165) defines enamel defects as deficiencies of enamel thickness initiated during enamel matrix secretion. These defects can be caused by a variety of factors including dietary deficiency, childhood fevers and infections (Hillson 2000, 250). They do not remodel and can be used as non-specific stress indicators (Chapter 3.10). To determine the timing of these interruptions some researchers directly measure the distance between the hypoplastic defect and the cemento-enamel junction. During the course of analysis, the position of any hypoplastic defect on the tooth surface was categorised by visual observation of the third of the crown in which the defect occurred, providing a broad developmental category.

At St Mary Spital, in common with virtually every other site in Britain, the anterior teeth were most frequently affected by hypoplastic defects. The distribution of hypoplastic defects by tooth type is shown in Fig 36, and it can be seen that canine teeth are the most commonly affected, followed by third premolars and lateral incisors. Overall, 13.4% of all teeth showed defects, and this figure is identical in males and females. Table 29 shows the distribution of enamel hypoplasia for males and females across all periods. Maxillary canines showed hypoplastic defects in 21.6–29.8% of teeth, whereas a much higher frequency (27.1–32.9%) was observed in the mandibular canines (Fig 37).

The distribution and severity of enamel hypoplastic defects are given in Tables 30–3 (permanent teeth only). Here, all four quadrants of the dentition have been pooled, and the following recording grades have been used: linear 1 = just discernable, linear 2 = clear groove on tooth surface, linear 3 = gross defects (ridges/dentine exposed).

Only minor sex differences were observed. Males were more commonly affected than females in periods 14 and 15: 14.9% and 14.8% compared to 12.3% and 13.1% (Table 30; Table 31). During period 16 this trend is reversed, with females showing a higher frequency (13.8%) than males (12.7%) (Table 32). The overall frequency was almost equally distributed by period 17, with males and females showing respectively 12.1% and 12.0% of teeth with hypoplastic defects. There was a statistically significant difference between burial types ABC and D (χ^2 = 18.2, df = 1, p ≤ 0.001) and this may be a product of type ABC being more strongly affected by selective mortality than type D (Fig 38; Fig 39).

Out of a total of 2327 deciduous teeth, only 7 (0.3%) showed any evidence of enamel hypoplastic defects. This very low figure is probably the result of scoring error. There was a greater degree of evidence for hypoplastic defects in older

Results

Table 28 Distribution of adult caries by period, burial type, sex and tooth type

Period	Burial type	Sex	\multicolumn{8}{c	}{Tooth type (FDI)}	Total
			1	2	3	4	5	6	7	8	
14	ABC	male affected	4	5	13	24	32	38	38	30	184
		male present	285	302	319	319	300	237	256	216	2234
		%	1.4	1.7	4.1	7.5	10.7	16.0	14.8	13.9	8.2
14	D	male affected	1	2	9	11	19	27	30	20	119
		male present	150	155	174	169	154	141	144	111	1198
		%	0.7	1.3	5.2	6.5	12.3	19.1	20.8	18.0	9.9
14	ABC	female affected	2	4	8	14	20	39	34	19	140
		female present	216	230	248	242	233	190	205	159	1723
		%	0.9	1.7	3.2	5.8	8.6	20.5	16.6	11.9	8.1
14	D	female affected	1	5	8	5	11	25	29	14	98
		female present	121	137	144	140	131	110	129	106	1018
		%	0.8	3.6	5.6	3.6	8.4	22.7	22.5	13.2	9.6
15	ABC	male affected	4	8	14	29	53	66	64	34	272
		male present	368	407	441	449	433	373	389	289	3149
		%	1.1	2.0	3.2	6.5	12.2	17.7	16.5	11.8	8.6
15	D	male affected	11	15	19	31	57	97	115	65	410
		male present	595	635	681	685	666	551	624	460	4897
		%	1.8	2.4	2.8	4.5	8.6	17.6	18.4	14.1	8.4
15	ABC	female affected	9	19	19	34	46	63	50	27	267
		female present	351	383	428	411	389	313	324	215	2814
		%	2.6	5.0	4.4	8.3	11.8	20.1	15.4	12.6	9.5
15	D	female affected	11	21	24	44	83	127	141	87	538
		female present	681	735	795	776	749	616	687	468	5507
		%	1.6	2.9	3.0	5.7	11.1	20.6	20.5	18.6	9.8
16	ABC	male affected	45	48	109	129	197	203	228	121	1080
		male present	1208	1289	1414	1368	1322	991	1115	812	9519
		%	3.7	3.7	7.7	9.4	14.9	20.5	20.4	14.9	11.3
16	D	male affected	14	30	53	89	168	226	231	167	978
		male present	1299	1383	1502	1459	1381	1138	1273	974	10,409
		%	1.1	2.2	3.5	6.1	12.2	19.9	18.1	17.1	9.4
16	ABC	female affected	35	51	71	110	134	195	217	124	937
		female present	968	1048	1147	1123	1052	891	952	631	7812
		%	3.6	4.9	6.2	9.8	12.7	21.9	22.8	19.7	12.0
16	D	female affected	18	26	52	102	139	207	230	141	915
		female present	1215	1320	1432	1413	1326	1099	1182	878	9865
		%	1.5	2	3.6	7.2	10.5	18.8	19.5	16.1	9.3
17	ABC	male affected	33	32	55	64	88	105	101	77	555
		male present	491	549	590	567	530	432	478	385	4022
		%	6.7	5.8	9.3	11.3	16.6	24.3	21.1	20.0	13.8
17	D	male affected	1	1	4	10	15	24	24	12	91
		male present	132	143	150	143	135	100	114	88	1005
		%	0.8	0.7	2.7	7.0	11.1	24.0	21.1	13.6	9.1
17	ABC	female affected	22	25	32	63	71	77	87	50	427
		female present	341	352	393	393	377	278	322	188	2644
		%	6.5	7.1	8.1	16.0	18.8	27.7	27.0	26.6	16.1
17	D	female affected	1	0	2	4	12	21	17	11	68
		female present	95	109	109	112	106	92	97	69	789
		%	1.1	-	1.8	3.6	11.3	22.8	17.5	15.9	8.6

Dental disease

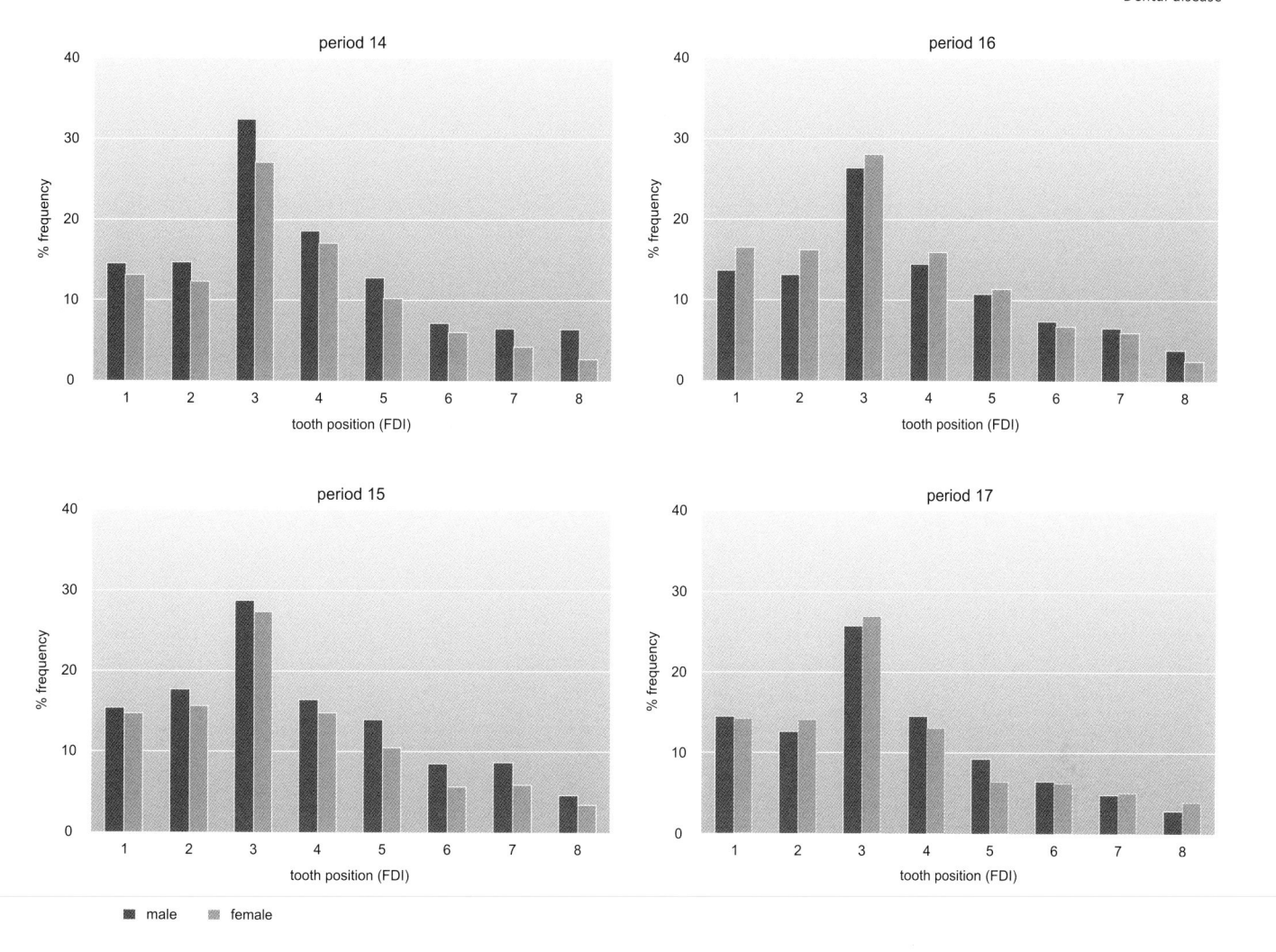

Fig 36 Percentage frequency distribution of teeth showing enamel hypoplastic defects, by period and sex

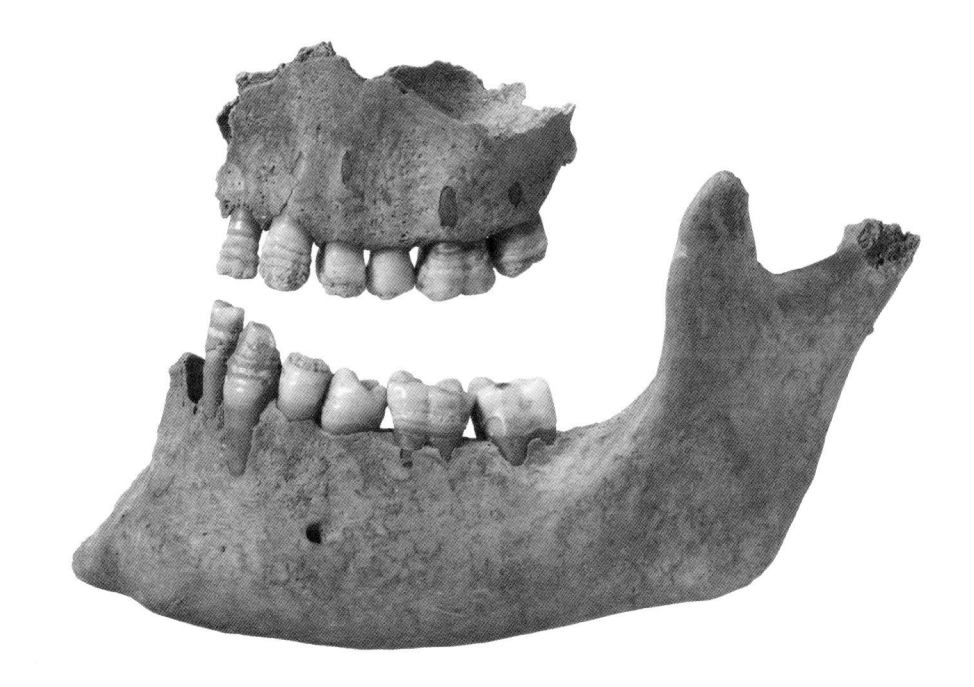

Fig 37 Enamel hypoplastic defects in the mandibular and maxillary dentition of 18–25-year-old female [12886] from period 15 (scale c 1:1)

Results

Table 29 Distribution of adult enamel hypoplastic defects by burial type and sex

Period	Burial type	Sex	1	2	3	4	5	6	7	8	Total
						Tooth type (FDI)					
14	ABC	male affected	29	35	98	60	38	16	22	18	316
		male present	285	302	319	319	300	237	256	216	2234
		%	10.2	11.6	30.7	18.8	12.7	6.8	8.6	8.3	14.1
14	D	male affected	34	32	62	30	19	10	3	3	193
		male present	150	155	174	169	154	141	144	111	1198
		%	22.7	20.6	35.6	17.8	12.3	7.1	2.1	2.7	16.1
14	ABC	female affected	33	32	73	49	27	9	4	4	231
		female present	216	230	248	242	233	190	205	159	1723
		%	15.3	13.9	29.4	20.2	11.6	4.7	2.0	2.5	13.4
14	D	female affected	11	15	37	17	12	10	10	3	115
		female present	121	137	144	140	131	110	129	106	1018
		%	9.1	10.9	25.7	12.1	9.2	9.1	7.8	2.8	11.3
15	ABC	male affected	68	84	124	75	50	25	24	9	459
		male present	368	407	441	449	433	373	389	289	3149
		%	18.5	20.6	28.1	16.7	11.5	6.7	6.2	3.1	14.6
15	D	male affected	81	102	202	112	103	54	63	27	744
		male present	595	635	681	685	666	551	624	460	4897
		%	13.6	16.1	29.7	16.4	15.5	9.8	10.1	5.9	15.2
15	ABC	female affected	41	48	112	60	43	22	20	10	356
		female present	351	383	428	411	389	313	324	215	2814
		%	11.7	12.5	26.2	14.6	11.1	7.0	6.2	4.7	12.7
15	D	female affected	114	130	241	121	78	30	43	14	771
		female present	681	735	795	776	749	616	687	468	5507
		%	16.7	17.7	30.3	15.6	10.4	4.9	6.3	3.0	14.0
16	ABC	male affected	135	151	332	197	133	73	76	23	1120
		male present	1208	1289	1414	1368	1322	991	1115	812	9519
		%	11.2	11.7	23.5	14.4	10.1	7.4	6.8	2.8	11.8
16	D	male affected	207	205	441	212	160	85	81	45	1436
		male present	1299	1383	1502	1459	1381	1138	1273	974	10,409
		%	15.9	14.8	29.4	14.5	11.6	7.5	6.4	4.6	13.8
16	ABC	female affected	160	174	303	164	107	61	46	15	1030
		female present	968	1048	1147	1123	1052	891	952	631	7812
		%	16.5	16.6	26.4	14.6	10.2	6.8	4.8	2.4	13.2
16	D	female affected	199	209	421	239	164	75	83	23	1413
		female present	1215	1320	1432	1413	1326	1099	1182	878	9865
		%	16.4	15.8	29.4	16.9	12.4	6.8	7.0	2.6	14.3
17	ABC	male affected	66	69	151	88	53	30	25	13	495
		male present	491	549	590	567	530	432	478	385	4022
		%	13.4	12.6	25.6	15.5	10	6.9	5.2	3.4	12.3
17	D	male affected	25	18	39	15	8	10	9	2	126
		male present	132	143	150	143	135	100	114	88	1005
		%	18.9	12.6	26.0	10.5	5.9	10.0	7.9	2.3	12.5
17	ABC	female affected	51	49	96	50	23	19	16	5	309
		female present	341	352	393	393	377	278	322	188	2644
		%	15.0	13.9	24.4	12.7	6.1	6.8	5.0	2.7	11.7
17	D	female affected	11	16	39	16	8	4	5	5	104
		female present	95	109	109	112	106	92	97	69	789
		%	11.6	14.7	35.8	14.3	7.5	4.3	5.2	7.2	13.2

Table 30 Distribution and severity of enamel hypoplastic defects in period 14

	Tooth type	1	2	3	4	5	6	7	8	Total
Males	total teeth	435	458	494	490	456	379	402	329	3443
	linear 1	38	42	93	51	43	12	16	13	308
	linear 2	23	22	65	39	13	14	10	7	193
	linear 3	2	3	2	1	1	0	0	0	9
	pits	0	0	0	0	1	1	0	1	3
	total teeth hypoplastic	63	67	160	91	58	27	26	21	513
	% teeth hypoplastic	14.5	14.6	32.4	18.6	12.7	7.1	6.5	6.4	14.9
Females	total teeth	337	367	392	382	364	300	334	265	2741
	linear 1	36	36	52	42	26	3	8	2	205
	linear 2	8	9	54	23	11	13	3	3	124
	linear 3	0	0	0	0	0	0	0	0	0
	pits	0	0	0	0	0	2	3	2	7
	total teeth hypoplastic	44	45	106	65	37	18	14	7	336
	% teeth hypoplastic	13.1	12.3	27.0	17.0	10.2	6.0	4.2	2.6	12.3

Table 31 Distribution and severity of enamel hypoplastic defects in period 15

	Tooth type	1	2	3	4	5	6	7	8	Total
Males	total teeth	963	1042	1122	1134	1099	924	1013	749	8046
	linear 1	110	143	181	127	115	36	54	22	788
	linear 2	35	38	130	56	38	38	28	9	372
	linear 3	3	2	5	1	0	0	1	0	12
	pits	0	1	6	2	0	4	4	3	20
	total teeth hypoplastic	148	184	322	186	153	78	87	34	1192
	% teeth hypoplastic	15.4	17.7	28.7	16.4	13.9	8.4	8.6	4.5	14.8
Females	total teeth	1035	1121	1228	1192	1140	932	1015	685	8348
	linear 1	112	128	187	115	90	26	32	12	702
	linear 2	40	44	139	57	23	19	18	8	348
	linear 3	0	3	9	3	5	5	1	0	26
	pits	0	0	0	1	1	2	8	3	15
	total teeth hypoplastic	152	175	335	176	119	52	59	23	1091
	% teeth hypoplastic	14.7	15.6	27.3	14.8	10.4	5.6	5.8	3.4	13.1

Table 32 Distribution and severity of enamel hypoplastic defects in period 16

	Tooth type	1	2	3	4	5	6	7	8	Total
Males	total teeth	2509	2675	2919	2831	2707	2133	2392	1789	19,955
	linear 1	227	220	428	285	225	86	91	34	1596
	linear 2	97	116	317	112	60	61	40	19	822
	linear 3	17	14	23	10	4	6	4	0	78
	pits	0	0	1	1	1	4	21	15	43
	total teeth hypoplastic	341	350	769	408	290	157	156	68	2539
	% teeth hypoplastic	13.6	13.1	26.3	14.4	10.7	7.4	6.5	3.8	12.7
Females	total teeth	2187	2372	2583	2540	2382	1991	2137	1513	17,705
	linear 1	249	268	403	288	221	74	75	20	1598
	linear 2	94	100	295	105	48	53	43	15	753
	linear 3	16	10	17	6	1	7	0	0	57
	pits	1	5	9	4	0	0	9	1	29
	total teeth hypoplastic	360	383	724	403	270	134	127	36	2437
	% teeth hypoplastic	16.5	16.1	28	15.9	11.3	6.7	5.9	2.4	13.8

Results

Table 33 Distribution and severity of enamel hypoplastic defects in period 17

	Tooth type	1	2	3	4	5	6	7	8	Total
Males	total teeth	623	692	740	710	665	532	592	473	5027
	linear 1	65	60	95	74	50	8	20	6	378
	linear 2	19	22	87	28	11	20	6	5	198
	linear 3	4	2	3	1	0	4	0	0	14
	pits	2	3	5	0	0	2	2	2	16
	total teeth hypoplastic	**90**	**87**	**190**	**103**	**61**	**34**	**28**	**13**	**606**
	% teeth hypoplastic	**14.4**	**12.6**	**25.7**	**14.5**	**9.2**	**6.4**	**4.7**	**2.7**	**12.1**
Females	total teeth	436	461	502	505	483	370	419	257	3433
	linear 1	29	44	73	38	24	11	13	6	238
	linear 2	20	18	51	27	7	9	6	1	139
	linear 3	10	3	10	1	0	2	1	0	27
	pits	3	0	1	0	0	1	1	3	9
	total teeth hypoplastic	**62**	**65**	**135**	**66**	**31**	**23**	**21**	**10**	**413**
	% teeth hypoplastic	**14.2**	**14.1**	**26.9**	**13.1**	**6.4**	**6.2**	**5.0**	**3.9**	**12.0**

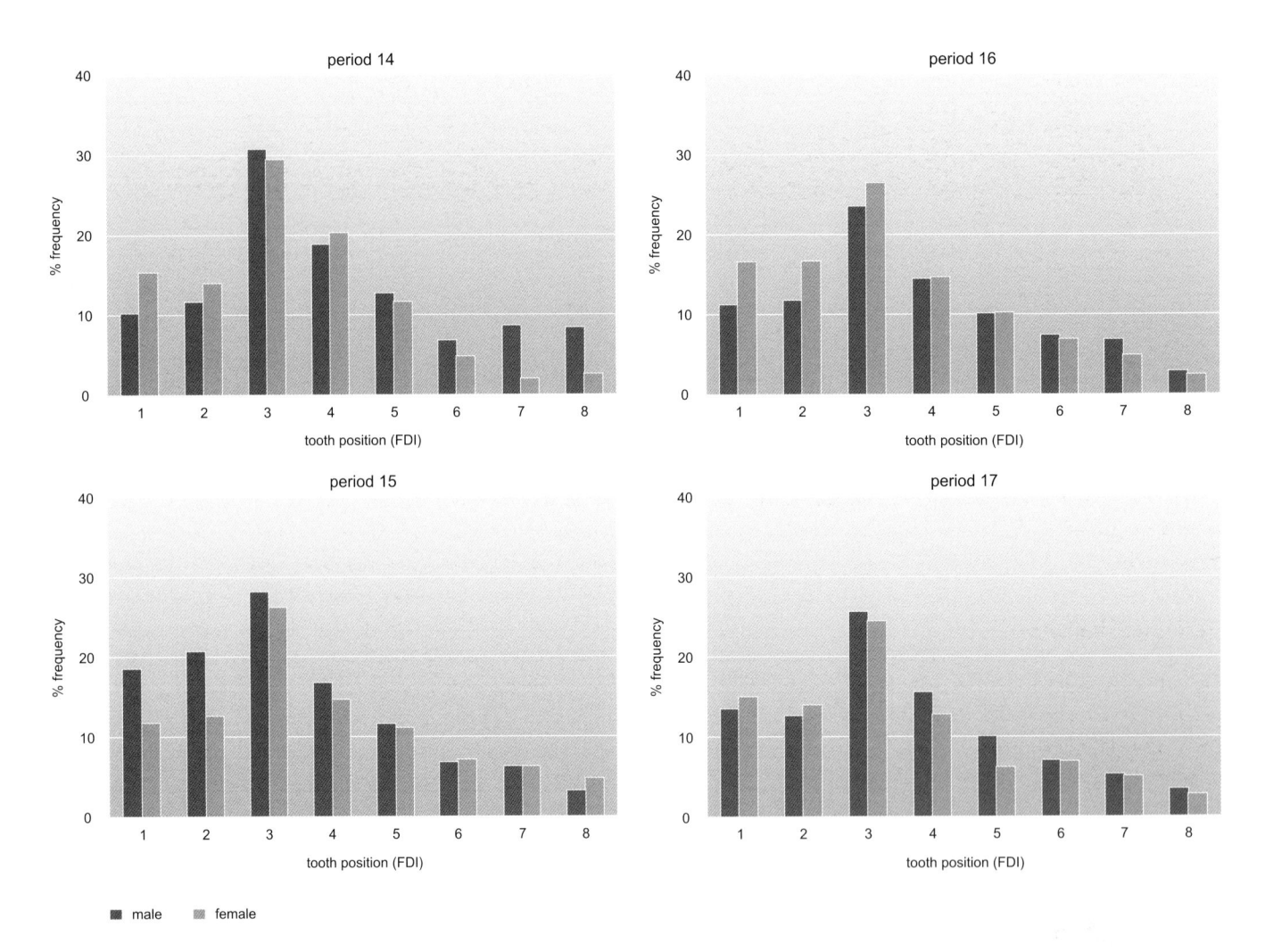

Fig 38 Distribution of teeth with enamel hypoplastic defects in burial type ABC

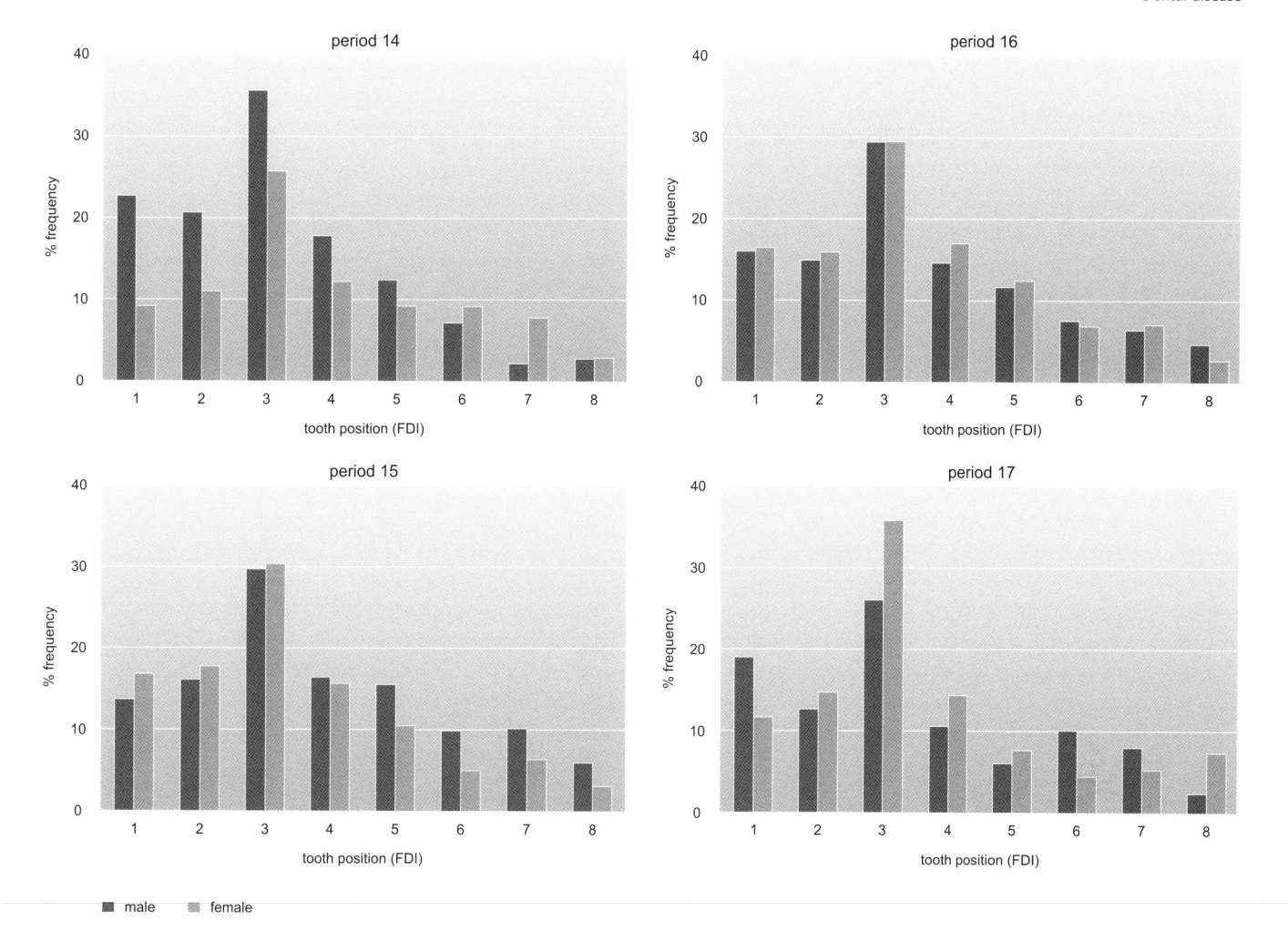

Fig 39 Distribution of teeth with enamel hypoplastic defects in burial type D

children. If we compare the frequencies in canine teeth only, then in period 14, 25.8% (31/120) are hypoplastic, rising to 35.5% (158/445) in period 16. This rate remains fairly constant at 46.5% (301/348) and 42% (66/157) in periods 16 and 17 respectively.

Periapical lesions

One of the most common causes of periapical lesions is when oral bacteria have gained access to the pulp chamber of the tooth, usually following caries. The by-products of the ensuing inflammation (pus) then extrude through the alveolar bone, leaving a perforation.

The frequencies of periapical lesions (cavities resulting from dental abscesses) varied from 2.5% to 3.3% of available tooth positions, and no major differences emerged through periods 14–17 (Fig 29). The overall frequency was 2.7% (2466 lesions/92,259 tooth positions). The distribution of the lesions within the dental arcade is shown in Fig 29 and it can be seen that they occur most frequently at first molar positions, correlating with the high frequency of caries seen in these teeth.

In the majority of cases, the lesion was associated with a carious cavity in the adjacent tooth (Fig 40). Drainage into the maxillary sinus was observed in 1.2% of caries-derived lesions

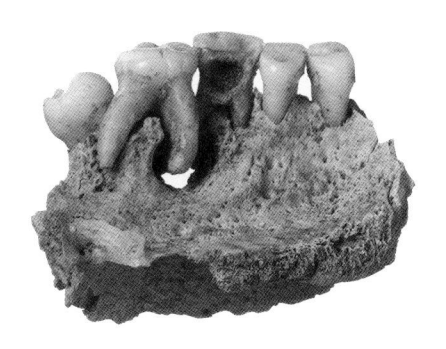

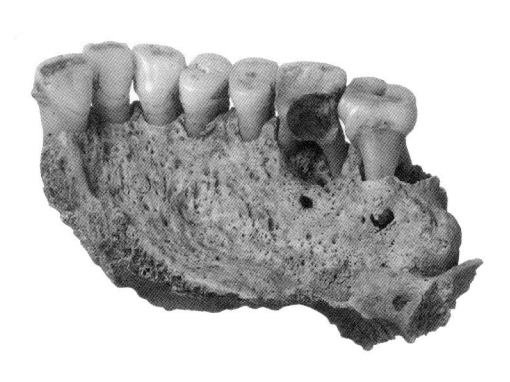

Fig 40 Caries and associated periapical lesions in 18–25-year-old male [1055] from period 15 (scale c 1:1)

Results

(30/2466) and 1.4% of pulpal exposures (35/2466), although these figures are underestimates of the true prevalence because it was not possible to routinely examine the maxillary sinus in intact skulls. In caries-derived periapical lesions, the direction of drainage was most commonly external (54.5–65.6%) with a much lower internal drainage frequency (7.1–8.9%). A smaller number of lesions were caused by advanced dental wear exposing the pulp chamber, and the reverse pattern was seen with predominantly internally draining lesions (15.4–26.3%), and a lower frequency of external drainage (3.5–6.7%) (Table 34).

Calculus

Bacterial plaque can build up on tooth surfaces and when left to accumulate can become mineralised, resulting in a calculus deposit. Although dietary factors can predispose to the formation of calculus, non-dietary factors can affect its severity, such as a lack of oral hygiene (Lieverse 1999).

Data from all four quadrants were pooled and demonstrated that the highest frequencies of calculus deposits (93.2–97.1%) were seen in the mandibular incisors (Tables 35–8). To some extent this is to be expected because calculus is preferentially deposited in proximity to the openings into the mouth of certain major salivary gland ducts. As a result, calculus accumulates on the buccal surfaces of the upper teeth and lingual surfaces of the lower front teeth, as seen here. This type of calculus deposit also tends to be supra-gingival (above the gum line) and this is also reflected in the relatively higher frequency of supra-gingival deposits towards the front of the mouth.

Within the study sample, 83.6% (60,092/71,883) of adult teeth were found to have calculus deposits. The supra-gingival form of calculus displayed a slightly higher rate in males over all periods (female 18,033/32,227: 56.0%; male 21,430/36,471: 58.8%; χ^2 = 54.98, df = 1, p ≤ 0.001). When male and female rates were combined, the true prevalence was 57.4% (39,463/68,698), with a significant increase from period 14 (3434/6184: 55.5%) to period 15 (9405/16,394: 57.4%) (χ^2 = 6.18, df = 1, p ≤ 0.025) (Fig 41).

More female teeth (8882/32,227: 27.6%) were affected by sub-gingival calculus at St Mary Spital than male teeth (8668/36,471: 23.8%) (χ^2 = 129.47, df = 1, p ≤ 0.001). When male and female teeth were combined, the true prevalence was

Table 34 Number of periapical lesions in adult dentitions by period, showing underlying cause and direction of drainage

Period	Total periapical lesions	Caries-related						Pulp exposure						No pathology or post-mortem loss					
		External	%	Internal	%	Sinus	%	External	%	Internal	%	Sinus	%	External	%	Internal	%	Sinus	%
14	266	145	54.5	22	8.3	0	–	17	6.4	70	26.3	4	1.5	7	2.6	0	–	1	0.4
15	534	294	55.1	47	8.8	12	2.2	36	6.7	113	21.2	12	2.2	12	2.2	3	0.6	5	0.9
16	1297	828	63.8	92	7.1	15	1.2	53	4.1	256	19.7	8	0.6	35	2.7	3	0.2	7	0.5
17	369	242	65.6	33	8.9	3	0.8	13	3.5	57	15.4	11	3	10	2.7	0	–	0	–
Total	2466	1509	61.2	194	7.9	30	1.2	119	4.8	496	20.1	35	1.4	64	2.6	6	0.2	13	0.5

Table 35 Frequency and location of calculus deposits in period 14 adults by sex

	Tooth position	1	2	3	4	5	6	7	8	Total
Males	teeth present	435	458	494	490	456	379	402	329	3443
	teeth with calculus	390	412	442	405	361	318	338	282	2948
	% calculus	89.7	90.0	89.5	82.7	79.2	83.9	84.1	85.7	85.6
	deposit sub-gingival	108	113	128	133	111	164	145	102	1004
	% sub-gingival	27.7	27.4	29.0	32.8	30.7	51.6	42.9	36.2	34.1
Females	teeth present	337	367	392	382	364	300	334	265	2741
	teeth with calculus	291	318	331	307	278	238	263	203	2229
	% calculus	86.4	86.6	84.4	80.4	76.4	79.3	78.7	76.6	81.3
	deposit sub-gingival	86	89	84	97	80	119	122	62	739
	% sub-gingival	29.6	28.0	25.4	31.6	28.8	50.0	46.4	30.5	33.2
Total sexed adults	teeth present	772	825	886	872	820	679	736	594	6184
	teeth with calculus	681	730	773	712	639	556	601	485	5177
	% calculus	88.2	88.5	87.2	81.7	77.9	81.9	81.7	81.6	83.7
	deposit sub-gingival	194	202	212	230	191	283	267	164	1743
	% sub-gingival	28.5	27.7	27.4	32.3	29.9	50.9	44.4	33.8	33.7

Table 36 Frequency and location of calculus deposits in period 15 adults by sex

	Tooth position	1	2	3	4	5	6	7	8	Total
Males	teeth present	963	1042	1122	1134	1099	924	1013	749	8046
	teeth with calculus	867	925	954	932	845	741	781	501	6546
	% calculus	90.0	88.8	85.0	82.2	76.9	80.2	77.1	66.9	81.4
	deposit sub-gingival	213	220	205	266	216	301	290	142	1853
	% sub-gingival	24.6	23.8	21.5	28.5	25.6	40.6	37.1	28.3	28.3
Females	teeth present	1035	1121	1228	1192	1140	932	1015	685	8348
	teeth with calculus	951	1002	1063	977	896	806	829	531	7055
	% calculus	91.9	89.4	86.6	82.0	78.6	86.5	81.7	77.5	84.5
	deposit sub-gingival	287	289	310	320	279	356	334	168	2343
	% sub-gingival	30.2	28.8	29.2	32.8	31.1	44.2	40.3	31.6	33.2
Total sexed adults	teeth present	1998	2163	2350	2326	2239	1856	2028	1434	16,394
	teeth with calculus	1818	1927	2017	1909	1741	1547	1610	1032	13,601
	% calculus	91.0	89.1	85.8	82.1	77.8	83.4	79.4	72.0	83.0
	deposit sub-gingival	500	509	515	586	495	657	624	310	4196
	% sub-gingival	27.5	26.4	25.5	30.7	28.4	42.5	38.8	30.0	30.9

Table 37 Frequency and location of calculus deposits in period 16 adults by sex

	Tooth position	1	2	3	4	5	6	7	8	Total
Males	teeth present	2509	2675	2919	2831	2707	2133	2392	1789	19,955
	teeth with calculus	2323	2406	2536	2311	2085	1749	1936	1353	16,699
	% calculus	92.6	89.9	86.9	81.6	77.0	82.0	80.9	75.6	83.7
	deposit sub-gingival	578	566	607	661	537	733	732	407	4821
	% sub-gingival	24.9	23.5	23.9	28.6	25.8	41.9	37.8	30.1	28.9
Females	teeth present	2187	2372	2583	2540	2382	1991	2137	1513	17,705
	teeth with calculus	1963	2115	2221	2081	1875	1684	1780	1146	14,865
	% calculus	89.8	89.2	86.0	81.9	78.7	84.6	83.3	75.7	84.0
	deposit sub-gingival	589	620	666	683	589	764	713	364	4988
	% sub-gingival	30.0	29.3	30.0	32.8	31.4	45.4	40.1	31.8	33.6
Total sexed adults	teeth present	4696	5047	5502	5371	5089	4124	4529	3302	37,660
	teeth with calculus	4286	4521	4757	4392	3960	3433	3716	2499	31,564
	% calculus	91.3	89.6	86.5	81.8	77.8	83.2	82.0	75.7	83.8
	deposit sub-gingival	1167	1186	1273	1344	1126	1497	1445	771	9809
	% sub-gingival	27.2	26.2	26.8	30.6	28.4	43.6	38.9	30.9	31.1

Table 38 Frequency and location of calculus deposits in period 17 adults by sex

	Tooth position	1	2	3	4	5	6	7	8	Total
Males	teeth present	623	692	740	710	665	532	592	473	5027
	teeth with calculus	536	592	607	530	476	411	438	315	3905
	% calculus	86.0	85.5	82.0	74.6	71.6	77.3	74.0	66.6	77.7
	deposit sub-gingival	118	121	125	140	106	168	144	68	990
	% sub-gingival	22.0	20.4	20.6	26.4	22.3	40.9	32.9	21.6	25.4
Females	teeth present	436	461	502	505	483	370	419	257	3433
	teeth with calculus	388	395	425	376	369	294	328	191	2766
	% calculus	89.0	85.7	84.7	74.5	76.4	79.5	78.3	74.3	80.6
	deposit sub-gingival	105	101	109	113	110	108	110	56	812
	% sub-gingival	27.1	25.6	25.6	30.1	29.8	36.7	33.5	29.3	29.4
Total sexed adults	teeth present	1059	1153	1242	1215	1148	902	1011	730	8460
	teeth with calculus	924	987	1032	906	845	705	766	506	6671
	% calculus	87.3	85.6	83.1	74.6	73.6	78.2	75.8	69.3	78.9
	deposit sub-gingival	223	222	234	253	216	276	254	124	1802
	% sub-gingival	24.1	22.5	22.7	27.9	25.6	39.1	33.2	24.5	27.0

Fig 41 True prevalence rate of adult supra-gingival calculus

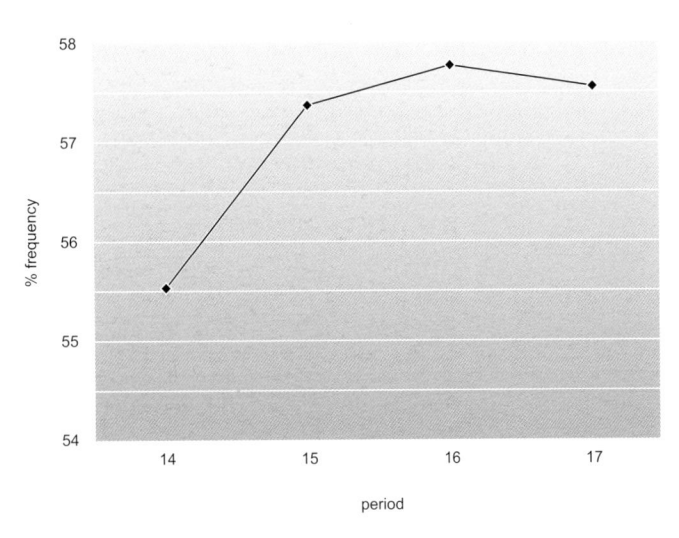

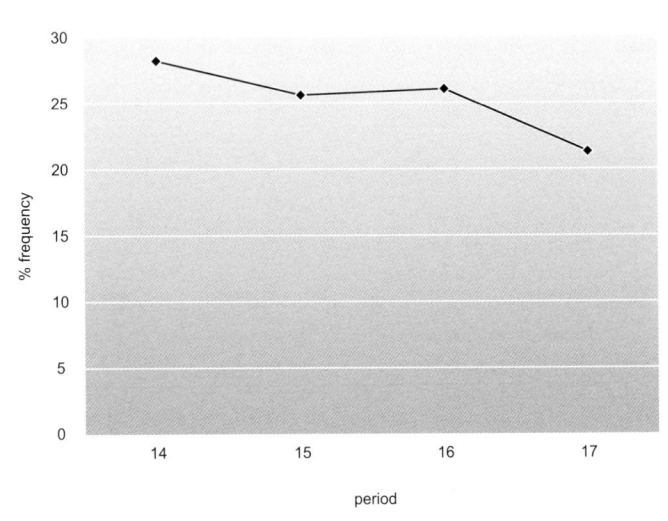

Fig 42 True prevalence rate of adult sub-gingival calculus

25.5% (17,550/68,698). The frequency fell from 28.2% (1743/6184) in period 14 to 21.3% (1802/8460) in period 17. The changes from periods 14 to 15 (χ^2 = 15.55, df = 1, p ≤ 0.001) and from periods 16 to 17 (χ^2 = 82.60, df = 1, p ≤ 0.025) were statistically significant (Fig 42).

Overall the frequencies of calculus deposits by tooth in each period varied little and there were no striking differences in the frequencies of teeth affected; there is a more or less similar distribution of calculus deposits throughout periods 14–17. However, when males and females are considered separately, the location of calculus deposits begins to alter slightly. Fig 43 shows the distribution of calculus on tooth surfaces and reveals that in period 14 males and females are affected equally; however, in the later periods (15–17) females show 4–5% more sub-gingival calculus than males. This can be partly explained by the fact that these periods contain a larger proportion of older females who are more likely to have accrued calculus, but Hillson (1996, 259) notes that in living populations males show more and heavier supra-gingival deposits than females. Overall, the highest frequencies of sub-gingival calculus are seen in first molar teeth, closely followed by second and third molars.

Ante-mortem tooth loss

The overall frequency of ante-mortem tooth loss was 11.9% (10,985/92,259 tooth positions). From period 14 to period 17 the frequency ranged from 9.7% to 14.1% for all teeth (see Tables 21–4). Fig 29 clearly shows that the highest frequencies occurred in first molar teeth, closely followed by second and third molars. The involvement of the first molar ranged from 35.0% to 51.0%, seen in period 17. This pattern is related to the high frequencies of carious lesions seen at these tooth positions.

To examine any possible changes through time, an average was taken of all four first molars (16, 26, 36 and 46) in each period. This pointed to an increase over time, with periods 14 and 15 having an average first molar loss of 25%, increasing to 29% in period 16 and to 32% in period 17. This gradual increase can be explained as being a direct consequence of the increase in carious cavities also seen in the first molar teeth.

Periodontal disease

Periodontal disease is caused by inflammation of the gingivae (gums) which can lead secondarily to destruction of the underlying alveolar bone. The inflammation of the gingivae is often related to a variety of oral bacteria residing in calculus deposits; Hildebolt and Molnar (1991) have pointed out that more than 40 bacterial taxa are associated with periodontal disease.

To examine this condition, destruction of the bony alveolar margin was visually graded (Chapter 2.2), and roughly half of all tooth positions (46–52%) were found to show some evidence of alveolar recession. It is only the more advanced levels of soft tissue inflammation that produce a bony effect, such as the destruction of the alveolar margin, or loosening of the periodontal ligament that anchors teeth in their sockets (Hillson 2000, 268).

The overall adult rate of periodontal disease per tooth socket was 50.2% (46,322/92,259). The prevalence rate fell to a significant extent in period 17 (period 16 25,737/50,649: 50.8%; period 17 5464/11,887: 46.0%; χ^2 = 90.52, df = 1, p ≤ 0.001) (Table 39; Fig 44). The highest frequencies of tooth positions showing periodontal disease were located around the first premolars (53.2–60.6%) followed by canine teeth (52.8–56.6%) (Table 39). No striking pattern emerges from the periodontitis data other than that anterior teeth are more affected than posterior teeth (Fig 45).

Dental disease

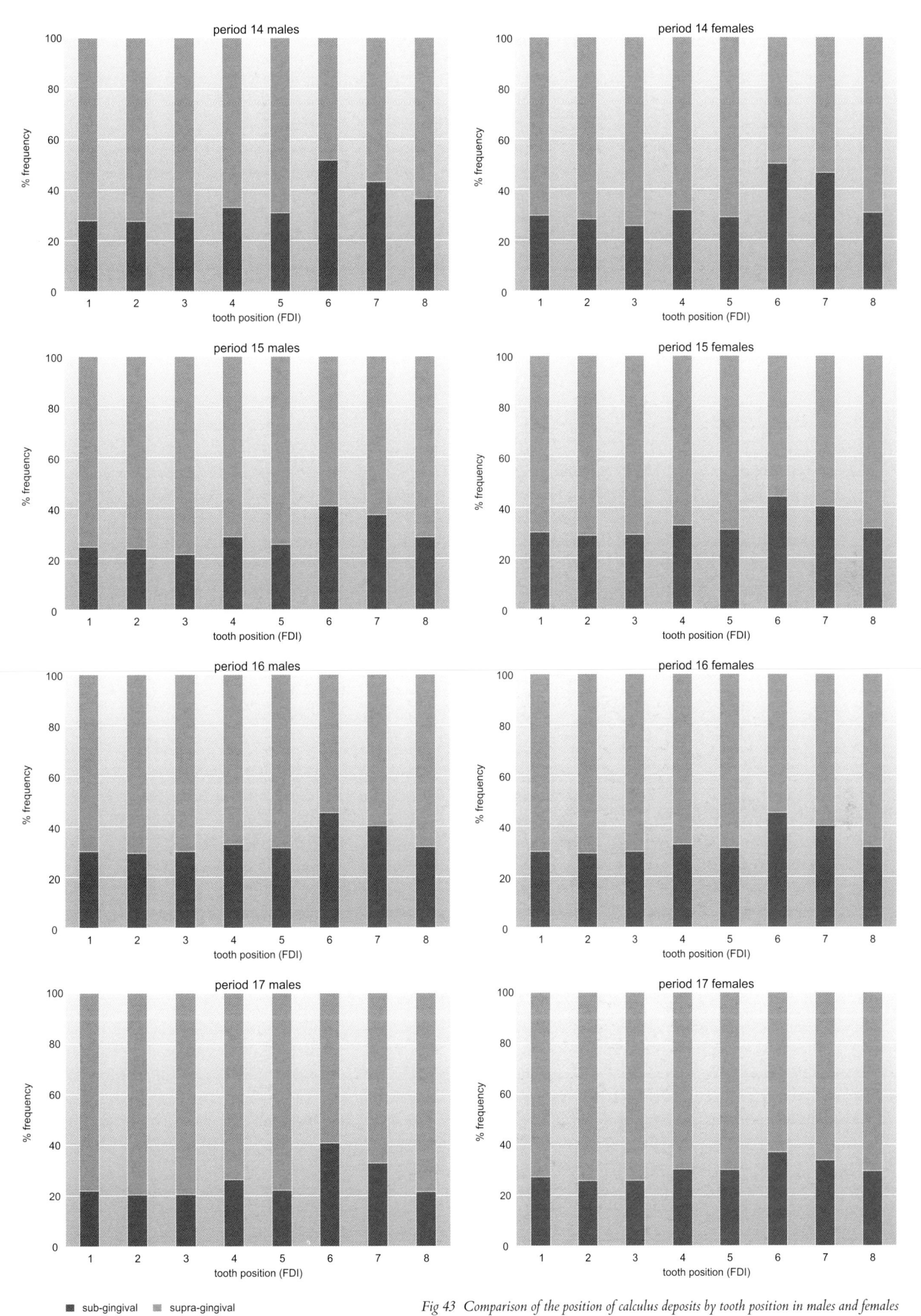

Fig 43 Comparison of the position of calculus deposits by tooth position in males and females

Table 39 Distribution of periodontitis by period

Period	Tooth position	1	2	3	4	5	6	7	8	Total
14	total affected	559	563	585	614	528	478	537	366	4230
	tooth positions available	1022	1027	1034	1032	1024	1029	1013	979	8160
	% frequency	54.7	54.8	56.6	59.5	51.6	46.5	53.0	37.4	51.8
15	total affected	1287	1439	1509	1628	1464	1354	1383	827	10,891
	tooth positions available	2696	2726	2757	2757	2751	2713	2666	2497	21,563
	% frequency	47.7	52.8	54.7	59.0	53.2	49.9	51.9	33.1	50.5
16	total affected	3194	3434	3619	3909	3467	3061	3184	1869	25,737
	tooth positions available	6353	6432	6497	6446	6421	6380	6260	5860	50,649
	% frequency	50.3	53.4	55.7	60.6	54.0	48.0	50.9	31.9	50.8
17	total affected	657	758	795	805	743	633	654	419	5464
	tooth positions available	1487	1490	1507	1512	1510	1513	1485	1383	11,887
	% frequency	44.2	50.9	52.8	53.2	49.2	41.8	44.0	30.3	46.0

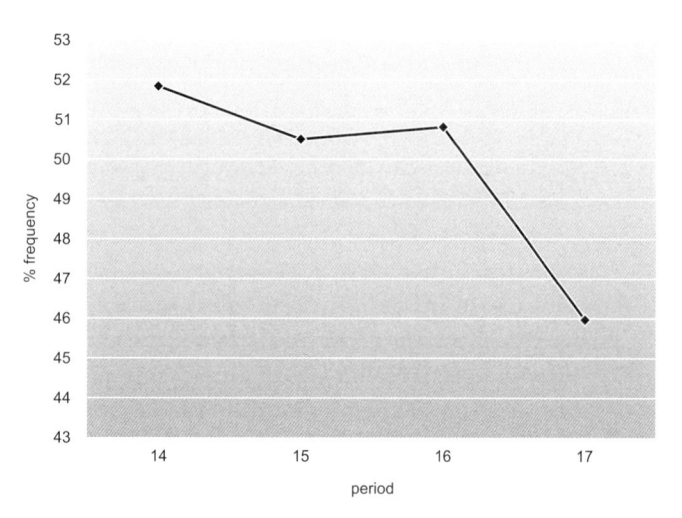

Fig 44 True prevalence rate of adult periodontal disease by period

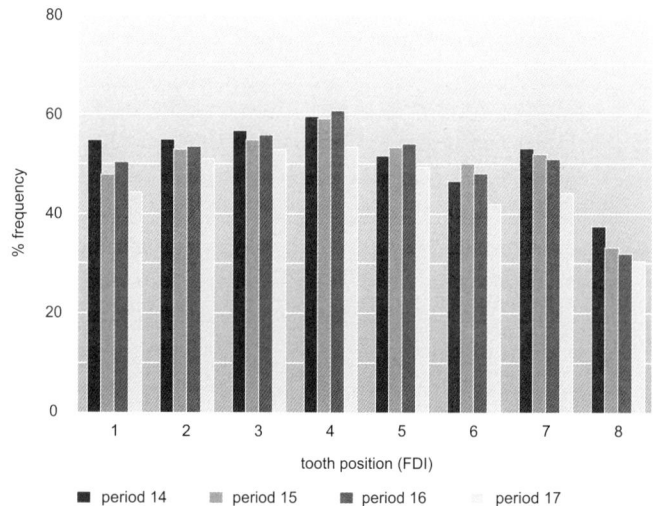

Fig 45 Distribution of periodontal disease

3.7 Joint disease

Amy Gray Jones, Rebecca Redfern and Don Walker

This section presents prevalence rates for the idiopathic degenerative joint diseases of the body (including the spine), the seronegative spondyloarthropathies (ankylosing spondylitis, Reiter's disease and psoriatic arthropathy), erosive arthropathies (rheumatoid arthritis and gout) and other osteoarthopathies such as ochronotic arthropathy, Charcot joint, joint ankylosis, rotator cuff disease and diffuse idiopathic skeletal hyperostosis (DISH).

Extra-spinal osteoarthritis

Crude prevalence rates presented here are based on osteoarthritis in any extra-spinal synovial joint (including the small joints of hands and feet) diagnosed by the presence of eburnation only. They do not include cases where osteoarthritic changes secondary to other pathology, such as trauma or developmental dysplasia, were seen.

The crude prevalence varied between 5.4% (period 15, 75/1390) and 7.1% (period 16, 202/2835) over the period of use of the cemetery, with a fall (from 6.1%: 31/512) from period 14 to period 15 (though this is not statistically significant) and a significant rise between periods 15 and 16 (χ^2 = 4.55, df = 1, $p \leq 0.05$) (Fig 46).

Overall, burial type ABC had a higher crude prevalence of extra-spinal osteoarthritis (210/2775: 7.6%) than type D (139/2612: 5.3%) (χ^2 = 11.20, df = 1, $p \leq 0.001$) (Fig 47).

There was a statistically significant rise in osteoarthritis in burial type ABC from period 15 (30/510: 5.9%) to period 16 (121/1392: 8.7%) (χ^2 = 4.03, df = 1, $p \leq 0.05$). The prevalence was higher than that in period 16, burial type D (5.6%) (χ^2 = 10.15, df = 1, $p \leq 0.01$). Although the crude prevalence rate of extra-spinal osteoarthritis was also higher in burial type ABC in

Joint disease

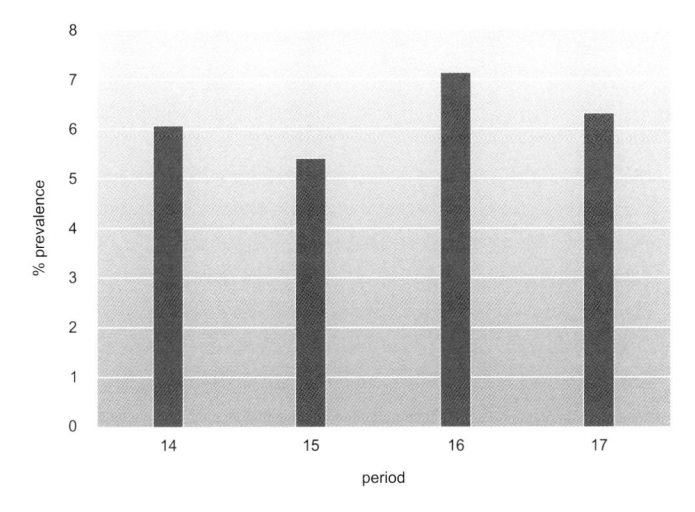

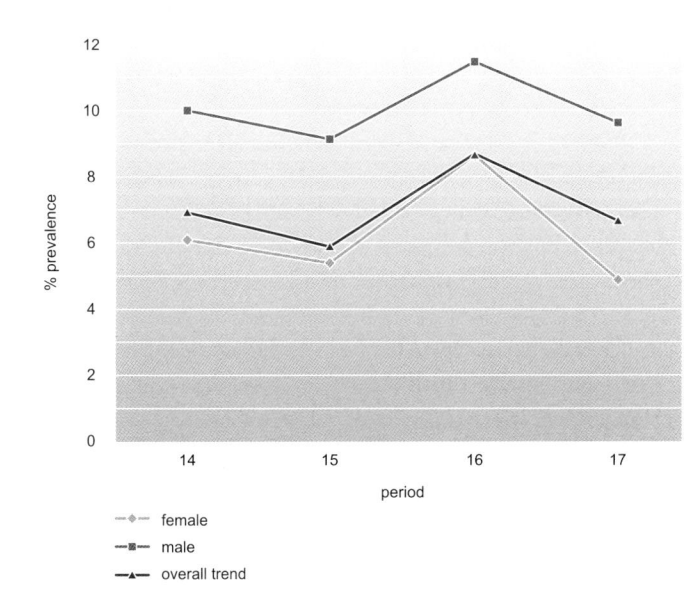

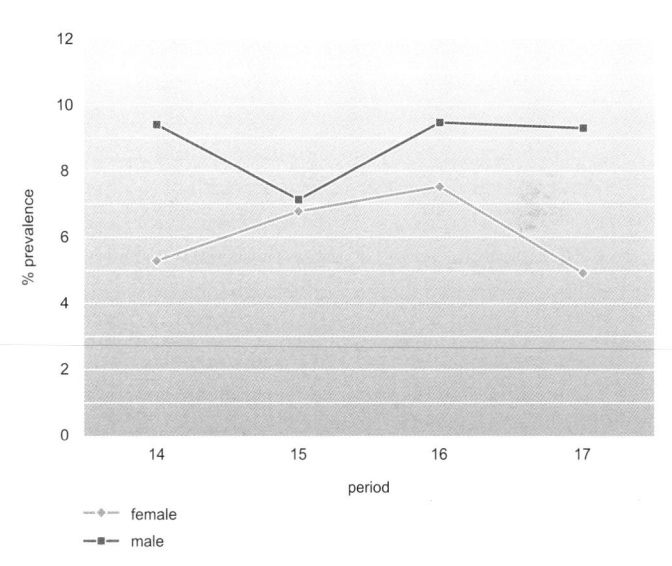

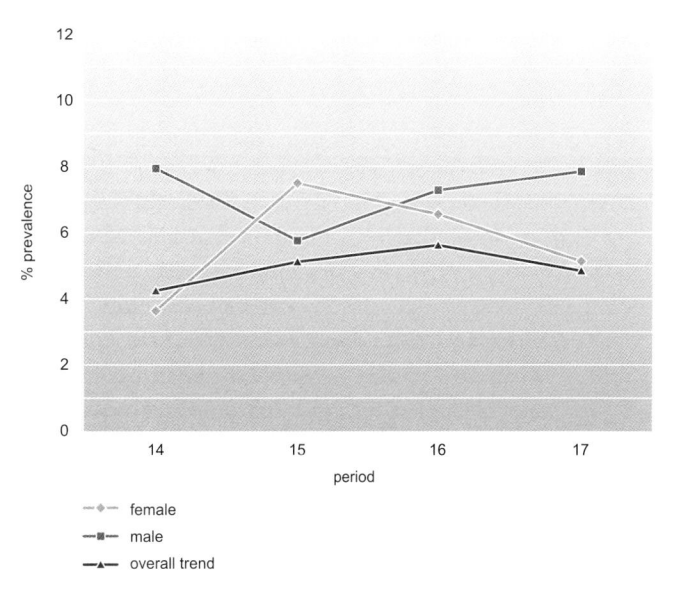

Fig 46 Crude prevalence rate of extra-spinal osteoarthritis by period

the other three periods, none of these differences was significant. The prevalence of osteoarthritis in burial type D remained relatively constant over time. For both burial types, there was little difference between periods 14 and 17.

Overall, males had a higher prevalence of extra-spinal osteoarthritis (199/2237: 8.9%) than females (129/1883: 6.8%) (χ^2 = 5.84, df = 1, p ≤ 0.025). However, there were no significant differences between the sexes in each individual period, and in period 15 the crude prevalence rates were similar (male 38/532: 7.1%, female 34/501: 6.8%) (Fig 48).

In burial type ABC, male and female rates of osteoarthritis followed similar trends over time, with males having a higher overall prevalence (male 131/1246: 10.5%, female 65/920: 7.1%) (χ^2 = 7.65, df = 1, p ≤ 0.01). The differences between the sexes in each individual period were not statistically significant (Fig 49). There were no significant changes over time in burial type ABC males or females. The general trend saw a fall from period

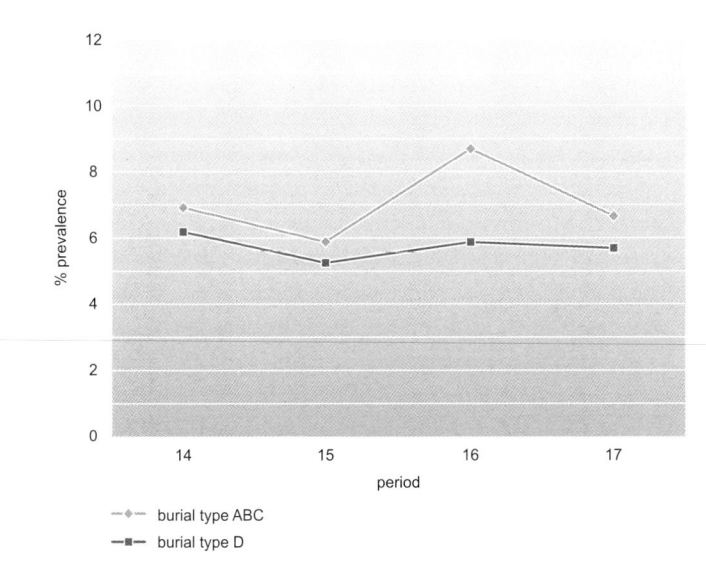

Fig 47 Crude prevalence rate of extra-spinal osteoarthritis by burial type

Fig 48 Crude prevalence rate of extra-spinal osteoarthritis by sex

Fig 49 Crude prevalence rate of extra-spinal osteoarthritis in burial type ABC

Fig 50 Crude prevalence rate of extra-spinal osteoarthritis in burial type D

Results

14 to 15 followed by a rise in period 16 and a fall in period 17.

In burial type D the overall trend differed from that in burial type ABC. The prevalence of extra-spinal osteoarthritis did not vary significantly over time. Male prevalence was higher than female in both period 14 (male 5/63: 7.9%; female 2/55: 3.6%) and period 17 (male 4/51: 7.8%; female 2/39: 5.1%), but the data set was too small to test for significance. The most similarity between the sexes was found in periods 15 and 16. Overall the male prevalence by period curve followed the opposite trend to that of the female curve, in contrast to the more homogeneous nature of the graph for burial type ABC. However, unlike burial type ABC, there was no significant difference between overall male (68/991: 6.9%) and female (64/963: 6.6%) prevalence in burial type D (Fig 50).

When each sex was compared by burial type, males from burial type ABC (131/1246: 10.5%) had a higher prevalence of extra-spinal osteoarthritis than males from burial type D (68/991: 6.9%) (χ^2 = 9.08, df = 1, p ≤ 0.01). The same was true for females, although the difference was not significant (burial type ABC 65/920: 7.1%; burial type D 64/963: 6.6%). For males, the variation between burial types was evident throughout all periods of the cemetery, with a statistically significant difference in period 16 (burial type ABC 72/628: 11.5%; burial type D 41/564: 7.3%) (χ^2 = 6.09, df = 1, p ≤ 0.05) (Fig 51). There was more inconsistency in the female sample comparison, although none of the differences by individual period was statistically significant (Fig 52).

In each period it was clear that the prevalence of extra-spinal osteoarthritis increased with age (Fig 53). The majority of adult individuals affected were over 36 years of age, and there was no significant variation in the crude prevalence for this age range across the periods. There was also no significant variation in the 26–35-year age range over the use of the cemetery. Osteoarthritis was rarely found in individuals below this age range. Young adults (18–25 years) were only affected in period 15 (1/263: 0.4%) and period 16 (3/508: 0.6%). Only one subadult aged 6–11 years from period 16 (1/187: 0.5%) [17736] had evidence of extra-spinal osteoarthritis (in the right radiocarpal joint).

In period 14, no 18–25-year-olds were affected and there was a steady rise in prevalence with increasing age (though chi-square testing demonstrated that increases between successive age categories were not significant). However, the difference between 26–35 years (6%: 9/150) and older adulthood (≥46 years: 17.5%: 7/40) was significant (χ^2 = 5.41, df = 1, p ≤ 0.025); 11.2% of adults aged 36–45 years were affected (15/134).

In period 15, one 18–25-year-old had extra-spinal osteoarthritis (1/263: 0.4%). Prevalence increased with age, and each successive rise from 26–35 years (8/399: 2.0%) onward was found to be statistically significant: to 36–45 years (41/301: 13.6%) (χ^2 = 35.56, df = 1, p ≤ 0.001), and from 36–45 years to ≥46 years (21/95: 22.1%) (χ^2 = 3.94, df = 1, p ≤ 0.05). Although the rate in 26–35-year-olds (2.0%) appeared to be low when compared to other periods, it was not found to be significantly different from them. This was also the case with the other age categories.

In period 16, there was a higher overall prevalence of extra-spinal osteoarthritis when compared to period 15. In addition to a 6–11-year-old subadult [17736], three 18–25-year-olds were affected (3/508: 0.6%), a slight (but not significant) increase from period 15. Again, prevalence increased with age, and each successive increase from 26–35 years (37/814: 4.5%) onward was found to be statistically significant: to 36–45 years (91/645: 14.1%) (χ^2 = 41.12, df = 1, p ≤ 0.001), and from 36–45 years to ≥46 years (62/244: 25.4%) (χ^2 = 15.87, df = 1, p ≤ 0.001).

The pattern of extra-spinal osteoarthritis by age in period 17 was very similar to that in period 14. Prevalence rose with age and the increase from 26–35 years (11/183: 6%) to 36–45 years (19/139: 13.7%) was statistically significant (χ^2 = 5.48, df = 1, p ≤ 0.025), though the increase in the next age group was not significant (≥46 years, 11/63: 17.5%). No individuals under 26 years were affected.

Comparison of results by age and sex did not include those individuals categorised as 'adult', as specific age could not be

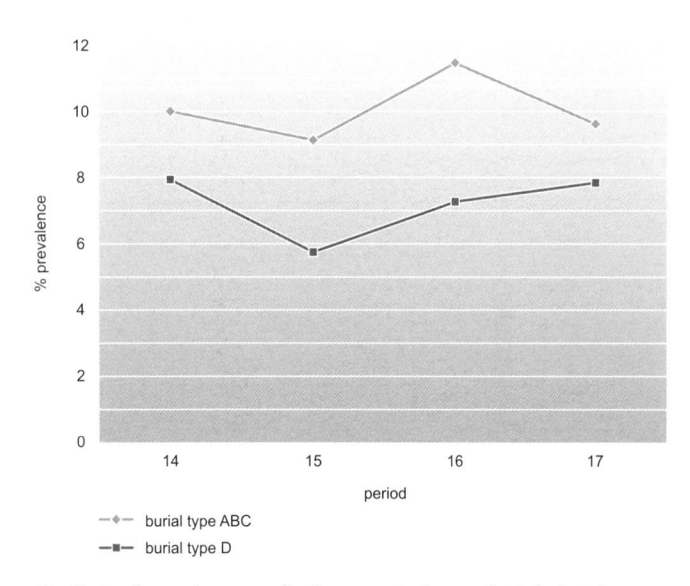

Fig 51 Crude prevalence rate of male extra-spinal osteoarthritis by burial type

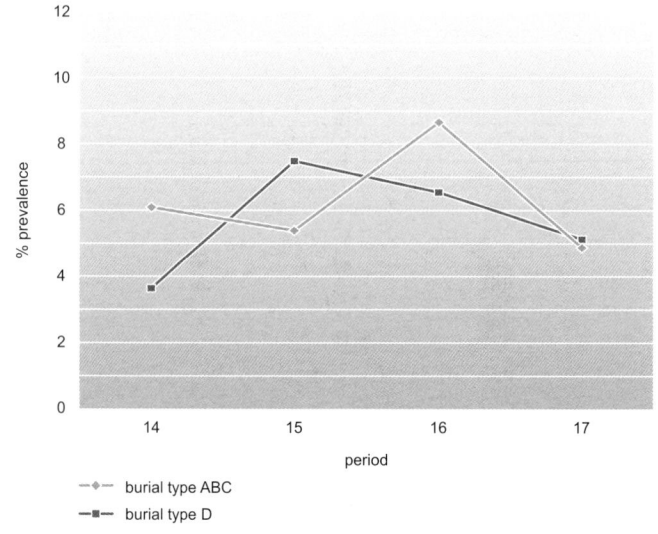

Fig 52 Crude prevalence rate of female extra-spinal osteoarthritis by burial type

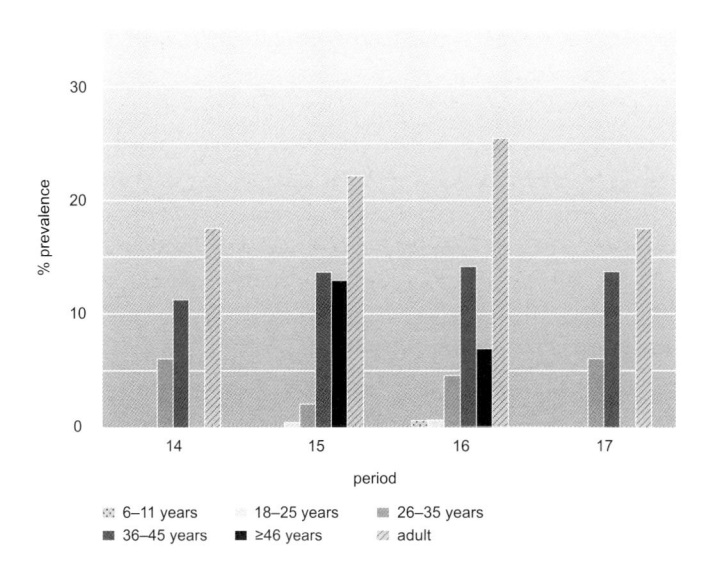

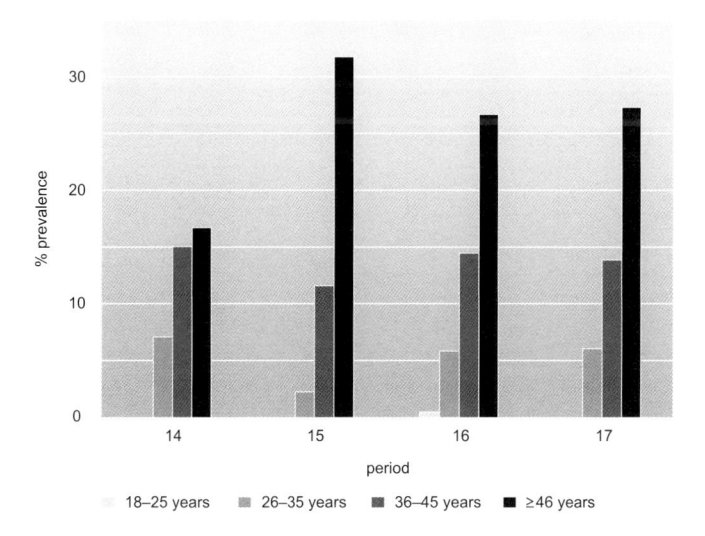

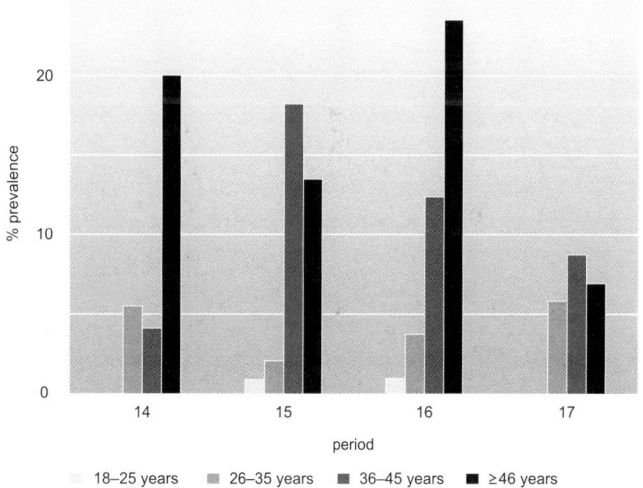

Fig 53 Crude prevalence rate of extra-spinal osteoarthritis by age

assigned. Male prevalence of extra-spinal osteoarthritis in each period increased with age. Only in period 16 was an 18–25-year-old male affected (1/253: 0.4%) (Fig 54). In period 14, prevalence increased with age, though each rise was not found to be statistically significant. While 18–25-year-old males were not affected, the rate among 26–35-year-old (5/71: 7.0%) and 36–45-year-old males (12/80: 15.0%) was similar to all other periods. Older males (≥46 years) had a lower prevalence (4/24: 16.7%) than in the following periods (though not to a statistically significant extent).

In period 15, prevalence again increased with age. Fewer 26–35-year-old males were affected (4/184: 2.2%) than in period 14 (though low frequencies prevented statistical testing). In this period 11.5% (19/165) of 36–45-year-old males and 31.7% (13/41) of ≥46-year-old males were affected, the increase with age being statistically significant (χ^2 = 10.20, df = 1, p ≤ 0.01).

Prevalence once again increased with age in period 16. One 18–25-year-old male was affected, 26–35-year-old males had a rate of 5.8% (23/397), and 36–45-year-old males a rate of 14.4% (53/368), similar to periods 14 and 17, and a statistically significant difference (χ^2 = 15.82, df = 1, p ≤ 0.001). Among older males (≥46 years) 26.6% (33/124) were affected, and again this rise was statistically significant (χ^2 = 9.59, df = 1, p ≤ 0.01).

In period 17, prevalence again increased with age (though not to a statistically significant extent) and the rise in each age group was similar to period 16: 6% (6/100) of 26–35-year-old males, 13.8% (12/87) of 36–45-year-old males, and 27.3% (9/33) of males ≥46 years were affected.

Although the pattern of female extra-spinal osteoarthritis was similar to that of males, there was more variation in prevalence across the age categories. This particularly applied to the distributions in periods 14 and 17, although the observed frequencies and sample sizes were relatively small. Periods 15 and 16 had more typical distributions. There were no statistically significant differences between periods. Only three 18–25-year-old adults in total, from periods 15 (1/120: 0.8%) and 16 (2/220: 0.9%), were affected by extra-spinal osteoarthritis (Fig 55).

In period 14, nine females (9/170: 5.3%) were affected by extra-spinal osteoarthritis. This included 5.5% (4/73) of 26–35-year-old females, 4.1% (2/49) of 36–45-year-old females and 20.0% (3/15) of females aged ≥46 years. The frequencies were too small for statistical testing. No 18–25-year-old females were affected (0/31).

In period 15, one 18–25-year-old female (1/120: 0.8%) was affected. Two per cent (4/196) of 26–35-year-old females and 18.2% (22/121) of 36–45-year-old females were affected, the latter being the highest rate for this age group, though not to a statistically significant extent. The prevalence decreased slightly in females aged ≥46 years to 13.5% (7/52).

In period 16, prevalence rose with age, and apart from the change from 18–25 years to 26–35 years, all these increases were shown to be statistically significant. Two 18–25-year-old females (2/220: 0.9%) were affected. The prevalence rose from 3.7% (14/378) in 26–35-year-old females to 12.4% (31/251) at 36–45 years (χ^2 = 17.0, df = 1, p ≤ 0.001). A further significant increase occurred in females ≥46 years (27/115: 23.5%) (χ^2 = 7.32, df = 1, p ≤ 0.01).

Fig 54 Crude prevalence rate of male extra-spinal osteoarthritis by age

Fig 55 Crude prevalence rate of female extra-spinal osteoarthritis by age

Results

In period 17, ten females (10/203: 4.9%) were affected: 5.8% (4/69) of 25–36-year-old females, rising with age to 8.7% (4/46) of 36–45-year-old females, and then to 6.9% (2/29) of females ≥46 years. Statistical significance was not tested due to the low frequencies (Table 40).

When male and female results by age were compared, the rates at 26–35 years were similar, while the prevalence at 36–45 years and ≥46 years was slightly lower for females than for males. Three 18–25-year-old females were affected, compared to only one 18–25-year-old male. In period 14, the rate at 36–45 years was lower for females, 4.1% compared to 15.0% of males. In period 15, there was a similar rate at 26–35 years for both sexes. A higher prevalence was found in 36–45-year-old females than in males, but the difference was not statistically significant. Males ≥46 years (13/41: 31.7%) were significantly more frequently affected than females of the same age group (7/52: 13.5%) (χ^2 = 4.52, df = 1, p ≤ 0.05). In period 16, there were similar rates and distributions in affected males and females from each age category and no significant differences between the sexes. In period 17, there were fewer females aged 36–45 years and ≥46 years females affected than males, but the frequencies were too small to test.

For males within burial type ABC, the prevalence of extra-spinal osteoarthritis increased with age (Fig 56). This could not be tested in period 14 due to low frequencies. However, there was a statistically significant rise in period 15 from 36–45 years (10/68: 14.7%) to ≥46 years (7/16: 43.8%) (χ^2 = 6.77, df = 1, p ≤ 0.01). In period 16, there was an increase from 26–35 years (13/213: 6.1%) to 36–45 years (36/205: 17.6%) (χ^2 = 13.25, df = 1, p ≤ 0.001). There was also a rise from 36–45 years to ≥46 years (20/63: 31.7%) (χ^2 = 5.87, df = 1, p ≤ 0.025).

Any variation in the rates of extra-spinal osteoarthritis in each category over time, such as the higher prevalence in ≥46 years males in period 15 compared to other periods and the lower prevalence of 26–35-year-olds in period 15, could not be shown to be statistically significant.

The prevalence of extra-spinal osteoarthritis in females

Table 40 Crude prevalence rate of extra-spinal osteoarthritis (OA) by age and sex

	Age (years)	Period 14 No. OA %	Period 15 No. OA %	Period 16 No. OA %	Period 17 No. OA %
Male	18–25	37 0 –	129 0 –	253 1 0.4	62 0 –
	26–35	71 5 7.0	259 4 1.5	397 23 5.8	100 6 6.0
	36–45	80 12 15.0	165 19 11.5	368 53 14.4	187 2 13.8
	≥46	24 4 16.7	41 13 31.7	124 33 26.6	33 9 27.3
Female	18–25	31 0 –	120 1 0.8	220 2 0.9	57 0 –
	26–35	73 4 5.5	196 4 2.0	378 14 3.7	69 4 5.8
	36–45	49 2 4.1	121 22 18.2	251 31 12.4	46 4 8.7
	≥46	15 3 20.0	52 7 13.5	115 27 23.5	29 2 6.9

increased with age in each period for burial type ABC (Fig 57). This rise was statistically significant in period 16, for both the increase from 26–35 years to 36–45 years, from 4.5% to 12.4% (χ^2 = 6.26, df = 1, p ≤ 0.025), and for the increase from 36–45 to ≥46 years, to 30% (χ^2 = 7.58, df = 1, p ≤ 0.01). The increases in periods 14, 15 and 17 could not be tested due to low observed frequencies. The same was true of variation over time. The prevalence of joint disease in females aged 26–35 years was fairly constant, though none was affected in period 15. In 36–45-year-old females there was an increase from period 14 to 15 and then a slight decrease in the following periods. The prevalence of extra-spinal osteoarthritis in females ≥46 years appeared to increase in period 16 compared to earlier periods and then decrease in period 17. Overall, there were significantly more males than females with extra-spinal osteoarthritis in burial type ABC.

Among males from burial type D, the prevalence of osteoarthritis generally increased with age. Although no ≥46-year-old males were affected, there were only five individuals within the age category. In period 14, there was a rise from

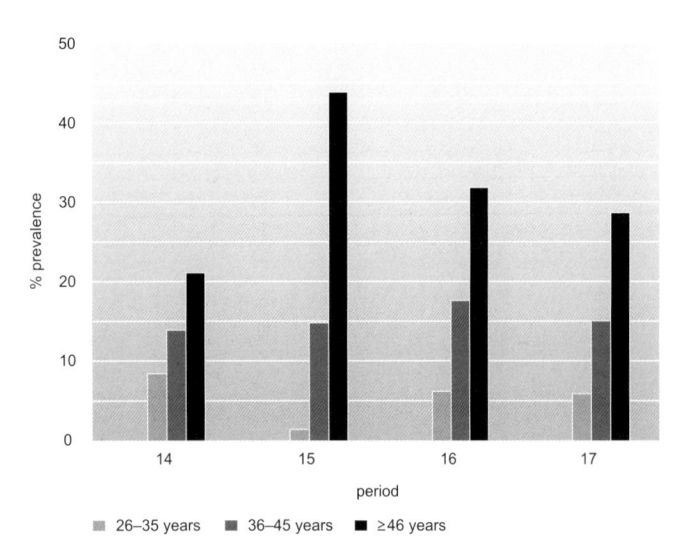

Fig 56 Crude prevalence rate of male extra-spinal osteoarthritis by age in burial type ABC

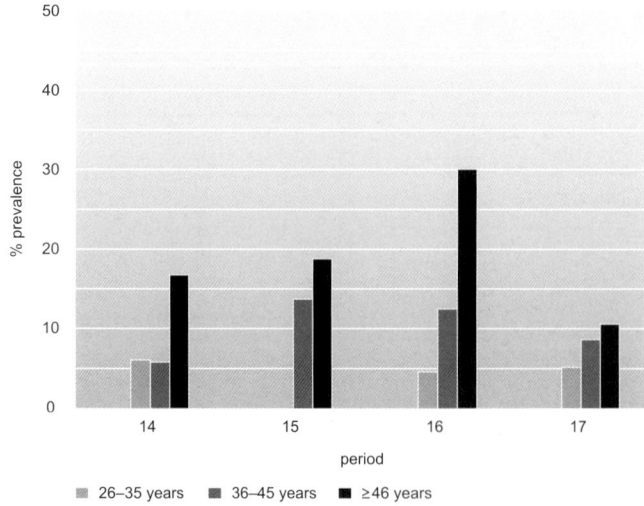

Fig 57 Crude prevalence rate of female extra-spinal osteoarthritis by age in burial type ABC

26–35 years (1/23: 4.3%) to 36–45 years (4/22: 18.2%), though the frequencies were too small for significance testing. In period 15, there was a statistically significant increase from 36–45-year-old males (9/97: 9.3%) to males aged ≥46 years (6/25: 24%) (χ^2 = 3.99, df = 1, p ≤ 0.05). In period 16, there was a statistically significant rise from 36–45 years (17/163: 10.4%) to ≥46 years (13/61: 21.3%) (χ^2 = 4.53, df = 1, p ≤ 0.05) (Fig 58).

There were very few females with osteoarthritis in periods 14 and 17 (two in each). Prevalence of osteoarthritis in females in periods 15 and 16 generally increased with age, and the rise in period 16 was statistically significant between 26–35 years (6/201: 3%) and 36–45 years (16/130: 12.3%) (χ^2 = 11.1, df = 1, p ≤ 0.001) (Fig 59).

There was no significant difference between the overall crude prevalence of extra-spinal osteoarthritis in males and females in burial type D.

True prevalence by period is shown in Tables 41–5. Due to the volume of data, only categories where one or more joints were affected are presented here. No subadults were affected.

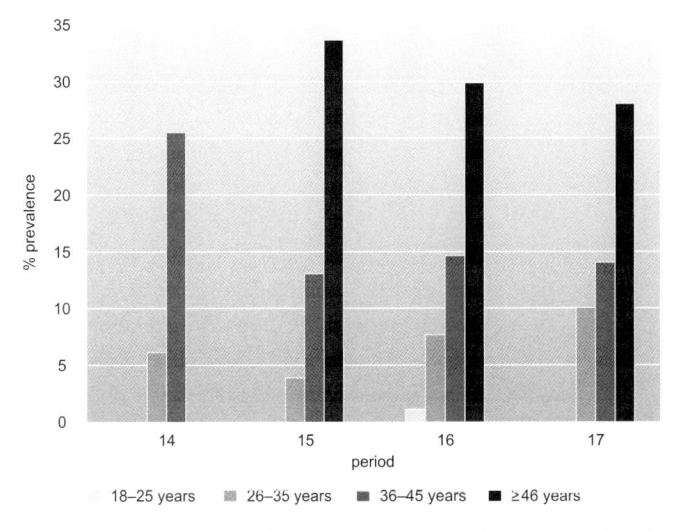

Fig 58 Crude prevalence rate of male extra-spinal osteoarthritis by age in burial type D

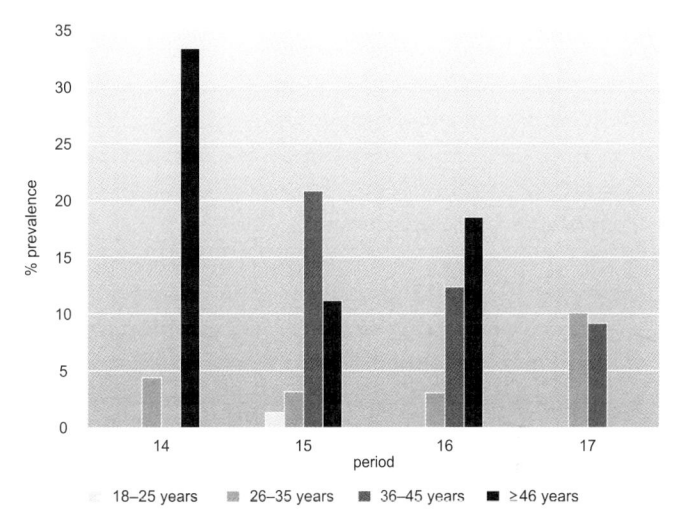

Fig 59 Crude prevalence rate of female extra-spinal osteoarthritis by age in burial type D

Table 41 True prevalence rate of extra-spinal osteoarthritis for affected joints in period 14

Joint	Sex	Age (years)	Burial type ABC No. present	No. affected	% affected	Burial type D No. present	No. affected	% affected	Total No. present	No. affected	% affected
Left acromioclavicular	female	26–35	29	0	-	15	1	6.7	44	1	2.3
Left acromioclavicular	female	36–45	19	1	5.3	10	0	0	29	1	3.4
Left acromioclavicular	male	≥46	13	2	15.4	4	4	100.0	17	6	35.3
Left acromioclavicular	male	36–45	36	3	8.3	18	2	11.1	54	5	9.3
Right acromioclavicular	female	26–35	35	1	2.9	16	0	-	51	1	2.0
Right acromioclavicular	male	≥46	14	2	14.3	3	0	-	17	2	11.8
Right acromioclavicular	male	36–45	40	4	10.0	18	2	11.1	58	6	10.3
Left coxal	female	26–35	40	1	2.5	22	0	-	62	1	1.6
Left coxal	female	adult	1	1	100.0	0	0	-	1	1	100.0
Left coxal	male	36–45	45	1	2.2	21	0	-	66	1	1.5
Right coxal	female	≥46	12	1	8.3	2	0	-	14	1	7.1
Right distal radioulnar	male	26–35	37	1	2.7	18	0	-	55	1	1.8
Right femoropatellar	female	26–35	35	1	2.9	19	0	-	54	1	1.9
Left glenohumeral	male	36–45	41	0	-	19	1	5.3	60	1	1.7
Right glenohumeral	male	≥46	13	1	7.7	4	0	-	17	1	5.9
Left humeroradial	male	≥46	17	1	5.9	4	0	-	21	1	4.8
Left humeroradial	male	36–45	42	1	2.4	17	0	-	59	1	1.7
Right humeroradial	male	≥46	15	1	6.7	4	0	-	19	1	5.3
Right humeroradial	male	26–35	39	1	2.6	19	1	5.3	58	2	3.4
Left humeroulnar	male	36–45	44	1	2.3	19	0	-	63	1	1.6
Right proximal radioulnar	male	26–35	39	1	2.6	19	0	-	58	1	1.7
Radiocarpal: for left lunate	male	26–35	36	1	2.8	20	0	-	56	1	1.8
Radiocarpal: for right lunate	male	26–35	34	1	2.9	18	0	-	52	1	1.9
Radiocarpal: for left scaphoid	male	26–35	35	1	2.9	19	0	-	54	1	1.9
Left sternoclavicular	male	36–45	41	1	2.4	17	0	-	58	1	1.7
Right sternoclavicular	male	36–45	41	1	2.4	16	0	-	57	1	1.8

Results

Table 42 True prevalence rate of extra-spinal osteoarthritis for affected joints in period 15

Joint	Sex	Age (years)	Burial type ABC No. present	No. affected	% affected	Burial type D No. present	No. affected	% affected	Total No. present	No. affected	% affected
Left sternoclavicular	male	36–45	42	0	-	74	1	1.4	116	1	0.9
Left sternoclavicular	intermediate	≥46	1	0	-	1	1	100.0	2	1	50.0
Right sternoclavicular	male	36–45	41	0	-	77	1	1.3	118	1	0.8
Left acromioclavicular	male	36–45	43	1	2.3	67	1	1.5	110	2	1.8
Left acromioclavicular	female	36–45	26	0	-	42	1	2.4	68	1	1.5
Left acromioclavicular	undetermined	adult	0	0	-	1	1	100.0	1	1	100.0
Right acromioclavicular	male	36–45	41	1	2.4	68	4	5.9	109	5	4.6
Right acromioclavicular	male	adult	3	0	-	1	0	-	4	0	-
Right acromioclavicular	female	36–45	28	1	3.6	45	2	4.4	73	3	4.1
Left glenohumeral	female	26–35	55	0	-	109	1	0.9	164	1	0.6
Right glenohumeral	female	36–45	34	0	-	57	1	1.8	91	1	1.1
Right glenohumeral	female	≥46	13	1	7.7	26	0	-	39	1	2.6
Left humeroradial	male	36–45	49	1	2	82	1	1.2	131	2	1.5
Left humeroradial	male	≥46	12	0	-	21	1	4.8	33	1	3.0
Right humeroradial	male	36–45	52	1	1.9	76	0	-	128	1	0.8
Right humeroradial	male	≥46	12	1	8.3	18	0	-	30	1	3.3
Right humeroradial	female	36–45	34	2	5.9	50	0	-	84	2	2.4
Left distal radioulnar	intermediate	adult	1	1	100.0	2	0	-	3	1	33.3
Right distal radioulnar	female	36–45	28	0	-	47	1	2.1	75	1	1.3
Radiocarpal: for left lunate	male	36–45	40	1	2.5	65	0	-	105	1	1.0
Radiocarpal: for left lunate	male	adult	3	1	33.3		0	-	3	1	33.3
Radiocarpal: for left lunate	female	≥46	11	0	-	22	1	4.5	33	1	3.0
Radiocarpal: for right lunate	female	≥46	8	0	-	20	1	5.0	28	1	3.6
Radiocarpal: for left scaphoid	male	36–45	38	1	2.6	63	1	1.6	101	2	2.0
Radiocarpal: for left scaphoid	male	adult	3	1	33.3		0	-	3	1	33.3
Radiocarpal: for right scaphoid	male	36–45	44	1	2.3	64	0	-	108	0	-
Radiocarpal: for right scaphoid	male	≥46	13	1	7.7	14	0	-	27	0	-
Radiocarpal: for right scaphoid	intermediate	≥46	0	0	-	1	1	100.0	1	1	100.0
Radiocarpal: for right scaphoid	female	≥46	7	0	-	19	1	5.3	26	0	-
Left coxal	male	26–35	62	0	-	95	1	1.1	157	1	0.6
Left coxal	male	≥46	14	1	7.1	22	1	4.5	36	2	5.6
Left coxal	female	36–45	38	0	-	65	1	1.5	103	1	1.0
Left coxal	female	≥46	16	1	6.3	30	1	3.3	46	2	4.3
Right coxal	male	26–35	60	0	-	89	1	1.1	149	1	0.7
Right coxal	male	≥46	15	2	13.3	21	0	-	36	2	5.6
Right coxal	male	adult	4	1	25.0	4	0	-	8	1	12.5
Right coxal	female	36–45	39	0	-	61	2	3.3	100	2	2.0
Left femoropatellar	male	26–35	51	1	2.0	80	0	-	131	1	0.8
Left femoropatellar	male	≥46	12	0	-	19	1	5.3	31	1	3.2
Left femoropatellar	female	26–35	49	0	-	97	2	2.1	146	2	1.4
Left femoropatellar	female	36–45	33	0	-	47	2	4.3	80	2	2.5
Right femoropatellar	female	26–35	45	0	-	98	1	1.0	143	1	0.7
Right femoropatellar	female	36–45	32	1	3.1	46	1	2.2	78	2	2.6
Femorotibial: left lateral	male	≥46	13	0	-	19	1	5.3	32	1	3.1
Femorotibial: right lateral	male	36–45	46	0	-	73	1	1.4	119	1	0.8
Femorotibial: left medial	female	36–45	33	1	3.0	51	0	-	84	1	1.2

Joint disease

Table 43 True prevalence rate of extra-spinal osteoarthritis for affected joints in period 16

Joint	Sex	Age (years)	Burial type ABC No. present	Burial type ABC No. affected	Burial type ABC % affected	Burial type D No. present	Burial type D No. affected	Burial type D % affected	Total No. present	Total No. affected	Total % affected
Left sternoclavicular	male	26–35	146	0	-	133	1	0.8	279	1	0.4
Right sternoclavicular	male	26–35	137	0	-	143	1	0.7	280	1	0.4
Right sternoclavicular	male	36–45	156	1	0.6	122	1	0.8	278	2	0.7
Right sternoclavicular	male	≥46	44	3	6.8	44	0	-	88	3	3.4
Left acromioclavicular	male	26–35	123	0	-	126	1	0.8	249	1	0.4
Left acromioclavicular	male	36–45	147	2	1.4	111	3	2.7	258	5	1.9
Left acromioclavicular	male	≥46	40	2	5.0	46	5	10.9	86	7	8.1
Left acromioclavicular	male	adult	15	1	6.7	7	0	-	22	1	4.5
Left acromioclavicular	female	26–35	103	1	1.0	135	1	0.7	238	2	0.8
Left acromioclavicular	female	36–45	77	1	1.3	88	1	1.1	165	2	1.2
Left acromioclavicular	female	≥46	29	1	3.4	42	1	2.4	71	2	2.8
Right acromioclavicular	male	36–45	146	6	4.1	111	1	0.9	257	7	2.7
Right acromioclavicular	male	≥46	43	3	7.0	48	5	10.4	91	8	8.8
Right acromioclavicular	intermediate	adult	3	1	33.3	2	0	-	5	1	20
Right acromioclavicular	female	26–35	103	1	1.0	134	2	1.5	237	3	1.3
Right acromioclavicular	female	36–45	77	0	-	93	2	2.2	170	2	1.2
Right acromioclavicular	female	≥46	25	0	-	51	2	3.9	76	2	2.6
Left glenohumeral	male	26–35	168	2	1.2	149	0	-	317	2	0.6
Left glenohumeral	male	36–45	175	1	0.6	137	0	-	312	1	0.3
Left glenohumeral	male	≥46	50	1	2.0	51	0	-	101	1	1.0
Left glenohumeral	female	36–45	93	2	2.2	105	1	1.0	198	3	1.5
Left glenohumeral	female	≥46	43	1	2.3	55	0	-	98	1	1.0
Left humeroulnar	male	36–45	177	1	0.6	138	1	0.7	315	2	0.6
Left humeroulnar	female	≥46	44	1	2.3	58	1	1.7	102	2	2.0
Right humeroulnar	male	adult	19	1	5.3	12	0	-	31	1	3.2
Right humeroulnar	female	≥46	44	1	2.3	58	0	-	102	1	1.0
Left humeroradial	male	26–35	162	2	1.2	149	0	-	311	2	0.6
Left humeroradial	male	36–45	170	3	1.8	132	3	2.3	302	6	2.0
Left humeroradial	male	≥46	54	2	3.7	53	1	1.9	107	3	2.8
Left humeroradial	intermediate	adult	4	1	25.0	4	0	-	8	1	12.5
Left humeroradial	female	36–45	95	1	1.1	100	2	2.0	195	3	1.5
Left humeroradial	female	≥46	40	1	2.5	52	3	5.8	92	4	4.3
Left humeroradial	female	adult	13	1	7.7	14	0	-	27	1	3.7
Right humeroradial	male	26–35	155	2	1.3	152	0	-	307	2	0.6
Right humeroradial	male	36–45	171	4	2.3	133	1	0.8	304	5	1.6
Right humeroradial	male	≥46	53	2	3.8	51	1	2.0	104	3	2.9
Right humeroradial	intermediate	36–45	13	0	-	4	1	25.0	17	1	5.9
Right humeroradial	intermediate	adult	3	1	33.3	3	0	-	6	1	16.7
Right humeroradial	female	36–45	93	3	3.2	103	1	1.0	196	4	2.0
Right humeroradial	female	≥46	43	2	4.7	52	1	1.9	95	3	3.2
Right humeroradial	female	adult	15	1	6.7	12	0	-	27	1	3.7
Right proximal radioulnar	female	36–45	98	1	1.0	110	0	-	208	1	0.5
Left distal radioulnar	male	26–35	141	1	0.7	142	1	0.7	283	2	0.7
Left distal radioulnar	male	36–45	157	2	1.3	122	1	0.8	279	3	1.1
Left distal radioulnar	male	≥46	48	2	4.2	54	2	3.7	102	4	3.9
Left distal radioulnar	female	26–35	113	1	0.9	136	0	-	249	1	0.4
Left distal radioulnar	female	36–45	81	0	-	89	1	1.1	170	1	0.6
Right distal radioulnar	male	26–35	144	1	0.7	145	0	-	289	1	0.3
Right distal radioulnar	male	36–45	155	0	-	127	3	2.4	282	3	1.1
Right distal radioulnar	male	≥46	43	3	7.0	47	0	-	90	3	3.3
Right distal radioulnar	female	18–25	63	1	1.6	74	0	-	137	1	0.7
Right distal radioulnar	female	26–35	122	1	0.8	136	0	-	258	1	0.4
Right distal radioulnar	female	36–45	80	0	-	93	1	1.1	173	1	0.6
Radiocarpal: for left lunate	male	≥46	45	3	6.7	50	0	-	95	3	3.2
Radiocarpal: for right lunate	male	36–45	146	0	-	116	2	1.7	262	2	0.8
Radiocarpal: for right lunate	male	≥46	40	1	2.5	44	0	-	84	1	1.2
Radiocarpal: for left scaphoid	male	26–35	125	1	0.8	131	0	-	256	1	0.4
Radiocarpal: for left scaphoid	male	36–45	148	1	0.7	113	0	-	261	1	0.4
Radiocarpal: for left scaphoid	male	≥46	44	3	6.8	48	0	-	92	3	3.3
Radiocarpal: for right scaphoid	male	26–35	128	0	-	139	1	0.7	267	1	0.4
Radiocarpal: for right scaphoid	male	≥46	40	1	2.5	44	0	-	84	1	1.2

Results

Table 44 True prevalence rate of extra-spinal osteoarthritis for affected joints in period 17

Joint	Sex	Age (years)	Burial type ABC No. present	Burial type ABC No. affected	Burial type ABC % affected	Burial type D No. present	Burial type D No. affected	Burial type D % affected	Total No. present	Total No. affected	Total % affected
Right sternoclavicular	male	36–45	56	1	1.8	16	0	-	72	1	1.4
Right sternoclavicular	male	≥46	26	0	-	5	1	20.0	31	1	3.2
Left acromioclavicular	male	36–45	58	2	3.4	17	0	-	75	2	2.7
Left acromioclavicular	female	36–45	19	1	5.3	7	0	-	26	1	3.8
Right acromioclavicular	male	36–45	54	1	1.9	16	0	-	70	1	1.4
Right acromioclavicular	male	≥46	26	1	3.8	5	0	-	31	1	3.2
Right acromioclavicular	intermediate	36–45	3	1	33.3	1	0	-	4	1	25
Right acromioclavicular	female	26–35	40	1	2.5	7	0	-	47	1	2.1
Right acromioclavicular	female	36–45	26	1	3.8	6	0	-	32	1	3.1
Left glenohumeral	male	36–45	61	1	1.6	18	0	-	79	1	1.3
Left glenohumeral	female	36–45	31	1	3.2	8	0	-	39	1	2.6
Right glenohumeral	male	36–45	58	1	1.7	19	0	-	77	1	1.3
Right glenohumeral	male	≥46	25	1	4.0	5	0	-	30	1	3.3
Left humeroradial	male	≥46	25	1	4.0	5	0	-	30	1	3.3
Left humeroradial	female	26–35	52	1	1.9	8	0	-	60	1	1.7
Left humeroradial	female	≥46	15	1	6.7	9	0	-	24	1	4.2
Right humeroradial	male	26–35	75	1	1.3	13	1	7.7	88	2	2.3
Right humeroradial	male	36–45	52	1	1.9	20	0	-	72	1	1.4
Right humeroradial	male	≥46	27	1	3.7	5	0	-	32	1	3.1
Right humeroradial	female	26–35	50	1	2.0	9	0	-	59	1	1.7
Left humeroulnar	female	18–25	38	1	2.6	6	0	-	44	1	2.3
Left humeroulnar	female	26–35	52	1	1.9	9	0	-	61	1	1.6
Right humeroulnar	male	36–45	53	1	1.9	20	0	-	73	1	1.4
Right humeroulnar	female	26–35	52	1	1.9	9	0	-	61	1	1.6
Left distal radioulnar	male	36–45	46	0	-	17	1	5.9	63	1	1.6
Left distal radioulnar	male	≥46	26	2	7.7	5	0	-	31	2	6.5
Right distal radioulnar	male	26–35	69	1	1.4	12	0	-	81	1	1.2
Right distal radioulnar	male	≥46	26	1	3.8	4	0	-	30	1	3.3
Right distal radioulnar	female	36–45	27	1	3.7	8	0	-	35	1	2.9
Radiocarpal: for left lunate	male	≥46	25	1	4.0	5	0	-	30	1	3.3
Radiocarpal: for right lunate	male	≥46	25	1	4.0	3	0	-	28	1	3.6
Radiocarpal: for left scaphoid	male	≥46	24	1	4.2	5	0	-	29	1	3.4
Radiocarpal: for right scaphoid	male	≥46	25	2	8.0	3	0	-	28	2	7.1
Left coxal	male	26–35	77	1	1.3	14	0	-	91	1	1.1
Left coxal	male	36–45	57	1	1.8	19	0	-	76	1	1.3
Left coxal	male	≥46	28	1	3.6	5	0	-	33	1	3.0
Right coxal	male	26–35	77	1	1.3	14	0	-	91	1	1.1
Right coxal	male	36–45	57	1	1.8	20	0	-	77	1	1.3
Right coxal	male	≥46	28	1	3.6	5	0	-	33	1	3.0
Right coxal	female	26–35	52	1	1.9	10	0	-	62	1	1.6
Right coxal	female	≥46	19	1	5.3	10	0	-	29	1	3.4
Left femoropatellar	male	≥46	25	1	4.0	5	0	-	30	1	3.3
Left femoropatellar	female	36–45	27	1	3.7	10	0	-	37	1	2.7
Right femoropatellar	male	36–45	50	0	-	19	1	5.3	69	1	1.4
Right femoropatellar	male	≥46	25	1	4.0	5	0	-	30	1	3.3
Right femoropatellar	female	≥46	16	1	6.3	10	0	-	26	1	3.8
Femorotibial: left lateral	male	≥46	25	1	4.0	5	0	-	30	1	3.3
Femorotibial: left lateral	intermediate	36–45	4	1	25.0	1	0	-	5	1	20.0
Femorotibial: left lateral	female	36–45	27	1	3.7	10	0	-	37	1	2.7
Femorotibial: right lateral	male	≥46	26	1	3.8	5	1	20.0	31	2	6.5
Femorotibial: right lateral	intermediate	36–45	3	1	33.3	1	0	-	4	1	25
Femorotibial: right lateral	female	36–45	27	1	3.7	10	0	-	37	1	2.7
Femorotibial: right medial	male	36–45	50	1	2.0	18	0	-	68	1	1.5
Femorotibial: right medial	male	≥46	25	1	4.0	5	0	-	30	1	3.3
Femorotibial: right medial	female	36–45	28	2	7.1	10	0	-	38	2	5.3
Right talocrural	female	26–35	41	1	2.4	8	0	-	49	1	2.0

Joint disease

Table 45 Total true prevalence rate of extra-spinal osteoarthritis for affected joints

Joint	Sex	Age (years)	Burial type ABC No. present	No. affected	% affected	Burial type D No. present	No. affected	% affected	Total No. present	No. affected	% affected
Right sternoclavicular	male	36–45	56	1	1.8	16	0	-	72	1	1.4
Left sternoclavicular	male	26–35	360	0	-	258	1	0.4	618	1	0.2
Left sternoclavicular	male	36–45	330	1	0.3	237	1	0.4	567	1	0.2
Left sternoclavicular	intermediate	≥46	5	0	-	1	1	100.0	6	1	16.7
Right sternoclavicular	male	26–35	296	0	-	247	1	0.4	543	1	0.2
Right sternoclavicular	male	36–45	294	3	1.0	231	2	0.9	525	4	0.8
Right sternoclavicular	male	≥46	95	3	3.2	72	1	1.4	167	4	2.4
Left acromioclavicular	male	26–35	274	0	-	221	1	0.5	495	1	0.2
Left acromioclavicular	male	36–45	284	8	2.8	213	6	2.8	497	14	2.8
Left acromioclavicular	male	≥46	84	4	4.8	69	9	13.0	153	13	8.5
Left acromioclavicular	male	adult	30	1	3.3	10	0	-	40	1	2.5
Left acromioclavicular	female	26–35	214	1	0.5	241	2	0.8	455	3	0.7
Left acromioclavicular	female	36–45	141	3	2.1	147	2	1.4	288	5	1.7
Left acromioclavicular	female	≥46	57	1	1.8	75	1	1.3	132	2	1.5
Left acromioclavicular	undetermined	adult	2	0	-	2	1	50.0	4	1	25.0
Right acromioclavicular	male	36–45	281	12	4.3	213	7	3.3	494	19	3.8
Right acromioclavicular	male	≥46	94	6	6.4	74	5	6.8	168	11	6.5
Right acromioclavicular	male	adult	29	0	-	9	2	22.2	38	2	5.3
Right acromioclavicular	intermediate	36–45	18	1	5.6	9	0	-	27	1	3.7
Right acromioclavicular	intermediate	adult	3	1	33.3	2	0	-	5	1	20.0
Right acromioclavicular	female	26–35	224	3	1.3	245	2	0.8	469	5	1.1
Right acromioclavicular	female	36–45	154	2	1.3	154	4	2.6	308	6	1.9
Right acromioclavicular	female	≥46	54	0	-	84	2	2.4	138	2	1.4
Left glenohumeral	male	26–35	340	2	0.6	260	0	-	600	2	0.3
Left glenohumeral	male	36–45	332	2	0.6	260	1	0.4	592	3	0.5
Left glenohumeral	male	≥46	101	1	1.0	81	0	-	182	1	0.5
Left glenohumeral	female	26–35	283	0	-	305	1	0.3	588	1	0.2
Left glenohumeral	female	36–45	184	3	1.6	178	1	0.6	362	4	1.1
Left glenohumeral	female	≥46	81	1	1.2	94	0	-	175	1	0.6
Right glenohumeral	male	36–45	324	1	0.3	262	0	-	586	1	0.2
Right glenohumeral	male	≥46	103	2	1.9	79	0	-	182	2	1.1
Right glenohumeral	female	36–45	182	0	-	185	1	0.5	367	1	0.3
Right glenohumeral	female	≥46	80	1	1.3	95	0	-	175	1	0.6
Left humeroradial	male	36–45	321	3	0.9	256	2	0.8	577	5	0.9
Left humeroradial	male	≥46	111	2	1.8	87	1	1.1	198	3	1.5
Left humeroradial	female	26–35	280	1	0.4	302	0	-	582	1	0.2
Left humeroradial	female	≥46	78	2	2.6	95	1	1.1	173	3	1.7
Right humeroradial	male	26–35	334	2	0.6	273	2	0.7	607	4	0.7
Right humeroradial	male	36–45	321	2	0.6	255	0	-	576	2	0.3
Right humeroradial	male	≥46	109	3	2.8	81	0	-	190	3	1.6
Right humeroradial	male	adult	35	1	2.9	14	0	-	49	1	2.0
Right humeroradial	female	26–35	286	1	0.3	301	0	-	587	1	0.2
Right humeroradial	female	36–45	189	2	1.1	178	0	-	367	2	0.5
Right humeroradial	female	≥46	81	1	1.2	95	0	-	176	1	0.6
Left humeroulnar	male	26–35	348	2	0.6	274	0	-	622	2	0.3
Left humeroulnar	male	36–45	320	4	1.3	255	3	1.2	575	7	1.2
Left humeroulnar	male	≥46	111	2	1.8	83	1	1.2	194	3	1.5
Left humeroulnar	intermediate	adult	5	1	20.0	6	0	-	11	1	9.1
Left humeroulnar	female	18–25	155	1	0.6	170	0	-	325	1	0.3
Left humeroulnar	female	26–35	277	1	0.4	295	0	-	572	1	0.2
Left humeroulnar	female	36–45	188	1	0.5	180	2	1.1	368	3	0.8
Left humeroulnar	female	≥46	80	1	1.3	92	3	3.3	172	4	2.3
Left humeroulnar	female	adult	15	1	6.7	19	0	-	34	1	2.9
Right humeroulnar	male	26–35	331	2	0.6	270	0	-	601	2	0.3
Right humeroulnar	male	36–45	321	5	1.6	258	1	0.4	579	6	1.0
Right humeroulnar	male	≥46	108	2	1.9	78	1	1.3	186	3	1.6
Right humeroulnar	intermediate	36–45	22	0	-	13	1	7.7	35	1	2.9
Right humeroulnar	intermediate	adult	4	1	25.0	6	0	-	10	1	10.0
Right humeroulnar	female	26–35	283	1	0.4	294	0	-	577	1	0.2
Right humeroulnar	female	36–45	186	3	1.6	178	1	0.6	364	4	1.1
Right humeroulnar	female	≥46	81	2	2.5	92	1	1.1	173	3	1.7
Right humeroulnar	female	adult	16	1	6.3	20	0	-	36	1	2.8
Right proximal radioulnar	male	26–35	321	1	0.3	265	0	-	586	1	0.2
Right proximal radioulnar	female	36–45	189	1	0.5	182	0	-	371	1	0.3

Results

Table 45 (cont)

			Burial type ABC			Burial type D			Total		
Joint	Sex	Age (years)	No. present	No. affected	% affected	No. present	No. affected	% affected	No. present	No. affected	% affected
Left distal radioulnar	male	26–35	304	1	0.3	248	1	0.4	552	2	0.4
Left distal radioulnar	male	36–45	286	2	0.7	229	2	0.9	515	4	0.8
Left distal radioulnar	male	≥46	100	4	4.0	80	2	2.5	180	6	3.3
Left distal radioulnar	intermediate	adult	4	1	25.0	5	0	-	9	1	11.1
Left distal radioulnar	female	26–35	230	1	0.4	249	0	-	479	1	0.2
Left distal radioulnar	female	36–45	161	0	-	158	1	0.6	319	1	0.3
Right distal radioulnar	male	26–35	297	3	1.0	245	0	-	542	3	0.6
Right distal radioulnar	male	36–45	292	0	-	238	3	1.3	530	3	0.6
Right distal radioulnar	male	≥46	97	4	4.1	71	0	-	168	4	2.4
Right distal radioulnar	female	18–25	119	1	0.8	138	0	-	257	1	0.4
Right distal radioulnar	female	26–35	248	1	0.4	247	0	-	495	1	0.2
Right distal radioulnar	female	36–45	158	1	0.6	154	2	1.3	312	3	1.0
Radiocarpal: for left lunate	male	26–35	281	1	0.4	232	0	-	513	1	0.2
Radiocarpal: for left lunate	male	36–45	276	1	0.4	212	0	-	488	1	0.2
Radiocarpal: for left lunate	male	≥46	95	4	4.2	73	0	-	168	4	2.4
Radiocarpal: for left lunate	male	adult	19	1	5.3	9	0	-	28	1	3.6
Radiocarpal: for left lunate	female	≥46	66	0	-	73	1	1.4	139	1	0.7
Radiocarpal: for right lunate	male	26–35	271	1	0.4	236	0	-	507	1	0.2
Radiocarpal: for right lunate	male	36–45	280	0	-	219	2	0.9	499	2	0.4
Radiocarpal: for right lunate	male	≥46	93	2	2.2	64	0	-	157	2	1.3
Radiocarpal: for right lunate	female	≥46	64	0	-	72	1	1.4	136	1	0.7
Radiocarpal: for left scaphoid	male	26–35	276	2	0.7	227	0	-	503	2	0.4
Radiocarpal: for left scaphoid	male	36–45	270	2	0.7	208	1	0.5	478	3	0.6
Radiocarpal: for left scaphoid	male	≥46	91	4	4.4	71	0	-	162	4	2.5
Radiocarpal: for left scaphoid	male	adult	19	1	5.3	10	0	-	29	1	3.4
Radiocarpal: for right scaphoid	male	26–35	272	0	-	236	1	0.4	508	1	0.2
Radiocarpal: for right scaphoid	male	36–45	276	1	0.4	220	0	-	496	1	0.2
Radiocarpal: for right scaphoid	male	≥46	93	4	4.3	64	0	-	157	3	1.9
Radiocarpal: for right scaphoid	intermediate	≥46	4	0	-	1	1	100.0	5	1	20
Radiocarpal: for right scaphoid	female	≥46	52	0	-	62	1	1.6	114	1	0.9
Left sacroiliac	male	36–45	324	0	-	259	1	0.4	583	1	0.2
Right sacroiliac	male	≥46	106	1	0.9	81	0	-	187	1	0.5
Left coxal	male	26–35	355	1	0.3	292	3	1.0	647	4	0.6
Left coxal	male	36–45	341	6	1.8	270	0	-	611	6	1.0
Left coxal	male	≥46	117	2	1.7	89	1	1.1	206	3	1.5
Left coxal	male	adult	18	1	5.6	17	0	-	35	1	2.9
Left coxal	female	26–35	308	1	0.3	322	0	-	630	1	0.2
Left coxal	female	36–45	204	0	-	203	2	1.0	407	2	0.5
Left coxal	female	≥46	89	3	3.4	101	3	3.0	190	6	3.2
Left coxal	female	adult	12	1	8.3	16	0	-	28	1	3.6
Right coxal	male	26–35	355	2	0.6	286	3	1.0	641	5	0.8
Right coxal	male	36–45	344	3	0.9	272	1	0.4	616	4	0.6
Right coxal	male	≥46	114	4	3.5	87	0	-	201	4	2.0
Right coxal	male	adult	20	2	10.0	16	0	-	36	2	5.6
Right coxal	female	26–35	292	1	0.3	324	0	-	616	1	0.2
Right coxal	female	36–45	211	1	0.5	199	2	1.0	410	3	0.7
Right coxal	female	≥46	91	2	2.2	103	1	1.0	194	3	1.5
Left femoropatellar	male	26–35	302	2	0.7	250	0	-	552	1	0.2
Left femoropatellar	male	36–45	302	4	1.3	210	0	-	512	4	0.8
Left femoropatellar	male	≥46	100	4	4.0	77	3	3.9	177	2	1.1
Left femoropatellar	female	26–35	248	0	-	269	2	0.7	517	2	0.4
Left femoropatellar	female	36–45	170	3	1.8	152	2	1.3	322	3	0.9
Left femoropatellar	female	≥46	82	3	3.7	86	0	-	168	3	1.8
Right femoropatellar	male	36–45	302	1	0.3	228	1	0.4	530	2	0.4
Right femoropatellar	male	≥46	99	3	3.0	77	1	1.3	176	4	2.3
Right femoropatellar	female	26–35	252	2	0.8	269	2	0.7	521	4	0.8
Right femoropatellar	female	36–45	172	1	0.6	156	1	0.6	328	2	0.6
Right femoropatellar	female	≥46	80	4	5.0	86	0	-	166	4	2.4
Femorotibial: left lateral	male	≥46	100	2	2.0	75	1	1.3	175	2	1.1
Femorotibial: left lateral	intermediate	36–45	23	1	4.3	14	0	-	37	1	2.7
Femorotibial: left lateral	female	26–35	254	1	0.4	263	0	-	517	1	0.2
Femorotibial: left lateral	female	36–45	173	1	0.6	157	1	0.6	330	1	0.3
Femorotibial: left lateral	female	≥46	79	1	1.3	79	1	1.3	158	2	1.3
Femorotibial: right lateral	male	36–45	304	2	0.7	229	1	0.4	533	1	0.2

Table 45 (cont)

			Burial type ABC			Burial type D			Total		
Joint	Sex	Age (years)	No. present	No. affected	% affected	No. present	No. affected	% affected	No. present	No. affected	% affected
Femorotibial: right lateral	male	≥46	101	1	1.0	78	3	3.8	179	2	1.1
Femorotibial: right lateral	intermediate	36–45	21	2	9.5	13	0	-	34	1	2.9
Femorotibial: right lateral	female	36–45	176	3	1.7	154	1	0.6	330	1	0.3
Femorotibial: right lateral	female	≥46	81	1	1.2	83	2	2.4	164	3	1.8
Femorotibial: left medial	male	26–35	314	0	-	249	1	0.4	563	1	0.2
Femorotibial: left medial	male	≥46	102	1	1.0	77	0	-	179	1	0.6
Femorotibial: left medial	female	26–35	253	1	0.4	259	0	-	512	1	0.2
Femorotibial: left medial	female	36–45	173	1	0.6	155	1	0.6	328	1	0.3
Femorotibial: left medial	undetermined	36–45	3	1	33.3	0	0	-	3	1	33.3
Femorotibial: right medial	male	26–35	309	0	-	241	1	0.4	550	1	0.2
Femorotibial: right medial	male	36–45	303	2	0.7	229	0	-	532	1	0.2
Femorotibial: right medial	male	≥46	101	2	2.0	78	1	1.3	179	1	0.6
Femorotibial: right medial	female	36–45	179	2	1.1	151	0	-	330	2	0.6
Femorotibial: right medial	female	≥46	80	1	1.3	85	1	1.2	165	2	1.2
Right talocrural	male	36–45	255	0	-	197	1	0.5	452	1	0.2
Right talocrural	female	26–35	217	1	0.5	229	1	0.4	446	1	0.2

Charcot joint

Only one individual was recorded with a Charcot joint, a ≥46-year-old adult female [2893] from burial type ABC in period 17 (Ortner 2003, 129). The sternal end of the right clavicle was affected with proliferative growth at the sternal facet and large and deep smooth-edged erosions penetrating the subchondral bone (Table 46).

Ochronotic osteoarthropathy

A 36–45-year-old female [10095] from burial type ABC in period 16 was recorded with this rare form of osteoarthropathy (Fig 60; Table 46). The intervertebral joint disease consisted of degenerative changes to the zygapophyseal, uncovertebral, intervertebral, costovertebral and costotransverse joints. The cervical vertebrae were the most affected, and the ninth to 12th thoracic vertebrae had fused in two pairs. Dense bone with an ivory-like texture was present on the vertebral endplates throughout the thoracic and lumbar spinal column, fusing the fourth and fifth, ninth and tenth, and 11th and 12th thoracic vertebrae. Bilateral diarthrodial joint disease was present in the temporomandibular, sternoclavicular, acromioclavicular and elbow joints. The left hip joint had severe metabolic osteoarthritic changes consisting of subchondral cysts, obliteration of the articular surface, marginal osteophytosis and new bone formation to the anterior aspect of the proximal femur, acetabulum and ischium.

Table 46 Crude prevalence rates of specific osteoarthropathies by period, sex and burial type

Period	Burial type	Sex	No. individuals	Charcot joint	% affected	Ochronotic osteoarthropathy	% affected	Ankylosis	% affected
14	ABC	male	160	0	-	0	-	1	0.6
		female	115	0	-	0	-	1	0.9
	D	male	63	0	-	0	-	0	-
		female	55	0	-	0	-	0	-
15	ABC	male	219	0	-	0	-	3	1.4
		female	167	0	-	0	-	1	0.6
	D	male	313	0	-	0	-	1	0.3
		female	334	0	-	0	-	2	0.3
16	ABC	male	628	0	-	0	-	9	1.4
		female	474	0	-	1	0.2	1	0.2
	D	male	564	0	-	0	-	11	1.9
		female	535	0	-	0	-	2	0.4
17	ABC	male	239	0	-	0	-	3	1.3
		female	164	1	0.6	0	-	0	-
	D	male	51	0	-	0	-	5	9.8
		female	39	0	-	0	-	0	-

Fig 60 Ochronotic osteoarthropathy in 36–45-year-old female [10095] from period 16, burial type ABC (scale c 1:1)

Ankylosis

Joint ankylosis was recorded in all periods (Table 46). More males (33/2237: 1.5%) than females were affected (7/1883: 0.4%), and the majority of individuals affected were in burial type ABC. Ankylosis predominantly affected the sacroiliac joint, particularly in males, and period 16 had the highest number of individuals affected (23).

Rotator cuff injuries

Degenerative changes to the greater and lesser tuberosities of the humerus and humeral head were recorded as rotator cuff injuries (Apley and Solomon 2000, 114–15; Rogers and Waldron 1995, 42). A total of 111 individuals with this condition were recorded (111/5387: 2.1%); the majority (55/111: 49.5%) were from period 16, and adults from 26–35 years to ≥46 years were affected. The majority of affected individuals were from burial type ABC (62/111: 55.9%) (Table 47).

The highest prevalence rate was observed in period 14 for intermediate 36–45-year-old adults (1/5: 20.0%), although this is a result of the low number of individuals in that age group. More meaningful data were observed in ≥46-year-old adult males in period 17 (4/33: 12.1%) and in females of the same age in period 16 (9/115: 7.8%).

In period 15 the difference between the number of males and females with rotator cuff injuries was found to be statistically significant (df = 1, p ≤ 0.001). In females, the difference between the numbers of individuals affected was found to be statistically significant between periods 15 and 16 (df = 1, p ≤ 0.001).

Diffuse idiopathic skeletal hyperostosis (DISH)

DISH is a condition that has only been recognised relatively recently, both clinically and in palaeopathological contexts. The main manifestations are bony proliferations on the margins of the vertebral bodies that fuse together, causing the spine to become rigid. Ossifications also occur elsewhere in the skeleton at sites of ligament and muscle attachment.

In terms of skeletal involvement, it is the vertebral changes that are most characteristic of DISH: blocks of ankylosed (fused) vertebrae have the appearance of melted candle wax dripped down the bodies, usually on the right side.

In total 34 individuals (34/5387: 0.6%), predominantly males, were affected in all periods, the most heavily affected age group being 36–45-year-olds. There were no statistically significantly differences found between the total number of males and females affected, between males with or without DISH, and between males from different burial types. In both

Table 47 Crude prevalence rate of rotator cuff disease by period, sex and burial type

Period	Burial type	Sex	No. individuals	No. affected	%
14	ABC	male	160	4	2.5
		female	115	3	2.6
		intermediate	16	1	6.25
	D	male	63	3	4.8
		female	55	0	-
		intermediate	5	0	-
15	ABC	male	219	10	4.6
		female	167	5	3.0
		intermediate	17	0	-
	D	male	313	6	1.9
		female	334	7	2.1
		intermediate	29	2	6.9
16	ABC	male	628	15	2.4
		female	474	11	2.3
		intermediate	71	0	-
	D	male	564	16	2.8
		female	535	12	2.2
		intermediate	39	1	2.6
17	ABC	male	239	9	3.8
		female	164	3	1.8
		intermediate	24	1	4.2
	D	male	51	2	3.9
		female	39	0	-
		intermediate	4	0	-

burial types, the highest crude prevalence rates were observed in period 17, for ≥46-year-old males (2/33: 6.1%), and in period 14, for 36–45-year-old males (4/80: 5%) (Fig 61).

The crude prevalence rates are summarised in Table 48. In period 14, five males were affected (36–45-year-old and ≥46-year-old adults), equally distributed between burial types (ABC 3/160: 1.9%; D 2/63: 3.2%).

In period 15, 15 individuals (15/1390: 1.1%) were affected (eight males and seven females). The majority of individuals were 36–45-year-old and ≥46-year-old adults. Only one female was aged 26–35 years. No statistically significant differences were found.

From period 16, nine individuals were affected (9/2835: 0.3%), the majority (seven) from burial type D (males 3/564, 0.5%; females 4/535, 0.7%).

In period 17, five males were affected (5/650: 0.1%). All were from burial type ABC (5/239: 2.1%), and no statistically significant difference was found between the numbers of males with or without DISH. Three affected males were aged 36–45 years (3/67: 4.5%) and two were aged ≥46 years (2/28: 7.2%).

The majority of affected individuals were ≥46-year-old and 36–45-year-old adults. No statistical significance was found between males with or without DISH.

Erosive osteoarthropathies

A total of 31 individuals had non-specific erosive osteoarthropathies, and these predominantly affected hand and foot bones and the sacroiliac joint. Affected individuals were observed in all periods, predominantly from burial type ABC, and the majority were male (Table 49).

Rheumatoid arthritis

Two males had osseous changes diagnostic of rheumatoid arthritis (2/5387: <0.1%). In period 15, 18–25-year-old male [11371] from burial type ABC had changes to the ankle, knee, hip, wrist, hand, elbow, shoulder and temporomandibular joints: 1.9% of 18–25-year-old males in this burial type (1/53) and 0.5% of all males from burial type ABC in this period (1/219) (Fig 62). In period 16, ≥46-year-old male [17863] from burial type ABC had changes to the cervical vertebrae and two foot phalanges, a prevalence of 1.6% for this age and sex group (1/63) and 0.2% of all males from burial type ABC in this period (1/628). Two further possible cases were noted (Table 49).

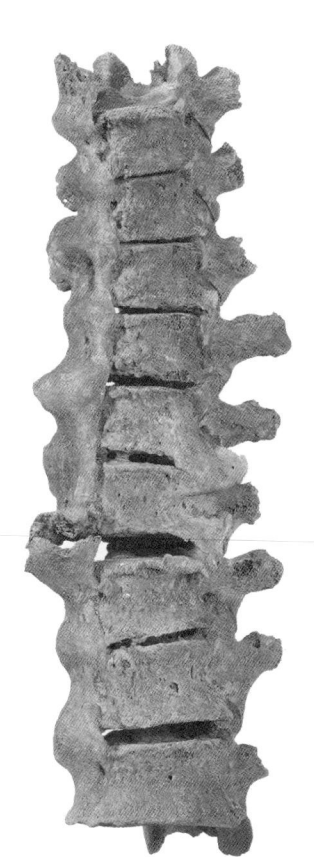

Fig 61 DISH in the thoracolumbar spine of 36–45-year-old male [12498] from period 15, burial type ABC (scale c 1:2)

Table 48 Crude prevalence rate of DISH by period, sex and burial type

Period	Burial type	Sex	No. individuals	No. affected	%
14	ABC	male	160	3	1.9
		female	115	0	-
	D	male	63	2	3.2
		female	55	0	-
15	ABC	male	219	6	2.7
		female	167	2	0.1
	D	male	313	2	0.6
		female	334	5	1.5
16	ABC	male	628	2	0.3
		female	474	0	-
	D	male	564	3	0.5
		female	535	4	0.7
17	ABC	male	239	5	2.1
		female	164	0	-
	D	male	51	0	-
		female	39	0	-

Fig 62 View of the distal articular surfaces of the radii with evidence for rheumatoid osteoarthritis in 18–25-year-old male [11371] from period 15, burial type ABC (scale c 2:1)

Results

Table 49 Crude prevalence rate of erosive osteoarthropathies by period, sex and burial type

Period	Burial type	Sex	No. individuals	Erosive arthopathy	% affected	Rheumatoid arthritis	% affected	Possible rheumatoid arthritis	% affected	Gout	% affected
14	ABC	male	160	2	1.25	0	-	0	-	0	-
		female	115	0	-	0	-	0	-	0	-
	D	male	63	0	-	0	-	0	-	0	-
		female	55	0	-	0	-	0	-	0	-
15	ABC	male	219	2	0.9	1	0.5	1	0.5	0	-
		female	167	0	-	0	-	0	-	0	-
	D	male	313	1	0.3	0	-	0	-	0	-
		female	334	1	0.3	0	-	0	-	1	0.3
16	ABC	male	628	8	1.3	1	0.2	0	-	1	0.2
		female	474	5	1.0	0	-	0	-	0	-
		intermediate	71	1	1.4	0	-	0	-	0	-
	D	male	564	4	0.7	0	-	0	-	0	-
		female	535	4	0.7	0	-	1	0.2	0	-
		intermediate	39	0	-	0	-	0	-	0	-
17	ABC	male	239	1	0.4	0	-	0	-	0	-
		female	164	2	1.2	0	-	0	-	0	-
	D	male	51	0	-	0	-	0	-	0	-
		female	39	0	-	0	-	0	-	0	-

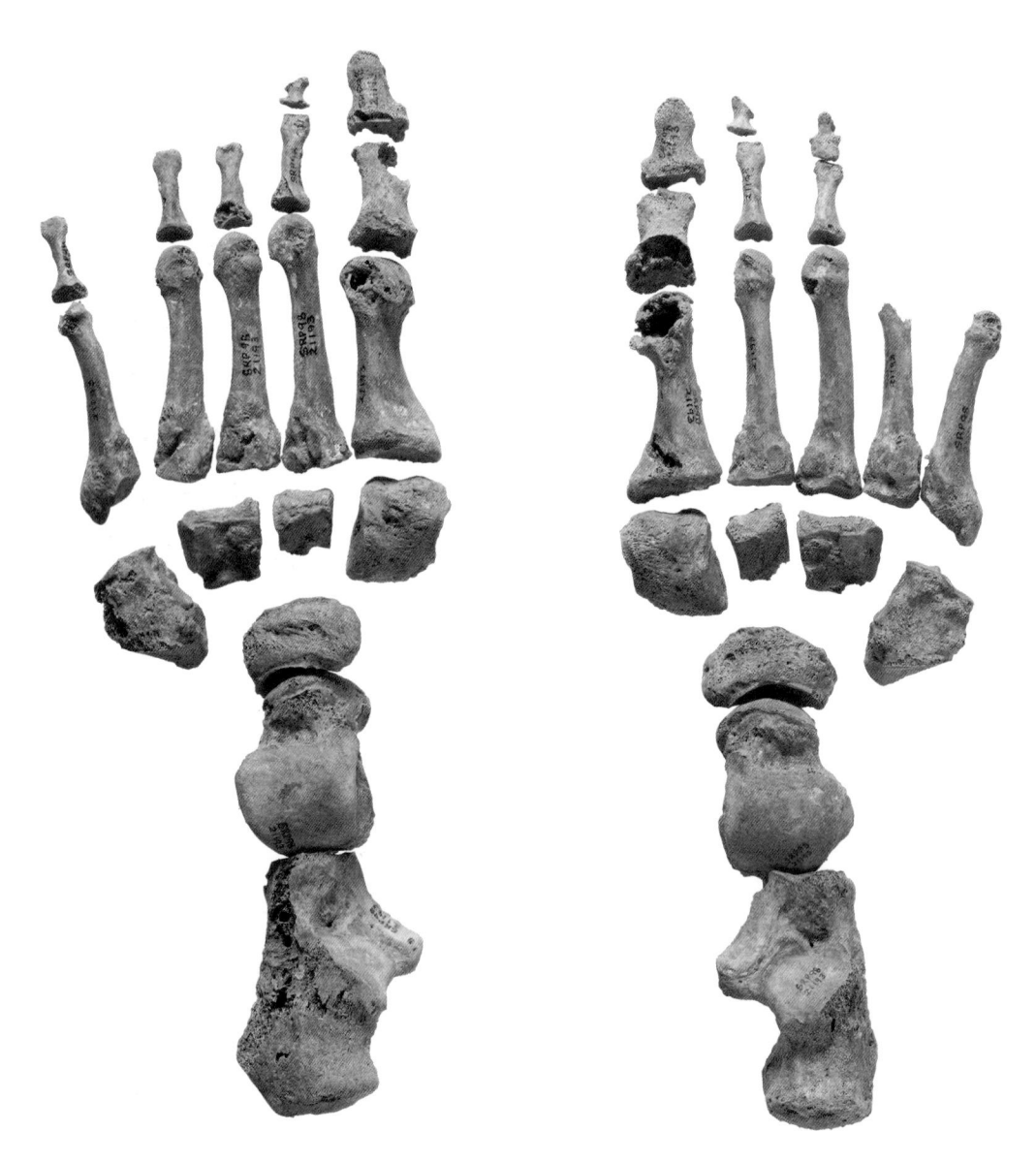

Fig 63 Erosive changes suggestive of gout in the foot elements of 18–25-year-old female [21193] from period 15, burial type D (scale c 1:2)

Gout

Two individuals were observed to have osseous changes indicative of gout in the bones of their feet. In period 15, 18–25-year-old female [21193] from burial type D was affected, 1.2% of this age and sex group in burial type D (1/81) (Fig 63). A 36–45-year-old male from period 16, burial type ABC was also affected; 0.5% of 36–45-year-old males in this burial type (1/205).

Seronegative osteoarthropathies

Three males in period 16 (3/628: 0.5%) presented with seronegative osteoarthritic changes to the cervical, thoracic and lumbar vertebrae, metacarpals, foot and hand phalanges, and ulna, which could not be further diagnosed (0.1% of the total sample: 3/5387). One 36–45-year-old male from burial type D (1/163 males of this age and burial type: 0.6%) and two ≥46-year-old males from burial type ABC (2/63: 3.2%) were affected (Table 50).

Ankylosing spondylitis

Four males from periods 16 and 17 presented with spinal changes possibly diagnostic of ankylosing spondylitis (4/5387: 0.1%) (Table 50). In period 16, two 36–45-year-old individuals, 0.2% of all males in this period (2/1192), were affected, one in each burial type (ABC 1/205: 0.5%; D 1/163: 0.6%). Male [29189], from burial type D, displayed the most extensive changes in the sample, as the cervical, thoracic and lumbar vertebrae, sacroiliac joints and trapezium were affected. In period 17 two males from burial type ABC were affected (2/290: 0.7%): ≥46-year-old adult [8962] (Fig 64), and [29185], who was of undetermined age.

Psoriatic osteoarthritis

Two individuals were affected by joint changes indicative of psoriatic osteoarthritis in periods 14 and 16 (2/5387: <0.1%) (Table 50). In period 14, ≥46-year-old female [13614] from burial type ABC (1/12 females of this age and burial type: 8.3%) had extensive degeneration (porosity, eburnation and osteophytosis) and bony erosion with adjacent proliferative changes of the joint surfaces and margins of the appendicular and axial skeleton, with the right side of the skeleton predominantly affected. The bones affected are the clavicle, humerus, radius and ulna, two metacarpals and a hand phalanx, six ribs, ilium, and the spinal column from the right occipital condyle to the first sacral body. In period 16, 36–45-year-old male [20142] from burial type D had diagnostic changes to one proximal-intermediate joint of a hand phalanx (Rogers and Waldron 1995, 77), 0.6% of males of this age and burial type (1/163).

Fig 64 A seronegative spondyloarthropathy in the thoracolumbar spine of ≥46-year-old adult male [8962] from period 17, burial type ABC (scale c 1:2)

Table 50 Crude prevalence rate of seronegative osteoarthropathies by period, sex and burial type

Period	Burial type	Sex	No. individuals	Ankylosing spondylitis	% affected	Psoriatic arthropathy	% affected	Reiter's disease	% affected	Non-specific seronegative spondylarthropathy	% affected
14	ABC	female	115	0	-	1	0.9	0	-	0	-
	D	female	55	0	-	0	-	0	-	0	-
16	ABC	male	628	1	0.2	0	-	0	-	2	0.3
	D	male	564	1	0.2	1	0.2	1	0.2	1	0.2
17	ABC	male	239	2	0.8	0	-	0	-	0	-
	D	male	51	0	-	0	-	0	-	0	-

Reiter's disease

A 36–45-year-old male [2539] from period 16, burial type D (1/163 males of this age and burial type: 0.6%), had evidence for Reiter's disease, which affected the calcanei, metatarsals and one right foot proximal phalange (Table 50). The changes consisted of marginal and central joint erosions with associated new bone formation. Reiter's disease was diagnosed because the lower extremity was affected and the lesions were asymmetrical (Rogers and Waldron 1995, 77). This case represents <0.1% of the entire sample (1/5387), 0.3% of the males aged 36–45 years in this period (1/368) and 0.1% of all males in period 16 (1/1192).

Other osteoarthropathies

Six adults ranging from 18–25 years to ≥46 years old were affected by joint changes which could not be definitely assigned to a specific disease (6/5387: 0.1%) (Table 51). The majority (four) were from burial type ABC and no individuals from period 14 were affected. The most frequently affected element was the first metatarsal.

Spinal joint disease

Spinal joint disease observed included evidence of osteoarthritis, osteophytosis, intervertebral disc disease, Schmorl's nodes and fusion. The crude prevalence of spinal joint disease of the sample was 62.4%: 3361/5387 individuals.

Subadult joint disease

In total 106 subadults (106/1027: 10.3%) displayed evidence of spinal joint disease. Two subadult age groups were affected: 6–11 years (3/348: 0.9%) and 12–17 years (103/544: 18.9%), a total of 11.9% from these age groups (106/892). The majority of these individuals had Schmorl's nodes (11.4% of 6–17-year-olds), which affected 9.9% (102/1027) of the total subadult sample.

For 12–17-year-olds, there was a significant difference in the prevalence of spinal joint disease between burial types ABC (51/221: 23.1%) and D (52/323: 16.1%) (χ^2 = 4.16, df = 1, p ≤ 0.05). The 12–17-year-olds within burial type ABC may have engaged in more strenuous activity than those in type D (although the prevalence for burial type ABC drops in period 16) (Fig 65). However, Schmorl's nodes may also result from other disease processes, such as Scheuermann's disease, osteoporosis, hyperparathyroidism, infection or neoplasm (Resnick 2002, 1430).

There is no evidence of a similar variation between the burial types in the next age range (18–25 years of age). Both burial types ABC (308/502: 61.3%) and D (282/477: 59.1%) show large increases in prevalence at this age. This suggests that the level of spinal joint disease in 12–17-year-olds varied between the two sample populations. Any evidence of a similar trend in young adulthood may have been obscured by the generally high rate of spinal joint disease.

Table 51 *Crude prevalence rate of non-specific osteoarthropathies by period, sex and burial type*

Period	Burial type	Sex	No. individuals	No. affected	% affected
14	ABC	male	160	0	-
		female	115	0	-
	D	male	63	0	-
		female	55	0	-
15	ABC	male	219	1	0.5
		female	167	0	-
	D	male	313	1	0.3
		female	334	1	0.3
16	ABC	male	628	0	-
		female	474	1	0.2
	D	male	564	0	-
		female	535	0	-
17	ABC	male	239	2	0.8
		female	164	0	-
	D	male	51	0	-
		female	39	0	-

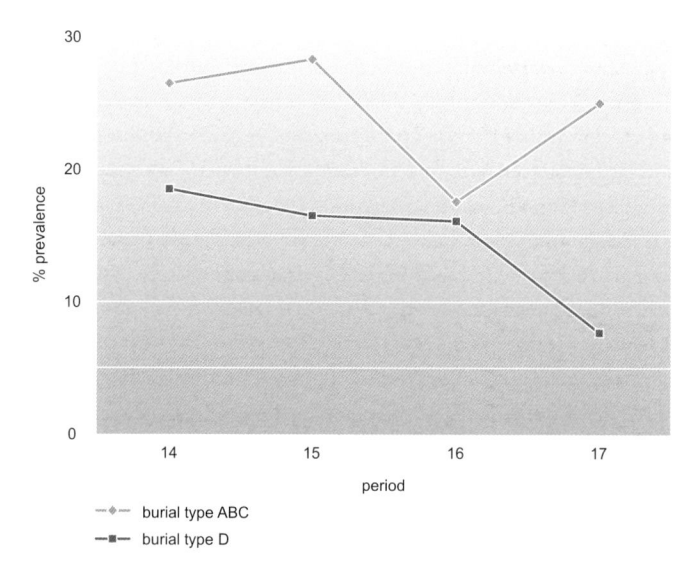

Fig 65 *Crude prevalence rate of spinal joint disease in 12–17-year-olds by period and burial type*

The majority of 12–17-year-olds affected by spinal joint disease had Schmorl's nodes (100/103: 97.1%); 14.6% (15/103) displayed other forms of lesion. The variation between the burial types was therefore due to a higher prevalence of Schmorl's nodes in burial type ABC.

Adult joint disease

There was a high crude prevalence of spinal joint disease in adult individuals (3255/4360: 74.7%). This prevalence increased with age except for the oldest age group (≥46 years). As the accurate ageing of older adults is problematical, this was possibly caused by the misallocation of individuals to the older categories. The overall trend was one of growing numbers of individuals with spinal joint disease in each successive age

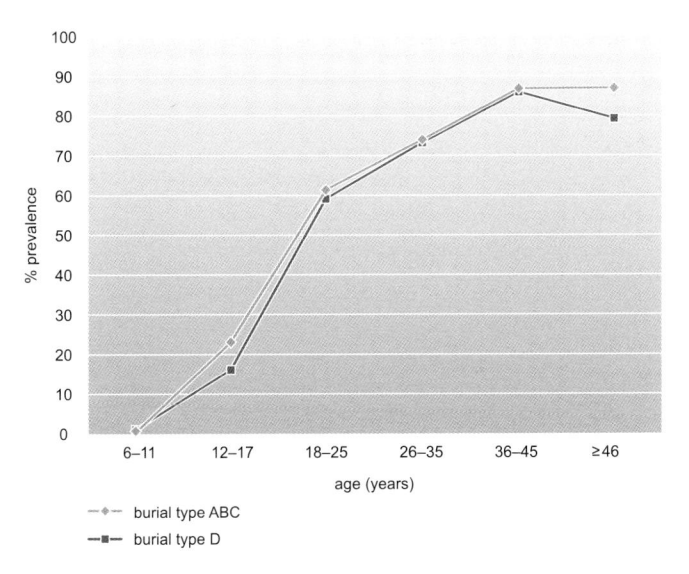

Fig 66 Crude prevalence rate of vertebral joint disease by age

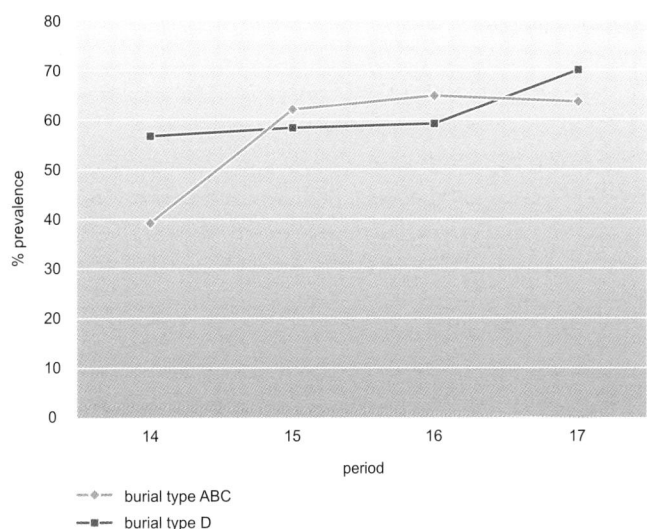

Fig 67 Crude prevalence rate of vertebral joint disease by period in 18–25-year-olds

category. Apart from the anomaly discussed above in the 12–17-year-old sample, there was little variation in the pattern of increased prevalence between burial types. Both displayed sharp increases in vertebral joint disease in the 18–25-year age group (Fig 66). However, in period 14 there was a lower prevalence in 18–25-year-olds from burial type ABC (20/51: 39.2%) than in those from burial type D (17/30: 56.7%) (χ^2 = 7.07, df = 1, p ≤ 0.01) (Fig 67).

Spinal joint disease affected 70.4% (1325/1883) of females and 79.3% (1773/2237) of males (crude prevalence per individual), a statistically significant difference between the sexes (χ^2 = 43.33, df = 1, p ≤ 0.001). Males were more frequently affected than females in both burial type ABC (χ^2 = 22.50, df = 1, p ≤ 0.001) and D (χ^2 = 19.24, df = 1, p ≤ 0.001) (Table 52).

For males in period 14, there was a significantly higher crude prevalence of vertebral joint disease in burial type D than in type ABC (Table 53). While there was little change in prevalence in burial type ABC over time, there was a distinct U-shape to the curve for burial type D, with high frequencies for periods 14 and 17, and an apparent reduction (though not statistically significant) in periods 15 and 16. The latter two periods represent the main phases of mass burial at St Mary Spital (Fig 68).

For female individuals, there was no discernable variation in crude prevalence rate by period or burial type (Table 54).

Table 52 Crude prevalence rate of vertebral joint disease by sex and burial type

Burial type	Female No.	Affected	%	Male No.	Affected	%
ABC	920	658	71.5	1246	1000	80.3
D	963	667	69.3	991	773	78.0
Total	1883	1325	70.4	2237	1773	79.3

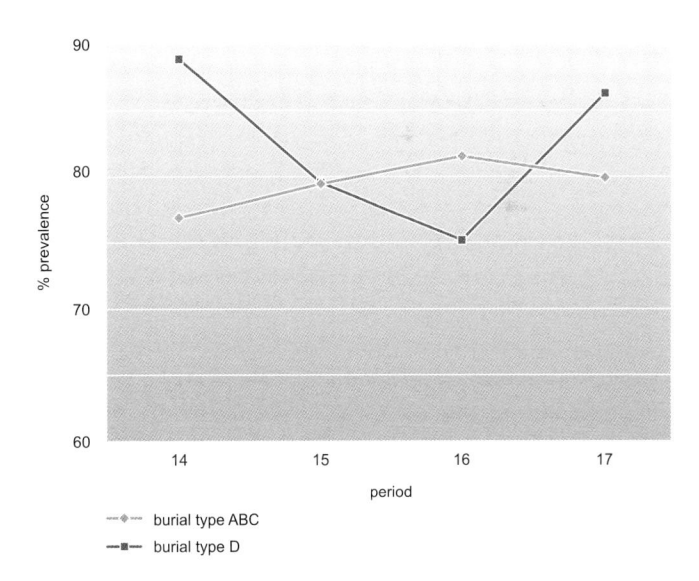

Fig 68 Crude prevalence rate of male vertebral joint disease by burial type and period

Table 53 Crude prevalence rate of male vertebral joint disease by burial type and period

Burial type	Period 14 No.	Affected	%	Period 15 No.	Affected	%	Period 16 No.	Affected	%	Period 17 No.	Affected	%	Total No.	Affected	%
ABC	160	123	76.9	219	174	79.5	628	512	81.5	239	191	79.9	1246	1000	80.3
D	63	56	88.9	313	249	79.6	564	424	75.2	51	44	86.3	991	773	78.0
Total	223	179	80.3	532	423	79.5	1192	936	78.5	290	235	81.0	2237	1773	79.3

Table 54 Crude prevalence rate of female vertebral joint disease by burial type and period

Burial type	Period 14 No.	Affected	%	Period 15 No.	Affected	%	Period 16 No.	Affected	%	Period 17 No.	Affected	%	Total No.	Affected	%
ABC	115	80	69.6	167	119	71.3	474	345	72.8	164	114	69.5	920	658	71.5
D	55	37	67.3	334	232	69.5	535	370	69.2	39	28	71.8	963	667	69.3
Total	170	117	68.8	501	351	70.1	1009	715	70.9	203	142	70.0	1883	1325	70.4

When the sexes from burial type ABC were compared, both followed similar patterns of variation throughout the use of the cemetery. The graph shows a slight rise in prevalence up to period 16, followed by a fall in period 17. However, none of these temporal changes was statistically significant (Fig 69). In burial type D, the female prevalence varied little over time, while the male pattern displayed the aforementioned U-shaped curve (Fig 70). For both burial types, the male crude prevalence of vertebral joint disease was significantly higher than the female prevalence throughout all periods of the cemetery.

Male vertebral joint disease was also analysed by type of lesion. Table 55 displays the number of spines affected as a

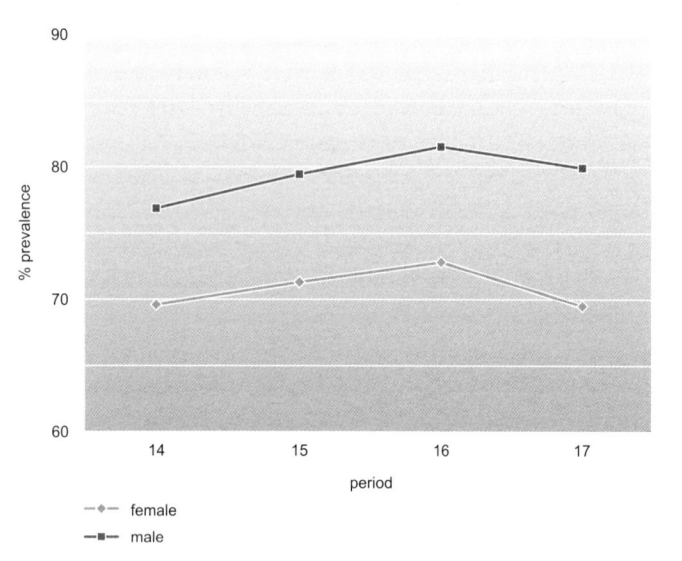

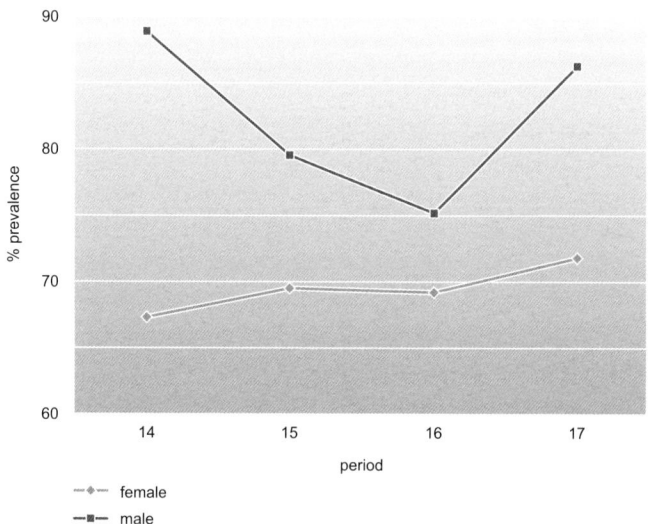

Fig 69 Crude prevalence rate of vertebral joint disease by sex in burial type ABC

Fig 70 Crude prevalence rate of vertebral joint disease by sex in burial type D

Table 55 Crude prevalence rate of male vertebral lesions by period

	Period 14 No.	Affected	%	Period 15 No.	Affected	%	Period 16 No.	Affected	%	Period 17 No.	Affected	%
Atlantoaxial joints	223	14	6.3	532	20	3.8	1192	57	4.8	290	12	4.1
Apophyseal joints	223	62	27.8	532	122	22.9	1192	284	23.8	290	79	27.2
Intervertebral disc disease	223	92	41.3	532	207	38.9	1192	456	38.3	290	126	43.4
Intervertebral osteophytosis	223	132	59.2	532	295	55.5	1192	642	53.9	290	154	53.1
Schmorl's nodes	223	133	59.6	532	313	58.8	1192	725	60.8	290	185	63.8
Fusion	223	8	3.6	532	13	2.4	1192	36	3.0	290	6	2.1

Joint disease

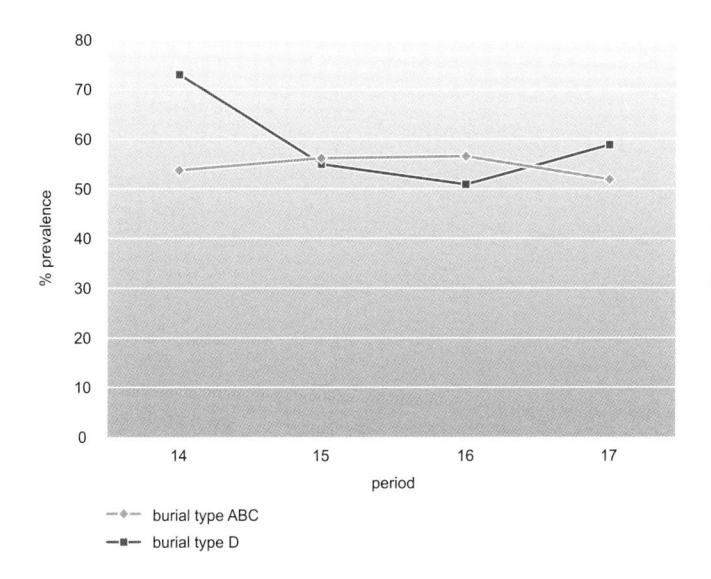

Fig 71 Crude prevalence rate of male intervertebral osteophytosis by burial type and period

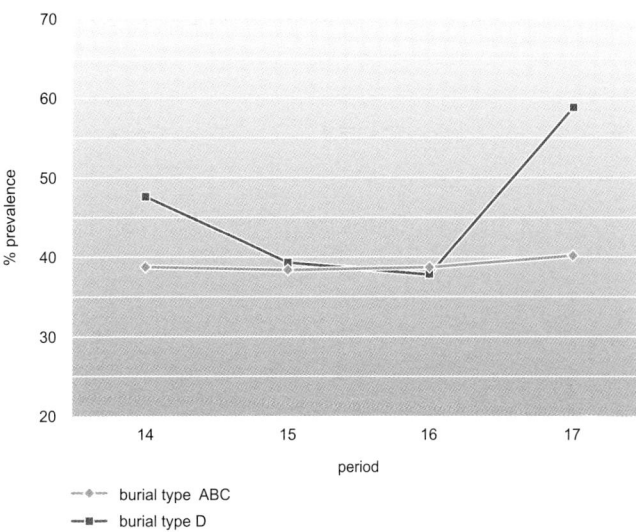

Fig 72 Crude prevalence rate of male intervertebral disc disease by burial type and period

percentage of all male individuals in each period. There was a higher prevalence of intervertebral osteophytosis in burial type D than in type ABC (χ^2 = 6.95, df = 1, p ≤ 0.01) (Fig 71).

The prevalence of male intervertebral disc disease in period 17 was higher in burial type D than in burial type ABC (χ^2 = 5.95, df = 1, p ≤ 0.05) (Fig 72), and the same was true of male apophyseal joint osteoarthritis (χ^2 = 4.48, df = 1, p ≤ 0.05) (Fig 73).

Female vertebral joint disease was also analysed by type of lesion (Table 56). In some respects, the female data mirrored those for males. In period 17, there was a significantly higher prevalence of intervertebral disc disease in burial type D than in burial type ABC (χ^2 = 4.57, df = 1, p ≤ 0.05) (Fig 74). This was also true of apophyseal joint osteoarthritis (χ^2 = 9.36, df = 1, p ≤ 0.01) (Fig 75).

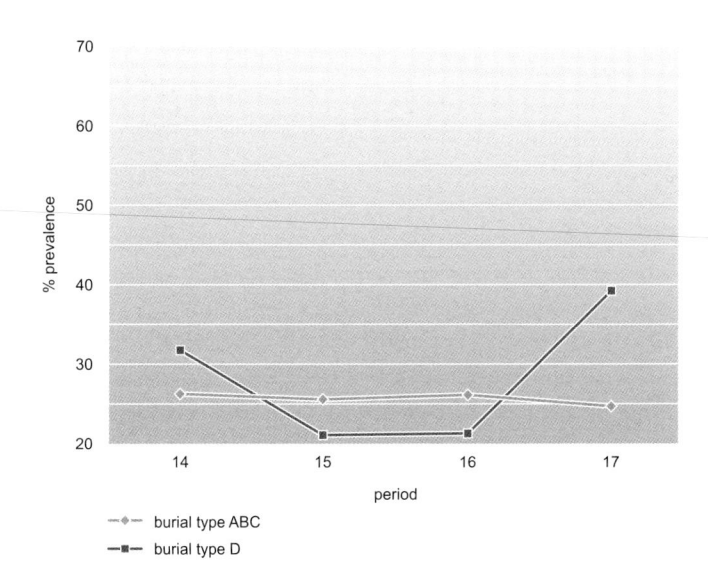

Fig 73 Crude prevalence rate of male apophyseal joint osteoarthritis by burial type and period

Table 56 Crude prevalence rate of female vertebral lesions by period

	Period 14			Period 15			Period 16			Period 17		
	No.	Affected	%	No.	Affected	%	No.	Affected	%	No.	Affected	%
Atlantoaxial joints	170	5	2.9	501	16	3.2	1009	44	4.4	203	7	3.4
Apophyseal joints	170	34	20.0	501	101	20.2	1009	205	20.3	203	38	18.7
Intervertebral disc disease	170	59	34.7	501	160	31.9	1009	366	36.3	203	60	29.6
Intervertebral osteophytosis	170	94	55.3	501	262	52.3	1009	514	50.9	203	91	44.8
Schmorl's nodes	170	81	47.6	501	208	41.5	1009	434	43.0	203	98	48.3
Fusion	170	2	1.2	501	7	1.4	1009	18	1.8	203	2	1.0

79

Results

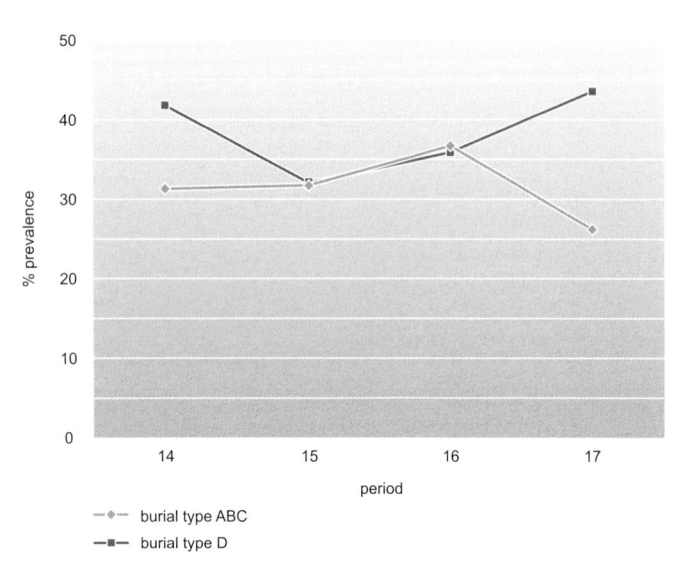

Fig 74 Crude prevalence rate of female intervertebral disc disease by burial type and period

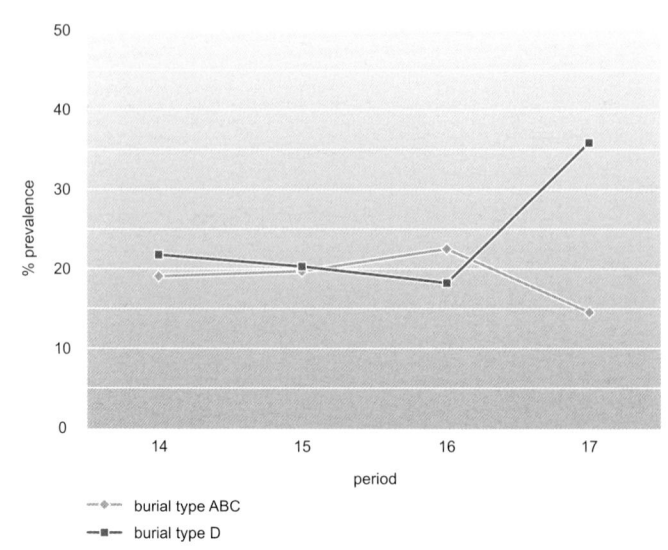

Fig 75 Crude prevalence rate of female apophyseal joint osteoarthritis by burial type and period

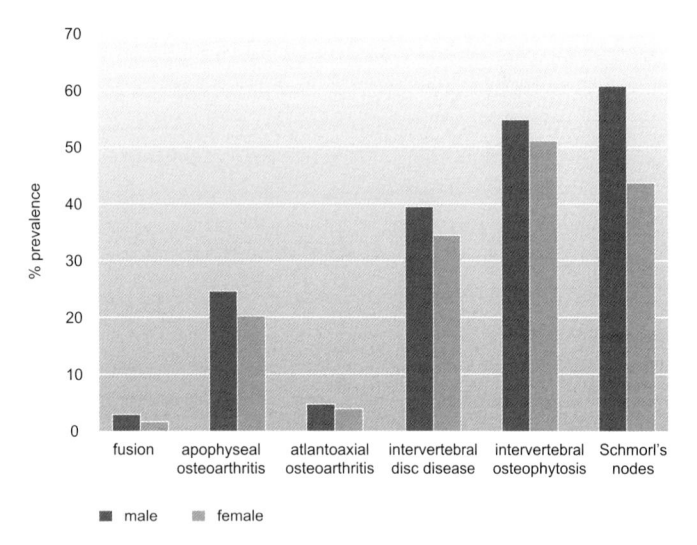

Fig 76 Crude prevalence rate of vertebral joint disease in males and females by lesion type

When the crude prevalence of each type of vertebral lesion was compared by sex, it was found that male individuals were significantly more affected by Schmorl's nodes (χ^2 = 118.80, df = 1, p ≤ 0.001), intervertebral disc disease (χ^2 = 11.53, df = 1, p ≤ 0.001), fusion (χ^2 = 7.63, df = 1, p ≤ 0.01), apophyseal joint osteoarthritis (χ^2 = 11.25, df = 1, p ≤ 0.001) and intervertebral osteophytosis (χ^2 = 5.43, df = 1, p ≤ 0.05) (Fig 76). There was no significant variation by burial type.

Among males, the thoracic spine was most commonly affected by joint disease (Table 57). The only variation between burial types was found in the period 14 cervical spine, where more males from burial type D were affected compared to those in burial type ABC (χ^2 = 6.05, df = 1, p ≤ 0.05). In general, there was more variation in the male sample from burial type D than that from burial type ABC. The relative cervical, thoracic and lumbar frequencies of joint disease in the burial type D sample appear to have changed over the period of use of the cemetery (from period 14 to period 17), while for periods 15 and 16 there was little variation (Fig 77; Fig 78).

As for males, females were most frequently affected by vertebral joint disease in the thoracic spine (Table 58). Again, the most variation in relative spinal disease frequencies was found in burial type D. As with the male sample, the burial type D female samples in periods 15 and 16 produced similar results (Fig 79; Fig 80).

Although male vertebral joint disease crude prevalence rates were generally higher than female rates, there was less variation in the cervical spine. Burial type ABC again provided a contrast with type D. In the former, males and females revealed a similar

Table 57 Crude prevalence rate of male joint disease by spinal segment

Burial type	Cervical No.	Affected	%	Thoracic No.	Affected	%	Lumbar No.	Affected	%
ABC	1246	393	31.5	1246	907	72.8	1246	604	48.5
D	991	281	28.4	991	702	70.8	991	483	48.7
Total	2237	674	30.1	2237	1609	71.9	2237	1087	48.6

Joint disease

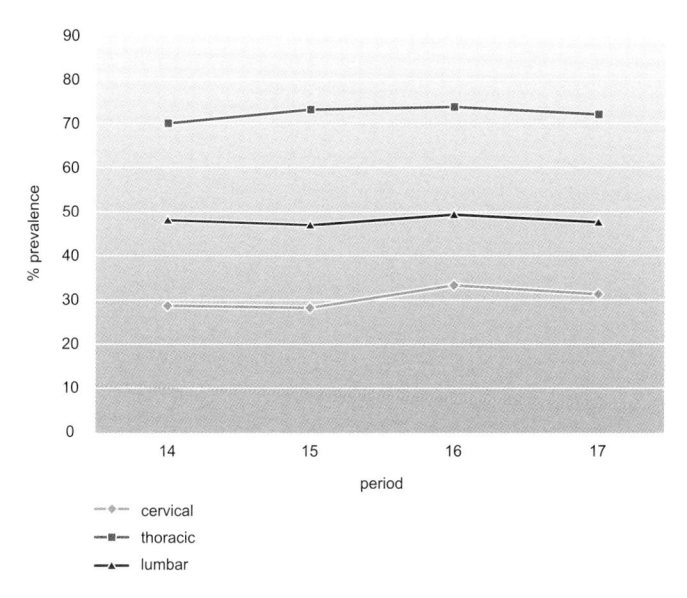

Fig 77 Crude prevalence rate of male joint disease by spinal segment in burial type ABC

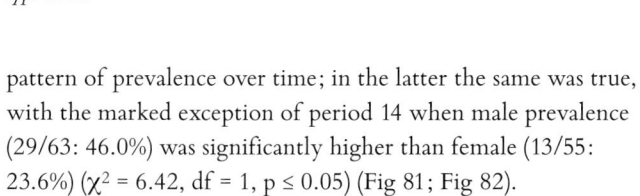

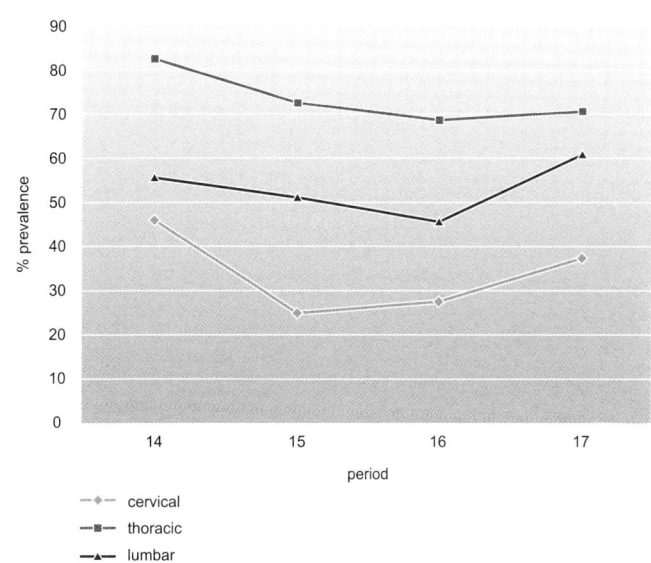

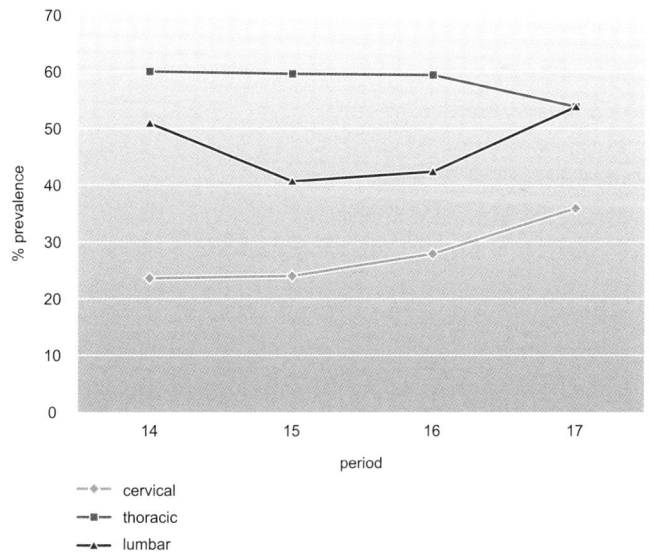

Fig 78 Crude prevalence rate of male joint disease by spinal segment in burial type D

pattern of prevalence over time; in the latter the same was true, with the marked exception of period 14 when male prevalence (29/63: 46.0%) was significantly higher than female (13/55: 23.6%) (χ^2 = 6.42, df = 1, p ≤ 0.05) (Fig 81; Fig 82).

True prevalence rates of Schmorl's nodes peaked in the lower thoracic spine (Table 59). True prevalence rates of Schmorl's nodes by period, regardless of age or sex, are summarised in Tables 60–3.

Table 58 Crude prevalence rate of female joint disease by spinal segment

Burial type	Cervical No.	Affected	%	Thoracic No.	Affected	%	Lumbar No.	Affected	%
ABC	920	255	27.7	920	561	61.0	920	401	43.6
D	963	256	26.6	963	571	59.3	963	412	42.8
Total	1883	511	27.1	1883	1132	60.1	1883	813	43.2

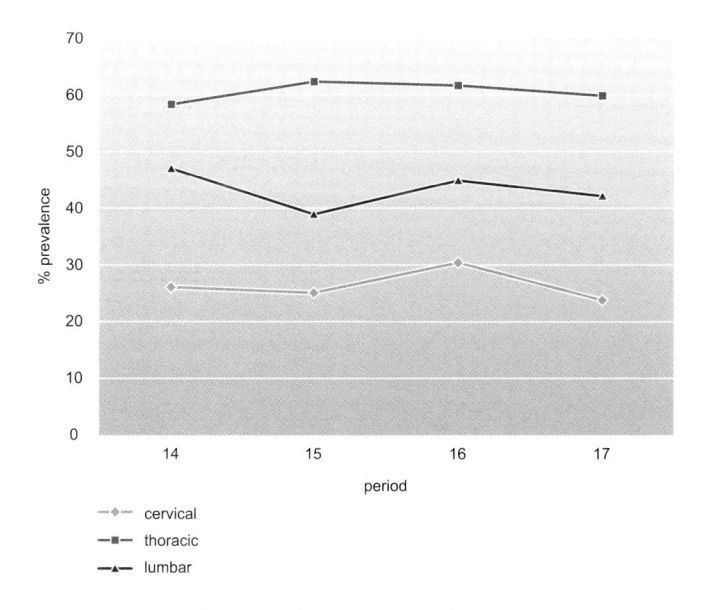

Fig 79 Crude prevalence rate of female joint disease by spinal segment in burial type ABC

Fig 80 Crude prevalence rate of female joint disease by spinal segment in burial type D

Results

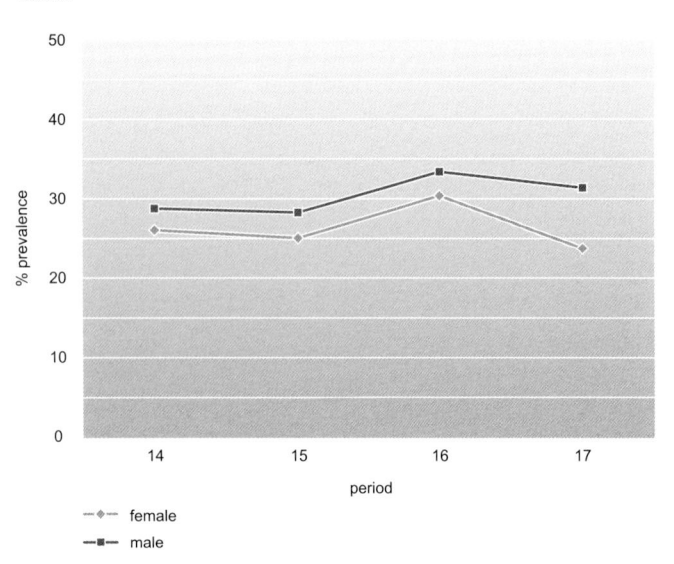

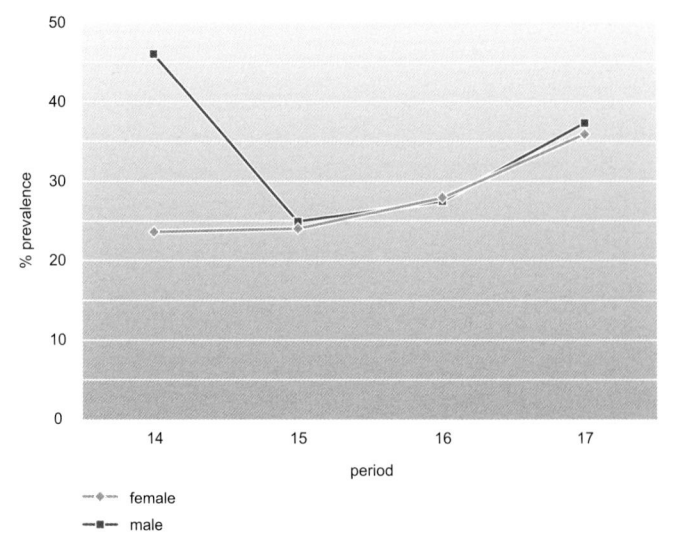

Fig 81 Crude prevalence rate of joint disease by cervical spine segment, sex and period in burial type ABC

Fig 82 Crude prevalence rate of joint disease by cervical spine segment, sex and period in burial type D

Table 59 True prevalence rates of Schmorl's nodes (SN) (C = cervical, T = thoracic, L = lumbar, S = sacral)

			Period 14						Period 15						Period 16						Period 17					
			Burial type ABC			Burial type D			Burial type ABC			Burial type D			Burial type ABC			Burial type D			Burial type ABC			Burial type D		
Vertebral joint	Age (years)	Sex	No.	SN	%	No.	SN	%	No.	SN	%	No.	SN	%	No.	SN	%	No.	SN	%	No.	SN	%	No.	SN	%
C2–3	26–35	male	33	0	-	18	0	-	49	0	-	76	0	-	148	0	-	146	0	-	69	1	1.4	11	0	-
C4–5	12–17	subadult	25	0	-	23	0	-	49	0	-	84	0	-	68	0	-	141	1	0.7	33	0	-	11	0	-
C4–5	18–25	male	15	0	-	9	0	-	33	1	3.0	50	0	-	94	0	-	108	0	-	42	0	-	9	0	-
C4–5	36–45	male	36	0	-	20	0	-	42	0	-	68	0	-	152	1	0.7	130	0	-	57	0	-	15	0	-
C5–6	12–17	subadult	27	0	-	23	0	-	48	0	-	88	0	-	68	0	-	143	1	0.7	33	0	-	12	0	-
C5–6	18–25	male	15	0	-	10	0	-	40	1	2.5	51	1	2.0	92	0	-	107	0	-	43	0	-	9	0	-
C5–6	26–35	female	35	0	-	22	0	-	51	0	-	101	0	-	120	1	0.8	153	3	2.0	48	0	-	9	0	-
C5–6	26–35	male	34	0	-	16	0	-	51	0	-	72	0	-	151	1	0.7	138	0	-	72	0	-	11	0	-
C5–6	36–45	male	39	0	-	20	0	-	46	0	-	75	0	-	155	1	0.6	132	1	0.8	58	0	-	16	0	-
C5–6	≥46	female	11	0	-	3	0	-	13	0	-	28	0	-	40	1	2.5	51	0	-	15	0	-	10	0	-
C5–6	adult	female	0	0	-	0	0	-	1	0	-	8	0	-	19	1	5.3	12	0	-	1	0	-	0	0	-
C5–6	adult	male	6	0	-	1	0	-	4	0	-	4	0	-	22	0	-	17	1	5.9	6	0	-	1	0	-
C6–7	12–17	subadult	26	0	-	23	0	-	49	0	-	87	0	-	74	0	-	141	1	0.7	33	0	-	12	0	-
C6–7	18–25	female	11	0	-	11	0	-	30	0	-	58	0	-	81	1	1.2	99	0	-	42	0	-	5	0	-
C6–7	18–25	male	17	0	-	11	0	-	45	1	2.2	51	1	2.0	93	1	1.1	113	0	-	45	0	-	10	0	-
C6–7	26–35	female	36	0	-	22	0	-	53	0	-	104	0	-	129	1	0.8	160	2	1.3	49	0	-	9	0	-
C6–7	26–35	male	34	0	-	17	0	-	52	0	-	77	1	1.3	152	2	1.3	148	0	-	70	0	-	10	0	-
C6–7	36–45	male	38	0	-	21	0	-	48	0	-	78	0	-	161	1	0.6	136	0	-	56	1	1.8	17	0	-
C6–7	≥46	male	16	2	12.5	4	0	-	9	0	-	22	1	4.5	55	0	-	50	0	-	24	0	-	5	0	-
C6–7	adult	male	6	0	-	1	0	-	5	0	-	4	0	-	21	0	-	15	1	6.7	6	0	-	1	0	-
C7–T1	12–17	subadult	28	0	-	24	0	-	49	0	-	93	0	-	75	0	-	147	1	0.7	34	0	-	13	0	-
C7–T1	18–25	female	13	0	-	13	0	-	28	0	-	61	0	-	89	1	1.1	105	0	-	41	0	-	6	0	-
C7–T1	18–25	male	19	0	-	11	0	-	46	0	-	55	1	1.8	99	1	1.0	113	0	-	48	0	-	10	0	-
C7–T1	26–35	female	36	0	-	21	0	-	56	0	-	109	0	-	142	0	-	174	1	0.6	53	0	-	9	0	-
C7–T1	26–35	male	36	0	-	19	0	-	56	0	-	87	0	-	162	1	0.6	151	0	-	72	0	-	11	0	-
C7–T1	36–45	male	40	0	-	22	0	-	51	0	-	85	0	-	170	1	0.6	137	0	-	59	0	-	18	0	-
T1–2	18–25	male	19	0	-	12	0	-	45	0	-	58	1	1.7	101	1	1.0	118	0	-	53	0	-	8	0	-
T1–2	26–35	female	40	0	-	21	0	-	55	0	-	109	0	-	137	0	-	173	1	0.6	52	0	-	9	0	-
T1–2	26–35	male	38	0	-	20	0	-	56	0	-	87	0	-	161	0	-	154	0	-	76	0	-	11	1	9.1
T1–2	36–45	male	40	0	-	22	0	-	49	0	-	90	1	1.1	173	1	0.6	136	2	1.5	59	0	-	19	0	-
T1–2	≥46	male	16	0	-	4	0	-	10	0	-	24	1	4.2	56	0	-	53	0	-	23	0	-	5	0	-
T2–3	18–25	female	14	0	-	13	0	-	31	0	-	62	0	-	90	0	-	103	1	1.0	37	0	-	6	0	-
T2–3	18–25	intermediate	4	0	-	4	0	-	5	0	-	4	0	-	16	1	6.3	10	0	-	6	0	-	1	0	-
T2–3	18–25	male	19	0	-	12	0	-	45	0	-	60	1	1.7	98	1	1.0	123	1	0.8	43	0	-	9	0	-
T2–3	26–35	female	41	0	-	22	0	-	56	0	-	111	0	-	139	1	0.7	180	2	1.1	49	1	2.0	9	0	-
T2–3	26–35	male	40	0	-	21	0	-	56	0	-	87	0	-	159	1	0.6	156	0	-	69	0	-	11	1	9.1
T2–3	36–45	male	41	0	-	22	0	-	49	0	-	88	1	1.1	178	1	0.6	139	0	-	59	0	-	16	0	-
T2–3	adult	male	5	0	-	0	0	-	5	0	-	4	0	-	22	0	-	16	1	6.3	6	0	-	1	0	-

Table 59 (cont)

Vertebral joint	Age (years)	Sex	Period 14 Burial type ABC No. SN %	Period 14 Burial type D No. SN %	Period 15 Burial type ABC No. SN %	Period 15 Burial type D No. SN %	Period 16 Burial type ABC No. SN %	Period 16 Burial type D No. SN %	Period 17 Burial type ABC No. SN %	Period 17 Burial type D No. SN %
T3–4	12–17	subadult	32 0 -	24 0 -	52 0 -	98 0 -	80 0 -	148 2 1.4	34 0 -	13 0 -
T3–4	18–25	female	14 0 -	14 0 -	31 0 -	62 0 -	93 0 -	104 1 1.0	42 0 -	6 0 -
T3–4	18–25	intermediate	4 0 -	4 0 -	5 0 -	4 0 -	15 1 6.7	11 0 -	7 0 -	1 0 -
T3–4	18–25	male	21 0 -	12 0 -	44 0 -	62 2 3.2	99 5 5.1	125 3 2.4	49 0 -	10 0 -
T3–4	26–35	female	42 0 -	22 0 -	57 0 -	111 1 0.9	144 2 1.4	180 3 1.7	55 1 1.8	9 0 -
T3–4	26–35	intermediate	4 0 -	0 0 -	7 0 -	6 1 16.7	18 0 -	13 0 -	7 0 -	1 0 -
T3–4	26–35	male	37 1 2.7	21 0 -	55 0 -	88 3 3.4	164 3 1.8	159 0 -	76 1 1.3	11 1 9.1
T3–4	26–35	undetermined	0 0 -	0 0 -	2 0 -	2 1 50.0	0 0 -	1 0 -	2 0 -	0 0 -
T3–4	36–45	female	27 0 -	14 0 -	41 0 -	61 0 -	104 1 1.0	118 1 0.8	34 0 -	8 0 -
T3–4	36–45	male	43 1 2.3	22 1 4.5	52 1 1.9	86 2 2.3	179 4 2.2	142 5 3.5	60 3 5.0	20 0 -
T3–4	≥46	female	12 0 -	2 0 -	15 0 -	29 0 -	45 1 2.2	53 3 5.7	16 0 -	9 0 -
T3–4	≥46	intermediate	1 0 -	0 0 -	1 0 -	1 1 100.0	2 0 -	0 0 -	1 0 -	0 0 -
T3–4	≥46	male	17 0 -	4 0 -	10 1 10.0	22 0 -	55 2 3.6	55 4 7.3	6 0 -	5 0 -
T3–4	adult	male	5 0 -	0 0 -	5 1 20.0	4 0 -	21 0 -	15 0 -	5 0 -	1 0 -
T4–5	12–17	subadult	31 1 3.2	23 0 -	54 2 3.7	98 1 1.0	78 1 1.3	154 3 1.9	36 0 -	13 0 -
T4–5	18–25	female	14 0 -	14 0 -	32 2 6.3	63 1 1.6	90 3 3.3	104 3 2.9	40 3 7.5	6 0 -
T4–5	18–25	intermediate	4 0 -	4 0 -	5 1 20.0	4 0 -	14 1 7.1	11 1 9.1	7 0 -	1 0 -
T4–5	18–25	male	21 0 -	12 0 -	44 4 9.1	62 6 9.7	99 11 11.1	126 14 11.1	48 0 -	11 1 9.1
T4–5	26–35	female	43 3 7.0	22 1 4.5	57 0 -	113 3 2.7	144 7 4.9	183 8 4.4	55 1 1.8	9 0 -
T4–5	26–35	intermediate	5 0 -	0 0 -	7 0 -	6 1 16.7	18 0 -	13 0 -	7 1 14.3	2 0 -
T4–5	26–35	male	41 1 2.4	21 3 14.3	56 4 7.1	85 11 12.9	169 16 9.5	158 10 6.3	76 6 7.9	12 1 8.3
T4–5	26–35	undetermined	1 0 -	0 0 -	2 0 -	2 1 50.0	0 0 -	2 0 -	2 0 -	0 0 -
T4–5	36–45	female	29 1 3.4	14 1 7.1	40 1 2.5	62 3 4.8	106 5 4.7	121 2 1.7	34 1 2.9	9 1 11.1
T4–5	36–45	intermediate	3 0 -	0 0 -	1 0 -	10 1 10.0	13 0 -	7 0 -	4 0 -	1 0 -
T4–5	36–45	male	45 5 11.1	21 1 4.8	53 6 11.3	86 6 7.0	178 14 7.9	142 11 7.7	61 4 6.6	20 1 5.0
T4–5	≥46	female	12 0 -	2 0 -	14 0 -	30 2 6.7	46 2 4.3	53 3 5.7	16 1 6.3	10 0 -
T4–5	≥46	male	18 2 11.1	4 1 25.0	11 2 18.2	22 1 4.5	57 2 3.5	55 4 7.3	25 0 -	5 0 -
T4–5	adult	female	0 0 -	1 0 -	2 0 -	8 0 -	19 0 -	13 1 7.7	2 0 -	0 0 -
T4–5	adult	male	5 0 -	0 0 -	5 0 -	4 0 -	19 1 5.3	12 0 -	7 1 14.3	0 0 -
T5–6	12–17	subadult	31 2 6.5	23 2 8.7	53 3 5.7	97 5 5.2	79 2 2.5	153 7 4.6	35 1 2.9	13 0 -
T5–6	18–25	female	14 0 -	14 3 21.4	31 4 12.9	62 6 9.7	90 7 7.8	105 10 9.5	40 8 20.0	6 3 50.0
T5–6	18–25	intermediate	4 0 -	4 0 -	5 1 20.0	4 2 50.0	14 2 14.3	11 3 27.3	7 1 14.3	1 0 -
T5–6	18–25	male	21 2 9.5	12 1 8.3	44 9 20.5	62 17 27.4	101 18 17.8	128 33 25.8	50 3 6.0	11 3 27.3
T5–6	26–35	female	43 5 11.6	22 2 9.1	56 4 7.1	111 6 5.4	143 17 11.9	185 16 8.6	56 7 12.5	9 0 -
T5–6	26–35	intermediate	5 2 40.0	0 0 -	7 7 -	6 1 16.7	18 3 16.7	12 4 33.3	8 1 12.5	2 0 -
T5–6	26–35	male	40 5 12.5	21 5 23.8	56 9 16.1	82 10 12.2	173 39 22.5	158 22 13.9	77 17 22.1	13 0 -
T5–6	26–35	undetermined	1 0 -	0 0 -	2 2 -	2 1 50.0	0 0 -	2 0 -	2 0 -	0 0 -
T5–6	36–45	female	29 3 10.3	13 0 -	39 3 7.7	62 7 11.3	107 13 12.1	123 10 8.1	34 2 5.9	9 1 11.1
T5–6	36–45	intermediate	3 0 -	0 0 -	1 1 -	11 2 18.2	13 1 7.7	7 1 14.3	5 0 -	1 0 -
T5–6	36–45	male	46 5 10.9	22 5 22.7	55 12 21.8	88 12 13.6	178 32 18.0	142 21 14.8	62 11 17.7	20 1 5.0
T5–6	≥46	female	12 0 -	2 0 -	15 1 6.7	31 3 9.7	45 6 13.3	53 8 15.1	15 1 6.7	10 1 10.0
T5–6	≥46	intermediate	0 0 -	0 0 -	1 0 -	1 1 -	2 1 50.0	0 0 -	1 0 -	0 0 -
T5–6	≥46	male	18 2 11.1	4 2 50.0	11 2 18.2	21 2 9.5	56 5 8.9	56 9 16.1	25 0 -	5 0 -
T5–6	adult	female	0 0 -	1 0 -	1 1 -	7 2 28.6	18 0 -	13 0 -	2 0 -	0 0 -
T5–6	adult	intermediate	0 0 -	0 0 -	0 0 -	1 0 -	4 2 50.0	3 0 -	1 0 -	0 0 -
T5–6	adult	male	5 0 -	0 0 -	5 1 20.0	5 5 -	16 3 18.8	11 2 18.2	7 2 28.6	1 0 -
T6–7	12–17	subadult	32 4 12.5	23 2 8.7	53 8 15.1	98 7 7.1	84 7 8.3	155 10 6.5	35 2 5.7	13 0 -
T6–7	18–25	female	13 1 7.7	13 3 23.1	32 3 9.4	62 13 21.0	90 21 23.3	105 23 21.9	40 14 35.0	6 3 50.0
T6–7	18–25	intermediate	4 0 -	4 0 -	5 3 60.0	4 1 25.0	15 3 20.0	11 1 9.1	6 2 33.3	1 0 -
T6–7	18–25	male	20 2 10.0	12 4 33.3	45 18 40.0	62 24 38.7	100 33 33.0	127 40 31.5	50 16 32.0	11 4 36.4
T6–7	26–35	female	43 10 23.3	22 3 13.6	57 11 19.3	113 13 11.5	144 30 20.8	183 31 16.9	56 9 16.1	9 0 -
T6–7	26–35	intermediate	5 1 20.0	0 0 -	7 1 14.3	6 2 33.3	17 6 35.3	12 5 41.7	8 3 37.5	2 0 -
T6–7	26–35	male	41 10 24.4	21 8 38.1	58 20 34.5	80 20 25.0	179 60 33.5	157 48 30.6	78 25 32.1	13 2 15.4
T6–7	26–35	undetermined	1 0 -	0 0 -	2 0 -	2 1 50.0	0 0 -	2 0 -	2 0 -	0 0 -
T6–7	36–45	female	29 10 34.5	14 2 14.3	38 5 13.2	62 17 27.4	108 19 17.6	123 23 18.7	33 6 18.2	9 4 44.4
T6–7	36–45	intermediate	3 0 -	0 0 -	1 0 -	10 4 40.0	14 2 14.3	7 1 14.3	4 0 -	1 0 -
T6–7	36–45	male	47 17 36.2	22 4 18.2	57 16 28.1	89 17 19.1	180 48 26.7	139 30 21.6	62 17 27.4	20 3 15.0
T6–7	36–45	undetermined	0 0 -	0 0 -	1 1 100.0	0 0 -	1 0 -	0 0 -	0 0 -	0 0 -
T6–7	≥46	female	12 0 -	2 0 -	15 1 6.7	32 7 21.9	42 6 14.3	53 14 26.4	16 4 25.0	10 2 20.0
T6–7	≥46	intermediate	1 0 -	0 0 -	1 0 -	1 0 -	2 1 50.0	0 0 -	1 1 100.0	0 0 -
T6–7	≥46	male	18 4 22.2	4 1 25.0	11 2 18.2	22 4 18.2	57 15 26.3	56 14 25.0	26 10 38.5	5 0 -
T6–7	adult	female	0 0 -	1 0 -	1 0 -	8 0 -	18 3 16.7	12 0 -	2 0 -	0 0 -
T6–7	adult	intermediate	0 0 -	0 0 -	0 0 -	1 0 -	4 3 75.0	3 1 33.3	1 0 -	0 0 -
T6–7	adult	male	5 0 -	0 0 -	5 2 40.0	5 0 -	16 3 18.8	11 2 18.2	7 4 57.1	1 0 -

Results

Table 59 (cont)

| | | | Period 14 ||| Period 14 ||| Period 15 ||| Period 15 ||| Period 16 ||| Period 16 ||| Period 17 ||| Period 17 |||
| | | | Burial type ABC ||| Burial type D ||| Burial type ABC ||| Burial type D ||| Burial type ABC ||| Burial type D ||| Burial type ABC ||| Burial type D |||
Vertebral joint	Age (years)	Sex	No.	SN	%	No.	SN	%	No.	SN	%	No.	SN	%	No.	SN	%	No.	SN	%	No.	SN	%	No.	SN	%
T6–7	adult	undetermined	0	0	-	0	0	-	0	0	-	1	0	-	2	0	-	0	0	-	1	1	100.0	0	0	-
T7–8	12–17	subadult	32	4	12.5	23	2	8.7	53	10	18.9	97	11	11.3	83	4	4.8	153	14	9.2	36	4	11.1	13	0	-
T7–8	18–25	female	14	2	14.3	13	4	30.8	32	6	18.8	60	14	23.3	90	21	23.3	105	30	28.6	40	16	40.0	6	3	50.0
T7–8	18–25	intermediate	4	0	-	4	1	25.0	5	2	40.0	4	1	25.0	16	4	25.0	11	4	36.4	6	2	33.3	1	1	100.0
T7–8	18–25	male	19	5	26.3	12	3	25.0	44	19	43.2	64	29	45.3	102	40	39.2	126	52	41.3	49	23	46.9	10	4	40.0
T7–8	26–35	female	44	10	22.7	22	6	27.3	59	13	22.0	111	20	18.0	145	38	26.2	183	33	18.0	55	12	21.8	8	1	12.5
T7–8	26–35	intermediate	5	2	40.0	0	0	-	7	3	42.9	6	3	50.0	17	7	41.2	13	5	38.5	8	4	50.0	2	0	-
T7–8	26–35	male	42	17	40.5	21	7	33.3	58	21	36.2	81	30	37.0	179	79	44.1	158	63	39.9	77	36	46.8	13	3	23.1
T7–8	36–45	female	31	12	38.7	14	5	35.7	40	7	17.5	64	18	28.1	105	23	21.9	123	23	18.7	33	5	15.2	8	2	25.0
T7–8	36–45	intermediate	3	0	-	0	0	-	1	0	-	9	2	22.2	14	2	14.3	7	2	28.6	4	1	25.0	1	0	-
T7–8	36–45	male	47	22	46.8	22	9	40.9	56	19	33.9	88	28	31.8	184	62	33.7	138	43	31.2	60	22	36.7	20	5	25.0
T7–8	≥46	female	12	1	8.3	2	1	50.0	16	1	6.3	32	6	18.8	43	8	18.6	53	16	30.2	15	3	20.0	10	2	20.0
T7–8	≥46	intermediate	1	0	-	0	0	-	1	0	-	1	1	100.0	2	0	-	0	0	-	1	1	100.0	0	0	-
T7–8	≥46	male	18	5	27.8	4	0	-	10	1	10.0	21	9	42.9	58	11	19.0	56	18	32.1	26	9	34.6	5	0	-
T7–8	adult	female	0	0	-	1	0	-	1	0	-	8	1	12.5	17	1	5.9	12	1	8.3	0	0	-	0	0	-
T7–8	adult	intermediate	0	0	-	0	0	-	0	0	-	2	0	-	4	3	75.0	3	0	-	1	0	-	0	0	-
T7–8	adult	male	5	0	-	0	0	-	5	2	40.0	2	0	-	17	4	23.5	12	2	16.7	7	4	57.1	1	0	-
T7–8	adult	undetermined	0	0	-	0	0	-	0	0	-	1	0	-	2	0	-	0	0	-	2	1	50.0	0	0	-
T8–9	12–17	subadult	30	3	10.0	23	3	13.0	53	9	17.0	93	10	10.8	80	7	8.8	154	12	7.8	36	5	13.9	13	0	-
T8–9	18–25	female	14	2	14.3	12	3	25.0	33	5	15.2	57	13	22.8	89	20	22.5	104	23	22.1	41	14	34.1	7	3	42.9
T8–9	18–25	intermediate	4	0	-	4	0	-	5	1	20.0	4	2	50.0	17	5	29.4	11	4	36.4	6	1	16.7	1	1	100.0
T8–9	18–25	male	20	6	30.0	12	4	33.3	44	25	56.8	64	32	50.0	104	42	40.4	128	53	41.4	49	19	38.8	10	7	70.0
T8–9	18–25	undetermined	3	0	-	0	0	-	2	0	-	0	0	-	1	0	-	2	1	50.0	0	0	-	0	0	-
T8–9	26–35	female	45	10	22.2	21	4	19.0	59	13	22.0	117	19	16.2	149	38	25.5	179	34	19.0	54	9	16.7	8	0	-
T8–9	26–35	intermediate	5	1	20.0	0	0	-	7	1	14.3	7	3	42.9	18	5	27.8	13	4	30.8	7	4	57.1	2	0	-
T8–9	26–35	male	42	19	45.2	19	8	42.1	59	23	39.0	81	33	40.7	181	84	46.4	160	55	34.4	77	38	49.4	13	4	30.8
T8–9	26–35	undetermined	1	0	-	0	0	-	2	1	50.0	2	1	50.0	0	0	-	2	0	-	2	1	50.0	0	0	-
T8–9	36–45	female	29	9	31.0	14	4	28.6	40	6	15.0	65	20	30.8	106	17	16.0	122	28	23.0	33	6	18.2	9	2	22.2
T8–9	36–45	intermediate	3	0	-	0	0	-	1	0	-	9	4	44.4	14	2	14.3	8	2	25.0	4	1	25.0	1	0	-
T8–9	36–45	male	46	21	45.7	22	8	36.4	57	22	38.6	88	29	33.0	186	66	35.5	143	47	32.9	60	25	41.7	20	5	25.0
T8–9	≥46	female	12	2	16.7	2	0	-	16	2	12.5	32	7	21.9	41	9	22.0	56	8	14.3	15	3	20.0	10	2	20.0
T8–9	≥46	intermediate	1	0	-	0	0	-	0	0	-	1	0	-	2	0	-	0	0	-	1	1	100.0	0	0	-
T8–9	≥46	male	18	5	27.8	4	2	50.0	10	2	20.0	21	9	42.9	58	14	24.1	57	23	40.4	27	7	25.9	5	2	40.0
T8–9	adult	female	0	0	-	1	0	-	1	0	-	8	1	12.5	17	4	23.5	12	1	8.3	2	0	-	0	0	-
T8–9	adult	intermediate	0	0	-	0	0	-	0	0	-	2	1	50.0	4	2	50.0	4	0	-	1	0	-	0	0	-
T8–9	adult	male	5	0	-	0	0	-	5	3	60.0	4	0	-	16	6	37.5	13	4	30.8	7	3	42.9	1	0	-
T8–9	adult	undetermined	0	0	-	0	0	-	0	0	-	1	0	-	2	0	-	0	0	-	1	1	100.0	0	0	-
T9–10	12–17	subadult	29	6	20.7	23	1	4.3	53	8	15.1	94	12	12.8	77	10	13.0	150	8	5.3	36	4	11.1	13	0	-
T9–10	18–25	female	14	2	14.3	12	2	16.7	33	6	18.2	61	11	18.0	87	23	26.4	101	19	18.8	41	13	31.7	7	3	42.9
T9–10	18–25	intermediate	4	0	-	4	1	25.0	5	2	40.0	4	2	50.0	17	3	17.6	11	5	45.5	6	2	33.3	1	1	100.0
T9–10	18–25	male	19	5	26.3	11	5	45.5	45	26	57.8	63	30	47.6	104	47	45.2	128	50	39.1	49	21	42.9	11	7	63.6
T9–10	26–35	female	44	11	25.0	21	2	9.5	58	10	17.2	114	19	16.7	148	35	23.6	181	28	15.5	54	15	27.8	8	0	-
T9–10	26–35	intermediate	4	2	50.0	0	0	-	7	1	14.3	6	2	33.3	18	6	33.3	13	3	23.1	7	4	57.1	1	0	-
T9–10	26–35	male	44	19	43.2	19	7	36.8	60	20	33.3	83	28	33.7	183	89	48.6	162	52	32.1	78	37	47.4	13	4	30.8
T9–10	36–45	female	28	7	25.0	13	2	15.4	39	6	15.4	63	13	20.6	106	20	18.9	119	26	21.8	34	7	20.6	9	1	11.1
T9–10	36–45	intermediate	3	0	-	1	0	-	1	0	-	9	3	33.3	14	4	28.6	8	2	25.0	4	2	50.0	1	0	-
T9–10	36–45	male	46	18	39.1	22	7	31.8	57	18	31.6	89	25	28.1	187	74	39.6	144	42	29.2	57	22	38.6	20	4	20.0
T9–10	36–45	undetermined	0	0	-	0	0	-	2	1	50.0	0	0	-	1	1	100.0	0	0	-	0	0	-	0	0	-
T9–10	≥46	female	11	1	9.1	2	0	-	16	4	25.0	32	5	15.6	43	6	14.0	60	10	16.7	14	3	21.4	10	1	10.0
T9–10	≥46	intermediate	1	0	-	0	0	-	0	0	-	1	1	100	2	0	-	0	0	-	1	1	100.0	0	0	-
T9–10	≥46	male	18	7	38.9	4	2	50.0	10	1	10.0	22	10	45.5	58	13	22.4	58	23	39.7	26	9	34.6	5	1	20.0
T9–10	adult	female	0	0	-	1	0	-	2	0	-	7	2	28.6	17	2	11.8	12	2	16.7	2	1	50.0	0	0	-
T9–10	adult	intermediate	0	0	-	0	0	-	0	0	-	2	1	50.0	3	2	66.7	3	0	-	0	0	-	0	0	-
T9–10	adult	male	4	0	-	0	0	-	5	2	40.0	4	1	25.0	14	4	28.6	12	3	25.0	7	3	42.9	1	0	-
T10–11	12–17	subadult	29	5	17.2	22	1	4.5	54	9	16.7	94	9	9.6	78	8	10.3	150	9	6.0	36	5	13.9	13	0	-
T10–11	18–25	female	13	2	15.4	13	3	23.1	32	7	21.9	61	9	14.8	89	24	27.0	101	20	19.8	41	12	29.3	7	4	57.1
T10–11	18–25	intermediate	4	0	-	4	0	-	5	2	40.0	4	1	25.0	17	6	35.3	11	4	36.4	6	1	16.7	1	1	100.0
T10–11	18–25	male	20	2	10.0	11	3	27.3	43	23	53.5	63	28	44.4	103	41	39.8	128	51	39.8	47	17	36.2	11	7	63.6
T10–11	18–25	undetermined	3	0	-	0	0	-	1	0	-	0	0	-	1	0	-	2	1	50.0	0	0	-	0	0	-
T10–11	26–35	female	46	10	21.7	21	3	14.3	57	12	21.1	116	15	12.9	149	38	25.5	183	25	13.7	53	16	30.2	8	0	-
T10–11	26–35	intermediate	5	2	40.0	0	0	-	7	1	14.3	6	1	16.7	18	9	50.0	12	4	33.3	7	2	28.6	1	0	-
T10–11	26–35	male	44	14	31.8	19	7	36.8	60	25	41.7	84	34	40.5	183	75	41.0	161	49	30.4	79	35	44.3	13	4	30.8
T10–11	26–35	undetermined	0	0	-	0	0	-	1	0	-	2	0	-	0	0	-	2	1	50.0	2	0	-	0	0	-
T10–11	36–45	female	26	6	23.1	13	2	15.4	39	8	20.5	64	9	14.1	105	16	15.2	119	22	18.5	35	8	22.9	9	4	44.4

Table 59 (cont)

Vertebral joint	Age (years)	Sex	Period 14 Burial type ABC No.	SN	%	Period 14 Burial type D No.	SN	%	Period 15 Burial type ABC No.	SN	%	Period 15 Burial type D No.	SN	%	Period 16 Burial type ABC No.	SN	%	Period 16 Burial type D No.	SN	%	Period 17 Burial type ABC No.	SN	%	Period 17 Burial type D No.	SN	%
T10–11	36–45	intermediate	3	0	-	1	0	-	1	0	-	10	3	30.0	16	3	18.8	8	2	25.0	4	1	25.0	1	0	-
T10–11	36–45	male	46	18	39.1	22	8	36.4	61	23	37.7	89	24	27.0	191	64	33.5	144	49	34.0	60	24	40.0	20	5	25.0
T10–11	≥46	female	11	3	27.3	2	0	-	15	3	20.0	32	3	9.4	42	8	19.0	61	8	13.1	13	1	7.7	10	1	10.0
T10–11	≥46	intermediate	1	0	-	0	0	-	0	0	-	1	0	-	2	0	-	0	0	-	1	1	100.0	0	0	-
T10–11	≥46	male	18	9	50.0	4	3	75.0	10	2	20.0	22	9	40.9	57	19	33.3	58	14	24.1	27	7	25.9	5	3	60.0
T10–11	adult	female	0	0	-	1	0	-	2	0	-	7	2	28.6	16	1	6.3	12	3	25.0	2	0	-	0	0	-
T10–11	adult	intermediate	0	0	-	0	0	-	0	0	-	3	1	33.3	4	2	50.0	3	0	-	0	0	-	0	0	-
T10–11	adult	male	3	0	-	0	0	-	3	1	33.3	4	0	-	12	3	25.0	13	3	23.1	7	4	57.1	1	1	100.0
T11–12	6–11	subadult	6	0	-	9	0	-	22	0	-	60	0	-	75	0	-	85	2	2.4	18	0	-	11	0	-
T11–12	12–17	subadult	26	4	15.4	21	3	14.3	54	6	11.1	96	8	8.3	80	8	10.0	148	12	8.1	36	6	16.7	13	0	-
T11–12	18–25	female	14	1	7.1	14	4	28.6	34	5	14.7	61	11	18.0	87	22	25.3	101	19	18.8	43	17	39.5	7	3	42.9
T11–12	18–25	intermediate	4	0	-	4	0	-	5	1	20.0	4	2	50.0	18	8	44.4	10	4	40.0	6	1	16.7	1	1	100.0
T11–12	18–25	male	21	6	28.6	11	6	54.5	45	23	51.1	64	28	43.8	103	41	39.8	129	57	44.2	46	15	32.6	11	6	54.5
T11–12	18–25	undetermined	3	0	-	0	0	-	1	1	100.0	0	0	-	1	0	-	2	0	-	0	0	-	0	0	-
T11–12	26–35	female	47	13	27.7	22	6	27.3	58	13	22.4	120	24	20.0	152	39	25.7	185	35	18.9	52	17	32.7	10	2	20
T11–12	26–35	intermediate	5	1	20.0	0	0	-	7	1	14.3	6	0	-	17	8	47.1	12	2	16.7	7	2	28.6	1	0	-
T11–12	26–35	male	43	20	46.5	20	9	45.0	60	29	48.3	85	33	38.8	181	88	48.6	157	58	36.9	78	38	48.7	13	4	30.8
T11–12	26–35	undetermined	1	0	-	0	0	-	1	0	-	2	1	50.0	0	0	-	2	2	100.0	2	1	50.0	0	0	-
T11–12	36–45	female	26	5	19.2	14	2	14.3	39	7	17.9	64	19	29.7	104	17	16.3	119	21	17.6	34	13	38.2	9	2	22.2
T11–12	36–45	intermediate	3	1	33.3	1	0	-	1	0	-	10	5	50.0	15	4	26.7	8	3	37.5	4	2	50.0	1	0	-
T11–12	36–45	male	46	16	34.8	22	7	31.8	62	29	46.8	89	32	36.0	191	78	40.8	146	54	37.0	59	19	32.2	20	7	35.0
T11–12	36–45	undetermined	0	0	-	0	0	-	2	1	50.0	0	0	-	2	1	50.0	0	0	-	0	0	-	0	0	-
T11–12	≥46	female	11	2	18.2	2	1	50.0	15	2	13.3	30	6	20.0	42	10	23.8	60	9	15.0	14	2	14.3	9	1	11.1
T11–12	≥46	intermediate	1	0	-	0	0	-	0	0	-	1	1	100	2	1	50.0	0	0	-	1	1	100.0	0	0	-
T11–12	≥46	male	18	8	44.4	4	1	25.0	12	3	25.0	22	9	40.9	58	20	34.5	55	23	41.8	27	11	40.7	5	3	60.0
T11–12	adult	female	0	0	-	1	0	-	2	0	-	6	3	50.0	15	0	-	12	4	33.3	1	0	-	0	0	-
T11–12	adult	intermediate	0	0	-	0	0	-	0	0	-	3	2	66.7	4	2	50.0	3	0	-	0	0	-	0	0	-
T11–12	adult	male	3	0	-	0	0	-	3	0	-	3	0	-	16	4	25.0	14	1	7.1	7	3	42.9	1	0	-
T11–12	adult	undetermined	0	0	-	0	0	-	0	0	-	1	0	-	0	0	-	0	0	-	1	1	100.0	0	0	-
T12–L1	12–17	subadult	26	3	11.5	23	3	13.0	52	7	13.5	97	4	4.1	79	8	10.1	157	8	5.1	36	2	5.6	13	1	7.7
T12–L1	18–25	female	16	1	6.3	13	3	23.1	35	4	11.4	64	12	18.8	92	18	19.6	109	15	13.8	43	12	27.9	7	2	28.6
T12–L1	18–25	intermediate	4	1	25.0	4	1	25.0	4	1	25.0	4	1	25.0	18	6	33.3	10	2	20.0	6	0	-	1	0	-
T12–L1	18–25	male	21	4	19.0	11	4	36.4	46	16	34.8	65	20	30.8	105	24	22.9	130	44	33.8	45	11	24.4	11	1	9.1
T12–L1	18–25	undetermined	3	0	-	0	0	-	2	1	50.0	0	0	-	1	0	-	2	0	-	1	0	-	1	0	-
T12–L1	26–35	female	47	9	19.1	23	2	8.7	59	9	15.3	122	23	18.9	153	21	13.7	191	24	12.6	53	7	13.2	10	2	20.0
T12–L1	26–35	intermediate	5	1	20.0	0	0	-	7	1	14.3	6	0	-	20	7	35.0	11	4	36.4	7	0	-	1	0	-
T12–L1	26–35	male	44	12	27.3	22	7	31.8	59	18	30.5	87	33	37.9	184	60	32.6	161	31	19.3	80	27	33.8	13	4	30.8
T12–L1	26–35	undetermined	1	0	-	0	0	-	1	0	-	2	1	50.0	0	0	-	2	0	-	2	1	50.0	0	0	-
T12–L1	36–45	female	30	4	13.3	14	2	14.3	39	7	17.9	64	13	20.3	108	14	13.0	118	18	15.3	35	6	17.1	10	3	30.0
T12–L1	36–45	intermediate	3	0	-	1	0	-	1	0	-	10	4	40.0	16	4	25.0	8	2	25.0	4	0	-	1	0	-
T12–L1	36–45	male	47	10	21.3	21	5	23.8	63	22	34.9	88	22	25.0	194	52	26.8	148	36	24.3	58	15	25.9	20	3	15.0
T12–L1	36–45	undetermined	0	0	-	0	0	-	2	1	50.0	0	0	-	2	1	50.0	0	0	-	0	0	-	0	0	-
T12–L1	≥46	female	12	0	-	2	0	-	15	2	13.3	30	4	13.3	46	5	10.9	62	6	9.7	16	2	12.5	9	1	11.1
T12–L1	≥46	intermediate	1	0	-	0	0	-	0	0	-	1	1	100	2	0	-	0	0	-	1	0	-	0	0	-
T12–L1	≥46	male	19	5	26.3	4	2	50.0	12	3	25.0	22	4	18.2	58	13	22.4	58	13	22.4	28	5	17.9	5	3	60.0
T12–L1	adult	female	0	0	-	1	0	-	2	0	-	6	1	16.7	13	0	-	13	2	15.4	1	0	-	0	0	-
T12–L1	adult	intermediate	0	0	-	0	0	-	0	0	-	2	1	50.0	4	1	25.0	5	2	40.0	0	0	-	0	0	-
T12–L1	adult	male	3	0	-	0	0	-	3	0	-	3	0	-	19	1	5.3	13	1	7.7	6	2	33.3	1	0	-
L1–2	12–17	subadult	25	2	8.0	23	2	8.7	50	4	8.0	99	7	7.1	80	4	5.0	158	9	5.7	34	3	8.8	13	0	-
L1–2	18–25	female	16	0	-	13	2	15.4	35	6	17.1	66	11	16.7	95	27	28.4	106	14	13.2	43	12	27.9	7	1	14.3
L1–2	18–25	intermediate	4	0	-	4	1	25.0	5	1	20.0	4	2	50.0	18	5	27.8	10	2	20.0	6	0	-	1	1	100.0
L1–2	18–25	male	21	6	28.6	11	1	9.1	45	13	28.9	66	20	30.3	107	28	26.2	130	30	23.1	46	6	13.0	11	2	18.2
L1–2	18–25	undetermined	3	0	-	0	0	-	2	1	50.0	0	0	-	1	0	-	2	0	-	0	0	-	0	0	-
L1–2	26–35	female	45	10	22.2	23	4	17.4	56	10	17.9	120	17	14.2	154	16	10.4	188	26	13.8	52	9	17.3	10	4	40.0
L1–2	26–35	intermediate	5	2	40.0	0	0	-	7	1	14.3	7	2	28.6	19	5	26.3	13	5	38.5	8	0	-	1	0	-
L1–2	26–35	male	45	13	28.9	22	6	27.3	61	14	23.0	91	27	29.7	186	43	23.1	163	29	17.8	81	20	24.7	13	3	23.1
L1–2	36–45	female	30	3	10.0	13	2	15.4	41	4	9.8	64	9	14.1	110	16	14.5	116	17	14.7	34	6	17.6	10	4	40.0
L1–2	36–45	intermediate	3	0	-	1	0	-	1	0	-	9	4	44.4	16	4	25.0	8	0	-	4	1	25.0	1	0	-
L1–2	36–45	male	48	10	20.8	20	6	30.0	63	13	20.6	88	19	21.6	190	37	19.5	147	37	25.2	58	15	25.9	20	4	20.0
L1–2	36–45	undetermined	0	0	-	0	0	-	2	1	50.0	0	0	-	2	1	50.0	0	0	-	0	0	-	0	0	-
L1–2	≥46	female	12	1	8.3	2	2	100.0	14	2	14.3	30	4	13.3	46	8	17.4	61	4	6.6	17	1	5.9	10	1	10.0
L1–2	≥46	intermediate	1	0	-	0	0	-	0	0	-	1	1	100	2	0	-	0	0	-	1	0	-	0	0	-
L1–2	≥46	male	19	4	21.1	4	2	50.0	12	1	8.3	21	3	14.3	58	8	13.8	59	12	20.3	28	6	21.4	5	2	40.0
L1–2	adult	female	0	0	-	1	0	-	1	0	-	6	2	33.3	11	2	18.2	14	1	7.1	1	0	-	0	0	-

Results

Table 59 (cont)

| | | | Period 14 ||||||Period 15 ||||||Period 16 ||||||Period 17 ||||||
| | | | Burial type ABC ||| Burial type D ||| Burial type ABC ||| Burial type D ||| Burial type ABC ||| Burial type D ||| Burial type ABC ||| Burial type D |||
Vertebral joint	Age (years)	Sex	No.	SN	%	No.	SN	%	No.	SN	%	No.	SN	%	No.	SN	%	No.	SN	%	No.	SN	%	No.	SN	%
L1–2	adult	intermediate	0	0	-	0	0	-	0	0	-	2	1	50.0	3	0	-	5	1	20.0	0	0	-	0	0	-
L1–2	adult	male	3	0	-	0	0	-	3	0	-	2	0	-	12	1	8.3	14	1	7.1	6	1	16.7	1	0	-
L2–3	12–17	subadult	25	3	12.0	24	2	8.3	50	3	6.0	102	5	4.9	79	4	5.1	159	8	5.0	35	3	8.6	13	0	-
L2–3	18–25	female	14	1	7.1	13	2	15.4	34	4	11.8	62	11	17.7	94	16	17.0	105	14	13.3	44	11	25.0	7	1	14.3
L2–3	18–25	intermediate	4	0	-	0	0	-	5	5	-	4	2	50.0	19	4	21.1	10	0	-	6	0	-	1	1	100.0
L2–3	18–25	male	20	5	25.0	11	1	9.1	46	11	23.9	66	20	30.3	104	22	21.2	129	31	24.0	44	6	13.6	11	2	18.2
L2–3	26–35	female	45	12	26.7	23	5	21.7	55	11	20.0	119	14	11.8	156	19	12.2	186	24	12.9	55	7	12.7	10	4	40.0
L2–3	26–35	intermediate	5	2	40.0	0	0	-	6	1	16.7	7	1	14.3	19	5	26.3	13	3	23.1	8	1	12.5	1	0	-
L2–3	26–35	male	44	11	25.0	22	6	27.3	61	10	16.4	91	24	26.4	184	38	20.7	164	25	15.2	80	14	17.5	14	1	7.1
L2–3	36–45	female	28	6	21.4	13	1	7.7	41	5	12.2	66	11	16.7	114	15	13.2	119	15	12.6	34	4	11.8	11	4	36.4
L2–3	36–45	intermediate	4	0	-	0	0	-	1	1	-	9	4	44.4	16	4	25.0	8	2	25.0	4	1	25.0	1	0	-
L2–3	36–45	male	49	11	22.4	20	3	15.0	63	13	20.6	89	18	20.2	190	35	18.4	148	29	19.6	59	14	23.7	20	2	10.0
L2–3	36–45	undetermined	0	0	-	0	0	-	2	1	50.0	0	0	-	2	1	50.0	0	0	-	0	0	-	0	0	-
L2–3	≥46	female	12	1	8.3	2	1	50.0	14	3	21.4	31	2	6.5	46	10	21.7	62	5	8.1	16	0	-	10	2	20.0
L2–3	≥46	male	19	3	15.8	4	1	25.0	11	1	9.1	22	3	13.6	60	9	15.0	58	9	15.5	28	5	17.9	5	2	40.0
L2–3	adult	female	0	0	-	1	0	-	2	0	-	6	0	-	10	2	20.0	13	0	-	0	0	-	0	0	-
L2–3	adult	intermediate	0	0	-	0	0	-	0	0	-	2	0	-	3	0	-	3	1	33.3	0	0	-	0	0	-
L2–3	adult	male	3	0	-	0	0	-	3	0	-	1	0	-	12	1	8.3	12	0	-	6	0	-	1	0	-
L3–4	12–17	subadult	24	2	8.3	24	0	-	51	3	5.9	98	3	3.1	81	4	4.9	152	3	2.0	35	2	5.7	13	0	-
L3–4	18–25	female	14	1	7.1	13	2	15.4	33	3	9.1	62	9	14.5	91	13	14.3	106	11	10.4	42	7	16.7	7	1	14.3
L3–4	18–25	intermediate	4	0	-	4	1	25.0	4	0	-	5	0	-	19	2	10.5	10	0	-	6	0	-	1	1	100.0
L3–4	18–25	male	20	3	15.0	11	2	18.2	47	7	14.9	66	18	27.3	104	13	12.5	126	25	19.8	43	4	9.3	11	2	18.2
L3–4	18–25	undetermined	3	1	33.3	0	0	-	0	0	-	1	0	-	1	0	-	2	0	-	0	0	-	0	0	-
L3–4	26–35	female	45	11	24.4	23	4	17.4	54	9	16.7	118	10	8.5	154	12	7.8	186	20	10.8	55	9	16.4	10	2	20.0
L3–4	26–35	intermediate	5	0	-	0	0	-	6	1	16.7	7	2	28.6	20	5	25.0	13	2	15.4	8	0	-	1	0	-
L3–4	26–35	male	44	9	20.5	22	8	36.4	61	7	11.5	91	13	14.3	184	31	16.8	164	20	12.2	80	15	18.8	14	3	21.4
L3–4	36–45	female	29	2	6.9	13	0	-	41	5	12.2	62	4	6.5	113	10	8.8	118	10	8.5	34	4	11.8	11	3	27.3
L3–4	36–45	intermediate	4	0	-	1	0	-	1	0	-	9	3	33.3	13	2	15.4	8	1	12.5	4	0	-	1	0	-
L3–4	36–45	male	49	6	12.2	20	4	20.0	61	10	16.4	88	10	11.4	186	22	11.8	150	25	16.7	58	9	15.5	20	2	10.0
L3–4	≥46	female	11	1	9.1	2	2	100.0	13	3	23.1	31	2	6.5	46	9	19.6	63	3	4.8	17	1	5.9	9	0	-
L3–4	≥46	male	19	2	10.5	4	0	-	13	0	-	22	1	4.5	59	6	10.2	57	6	10.5	28	3	10.7	5	1	20.0
L3–4	adult	female	0	0	-	1	0	-	1	0	-	4	0	-	8	1	12.5	12	0	-	1	0	-	0	0	-
L3–4	adult	intermediate	0	0	-	0	0	-	0	0	-	2	1	50.0	2	0	-	3	1	33.3	0	0	-	0	0	-
L3–4	adult	male	3	0	-	0	0	-	3	0	-	1	0	-	12	1	8.3	10	0	-	5	0	-	1	0	-
L4–5	12–17	subadult	24	2	8.3	24	0	-	51	1	2.0	94	1	1.1	79	2	2.5	153	3	2.0	35	2	5.7	13	0	-
L4–5	18–25	female	11	0	-	13	2	15.4	32	0	-	61	2	3.3	89	5	5.6	104	5	4.8	42	5	11.9	8	0	-
L4–5	18–25	intermediate	3	0	-	4	0	-	4	0	-	5	0	-	19	2	10.5	10	0	-	6	0	-	1	0	-
L4–5	18–25	male	20	2	10.0	11	0	-	45	1	2.2	66	8	12.1	102	7	6.9	125	5	4.0	42	0	-	10	1	10.0
L4–5	18–25	undetermined	3	1	33.3	0	0	-	0	0	-	0	0	-	1	0	-	2	0	-	0	0	-	0	0	-
L4–5	26–35	female	40	0	-	23	0	-	53	3	5.7	120	4	3.3	154	7	4.5	188	5	2.7	55	3	5.5	10	2	20.0
L4–5	26–35	intermediate	5	0	-	0	0	-	6	1	16.7	7	1	14.3	20	2	10.0	13	0	-	8	0	-	1	0	-
L4–5	26–35	male	44	2	4.5	21	4	19.0	62	3	4.8	90	4	4.4	181	17	9.4	162	7	4.3	78	6	7.7	14	0	-
L4–5	36–45	female	30	2	6.7	13	0	-	38	3	7.9	61	2	3.3	113	8	7.1	117	4	3.4	34	1	2.9	11	0	-
L4–5	36–45	intermediate	4	0	-	1	0	-	1	0	-	9	0	-	13	1	7.7	8	0	-	4	0	-	1	0	-
L4–5	36–45	male	47	1	2.1	21	3	14.3	60	3	5.0	88	6	6.8	183	8	4.4	149	12	8.1	58	4	6.9	20	2	10.0
L4–5	≥46	female	11	0	-	2	0	-	12	0	-	30	0	-	46	3	6.5	60	3	5.0	17	1	5.9	10	0	-
L4–5	≥46	male	19	0	-	5	0	-	14	0	-	21	1	4.8	55	1	1.8	58	4	6.9	28	3	10.7	5	0	-
L4–5	adult	female	0	0	-	1	0	-	1	0	-	3	1	33.3	8	0	-	11	0	-	0	0	-	0	0	-
L5–S1	12–17	subadult	26	0	-	24	0	-	51	0	-	94	0	-	80	0	-	157	1	0.6	34	0	-	13	0	-
L5–S1	18–25	female	11	0	-	13	0	-	34	0	-	65	0	-	92	1	1.1	105	0	-	42	2	4.8	8	0	-
L5–S1	18–25	male	19	0	-	11	0	-	46	0	-	67	0	-	102	2	2.0	123	1	0.8	42	0	-	11	1	9.1
L5–S1	26–35	female	40	1	2.5	23	0	-	55	0	-	121	0	-	154	0	-	191	2	1.0	56	0	-	10	0	-
L5–S1	26–35	male	43	1	2.3	22	0	-	63	0	-	92	0	-	179	3	1.7	166	2	1.2	79	3	3.8	14	0	-
L5–S1	36–45	female	29	0	-	14	0	-	40	0	-	63	0	-	113	3	2.7	122	1	0.8	34	0	-	11	0	-
L5–S1	36–45	male	19	0	-	5	0	-	61	0	-	87	2	2.3	187	2	1.1	149	0	-	58	1	1.7	20	0	-
L5–S1	≥46	female	11	0	-	2	0	-	12	0	-	31	0	-	46	2	4.3	62	0	-	17	0	-	10	0	-
L5–S1	adult	intermediate	0	0	-	0	0	-	0	0	-	2	1	50.0	2	0	-	3	0	-	0	0	-	0	0	-

Joint disease

Table 60 Summary of prevalence of Schmorl's nodes by vertebral joint in period 14

	Burial type ABC			Burial type D		
Vertebral joint	No.	Affected	%	No.	Affected	%
Occ–C1	244	0	–	132	0	–
C1–2	225	0	–	127	0	–
C2–3	230	0	–	124	0	–
C3–4	236	0	–	129	0	–
C4–5	240	0	–	129	0	–
C5–6	244	0	–	133	0	–
C6–7	242	2	0.8	136	0	–
C7–T1	258	0	–	142	0	–
T1–2	265	0	–	147	0	–
T2–3	269	0	–	148	0	–
T3–4	273	2	0.7	149	1	0.7
T4–5	284	13	4.6	149	7	4.7
T5–6	285	26	9.1	149	20	13.4
T6–7	286	59	20.6	149	27	18.1
T7–8	290	80	27.6	149	38	25.5
T8–9	287	78	27.2	145	36	24.8
T9–10	284	78	27.5	143	29	20.3
T10–11	282	71	25.2	143	30	21.0
T11–12	281	77	27.4	145	39	26.9
T12–L1	292	50	17.1	148	28	18.9
L1–2	291	51	17.5	147	28	19.0
L2–3	289	55	19.0	143	22	15.4
L3–4	288	38	13.2	148	23	15.5
L4–5	277	10	3.6	149	9	6.0
L5–S1	279	2	0.7	149	0	–
S5–1st coccyx	175	0	–	84	0	–
Total	6896	692	10.0	3636	337	9.3

Table 61 Summary of prevalence of Schmorl's nodes by vertebral joint in period 15

	Burial type ABC			Burial type D		
Vertebral joint	No.	Affected	%	No.	Affected	%
Occ–C1	378	0	–	662	0	–
C1–2	351	0	–	624	0	–
C2–3	361	0	–	620	0	–
C3–4	351	0	–	607	0	–
C4–5	364	1	0.3	606	0	–
C5–6	374	1	0.3	638	1	0.2
C6–7	388	1	0.3	656	3	0.5
C7–T1	405	0	–	700	1	0.1
T1–2	404	0	–	709	3	0.4
T2–3	405	0	–	717	2	0.3
T3–4	408	3	0.7	721	11	1.5
T4–5	413	22	5.3	723	37	5.1
T5–6	412	49	11.9	715	76	10.6
T6–7	418	91	21.8	721	130	18.0
T7–8	418	104	24.9	720	173	24.0
T8–9	421	113	26.8	722	184	25.5
T9–10	421	105	24.9	723	165	22.8
T10–11	418	116	27.8	729	148	20.3
T11–12	427	121	28.3	730	184	25.2
T12–L1	431	92	21.3	738	144	19.5
L1–2	427	71	16.6	747	129	17.3
L2–3	422	63	14.9	750	115	15.3
L3–4	419	48	11.5	740	76	10.3
L4–5	412	15	3.6	728	30	4.1
L5–S1	420	0	–	743	3	0.4
S5–1st coccyx	239	0	–	435	0	–
Total	10,307	1016	9.9	17,924	1615	9.0

Table 62 Summary of prevalence of Schmorl's nodes by vertebral joint in period 16

	Burial type ABC			Burial type D		
Vertebral joint	No.	Affected	%	No.	Affected	%
Occ–C1	1099	0	–	1205	0	–
C1–2	1012	0	–	1124	0	–
C2–3	1007	0	–	1117	0	–
C3–4	991	0	–	1090	0	–
C4–5	986	1	0.1	1091	1	0.1
C5–6	1012	5	0.5	1121	6	0.5
C6–7	1039	6	0.6	1151	4	0.3
C7–T1	1098	4	0.4	1186	2	0.2
T1–2	1099	2	0.2	1189	3	0.3
T2–3	1109	5	0.5	1222	5	0.4
T3–4	1138	19	1.7	1235	22	1.8
T4–5	1141	63	5.5	1247	60	4.8
T5–6	1141	151	13.2	1256	146	11.6
T6–7	1152	260	22.6	1253	243	19.4
T7–8	1157	307	26.5	1248	306	24.5
T8–9	1168	321	27.5	1262	299	23.7
T9–10	1163	339	29.1	1265	273	21.6
T10–11	1172	317	27.0	1269	265	20.9
T11–12	1174	351	29.9	1262	306	24.2
T12–L1	1200	235	19.6	1300	208	16.0
L1–2	1193	205	17.2	1293	188	14.5
L2–3	1198	185	15.4	1287	166	12.9
L3–4	1181	131	11.1	1275	127	10.0
L4–5	1158	63	5.4	1271	48	3.8
L5–S1	1165	13	1.1	1288	7	0.5
S5–1st coccyx	658	0	–	729	0	–
Total	28,611	2983	10.4	31,236	2685	8.6

Table 63 Summary of prevalence of Schmorl's nodes by vertebral joint in period 17

	Burial type ABC			Burial type D		
Vertebral joint	No.	Affected	%	No.	Affected	%
Occ–C1	437	0	–	106	0	–
C1–2	409	0	–	98	0	–
C2–3	413	1	0.2	98	0	–
C3–4	408	0	–	96	0	–
C4–5	407	0	–	98	0	–
C5–6	451	0	–	103	0	–
C6–7	420	1	0.2	101	0	–
C7–T1	434	0	–	107	0	–
T1–2	433	0	–	104	1	1.0
T2–3	412	1	0.2	98	1	1.0
T3–4	443	5	1.1	107	1	0.9
T4–5	446	18	4.0	111	4	3.6
T5–6	454	54	11.9	113	9	8.0
T6–7	456	114	25.0	113	18	15.9
T7–8	448	143	31.9	110	21	19.1
T8–9	450	138	30.7	110	26	23.6
T9–10	444	144	32.4	110	22	20.0
T10–11	446	134	30.0	110	30	27.3
T11–12	442	149	33.7	112	29	25.9
T12–L1	446	90	20.2	113	20	17.7
L1–2	447	80	17.9	114	22	19.3
L2–3	447	66	14.8	117	19	16.2
L3–4	442	54	12.2	116	15	12.9
L4–5	432	25	5.8	116	5	4.3
L5–S1	435	6	1.4	118	1	0.8
S5–1st coccyx	292	0	–	79	0	–
Total	11,194	1223	10.9	2778	244	8.8

87

3.8 Trauma

Don Walker

When the data from all traumatic lesions (fractures, soft tissue injuries and dislocations) to all parts of the skeleton were compiled, the crude prevalence rate of trauma at St Mary Spital was 22.5% (1214/5387). Males suffered a higher crude prevalence of injury when compared to females (χ^2 = 62.14, df = 1, p ≤ 0.001) (Table 64).

All fractures

The majority of recorded injuries were bone fractures, for which the crude prevalence rate was 20.9% (1125/5387). The frequency of bone fracture increased with age, although the rate of increase had slowed by older adulthood (Fig 83). Males were more frequently affected by bone fracture than females (χ^2 = 56.67, df = 1, p ≤ 0.001) (Table 65); when analysed by age and sex, male fracture prevalence was found to be significantly higher than that of females within each adult age category (Fig 84; Table 66; Table 67).

Table 64 Trauma crude prevalence summary

	No.	Affected	%
All individuals	5387	1214	22.5
Female	1883	404	21.4
Male	2237	726	32.4
Subadult	1027	35	3.4

Table 65 Fracture crude prevalence summary

	No.	Affected	%
All individuals	5387	1125	20.9
Female	1883	375	19.9
Male	2237	675	30.2
Subadult	1027	32	3.1

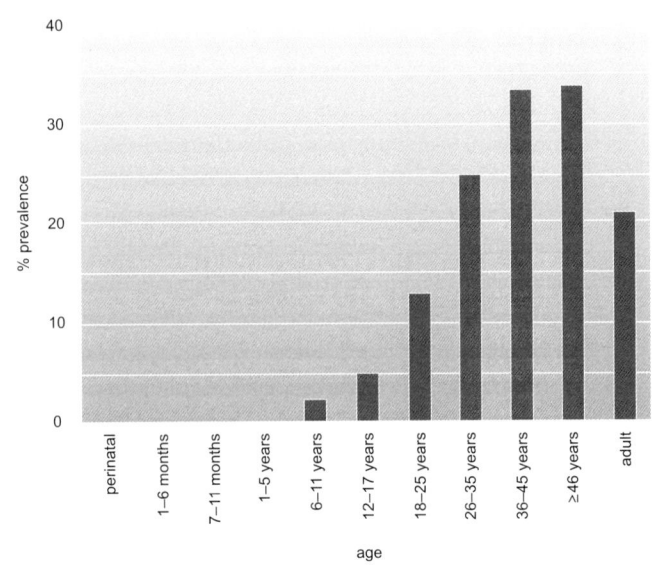

Fig 83 Crude prevalence rate of fracture by age group

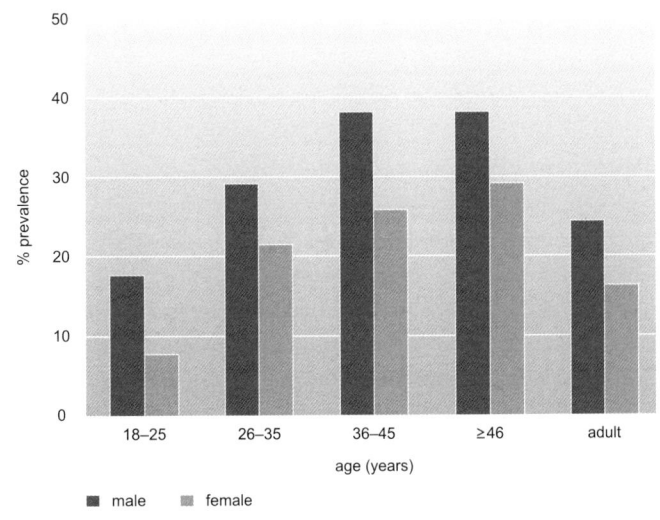

Fig 84 Crude prevalence rate of adult fracture by age and sex

Table 66 Crude prevalence rate of fracture by age and sex

Age (years)	Female No.	Affected	%	Male No.	Affected	%	Intermediate No.	Affected	%	Undetermined No.	Affected	%	Subadult No.	Affected	%	Total No.	Affected	%
6–11	0	0	-	0	0	-	0	0	-	0	0	-	348	7	2.0	348	7	2.0
12–17	0	0	-	0	0	-	0	0	-	0	0	-	544	25	4.6	544	25	4.6
18–25	428	32	7.5	481	85	17.7	62	6	9.7	8	0	-	0	0	-	979	123	12.6
26–35	716	152	21.2	752	219	29.1	69	10	14.5	9	2	22.2	0	0	-	1546	383	24.8
36–45	467	120	25.7	700	266	38.0	48	14	29.2	4	2	50.0	0	0	-	1219	402	33.0
≥46	211	61	28.9	222	85	38.3	7	3	42.9	2	0	-	0	0	-	442	149	33.7
Adult	61	10	16.4	82	20	24.4	19	3	15.8	12	3	25.0	0	0	-	174	36	20.7

Table 67 Statistical testing (χ²) of fracture crude prevalence rate by age and sex

Age (years)	Female No.	Affected	%	Male No.	Affected	%	χ² df = 1, p ≤ 0.001
18–25	428	32	7.5	481	85	17.7	20.99
26–35	716	152	21.2	752	219	29.1	12.10
36–45	467	120	25.7	700	266	38.0	18.67
≥46	211	61	28.9	222	85	38.3	4.26

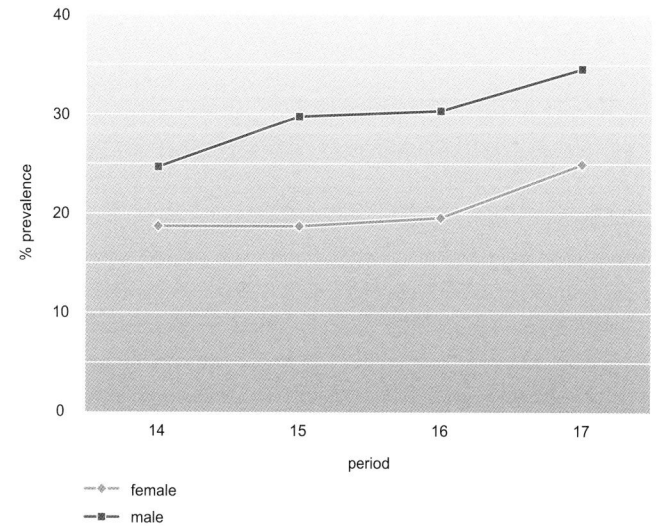

The crude prevalence rate of fracture within the sample increased throughout the period of use of the cemetery. The prevalence in period 17 was significantly higher than that in period 14 (χ^2 = 8.44, df = 1, p ≤ 0.01). The largest increase (4.0%) was from period 16 to period 17 (χ^2 = 5.01, df = 1, p ≤ 0.05). This suggests that London became a more dangerous place to live throughout the course of the medieval period, with a significant rise in fracture risk in the 15th century (Table 68; Fig 85). Male fracture rates were higher than female throughout the study period (Fig 86).

An increase in crude prevalence of fractures over time was evident in both burial type ABC (χ^2 = 4.52, df = 1, p ≤ 0.05) and D (χ^2 = 4.31, df = 1, p ≤ 0.05) (Table 68; Fig 87). Females displayed a general increase in fractures over time in both burial types. The prevalence in type ABC rose significantly (9.4%) from period 15 to period 17 (χ^2 = 4.75, df = 1, p ≤ 0.05). In burial type D, there was an increase of 12.9% from period 16 to period 17 (χ^2 = 3.91, df = 1, p ≤ 0.05) (Table 69; Fig 88).

The crude prevalence of males with fractures increased by 9.8% from period 14 to period 17 (χ^2 = 5.76, df = 1, p ≤ 0.025). The pattern of change in both burial types was very similar over all four periods, with a reduction in the rate of increase from period 15 to 16. The evidence suggests that, at least as far as crude prevalence rates are concerned, males in burial types ABC and D had similar fracture risks throughout the period of use of the cemetery (Table 70) (Fig 89).

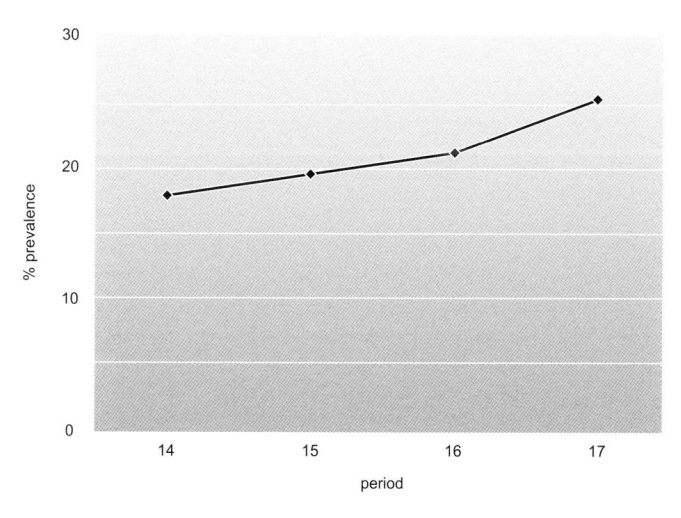

Table 68 Crude prevalence rate of fracture by period and burial type

Burial type	Period 14 No.	Affected	%	Period 15 No.	Affected	%	Period 16 No.	Affected	%	Period 17 No.	Affected	%	Total No.	Affected	%
ABC	347	65	18.7	510	98	19.2	1392	313	22.5	526	130	24.7	2775	606	21.8
D	165	27	16.4	880	175	19.9	1443	284	19.7	124	33	26.6	2612	519	19.9
Total	512	92	18.0	1390	273	19.6	2835	597	21.1	650	163	25.1	5387	1125	20.9

Fig 85 Crude prevalence rate of fracture by period

Fig 86 Crude prevalence rate of fracture by sex

Results

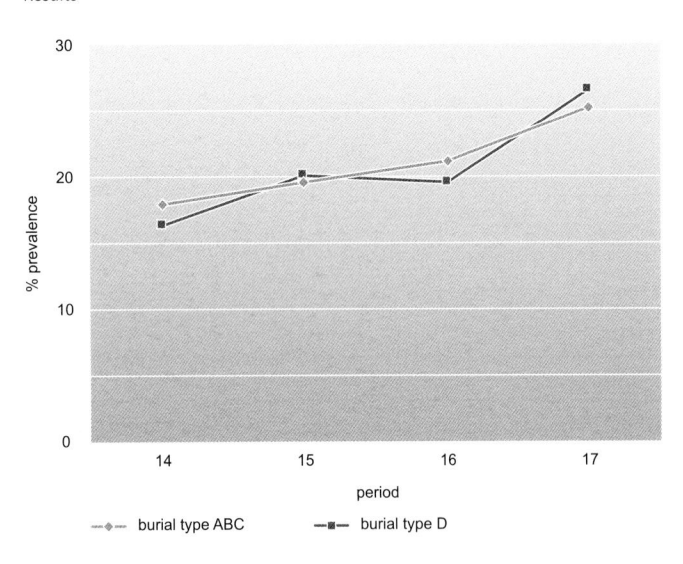

Fig 87 Crude prevalence rate of fracture by period and burial type

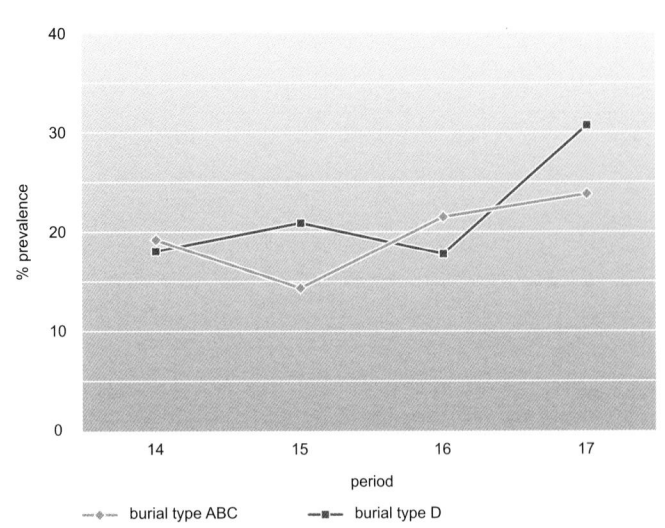

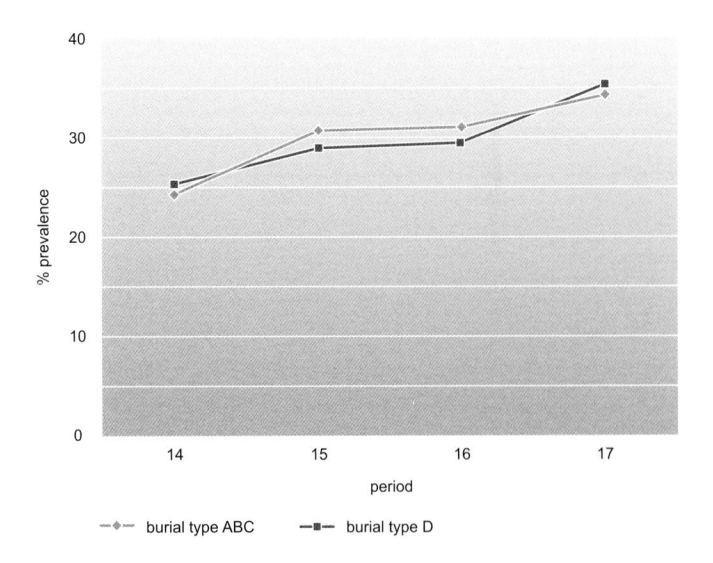

Fig 88 Crude prevalence rate of female fracture by period and burial type

Table 69 *Crude prevalence of female fracture by period and burial type*

Burial type	Period 14 No.	Affected	%	Period 15 No.	Affected	%	Period 16 No.	Affected	%	Period 17 No.	Affected	%	Total No.	Affected	%
ABC	115	22	19.1	167	24	14.4	474	102	21.5	164	39	23.8	920	187	20.3
D	55	10	18.2	334	70	21.0	535	96	17.9	39	12	30.8	963	188	19.5
Total	170	32	18.8	501	94	18.8	1009	198	19.6	203	51	25.1	1883	375	19.9

Table 70 *Crude prevalence of male fracture by period and burial type*

Burial type	Period 14 No.	Affected	%	Period 15 No.	Affected	%	Period 16 No.	Affected	%	Period 17 No.	Affected	%	Total No.	Affected	%
ABC	160	39	24.4	219	67	30.6	628	196	31.2	239	82	34.3	1246	384	30.8
D	63	16	25.4	313	91	29.1	564	166	29.4	51	18	35.3	991	291	29.4
Total	223	55	24.7	532	158	29.7	1192	362	30.4	290	100	34.5	2237	675	30.2

Male fracture prevalence was higher than female for both burial types ABC and D, throughout all periods of the cemetery's use. In burial type ABC, significantly higher male rates were evident in period 15 (χ^2 = 13.84, df = 1, p ≤ 0.001), period 16 (χ^2 = 12.86, df = 1, p ≤ 0.001) and period 17 (χ^2 = 5.13, df = 1, p ≤ 0.025). In burial type D, significantly higher male rates were found in period 15 (χ^2 = 5.69, df = 1, p ≤ 0.025) and period 16 (χ^2 = 20.00, df = 1, p ≤ 0.001) (Fig 90; Fig 91).

The burial sample from St Mary Spital produced a true prevalence rate of fracture of 0.4%. A significantly higher number of male elements were fractured when compared to female elements (χ^2 = 140.98, df = 1, p ≤ 0.001). Only 0.1% of subadult bones were affected (Table 71). The percentage of fractured elements increased significantly from period 16 to period 17 (χ^2 = 1617.92, df = 1, p ≤ 0.001). Periods 14 to 16 had a very similar prevalence (Table 72).

Fig 89 Crude prevalence rate of male fracture by period and burial type

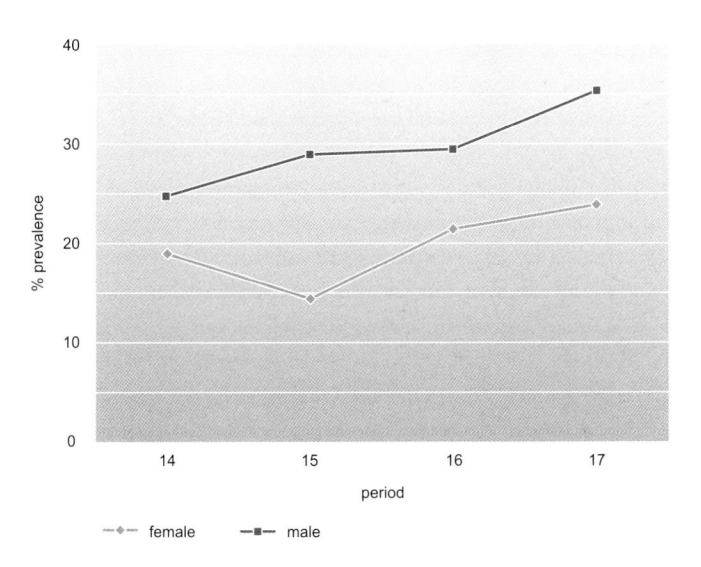

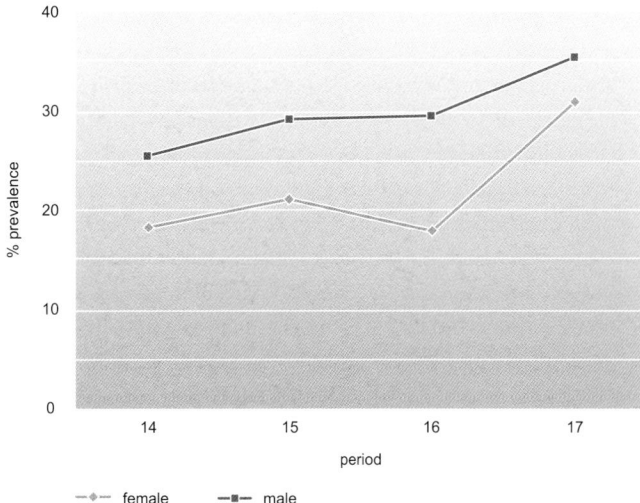

Fig 90 Crude prevalence rate of male and female fracture in burial type ABC

Fig 91 Crude prevalence rate of male and female fracture in burial type D

Table 71 Fracture true prevalence summary

	Elements	Affected	%
All individuals	616,245	2394	0.4
Female	192,459	732	0.4
Male	239,047	1538	0.6
Subadult	92,266	48	0.1

Table 72 True prevalence of fracture by period

Period	Elements	Affected	%
14	56,011	222	0.4
15	151,886	581	0.4
16	329,125	1208	0.4
17	79,223	383	0.5

Table 73 Skull fracture crude prevalence summary

	No.	Affected	%
All individuals	5387	157	2.9
Female	1883	51	2.7
Male	2237	98	4.4
Subadult	1027	7	0.7

Skull fractures

More male individuals than females suffered skull fractures ($\chi^2 = 7.82$, df = 1, p ≤ 0.01) (Table 73). Very few individuals (27/5387: 0.5%) displayed evidence of sharp force trauma to the cranium. Most sharp force injuries were found in males (20/2237: 0.9%) with only six females affected (6/1883: 0.3%) ($\chi^2 = 5.40$, df = 1, p ≤ 0.02). For much of this analysis, the skull was divided into two parts, the cranial vault (frontals, parietals, supraoccipital, squamous temporals, greater wings of sphenoid) and the face (maxilla, nasal, zygomatic and mandible).

More males had fractures to the cranial vault ($\chi^2 = 11.73$, df = 1, p ≤ 0.001), and males were also more frequently affected by blunt force ($\chi^2 = 6.39$, df = 1, p ≤ 0.025) and sharp force ($\chi^2 = 5.40$, df = 1, p ≤ 0.025) fractures to the cranial vault. There was also a higher prevalence of facial fractures in males than in females, though not to a statistically significant extent. Dental fractures were evenly distributed (Table 74; Fig 92).

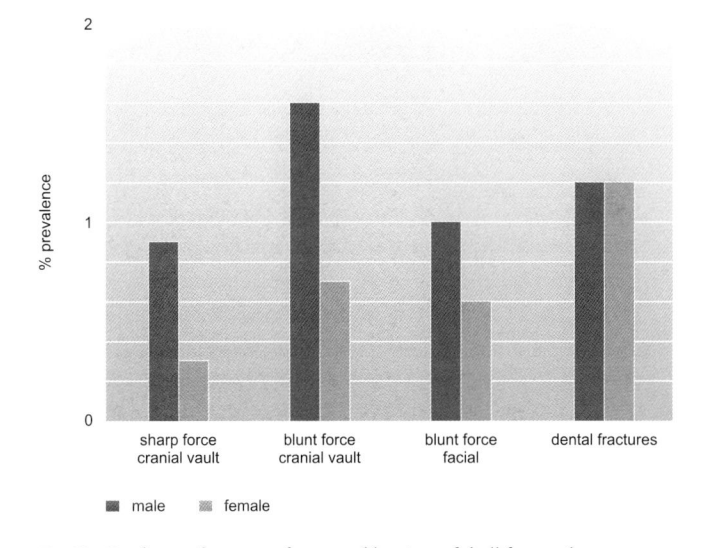

Fig 92 Crude prevalence rate of types and locations of skull fracture by sex

Table 74 Crude prevalence rate of skull fracture by location and sex

			Female			Male	
Location	Fracture type	No.	Affected	%	No.	Affected	%
Cranial vault	all	1883	20	1.1	2237	56	2.5
Cranial vault	blunt force	1883	14	0.7	2237	36	1.6
Cranial vault	sharp force	1883	6	0.3	2237	20	0.9
Facial	all	1883	11	0.6	2237	23	1.0
Dental	tooth	1883	23	1.2	2237	26	1.2

Results

In period 16, more males in burial type ABC suffered cranial vault fractures (24/628: 3.8%) than males in burial type D (10/564: 1.8%) (χ^2 = 4.50, df = 1, p ≤ 0.05). In the other periods, the numbers were too small to test. The true prevalence rate of cranial vault fracture was higher in males than in females (χ^2 = 16.65, df = 1, p ≤ 0.001) (Table 75).

Over half of all cranial vault fractures were distributed in the parietal bones (Fig 93), with a true prevalence rate of 0.7% (61/8264). The second most common type of fracture was to the frontal bone (40/7829: 0.5%). The occipital was rarely involved (2/4076: 0.1%).

The male data display an increase in fractures to the cranial vault from period 15 to period 16 (period 15 9/3008: 0.3%; period 16 49/7529: 0.7%) (χ^2 = 4.85, df = 1, p ≤ 0.05) (Table 76). This suggests that levels of interpersonal violence may have risen with the economic and social upheaval of the late 13th and 14th centuries (competition for resources, wars, famine and plague). The frequency did not fall in period 17, reflecting the general increase in fracture rates over time. These results were not reflected in the female data. However, the numbers affected were too small to produce reliable temporal information (Fig 94).

When examined by burial type, the graphed data produce variations between burial types ABC and D. Although most of this data subset is too small to test for significance, these graphs may reflect divergent trends in the prevalence of cranial vault fractures (Fig 95; Fig 96).

Table 75 *Cranial vault fracture true prevalence summary*

	Elements	Affected	%
All	33,797	108	0.3
Female	12,186	27	0.2
Male	13,764	74	0.5
Subadult	6676	4	0.1

Table 76 *True prevalence rate of male cranial vault fracture by period*

Period	Elements	Affected	%
14	1284	2	0.2
15	3008	9	0.3
16	7529	49	0.7
17	1943	14	0.7

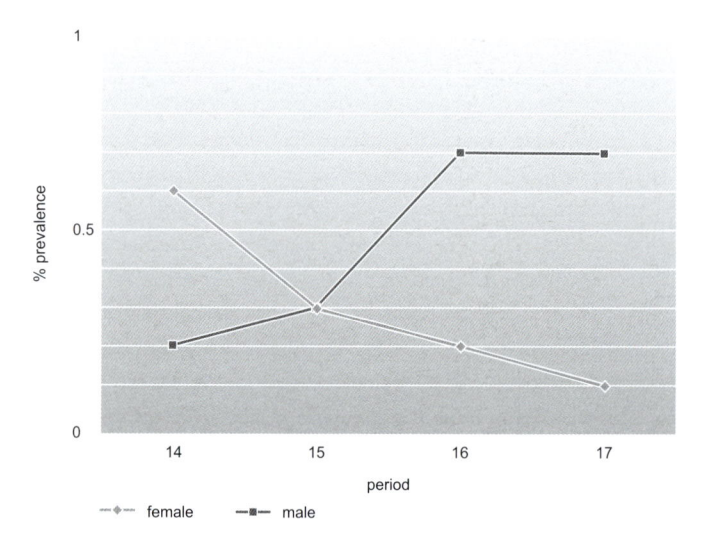

Fig 93 *Cranial vault fracture distribution*

Fig 94 *True prevalence rate of cranial vault fracture by period*

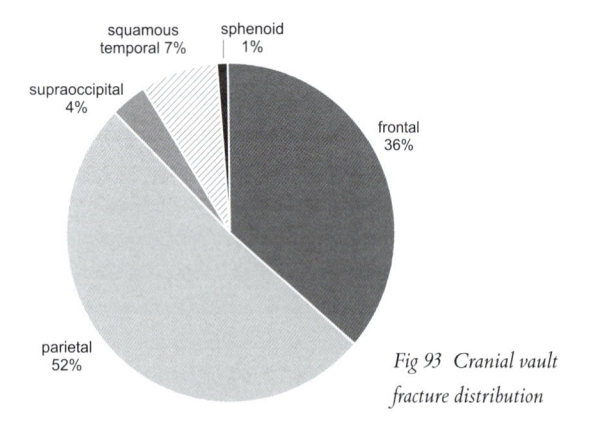

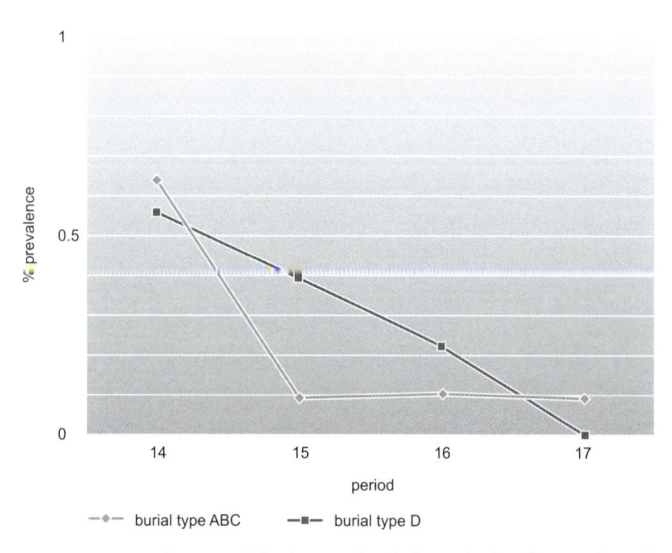

Fig 95 *True prevalence rate of female cranial vault fracture by burial type and period*

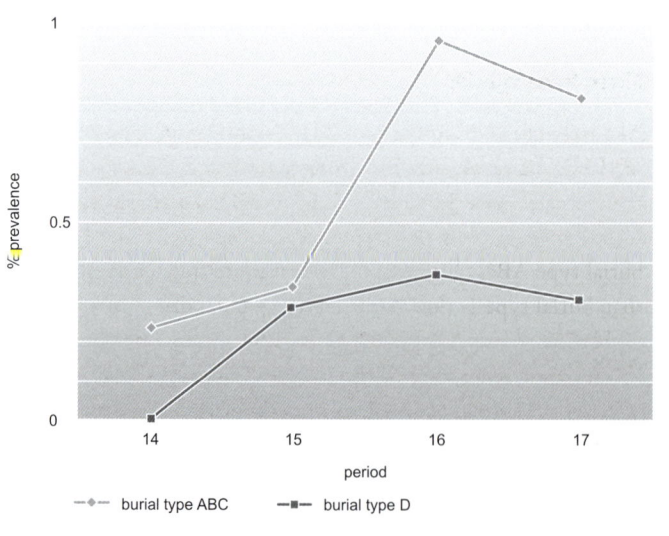

Fig 96 *True prevalence rate of male cranial vault fracture by burial type and period*

The rise in male cranial vault fractures in period 16 was restricted to the sample from burial type ABC. The prevalence rate of 1.0% (36/3760) was significantly higher than that for burial type D (13/3769: 0.3%) (χ^2 = 10.92, df = 1, p ≤ 0.001), which remained unchanged from period 15 (5/1835: 0.3%). Period 17 males exhibited a similar pattern, although the raw data were too few to test (burial type ABC 13/1594: 0.8%; burial type D 1/349: 0.3%). It therefore appears that the increase in male cranial vault fractures in period 16 was a result of a rise in the group from burial type ABC rather than burial type D. The male individuals from burial type ABC may have been exposed to an increased level of interpersonal violence when compared with those in burial type D (Fig 97).

There was a higher rate of male frontal bone fracture in burial type ABC for period 16 (17/881: 1.9%) than in burial type D (5/861: 0.6%) (χ^2 = 6.35, df = 1, p ≤ 0.025). The parietal bone rate was also higher (burial type ABC 16/947: 1.7%; burial type D 8/892: 0.9%), though not to a statistically significant extent (Fig 98; Fig 99).

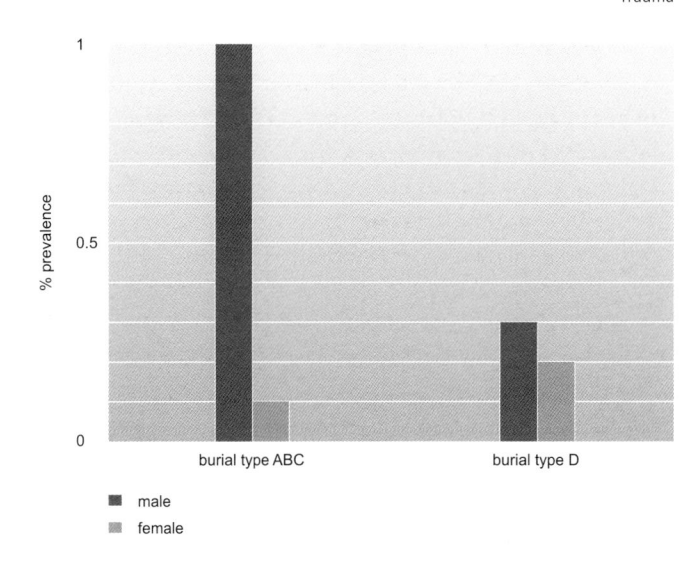

Fig 97 True prevalence rate of cranial vault fracture in period 16 by sex and burial type

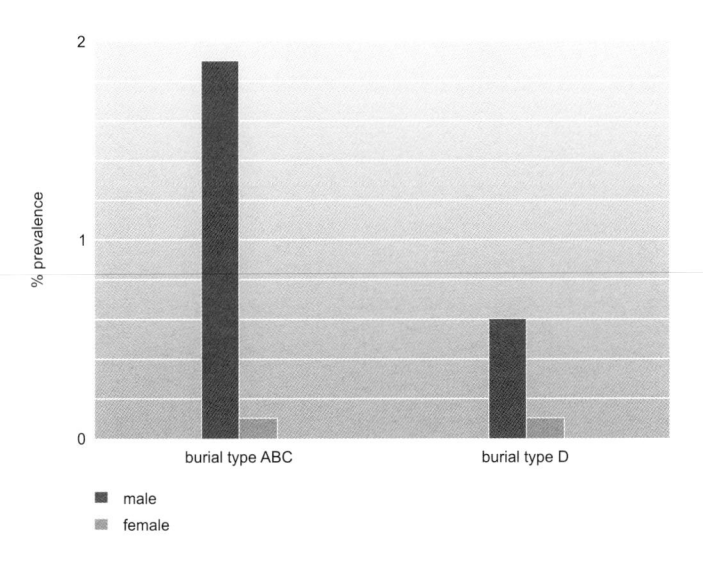

Fig 98 True prevalence rate of frontal bone fracture in period 16 by sex and burial type

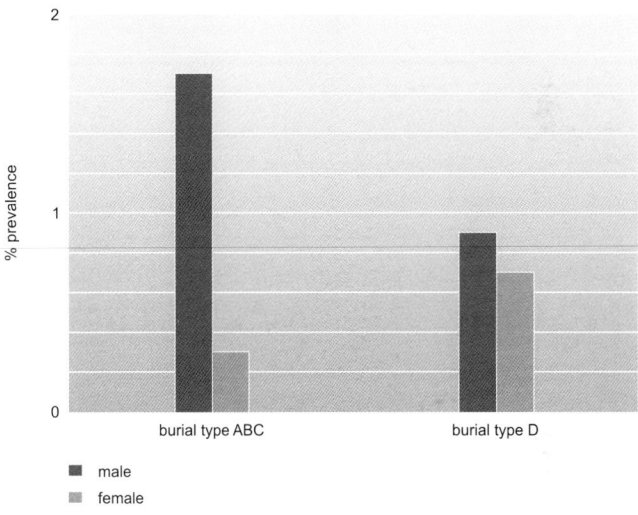

Fig 99 True prevalence rate of parietal bone fracture in period 16 by sex and burial type

Sharp force injuries

Although the overall true prevalence rate of sharp force fracture of the cranial vault was low, males were affected more often than females (χ^2 = 14.06, df = 1, p ≤ 0.001). There was also some variation identified in period 16, where the sample from burial type ABC (20/8392: 0.2%) was more frequently affected than burial type D (9/9747: 0.1%) (χ^2 = 6.02, df = 1, p ≤ 0.025) (Table 77).

Sharp force fracture of the cranial vault most usually affected the frontal and parietal bones (Fig 100). The left side was more commonly affected, especially on the male parietal bone, though not to a statistically significant extent (Fig 101).

Sharp force injuries are more commonly associated with interpersonal violence and support the evidence above, which suggests there was an increase in injuries caused by interpersonal violence in males in period 16 when compared to the previous periods, and that this increase was restricted to individuals in burial type ABC. There was no evidence of such an increase in burial type D.

Table 77 True prevalence summary of cranial vault sharp force fracture

	Elements	Affected	%
All individuals	33,797	39	0.1
Female	12,186	6	0.1
Male	13,764	31	0.2

Results

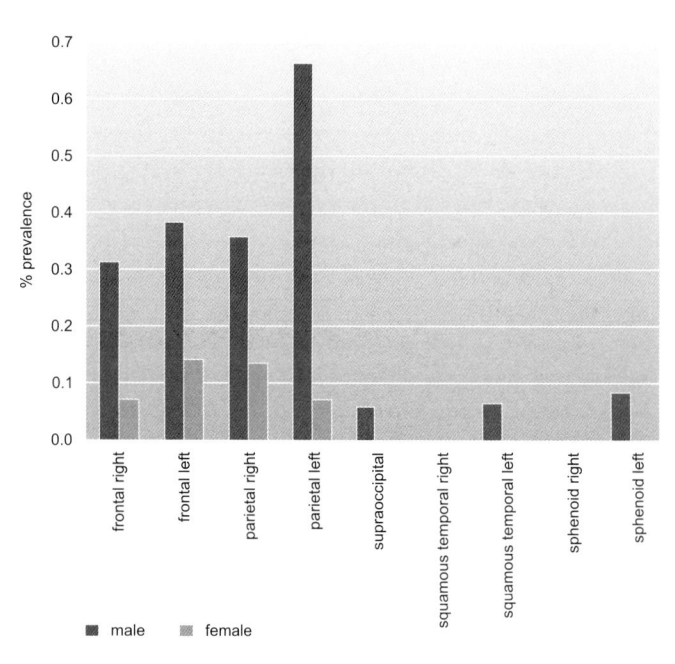

Fig 100 Sharp force injury to the cranium of 26–35-year-old male [9488] from period 17, burial type ABC (scale c 1:2)

Fig 101 True prevalence rate of cranial vault sharp force fracture

Blunt force injuries

There was a higher prevalence of blunt force fracture to the cranial vault in males than in females (χ^2 = 5.15, df = 1, p ≤ 0.025) (Table 78; Fig 102). There was a gradual increase in male blunt force cranial vault fracture throughout the use of the cemetery, with a statistically significant increase from period 15 (5/3008: 0.2%) to period 17 (12/1943: 0.6%) (χ^2 = 7.03, df = 1, p ≤ 0.01). In contrast, female rates fell throughout, with a significant reduction between period 14 (6/978: 0.6%) and period 16 (8/6757: 0.1%) (χ^2 = 11.59, df = 1, p ≤ 0.001) (Fig 103).

When male frontal and parietal bones from period 16 were combined, there was a higher prevalence of blunt force cranial vault fracture in burial type ABC (19/1828: 1.0%) than in burial type D (5/1753: 0.3) (χ^2 = 5.34, df = 1, p ≤ 0.025) (Fig 104). In period 16 there was therefore a higher rate of cranial vault fracture (both sharp and blunt force) in burial type ABC than in burial type D.

Table 78 True prevalence summary of cranial vault blunt force fracture

	Elements present	Affected	%
All	33,797	70	0.2
Female	12,186	21	0.2
Male	13,764	43	0.3
Subadult	6676	5	0.1

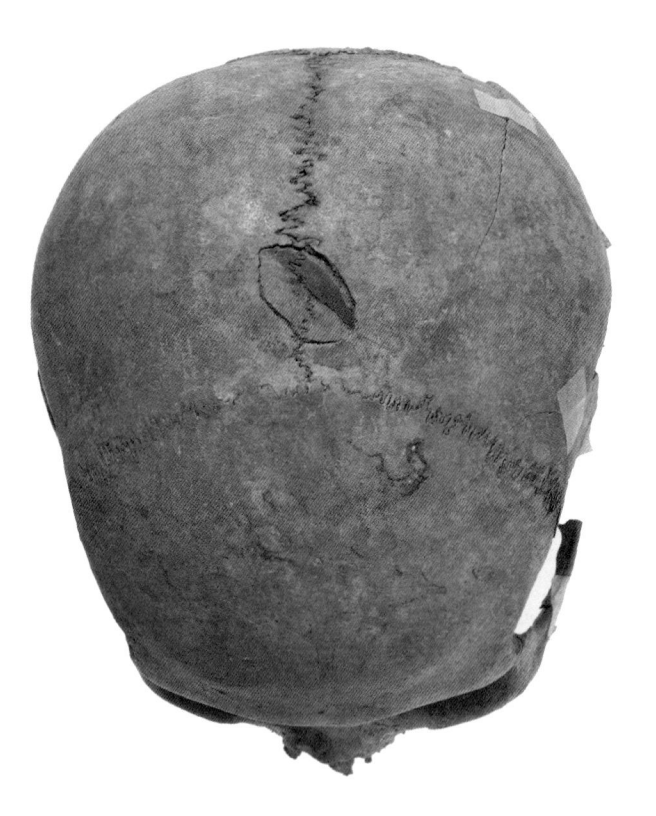

Fig 102 Peri-mortem blunt force cranial injury in 36–45-year-old female [3243] from period 15, burial type D (scale c 1:2)

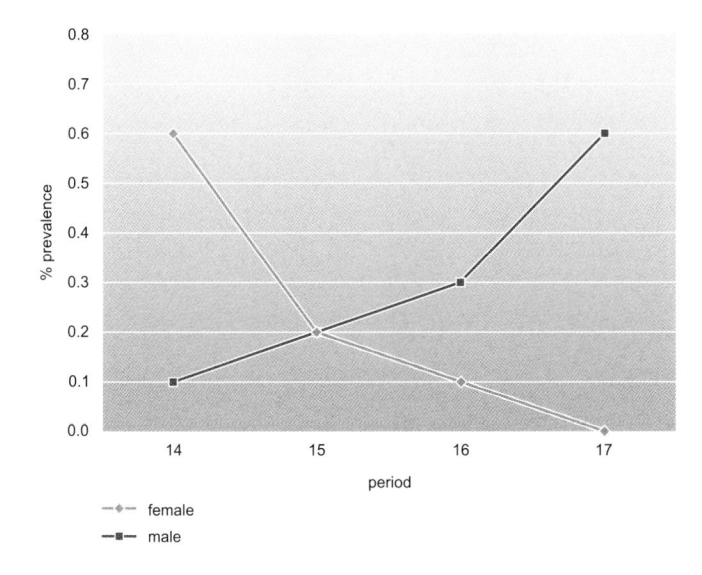

Fig 103 True prevalence rate of cranial vault blunt force fracture by sex and period

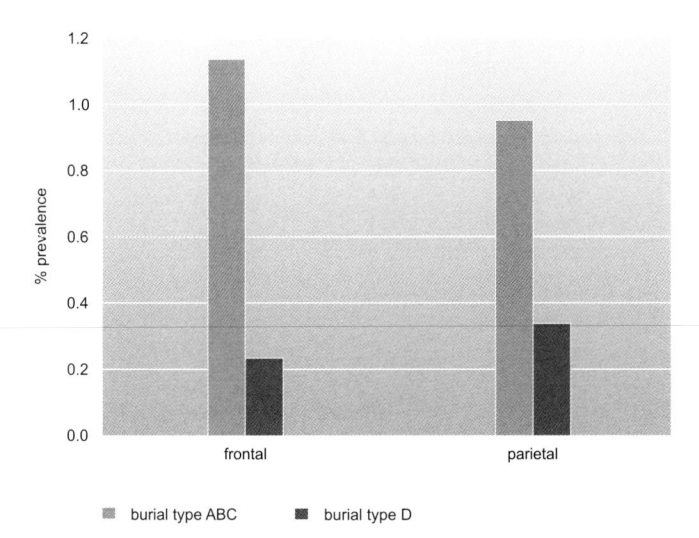

Fig 104 True prevalence rates of male frontal and parietal blunt force fracture in period 16 by burial type

Facial injuries

There was a higher prevalence of blunt force facial fractures (maxilla, nasal, zygomatic bones and mandible) in males than in females (χ^2 = 6.06, df = 1, p ≤ 0.025). Of 52 facial fractures, 26 (50%) were on the right side of the face, and 26 (50%) on the left. The data subset was too small to trace by period (Table 79).

Table 79 True prevalence summary of facial blunt force fracture

	Elements present	Affected	%
All	25,222	52	0.2
Female	9193	15	0.2
Male	10,540	36	0.3
Subadult	4621	1	<0.1

Dental fractures

While males suffered higher crude prevalence rates of fracture to the face and cranial vault than females, dental fracture rates showed no variation between the sexes (total 51/5387: 0.9%; female 23/1883: 1.2%; male 26/2237: 1.2%).

Of those individuals with dental fractures, 13 (13/51: 25.5%) also had skull fractures, while 9.1% (108/1183) of individuals without dental fractures had skull fractures. A greater percentage of individuals with dental fractures therefore also had skull fractures than those without dental fractures (χ^2 = 14.80, df = 1, p ≤ 0.001). There was a relationship between skull fracture and dental fracture. The increased female-to-male ratio of dental fracture relative to the female-to-male ratio of skull fracture may have been due to gender-related mechanism. Female individuals with dental fractures were less likely to have fractures to the skull than males with dental fractures.

There was a slightly higher true prevalence rate of dental fracture in males, but not to a statistically significant extent (Table 80). There were also no significant differences between sides (right 38/34,365 teeth: 0.1%; left 49/34,333 teeth: 0.1%), or between upper and lower jaws (maxilla 46/31,843 teeth: 0.1%; mandible 41/36,855 teeth: 0.1%).

Long bone fractures

The total long bone shaft fracture true prevalence rate (humerus, radius, ulna, femur, tibia and fibula) was 1.1% (550/48,749) (Table 81). Forearm bones were most affected, with a significantly larger number of ulna fractures (172/8537: 2.0%) when compared to the radius (119/8476: 1.4%) (χ^2 = 9.44, df = 1, p ≤ 0.01).

Table 80 Dental fracture true prevalence summary

	Teeth present	Affected	%
All	71,883	95	0.1
Female	32,227	34	0.1
Male	36,471	52	0.1

Table 81 True prevalence rates of long bone fractures

Bone	Elements present	Elements affected	%
Humerus	8739	74	0.8
Radius	8476	119	1.4
Ulna	8537	172	2.0
Femur	8471	23	0.3
Tibia	7453	81	1.1
Fibula	7073	81	1.1
Total	48,749	550	1.1

Results

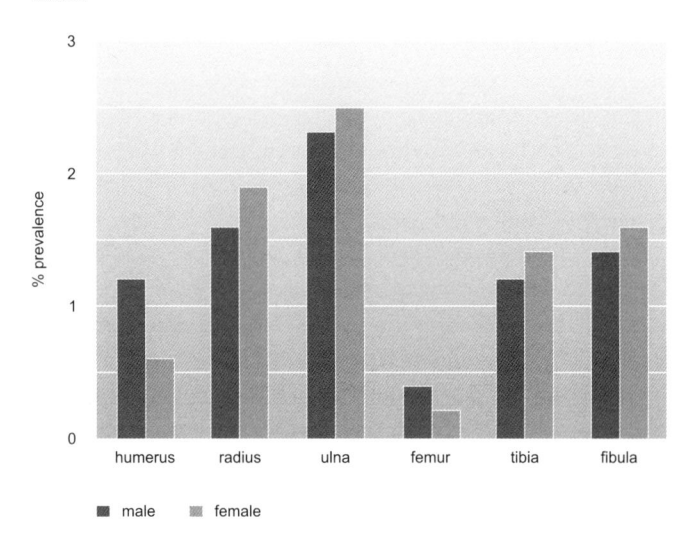

Fig 105 True prevalence rates of long bone fractures by sex

The humerus was the only single bone fracture to vary significantly between the sexes, with a higher fracture rate in the male sample (44/3606: 1.2%) than in the female sample (19/3089: 0.6%) (χ^2 = 6.53, df = 1, p ≤ 0.01) (Fig 105). However, 18.0% (132/732) of all female fractures were located in the radius or ulna. Male forearms were less frequently affected (140/1538: 9.1%) (χ^2 = 37.50, df = 1, p ≤ 0.01).

Some variation was encountered when the data were analysed by period and burial type. In burial type ABC, when periods 15 and 16 were combined, there was a greater rate of ulna shaft fracture in males (35/1313: 2.7%) than in females (15/1016: 1.5%) (χ^2 = 3.86, df = 1, p ≤ 0.05). However, in period 17 the opposite was true. This was due to an increase in ulna shaft fractures in females (15/265: 5.7%) rather than a decrease in male rates (9/389: 2.3%) (χ^2 = 4.99, df = 1, p ≤ 0.025).

In burial type D, in periods 15 and 16, female and male ulna shaft fracture rates were similar (period 15 – female 9/505: 1.8%, male 10/489: 2.0%; period 16 – female 25/930: 2.7%, male 20/972: 2.1%). For periods 15–16, ulna shaft fractures were therefore equally distributed between the sexes in burial type D, while males had a higher rate in burial type ABC. In period 17, there was a general rise in the rate of ulna shaft fracture (as there was with fractures in general), which was particularly evident in the female sample.

Ulna shaft fractures displayed interesting variation, especially in periods 15 and 16 where the larger data subsets allowed more detailed investigation. In general, the prevalence of female ulna shaft fractures (and to a certain degree female radius shaft fractures) in burial type D was higher than in type ABC. For males, the opposite was true (Fig 106).

While male fracture rates were much higher than female rates in burial type ABC, they were more equal in burial type D. However, female rates of radial trauma in burial type D were higher than in males (though this was not statistically significant). There was therefore more variation in ulna shaft fracture frequency between the sexes in burial type ABC than in burial type D (Fig 107; Fig 108).

All long bones, except the femur, were fractured more

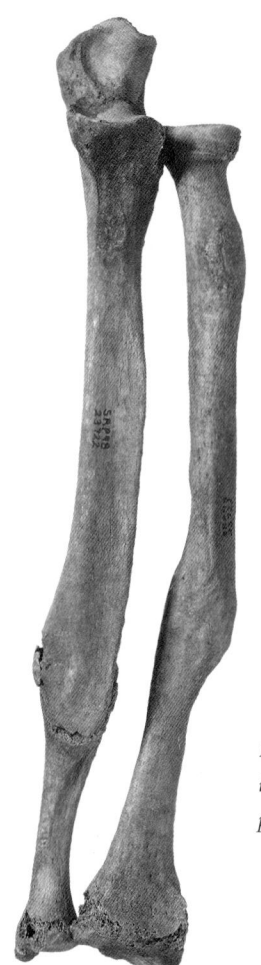

Fig 106 Healed radial and ulna fractures in 36–45-year-old male [23722] from period 14, burial type D (scale c 1:2)

frequently on the left side (Fig 109) (Chapter 4.1). Left ulna shafts were more frequently fractured than right, both overall and when divided by sex (Table 82). Left male humerus shafts (30/1816: 1.6%) were also found to be more frequently affected than right male humeri (14/1790: 0.8%) (χ^2 = 5.66, df = 1, p ≤ 0.025).

Though not included in the overall long bone shaft analysis, clavicle shafts were found to be fractured more frequently in males (36/3496: 1.0%) than females (16/3011: 0.5%) (χ^2 = 4.89, df = 1, p ≤ 0.05), and left clavicles (35/4151: 0.8%) were affected more often than right (20/4187: 0.5%) (χ^2 = 4.25, df = 1, p ≤ 0.05).

The distal segments of long bone shafts were most frequently fractured. In female upper limbs, only 0.1% (18/12,021) of proximal shafts were affected, compared to 0.3% (34/12,187) of midshafts and 0.8% (94/11,772) of distal shafts. The difference between midshaft fractures and distal shaft fractures was significant (χ^2 = 30.41, df = 1, p ≤ 0.001) (Fig 110). Female radii were more often fractured in the distal shaft (35/2899: 1.2%) than the midshaft (8/3063: 0.3%) (χ^2 = 18.62, df = 1, p ≤ 0.001), as were female ulnae (midshaft fractures 19/3044: 0.6%; distal shaft fractures 43/2790: 1.5%; χ^2 = 11.64, df = 1, p ≤ 0.001).

Male long bone shafts were similarly affected, with distal shafts (128/13,939: 0.9%) fractured more frequently than midshafts (38/14,264: 0.3%) (χ^2 = 51.20, df = 1, p ≤ 0.001). Proximal shafts were again least affected (23/14,133: 0.2%)

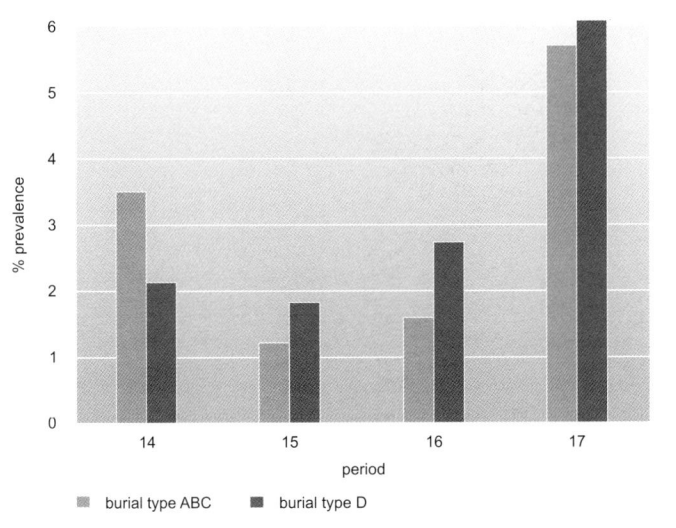

Fig 107 True prevalence rates of female ulna fractures by period and burial type

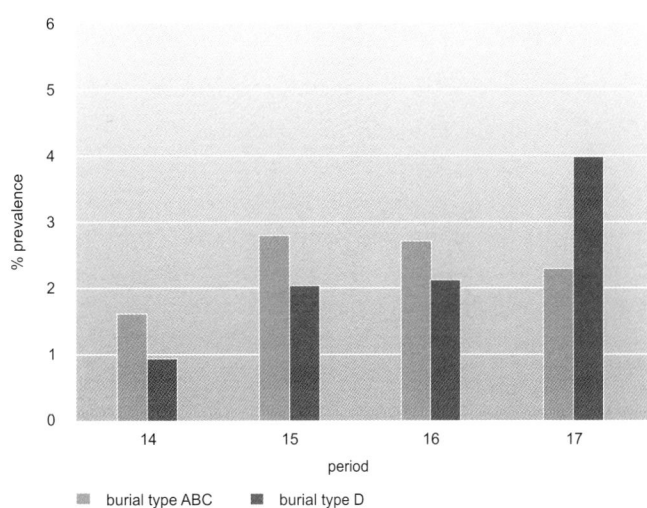

Fig 108 True prevalence rates of male ulna fractures by period and burial type

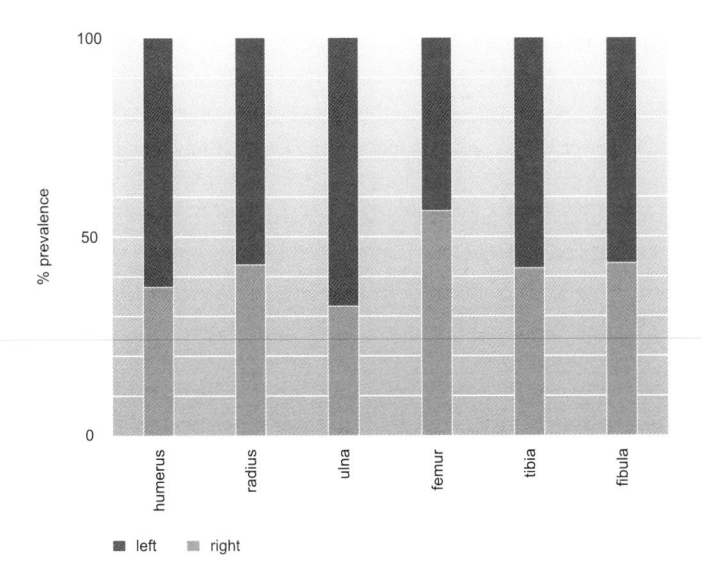

Fig 109 True prevalence rates of long bone fractures by side

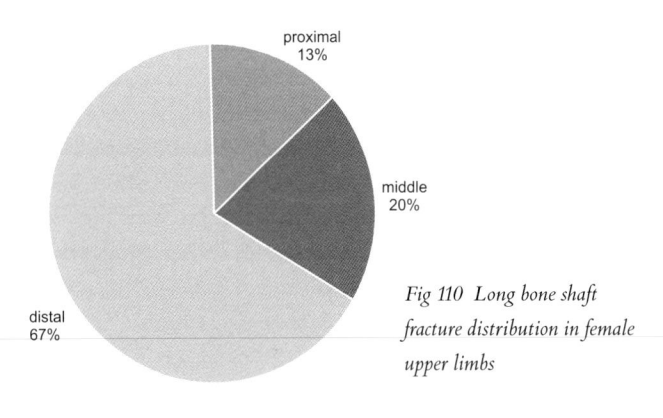

Fig 110 Long bone shaft fracture distribution in female upper limbs

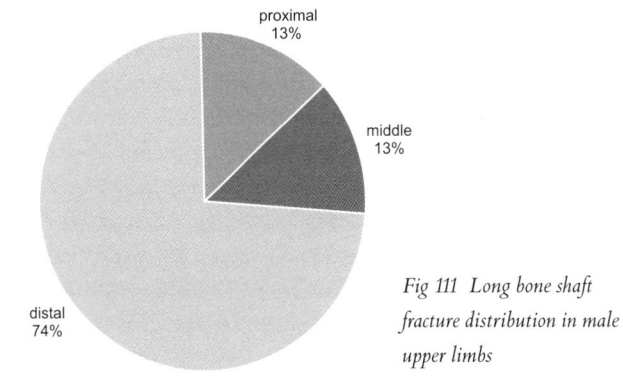

Fig 111 Long bone shaft fracture distribution in male upper limbs

Table 82 Ulna shaft fractures by side

	Side	Elements present	Affected	%	χ^2 df = 1
All	right	4281	57	1.3	20.31, p ≤ 0.001
	left	4256	115	2.7	
Female	right	1532	24	1.6	21.48, p ≤ 0.001
	left	1503	52	3.5	
Male	right	1782	28	1.6	8.81, p ≤ 0.01
	left	1794	55	3.1	

(Fig 111). As in the female forearm, male radii were more often fractured in the distal shaft (33/3438: 1.0%) than in the midshaft (8/3565: 0.2%) (χ^2 = 16.26, df = 1, p ≤ 0.001), as were male ulnae (midshaft fractures 14/3580: 0.3%; distal shaft fractures 55/3380: 1.6%; χ^2 = 27.07, df = 1, p ≤ 0.001). Male humeri were fractured more frequently in the distal shafts (23/3599: 0.6%) than in the proximal shafts (6/3524: 0.2%) (χ^2 = 9.65, df = 1, p ≤ 0.01).

Male left distal ulna shafts (36/1701: 2.1%) were fractured more frequently than male right ulna distal shafts (19/1679: 1.1%) (χ^2 = 5.12, df = 1, p ≤ 0.025). Female ulna distal shafts were also fractured more frequently on the left side (27/1378: 2.0%) than on the right (16/1412: 1.1%), but not to a statistically significant extent. Male and female distal radial shafts were also fractured more frequently on the left side, though not to a statistically significant extent (female right 14/1466: 0.9%; female left 21/1433: 1.5%; male right 14/1702: 0.8%, male left 19/1736: 1.1%).

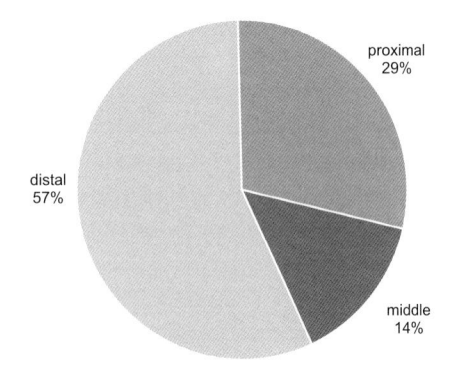

Fig 112 Long bone shaft fracture distribution in female lower limbs

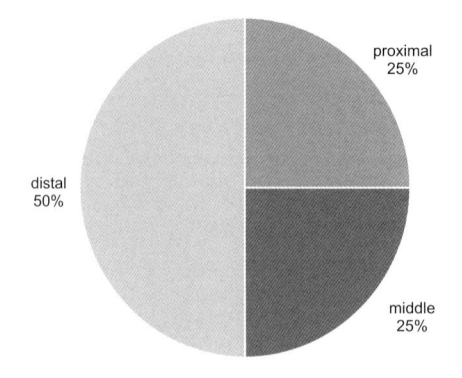

Fig 113 Long bone shaft fracture distribution in male lower limbs

In summary, forearm fractures were concentrated on the distal shafts and were more often found on the left side.

In the lower limbs, females were affected more in the distal shafts (34/7990: 0.4%) than the proximal shafts (16/8308: 0.2%) (χ^2 = 7.23, df = 1, p ≤ 0.01). Midshafts were least often fractured (8/8238: 0.1%) (Fig 112). The distal shafts of female tibiae (13/2595: 0.5%) were more frequently affected than the midshafts (5/2693: 0.2%) (χ^2 = 3.87, df = 1, p ≤ 0.05). In the lower limbs of males, distal shafts (34/9356: 0.4%) were fractured significantly more often than proximal shafts (18/9757: 0.2%) (χ^2 = 5.63, df = 1, p ≤ 0.025) and midshafts (15/9621: 0.2%) (Fig 113).

Joint fractures

The true prevalence rate of extra-spinal joint fracture at St Mary Spital was 0.1% (124/114,205). The joint with the highest frequency of fracture was the talocrural (29/6306: 0.5%), which was significantly more often affected than the second highest, the radiocarpal (for scaphoid) joint (13/6096: 0.2%) (χ^2 = 5.59, df = 1, p ≤ 0.025) (Fig 114).

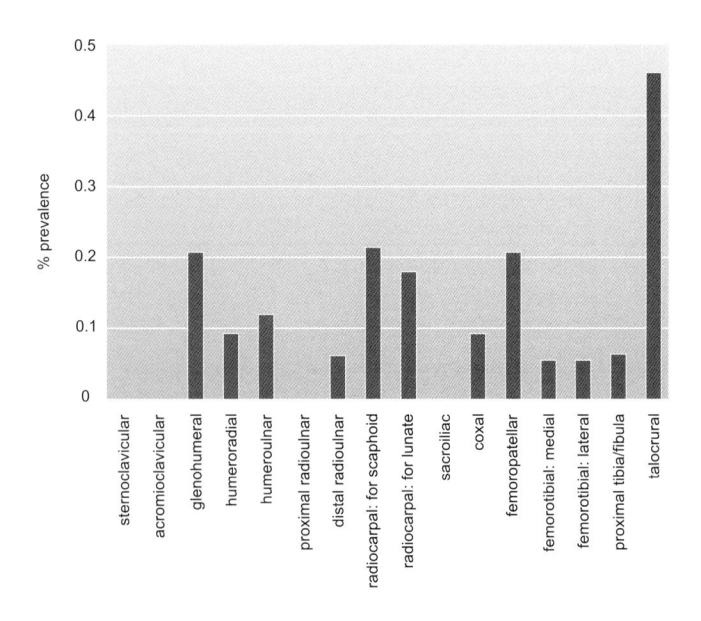

Fig 114 True prevalence rates of joint fractures

Vertebral fractures

Vertebral body fractures

This section includes only those fractures which are believed to result from traumatic incidents. Those thought to relate to metabolic conditions (ie osteoporosis or osteomalacia) are included in section 3.10, while examples of Scheuermann's disease are detailed under circulatory disease (3.12). The relationship between vertebral body fracture and osteoporosis is not fully understood, so the results must be treated with caution, especially when elderly females are involved (Resnick 2002, 1833).

In clinical studies, the four most common forms of spinal injury involve seatbelt-type injuries, fracture-dislocations, compression fractures and burst fractures (McRae 2003, 351). The majority of vertebral body fractures within the Spitalfields sample also involved compression, often resulting in anterior wedging. This form of injury is often caused by falls on to the feet or base of the spine (Dandy and Edwards 1998, 155; Galloway 1999, 96).

The overall true prevalence rate of fractures to the vertebral body was 0.5% (524/114,504) (Table 83). When analysed by individual vertebrae, the 12th thoracic vertebra was most frequently affected (60/4248: 1.4%) (Table 83; Fig 115). Further peaks were identified at the fourth lumbar and second to fourth coccygeal vertebrae.

Table 83 True prevalence rate of vertebral body fractures by spinal segment

Spine	Elements present	Affected	%
Cervical	25,301	7	<0.1
Thoracic	50,334	304	0.6
Lumbar	21,331	198	0.9
Sacral	16,216	12	0.1
Coccygeal	1322	3	0.2
Total	114,504	524	0.5

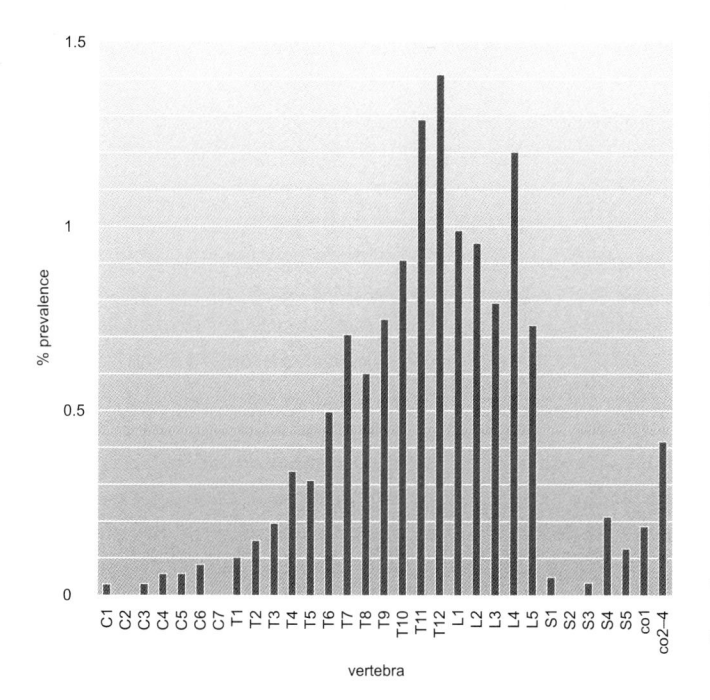

Fig 115 True prevalence rates of vertebral body fracture (C = cervical, T= thoracic, L = lumbar, S = sacral, co = coccygeal)

Table 84 True prevalence rates of vertebral body fractures by period

Period	Elements present	Affected	%
14	10,923	65	0.6
15	28,925	159	0.5
16	60,302	221	0.4
17	14,354	79	0.6

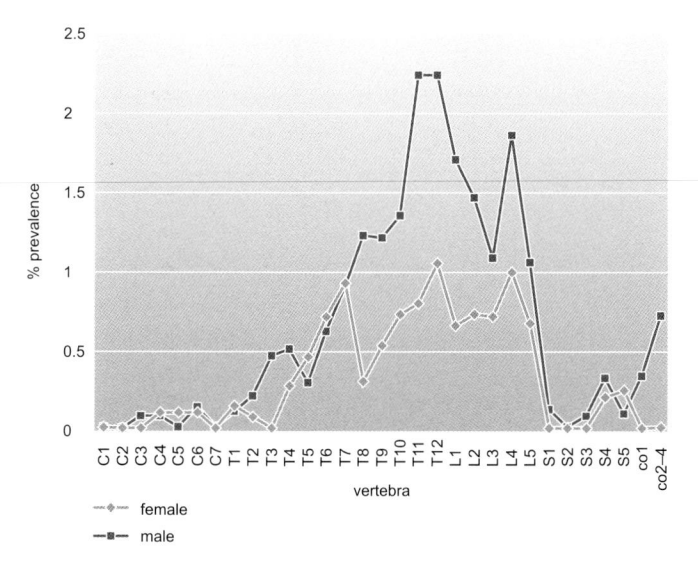

Fig 116 True prevalence rates of vertebral body fractures by sex (C = cervical, T= thoracic, L = lumbar, S = sacral, co = coccygeal)

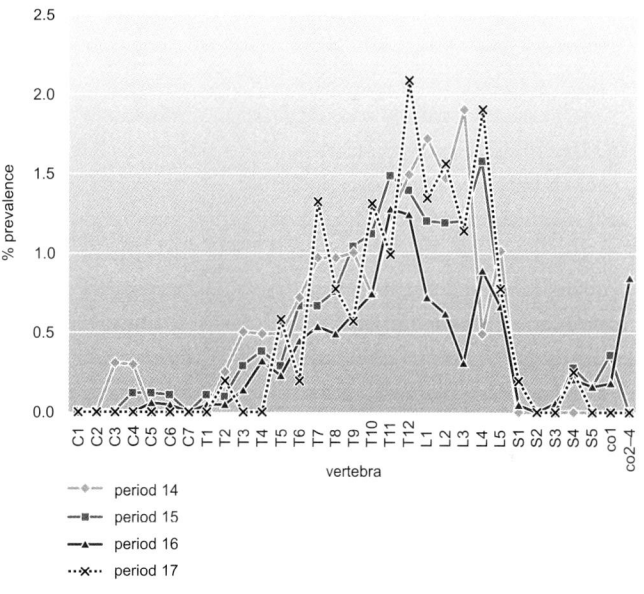

Fig 117 True prevalence rates of vertebral body fractures by period (C = cervical, T= thoracic, L = lumbar, S = sacral, co = coccygeal)

There was a higher rate of vertebral body fracture in males (348/49,538: 0.7%) than females (152/41,205: 0.4%) (χ^2 = 45.69, df = 1, p ≤ 0.001) (Fig 116): this was true for both thoracic vertebral body fracture (male 203/21,576: 0.9%; female 89/18,206: 0.5%; χ^2 = 27.69, df = 1, p ≤ 0.001) and the lumbar spine (male 131/9189: 1.4%; female 56/7628: 0.7%; χ^2 = 18.12, df = 1, p ≤ 0.001). Males were found to have a significantly higher fracture prevalence in the 12th thoracic vertebra (male 41/1833: 2.2%; female 16/1519: 1.1%; χ^2 = 6.96, df = 1, p ≤ 0.01) and fourth lumbar vertebra (male 34/1831: 1.9%; female 15/1523: 1.0%; χ^2 = 6.96, df = 1, p ≤ 0.01).

When analysed over time, the frequency of period 16 vertebral body fractures was found to be lower than that of the other periods (period 14 χ^2 = 12.08, df = 1, p ≤ 0.001; period 15 χ^2 = 15.47, df = 1, p ≤ 0.001; period 17 χ^2 = 9.79, df = 1, p ≤ 0.01) (Table 84; Fig 117). The decrease in frequency that followed period 15 was due to an even reduction in both burial types: ABC period 15, 55/10,486: 0.5%; period 16, 107/28,782: 0.4% (χ^2 = 4.36, df = 1, p ≤ 0.05); D period 15, 104/18,439: 0.6%, period 16, 114/31,520: 0.4% (χ^2 = 11.51, df = 1, p ≤ 0.001). This decrease in both burial types in period 16 occurred in males (period 15 110/11,356: 1.0%; period 16 139/26,446: 0.5%; χ^2 = 23.83, df = 1, p ≤ 0.001), but not in females. In period 17, both female and male rates rose.

Neural arch fractures

Clay shoveller's fractures occur in the spinous processes of lower cervical and upper thoracic vertebrae. They are usually the result of avulsion by the supraspinous ligament due to hyperflexion in this area of the spine, although they can also be caused by direct blows (Resnick 2002, 2975). Overall within the sample, the first thoracic vertebra was most often affected (Table 85). The crude prevalence of clay shoveller's fractures was higher in males than females (Table 86). Adults from different age ranges were equally affected.

Results

Table 85 True prevalence rate of clay shoveller's fractures

Vertebra	Elements present	Affected	%
C6	3590	1	<0.1
C7	3647	7	0.2
T1	3854	15	0.4
T2	3892	2	0.1
T4	3817	1	<0.1

Table 86 Crude prevalence rate of clay shoveller's fractures by sex

	Elements present	Affected	%
Total	5387	26	0.5
Female	1883	3	0.2
Male	2237	23	1.0

There was a single fracture of a C1 arch in later middle-aged female [25087], possibly a Jefferson fracture caused by compressive axial loading (Resnick 2002, 2959). Five apophyseal facet fractures were recorded. They were all in males, and all in the thoracic and lumbar spine.

Subadult fractures

The crude prevalence rate of subadult bone fracture was 3.2% (33/1027). Only individuals within age categories 6–11 years (8/348: 2.3%) and 12–17 years (25/544: 4.6%) were affected. There was no evidence of bone fracture in individuals below 6 years of age. The duration of the youngest adult age category (18–25 years) is slightly longer than that preceding it, but the substantial increase in fractures to 12.6% (123/979) of individuals in this category suggests that injury risk increased throughout youth and into early adulthood. However, to some extent this is mitigated by the more active remodelling of subadult bone. Young individuals who suffer skeletal injuries

Table 87 Crude prevalence of subadult fracture by period

	6–11 years			12–17 years			Total (all subadults)		
	No.	Affected	%	No.	Affected	%	No.	Affected	%
Period 14	21	1	4.8	61	1	1.6	94	2	2.1
Period 15	103	2	1.9	169	6	3.6	301	8	2.7
Period 16	187	3	1.6	265	17	6.4	508	20	3.9
Period 17	37	2	5.4	49	1	2.0	124	3	2.4
Total	348	8	2.3	544	25	4.6	1027	33	3.2

Table 88 Crude prevalence of subadult fracture in period 16 by burial type

Burial type	No.	Affected	%
ABC	178	6	3.4
D	274	14	5.1

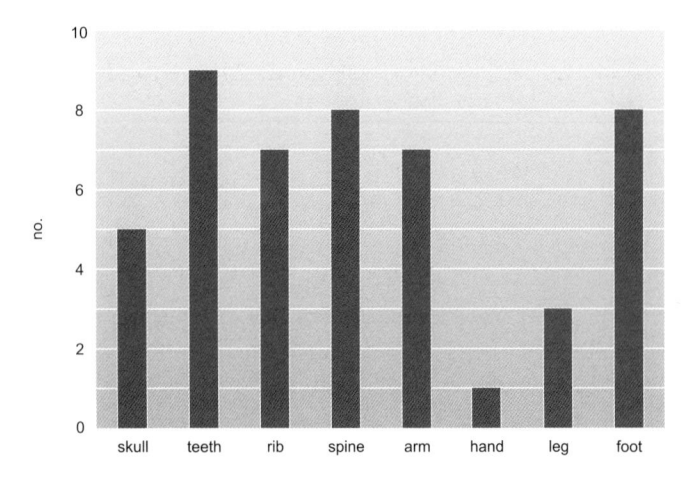

Fig 118 Frequency of fractures in subadults

potentially reveal less evidence of such, due to relatively rapid healing in comparison with adult individuals.

The number of individuals aged 6–17 years at death who were affected by bone fracture increased from period 14 to period 16, with a slight decrease in period 17, although none of these variations was statistically significant (Table 87). In period 16, a larger number of subadults from burial type D were affected than in burial type ABC, though again this difference was not statistically significant (Table 88).

The true prevalence rate of subadult bone fracture was 0.1% (48/92,266). The distribution of fractures around the body was not dissimilar to that found in adults, although the high level of foot involvement may be a product of the relatively low number of fractures (48) (Fig 118).

Some of the fractures identified on adult skeletons were types that often affect subadult individuals and may have been a consequence of fracture prior to adulthood (<18 years). These included fracture separations of epiphyseal plates and greenstick fractures. While these fractures were included in the analysis of adult fractures, they were also examined separately (Fig 119). Fifty-two adult males (52/2237: 2.3%) displayed subadult-type fractures, compared to 1.3% (24/1883) of adult females ($\chi^2 = 6.22$, df = 1, $p \leq 0.01$).

Out of a total of 105 subadult-type fractures, 35 (33.3%)

affected the humerus. Of these, 14 involved the disruption of the proximal growth plate; 17 were found at the distal end of the humerus, all but three on the left side. The single most commonly identified lesion was the avulsion of the medial epicondyle (12 examples) which can be caused by falls on to the elbow or extended forearm, by throwing, sudden valgus strain or a fall on to an outstretched hand (Galloway 1999, 132; Resnick 2002, 2743, 2827). All but three of these affected male humeri, and when calculated as a true prevalence of distal humerus shafts there was a larger frequency on the left side (right 2/1800: 0.1%; left 7/1801: 0.4%) (Fig 120).

Injury recidivism

Clinical studies on modern populations have identified 'injury recidivists' as individuals from low-status groups who are most likely to suffer repeat episodes of serious injury due to interpersonal violence (Judd 2002a, 90–1). For the purposes of this analysis, individuals with two or more injuries were studied in an attempt to identify high-risk groups within the sample. All traumatic lesions – fractures, soft tissue injuries and dislocations – were included. Unfortunately, it is rarely possible to determine the age at which traumatic episodes have occurred in healed injuries from archaeological samples, and this hinders the differentiation of single episodes of multiple trauma from multiple episodes of trauma. This was mitigated to a certain extent by counting separate injuries which were judged to have resulted from a single incident as single injuries. One example of this would be an individual with a fracture to one or more ribs in close anatomical proximity to a separate fracture in the scapular blade. In such cases there is a high probability that all injuries were caused by the same incident, a blow to, or a fall on to, the upper back. Similarly, a severe fracture to a long bone may cause damage to neighbouring soft tissue, so where fractures and soft tissue injuries are closely associated, they have been interpreted as a single episode of trauma. Some injuries can be caused by a number of different mechanisms, which may result from either accidental trauma or interpersonal violence, so care must be taken in the interpretation of studies of multiple injuries within archaeological samples.

There was a higher crude prevalence of males with multiple injury (245/2237: 11.0%) than females (102/1883: 5.4%), both

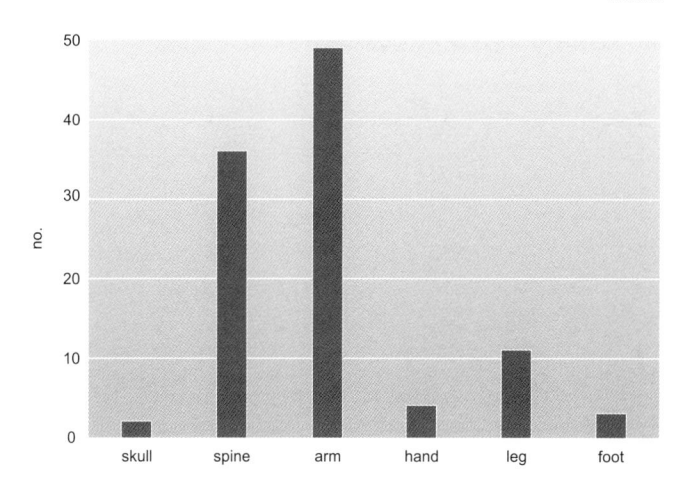

Fig 119 Frequency of subadult fractures in adults

Fig 120 Subadult humeral fracture in 18–25-year-old male [14945] from period 14, burial type ABC, showing disruption of proximal growth plate (scale c 1:1)

overall and for each age range. In total, 6.8% of individuals (364/5387) had suffered multiple injuries (Table 89; Table 90).

In period 17 there was a significant increase in the percentage of adults with multiple injuries. This mirrored the

Table 89 Injuries in sexed adults by age

	Single injury			Multiple injuries			No injuries			Number of individuals		
Age (years)	Female	Male	Total	Female	Male	Total	Female	Male	Total	Female	Male	Total
18–25	31	68	99	5	20	25	392	393	785	428	481	909
26–35	126	172	298	38	64	102	552	516	1068	716	752	1468
36–45	88	174	262	39	116	155	340	410	750	467	700	1167
≥46	45	53	98	20	37	57	146	132	278	211	222	433
Adult	12	14	26	0	8	8	49	60	109	61	82	143
Total	302	481	783	102	245	347	1479	1511	2990	1883	2237	4120

Results

Table 90 Crude prevalence rate of multiple injury by age and sex

Age (years)	Female No.	Affected	%	Male No.	Affected	%	χ^2 df = 1
18–25	428	5	1.2	481	20	4.2	7.57, $p \leq 0.01$
26–35	716	38	5.3	752	64	8.5	5.82, $p \leq 0.025$
36–45	467	39	8.4	700	116	16.6	16.43, $p \leq 0.001$
≥46	211	20	9.5	222	37	16.7	4.89, $p \leq 0.05$
Adult	61	0	-	82	8	9.8	-
Total	1883	102	5.4	2237	245	11.0	40.61, $p \leq 0.001$

increase in fracture crude prevalence over the same time period, and was evident in both burial types (ABC: period 16 86/1183: 7.3%; period 17 51/431: 11.8%; χ^2 = 8.47, df = 1, $p \leq 0.01$; D: period 16 87/1144: 7.6%; period 17 14/95: 14.7%; χ^2 = 5.96, df = 1, $p \leq 0.025$). More individuals suffered fractures and multiple injuries in period 17 (Fig 121).

A greater percentage of females with multiple injuries (69/102: 67.6%) suffered long bone injuries when compared to males (127/245: 51.8%) (χ^2 = 7.32, df = 1, $p \leq 0.001$) (Fig 122). In contrast, males exhibited higher levels of spinal fractures, especially from 18 to 35 years of age (female 9/43: 20.9%, male 33/84: 39.3%; χ^2 = 4.33, df = 1, $p \leq 0.05$) (Fig 123).

Skull involvement in females with multiple injuries (21/102: 20.6%) was similar to that of males (51/245: 20.8%). This was not the case with overall skull fracture crude or true prevalence rates, and suggests that females with multiple injuries (unlike those with single injuries) were as likely to have skull fractures as males.

Zonal fracture distribution

This analysis studied the relative frequency of fracture in different areas of the skeleton: the skull, ribs, spine, arms, hands, legs and feet. This method was employed as a tool for observing possible variations in the bodily distribution of injury by age, sex and period. Fractures from the scapulae and clavicles were included in the arms, those in the sternum were added to the ribs, and fractures in the os coxae were grouped with the legs (Fig 124). For the purposes of this study, teeth were not included in the count, as they may have artificially increased the skull rate (13/51:

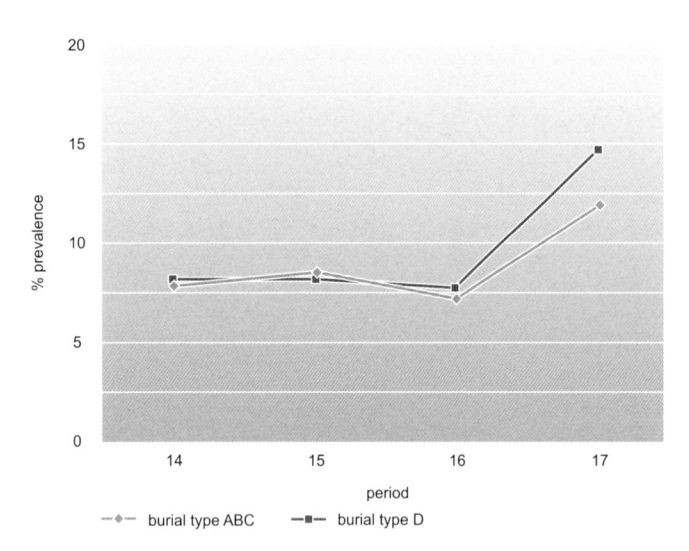

Fig 121 Adults with multiple injuries by period and burial type

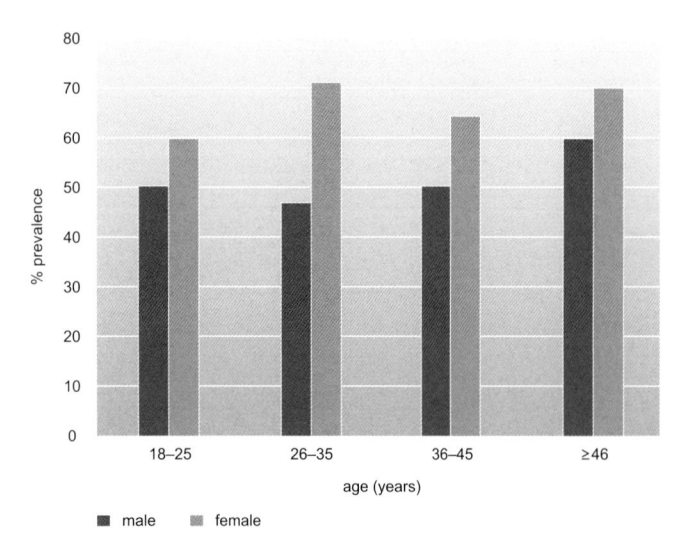

Fig 122 Proportion of individuals with multiple injuries including long bone involvement, by sex and age group

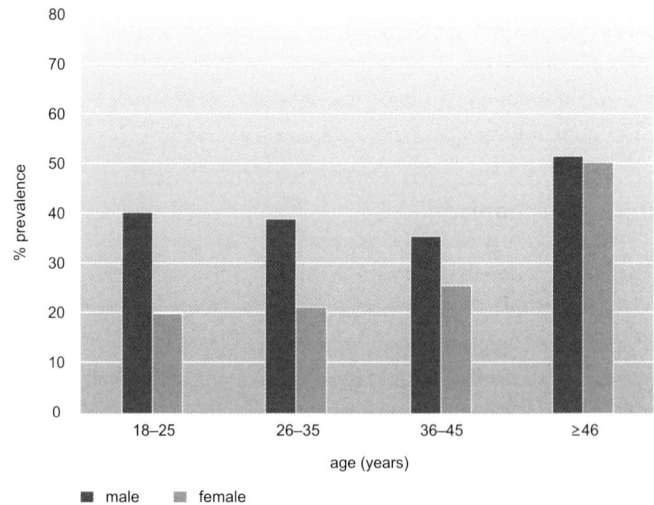

Fig 123 Proportion of individuals with multiple injuries including spinal involvement, by sex and age group

25.5% of individuals with dental fractures also had skull fractures, and multiple dental fractures were common).

When analysed by period, a number of trends were identified. These included a rise in the relative frequency of rib fractures throughout the study period (period 14 34/201: 16.9%; period 17 124/377: 33.0%; $\chi^2 = 17.00$, df = 1, $p \leq 0.001$). The opposite trend was found in the spine, where the relative frequency of vertebral fracture fell (period 14 68/206: 33.0; period 17 83/377: 22.0; $\chi^2 = 8.39$, df = 1, $p \leq 0.01$). The high relative frequency of foot fracture in period 14 resulted from an anomalous increase caused by feet with multiple fractures (Fig 125).

When the distribution of fractures was studied by sex, females were found to have a greater relative frequency of arm fracture (172/698: 24.6%) than males (245/1486: 16.5%) ($\chi^2 = 20.44$, df = 1, $p \leq 0.001$), and therefore had a higher proportion of arm fractures relative to fractures in other areas of the skeleton. The same was true of fractures in the legs, where females had a higher relative frequency (88/698: 12.6%) than males (117/1486: 7.9%) ($\chi^2 = 12.51$, df = 1, $p \leq 0.001$). By contrast, there was a higher relative fracture frequency of ribs in males (439/1486: 29.5%) than females (162/698: 23.2%) ($\chi^2 = 9.55$, df = 1, $p \leq 0.01$) (Fig 126).

In period 15 females, there was a higher relative fracture frequency in the ribs of the sample from burial type ABC (17/57: 29.8%) than in those from burial type D (17/121: 14.0%) ($\chi^2 = 6.23$, df = 1, $p \leq 0.025$). The same was true of period 16 (ABC 54/170: 31.8%; D 35/177: 19.8%; $\chi^2 = 6.54$, df = 1, $p \leq 0.025$). In period 16, there was an greater proportion of female arm fractures relative to the remainder of the skeleton in burial type D (55/177: 31.1%) than in burial type ABC (36/170: 21.2%) ($\chi^2 = 4.39$, df = 1, $p \leq 0.05$). When periods 15 and 16 were combined, there were statistically significant increases in the proportion of female skull and arm fractures in burial type D and in the proportion of female rib and hand fractures in burial type ABC (Fig 127; Fig 128).

In period 16, there was a higher proportion of male vertebral fractures in burial type D (80/325: 24.6%) than in type ABC (73/438: 16.7%) ($\chi^2 = 7.35$, df = 1, $p \leq 0.01$).

The relative frequency of fractures in subadults was at least partially a product of the low overall number of identified fractures. The results were probably also influenced by varying macroscopic survival of different fracture types in subadult and adult bone following remodelling (Fig 129).

Injury mechanism

The most commonly identified fracture type was oblique (180/297: 60.6% of recorded fracture types), followed by transverse (63/297: 21.2%). This suggests that most fractures were due to indirect force. Together, oblique and transverse fractures made up 81.8% (243/297) of recorded fracture types (Fig 130).

This section only includes fractures where the mechanism of injury could be identified. Many fractures had more than one possible mechanism, and where this occurred the fracture was included in all possible groups. Of identified fractures, 31.8% (277/870) resulted from direct force, 38.2% (332/870) from falls on to the forearm, elbow or hand, and 22.3% (194/870) from falls on to an outstretched hand (FOOSH) alone. A total of 14.7% (128/870) resulted from twisting and torsion of the lower

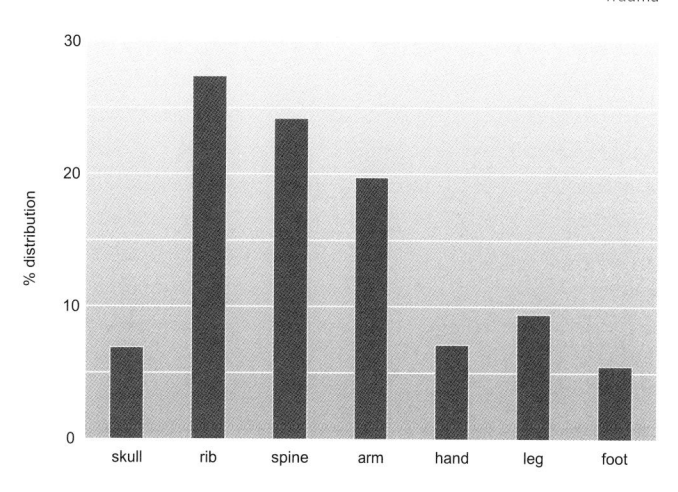

Fig 124 Distribution of adult fractures by zone

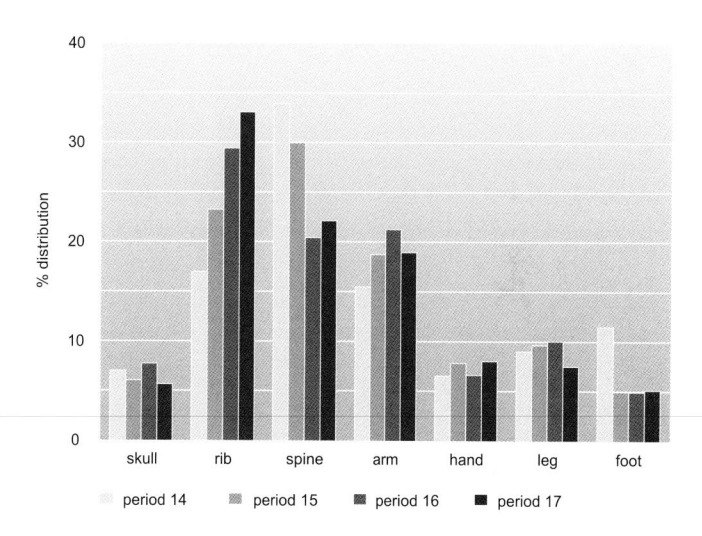

Fig 125 Distribution of adult fractures by period

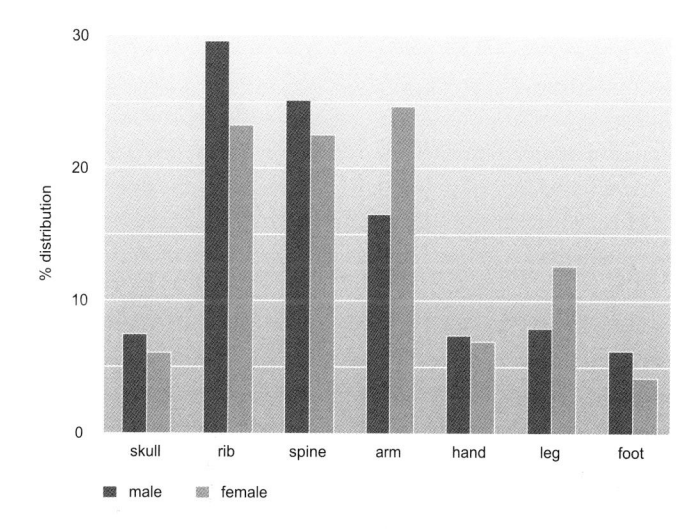

Fig 126 Distribution of adult fractures by sex

Results

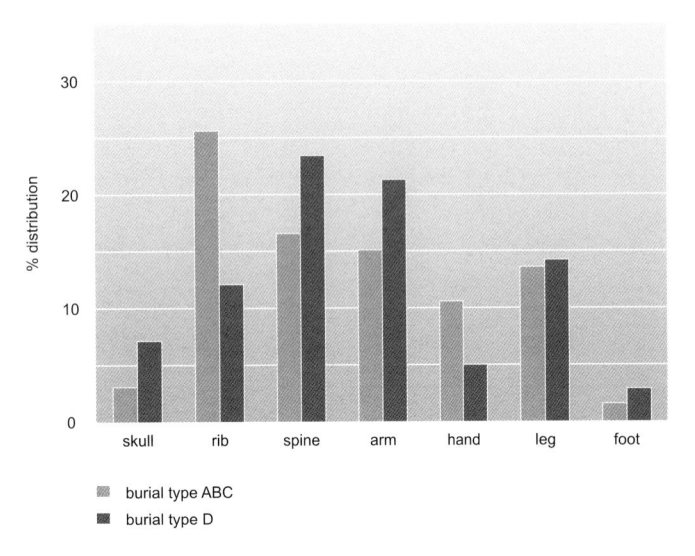

Fig 127 Female fracture distribution by burial type in period 15

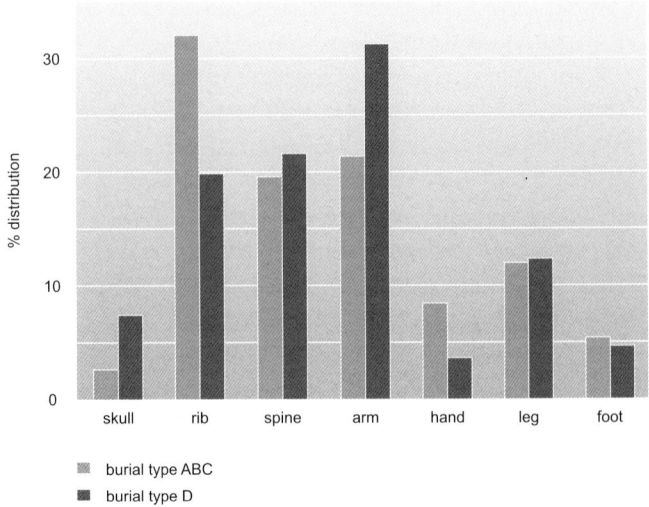

Fig 128 Female fracture distribution by burial type in period 16

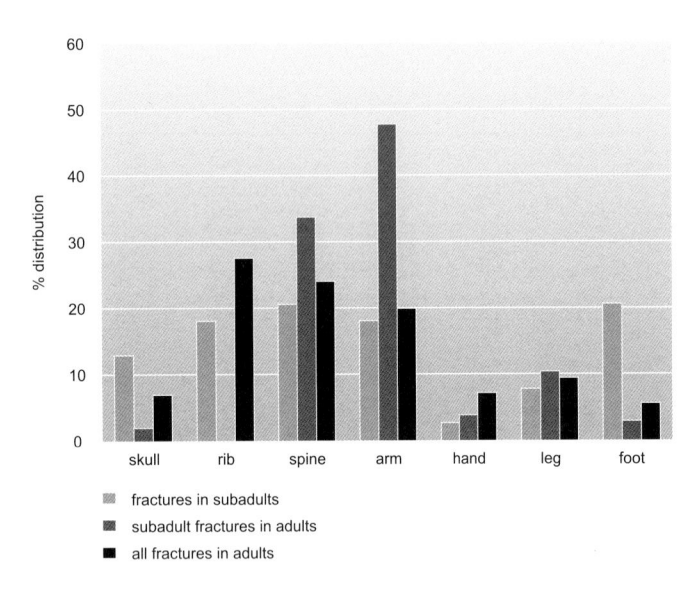

Fig 129 Distribution of adult and subadult fractures

Fig 130 Long bone shaft fracture type

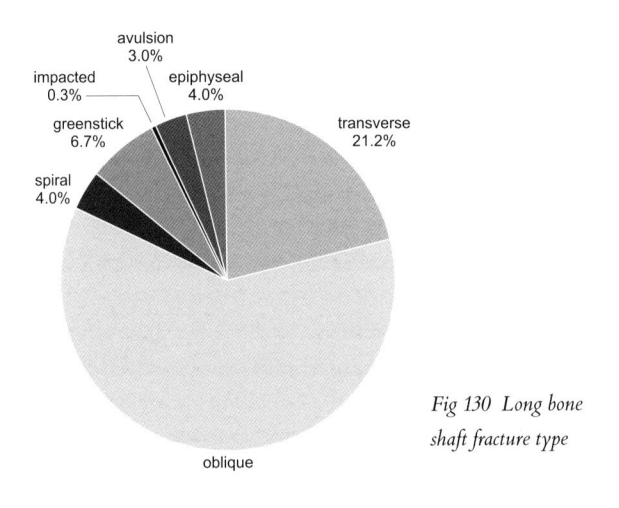

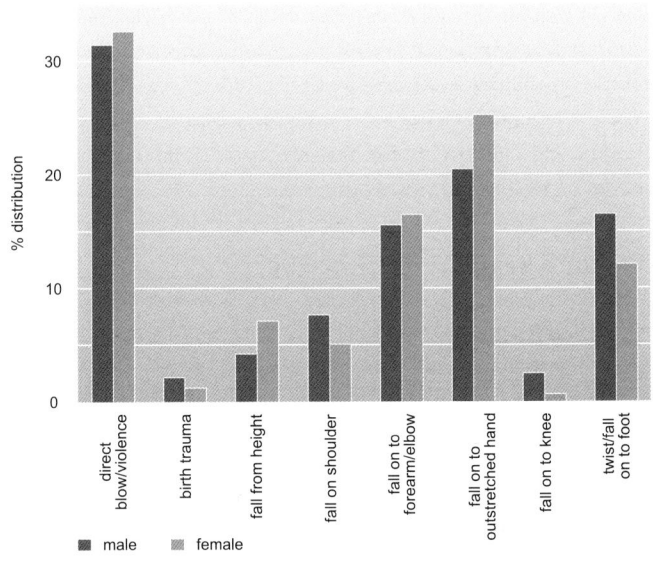

Fig 131 Distribution of identified injury mechanism

limb or from a fall on to a foot. There was no overall variation by sex (Fig 131).

In total, 46.4% (123/265) of direct blows to the post-cranial skeleton occurred in the forearm. As a percentage of direct force fractures, females were more often affected in the forearm (61/111: 55.0%) than males (70/164: 42.7%) (Fig 132).

Seventeen (17/157: 10.8%) individuals with skull fractures displayed evidence of direct ulna shaft fracture, compared to 12.4% (120/968) of individuals without skull fractures. Transverse fractures were more common in female ulna shafts (30/3035: 1.0%) than in male (15/3576: 0.4%) ($\chi^2 = 7.86$, df = 1, $p \leq 0.01$). When male and female fractures were combined, the left side was far more frequently affected (37/3297: 1.1%) than the right (8/3314: 0.2%) ($\chi^2 = 18.97$, df = 1, $p \leq 0.001$). In addition, a larger percentage of total female bone fractures were attributed to direct ulna shaft fractures (48/732: 6.6%) when compared to male bone fractures (60/1538: 3.9%) ($\chi^2 = 7.72$, df = 1, $p \leq 0.01$).

When analysed by period, the frequency of direct ulna shaft fracture in females was higher than in males in period 16

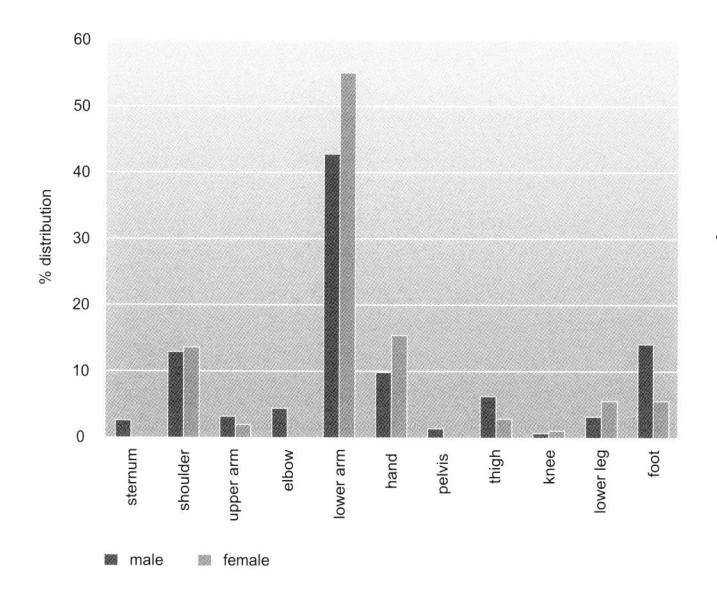

Fig 132 Distribution of direct force injuries

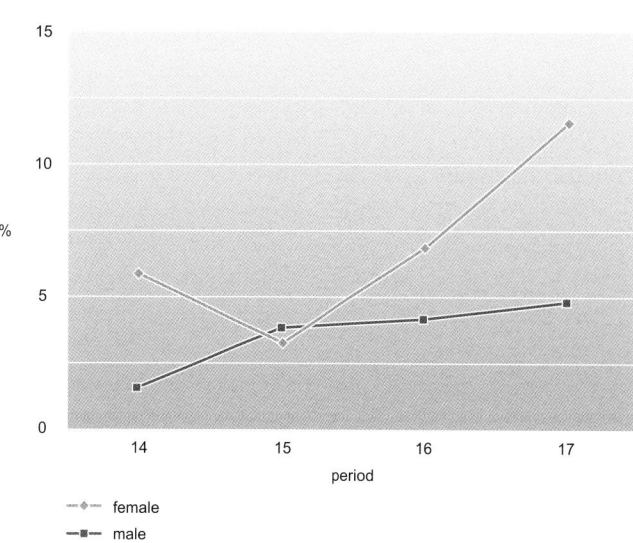

Fig 133 Frequency of direct ulna shaft fractures as a percentage of bone fractures

(female 25/367: 6.8%; male 32/785: 4.1%; χ^2 = 3.98, df = 1, p ≤ 0.05) and period 17 (female 13/113: 11.5%; male 12/248: 4.8%; χ^2 = 5.35, df = 1, p ≤ 0.025). There was no difference in period 15, and in period 14 the sample size was too small to test. The female rate rose significantly from period 15 to 17 (period 15 6/184: 3.3%; period 17 13/113: 11.5%; χ^2 = 7.94, df = 1, p ≤ 0.01) (Fig 133).

When female direct ulna shaft fractures were examined by both period and burial type, the evidence suggested that burial type D largely accounted for the fall in female prevalence from period 14 to 15, and the rise from period 15 to 17. In period 16, females from burial type D (19/186: 10.2%) were found to have a significantly higher frequency of fracture than those from burial type ABC (6/181: 3.3%) (χ^2 = 6.88, df = 1, p ≤ 0.01). This also appeared to be the case in periods 14 and 17, but the data were too few to test. It was therefore the females in burial type D that were causing the sex differences. Period 15 was the exception to this rule, with equal male and female prevalence, and no variation between the females in the two burial types (Fig 134).

Fracture healing and treatment

Unhealed fractures

This section includes fractures where the bone was still in the process of healing at the time of death. This was irrespective of union or non-union. Out of a total of 2394 fractured bones, 101 (4.2%) were still in the process of healing at the time of death. Scapulae (8/8196: 0.1%) were most often affected, followed by ribs (52/87,059: 0.1%). Males were more frequently affected than females, though not to a statistically significant extent (Table 91).

Females with fractures died during healing more frequently than males, though not to a statistically significant extent (Table 92). This was most evident in the ≥46 age range (females 5/61:

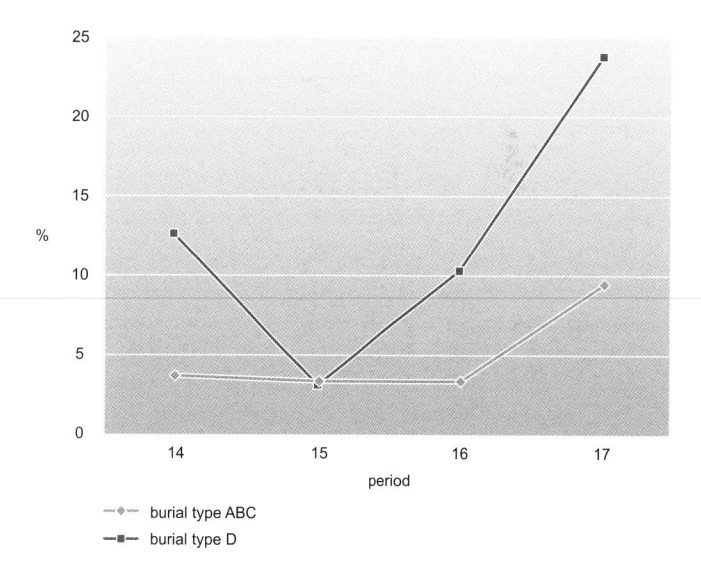

Fig 134 Frequency of female direct ulna shaft fractures by period and burial type, as a percentage of bone fractures

Table 91 Individuals with unhealed fractures

	No.	Affected	%
All individuals	5387	64	1.2
Female	1883	24	1.3
Male	2237	35	1.6

Table 92 Individuals with unhealed fractures as a proportion of those with fractures

	No. with fractures	No. with unhealed fractures	%
Total	1125	64	5.7
Female	375	24	6.4
Male	675	35	5.2

Results

8.2%; males 1/85: 1.2%). It is possible that older adult females who suffered fractures were more likely than males to die before their fractures had healed. However, the absence of fractures in the wrists, hips and spines of the five affected females suggests that this was not related to osteoporosis.

Of 64 individuals with unhealed fractures at death, 26 (40.6%) had rib fractures. This may have been due to the life-threatening nature of soft tissue injuries associated with breach of the rib cage. The scapula, often associated with rib fractures, was the second most frequently involved bone (8/64: 12.5%).

Fractures to the cranium are often associated with unhealed or peri-mortem injuries, but not at St Mary Spital. Only three individuals (3/5387: 0.1%) were identified with unhealed cranial fractures, two female (2/1883: 0.1%) and one male (1/2237: <0.1%).

Fracture complications

The calculation of true prevalence rates of long bone fractures leading to complications and other post-traumatic effects incorporated deformity, non-union, osteoarthritis, infection, nerve damage and avascular necrosis. In the case of osteoarthritis, lesions were only recorded as being as a result of fracture complication when they were isolated to the adjacent joints of the affected bone. Individuals with generalised osteoarthritis were not included. The same principle applied to infection, which was recorded as a complication when it was isolated to the area of fracture. The tibia was the bone most affected by fracture-related complications; the ulna and fibula were the least affected. More female fractured tibiae were affected by complications (16/38: 42.1%) than those of males (6/39: 15.4%) (χ^2 = 6.73, df = 1, p ≤ 0.01) (Table 93).

Fracture deformity was measured in long bones only, and therefore, solely for the purpose of the calculation of complications by total number of fractured bones, deformity was excluded from the analysis (Table 94). Males and females were equally affected (Table 95).

The ulna was the long bone with the highest prevalence of non-union (16/172: 9.3%). The other long bones affected were the radius (3/119: 2.5%) and the tibia (1/81: 1.2%).

The analysis of secondary infection revealed that the tibia (10/81: 12.3%) was the most commonly affected long bone, for both periostitis (6/81: 7.4%) and osteomyelitis (4/81: 4.9%), though not to a statistically significant extent.

Osteoarthritis can develop in the joints of malaligned healed bones due to repetitive irregular function. The damaged bone can change the forces acting through a joint by influencing the relative biomechanical actions of the musculature surrounding it. This may result in irregular movement in at least one of the associated joints which, over a period of time, can lead to the development of joint disease, and occasionally to ankylosis (Lovell 1997, 147). At St Mary Spital, 2.9% (70/2394) of all fractured bones were affected by osteoarthritis which appeared to be secondary to injury, rather than the result of a specific joint disease before the injury. The most commonly affected long bones were the radius (13/119: 10.9%) and the humerus

Table 93 Long bone fractures with complications

	No.	Complications	%
Humerus	74	17	23.0
Radius	119	27	22.7
Ulna	172	27	15.7
Femur	23	5	21.7
Tibia	81	23	28.4
Fibula	81	6	7.4
Total	550	105	19.1

Table 94 Complications as a percentage of all fractured bones (n = 2394)

Complication	Elements with complications	%
Osteoarthritis	70	2.9
Non-union	79	3.3
Infection	28	1.2
Avascular necrosis	4	0.2
Nerve damage	5	0.2

Table 95 Complications as a percentage of all fractured bones by sex

Complication	Female (n = 732) Affected	%	Male (n = 1538) Affected	%
Osteoarthritis	20	2.7	46	3.0
Non-union	25	3.4	53	3.4
Infection	8	1.1	17	1.1
Avascular necrosis	2	0.3	2	0.1
Nerve damage	2	0.3	3	0.2

(7/74: 9.5%). These data reflect the low rate of unsuccessful healing within the burial sample.

Long bone deformity

Where radiographs were taken of long bones (humerus, radius, ulna, femur, tibia and fibula) (Chapter 2.2), measurements of linear deformity, overlap and apposition were recorded following Grauer and Roberts (1996). This method allowed the type and deformity of each fracture to be accurately assessed, without being hampered by macroscopic remodelling of the bone surface. Some bones were subjected to both antero-posterior and medio-lateral inspection, but the majority were only radiographed in a single view. Unfortunately, the results tell us little about the rate of success of fracture healing, as the bones recorded were radiographed on the basis of 'suspected fracture'. By their very nature, these examples were likely to show little deformity when compared to those bones that did not require radiographic diagnosis because they were obviously fractured. For example, mid- or distal shaft fractures of the ulna were rarely deformed to any great degree and, as a result, these

Table 96 Radiographic analysis of fractured long bones

Context	Bone	Segment	Fracture type	Linear angle	Overlap (mm)	Apposition (%)
[2586]	right ulna	middle	spiral	5° lateral	35	-
[3027]	right ulna	distal	transverse	10° medial	-	70
[3790]	right ulna	distal	unknown	10° medial	-	100
[5082]	right clavicle	middle	oblique	15° posterior	41	-
[6629]	right clavicle	middle	spiral	-	10	<50
[6721]	left tibia	distal	oblique	30° posterior	20	-
[6775]	right ulna	distal	transverse	10° posterior	-	50
[6775]	left radius	proximal	transverse	20° anterior	-	-
[6775]	left ulna	middle	transverse	5° medial	-	50
[6775]	left ulna	distal	transverse	5° lateral	5	-
[9579]	left radius	distal	transverse	20° lateral	10	60
[11291]	left radius	distal	transverse	20° lateral	15	-
[20112]	left ulna	distal	unknown	-	-	100
[21522]	left ulna	distal	oblique	-	14	75
[21593]	left ulna	middle	transverse	-	-	100
[23245]	right ulna	distal	unknown	5° posterior	-	100
[24030]	right clavicle	distal	unknown	30° posterior	21	100
[24185]	right ulna	distal	transverse	10° medial	-	80
[26580]	right radius	middle	transverse	25° medial	-	100
[27202]	right radius	middle	greenstick	20° medial	-	100
[27375]	right tibia	distal	unknown	5° medial	-	100
[29673]	right radius	middle	unknown	10° lateral	-	100
[30761]	right radius	middle	oblique	-	10	75
[30971]	left ulna	distal	transverse	5° posterior	-	100
[31639]	right ulna	distal	transverse	15° medial	-	75
[32480]	right ulna	distal	unknown	5° medial	-	100

were commonly radiographed in order to determine whether there was a true fracture line (Table 96).

All healed and united long bone fractures were assessed macroscopically to determine the presence and extent of linear and rotational deformity, overlap and apposition. This allowed the calculation of deformity rates for each bone. In order to assess the possible clinical significance of the results, they were compared with Roberts's model for successful and unsuccessful healing on radiographs (Grauer and Roberts 1996, 535). This involved the comparison of the data from each fracture with the tabulated figures representing unsuccessful healing in each long bone. For example, in the tibia healing was deemed to be unsuccessful if there was more than 15° linear deformity or more than 10mm overlap (ibid).

Out of a total of 550 long bone fractures, 279 (50.7%) were left with some degree of macroscopic deformity on the bone.

Table 97 Long bone fracture healing

	No. fractures	Deformity	%	Unsuccessful healing	%
Humerus	74	36	48.6	6	8.1
Radius	119	82	68.9	9	7.6
Ulna	172	75	43.6	6	3.5
Femur	23	17	73.9	4	17.4
Tibia	81	38	46.9	17	21.0
Fibula	81	31	38.3	5	6.2
Total	550	279	50.7	47	8.5

Only 47/550 (8.5%) were considered to have healed unsuccessfully (Grauer and Roberts 1996). The relatively high prevalence in the femur and tibia may have resulted in part from strong muscle contraction in the femur leading to problems for reduction of the fracture, and in part to walking before the fracture had fully healed. The ulna and fibula were least affected, perhaps due to the paired nature of bones in the lower arms and legs, where the radius and tibia respectively would act as natural splints (Table 97).

Females (127/235: 54.0%) and males (130/276: 47.1%) had similar rates of deformity, but a greater percentage of long bone fractures were judged to have healed unsuccessfully in females (29/235: 12.3%) than in males (14/276: 5.1%) (χ^2 = 8.70, df = 1, p ≤ 0.01). While approximately half of male and female fractured long bones were vulnerable to some deformity, female bones were more likely to be left with clinically significant deformity. None of the individual bones showed significant differences, although the results revealed higher rates of unsuccessful healing in female tibiae, fibulae and radii (Table 98; Table 99).

Female and male rates of unsuccessful healing were similar in period 14. In the other periods females rates were higher, though only period 16 had enough data to test the significance of difference (female 16/118: 13.6%; male 8/156: 5.1%; χ^2 = 5.97, df = 1, p ≤ 0.025). Treatment may have improved more for males than for females over time. The foundation of hospitals may or may not have contributed to an improvement in standards of fracture treatment. There was no evidence of variation by burial type.

Results

Table 98 Female long bone fracture healing

	No. fractures	Deformity	%	Unsuccessful healing	%
Humerus	19	12	63.2	2	10.5
Radius	56	39	69.6	6	10.7
Ulna	76	37	48.7	3	3.9
Femur	6	4	66.7	1	16.7
Tibia	38	22	57.9	14	36.8
Fibula	40	13	32.5	3	7.5
Total	235	127	54.0	29	12.3

Table 99 Male long bone fracture healing

	No. fractures	Deformity	%	Unsuccessful healing	%
Humerus	44	18	40.9	4	9.1
Radius	57	40	70.2	2	3.5
Ulna	83	32	38.6	2	2.4
Femur	14	10	71.4	2	14.3
Tibia	39	13	33.3	3	7.7
Fibula	39	17	43.6	1	2.6
Total	276	130	47.1	14	5.1

Soft tissue injuries

Males were more often affected by soft tissue injuries than females ($\chi^2 = 19.27$, df = 1, $p \leq 0.001$) (Table 100). Male rates were higher than female rates throughout adulthood, and in the 36–45 year age category they were significantly so (female 9/467: 1.9%; male 49/700: 7.0%; $\chi^2 = 15.26$, df = 1, $p \leq 0.001$) (Fig 135).

Table 100 Crude prevalence of soft tissue injury by sex

	No.	Affected	%
All individuals	5387	140	2.6
Females	1883	36	1.9
Males	2237	97	4.3
Subadults	1027	3	0.3

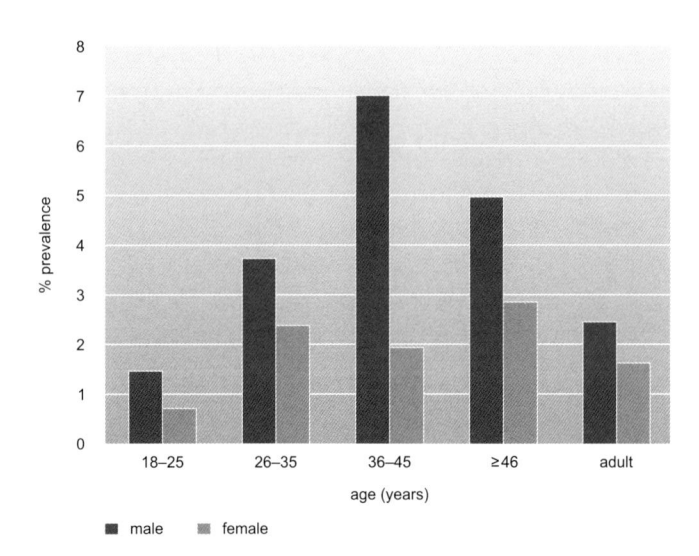

Fig 135 Crude prevalence of soft tissue injury by sex and age group

Table 101 Crude prevalence of dislocation by sex

	No.	Affected	%
All individuals	5387	54	1.0
Female	1883	19	1.0
Male	2237	32	1.4

Soft tissue calcification

Most soft tissue calcifications took the form of enthesopathic spurring at the site of tendon and ligament attachments, or around joint capsules (134/149: 89.9%). The remainder were due to myositis ossificans (8), ossified haematomas (6) and calcified lung tissue (1).

Dislocation

Males were more frequently affected by joint dislocation, though not to a statistically significant extent (Table 101). Fifty-eight dislocations were identified (Fig 136). Where true prevalence could be calculated, the most commonly affected joints were the fifth sacral to first coccygeal vertebrae (6/2691: 0.2%), the glenohumeral (12/8230: 0.1%) and the temporomandibular (10/7804: 0.1%). There was no significant variation by sex, age or period.

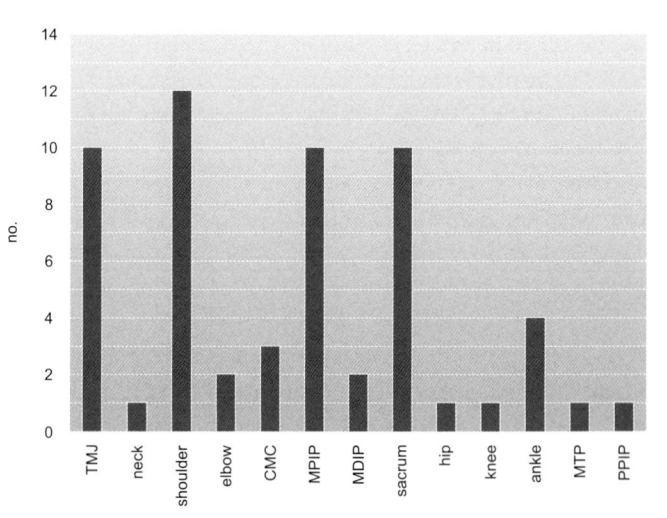

Fig 136 Frequency of dislocation by element or joint (TMJ = temporomandibular joint, CMC = carpo-metacarpal, MPIP = manual proximal interphalangeal, MDIP = manual distal interphalangeal, MTP = metatarso-phalangeal, PPIP = pedal proximal interphalangeal)

3.9 Infectious disease

Brian Connell, Amy Gray Jones, Rebecca Redfern and Don Walker

Infectious diseases represent one of most serious threats to health in urban communities. Broadly speaking, infectious disease can be classified into two groups. A specific infection is one where the bony changes observed are characteristic of one particular type of pathogenic organism, which in palaeopathological contexts usually refers to treponemal disease (eg venereal syphilis) or mycobacterial disease (eg tuberculosis and leprosy), while a non-specific infection is one where the lesions are common to a wide variety of pathogens.

Non-specific infection

Osteomyelitis and osteitis

Osteomyelitis is a non-specific infection caused by bacteria entering the body from a penetrating injury, a primary focus of infection, or trauma. The bacteria spread throughout the body via the bloodstream, and eventually destroy the inside of the bone and cause pus to be discharged into the surrounding tissue (Roberts and Manchester 2005, 168–72).

Given the size of the sample there were very few cases of osteomyelitis, in just 30 individuals (30/5387: 0.6%). No meaningful patterns were seen through the different periods of cemetery use; both subadults and adults are affected and both sexes. More males were affected in periods 15 and 16 in burial type D, but overall the difference in frequency between the two major burial types (ABC and D) was not significant ($\chi^2 = 0.83$, df = 1, $p \geq 0.05$).

There were slightly more cases of osteitis – a total of 50 (50/5387: 0.9%) were identified across periods 14–17. Both males and females were equally affected.

Not included in these figures are cases of sclerosing osteomyelitis of Garré. This particular form of osteomyelitis was identified in two males aged 36–45 years, the first case ([20825]) involving the right tibia and fibula and the second case the right femur ([34084]). The bones were expanded and covered in irregular sheets of sclerotic bone. Sclerotic and fusiform thickening is recognised as the predominant feature in this condition (Aufderheide and Rodríguez-Martín 1998, 178).

Periostitis

Periostitis is the result of a low-grade inflammatory response that causes the osteogenic layer of the periosteum to lay down new bone on the underlying cortex. This may result from infection by common bacteria (eg *Staphylococcus* or *Streptococcus* spp), systemic disease or minor trauma, and many consider it as a non-specific stress indicator. Periostitis is frequently seen in archaeological populations, particularly in the lower limbs.

Overall, there was a crude prevalence rate of 22.4% (1204/5387), just under a quarter of the total population. Both adults and subadults were affected, with a higher frequency of males and females affected in burial type ABC in periods 15 and 16 (Fig 137). Only in period 16 was this statistically significant ($\chi^2 = 6.46$, df = 3, $p \leq 0.05$). The distribution within the skeleton is predominantly in the lower limbs, and two-thirds (67.7%) of all cases were seen in the tibiae or fibulae. Overall, significantly higher frequencies of periostitis were found in burial type ABC than in burial type D ($\chi^2 = 19.7$, df = 1, $p \leq 0.001$).

Considering periostitis as a non-specific stress indicator (discussed further in Chapter 3.10 and Chapter 4.1), the result follows the same pattern as enamel hypoplasia in showing a higher frequency in burial type ABC. Again, this is probably a product of the population represented by this group being more strongly affected by selective mortality than that within burial type D.

Bone formative responses on the visceral surfaces of ribs are caused by inflammatory conditions in the lungs and pleural sacs. It has been suggested that periosteal lesions on visceral rib surfaces are indicative of pulmonary disease. Roberts (2000b, 152) has highlighted the need to consider the frequency of periostitis on rib surfaces as a possible indicator of pulmonary tuberculosis, pneumonia, cancer and bronchitis. Furthermore, studies on documented skeletal samples have demonstrated a correlation between the presence of rib lesions and those known to have died from tuberculosis (Roberts et al 1994; Kelley and Micozzi 1984). At present, there is some difficulty in verifying a direct relationship (Roberts et al 1998, 57) and the aetiology of periosteal rib lesions remains uncertain. Pfeiffer (1991, 197) suggested that rib lesions of this type are best interpreted as non-specific inflammatory periostitis. More recently Mays et al (2002b) have failed to find a direct correlation between the presence of these lesions and aDNA of *Mycobacterium tuberculosis*, but a non-correlation does not necessarily mean the person did not have tuberculosis.

Higher frequencies of rib lesions were observed in burial type ABC compared to burial type D ($\chi^2 = 6.45$, df = 1, $p \leq 0.05$). This compares well with the results for periostitis in general and is further evidence of selective mortality operating in burial type ABC. Subadults were affected more than adults in periods 14 and 15 and also more in burial type ABC.

Sinusitis

Maxillary sinusitis can be attributed to air pollution, although other factors such as congenital predisposition or a systemic susceptibility have been noted (Lewis et al 1995, 498). Sinusitis affected 89 individuals from across all four periods (Table 102). More females were affected than males ($\chi^2 = 4.55$, df = 1, $p \leq 0.05$).

There was little overall difference in frequencies between burial types ABC (48/2538: 1.9%) and D (41/2461: 1.7%) (Table 103). Period 16 saw the widest distribution among the population (in both burial types), with sinusitis more common in older age groups in both males and females (Fig 138). These data are only a crude indication of prevalence: the sinuses could not be systematically examined as there were a large

Results

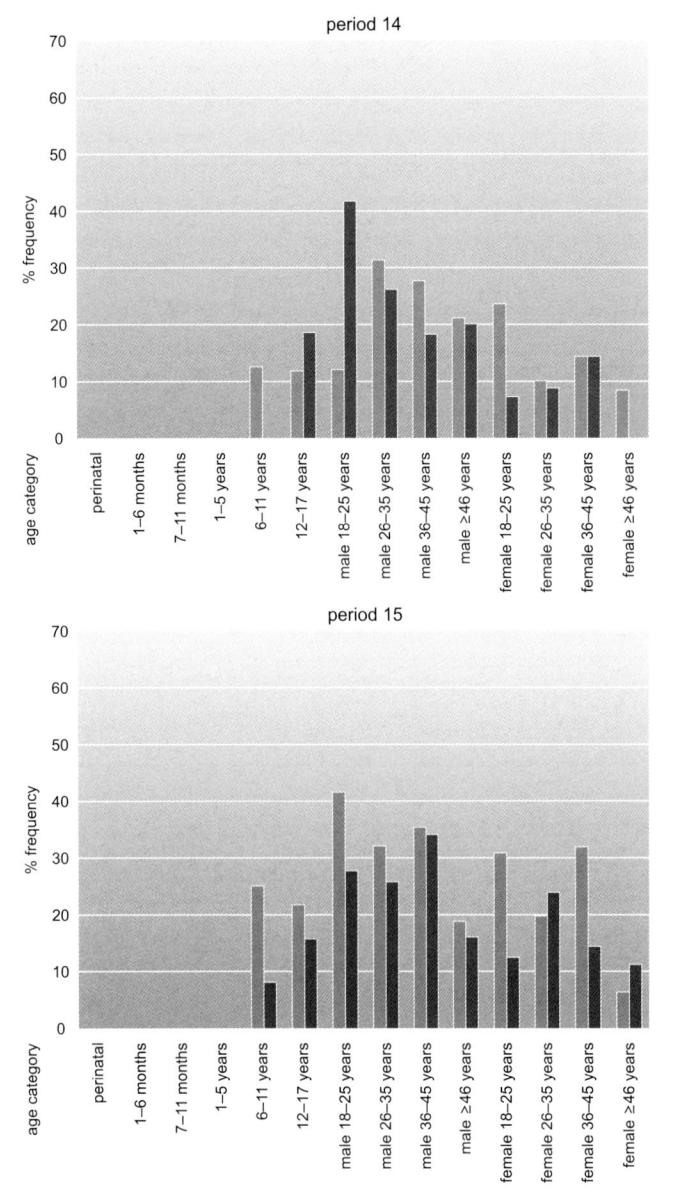

Fig 137 Comparison of frequency distribution of periostitis between burial types

Table 102 Crude prevalence rate of sinusitis by sex

	No. individuals	Affected	%
All individuals	5387	89	1.7
Female	1883	47	2.5
Male	2237	35	1.6

Table 103 Distribution of sinusitis by period and burial type

	Burial type ABC			Burial type D		
Period	No. individuals	No. affected	%	No. individuals	No. affected	%
14	315	4	1.3	158	0	–
15	474	16	3.4	832	14	1.7
16	1260	22	1.7	1353	25	1.8
17	489	6	1.2	118	2	1.7
Total	2538	48	1.9	2461	41	1.7

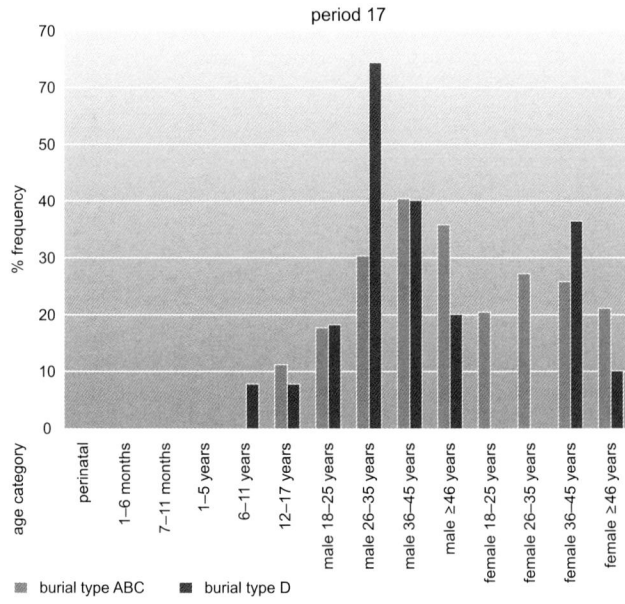

number of intact skulls.

A particularly severe example of chronic inflammation of the frontal sinuses was evident on the ectocranial glabella of 12–17-year-old [3263] from period 15, burial type D. A well-defined symmetrical expansion of bone projected from the area between the orbits, immediately superior to the nasal bones. The outer table swelled anteriorly, increasing the volume of both frontal sinuses. Four well-defined, smooth-edged perforations

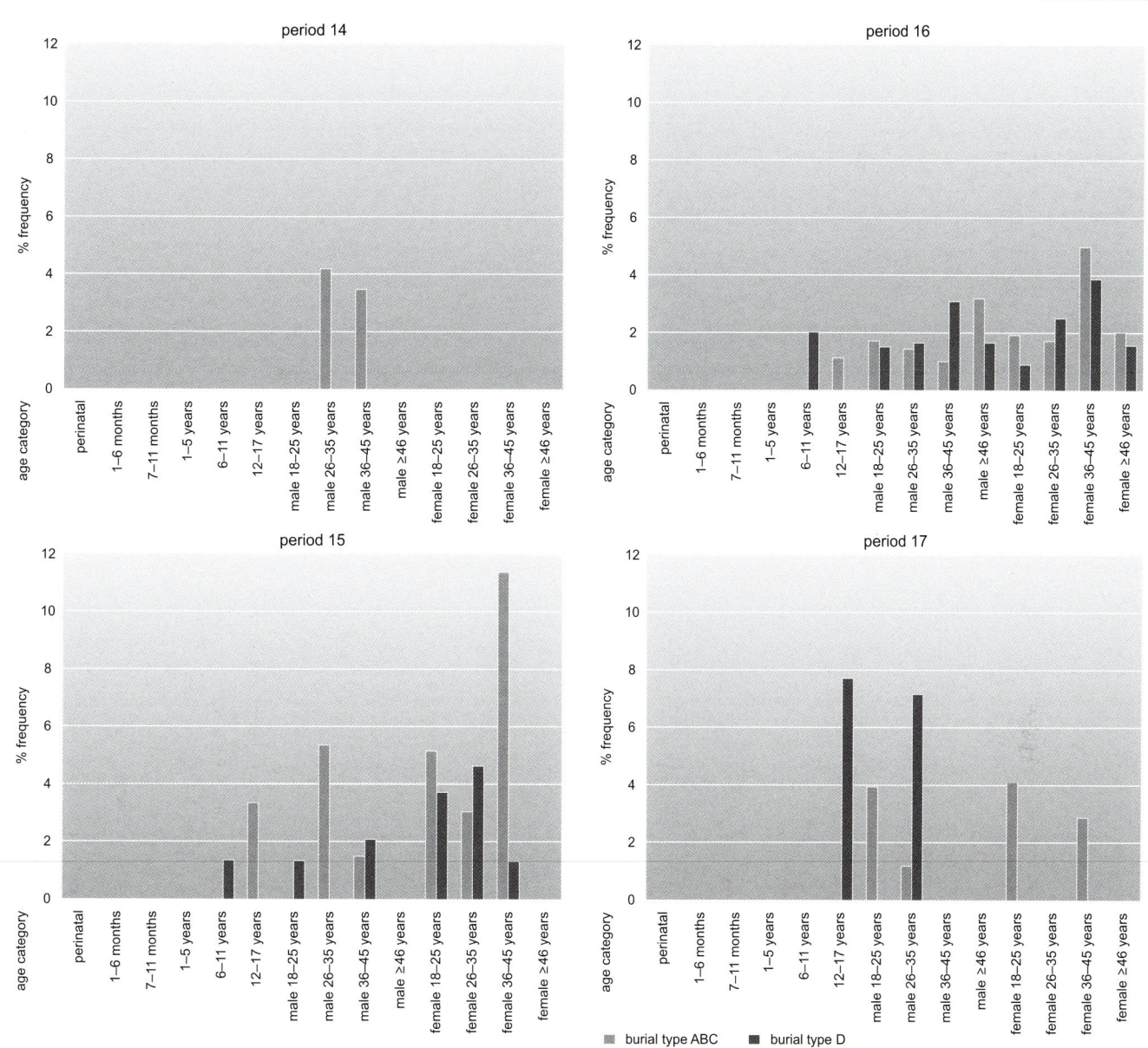

Fig 138 Comparison of frequency distribution of sinusitis between burial types

allowed communication between the ectocranial surface and the internal area of the sinus. They were large enough to allow viewing of an apparently still intact internal partition between the sinuses. The ectocranial surface of the glabella immediately inferior to these lesions was striated by a stellate pattern of small ridges, possibly reflecting the reaction of the *in vivo* bone to the gross swelling. Internal inspection of the frontal sinuses revealed no evidence of new bone growth.

Septic arthropathies

A septic arthropathy arises when a joint capsule becomes infected. This can arise as a result of direct spread from local tissues, haematogenous spread, or by direct implantation such as in a penetrating wound (Rogers and Waldron 1995, 87). Fourteen cases of septic joint changes were found. There were no septic arthropathies discovered in period 14 but four cases in period 15: one male and one probable male with right sacroiliac joint destruction ([23514] and [3645]; Fig 139), and two females

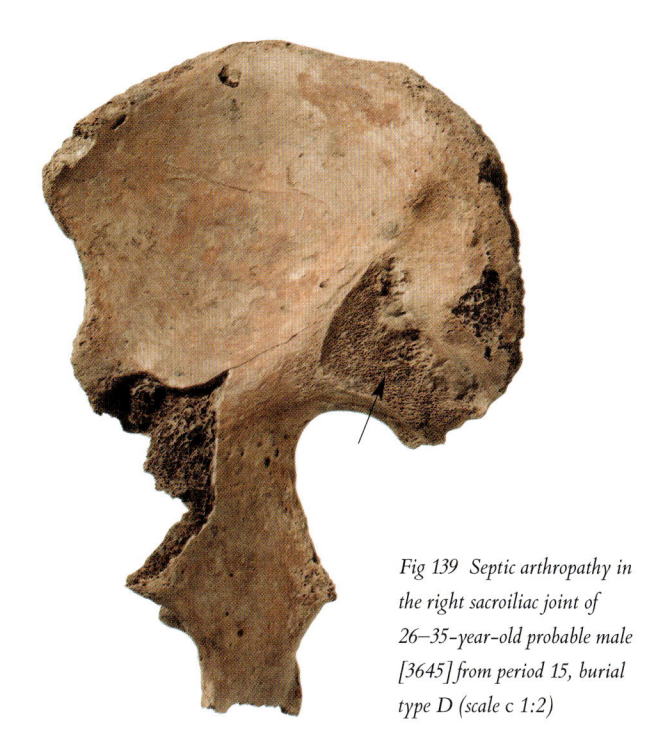

Fig 139 Septic arthropathy in the right sacroiliac joint of 26–35-year-old probable male [3645] from period 15, burial type D (scale c 1:2)

Results

([20988] and [21708]), one with a left sacroiliac joint destroyed and one with a right first metatarsal joint destroyed. All four individuals were from burial type D.

Nine further cases of septic arthropathy were seen in period 16. Interestingly, one was a subadult aged 12–17 years ([20621]) with right sacroiliac joint involvement. The adults consist of five females, all with one or both sacroiliac joints involved ([23675], [5503], [25814], [17459] and [29859]), and three males: [29158] with the left elbow involved, [31701] with the left knee joint involved and [31360] with the right sacroiliac joint involved. The high number of cases of sacroiliac joint involvement in period 16 should be treated warily as tuberculosis appears as a differential diagnosis for many individuals. There was an equal mix of septic arthropathies between burial types ABC and D.

In period 17 there was a single case in the left elbow of female [23567], from burial type ABC.

Specific infection

Leprosy

Two females (<0.1% of the total assemblage) had changes suggestive of tuberculoid leprosy, consisting of pencilling and resorption of the phalanges and metatarsals of the left foot.

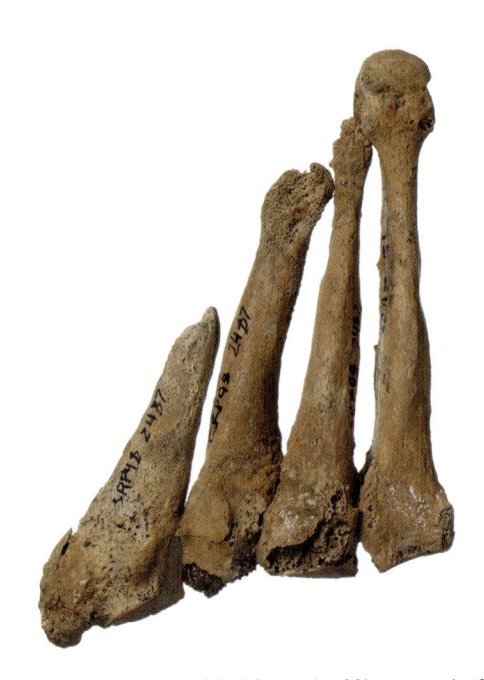

Fig 140 Superior view of the left second to fifth metatarsals of 26–35-year-old female [2487] from period 17, burial type D, with evidence for tuberculoid leprosy (scale c 1:1)

Neither one had rhinomaxillary changes, as is typical of this form of leprosy. This highly resistant form of leprosy is transmitted by skin contact, particularly between family members over a long period of time or by droplet-transfer (Aufderheide and Rodríguez-Martín 1998, 142–55). In period 16, 26–35-year-old female [19821] from burial type ABC (1/177: 0.6%) had destructive changes and achroosteolysis (destruction of the tips of the digits) of the second to fifth metatarsals and proximal phalanx, representing 0.3% of females from both burial types in this age group (1/378) and 0.1% of all females (1/1009) (Table 104). In period 17, 26–35-year-old female [2487] from burial type D (Fig 140) had destructive changes to the third to fifth metatarsal, one foot proximal phalanx, and two hand proximal phalanges, representing 10.0% of the females in this age group and burial type (1/10), 1.4% of the age and sex group for this period (1/69), and 0.5% of all females in period 17 (1/203).

Treponematosis

Treponematosis is defined as a chronic or subacute infection caused by micro-organisms called spirochetes of the genus *Treponema* (Aufderheide and Rodríguez-Martín 1998, 154).

Twenty-five individuals were diagnosed with treponemal disease, 0.5% (25/5387) of the recorded sample (Table 105). Skeletons showing evidence of treponemal infection were buried either as a single burial (23/25: 92%) or in a single layer multiple burial (2/25: 8%), burial type B. No recorded cases of treponematosis were associated with burial type D.

Pivotal to the understanding of this material is the dating, for without firm dating these cases cannot effectively contribute to clarifying bioarchaeological questions about the timing and epidemiology of the disease. Following the detailed stratigraphic analysis of the cemetery, a pilot study was undertaken at MOLA by Nick Holder to establish a general

Table 105 Distribution of treponemal infections by period

	No. affected						
Period	14	15	16	17	All periods	Total	%
Male	0	1	4	6	11	2237	0.5
Intermediate sex	0	0	0	0	0	205	-
Female	0	0	1	7	8	1883	0.4
Subadult	0	0	0	3	3	1027	0.3
Undetermined sex	0	1	0	2	3	35	8.6
Total	0	2	5	18	25	5387	0.5

Table 104 Crude prevalence rate of leprosy by period, sex and burial type

		Burial type ABC			Burial type D		
Period	Sex	No. individuals	No. affected	%	No. individuals	No. affected	%
16	female	474	1	0.2	535	0	-
17	female	164	0	-	39	1	2.6

pattern of grave alignment and burial sequence. The results from this study, which consisted of a provisional cemetery sequence, were then subjected to further, targeted high-precision radiocarbon dating (Chapter 1.1).

The first treponemal cases appear in period 15 (*c* 1200–50) and consist of two 26–35-year-olds, male [20360] and adult [22251] for whom sex could not be established. This gives a crude prevalence rate of 0.1% for period 15 (2/1390). Most significantly, these two cases are the earliest examples of this disease yet discovered in Britain. In period 16 (*c* 1250–*c* 1400) there is an increase in the number of cases. Five adults aged 18–45 years are affected (four males and one female), giving a crude prevalence rate of 0.2% (5/2835). However, it is not until period 17 (*c* 1400–1539) that a significant increase in cases occurs, clearly illustrated in Fig 141. This period contains 18 treponemal cases: six males, seven females, two unsexed adults and three subadults, with a crude prevalence rate of 2.8% (18/650). The three affected subadults were all buried in individual graves (burial type A).

Of the 25 cases of treponemal disease identified in the adult population, eight involved adult females, many of whom were within their childbearing years. If the treponemal disease found in this population during the 15th century is venereal, it follows that cases of congenital syphilis might be present in the subadult population. Congenital syphilis causes fatality in about 50% of affected foetuses (Aufderheide and Rodríguez-Martín 1998) and bone changes suggestive of the disease have been identified in foetal material from elsewhere in Europe; Pálfi et al (1992) described a probable case of congenital syphilis in a 7-month-old foetus from France.

The three subadults from period 17 with treponemal skeletal changes ([6974], [13715] and [20634]) are of particular interest as they present with changes consistent with tertiary stage disease. This diagnosis is based on the presence of a series of focal destructive lesions on the cranial vault associated with diffuse osteitis with evidence of overlying gumma. By far the most advanced stages of the disease are present in the skeleton of child [6974] aged 10–11 years (Fig 142). Here, the cranial vault had advanced and prolific caries sicca was accompanied by massive rhinomaxillary destruction. The destruction was so severe that the permanent canine teeth erupted at 45° to the normal alignment. The post-cranial skeleton was also severely affected, with all long bones showing widespread gummatous lesions (Fig 143). This individual is thought to be evidence of a congenital route of transmission.

A second subadult ([20634]) aged 16–17 years had cranial caries sicca and gummatous post-cranial lesions but was the only individual to present with dental changes with defective enamel formation on the permanent first molars. The cusps of these teeth form at or slightly before birth.

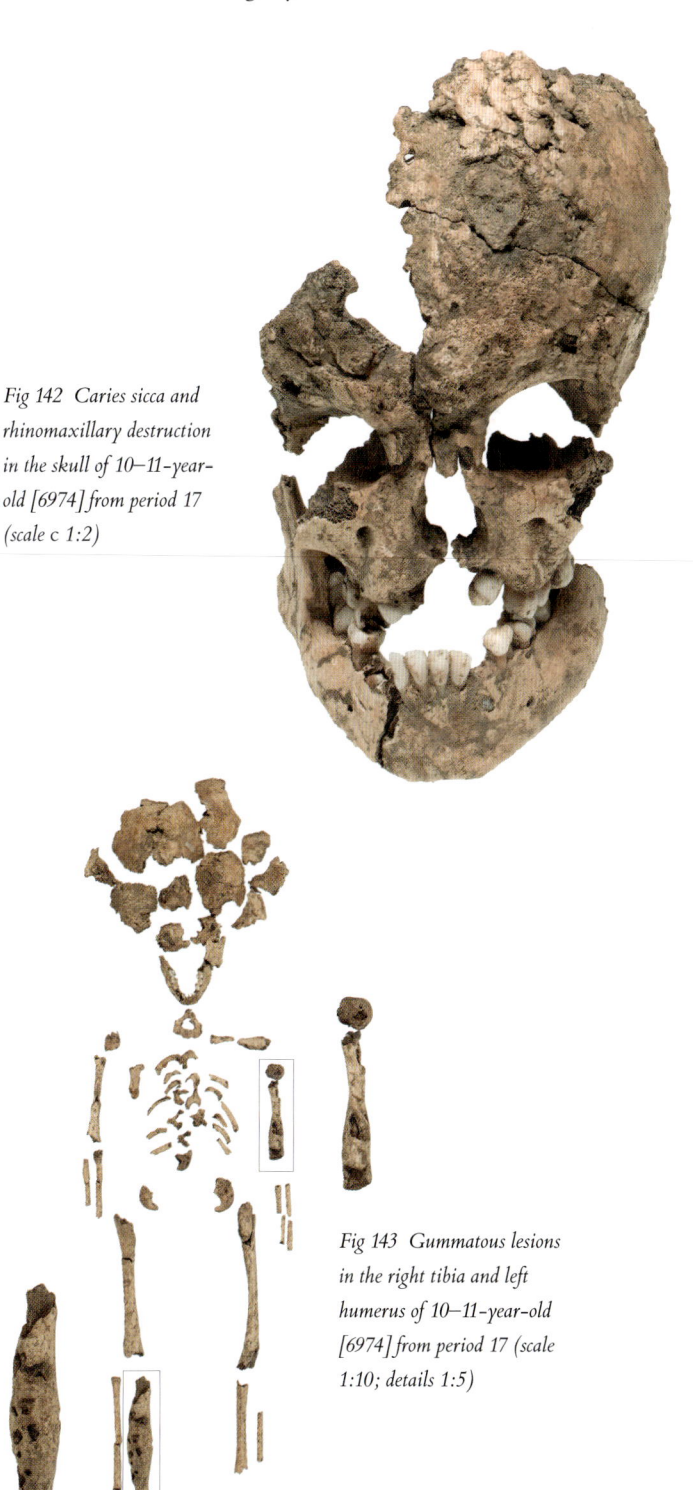

Fig 142 Caries sicca and rhinomaxillary destruction in the skull of 10–11-year-old [6974] from period 17 (scale c 1:2)

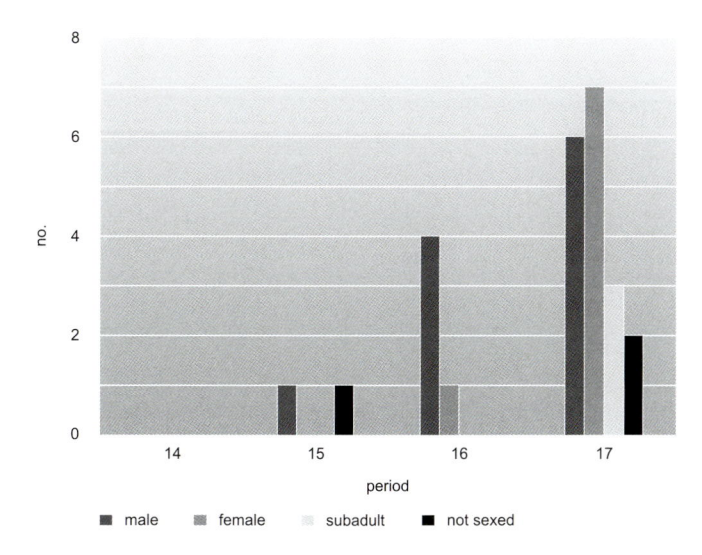

Fig 143 Gummatous lesions in the right tibia and left humerus of 10–11-year-old [6974] from period 17 (scale 1:10; details 1:5)

Fig 141 Number of treponemal infections by sex and period

Results

Tuberculosis

Tuberculosis is a chronic infectious disease caused by *Mycobacterium tuberculosis* and *Mycobacterium bovis*. *Mycobacterium tuberculosis* is transmitted via droplet infection from human to human, while *Mycobacterium bovis* is transmitted via the ingestion of meat and milk from animals, especially cattle, or via droplet infection. It is primarily a disease of the soft tissues, with only a minority of individuals showing skeletal involvement and identifiable in palaeopathology; data from the pre-antibiotic era suggest that bone changes are seen in only about 5–7% of cases (Steinbock 1976).

In total, 100 cases of tuberculosis were observed (1.9% of the total analysed sample): 36 males, 43 females, 16 subadults aged 6–17 years, and 5 adults of intermediate sex were affected (Table 106). The highest crude prevalence rates were observed in periods 14 and 16 (2.1% in each period) and period 15 (1.7%). Period 17 had the lowest crude prevalence rate (0.9%). The difference in the number of individuals affected in periods 16 and 17 was found to be statistically significant ($\chi^2 = 3.86$, df = 1, $p \leq 0.05$).

Overall more females (43/1883: 2.3%) than males (36/2237: 1.6%) were affected, but this was not a statistically significant result. No significant temporal differences were observed between the sexes, and both sexes displayed the same temporal pattern of disease prevalence. However, when both males and females in the same age group were affected, female prevalence rates are higher, particularly in periods 14 and 17 (Figs 144–6).

In period 14, a greater proportion of females (3/73: 4.1%) than males were affected in the 26–35-year age range. In the 36–45-year category, by contrast, there was a higher proportion of affected males (4/80: 5.0%) than females. Adults ≥46 years of both sexes were affected but the prevalence was higher in females (1/15: 6.7%) than males (1/24: 4.2%) (Fig 147).

In period 15, seven males (7/532: 1.3%) were affected. These were distributed among the younger age groups: prevalence decreased with increasing age, from 3.1% (4/129) of 18–25-year-old males to 1.1% (2/184) of 26–35-year-old males, and finally to 0.6% (1/165) of 36–45-year-olds. Ten females were affected in this period and again prevalence decreased with age: 4.2% of 18–25-year-olds (5/120) and 2.6% of 26–35-year-old females (5/196) were affected.

The pattern of prevalence decreasing with age was repeated when male and female data were combined. A higher percentage of females were affected than males in both younger adult categories (18–25 years and 26–35 years), but no affected females over 35 years were observed, compared to 0.6% of 36–45-year-old males.

Period 16 contained the greatest number of individuals from the site, and had the highest prevalence rates. Twenty-one males from all age groups were affected (21/1192: 1.8%), with the prevalence rate increasing slightly from 18–25 years to 36–45 years. Fewer 18–25-year-old males were affected (3/253: 1.2%) than in period 15, while the 26–35-year-old and 36–45-year-old males both showed a similar rate with about 2% affected, an increase from period 15. Only 0.8% (1/124) of ≥46-year-old

Table 106 *Overall crude prevalence rate of tuberculosis by sex or age*

	No. individuals	No. affected	%
All individuals	5387	100	1.9
Female	1883	43	2.3
Male	2237	36	1.6
Subadult	1027	16	1.6

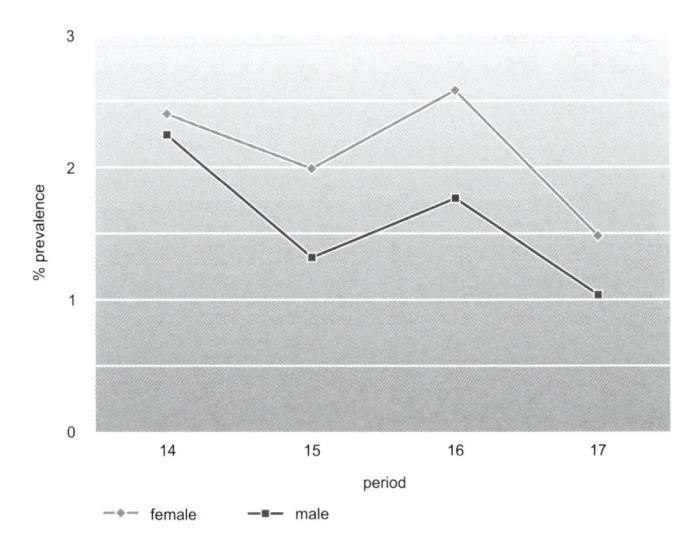

Fig 144 *Crude prevalence rate of tuberculosis by sex and period*

Fig 145 *Healed tuberculous lesions in the lumbar vertebrae of 36–45-year-old male [22806] from period 16, burial type ABC (scale c 1:2)*

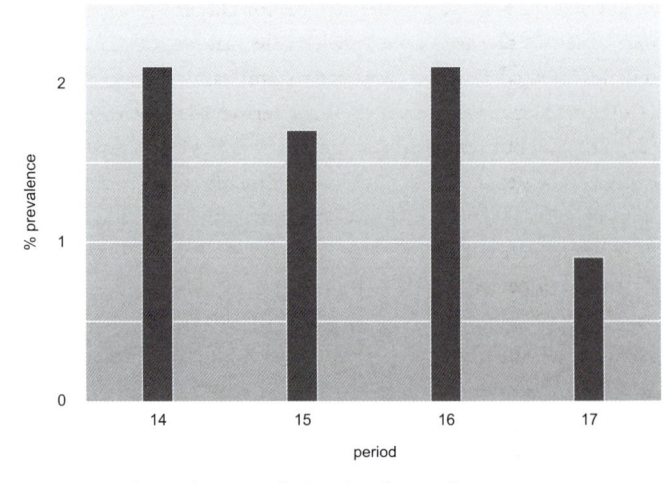

Fig 146 *Crude prevalence rate of tuberculosis by period*

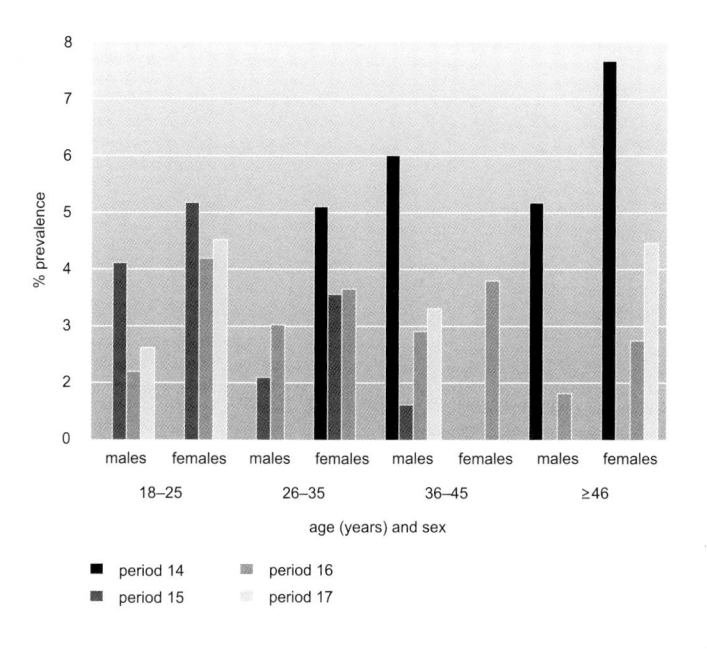

Fig 147 Crude prevalence rate of tuberculosis by age and sex

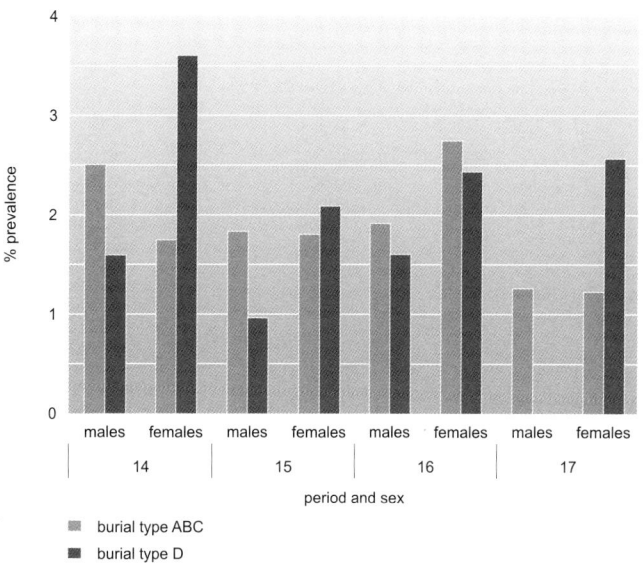

Fig 148 Crude prevalence rates of tuberculosis by sex, period and burial type

males were affected. For females, this period had the highest prevalence rate, at 2.6% (26/1009). All ages were affected and minor variations suggest that prevalence decreased with age, from 3.2% of 18–25-year-olds (7/220) to 1.7% of females aged ≥46 years (2/115).

In period 17, all age groups were affected; again the female prevalence rate was higher than that for males in all groups, and both sexes showed a decrease in prevalence throughout adulthood. In 18–25-year-old adults, a greater number of females were affected, more than males of the same age and more than other female age groups.

The lowest prevalence rates were observed in this period for both sexes, as only six individuals were affected (6/650: 0.9%). Three males were affected (3/290: 1.0%) from the 18–25 year and 36–45 year age groups, 1.6% (1/62) and 2.3% (2/87) respectively; this was a slight increase in these age groups from period 16. Among females, two 18–25-year-olds (2/57: 3.5%) and one ≥46-year-old (1/29: 3.4%) were affected.

In burial type ABC, the highest crude prevalence rates were observed in periods 14 and 16, as for the cemetery as a whole. Males had the highest prevalence rates for all periods apart from period 16 but the difference between the number of males and females affected was not statistically significant. In males, the crude prevalence rate decreased from period 14 to period 15 (2.5%–1.8%) but remained stable in period 16 (1.9%) and decreased in period 17 (1.3%). By contrast, the crude prevalence rate for females remained constant in periods 14 (1.7%) and 15 (1.8%) but increased in period 16 (2.7%); as for males the rate decreased in period 17 (1.2%) (Fig 148).

The crude prevalence rates of tuberculosis in burial type D appear different from the pattern observed in the cemetery as a whole, and in comparison to burial type ABC. The female prevalence rate is higher in all periods (females are the only sex affected in period 17) but this result is not statistically significant. In contrast to burial type ABC, the female crude prevalence rate is highest in period 14 (3.6%), decreases in period 15 (2.1%) and slightly increases (to 2.6%) in period 17. Burial type D females have a higher prevalence rate compared to those in ABC in periods 14 and 17, and in periods 15 and 16 both burial types have very similar rates of tuberculosis. The crude prevalence rate for males is lower in burial type D than in type ABC: the highest prevalence rates were observed in periods 14 and 16 (1.6% in both), which conforms to the pattern observed in the cemetery as a whole and in burial type ABC; and the prevalence rate decreases by 0.6% in period 15. Despite the differences in prevalence rates, no statistical significance was found between the numbers of individuals with tuberculosis in each burial type.

SKELETAL DISTRIBUTION OF TUBERCULOUS LESIONS IN SEXED ADULTS

The majority of individuals affected by tuberculosis displayed spinal changes (64/100: 64.0%), predominantly in the thoracolumbar vertebrae, and particularly the tenth thoracic and fifth lumbar vertebrae. The only vertebrae not to display destructive lesions were the atlas and axis. Extra-spinal evidence for tuberculosis was most frequently observed in burial type ABC, and in period 16, which correlates with the increase in crude prevalence rates in the cemetery as a whole during this period. More males had tubercular changes to the joints, such as the elbow and wrist (Fig 149; Fig 150). The skull, spine, clavicle, metacarpal, right ilium and left sacroiliac joint were affected in both sexes.

Female [27531] from period 16 (burial type ABC) had tubercular destruction of the cervical and thoracolumbar spine, rib lesions, and evidence for *lupus vulgaris*. The anterior half of the maxilla was obliterated by a large circular lesion, which had eroded alveolar process and part of the left palatine process, causing loss of the lateral central incisors, and resulting in a large communicating aperture from the cheek to the nasal and buccal cavities.

Fig 150 Tubercular infection of the left wrist of 36–45-year-old male [17394] from period 16, burial type ABC (scale c 1:1)

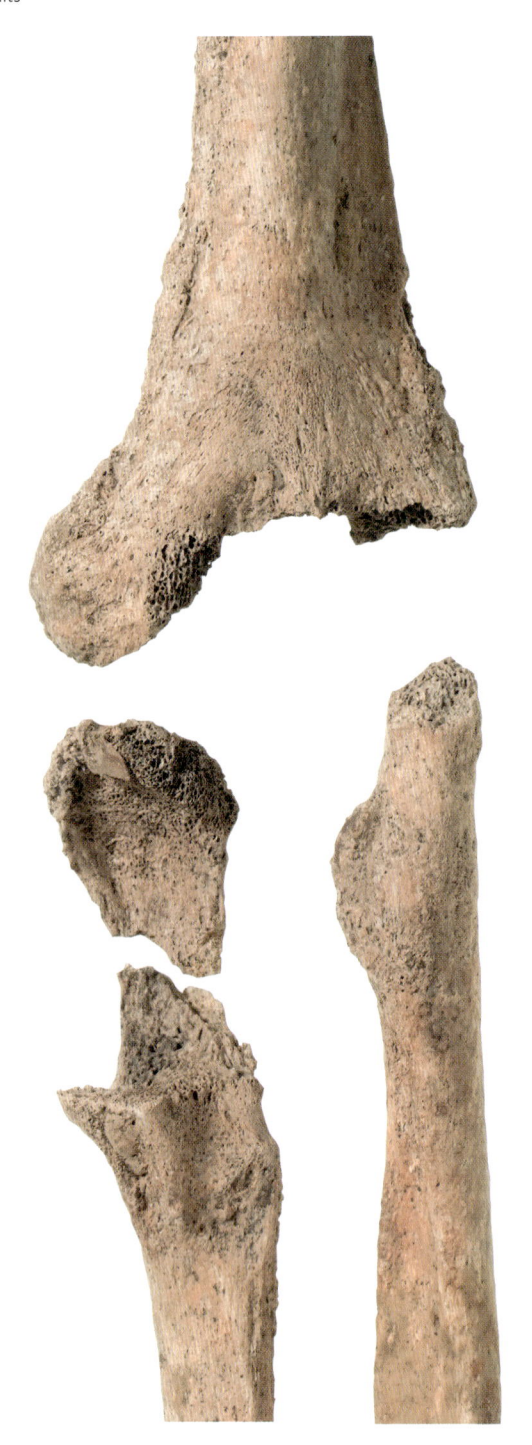

Fig 149 Tubercular infection of the left elbow of 26–35-year-old male [17273] from period 16, burial type ABC (scale c 1:1)

Fig 151 Active rib lesions in 12–17-year-old [22829] with Pott's disease of the thoracolumbar spine from period 15, burial type D (scale c 1:1)

RIB LESIONS AND TUBERCULOSIS

For all periods, 33 individuals (33/5387: 0.6%) had rib lesions and tubercular changes: 6 subadults (6/5387: 0.1%) (Fig 151), 13 males (13/5387: 0.2%), 11 females (11/5387: 0.2%) and 3 intermediate adults (3/5387: 0.1%). The difference between the number of males and females with rib lesions and tuberculosis was not statistically significant. The majority of individuals affected were in burial type D (20/5387: 0.4%; burial type ABC 13/5387: 0.2%). The greatest number of individuals (18/5387: 0.3%) was from period 16, which conforms to the overall disease distribution.

SUBADULT TUBERCULOSIS

Sixteen subadults had evidence for tuberculosis. There was no clear difference between burials types ABC (7/16) and D (9/16). The majority of individuals affected were 12–17-year-olds (10/16: 62.5%). The highest crude prevalence rates for this age group were observed in period 16 and the rates were constant in periods 14 and 15. Six individuals were 6–11 years old, and there were none from period 14 (Table 107).

Fourteen individuals had spinal changes present, and seven individuals also had cranial and post-cranial changes, particularly to the ribs. For example, 12–17-year-old [5426] (period 15,

Infectious disease

Table 107 Crude prevalence rate of tuberculosis in subadults by period and burial type

		6–11 years			12–17 years		
Period	Burial type	No. individuals	No. affected	%	No. individuals aged	No. affected	%
14	ABC	8	0	-	34	1	2.9
	D	13	0	-	27	0	-
15	ABC	28	1	3.6	60	0	-
	D	75	1	1.3	109	3	2.8
16	ABC	87	2	2.3	91	3	3.3
	D	100	2	2.0	174	3	2.3

Fig 152 Healed cranial lesion to the left parietal bone of 6–11-year-old [31901] from period 16, burial type ABC (scale c 1:1)

burial type D) had evidence for a healing tubercular infection. Destructive lesions were seen on the lumbar centra: on the second vertebra, these lesions perforated the posterior aspect of the centrum, and the third and fourth vertebrae had fused after extensive destruction of the left portion of the centra. Spicules of bone on the posterior aspect indicate that the infection may have been active at the time of death. Nine ribs had lamellar bone present to the visceral aspect of the head and neck, and the left hip joint was ankylosed; the femoral head was fused to the acetabulum (with trabecular continuity between the head and ilium) and the femoral head was collapsed on to the neck.

Two individuals in period 16 had cranial changes: a 6–11-year-old ([31901], burial type ABC) had destructive lesions present on the occipital and parietal bones, and a 12–17-year-old ([29986], burial type D) had changes to the mandible. Individual [31901] also had changes to the manubrium, clavicles and ribs, but no spinal changes were present (Fig 152). In other individuals, post-cranial changes affected the right elbow joint, hand phalanges, right hip and left sacroiliac joint.

Brucellosis

Brucellosis is a chronic infection caused by the bacterium *Brucella*. A zoonotic disease, brucellosis is usually passed to humans via ingestion of milk or meat products from infected animals, such as goats, sheep, pigs, cows and horses, or from close contact with their secretions, and hence is considered an occupational disease in those who work with such animals (Aufderheide and Rodríguez-Martín 1998, 192). Person-to-person transmission is uncommon and, as with tuberculosis infection, skeletal involvement is only present in about 10% of cases, where the vertebrae, especially the lumbar, are most commonly affected (ibid). Skeletal changes of brucellosis are difficult to differentiate from tuberculosis infection. Vertebral lesions begin with an abscess causing a lytic lesion in one or several vertebral bodies, often involving the intervertebral disc and spreading to adjacent vertebra. However, vertebral brucellosis does not usually cause paravertebral abscesses or the vertebral collapse observed in tuberculosis (ibid, 193).

Two males (2/5387: <0.1%) from period 16 had destructive spinal lesions to the lumbar vertebrae. The first male was aged between 18 and 25 years ([11849], burial type ABC) and had destructive lesions to the inferior aspect of the third lumbar centrum and the superior aspect of the fourth lumbar centrum (Fig 153). On both vertebrae, additional destructive lesions were

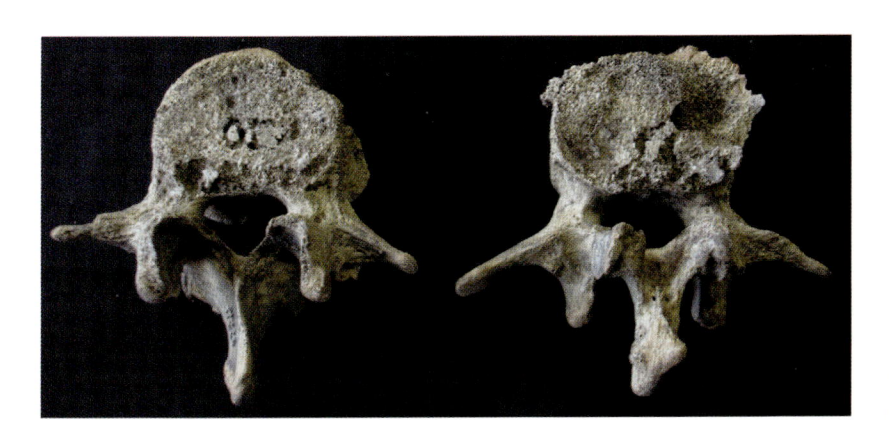

Fig 153 Evidence for brucellosis in the third and fourth lumbar vertebrae of 18–25-year-old male [11849] from period 16, burial type ABC (scale c 1:2)

also present to the lateral and anterior aspects and the left transverse processes. New bone formation associated with these lesions was present and there was also osteophyte formation. The second male ([26987], burial type D) was 36–45 years old, and had a large semicircular destructive lesion to the inferior aspect of the first lumbar vertebrae and a shallow circular destructive lesion on the posterior aspect of the second lumbar vertebra.

Tuberculosis/brucellosis

Eight individuals (8/5387: 0.1%) had lesions suggestive of either tuberculosis or brucellosis, but these changes could not be distinguished further. Three males (3/5387: 0.1%), three females (3/5387: 0.1%) and two 12–17-year-olds (2/5387: <0.1%) had spinal changes, in addition to rib and joint destruction. In all cases the spinal lesions were remodelling. The majority of cases (5/8: 62.5%) were from period 16 or burial type D (4/8: 50.0%) (Table 108).

In period 14, ≥46-year-old male [11291] (burial type ABC) had ankylosis of the right wrist joint; in period 15, two females from burial type D were affected ([26510] and [22202]), the younger of whom (18–25 years old) had a destructive lesion to a thoracolumbar vertebra, while a 36–45-year-old female had destructive lesions to the spine and left temporomandibular joint. In period 16, two 26–35-year-old males from burial type D were affected. The first, [26362], had destructive lesions to the ninth and tenth thoracic vertebrae and active new bone formation to six right rib heads; the second male [28269] had a large destructive lesion to the superior aspect of the 12th thoracic vertebra. One ≥46-year-old adult female was also affected ([3185], burial type D), displaying a destructive lesion to one vertebra and new bone formation to one rib head. Two 12–17-year-olds from period 16 also displayed changes: the first ([22212], burial type ABC) had destructive lesions to the sacroiliac joints and third to fourth lumbar vertebrae and the second ([25618], burial type D) had destructive lesions to the seventh cervical and 11th thoracic vertebrae and new bone formation to the heads of two left ribs.

Table 108 Crude prevalence rate of tuberculosis or brucellosis cases by period, burial type and sex or age

Period	Burial type	Sex or age	No. individuals	No. affected	%
14	ABC	male	160	1	0.6
	D		63	0	-
15	ABC	female	167	0	-
	D		334	2	0.6
16	ABC	male	628	0	-
		female	474	0	-
		subadult	209	1	0.5
	D	male	564	2	0.4
		female	535	1	0.2
		subadult	299	1	0.3

3.10 Nutritional and metabolic disease

Amy Gray Jones, Rebecca Redfern and Don Walker

Metabolic disease results from disturbances to the normal metabolic processes that occur during the growth and development of the body and can result from dietary insufficiencies, hormone imbalances or other disease. The prevalence of specific metabolic diseases was very low in all periods and was predominantly observed in subadults. Due to the small sample size, statistical tests could not be performed on the data set.

Scurvy

Four subadults (0.4% of all subadults; 0.1% (4/5387) of all individuals) from periods 15 to 17 had osseous lesions resulting from a deficiency in ascorbic acid (vitamin C) (Ortner and Eriksen 1997). Individuals from both burial types were affected (burial type ABC 1/456 subadults: 0.2%; burial type D 3/571 subadults: 0.5%) and period 17 had the highest prevalence rate (1/124 subadults: 0.8%) (Table 109).

Two individuals aged 6–11 years were affected, 0.6% of this age group (2/348): [26421] in period 15 (burial type D) had skull and post-cranial changes present, and in period 17 [3933] (burial type ABC) had skull changes present (Fig 154). Both cases had lesions that were active at the time of death.

Adolescents [32355] and [21042] (aged 12–17 years) from period 16, burial type D, were also affected, 0.4% of this age group (2/544). Only [32355] had post-cranial and skull changes present. The condition appears to have been remodelling at the time of death in both individuals.

Rickets

Five subadults, two adult males and one adult female (8/5387: 0.1%) showed evidence for vitamin D deficiency during childhood (Brickley and Ives 2008). The changes were remodelled in the adults and one subadult aged 6–11 years. In total, 0.2% of those from each burial type were affected (ABC 4/2275; D 4/2612). No individuals were affected in period 14; 0.1% of those from period 15 (1/1390); 0.2% of burials from period 16 (6/2835); and 0.2% from period 17 (1/650).

In period 15, 36–45-year-old male [15599] (burial type ABC) had anterior bowing of the femora, indicating healed rickets. The greatest numbers of affected subadults (four)

Table 109 Crude prevalence rate of scurvy in subadults

Period	Burial type	Age (years)	No. subadults	No. affected	%
15	D	6–11	301	1	0.3
16	D	12–17	508	2	0.4
17	ABC	6–11	124	1	0.8

Nutritional and metabolic disease

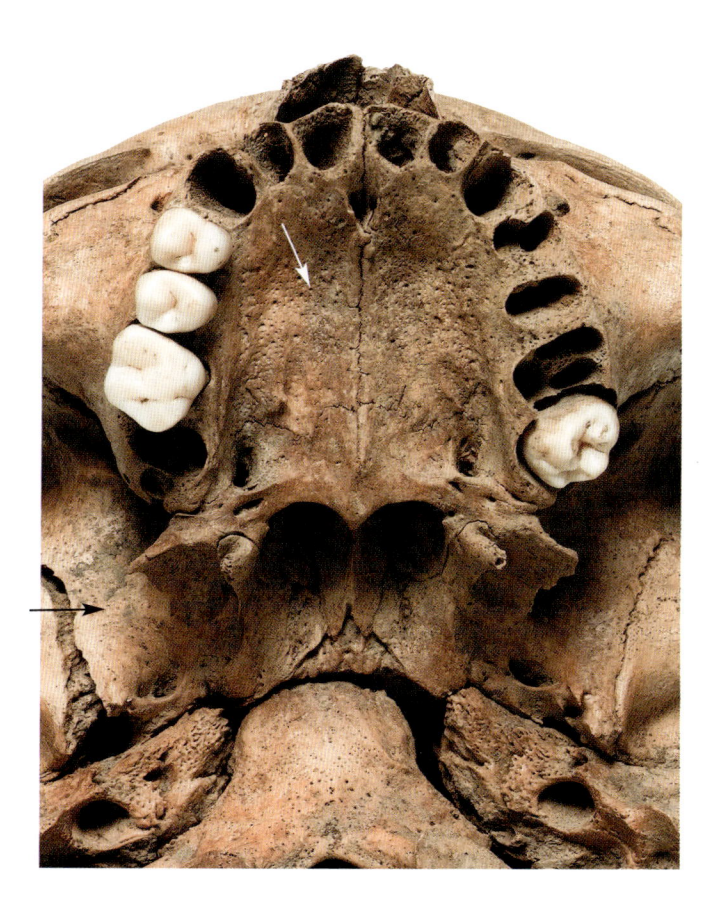

Fig 154 Scurvy in 6–11-year-old [3933] from period 17, burial type ABC, showing porosity on the greater wings of sphenoid and palate (scale c 1:1)

were from period 16. Two were aged 1–5 years: [8464] (burial type ABC) had skull and post-cranial changes and [18339] (burial type ABC) had post-cranial changes to the upper and lower limbs (Table 110; Fig 155). Two 6–11-year-olds in burial type D were affected; both individuals ([29118] and [31688]) had anterior bowing to the distal humeri. Two adults in burial type D had evidence of resolved rickets: a 26–35-year-old male [31257] had anterior bowing of the middle and distal segments of the humeri and a ≥46-year-old adult female [31639] had anterior bowing of the radii and femora. One 1–5-year-old [10373] from burial type ABC was affected in period 17, and had cranial and post-cranial changes present, which appear to show remodelling at the time of death. The crude prevalence for each age and sex group by period is shown in Table 110.

Table 110 Crude prevalence rate of rickets by age, sex and period

Period	Sex or age	No. individuals	No. affected	%
15	male	532	1	0.2
16	1–5 years	31	2	6.5
	6–11 years	187	2	1.1
	male	1192	1	0.1
	female	1009	1	0.1
17	1–5 years	11	1	9.1

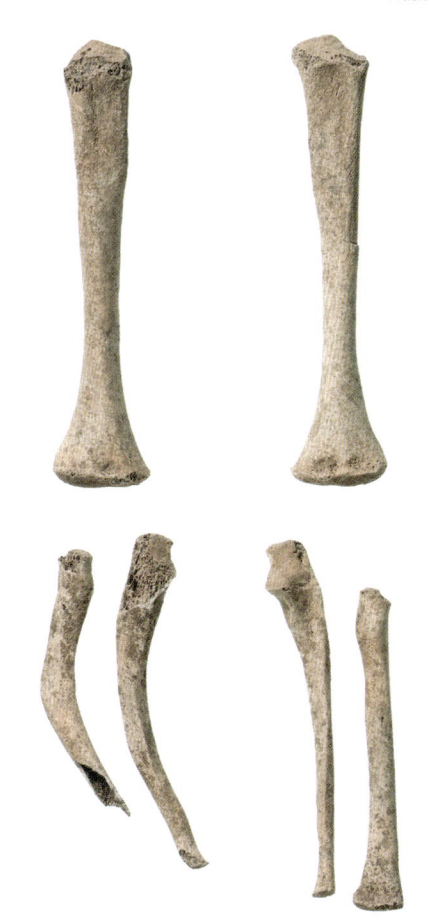

Fig 155 Rickets in 1–5-year-old [18339] from period 16, burial type ABC (scale c 1:2)

119

Results

Osteomalacia

Only one individual, a ≥46-year-old adult female [3699] from period 17 (burial type ABC), had post-cranial changes conforming to vitamin D deficiency with an onset in adulthood demonstrated by macroscopic and radiographic analysis (Brickley et al 2007). The axial and appendicular skeleton was affected, with all bone elements showing poor mineralisation (Fig 156). The female comprised <0.1% of all individuals in the sample (1/5387), 0.2% of all individuals from period 17 (1/650) and 3.4% of ≥46-year-old adult females in period 17 (1/29). The axial changes consisted of a healed compression fracture to the 12th thoracic vertebra and multiple healed and healing stress fractures to the ribs. The appendicular changes were multiple healed and healing stress fractures to the scapulae, and thinning of the cortical bone of the os coxae.

Cribra orbitalia

The majority of orbits did not display any evidence of cribra orbitalia, and the most frequently scored changes were grades 1 to 3 (Stuart-Macadam 1991).

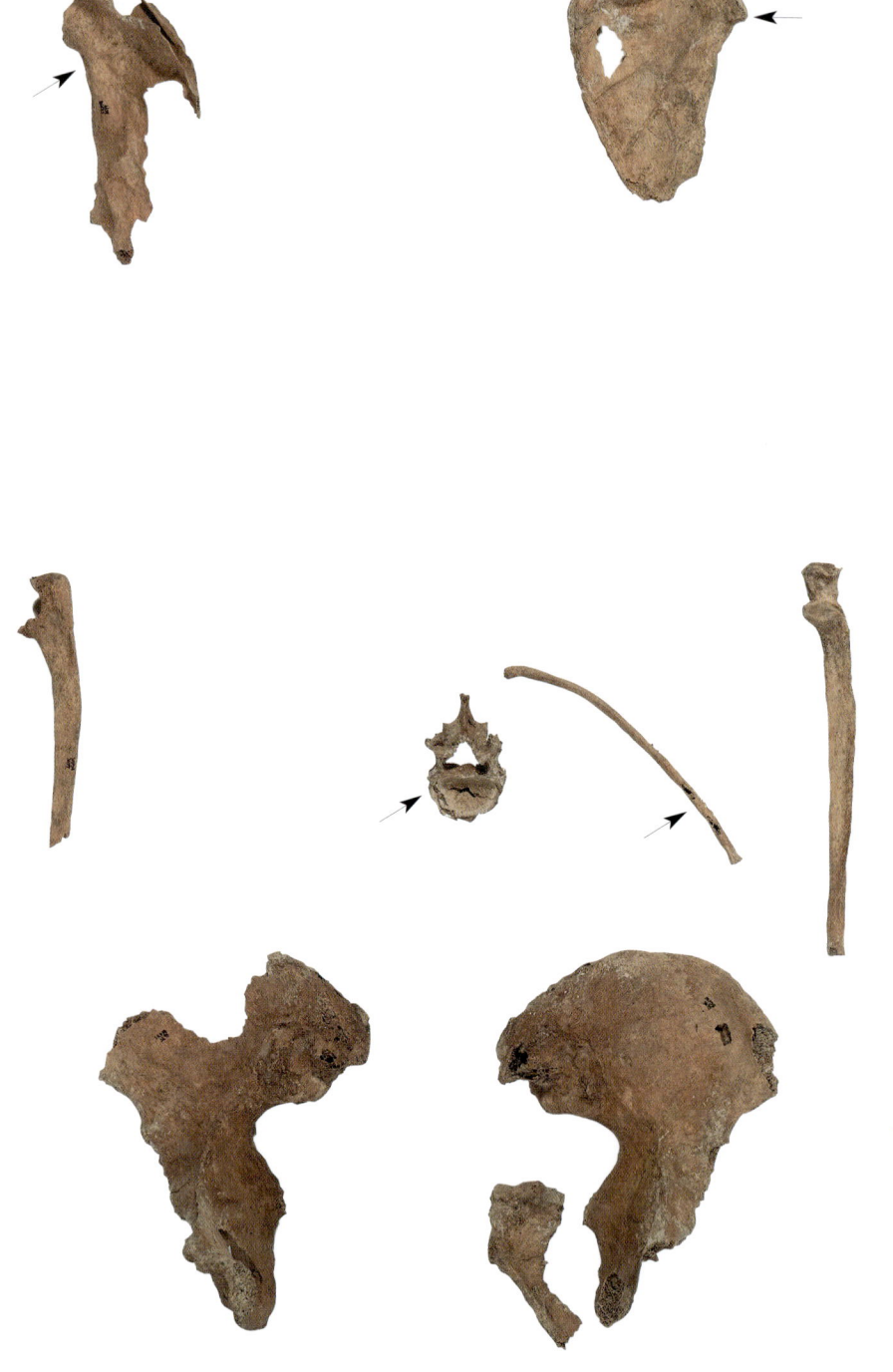

Fig 156 Changes to the axial and appendicular skeleton of ≥46-year-old adult female [3699] from period 17, burial type ABC, due to osteomalacia (scale c 1:4)

In period 14, the majority of orbits in all age and sex groups did not display any evidence of cribra orbitalia. The most frequently scored changes were grades 1 and 2. There were no marked differences between the sides affected. It should be noted that only a small number of intermediate adults displayed evidence of orbital changes (three in burial type D) and thus the rates are artificially high (Table 111). The highest prevalence rate observed in the right orbit was for burial type ABC females (25.4%), and in the left orbit for subadults from burial type D (27.8%). More male orbits were affected in burial type D (right: 40.4%; left: 40.9%) than in burial type ABC (right: 27.6%; left: 25.6%) (χ^2 = 5.48, df = 1, p ≤ 0.025).

As in period 14, the majority of those who were buried in period 15 did not display any evidence of cribra orbitalia, and the most frequently scored changes were grades 1 to 3. There were no marked differences between left and right orbits, although once intermediate adults were excluded, the highest prevalence rates were chiefly in right orbits in burial type ABC males (25.4%) and in left orbits in burial type ABC females (21.2%) (Table 112). When the overall prevalence of orbits affected by cribra orbitalia (grades 1 to 5) was considered, there was no variation by sex or burial type.

The majority of orbits in period 16 did not display any evidence of cribra orbitalia; the most frequently recorded changes were grades 1 and 2 (Table 113). The highest prevalence rates observed in right orbits were in burial type ABC males (23.7%), and in left orbits in burial type ABC females (20.6%). When the overall prevalence of orbits affected by cribra orbitalia (grades 1 to 5) was considered, males displayed a higher rate (right: 36.1%; left: 37.7%) than females (right: 30.5%; left: 33.5%) (χ^2 = 7.70, df = 1, p ≤ 0.01).

The most frequently recorded changes in those buried in period 17 were grade 1. A larger number of female orbits were affected by cribra orbitalia in burial type ABC (right: 28.7%; left: 31.7%) when compared to burial type D (right: 19.2%; left: 11.1%) (χ^2 = 4.89, df = 1, p ≤ 0.05). The highest prevalence rates were observed in right orbits for burial type ABC males (22.4%) and in left orbits for burial type ABC males (17.2%) (Table 114).

When male right and left orbits were combined, there was a significant difference in the true prevalence rate between periods 14 (83/264 orbits: 31.4%) and 15 (265/651: 40.7%) (χ^2 = 541.2, df = 1, p ≤ 0.01). The rate then fell between periods 16 and 17, from 36.9% (555/1504) to 31.4% (122/388), a statistically significant difference (χ^2 = 3.99, df = 1, p ≤ 0.05) (Fig 157). When female right and left orbits were combined, there was a significant fall in true prevalence rate between periods 14 (39.3%: 52/161) and 17 (27.1%: 70/258) (χ^2 = 11.62, df = 1, p ≤ 0.001) (Fig 158).

Table 111 True prevalence of cribra orbitalia in period 14 (grades as scored by Stuart-Macadam 1991)

Burial type	Sex or age	Grade	No.	Right (%)	No.	Left (%)
ABC	subadult	1	4	14.8	6	20.7
		2	3	11.1	3	10.3
		3	2	7.5	2	6.9
		4	2	7.4	3	10.3
	male	1	15	17.2	14	16.3
		2	7	8.0	4	4.6
		3	2	2.3	2	2.3
		4	0	-	2	2.3
	female	1	14	25.4	6	17.1
		2	3	5.4	4	11.4
		3	0	-	1	2.8
		4	1	1.8	1	2.8
	intermediate	4	1	100.0	1	12.5
D	subadult	1	2	6.1	1	2.8
		2	7	21.2	10	27.8
		3	5	15.1	6	16.7
		4	2	6.1	2	5.5
		5	3	9.1	4	11.1
	male	1	11	23.4	8	18.2
		2	4	8.5	5	11.4
		3	2	4.2	3	6.8
		4	2	4.2	2	4.5
	female	1	5	13.9	6	17.1
		2	3	8.3	4	11.4
		3	1	2.8	1	2.8
		4	1	2.8	1	2.8
	intermediate	1	2	50.0	2	66.7

Table 112 True prevalence of cribra orbitalia in period 15 (grades as scored by Stuart-Macadam 1991)

Burial type	Sex or age	Grade	No.	Right (%)	No.	Left (%)
ABC	subadult	1	3	6.1	6	11.3
		2	7	14.3	9	17.1
		3	6	12.2	8	15.1
		4	6	12.2	5	9.4
		5	2	4.1	2	3.8
	male	1	29	25.4	15	13.6
		2	3	2.6	8	7.3
		3	6	5.3	8	7.3
		4	2	1.7	2	1.8
	intermediate	1	3	27.3	3	30.0
		2	1	9.1	1	10.0
		3	1	9.1	2	20.0
	female	1	24	22.6	24	21.2
		2	13	12.3	14	12.4
		3	1	0.9	4	3.5
		4	5	4.7	8	7.1
		5	1	0.9	0	-
D	subadult	1	12	9.4	13	9.9
		2	18	14.2	17	13.1
		3	24	18.9	22	16.8
		4	8	6.3	10	7.6
		5	9	7.1	8	6.1
	male	1	25	13.0	33	16.9
		2	10	5.2	15	7.7
		3	10	5.2	8	4.1
		4	8	4.2	8	4.1
		5	0	-	1	0.5
	intermediate	1	7	36.8	4	22.2
		2	1	5.3	2	11.1
		3	3	15.8	3	16.7
		4	1	5.3	1	5.5
	female	1	46	22.2	40	18.9
		2	13	6.3	18	8.5
		3	13	6.3	14	6.6
		4	6	2.9	6	2.8

Results

Table 113 True prevalence of cribra orbitalia in period 16 (grades as scored by Stuart-Macadam 1991)

Burial type	Sex or age	Grade	No.	Right (%)	No.	Left (%)
ABC	subadult	1	12	11.2	14	13.1
		2	15	14.0	14	13.1
		3	14	13.1	12	11.1
		4	6	5.6	7	6.5
		5	3	2.8	3	2.8
	male	1	86	23.7	82	22.3
		2	28	7.7	33	9.1
		3	14	3.8	16	4.3
		4	5	1.4	9	2.4
		5	0	-	1	0.3
	intermediate	1	9	30.0	8	28.6
		2	5	16.7	3	10.7
		3	2	6.7	3	10.7
		4	2	6.7	3	10.7
	female	1	51	16.6	63	20.6
		2	26	8.5	17	5.6
		3	18	5.9	24	7.9
		4	5	1.6	6	2.1
D	subadult	1	34	19.6	27	16.1
		2	29	16.8	27	16.1
		3	22	12.7	20	11.8
		4	9	5.2	10	5.9
		5	1	0.6	3	1.8
	male	1	64	16.6	67	17.3
		2	41	10.6	47	12.1
		3	24	6.2	18	4.6
		4	8	2.1	12	3.1
	intermediate	1	5	20.8	4	16.0
		2	3	12.5	1	4.0
		3	1	4.2	1	4.0
		4	2	8.3	3	12.0
		5	1	4.2	1	4.0
	female	1	55	13.7	54	13.9
		2	35	8.7	36	9.3
		3	14	3.5	17	4.4
		4	12	3.1	15	3.9

Table 114 True prevalence of cribra orbitalia in period 17 (grades as scored by Stuart-Macadam 1991)

Burial type	Sex or age	Grade	No.	Right (%)	No.	Left (%)
ABC	subadult	1	5	10.4	9	17.3
		2	3	6.2	5	9.6
		3	7	14.6	5	9.6
		4	1	2.1	5	9.6
		5	2	4.2	1	1.9
	male	1	34	22.4	28	17.2
		2	8	5.3	13	8.1
		3	3	2.1	8	4.9
		4	1	0.6	1	0.6
	intermediate	1	2	16.7	2	18.2
		2	4	33.3	4	36.4
		3	1	8.3	0	-
	female	1	15	14.8	71	16.3
		2	10	9.9	17	10.6
		3	2	2.1	11	3.8
		4	2	2.1	4	1.1
D	subadult	1	0	-	2	7.7
		2	3	11.1	4	15.4
		3	4	14.8	4	15.4
		4	2	7.4	1	3.8
		5	1	3.7	1	3.8
	male	1	5	13.5	4	11.1
		2	3	8.1	3	8.3
		3	4	10.8	4	11.1
		4	2	5.4	1	2.8
	intermediate	1	0	-	0	-
		2	1	25.0	1	25.0
	female	1	2	7.7	1	3.7
		2	1	3.8	1	3.7
		3	1	3.8	1	3.7
		4	1	3.8	0	-

Fig 157 True prevalence rate of male cribra orbitalia by period

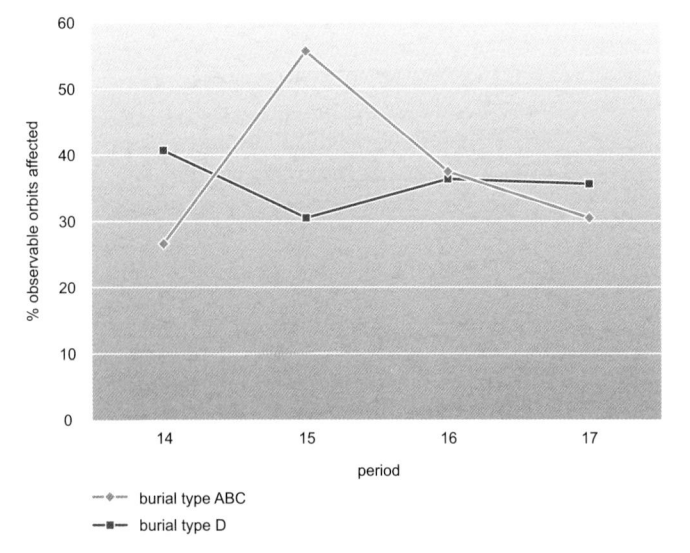

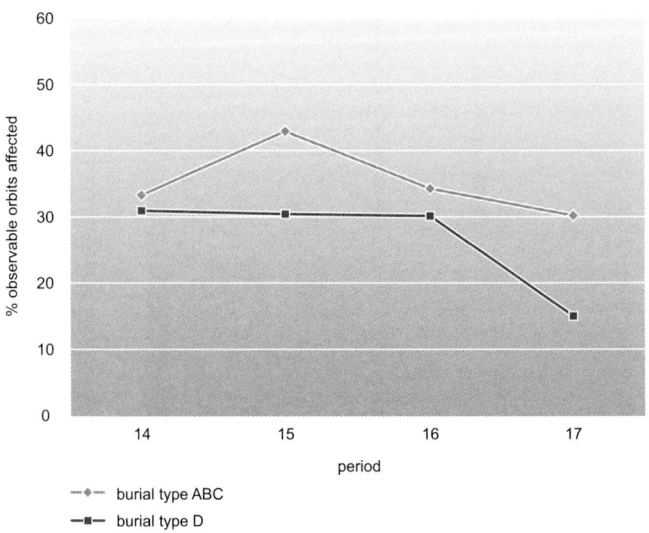

Fig 158 True prevalence rate of female cribra orbitalia by period

Porotic hyperostosis of the cranial vault

In this report, porotic hyperostosis refers to cranial vault lesions (rather than porosity observed in the orbits or on the long bone ends). This condition is considered to be associated with anaemia, infectious disease and high parasite burden (Goodman and Martin 2002, 27–31).

In period 14 individuals from both burial types were affected; the majority of the lesions observed were healing or healed and the parietal bones were the most frequently affected. In subadults of known age, porotic hyperostosis was only observed in 6–11 and 12–17-year-olds. The latter age group dominates the data set and has the highest prevalence rates, particularly to the parietal and occipital bones (Table 115).

Males from all age groups were affected. The highest prevalence rates for the frontal bone were observed in males of undetermined age from burial type ABC (2/14: 14.3%); for the right parietal bones in 26–35-year-old males from burial type D (8/18: 44.4%); in the left parietal bone of both 18–25-year-old males and males of undetermined age from burial type ABC (both 3/7: 42.9%) and for the occipital bone in adult males of undetermined age from burial type ABC (3/7: 42.9%). In females the highest prevalence rates were observed in ≥46-year-old adults from burial type D in the right and left parietal bones (both 1/3: 33.3%). For adults with intermediate characteristics, only the 26–35-year-old age group in burial type ABC was affected, as were 18–25-year-olds for burial type D (Table 115).

The difference between the numbers of females and males with porotic hyperostosis was significant for both burial type ABC (χ^2 = 11.77, df = 1, p ≤ 0.001) and burial type D (χ^2 = 4.80, df = 1, p ≤ 0.05).

In the assemblage from period 15, only healing or healed lesions were present. In subadults, the only age groups affected were 6–11 and 12–17-year-olds. The highest prevalence rates were observed in burial type ABC. In burial type D the highest prevalence rates were observed for the parietal bones of 12–17-year-olds (5/89: 5.6%). In males from burial type ABC only ≥46-year-old adults were affected, while in burial type D, cases were observed in all age groups. The parietal bones had the highest prevalence rates for both burial types. For intermediate adults from period 15, burial type ABC, only those of undetermined age were affected, and in burial type D, 18–25 and 36–45-year-olds were affected. Females in the 18–25 and 26–35-year-old age groups were affected in burial type ABC. The highest prevalence rates were observed for the right parietal bones (2/27: 7.4%). In burial type D, females from all age groups had porotic hyperostosis in the parietal and occipital bones (Table 116).

The difference between the numbers of females and males with porotic hyperostosis was significant for both burial types (burial type ABC χ^2 = 0.025, df = 1, p ≤ 0.025; burial type D χ^2 = 18.75, df = 1, p ≤ 0.001).

In period 16, the parietal bones were the most frequently affected elements. In subadults from burial type ABC, cases were only observed in 6–11 and 12–17-year-olds, and only 12–17-year-olds had the frontal, parietal and occipital bones affected. In burial type D, only 6–11-year-olds and 12–17-year-olds had all cranial bones affected and the highest prevalence rates were observed in the parietal bones of 12–17-year-olds (28/153: 18.5%). In males, frontal and occipital bones were least frequently affected. In burial type ABC the highest prevalence rates were observed in the parietal bones of 26–35-year-olds (both 31/160: 19.4%). In burial type D, the highest prevalence rates were also observed in the left (63/148: 42.6%) and right

Table 115 True prevalence rate of porotic hyperostosis in period 14

Burial type	Sex	Age (years)	Frontal bone No. present	Frontal bone No. affected	Frontal bone %	Right parietal bone No. present	Right parietal bone No. affected	Right parietal bone %	Left parietal bone No. present	Left parietal bone No. affected	Left parietal bone %	Occipital bone No present	Occipital bone No. affected	Occipital bone %
ABC	subadult	12–17	26	1	3.8	14	2	14.3	14	2	14.3	14	1	7.1
		≥18	1	0	-	1	1	100.0	1	1	100.0	1	0	-
	male	18–25	14	1	7.1	6	3	50.0	7	3	42.9	7	1	14.3
		26–35	40	3	7.5	23	8	34.8	23	8	34.9	24	6	25.0
		36–45	53	3	5.7	23	5	21.7	24	5	20.8	22	4	18.2
		≥46	26	2	7.7	14	4	28.6	14	4	28.6	14	4	28.6
		≥18	14	2	14.3	7	3	42.9	7	3	42.9	7	3	42.9
	female	26–35	44	2	4.5	22	3	13.6	23	4	17.4	22	0	-
		36–45	33	1	3.0	15	1	6.7	16	1	6.3	16	1	6.3
	intermediate	26–35	7	0	-	4	1	25.0	4	1	25.0	4	1	25.0
D	subadult	6–11	21	0	-	10	2	20.0	10	2	20.0	11	1	9.1
		12–17	48	3	6.3	24	7	29.2	24	7	29.2	24	7	29.2
	male	18–25	19	1	5.3	9	3	33.3	9	3	33.3	9	2	22.2
		26–35	37	5	13.5	18	8	44.4	19	8	42.1	19	8	42.1
		36–45	34	3	8.8	16	8	50.0	16	8	50.0	16	4	25.0
	female	18–25	0	0	-	9	1	11.1	8	1	12.5	9	1	11.1
		26–35	0	0	-	19	4	21.1	18	4	22.2	19	3	15.8
		36–45	0	0	-	8	1	12.5	8	1	12.5	0	0	-
		≥46	0	0	-	3	1	33.3	3	1	33.3	0	0	-
	intermediate	18–25	0	0	-	4	2	50.0	4	2	50.0	4	1	25.0

Results

Table 116 True prevalence rate of porotic hyperostosis in period 15

Burial type	Sex	Age (years)	Frontal bone No. present	Frontal bone No. affected	Frontal bone %	Right parietal bone No. present	Right parietal bone No. affected	Right parietal bone %	Left parietal bone No. present	Left parietal bone No. affected	Left parietal bone %	Occipital bone No. present	Occipital bone No. affected	Occipital bone %
ABC	subadult	6–11	0	0	–	19	1	5.3	19	1	5.3	20	1	5.0
		12–17	0	0	–	47	6	12.8	47	5	10.6	46	5	10.9
	female	18–25	158	2	1.3	27	2	7.4	56	3	5.4	29	1	3.4
		26–35	0	0	–	105	4	3.8	89	4	4.5	51	2	3.9
	male	≥46	0	0	–	9	1	11.1	9	1	11.1	9	1	11.1
	intermediate	≥18	2	1	50.0	1	1	100.0	1	1	100.0	1	1	100.0
D	subadult	6–11	0	0	–	59	2	3.4	58	2	3.4	59	1	1.7
		12–17	169	1	0.6	89	5	5.6	89	5	5.6	86	2	2.3
	male	18–25	93	2	2.2	49	16	32.7	48	16	33.3	48	10	20.8
		26–35	146	14	9.6	78	29	37.2	78	29	37.2	76	24	31.6
		36–45	129	15	11.6	67	27	40.3	67	27	40.3	67	25	37.3
		≥46	39	2	5.1	20	4	20.0	20	4	20.0	20	4	20.0
		≥18	12	2	16.7	6	3	50.0	6	3	50.0	6	3	50.0
	intermediate	18–25	10	1	10.0	5	2	40.0	5	2	40.0	3	1	33.3
		26–35	8	1	12.5	4	3	75.0	4	3	75.0	4	3	75.0
		36–45	19	1	5.3	10	5	50.0	9	5	55.6	10	4	40.0
	female	18–25	126	1	0.8	63	8	12.7	66	8	12.1	65	7	10.8
		26–35	177	2	1.1	93	14	15.1	91	15	16.5	91	8	8.8
		36–45	0	0	–	53	11	20.8	51	11	21.6	52	7	13.5
		≥46	0	0	–	26	3	11.5	26	3	11.5	24	2	8.3
		≥18	0	0	–	8	2	25.0	8	2	25.0	8	1	12.5

(62/148: 41.9%) parietal bones of this age group. Among females from burial type ABC, the parietal and occipital bones were most frequently affected, and 36–45 and ≥46-year-olds had the highest prevalence rates. In burial type D, the lowest female prevalence rates were observed for the frontal bone and the highest in the parietal bones. The highest female prevalence rate was observed in adults (≥18 years) from burial type D (4/18: 22.2%). In intermediate adults, the highest prevalence rates were observed in the right and left parietal bones of 18–25-year-olds from burial type D (5/11: 45.4%) (Table 117).

The difference between the number of females and males with porotic hyperostosis was significant for burial type ABC (χ^2 = 16.75, df = 1, p ≤ 0.01) and burial type D (χ^2 = 39.24, df = 1, p ≤ 0.001), and also between burial types in males (χ^2 = 5.5299, df = 1, p ≤ 0.001).

The parietal bones were also the most frequently affected cranial elements in period 17, and only healing or healed lesions were observed. In subadult individuals, only 6–11 and 12–17-year-olds were affected, the majority being from burial type ABC. For males from burial type ABC, the highest prevalence rates were observed in adult occipital bones (2/5: 40.0%). In burial type D, the highest prevalence rates were observed for the parietal bones (2/9: 22.2%). For burial type ABC females, the frontal bone was the least frequently affected bone (seen only in 18–25 and 26–35-year-old individuals) and the parietal bones were most often affected. The most frequently affected element was the occipital bone of 26–35-year-olds (5/46: 10.9%). Only 18–25 and 26–35-year-old females were affected in burial type D, the younger group having the highest prevalence rates. The high prevalence rates for intermediate adults from both burial types were because of the small number of observable elements (Table 118).

The difference between the number of females and males with porotic hyperostosis for period 17, burial type ABC was statistically significant (χ^2 = 13.66, df = 1, p ≤ 0.01) as was the difference between burial types for males (χ^2 = 5.17, df = 1, p ≤ 0.025).

Indicators of stress in subadults

The model of health, nutrition and adaptation presented by Goodman and Armelagos (1989) allows a researcher to investigate levels of stress in past communities, providing data that may not be obtained from environmental and cultural evidence, as skeletal remains provide an independent perspective of community well-being (Goodman et al 1988, 177). The model employs (among others) long bone growth, Harris lines, enamel hypoplastic defects, porotic hyperostosis (cranium and orbitalia roofs) and mortality rates (see also Larsen 1999, 29–61). An important feature of the model is the recognition that culture can act as a stressor or a buffer, often in conjunction with environmental stressors. The ability of an individual to cope with stress is influenced by his or her social status and health status; thus not all members of a community are at equal risk (Goodman and Armelagos 1989, 226; see also Wood et al 1992).

Due to the individual and population variation that affects Goodman and Armelagos's (1989) model, the use of non-specific indicators has been questioned, particularly in the light of studies indicating a wide range of causes for the formation of

Table 117 True prevalence rate of porotic hyperostosis in period 16

Burial type	Sex	Age (years)	Frontal bone No. present	No. affected	%	Right parietal bone No. present	No. affected	%	Left parietal bone No. present	No. affected	%	Occipital bone No present	No. affected	%
ABC	subadult	6–11	0	0	-	74	3	4.1	75	3	4.0	73	2	2.7
		12–17	130	5	3.8	72	9	12.5	70	9	12.9	70	7	10.0
	male	18–25	166	4	2.4	90	12	13.3	86	12	14.0	92	8	8.7
		26–35	284	13	4.6	160	31	19.4	160	31	19.4	158	24	15.2
		36–45	286	1	0.3	152	2	1.3	149	2	1.3	151	1	0.7
		≥46	96	1	1.0	53	1	1.9	51	1	2.0	51	1	2.0
	female	18–25	159	1	0.6	86	4	4.7	84	4	4.8	84	2	2.4
		26–35	0	0	-	134	7	5.2	137	7	5.1	135	2	1.5
		36–45	191	1	0.5	99	7	7.1	101	7	6.9	99	6	6.1
		≥46	0	0	-	42	3	7.1	43	3	7.0	42	2	4.8
		≥18	0	0	-	20	1	5.0	20	1	5.0	20	1	5.0
	intermediate	≥18	0	0	-	5	1	20.0	5	1	20.0	0	0	-
D	subadult	1–5	0	0	-	9	1	11.1	9	1	11.1	0	0	-
		6–11	126	1	0.8	82	8	9.8	81	8	9.9	80	6	7.5
		12–17	130	6	4.6	151	28	18.5	153	28	18.3	149	20	13.4
	male	18–25	206	13	6.3	107	31	29.1	107	32	29.9	108	31	28.7
		26–35	425	23	5.4	148	62	41.9	148	63	42.6	145	47	32.4
		36–45	248	16	6.4	125	44	35.2	125	44	35.2	126	36	28.6
		≥46	94	7	7.4	48	10	20.8	48	10	20.8	47	6	12.8
		≥18	32	3	9.4	18	6	33.3	18	6	33.3	15	5	33.3
	female	18–25	193	1	0.5	100	14	14.0	97	13	13.4	98	12	12.2
		26–35	320	3	0.9	162	33	20.4	163	32	19.6	161	20	12.4
		36–45	211	2	0.9	110	16	14.5	112	15	13.4	110	12	10.9
		≥46	107	1	0.9	54	4	7.4	54	4	7.4	53	3	5.7
		≥18	35	0	-	18	4	22.2	18	4	22.2	17	2	11.8
	intermediate	18–25	22	0	-	11	5	45.5	11	5	45.4	11	4	36.4
		26–35	16	1	6.3	8	2	25.0	8	2	25.0	8	0	-
		36–45	10	0	-	6	1	16.7	6	1	16.7	6	0	-
		≥18	8	1	12.5	4	1	25.0	4	1	25.0	4	1	25.0

Table 118 True prevalence rate of porotic hyperostosis in period 17

Burial type	Sex	Age (years)	Frontal bone No. present	No. affected	%	Right parietal bone No. present	No. affected	%	Left parietal bone No. present	No. affected	%	Occipital bone No present	No. affected	%
ABC	subadult	6–11	0	0	-	13	1	7.7	13	1	7.7	0	0	-
		12–17	12	3	25.0	12	8	66.7	12	8	66.7	12	7	58.3
	male	18–25	0	0	-	42	2	4.8	42	2	4.8	42	1	2.4
		26–35	0	0	-	67	3	4.5	66	3	4.5	65	3	4.6
		36–45	110	1	0.9	58	4	6.9	58	0	-	57	2	3.5
		≥18	0	0	-	6	2	33.3	6	2	33.3	5	2	40.0
	intermediate	18–25	7	1	14.3	5	1	20.0	5	1	20.0	4	1	25.0
		26–35	10	1	10.0	6	1	16.7	6	1	16.7	6	1	16.7
		≥18	0	0	-	1	1	100.0	1	1	100.0	1	1	100.0
	female	18–25	77	1	1.3	40	2	5.0	40	2	5.0	39	3	7.7
		26–35	87	2	2.3	47	5	10.6	48	5	10.4	46	5	10.9
		36–45	0	0	-	29	3	10.3	29	3	10.3	29	2	6.9
D	subadult	6–11	0	0	-	13	1	7.7	13	1	7.7	0	0	-
		12–17	0	0	-	12	1	8.3	12	1	8.3	0	0	-
	male	26–35	0	0	-	9	2	22.2	9	2	22.2	0	0	-
		36–45	0	0	-	17	2	11.8	16	2	12.5	0	0	-
		≥46	20	1	5.0	5	1	20.0	5	1	20.0	5	1	20.0
	intermediate	26–35	0	0	-	2	1	50.0	2	1	50.0	0	0	-
	female	18–25	8	1	12.5	4	1	25.0	4	1	25.0	5	1	20.0
		26–35	0	0	-	9	1	11.1	9	1	11.1	0	0	-

Results

such indicators. Lewis and Roberts's (1997) review of non-specific indicators of stress and their interpretations confirms multiple aetiologies, while cribra orbitalia may be caused by dietary deficiency, high parasite load or an adaptive response to infectious disease, all relating to ecological factors (Stuart-Macadam 1992). Ribot and Roberts, who examined indicators of stress in subadults, concluded that although they are the result of a combination of stressors and only have partially overlapping aetiologies, they could be successfully studied between populations of similar chronological, ecological and pathological backgrounds (1996, 78).

The most frequently employed indicators of stress are enamel hypoplastic defects, periosteal new bone formation and cribra orbitalia, and these have been employed when examining the subadult population from St Mary Spital (Table 119). The adult data for indicators of stress are presented separately by disease type (above, 3.6, 3.9, 3.10).

In period 14, only 12–17-year-olds had evidence for all three stress indicators. In the 1–5 year age group, indicators of stress (cribra orbitalia) were only observed in burial type ABC (1/5: 20.0%); those aged 6–11 years had higher prevalence rates of enamel hypoplastic defects in burial type D than type ABC. Individuals aged 12–17 years had higher crude prevalence rates in burial type D, the greatest disparity being observed for enamel hypoplasia. The difference between burial types in the number of 12–17-year-olds with an enamel hypoplastic defect was found to be statistically significant (χ^2 = 5.52, df = 1, $p \leq 0.025$).

In period 15, all three indicators were observed in individuals aged 6–17 years. The 6–11-year-olds from burial type ABC had a higher crude prevalence of periosteal new bone formation than those from burial type D. The difference between burial types in this period was found to be statistically significant (χ^2 = 4.64, df = 1, $p \leq 0.05$). Adolescents (12–17 years old) in burial type D had a higher prevalence of all indicators of stress than those from burial type ABC, with the exception of

Table 119 Crude prevalence of stress indicators in subadults by period and burial type

Period	Age (years)	Burial type	No. individuals	Enamel hypoplasia (permanent dentition) No. affected	%	Non-specific periosteal lesions No. affected	%	Cribra orbitalia No. affected	%
14	1–5	ABC	5	0	-	0	-	1	20.0
		D	0	0	-	0	-	0	-
		total	5	0	-	0	-	1	20.0
	6–11	ABC	8	3	37.5	1	12.5	0	-
		D	13	6	46.2	0	-	9	69.2
		total	21	9	42.9	1	4.8	9	42.9
	12–17	ABC	34	15	44.1	4	11.8	12	35.3
		D	27	20	74.1	5	18.5	14	51.9
		total	61	35	57.4	9	14.8	26	42.6
15	1–5	ABC	3	2	66.7	0	-	2	66.7
		D	8	1	12.5	0	-	3	37.5
		total	11	3	27.3	0	-	5	45.5
	6–11	ABC	28	9	32.1	7	25.0	12	42.9
		D	75	42	56.0	6	8.0	35	46.7
		total	103	51	49.5	13	12.6	47	45.6
	12–17	ABC	60	31	51.7	13	21.7	23	38.3
		D	109	65	59.6	17	15.6	44	40.4
		total	169	96	56.8	30	17.8	67	39.6
16	1–5	ABC	17	0	-	2	11.8	5	29.4
		D	14	1	7.1	2	14.3	2	14.3
		total	31	1	3.2	4	12.9	7	22.6
	6–11	ABC	87	41	47.1	8	9.2	26	29.9
		D	100	41	41.0	11	11.0	2	2.0
		total	187	82	43.9	19	10.2	28	15.0
	12–17	ABC	91	45	49.5	20	22.0	34	37.4
		D	174	97	55.7	19	10.9	72	41.4
		total	265	142	53.6	39	14.7	106	40.0
17	1–5	ABC	10	0	-	0	-	4	40.0
		D	1	0	-	0	-	0	-
		total	11	0	-	0	-	4	36.4
	6–11	ABC	24	13	54.2	0	-	12	50.0
		D	13	9	69.2	1	7.7	7	53.8
		total	37	22	59.5	1	2.7	19	51.4
	12–17	ABC	36	23	63.9	4	11.1	12	33.3
		D	13	9	69.2	1	7.7	6	46.2
		total	49	32	65.3	5	10.2	18	36.7

periosteal new bone formation.

In period 16, all three stress indicators were observed in subadults of all ages from burial type D. For those aged 6–11 years, a clear difference was observed between burial types for the rate of cribra orbitalia (burial type ABC 26/87: 29.9%; burial type D 2/100: 2.0%).

In period 17, those aged 1–5 years did not have evidence for enamel hypoplastic defects or periosteal new bone formation, and no stress indicators were observed in burial type D. In later childhood (6–11 years), periosteal new bone formation was not observed in burial type ABC, and the crude prevalence rate of all indicators was higher in burial type D than in burial type ABC. Adolescents were the only individuals to have all three indicators in both burial types. The crude prevalence rates of enamel hypoplastic defects and cribra orbitalia for this age group were higher in burial type D, while the rate of periosteal new bone formation was higher in burial type ABC.

The crude prevalence of indicators of stress shows clear age and burial type differences. Of all three indicators, periosteal new bone formation had the lowest rates in all periods and enamel hypoplastic defects had the highest. Individuals aged 12–17 years had the highest rates and were the only individuals to have all three indicators present in each period. This result is to be expected as this group had lived the longest, thereby allowing them to have sufficient opportunity to develop a bony or dental response to stress (Humphrey and King 2000). Rates of stress indicators for burial type ABC peaked in periods 15 and 17, and for burial type D in periods in 14 and 17 (Fig 159).

Osteoporosis

Four adults had skeletal changes conforming to osteoporosis (0.1% of the entire sample). The disease was only observed in periods 16 and 17, and in burial type ABC.

In period 16, two females were affected, 0.5% of all females in this period (2/1009). A 36–45-year-old [17861] displayed biparietal thinning (Ortner 2003, 412; cf Barnes 1994, 146–8) and a ≥46-year-old female [25907] had very lightweight long bones (Ortner 2003, 413).

In period 17, two 36–45-year-old males had axial and appendicular changes: [11288] had a healed Colles fracture to the distal left radius and osteoporotic changes to the spine, with compression and anterior wedging in the thoracic spine, and [20184] had 'cod-fish' vertebrae from the 11th thoracic to fourth lumbar vertebrae (Brickley and Ives 2008, 158–66).

3.11 Neoplastic disease

Don Walker

Evidence of neoplastic disease, in the form of bone and cartilage tumours, was identified in 132 individuals (132/5387: 2.5%). The majority of those affected were adults, with an

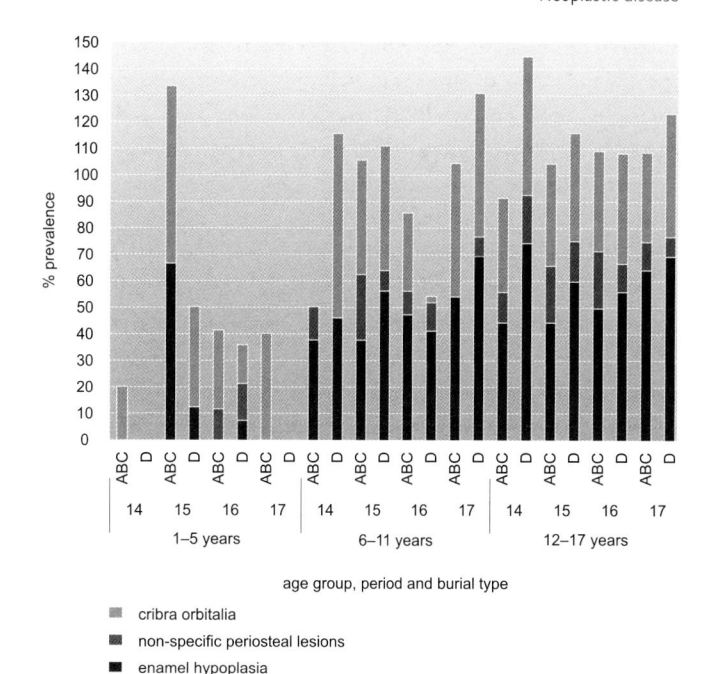

Fig 159 Temporal comparison of indicators of stress in subadults

increased frequency up to later middle age (36–45 years). Following this peak, the prevalence fell in those ≥46 years. While we might have expected to find the greatest frequency of neoplastic disease in the oldest age category, not all tumours are associated with advancing years, and the age distribution was partially dependent upon the relative frequencies of different types of neoplasm. Only seven subadults were affected, and no individuals younger than 6 years of age (Table 120; Fig 160).

Male crude prevalence was higher than female, but not to a statistically significant extent. The greatest variation was found in the 18–25-year-old age group, but the female frequency was too small to test (Table 121; Fig 161). There was no significant variation in crude prevalence rate by period (Fig 162).

Bone tissue neoplasia predominated in the sample (Table 122). More than half of all individuals with neoplasia (70/132: 53.3%) and 90.9% (70/77) of those with bone tissue neoplasia had osteoma. The majority of these had button osteoma on their crania (64/70: 91.4%), 48.5% of all individuals with neoplasia (64/132). Males and females were equally affected (Fig 163).

The majority of individuals with cartilage tissue neoplasia were affected by osteochondromas (33/39: 84.6%) (Fig 164). Males had a significantly higher prevalence of osteochondromas than females (female 5/1883: 0.3%; male 22/2237: 0.1%; $\chi^2 = 8.09$, df = 1, p ≤ 0.01), and it was this difference that accounted for the higher male frequency in the overall neoplastic disease crude prevalence rates (Fig 161).

The distribution of osteochondromas throughout the body demonstrated the predominance of the lower limbs, and especially the tibia (Fig 165). Of those individuals with neoplasms, 73.5% (97/132) had either button osteomas or osteochondromas (Fig 166; Fig 167).

Results

Table 120 Crude prevalence of neoplastic disease by age

Age	No.	Affected	%
Perinatal	68	0	-
1–6 months	2	0	-
7–11 months	2	0	-
1–5 years	58	0	-
6–11 years	348	2	0.6
12–17 years	544	5	0.9
Subadult	5	0	-
Total subadult	**1027**	**7**	**0.7**
18–25 years	979	14	1.4
26–35 years	1546	37	2.4
36–45 years	1219	53	4.3
≥46 years	442	16	3.6
Adult	174	5	2.9
Total adult	**4360**	**125**	**2.9**
Grand total	**5387**	**132**	**2.5**

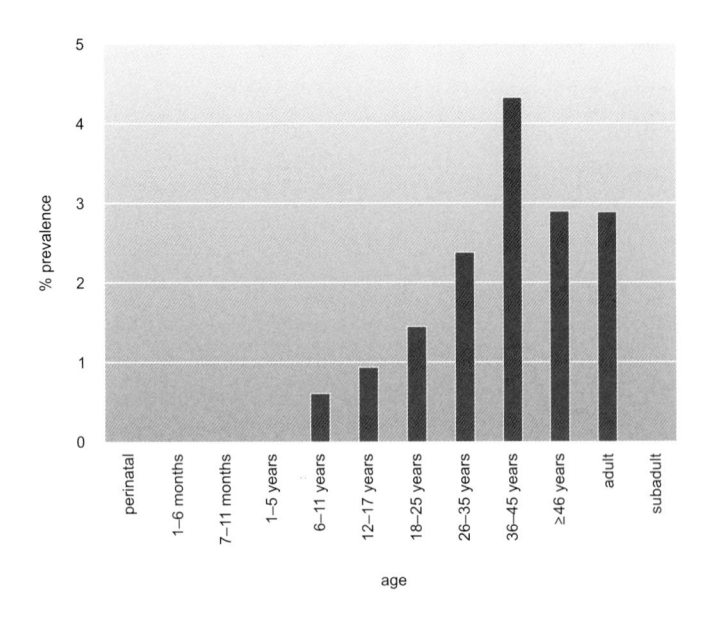

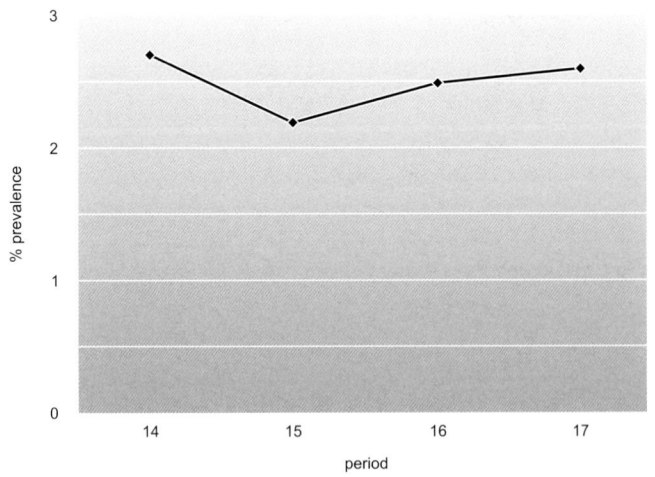

Fig 160 Crude prevalence rate of neoplastic disease by age

Table 121 Crude prevalence of neoplastic disease in adults by sex

	Female			Male			Intermediate			Undetermined			Total		
Age (years)	No.	Affected	%	No.	Affected	%	No.	Affected	%	No.	Affected	%	No.	Affected	%
18–25	428	3	0.7	481	11	2.3	62	0	-	8	0	-	979	14	1.4
26–35	716	17	2.4	752	20	2.7	69	0	-	9	0	-	1546	37	2.4
36–45	467	18	3.9	700	33	4.7	48	2	4.2	4	0	-	1219	53	4.3
≥46	211	6	2.8	222	10	4.5	7	0	-	2	0	-	442	16	3.6
Adult	61	1	1.6	82	2	2.4	19	2	10.5	12	0	-	174	5	2.9
Total	**1883**	**45**	**2.4**	**2237**	**76**	**3.4**	**205**	**4**	**2.0**	**35**	**0**	**-**	**4360**	**125**	**2.9**

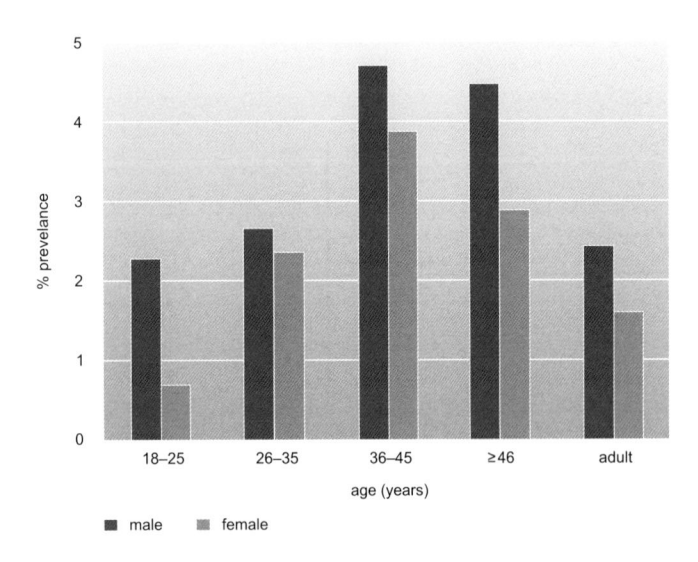

Fig 161 Crude prevalence rate of neoplastic disease in adults by sex

Fig 162 Crude prevalence rate of neoplastic disease by period

Neoplastic disease

Table 122 Distribution of different types of neoplasia

Type	No. with neoplasia	Affected	%
Bone tissue	132	77	58.3
Cartilage tissue	132	39	29.5
Other	132	16	12.1

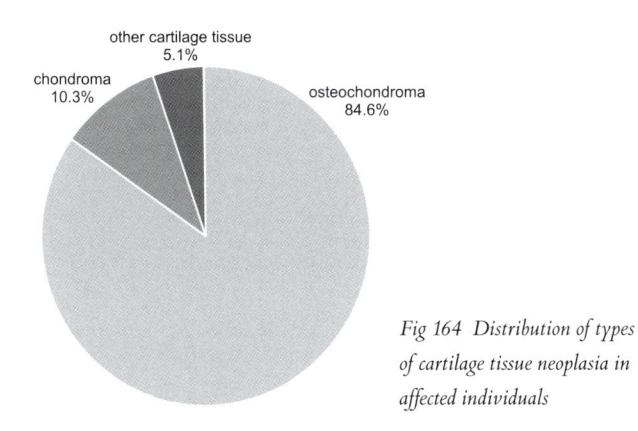

Fig 163 Distribution of types of bone tissue neoplasia by individual

Fig 164 Distribution of types of cartilage tissue neoplasia in affected individuals

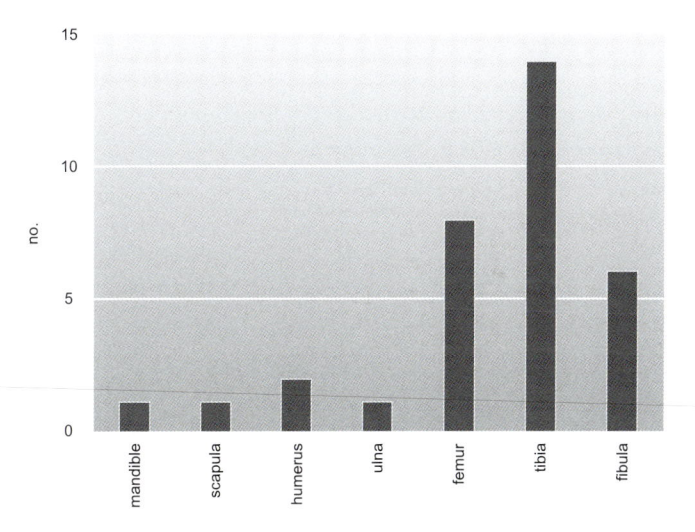

Fig 165 Distribution of osteochondromas in parts of the body

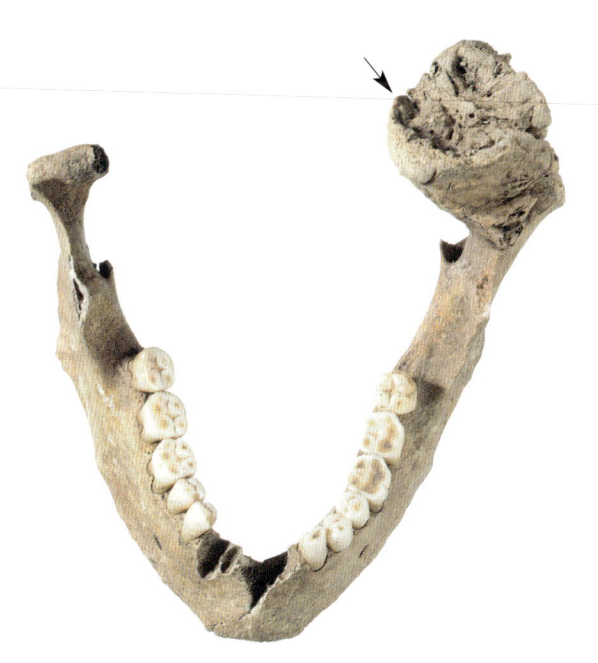

Fig 166 Osteochondroma in the left mandible of 36–45-year-old male [13279] from period 16, burial type ABC (scale c 1:2)

Fig 167 Osteochondroma with possible secondary malignancy (chondrosarcoma) of the right scapula of 26–35-year-old female [11661] from period 15, burial type D (scale c 1:1)

129

3.12 Circulatory disorders

Rebecca Redfern

Osteonecroses

Two individuals had osteonecrotic changes (2/2387: <0.1%) (Table 123). In period 15, 18–25-year-old male [25775] (burial type ABC) had bilateral changes to the humeral heads; and in period 16, 36–45-year-old female [34104] (burial type D) had multiple ischaemic necrosis to major joints (left hip, humeri and distal right tibia). The hip joint necrosis in this individual had resulted in joint instability, and the joint may have been subluxed. In subluxed hips, there is contact with the acetabulum but the joint can become completely dislocated (Shapiro 2002). On the left ilium there was a large oval depression, which suggests that the femur had articulated with this false facet. The true hip joint had developed osteoarthritis, indicating that the joint had been reduced (ie treated) and was used, despite secondary osteoarthritic changes limiting movement and causing slight anterior flexion.

Osteochondroses

Scheuermann's, Freiberg's and Perthes' diseases were observed in 0.5% of the assemblage (25/5387). In all cases the numbers of individuals affected were too small for chi-square tests to be undertaken (Table 124).

Table 123 Crude prevalence of osteonecroses by period

Period	Sex	No. individuals	No. affected	%
15	male	532	1	0.2
16	female	1009	1	0.1

Scheuermann's disease

This disease was recorded in individuals from periods 15 to 17. It affected ten individuals (10/5387: 0.2%), seven of whom were male and seven from burial type D. The condition was most common in period 17 (3/650: 0.5%) (Table 124). The most frequently affected elements were the sixth to 11th thoracic vertebrae.

A 26–35-year-old male [22764] (period 15, burial type D) had changes to the eighth to 11th thoracic vertebrae, which also show widening of the annulus fibrosus, Schmorl's nodes and irregularity in vertebral contour. The body and the neural arch of the tenth and 11th thoracic vertebrae were also fused but with the intervertebral disc space maintained, and the ninth and eighth thoracic vertebrae were joined by a large osteophyte on the right anterior surface. The centrum of the eighth thoracic vertebra had fused at a slight oblique angle, creating a small degree of scoliosis to the right. Fusion and scoliosis, when occurring at the same level as the kyphosis, are recognised in the clinical literature as being associated with Scheuermann's disease (Resnick 2002, 3725–8) (Fig 168).

Freiberg's disease

Two females from period 17 ([7726] and [3860]) had evidence for osteochondrosis of the head of the second metatarsal (2/5387: <0.1%) (Aufderheide and Rodríguez-Martín 1998, 86) (Table 124). In 36–45-year-old [3860], burial type D, the left foot proximal phalanx was also affected; the superior half of the distal articular surface was flattened and expanded, forming a circular area with a smooth-walled central depression. The proximal articular surface of the proximal phalanx also showed expansion and slight flattening. When the elements were articulated, the phalanx lay dorsiflexed on to the flattened area of the second metatarsal head (Fig 169).

Table 124 Crude prevalence of osteochondroses by period and burial type

Period	Sex or age	Burial type	No. individuals	Perthes' disease No. affected	%	Scheuermann's disease No. affected	%	Freiberg's disease No. affected	%
15	12–17 years	ABC	60	0	-	0	-	0	-
		D	109	1	0.9	0	-	0	-
	male	ABC	219	1	0.5	0	-	0	-
		D	313	1	0.3	3	1.0	0	-
16	male	ABC	628	6	1.0	1	0.2	0	-
		D	564	2	0.4	2	0.4	0	-
	female	ABC	474	0	-	1	0.2	0	-
		D	535	0	-	0	-	0	-
	intermediate	ABC	71	0	-	0	-	0	-
		D	39	1	2.6	0	-	0	-
17	male	ABC	239	0	-	0	-	0	-
		D	51	0	-	1	2.0	0	-
	female	ABC	164	1	0.6	1	0.6	1	0.6
		D	39	0	-	1	2.6	1	2.6

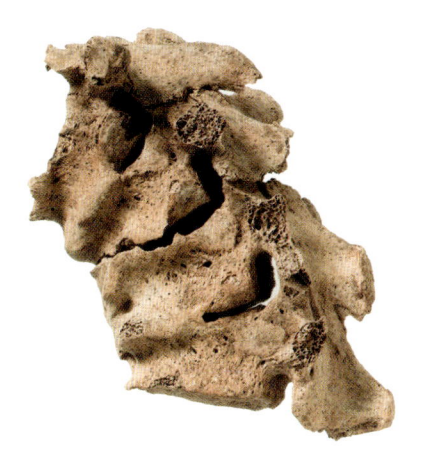

Fig 168 Multiple changes to the thoracic vertebrae in 26–35-year-old male [22764] from period 15, burial type D (scale c 1:2)

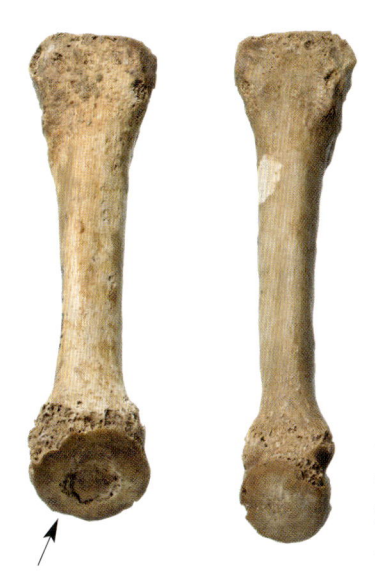

Fig 169 Right second metatarsal with Freiberg's disease in 36–45-year-old female [3860] from period 17, burial type D (scale c 1:1)

Perthes' disease

Thirteen individuals with Perthes' disease were recorded (13/5387: 0.2%), ten of whom were male (10/13: 76.9%). No individuals from period 14 were affected, and 12–17-year-olds were only affected in period 15. The right hip was predominantly affected and the majority of those affected were from burial type ABC. The greatest number of affected individuals were males from period 16 (8/1192: 0.7%) (Table 124).

Young adult male [23126] (period 14, burial type D) had evidence for late onset Perthes' disease (Aufderheide and Rodríguez-Martín 1998, 84). The left femoral head had flattened, causing severe expansion of the head diameter (it was 13.4mm larger than the right side); the fovea capitis had also enlarged, and the surgical neck had widened and reduced in vertical height, lying below the level of the superior point of the greater trochanter. The left acetabulum was within normal morphology and the lower limb elements showed biomechanical evidence for under-use, as the anterior-posterior width of the left femur and tibia was smaller than the right.

Osteochondritis dissecans

Osteochondritis dissecans was recorded in all periods and was observed in 123 individuals aged between 6 and ≥46 years, 2.3% of the population (123/5387). The proportion of individuals affected showed an increase from 1.6% in period 14 (8/512) to 2.6% in period 16 (75/2835) and subsequent decrease in period 17 (12/650: 1.8%) (Table 125). No statistically significant difference was observed between the number of affected males and females by burial type. Seventy-four male elements and 49 female elements were affected. The most frequently affected element was the humerus (23/123: 18.7%), followed by the femur and radius (20/123: 16.3%). For example, 18–25-year-old female [19443] (period 16, burial type D) had large remodelling oval defects on the medial femoral condyles.

Elements from the axial and appendicular skeleton were affected, ranging from the atlas and axis vertebrae to the scapula, first metatarsal and ulna. The most frequently affected joint surface was the humeroulnar trochlea (20/156 affected bones: 12.8%), followed by the humeroradial head (14/156 affected bones: 9.0%), and femorotibial lateral joint surface and talocalcaneal joints (14/156 affected bones: 9.0%). No statistical significance was found between burial types or sexes (Table 125).

Table 125 Crude prevalence of osteochondritis dissecans by period and burial type

Period	Sex or age	Burial type	No. individuals	No. affected	%
14	12–17 years	ABC	34	1	2.9
		D	27	1	3.7
	male	ABC	160	2	1.3
		D	63	3	4.8
	female	ABC	115	0	-
		D	55	1	1.8
15	6–11 years	ABC	28	0	-
		D	75	2	2.7
	12–17 years	ABC	60	3	5.0
		D	109	3	2.8
	male	ABC	219	7	3.2
		D	313	2	0.6
	female	ABC	167	3	1.8
		D	334	7	2.1
	intermediate	ABC	17	0	-
		D	29	1	3.4
16	6–11 years	ABC	87	2	2.3
		D	100	2	2.0
	12–17 years	ABC	91	2	2.2
		D	174	4	2.3
	male	ABC	628	20	3.2
		D	564	19	3.4
	female	ABC	474	11	2.3
		D	535	12	2.2
	intermediate	ABC	71	2	2.8
		D	39	1	2.6
17	male	ABC	239	6	2.5
		D	51	1	2.0
	female	ABC	164	4	2.4
		D	39	1	2.6

Results

Table 126 Crude prevalence of hypertrophic osteoarthropathy by period and burial type

Period	Sex	Burial type	No. individuals	No. affected	%
15	male	ABC	219	0	-
		D	313	2	0.6
	female	ABC	167	0	-
		D	334	1	0.3
16	female	ABC	474	1	0.2
		D	535	1	0.2

Hypertrophic osteoarthropathy

This disease, which may also be caused by circulatory and pulmonary disorders or neoplasms (Resnick 2002, 3564–96; eg Mays and Taylor 2002), was observed in periods 15 and 16 and affected five individuals (5/5387: 0.1%), predominantly from burial type D. More females (3/1883: 0.2%) than males (2/2237: 0.1%) were affected. Only in period 15 were both sexes affected, and the majority of affected individuals were in the 26–35-year-old age group (Table 126).

Young adult male [3483] (period 15, burial type D) had active periosteal new bone formation present to the axial and appendicular skeleton. On the long bones the periosteal new bone formation predominantly affected the mid and distal thirds of the diaphyses; on the clavicles, lamellar bone formation was present to the distal third of the diaphysis and the superior aspect of the acromion and body of the left scapula, adjacent to the glenoid cavity. On the right os coxa, remodelling woven bone was present to the inner surface of the ilium and the inner and outer surfaces of the pubis. On the outer surface of the left ischium there were small patches of remodelling woven bone. Other individuals had evidence of new bone formation to the metatarsals, tarsals, metacarpals and phalanges, for example 36–45-year-old female [19235] (period 16, burial type D).

3.13 Congenital and developmental abnormalities

Rebecca Redfern

Cranial anomalies

Seventeen individuals from periods 15 to 17 were affected (17/5387: 0.3%). A similar proportion of males (8/5387: 0.1%) and females (6/5387: 0.1%) were affected, in addition to two 12–17-year-olds (2/5387: <0.1%), and one intermediate adult (1/5387: <0.1%) (Table 127). Given the generally small data sets, further results have not been presented by period as in the previous sections, but rather by the nature of the condition observed.

Table 127 Crude prevalence of cranial anomalies by period and burial type

Period	Sex or age	Burial type	No. individuals	No. affected	%
15	12–17 years	ABC	60	0	-
		D	109	1	0.9
	male	ABC	219	1	0.5
		D	313	1	0.3
	female	ABC	167	0	-
		D	334	1	0.3
	intermediate	ABC	17	1	5.9
		D	29	0	-
16	male	ABC	628	2	0.3
		D	564	1	0.2
	female	ABC	474	4	0.8
		D	535	0	-
17	12–17 years	ABC	36	0	-
		D	13	1	7.7
	male	ABC	239	2	0.8
		D	51	1	2.0
	female	ABC	164	1	0.6
		D	39	0	-

Cranial hyperplasia

Cranial hyperplasia, a developmental disturbance which results in excessive growth or tissue development (Barnes 1994, 327), was observed in four individuals (4/5387: 0.1%) from periods 15 to 17. Where cranial elements could be sided, only the right was affected, and the most frequently affected bone was the supraoccipital. In female [13602] (period 17, burial type ABC) all the elements on the right side of the cranium and the supraoccipital were affected.

Sutural agenesis

Two males were affected by sutural agenesis (2/5387: <0.1%). In period 16, ≥46-year-old adult [31402] (burial type D) showed obliteration of the squamosal and temporosphenoid sutures, resulting in a very wide cranial breadth. In period 17, 36–45-year-old male [19564] (burial type D) had premature closure of the coronal and sagittal sutures, which resulted in oxycephaly. This condition has a high risk of associated mental impairment, intracranial pressure and possible ophthalmic complications (Renier et al 1997).

Bathrocrania

Bathrocrania was observed in 25 individuals, the majority of whom were male (15/25: 60.0%). In period 14 one female was affected (1/170 females in this period: 0.6%). In period 15 the majority of individuals affected were male (5/8: 62.5%); two 12–17-year-olds were also observed (2/169 of this age group and period: 1.2%). Period 16 had the greatest number of affected individuals (16/25: 64.0%), the majority of whom were male (10/16: 62.5%) (Table 128).

Table 128 Crude prevalence of bathrocrania by period

Period	Sex or age	No. individuals	No. affected	%
14	female	170	1	0.6
15	12–17 years	169	2	1.2
	male	532	5	0.9
	female	501	1	0.2
16	male	1192	10	0.8
	female	1009	5	0.5
	intermediate	110	1	0.9

Craniofacial anomalies

A range of craniofacial anomalies were observed in periods 15 and 16, affecting four individuals of both sexes (4/5387: 0.1%). The anomalies included clefting of the maxilla and palatine bones, fissural cysts, bilateral concha bullosa, and complete ossification and unification of the stylohyoid chain to the hyoid (Reichert's cartilage) (Barnes 1994, 206).

Clefting to the maxilla and palatine bones, fissural cysts and cephalocele were only observed in periods 16 and 17 and affected six individuals (6/5387: 0.1%): three males, two females and one 12–17-year-old. The latter, 12–17-year-old [2480] from period 17, burial type D (1/42: 2.4%) (Fig 170), had a unilateral cleft palate: the cleft occurred at the midline of the palate and in the alveolar bone, adjacent to the right first incisor. The right second incisor was congenitally absent. The clefting resulted in asymmetry of the nasal cavity. This would have been overlain by an associated soft tissue defect (a severe expression of a cleft lip).

Cephalocele (the protrusion of a part of the brain through an opening in the skull) was observed in female [22326] (burial type ABC), consisting of a large (39mm), depressed, circular lesion on the frontal bone with a small (5mm) perforation on the midline, penetrating both cranial tables.

Hemifacial microsomia type 1 (Barnes 1994, 161–3), a condition in which one side of the lower face fails to develop properly, was observed in periods 16 and 17. One subadult, five males and two females were affected (8/5387: 0.1%). In period 16, one 12–17-year-old (1/265: 0.4%), two females (2/1009: 0.2%) and four males (4/1192: 0.3%) were affected. In period 17 one male was affected (1/290: 0.3%). The majority of affected individuals (four) had died between the ages of 36 and 45 years, and no adults over this age were observed with this condition.

Nasal bone hypoplasia

Bilateral hypoplasia, sometimes severe, was the most frequently observed condition, though bilateral aplasia was also recorded. These conditions were only recorded in periods 15 and 16. In period 15, two males displayed bilateral hypoplasia (2/532: 0.4%). In period 16, one male (1/1192: 0.1%) had a severe form of the anomaly (Barnes 1994, 194), one female had bilateral hypoplasia (1/1009: 0.1%) and another had bilateral aplasia (1/1009: 0.1%).

Chromosomal disorders

Chromosomal disorders are rarely observed in ancient and modern populations, as the majority of affected embryos were miscarried. Survivors have changes to the soft tissue and/or skeleton which are caused by errors in chromosome pairs (known as syndromes) whose incidence is related to maternal age, underlying genetic factors and prenatal exposure to pollution (Roberts and Manchester 2005, 62; genome.gov 2011). The syndromes often involve multiple developmental anomalies: for example, individuals with partial trisomy have (among other features) craniofacial anomalies, syndactyly (the fusion of two or more digits) and delayed growth (Shashidhar et al 2003, 2).

Two individuals (2/5387: <0.1%) presented with multiple skeletal anomalies which were considered to be related to a chromosomal disorder. In period 15, male [15655] (burial type D) had bilateral changes to the frontal, maxilla, nasal, zygomatic and occipital bones and mandible. In period 16, 12–17-year-old [20924] (burial type D) had bilateral changes to the frontal and occipital bones. The anomalies seen in these individuals could not be assigned to a particular condition, as they are common to a range of disorders.

Spinal anomalies

Thirty-one individuals (31/5387: 0.6%) had spinal anomalies and a greater proportion of males (17/2237: 0.8%) than females (12/1883: 0.6%) were affected. One 12–17-year-old and one adult of intermediate sex were also affected (Table 129).

Fig 170 Anterior view of unilateral cleft palate in 12–17-year-old [2480] from period 17, burial type D (scale c 1:2)

Results

Table 129 Crude prevalence of spinal anomalies by period and burial type

Period	Burial type	Sex or age	No. individuals	Scoliosis No. affected	%	Kyphosis No. affected	%	Kyphoscoliosis No. affected	%
14	ABC	male	160	2	1.3	0	-	0	-
		female	115	1	0.9	1	0.9	0	-
15	ABC	12–17 years	60	0	-	1	1.7	0	-
		male	219	1	0.5	0	-	0	-
		female	167	2	1.2	0	-	0	-
	D	female	334	1	0.3	1	0.3	1	0.3
16	ABC	male	628	1	0.2	0	-	0	-
		female	474	2	0.4	0	-	0	-
		intermediate	71	1	1.4	0	-	0	-
	D	male	564	3	0.5	1	0.2	3	0.5
		female	535	2	0.4	0	-	0	-
17	ABC	male	239	4	1.7	0	-	2	0.8
		female	164	0	-	0	-	1	0.6

Kyphosis

Four individuals had kyphotic spinal changes to multiple vertebrae (4/5387: 0.1%) (Table 129). In period 14, one 26–35-year-old female was affected; 1/50 females in this age group from burial type ABC (2.0%), and 1/73 females in this age group from both burial types (1.4%). In period 15 a 12–17-year-old was affected; 1/60 from burial type ABC (1.7%) and 1/169 of this age group from both burial types combined (0.6%). In period 16 one 36–45-year-old male was affected, and represented 0.6% of the males in this age group from burial type D (1/163) and 0.3% of the group when burial types were combined (1/368).

The most frequently affected elements were the fifth to 12th thoracic vertebrae. The 12–17-year-old [30711] had a sagittal cleft to the fifth thoracic vertebra, while the sixth to ninth thoracic vertebrae had blocked neural arches and aplastic right pedicles. The severe (180°) kyphosis had been caused by ventral aplasia of the ninth thoracic vertebra centrum, hypoplasia of the fifth thoracic vertebra centrum and dorsal hemicentrum of the 11th thoracic vertebra. Secondary changes were present to the ribs, scapulae and clavicles, the lateral portions of which were spatulate. Other secondary changes included atrophy of the left femur in a 36–45-year-old female [11471] from period 16.

Kyphoscoliosis

This spinal anomaly was recorded in seven individuals (7/5387: 0.1%) from periods 15 to 17 (Table 129). The burial types were affected equally but more males (5/2237: 0.2%) than females (2/1883: 0.1%) were affected. Only in period 17 were both sexes affected (two male and one female). The highest prevalence rate was observed among the ≥46-year-old adult males from period 17, burial type ABC (1/28 males in this age group: 3.6%). However, this is a result of the low number of individuals in this age group (28). An 18–25-year-old female was also affected in this period, 1.7% of this age group (1/57). More meaningful prevalence rates were observed in periods 15 and 16, where pooled data showed that 0.8% of 18–25-year-old females (1/120) and 0.8% of ≥46-year-old males (1/124) were affected.

Young adult female [20488], from period 15 (burial type D), had severe kyphoscoliosis stretching from the second thoracic to the fifth lumbar vertebrae (Fig 171; Fig 172). The thoracic spine formed a block from the second to sixth vertebrae, fixed in extreme kyphosis, the second thoracic vertebral body being in contact with the left side of the anterior body of the sixth thoracic vertebra. The thoracic vertebrae also displayed hypoplasia of the left lateral centra and the seventh and eighth thoracic centra were concave, exaggerating the scoliosis. Hyperplasia of the anterior portions of the lumbar vertebrae and asymmetrical transverse processes were also seen. Such severe anomalies resulted in a narrowing of the intervertebral foramen and neural canal, and appeared to have caused paraplegia. This diagnosis is supported by the unusual burial position of this female, on her right side with both legs together, the femora at 90° to the long axis of the body and the lower legs flexed at a very sharp angle from the knee, causing the feet to be positioned close to the pelvis (Fig 173). This woman's skeleton was small and gracile but although her bones were thin, they were not atrophied; the muscle markings fell within normal variation considering her reduced size.

Scoliosis

Paralytic scoliosis (curvature of the spine due to imbalance and/or weakness of the supporting musculature) was observed in 20 individuals from all periods (20/5387: 0.4%): 0.1% of females (8/5387), 0.2% of males (11/5387) and one adult of intermediate sex (1/5387: <0.1%) (Table 129). This form of scoliosis predominantly affects the thoracolumbar region, and is caused by neurological disorders affecting the spinal muscles (Aufderheide and Rodríguez-Martín 1998, 67).

Congenital and developmental abnormalities

Both sexes were affected in all periods except period 17, where only males were affected. The highest prevalence rates were seen among 18–25-year-old males from period 14 (burial types ABC and D 2/37: 5.4%) and 26–35-year-olds of intermediate sex in period 16 (burial types ABC and D 1/37: 2.7%).

The cervical vertebrae were only affected in two males, one from period 16 and one from period 17. The first sacral vertebra was only affected in period 15 females but the thoracic spine was the most affected spinal segment, particularly the third to

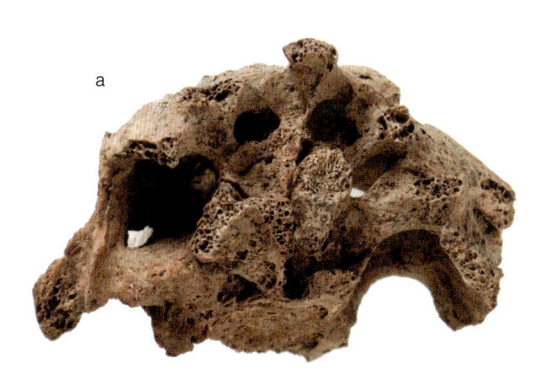

Fig 171 Kyphoscoliosis of the second to sixth thoracic vertebrae in 18–25-year-old female [20488] from period 15, burial type D: a – left lateral view; b – inferior view (scale c 1:1)

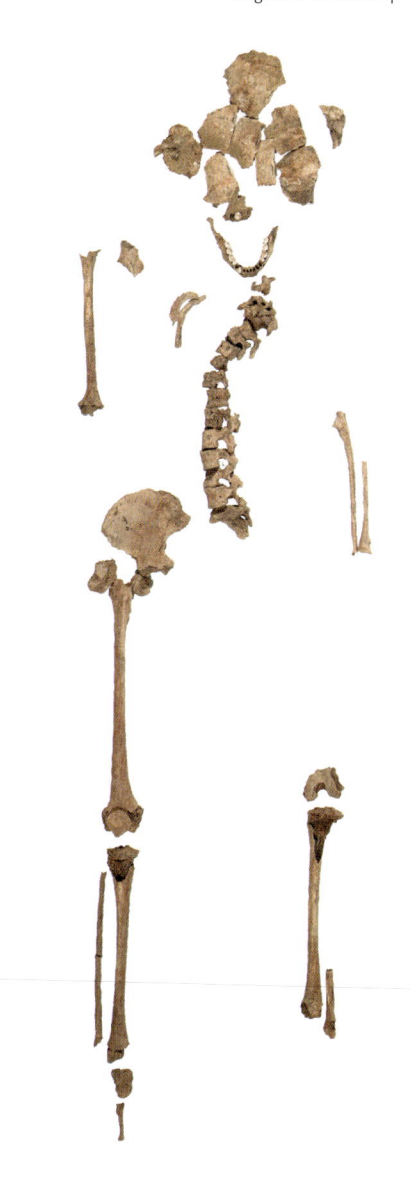

Fig 172 Kyphoscoliosis and limb atrophy in 18–25-year-old female [20488] from period 15, burial type D (scale c 1:10)

Fig 173 18–25-year-old female [20488] from period 15, burial type D, as excavated, showing the unusual burial position (0.2m scale)

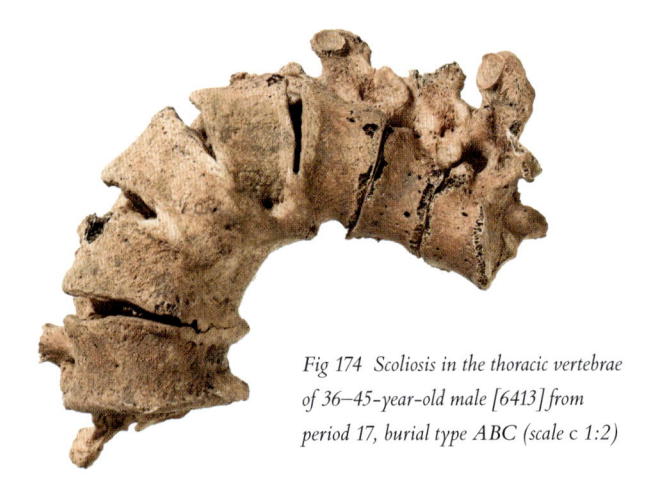

Results

Fig 174 Scoliosis in the thoracic vertebrae of 36–45-year-old male [6413] from period 17, burial type ABC (scale c 1:2)

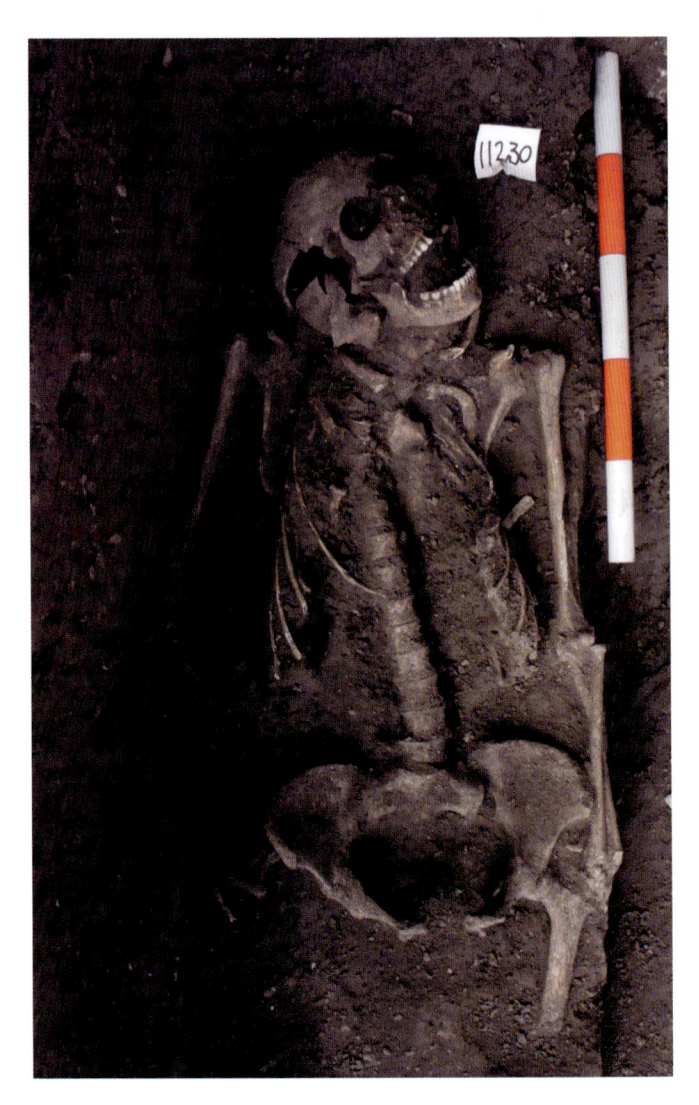

eighth vertebrae (Fig 174). The difference between the numbers of males and females affected was not statistically significant.

A 26–35-year-old female from period 16 ([11230], burial type ABC) had evidence for paralytic scoliotic changes from the atlas to the 12th thoracic vertebra, caused by hypoplasia of the vertebral bodies and/or neural arches (Fig 175). The scoliotic changes were severe in the cervical vertebrae and mild from the first to eighth thoracic vertebrae, with spinous processes of the ninth to 12th thoracic vertebrae displaying asymmetry. These changes resulted in the thoracic spine leaning to the left and the cervical spine to the right, creating a classic S shape. The vertebrae showed biomechanical adaptation to the scoliotic changes, as the spinous processes, costal facets and articular facets displayed asymmetry or atypical morphology. Seven ribs also displayed biomechanical adaptations, for example the first rib necks were angled by 30° in a superior direction, the heads being larger than normal. This female also had hypoplastic and biomechanical changes to other elements in the axial skeleton: the clavicles were asymmetrical, the left with an exaggerated S-shaped diaphysis with marked anterior projection of the mid third, and superior bowing. In comparison, the right clavicle had a relatively straight diaphysis. The left half of the manubrium was flatter and sloped laterally, with a larger and more posteriorly angulated left sternoclavicular notch. The mandible showed extreme hypoplasia of the right side, the left body extending posteriorly and angulated further from the midline than the right. Asymmetry of the palato-maxillary suture was present, the right posterior margin and right palatine being larger than the left. The right maxilla had a splayed appearance and the right maxillo-zygomatic articulation lay anterior of the normal orientation. Unfortunately, due to taphonomic damage of the temporal bones, only limited observation was possible. The right temporomandibular joint was larger, with a splayed appearance and the right temporal bone smaller than the left, but the mastoid process was more robust and rounded.

An 18–25-year-old male [6571] (period 14, burial type ABC) also displayed severe scoliosis in the thoracic spine. He was found buried in a crouched position, and had marked atrophy of the pelvic girdle, femora, tibiae and fibulae, although the long bones were of normal length. The femoral condyles showed a

Fig 175 26–35-year-old female [11230] with scoliosis, from period 16, burial type ABC, as excavated (0.5m scale)

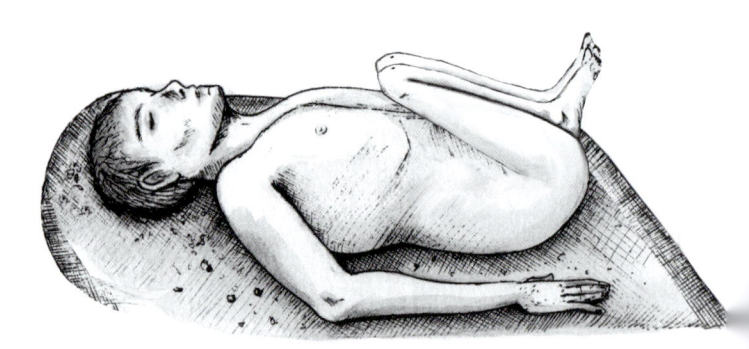

Fig 176 18–25-year-old male [6571] with scoliosis and lower limb atrophy, from period 14, burial type ABC, was buried in the crouched position his limbs held during life (burial reconstruction drawn by Hannah Faux)

pronounced transverse ridge on the articular surfaces and flattening to the posterior portion of the condyles. Such biomechanical changes to the lower limbs suggest that his knee joints were fixed in a semi-flexed position (Fig 176).

Spondylolysis

Spondylolysis may have both developmental and traumatic aetiologies but has been classified as a developmental anomaly here for the purpose of presenting the results. A total of 236 individuals were affected (236/5387: 4.4%): 5.0% of males (112/2237), 6.1% of females (114/1883), 0.9% of 12–17-year-olds (5/544) and 2.4% of adults of intermediate sex (5/205). No statistical significance was found between the number of males and females affected or in the location of the lesions (right, left or bilateral) (Table 130).

When both burial groups are combined, the right side was affected in 24 individuals (24/5387: 0.4%); more males (14/2237: 0.6%) than females (8/1883: 0.4%) were affected, together with one 12–17-year-old (1/544: 0.2%) and one intermediate adult (1/205: 0.5%). Separation had occurred at the interarticularis, with the exception of one female from period 15 where separation had occurred at the left lamina. The majority of individuals had the fifth lumbar vertebra affected (178/236 affected individuals: 75.4%), followed by the fourth lumbar vertebra (44/236: 18.6%); the first lumbar vertebra was affected in one female from period 17, burial type ABC (1/164 females in this group: 0.6%), at the right pars interarticularis.

Males were most frequently affected in all periods, apart from period 17. The highest crude prevalence was observed in 36–45-year-old females from period 17 (3/46: 6.5%), 26–35-year-olds of intermediate sex from period 16 (1/37: 2.7%) and 18–25-year-old males from period 14 (1/37: 2.7%).

The left side of the vertebrae was affected in 14 individuals (14/5387: 0.3%), with no difference in the number of males and females (both 6/5387: 0.1%). One 12–17-year-old (1/5387: <0.1%) and one intermediate adult were affected (1/5387: <0.1%). In all periods, apart from period 15, the separation had occurred at the pars interarticularis. The most frequently affected element was the fifth vertebra (9/14: 64.2%), followed by the third lumbar vertebra (3/14: 21.4%). However, the third lumbar vertebra was only affected in individuals from periods 16 and 17 and only in 12–17-year-olds, females and intermediate adults. Males were most frequently affected, and all cases observed were in the fifth lumbar vertebra. The greatest numbers of vertebrae affected were from period 15. The highest crude prevalence was observed in 18–25-year-old adults of intermediate sex (1/8: 12.5%) and 36–45-year-old females (1/46: 2.2%) from period 17. In period 15, females ≥46 years old (1/52: 1.9%) and 36–45-year-old males (3/165: 1.8%) were affected, and in period 14, 26–35-year-old females (1/73: 1.4%) were affected.

Table 130 Crude prevalence of spondylolysis by period and burial type

Period	Burial type	Sex or age	No. individuals	Right No. affected	%	Left No. affected	%	Bilateral No. affected	%
14	ABC	subadult	52	0	-	0	-	0	-
		male	160	1	0.6	0	-	7	4.4
		female	115	1	0.9	1	0.9	8	7.0
	D	subadult	42	0	-	0	-	0	-
		male	63	0	-	0	-	5	7.9
		female	55	0	-	0	-	4	7.3
15	ABC	subadult	100	0	-	0	-	0	-
		male	219	2	0.9	4	1.8	8	3.7
		female	167	1	0.6	1	0.6	8	4.8
		intermediate	17	0	-	0	-	0	-
	D	subadult	201	1	0.5	0	-	0	-
		male	313	3	1.0	1	0.3	14	4.5
		female	334	0	-	1	0.3	17	5.1
		intermediate	29	0	-	0	-	1	3.4
16	ABC	subadult	209	0	-	0	-	0	-
		male	628	4	0.6	0	-	29	4.6
		female	474	1	0.2	1	0.2	30	6.3
		intermediate	71	1	1.4	0	-	1	1.4
	D	subadult	299	0	-	1	0.3	2	0.7
		male	564	3	0.5	1	0.2	15	2.7
		female	535	2	0.4	1	0.2	22	4.1
		intermediate	39	0	-	0	-	1	2.6
17	ABC	subadult	95	0	-	0	-	1	1.1
		male	239	1	0.4	0	-	11	4.6
		female	164	3	1.8	1	0.6	9	5.5
		intermediate	24	0	-	1	4.2	0	-
	D	subadult	29	0	-	0	-	0	-
		male	51	0	-	0	-	3	5.9
		female	39	0	-	0	-	2	5.1
		intermediate	4	0	-	0	-	0	-

Results

The majority of individuals presented with bilateral separation (198/5387: 3.7%). More females (100/1883: 5.3%) than males (92/2237: 4.1%) were affected, and the condition was seen in just three 12–17-year-olds (3/544: 0.6%) and three intermediate adults (3/205: 1.5%). In all periods, the separation occurred at the interarticularis and in most individuals this occurred at the fifth (149/198: 75.2%) or fourth (40/198: 20.2%) lumbar vertebrae. Males and females had bilateral separation at the third lumbar vertebra but this occurred much less frequently than in the vertebrae below (5/198: 2.5%). Males were more frequently affected than females but only by eight more cases. Males and females were affected from the third to sixth lumbar vertebrae, 12–17-year-olds only in the fourth and fifth lumbar vertebrae, and only the fifth lumbar vertebrae was affected in intermediate adults. The highest overall crude prevalence rates were observed in 36–45-year-olds of intermediate sex from period 17 (1/6: 16.7%); 36–45-year-old males from period 14 (8/80: 10%); 36–45-year-old females from period 16 (21/251: 8.4%); 18–25-year-olds of intermediate sex from period 15 (1/12: 8.3%), and adult females in period 16 (3/45: 6.7%).

Spondylolisthesis

Spondylolisthesis was identified where one vertebral body had slipped forwards over another (Mays 2006c; Merbs 2001; Wiltse et al 1975). Nine individuals were affected (9/5387: 0.2%): four males (4/2237: 0.2%) and five females (5/1883: 0.3%) (Table 131; Fig 177).

Spondylolisthesis was only observed in periods 16 and 17; period 16 had the greatest range of vertebrae affected (third

Table 131 Crude prevalence rate of spondylolisthesis by period and burial type

Period	Burial type	Sex	Age (years)	No. individuals	No. affected	%
16	ABC	male	18–25	118	1	0.8
			36–45	205	0	-
			≥46	63	1	1.6
			All male	628	2	0.3
	D	male	18–25	135	0	-
			36–45	163	1	0.6
			≥46	61	0	-
			All male	564	1	0.2
		female	36–45	130	1	0.8
			≥46	65	2	3.1
			All female	535	3	0.6
17	ABC	male	≥46	28	1	3.6
			All male	239	1	0.4
		female	36–45	35	1	2.9
			All female	164	1	0.6
	D	female	36–45	11	1	9.1
			All female	39	1	2.6

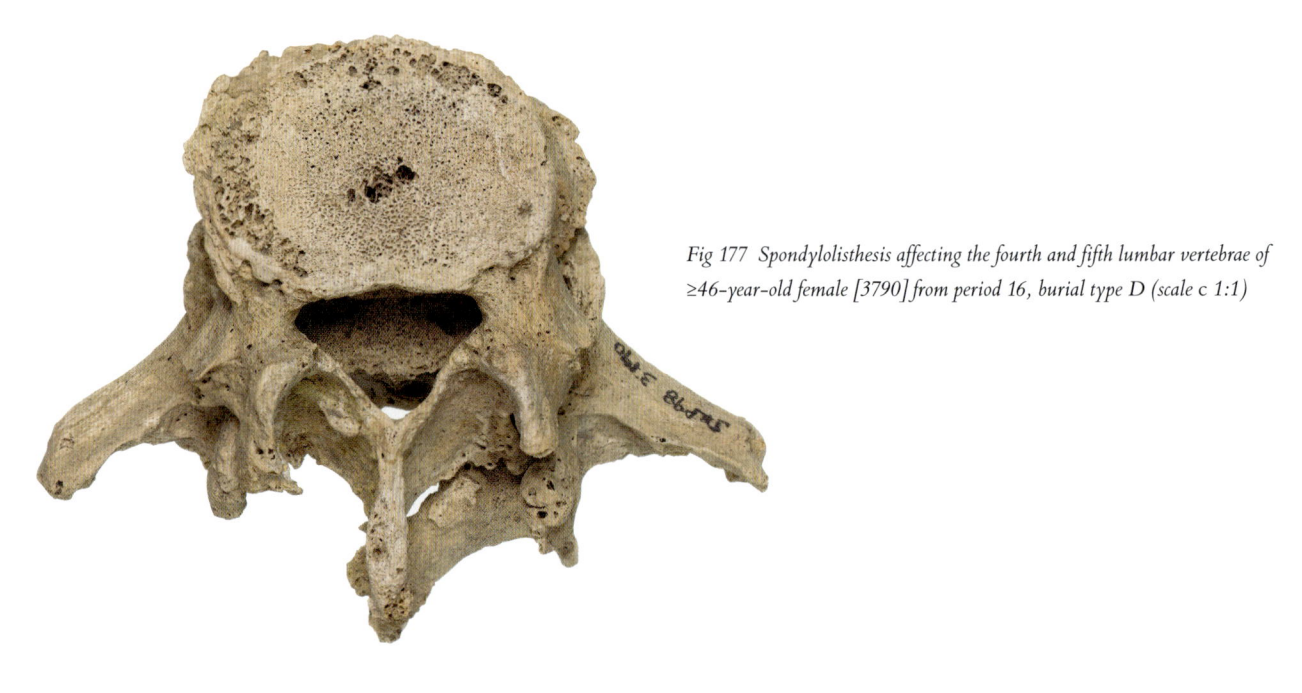

Fig 177 Spondylolisthesis affecting the fourth and fifth lumbar vertebrae of ≥46-year-old female [3790] from period 16, burial type D (scale c 1:1)

lumbar to first sacral vertebrae), whereas in period 17 only the fourth lumbar to first sacral vertebrae were affected. The fourth and fifth lumbar vertebrae were most often affected in both periods. The sixth lumbar and first sacral vertebrae were only affected in females from period 16. The highest crude prevalence rates were observed in period 17 in 36–45-year-old females (burial type D, 1/11: 9.1%) and ≥46-year-old males (burial type ABC, 1/28: 3.6%), and in period 16 in ≥46-year-old adult females, burial type D (2/65: 3.1%). When both burial types were combined, the highest crude prevalence rate was observed in 36–45-year-old females from period 17 (2/46: 4.3%).

Developmental delay of the vertebrae

Bifurcated (a narrow separation) and cleft (a wide separation) neural arches were the most frequently observed types of developmental delay for all ages and both sexes. Most frequently affected were the first, fourth and fifth sacral vertebrae. The highest prevalence rate for cleft neural arch was observed in the fifth sacral vertebra of subadults from period 16 (46/151: 30.5%). The true prevalence of both cranial (fusion in a superior direction) and caudal segmentation failure (fusion in an inferior direction) was low (Tables 132–5).

Cleft neural arches were most prevalent in the fifth sacral vertebra of males from period 16 (416/1058: 39.3%), while the highest rate for bifurcate neural arch (the arch divided by a narrow separation) was seen in the first sacral vertebra of males from period 16 (31/909: 3.4%).

Hypoplasia of the right transverse process was observed among males from period 16. The left transverse process was hypoplastic in a single atlas vertebra belonging to a male from period 16. Hyperplasia of the right transverse process was observed in one male from period 16, while the hyperplasia of the left transverse process was observed in a female from period 16.

One individual was present with multiple segmentation failures that resulted in considerable spinal deformity. A 36–45-year-old male [29335] had bifid spinous processes at the 11th and 12th thoracic vertebrae. These vertebrae and the first lumbar vertebra also had hypoplasia of the right intervertebral facets; the neural arches of these vertebrae were a block as the right side had failed to segment. The fifth lumbar vertebra was also posteriorly wedged, accompanied by spondylolysis, causing the anterior curve of the lumbar spine to deepen. These anomalies resulted in a series of osseous changes. The first and second, and third to fifth lumbar vertebrae were anteriorly and laterally fused by ligament ossification, and the posterior facet joints of the third to fifth lumbar vertebrae were also fused. The 11th thoracic vertebra was anteriorly wedged due to a fracture on the anterior portion of the superior endplate, which may have resulted from abnormal loading of the lower thoracic and lumbar spine. The fusion of the lumbar vertebrae may represent an attempt by the body to stabilise the lower spine. These congenital spinal anomalies were caused by developmental delay and segmentation failure (Barnes 1994, 66–7).

Border shifts

Border shifts represent a delay during morphogenesis (the stage in the early development of an embryo where differentiation of cells and tissues establishes the form and structure of the parts of the body) affecting the developmental unit that forms the intervertebral disc space and adjacent vertebral segments. The direction of change (cranial and/or caudal) also has a genetic component, and the expression of change is influenced by the timing of the delay (Barnes 1994, 79–80).

The sacrocaudal and lumbosacral borders were most frequently affected and males were more often affected than females (Table 136).

Table 132 True prevalence rate of segmentation failure in period 14

Sex or age	Anomaly	Cervical vertebrae No.	No. affected	%	Thoracic vertebrae No.	No. affected	%	Lumbar vertebrae No.	No. affected	%	Sacral vertebrae No.	No. affected	%	First coccygeal vertebrae No.	No. affected	%
Subadult	caudal segmentation failure	403	1	0.2	804	0	0.0	325	0	-	244	0	-	14	0	-
	cleft neural arch		0	-		0	0.0		2	0.6		28	11.5		0	-
	bifurcate neural arch		2	0.5		1	0.1		2	0.6		1	0.4		0	-
	left centrum hypoplasia		0	-		0	0.0		0	-		1	0.4		1	7.1
Male	cranial segmentation failure	994	0	-	2109	1	<0.1	917	0	-	721	2	0.3	59	0	-
	caudal segmentation failure		0	-		1	<0.1		0	-		0	-		0	-
	cleft neural arch		1	0.1		0	0.0		4	0.4		130	18.0		0	-
	bifurcate neural arch		3	0.3		0	0.0		1	0.1		3	0.4		0	-
	left centrum hypoplasia		0	-		0	0.0		2	0.2		0	-		0	-
Female	cranial segmentation failure	828	0	-	1699	0	0.0	700	1	0.1	543	0	-	34	0	-
	caudal segmentation failure		1	0.1		0	0.0		1	0.1		0	-		0	-
	cleft neural arch		0	-		0	0.0		3	0.4		64	11.8		0	-
	bifurcate neural arch		1	0.1		0	-		0	-		3	0.6		0	-
Intermediate	cleft neural arch	107	0	-	200	0	-	86	0	-	74	1	1.4	5	0	-
	bifurcate neural arch		1	0.9		0	-		0	-		9	12.2		0	-

Results

Table 133 True prevalence rate of segmentation failure in period 15

Sex or age	Anomaly	Cervical vertebrae No.	No. affected	%	Thoracic vertebrae No.	No. affected	%	Lumbar vertebrae No.	No. affected	%	Sacral vertebrae No.	No. affected	%	First coccygeal vertebrae No.	No. affected	%
Subadult	cranial segmentation failure	1330	0	-	2631	1	<0.1	1129	0	-	764	0	-	25	0	-
	caudal segmentation failure		0	-		1	<0.1		0	-		0	-		0	-
	cleft neural arch		2	0.2		0	-		0	-		77	10.1		0	-
	bifurcate neural arch		1	0.1		1	<0.1		3	0.3		16	2.1		0	-
Male	cranial segmentation failure	2324	1	<0.1	4932	1	<0.1	2150	2	0.1	1768	16	0.9	151	0	-
	caudal segmentation failure		2	0.1		1	<0.1		2	0.1		0	-		0	-
	cleft neural arch		1	<0.1		0	-		7	0.3		376	21.3		2	1.3
	bifurcate neural arch		15	0.6		0	-		2	0.1		25	1.4		0	-
	left centrum hypoplasia		0	-		0	-		1	0.1		1	0.1		0	-
Female	cranial segmentation failure	2404	2	0.1	4715	2	<0.1	1952	0	-	1458	0	-	94	0	-
	caudal segmentation failure		4	0.2		0	-		0	-		0	-		0	-
	cranial and caudal segmentation failure		0	-		1	<0.1		0	-		3	0.2		0	-
	cleft neural arch		0	-		0	-		4	0.2		215	14.7		1	1.1
	bifurcate neural arch		4	0.2		0	-		1	0.1		11	0.8		0	-
	right centrum hypoplasia		0	-		0	-		0	-		3	0.2		0	-
Intermediate	cranial segmentation failure	210	1	0.5	420	0	-	172	0	-	126	0	-	9	0	-
	caudal segmentation failure		1	0.5		0	-		0	-		0	-		0	-
	cleft neural arch		0	-		0	-		0	-		32	25.4		0	-
	bifurcate neural arch		0	-		0	-		0	-		2	1.6		0	-
	left centrum hypoplasia		0	-		0	-		0	-		1	0.8		0	-

Table 134 True prevalence rate of segmentation failure in period 16

Sex or age	Anomaly	Cervical vertebrae No.	No. affected	%	Thoracic vertebrae No.	No. affected	%	Lumbar vertebrae No.	No. affected	%	Sacral vertebrae No.	No. affected	%	First coccygeal vertebrae No.	No. affected	%
Subadult	cleft neural arch	2163	0	-	4220	0	-	1858	2	0.1	1304	106	8.1	46	0	-
	bifurcate neural arch		9	0.4		0	-		3	0.2		13	1.0		0	-
	right centrum hypoplasia		0	-		0	-		0	-		1	0.1		0	-
	left centrum hypoplasia		0	-		0	-		0	-		1	0.1		0	-
Male	cranial segmentation failure	5853	7	0.1	11,546	4	<0.1	4883	3	0.1	3771	2	0.1	317	0	-
	caudal segmentation failure		8	0.1		4	<0.1		3	0.1		0	-		0	-
	cranial and caudal segmentation failure		0	-		1	<0.1		3	0.1		3	0.1		0	-
	cleft neural arch		6	0.1		1	<0.1		10	0.2		743	19.7		1	0.3
	bifurcate neural arch		12	0.2		2	<0.1		8	0.2		52	1.4		0	-
	right transverse process hypoplasia		0	-		2	<0.1		1	<0.1		0	-		0	-
	left transverse process hypoplasia		1	<0.1		0	-		0	-		0	-		0	-
	right centrum hypoplasia		0	-		6	0.1		3	0.1		1	<0.1		0	-
	left centrum hypoplasia		0	-		6	0.1		4	0.1		2	0.1		0	-
	right transverse process hyperplasia		0	-		0	-		1	<0.1		0	-		0	-
Female	cranial segmentation failure	4930	1	<0.1	9779	4	<0.1	4108	1	-	3003	1	<0.1	170	0	-
	caudal segmentation failure		1	<0.1		3	<0.1		0	-		0	-		0	-
	cranial and caudal segmentation failure		0	-		2	<0.1		0	-		2	0.1		0	-
	cleft neural arch		2	<0.1		0	-		2	<0.1		418	13.9		0	-
	bifurcate neural arch		8	0.2		2	<0.1		1	<0.1		20	0.7		0	-
	left transverse process hyperplasia		0	-		0	-		1	<0.1		0	-		0	-
Intermediate	cranial segmentation failure	459	1	0.2	996	0	-	444	0	-	318	0	-	11	0	-
	caudal segmentation failure		1	0.2		0	-		0	-		0	-		0	-
	cleft neural arch		0	-		0	-		43	9.7		0	-		0	-
	bifurcate neural arch		1	0.2		0	-		1	0.2		0	-		0	-
	left transverse process hypoplasia		0	-		0	-		2	0.5		0	-		0	-

Table 135 True prevalence rate of segmentation failure in period 17

Sex or age	Anomaly	Cervical vertebrae No.	No. affected	%	Thoracic vertebrae No.	No. affected	%	Lumbar vertebrae No.	No. affected	%	Sacral vertebrae No.	No. affected	%
Subadult	cleft neural arch	500	0	-	901	0	-	378	2	0.5	291	21	7.2
	bifurcate neural arch		2	0.4		0	-		2	0.5		8	2.7
	right centrum hypoplasia		0	-		1	0.1		0	-		0	-
Male	cranial segmentation failure	1589	1	0.1	2989	0	-	1239	0	-	994	1	0.1
	caudal segmentation failure		1	0.1		0	-		0	-		0	-
	cleft neural arch		0	-		0	-		3	0.2		178	17.9
	bifurcate neural arch		3	0.2		0	<0.1		3	0.2		1	0.1
	right centrum hypoplasia		0	-		1	<0.1		0	-		0	-
	left centrum hypoplasia		0	-		0	-		2	0.2		1	0.1
Female	cranial segmentation failure	1037	1	0.1	2013	1	<0.1	868	0	-	751	2	0.3
	caudal segmentation failure		1	0.1		1	<0.1		0	-		0	-
	cleft neural arch		0	-		0	-		3	0.3		132	17.6
	bifurcate neural arch		1	0.1		0	-		0	-		5	0.7
Intermediate	cleft neural arch	128	0	-	266	0	-	107	0	-	101	18	17.8
	bifurcate neural arch		1	0.8		0	-		0	-		2	2.0

Table 136 True prevalence rate of border shifts, calculated as a percentage where one or both vertebrae at the border level were observable

Period	Border Sex or age	Occipitocervical No.	No. affected	%	Cervicothoracic No.	No. affected	%	Thoracolumbar No.	No. affected	%	Lumbosacral No.	No. affected	%	Sacrocaudal No.	No. affected	%
14	subadult	78	0	-	68	0	-	68	5	7.4	70	22	31.4	31	1	3.2
15		244	2	0.8	228	3	1.3	243	13	5.3	243	16	6.6	98	2	2.0
16		423	3	0.7	377	0	-	423	19	4.5	419	12	2.9	160	7	4.4
17		113	0	-	86	1	1.2	86	4	4.7	81	7	8.6	39	0	-
14	male	157	2	1.3	171	4	2.3	190	21	11.1	189	26	13.8	123	23	18.7
15		371	9	2.4	424	9	2.1	448	42	9.4	456	65	14.3	318	68	21.4
16		957	13	1.4	975	19	1.9	1073	83	7.7	1038	135	13.0	682	137	20.1
17		244	1	0.4	255	4	1.6	267	15	5.6	262	29	11.1	181	41	22.7
14	female	126	1	0.8	141	1	0.7	157	17	10.8	144	13	9.0	89	15	16.9
15		390	6	1.5	412	7	1.7	440	38	8.6	428	41	9.6	238	32	13.4
16		856	12	1.4	854	8	0.9	907	72	7.9	904	78	8.6	500	71	14.2
17		167	2	1.2	175	2	1.1	184	12	6.5	188	26	13.8	135	14	10.4
14	intermediate	17	0	-	16	1	6.3	18	2	11.1	18	3	16.7	13	0	-
15		37	0	-	38	0	-	35	5	14.3	35	8	22.9	21	6	28.6
16		69	5	7.2	78	2	2.6	94	4	4.3	90	9	10.0	46	3	6.5
17		19	1	5.3	23	0	-	21	1	4.8	23	2	8.7	15	3	20.0

In period 14, subadults exhibited no shifts at the occipitocervical and cervicothoracic borders. At the thoracolumbar border the most frequently observed shift was a transitional facet or facets on the 11th thoracic vertebra, while at the lumbosacral border it was an ala-like transverse process of the fifth lumbar vertebra articulating on the right or left side (partial sacralisation). At the sacrocaudal border, the only shift observed was the complete sacralisation of the first caudal vertebra.

At the lumbosacral border, males from period 14 presented with bilateral ala-like transverse processes of the sixth (supernumerary) lumbar vertebra, and partial sacralisation on the left transverse process of the fifth lumbar vertebra. The most frequent sacrocaudal border shifts were incomplete sacralisation of the first coccygeal vertebra and complete sacralisation of the first coccygeal vertebra. The least frequently affected borders were the occipitocervical (where only transverse basilar cleft and right paracondylar process were noted) and the cervicothoracic border, where bony tubercles or blunt bony projections representing an expression of cervical ribs, or complete cervical ribs with articular facets, were seen, together with stunted transverse process of the seventh cervical vertebra. At the thoracolumbar border the most frequently observed shift was transitional facets on the 11th thoracic vertebra and the least frequently seen was a hypoplastic 12th rib.

No occipitocervical and sacrocaudal border shifts were observed in intermediate adults. At the cervicothoracic border, the only observed shift was a bony tubercle representing an expression of a cervical rib, and at the thoracolumbar border an aplastic 12th rib (no rib facets on the 12th thoracic vertebra) and transitional facets on the 11th thoracic vertebra were observed. At the lumbosacral border, only three shifts were observed: partial (left) sacralisation of a fifth lumbar vertebra, non-articulating, non-ala-like wings in the sixth lumbar vertebra, and apophyseal joints and an anterior cleft in the first and second sacral vertebrae.

Among females in period 14, the only shifts at the occipitocervical border were a precondylar process, and at the cervicothoracic border a bony tubercle representing an expression of a cervical rib. At the thoracolumbar border the most common shift was the presence of transitional facets on the 11th thoracic vertebra, and at the lumbosacral the most frequently recorded shifts were partial (left) sacralisation of the fifth lumbar vertebra and partial (right) sacralisation of sixth lumbar vertebrae. At the sacrocaudal border, the most frequently observed shift was complete sacralisation of the first coccygeal vertebra.

In period 15, subadults were affected at the occipitocervical border with left and bilateral paracondylar processes. At the cervicothoracic border stunted transverse process on the seventh cervical vertebra and a bony tubercle representing a cervical rib were recorded. At the thoracolumbar border, the most frequently observed shift was transitional facets on the 11th thoracic vertebra, and at the lumbosacral border the most frequently observed shift was non-articulating, non-ala-like wings in the sixth lumbar vertebra. At the sacrocaudal border, the only observed shift was the complete sacralisation of the first coccygeal vertebra.

Among males from period 15, the most commonly observed shifts at the occipitocervical and cervicothoracic borders were bilateral paracondylar process, occipitalised atlas, and expressions of cervical ribs. At the thoracolumbar border, the most commonly observed shift was transitional facets on the 11th thoracic vertebra. The lumbosacral and sacrocaudal borders were the most frequently affected borders: at the lumbosacral border the most frequently observed shift was an anterior cleft between the first and second sacral vertebrae, and at the sacrocaudal border the complete sacralisation of the first coccygeal vertebra.

Adults of intermediate sex from period 15 were affected at the thoracolumbar (most frequently transitional facets on the 11th thoracic vertebra), lumbosacral and sacrocaudal borders (complete sacralisation of the first caudal vertebra).

In period 15 females, the most frequently observed shift at the occipitocervical border was the bilateral paracondylar process. At the thoracolumbar border the most frequently observed shifts were transitional facets on the 11th thoracic and first lumbar vertebrae. At the lumbosacral border partial (left) sacralisation and complete sacralisation of the fifth lumbar vertebra were most frequently observed.

In period 16 subadults, only three border shifts were observed at the occipitocervical border: precondylar facets, left and bilateral paracondylar process. At the thoracolumbar border the most frequently observed shift was transitional facets on the 11th thoracic vertebra, and at the lumbosacral border partial (left) sacralisation of the fifth lumbar vertebra. At the sacrocaudal border complete sacralisation of first coccygeal vertebra was observed.

For males in this period, the most frequently observed shifts at the occipitocervical border were paracondylar processes (right side and bilateral). At the cervicothoracic border the most frequently observed shift was a stunted transverse process on the seventh cervical vertebra, and at the thoracolumbar border the most recorded shifts were transitional facets on the 11th thoracic vertebra, the presence of a supernumerary (13th) thoracic vertebra and an aplastic 12th rib. At the lumbosacral border the most frequently observed shifts were an anterior cleft (with or without apophyseal joints) between the first and second sacral vertebrae, non-articulating, non-ala-like wings in the sixth lumbar vertebra and complete sacralisation of a sixth lumbar vertebra. At the sacrocaudal border the most frequently observed shifts were incomplete sacralisation of the first coccygeal vertebra and complete sacralisation of the first coccygeal vertebra.

For adults of intermediate sex from period 16, the only border shifts at the occipitocervical border were occipitalised atlas vertebrae and bilateral paracondylar process. At the cervicothoracic border the only observed shifts were stunted transverse process of the seventh cervical vertebra and the rudimentary first rib. At the thoracolumbar border, transitional facets on the 11th thoracic vertebra and the presence of a 13th thoracic vertebra were observed. For the lumbosacral border the most frequently occurring shifts were non-articulating, non-ala-like wings in the sixth lumbar vertebra and an anterior cleft between the first and second sacral vertebrae. At the sacrocaudal border the only shift type recorded was complete sacralisation of the first coccygeal vertebra.

Females in period 16 most frequently showed a left paracondylar process at the occipitocervical border. At the cervicothoracic border the most frequently observed shifts were a bony tubercle (an expression of a cervical rib) and complete cervical ribs. At the thoracolumbar border the most frequently observed shifts were transitional facets on the 11th thoracic and first lumbar vertebrae. At the lumbosacral border, the most frequently recorded shifts were partial (left) sacralisation of the fifth lumbar vertebra, non-articulating, non-ala-like wings in the sixth lumbar vertebra, and an anterior cleft between the first and second sacral vertebrae. At the sacrocaudal border, the most frequently recorded shifts were complete sacralisation of the first coccygeal vertebra, incomplete sacralisation of the first coccygeal vertebra and complete separation of the fifth sacral vertebra.

No occipitocervical and sacrocaudal border shifts were recorded in subadults from period 17. At the cervicothoracic border the only shift recorded was the cervical rib, and at the thoracolumbar border transitional facets on the 11th thoracic vertebra. At the lumbosacral border, the most frequently observed shifts were partial (left) sacralisation and non-articulating ala-like transverse process of the fifth lumbar vertebra, and non-articulating, non-ala-like wings in the sixth lumbar vertebra.

Among males from period 17, at the occipitocervical border the only recorded shift was an expression of occipital vertebra; at the cervicothoracic border the only observed shifts were expressions of cervical ribs. The most frequently observed shift at the thoracolumbar border was transitional facets on the 11th thoracic vertebra and hypoplastic 12th ribs. At the lumbosacral border, the most frequently observed shifts were an anterior cleft (with or without apophyseal joints) between the first and second sacral vertebrae, and complete sacralisation of a sixth (supernumerary) lumbar vertebra. At the sacrocaudal border, complete sacralisation of the first coccygeal vertebra, incomplete sacralisation of the first coccygeal vertebra and incomplete separation of the fifth sacral vertebra were observed.

Period 17 adults of intermediate sex were unaffected at the cervicothoracic border. At the occipitocervical border the only shift observed was bilateral paracondylar process and at the thoracolumbar border the only recorded shifts were transitional facets on the first lumbar vertebra. At the lumbosacral border, apophyseal joints and an anterior cleft were recorded between the first and second sacral vertebrae, and at the sacrocaudal border the only recorded shifts were the complete separation of the fifth sacral vertebra, incomplete sacralisation of the first coccygeal vertebra and complete sacralisation of first coccygeal vertebra.

Within females from period 17, the only observed shifts at the occipitocervical border were precondylar facets and a left paracondylar process; at the cervicothoracic border, a bony tubercle and complete cervical rib were observed. The most frequently observed shifts at the thoracolumbar border were transitional facets on the 11th thoracic vertebra and aplastic 12th rib. The most frequently observed lumbosacral border shifts were an anterior cleft between the first and second sacral vertebrae and partial (left) sacralisation of the fifth lumbar vertebra, and at the sacrocaudal border, the most frequently observed shifts were complete sacralisation of the first coccygeal vertebra and incomplete sacralisation of the first coccygeal vertebra.

Limb and joint anomalies

Limb anomalies were observed in five individuals and joint anomalies in 44 individuals. The results are summarised in Table 137 and Table 138.

Table 137 Crude prevalence rate of limb anomalies by period and burial type

Period	Burial type	Sex or age	No. individuals	Upper limb anomalies No. affected	%	Upper limb anomalies No. affected	%
15	ABC	male	219	0	-	1	0.5
16	ABC	6–11 years	87	0	-	1	1.1
		female	474	1	0.2	0	-
	D	female	535	0	-	1	0.2
17	D	12–17 years	13	1	7.7	0	-

Table 138 Crude prevalence rate of joint anomalies by period and burial type

Period	Burial type	Sex or age	No. individuals	Glenoid dysplasia No. affected	%	Hip dysplasia No. affected	%	Hip dislocation No. affected	%
14	ABC	male	160	0	-	1	0.6	1	0.6
		female	115	0	-	1	0.9	0	-
	D	male	63	0	-	0	-	0	-
		female	55	1	1.8	0	-	0	-
15	ABC	12–17 years	60	0	-	1	1.7	0	-
		male	219	0	-	2	0.9	0	-
		female	167	0	-	0	-	1	0.6
		intermediate	17	0	-	0	-	0	-
	D	12–17 years	109	0	-	0	-	0	-
		male	313	1	0.3	3	1.0	1	0.3
		female	334	0	-	1	0.3	1	0.3
		intermediate	29	0	-	2	6.9	0	-
16	ABC	12–17 years	91	0	-	0	-	0	-
		male	628	1	0.2	3	0.5	1	0.2
		female	474	0	-	2	0.4	1	0.2
	D	12–17 years	174	0	-	1	0.6	0	-
		male	564	0	-	6	1.1	1	0.2
		female	535	0	-	4	0.7	1	0.2
17	ABC	male	239	0	-	1	0.4	0	-
		female	164	0	-	3	1.8	0	-
	D	male	51	0	-	0	-	0	-
		female	39	0	-	1	2.6	1	2.6

Results

Glenoid cavity dysplasia

Three individuals with this condition were recorded, one each from periods 14, 15 and 16 (3/5387: 0.1%). Female [23734], burial type D, period 14, had bilateral changes (1/170 females in this period: 0.6%). In the remaining two males, 36–45-year-old [22136] from period 15, burial type D (1/532 males in period 15: 0.2%), and young adult [22587] from period 16, burial type ABC (1/1192 males in period 16: 0.1%), the right glenoid cavity was affected.

Congenital absence of the styloid process

Congenital absence was observed in one individual (1/5387: <0.1%), [17227], a 26–35-year-old male from period 16, burial type ABC (1/1192 males: 0.1%), where the styloid process of the left ulna was missing.

Limb hypoplasia

Two individuals were affected by limb hypoplasia in periods 16 and 17 (2/5387: <0.1%). In period 16 an adult female [7408], burial type ABC, had hypoplasia of the left ulna and radius, 0.2% of females in this burial type (1/474), while in period 17, 12–17-year-old [2917], burial type D, had hypoplasia of the left radius and ulna, 7.7% of all adolescents in this burial type (1/13).

Radioulnar synostosis

This was recorded in a 36–45-year-old female [16964] (1/5387: <0.1%) from period 16, burial type ABC, 4.8% of females from this age group and burial type (1/121) (Fig 178). The left ulna was ankylosed at the proximal joint surface and proximal third. The humeroulnar articular surface retained normal morphology but the radioulnar joint surface was not present, and the articular surface on the coronoid process extended on to the radial head. The ulna diaphysis showed extreme atrophy (just 30mm in circumference); unfortunately the distal joint surface was unobservable. The left radius lay in a pronated position; the head was superiorly dislocated and lying adjacent to the olecranon process, and the radial tuberosity was located inferior to the coronoid process on the pronated lateral border. The diaphysis of the radius showed no evidence for atrophy and the radiocarpal joint surfaces were normal. The distal radioulnar joint was unobservable.

Undiagnosed chromosomal disorder

A 26–35-year-old male ([14895], burial type ABC) from period 15 (1/5387: <0.1%) had an abnormally formed left ilium, 1.3% of males in this age group and burial type (1/75). The retroauricular area was 11.5mm thicker than the right and had a scooped ventral aspect; the iliac crest was shortened, flattened and thickened and the distance between the superior and inferior iliac spines shorter than normal. This male also had an asymmetrical cranium and widely spaced dentition with peg-like premolars. Such multiple defects are suggestive of a chromosomal disorder; however, the absence of soft tissue limits further identification (Shashidhar et al 2003; OMIM 2011).

Joint hypermobility syndrome

Bilateral knee joint changes were observed in 36–45-year-old female [3234] from period 16, burial type D, 0.8% of this age group and burial type (1/130) and <0.1% of the entire assemblage (1/5387). On the antero-lateral aspect of the distal third of both right and left diaphyses, there was a small circular depression located 6mm from the articular margin. The femoropatellar joint surfaces were oval in shape and on the antero-lateral aspect there was eburnation and subchondral pitting; the femorotibial joint surfaces had rugose lateral portions and the adductor tubercle was larger than normal. The tibial plateaux were posteriorly angulated in an oblique plane, and the left patella (the right was not present) had abnormal joint surfaces. Normal articular surfaces were present to the medial and lateral margins which had an arc of eburnation present. The supero-lateral margin consisted of dense trabecular bone.

Hip dysplasia

This hip anomaly was recorded in individuals from all periods. Type 1 change, consisting of a shallow depression in the lateral cortex of the ilium (Mitchell and Redfern 2008, 63), was most frequently observed; the right side was most often affected, and both sexes were equally involved (16 males, 12 females). Period 16 had the most affected individuals (Table 138).

One example of a bilateral anomaly was observed in 26–35-year-old female [12726] from period 15 (burial type D). The left acetabulum was dysplastic with early degenerative changes, and the right hip was subluxed with a dysplastic acetabular rim posterosuperiorly, which appears to have been

Fig 178 Lateral view of the proximal left radius and ulna of 36–45-year-old female [16964] from period 16, burial type ABC, showing congenital synostosis (scale c 1:1)

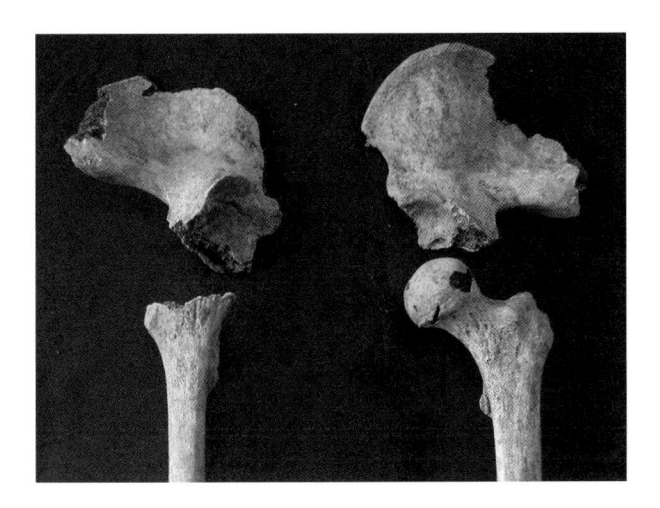

Fig 179 Anterior view of the ilia and femora of 26–35-year-old female [12726] from period 15, burial type D, illustrating the presence of bilateral hip anomaly (scale c 1:4)

Fig 180 Dislocation of the left hip, with a deep rounded cup (type 4 anomaly), in ≥46-year-old male [5970] from period 14, burial type ABC (scale c 1:2)

the weight-bearing surface (Fig 179). The subluxation resulted in 10mm of leg shortening, associated with mild disuse atrophy of the right femur. A number of defects were observed in the lumbar spine; the atlas and third cervical vertebrae were a block – joined because the embryonic precursors did not separate (Barnes 1994, 324) – and angled to the left; the seventh cervical to second thoracic vertebrae were congenitally fused; the first thoracic vertebra was a hemivertebra (only the left portion was present); and the left first and second ribs were bifid.

Hip dislocation

This hip anomaly was recorded in all periods. Types 1 (see above), 3 (a raised plaque of bone laid down proud of the iliac cortex) and 4 (a deep rounded cup; Fig 180) were observed (Mitchell and Redfern 2008, 63), and a total of nine individuals were affected (9/5387: 0.2%). Type 3 was most frequently observed, and overall side distribution was virtually equal (Table 138).

An example of a unilateral dislocation to the right hip joint was observed in 18–25-year-old female [3715] from period 15 (burial type ABC). A shallow false acetabulum located 33.8mm posterior to the anterior inferior iliac spine was formed from a circular raised plaque of dense bone 24mm in diameter. There was no evidence of secondary degeneration and this case was classified as type 2 – a fine layer of patchy new bone in the surface of the ilium without evidence of depression (Mitchell and Redfern 2008, 63). The right femoral head was mushroom-shaped and asymmetrical, with possible avascular necrosis on the superior aspect; the neck was shorter than normal and the lesser tuberosity long and flattened.

Hand and foot anomalies

Forty-two individuals from periods 14 to 17 had hand or foot anomalies (42/5387: 0.8%): four 12–17-year-olds (4/5387:

Table 139 Crude prevalence rate of hand and foot anomalies by period and burial type

Period	Burial type	Sex or age	No. individuals	No. affected	%
14	ABC	12–17 years	34	0	-
		male	160	3	1.9
		female	115	2	1.7
	D	12–17 years	27	1	3.7
		male	63	2	3.2
		female	55	0	-
15	ABC	12–17 years	60	2	3.3
		male	219	2	0.9
		female	167	0	-
	D	12–17 years	109	1	0.9
		male	313	6	1.9
		female	334	1	0.3
16	ABC	male	628	3	0.5
		female	474	2	0.4
		intermediate	71	0	-
	D	male	564	4	0.7
		female	535	6	1.1
		intermediate	39	1	2.6
17	ABC	male	239	1	0.4
		female	164	1	0.6
		intermediate	24	1	4.2
	D	male	51	2	3.9
		female	39	0	-
		intermediate	4	1	25.0

0.1%), 23 males (23/5387: 0.4%), 12 females (12/5387: 0.2%) and three intermediate adults (3/5387: 0.1%) (Table 139).

Phalangeal anomalies

One female from period 16 had ankylosed proximal and intermediate hand phalanges (1/5387: <0.1%).

Tarsal coalition

Calcaneo-navicular, cuboid-lateral cuneiform and lateral cuneiform-third metatarsal coalition was observed in ten individuals dated to periods 14 to 16 (10/5387: 0.2%), seven of whom were male. The most frequently observed form was fibrous coalition between the cuboid and lateral cuneiform.

Accessory ossicles were recorded in periods 15 and 16 in two males, four females and one intermediate individual; the majority of individuals affected were from period 16. The majority of cases were observed on the navicular bone, apart from one female right calcaneus (in period 16). More female elements (seven) than male (two) were affected.

Carpal anomalies

A range of carpal anomalies were observed in one male (1/2237: <0.1%) and five females (5/1883: 0.3%). In period 15, coalition of the capitate and third metacarpal and of the lunate and triquetral were observed in two females (2/1883: 0.1%). In period 16 one male (1/2237: <0.1%) and one female (1/1883: 0.1%) displayed absence of the hamulus, and in period 17, one male (1/2237: <0.1%) had coalition of the capitate and third metacarpal.

Foot anomalies

These were observed in two males from periods 15 and 16, and affected the left side (2/5387: <0.1%). Congenital talipes equinovarus was recorded in 18–25-year-old male [20417] from period 15 and affected the distal tibia, talus and calcaneus (1/2237 males: <0.1%) (Fig 181). Hindfoot valgus deformity was recorded in 18–25-year-old male ([22853] from period 16, and affected the calcaneus, talus and navicular (1/2237 males: <0.1%).

Fig 181 Congenital talipes equinovarus: medial view of the left calcaneus and talus of 18–25-year-old male [20417] from period 15, burial type ABC (scale c 1:1)

3.14 Miscellaneous pathological conditions

Rebecca Redfern

Hyperostosis frontalis interna (HFI)

Hyperostosis frontalis interna was recorded in all periods and affected a total of 22 adults (22/4360: 0.5%). As is to be expected, the frontal bone was most frequently involved; the parietal and occipital bones were only affected in periods 14 and 16. Also as expected, females were predominantly affected (18/1883: 1.0%), particularly the 36–45-year-old and ≥46-year-old age groups: the group with the highest number of affected elements was ≥46-year-old females from period 16 (4/115: 3.5%). Two males (2/2237: 0.1%) and two adults with intermediate sexual characteristics (2/205: 0.1%) also had changes present (Table 140).

Paget's disease of bone

Paget's disease of bone was identified following the methodology described in Powers (2008) with reference to Ortner (2003, 435), Aufderheide and Rodríguez-Martín (1998, 413), Salter (1999, 199) and Resnick (2002, 1947–95). The majority of cases were identified macroscopically and a minority were radiographed. Seventeen individuals from all periods were affected (17/5387: 0.3%): the greatest number of affected individuals was observed in period 16 (11/2835: 0.4%), and particularly in burial type ABC (Table 141). In both periods 14 and 15, one 36–45-year-old male was affected; in period 16, 36–45-year-old and ≥46-year-old adults of both sexes were affected; and in period 17, ≥46-year-old adults of both sexes were affected. No statistical difference was observed between burial types.

Table 140 Crude prevalence rate of HFI by period and burial type

Period	Burial type	Sex	No. individuals	No. affected	%
14	ABC	female	115	6	5.2
	D		55	0	-
15	ABC	male	219	0	-
		female	167	1	0.6
		intermediate	17	0	-
	D	male	313	2	0.6
		female	334	2	0.6
		intermediate	29	1	3.4
16	ABC	female	474	4	0.8
		intermediate	71	1	1.4
	D	female	535	4	0.7
		intermediate	39	0	-
17	ABC	female	164	1	0.6
	D		39	0	-

Table 141 Crude prevalence rate of Paget's disease of bone by period and burial type

Period	Burial type	Sex	No. individuals	No. affected	%
14	ABC	male	160	0	-
	D		63	1	1.6
15	ABC	male	219	2	0.9
	D		313	1	0.3
16	ABC	male	628	6	1.0
		female	474	1	0.2
	D	male	564	2	0.4
		female	535	2	0.4
17	ABC	male	239	1	0.4
		female	164	1	0.6
	D	male	51	0	-
		female	39	0	-

The majority of individuals only had a single element affected: for example, ≥46-year-old male [12251] (period 16, burial type D) had Pagetic changes to the right scapula, an element rarely affected by this disease process (Resnick 2002, 1961), and in 36–45-year-old male [14106] the tibia was affected (Fig 182). A small number of individuals had multiple elements affected, for example a 36–45-year-old male [14013] (period 16, burial type ABC) with osseous changes in the cranium, right humerus and os coxa.

Endocranial lesions

Eighty individuals were affected by endocranial new bone formation (80/5387: 1.5%): 1.0% of males (22/2237), 1.1% of females (21/1883), 0.5% of intermediate adults (1/205), 4.0% of 12–17-year-olds (22/544), 3.4% of 6–11-year-olds (12/348) and 3.4% of 1–5-year-olds (2/58).

A total of 143 skull bones were affected. The most frequently affected elements were the occipital (52/143: 36.4%) and frontal bones (40/143: 28.0%). In 138 bones, the type of lesion could be established. Capillary form lesions were the most commonly observed expression (63/138: 45.7%), followed by pitted (28/138: 20.3%) and hair-on-end lesions (19/138: 13.8%). Deposits of new bone and capillary lesions affected individuals aged 6–11 years, 12–17 years and in adulthood. The highest number of affected bones and recorded lesions was observed in males (43/143 bones: 30.1%) and 12–17-year-olds (39/143 bones: 27.3%). No statistically significant patterns of difference were found (Table 142).

Seven individuals from period 14 were affected (7/5387: 0.1%). The type of lesion most frequently seen in this period was capillary formation and the occipital bone was most commonly affected. Although 12–17-year-olds were predominantly affected, the highest crude prevalence was seen in young adults aged 18–25 years from burial type ABC (1/6: 16.7%).

Fig 182 Paget's disease of bone in the right tibia of 36–45-year-old male [14106] from period 15, burial type D (scale c 1:4)

Table 142 Crude prevalence rate of endocranial lesions by period and burial type

Period	Burial type	Sex or age	No. individuals	No. affected	%
14	ABC	12–17 years	34	3	8.8
		male	160	2	1.2
		intermediate	16	1	6.3
	D	12–17 years	27	1	3.7
		male	63	0	-
		intermediate	5	0	-
15	ABC	6–11 years	28	1	3.6
		12–17 years	60	0	-
		male	219	5	2.3
		female	167	2	1.2
	D	6–11 years	75	4	5.3
		12–17 years	109	6	5.5
		male	313	2	0.6
		female	334	1	0.3
16	ABC	6–11 years	87	5	5.7
		12–17 years	91	1	1.1
		male	628	5	0.8
		female	474	9	1.9
	D	6–11 years	100	0	-
		12–17 years	174	9	5.2
		male	564	3	0.5
		female	535	7	1.3
17	ABC	1–5 years	10	2	20.0
		6–11 years	24	2	8.3
		12–17 years	36	2	5.6
		male	239	5	2.1
		female	164	2	1.2
	D	1–5 years	13	0	-
		6–11 years	13	0	-
		12–17 years	13	0	-
		male	51	0	-
		female	39	0	-

Results

In period 15, 1.5% of individuals were affected (21/1390) and the most frequent type of lesion was capillary formation, particularly in later childhood (6–11 years). Of the 37 bones observed, the frontal and occipital bones were the most frequently affected elements (13/37: 35.1%) and of these, 36 bones could have the type of change established. The highest true prevalence rate was observed in capillary formation to the occipital bone in 6–11-year-olds (10/36: 27.8%). The highest crude prevalence rate (3/53 5.7%) was observed in the 18–25-year-old males from burial type ABC.

In period 16, 1.4% of individuals were affected (39/2835). The most frequent type of lesion was capillary formation, particularly among those aged 12–17 years. Of the 66 bones observed, the occipital (25/66: 37.9%) and frontal bones (16/66: 24.2%) were most frequently affected. The highest crude prevalence rate was observed in 6–11-year-olds from burial type ABC (5/87: 5.7%). The highest true prevalence rate was observed in deposits of new bone in the left parietal of 26–35-year-old intermediate individuals (1/22: 4.5%).

In period 17, 2.0% of individuals were affected (13/650), a greater proportion of males (5/290: 1.7%) than females (2/203: 1.0%). In total, 33 bones were affected. The most frequent type of lesion was capillary formation (17/33: 51.5%), and the frontal and occipital bones were most often affected (both 9/33: 27.3%). The highest crude prevalence rate for the period as a whole was observed in those aged 1–5 years (2/11: 18.2%).

Diaphyseal aclasia

Diaphyseal aclasia was identified in a 36–45-year-old male [19378] from period 15, burial type D: 1.0% of males of this age and burial type (1/97) and 0.2% of all males in period 15 (1/532). Multiple exostoses were present at the proximal and distal portions of the right humerus (1/406 male right humeri in this period: 0.2%), right tibia (1/353 male right tibiae in this period: 0.3%) and fibulae (1/344 male right fibulae: 0.3%; 1/349 male left fibulae: 0.3% in this period) (Fig 183).

The right humerus appeared to be foreshortened in the proximal segment and c 25mm shorter than the left bone. The exostosis projected from the antero-lateral aspect of the proximal segment, 28mm in length and 13mm wide. Post-mortem (taphonomic) damage showed trabecular and cortical continuity with the diaphysis was present. The proximal segment of the right tibia was expanded, giving a flared appearance, and there was anterior bowing. On the posterior aspect were a large exostosis (at least 31mm long) and two or three smaller exostoses (10mm long and 5mm wide). The fibulae had long exotoses projecting from the anterior and posterior aspects of the proximal segment, and there was a small exostosis on the medial aspect of the distal segment of the right fibula.

Fig 183 Diaphyseal aclasia indicated by multiple exostoses in the right humerus, right tibia and fibulae of 36–45-year-old male [19378] from period 15, burial type D (scale c 1:4)

4

St Mary Spital in context

This chapter discusses the osteological results from Spitalfields in the context of life in medieval London. Themes covered include the local environment, diet, childhood, risk of injury, impairment and treatment of the sick, evidence for continuity and change over the period of use of the cemetery, and comparison between the burial sample from Spitalfields and those from other medieval sites in London, Britain and Europe.

In this chapter, burials of type ABC are referred to as the attritional cemetery and those of burial type D as mass burials or the catastrophic cemetery.

4.1 Medieval London

Don Walker

Howe (1976, 1) states that the environment is 'the matrix of physical, biological and social circumstances surrounding man and affecting his well being'. The specific stimuli that act upon health can be divided into the physical-chemical (inorganic), biological (organic) and socio-cultural (human activity). If disease is defined as maladjustment to the environment, then the study of the location and condition of habitation can inform us of the circumstances of disease. Such studies depend upon the collection of environmental data from a wide range of sources, including human and animal bones, plant remains, molluscs and insects. Documentary evidence can help us to put these data into their historical context.

The impact of the environment plays an important role in the health of a population, and in a multitude of ways. Many of these factors result directly from human activity, such as pollution from industry, waste disposal, or smoke from domestic heating. Others are natural in source, including climate and terrain, though these can also be influenced by human activity. Biological factors include micro-organisms such as bacteria, viruses and protozoa which can enter the human body through ingestion, inhalation and open wounds. These organisms also react differently to changing environments, and their survival depends upon their adaptive capabilities (Howe 1976, 15).

The growth of towns allowed the transition to an urban lifestyle for many people. These changes would have had consequences for health in the past, as they do today (Schofield and Vince 2003, 232). Migrants moving from rural areas to crowded and polluted towns would have met a micro-environment which differed from that in which they were raised, and their future prospects depended on their ability to adapt. This chapter uses documentary and archaeological evidence to investigate the environment within medieval London with particular regard to the health of the St Mary Spital population.

Housing

Housing provides shelter from environmental extremes of weather, and allows a degree of privacy in densely occupied settlements, as well as a place where possessions can be stored,

St Mary Spital in context

children raised and everyday domestic activities such as cooking performed (Howe 1973, 2). Standards of housing are often determined by socio-economic status, with considerable differences between the rich and poor, and may present a significant health risk factor (Schell 1992, 138). It is possible to investigate both the status and the everyday lives of medieval Londoners by using an approach that incorporates osteological, architectural, environmental and documentary evidence.

As Munby (1987, 156) states, 'the fundamental nature of urban living is reflected in its buildings'. The design and proximity to each other of domestic structures, as well as the material remains within, are central to the investigation of urban life and provide a framework in which biological evidence can be interpreted. Unfortunately, pictorial sources are limited and many of the written records concentrate on the grander structures, which are also those most often recorded by archaeologists. Of the simple timber structures that housed the majority of the poor, evidence is far scarcer.

In London, the 13th century was a period of rapid growth, in which the city's population may have doubled in size. This led to an increase in the density of the street grid as existing plots were subdivided by the construction of new lanes, in response to the need for more housing (Thomas 2002, 66) (Fig 184). A further innovation occurred in the middle of the 13th century with the appearance of jettied buildings. Jettying was a timber-frame building technique where an upper floor of a structure projected beyond the floor immediately below. This maximised living space in crowded streets where little room was available at ground level (Fig 185).

The evidence points to an increasingly crowded environment in London before the crises of the 14th century. Most families lived in three rooms or fewer, and living space was cramped, leading to an increase in the amount and range of activity on the streets. Such an environment must have led to numerous neighbourly disputes, and put added strain on sanitary systems (Hanawalt 1993, 29–30).

Streets were often cambered and constructed of gravel with side ditches for drainage (Thomas 2002, 67). Apart from rainwater run-off, these ditches would have carried human waste and kitchen refuse (Hanawalt 1993, 29). While rainwater may have assisted in the flow of waste away from some areas, it may also have led to flooding and resulting overspill of foul-smelling matter on to streets and even into properties.

Nevertheless, for commercial reasons it was desirable to live in the centre of London, where shopping areas such as Cheapside provided a ready market for manufactured goods (Dyer 2002, 199). The streets at the centre of the city were crowded, with merchants, artisans and labourers alike seeking to take advantage of the greater opportunities for trading and employment. Merchants could expand their trading networks, while the poor could find casual labour.

It has been suggested that the high demand for centrally located property led to a growth in more marginal areas of the city and in the suburbs, where the poor could more easily afford

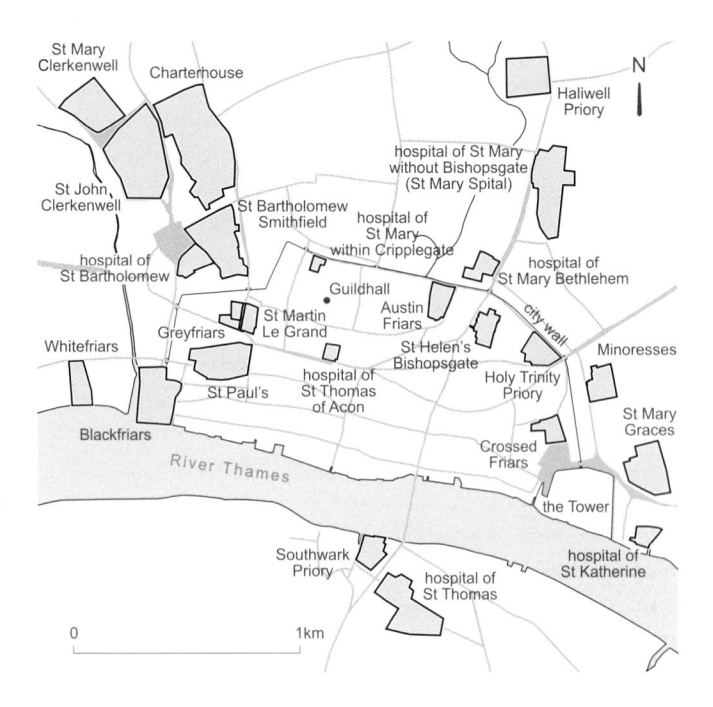

Fig 184 Plan of the medieval city of London, showing the precincts of the larger religious houses (scale 1:32,500)

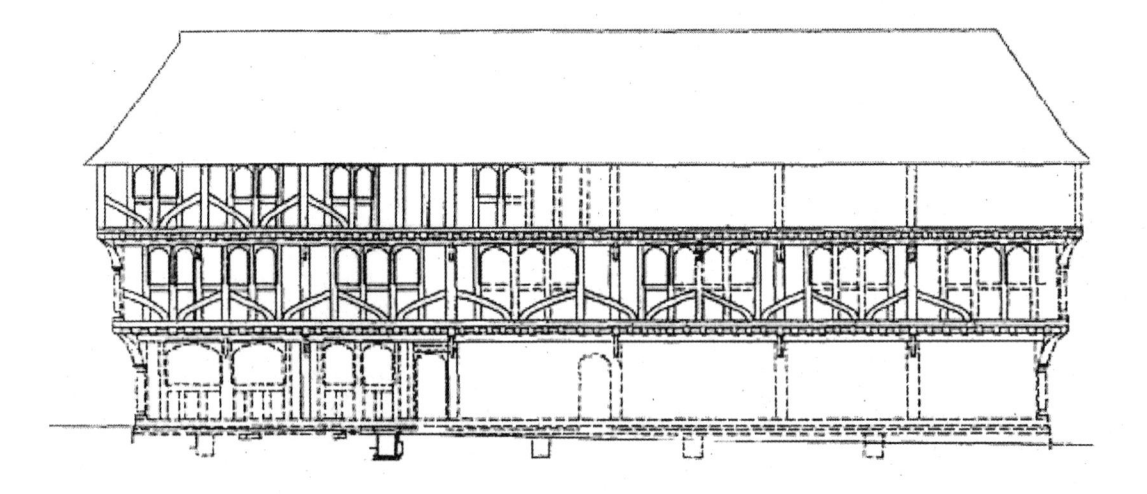

Fig 185 Diagram of a medieval jettied building from Canterbury (from Munby 1987, 163)

to live (Keene 1990, 115), and that as a result, living conditions in the suburbs were far from salubrious, as they lay outside the area governed by City of London ordinances (Grenville 1997, 193).

Even so, much of London's population probably spent the majority of the daylight hours in the centre of the city, where there was little physical separation between rich and poor (Holt and Rosser 1990, 15). This would have increased the risk of the spread of communicable infectious diseases, such as tuberculosis, influenza or measles. It was probably easier for the wealthy to escape some of the ills of the urban environment, whether by living within a large property in the town centre or in a house on purchased land outside the walls (Dyer 2002, 199). Escape to the countryside was particularly appealing during outbreaks of plague (Schofield and Vince 2003, 240).

In the course of the 13th century there was an increase in the use of stone in the construction of houses, although this was restricted to high-status buildings; the majority of structures remained timber-framed (Thomas 2002, 69) (Fig 186). The small houses of the poor were less likely to survive than large timber or stone buildings, and those that did were vulnerable to later works, such as the construction of cellars or street widening (Schofield and Vince 2003, 90). Fire was also responsible for the destruction of many timber structures, and in response to this hazard the use of thatch for roofing in London was banned in 1212, leading to an increase in the use of ceramic tiles (Thomas 2002, 71). Many of the poorest dwellings consisted of single-roomed houses with wattle walls, closely flanked by similar structures, with little room for expansion except upwards (Schofield and Vince 2003, 115). Those who could not afford to rent a room may have occupied temporary lean-to shacks, or squatted in empty properties (Hanawalt 1993, 27). Only a small proportion of the homeless could have hoped to receive lodging at hospitals such as St Mary Spital.

Some houses were built on stone foundations and contained two or more storeys. The upper floors were used for accommodation, and the ground floors were often shops (Thomas 2002, 111). While single room occupancy, often on the upper floor of a house, was an option for labourers, larger timber structures may have been shared by a number of families (Dyer 2002, 199). Understanding room use is therefore problematic. Research at Winchester has shown that early 14th-century houses, 4.6m square, were subdivided into smaller compartments that may indicate separate dwellings. In contrast, in York two-storey houses dating from 1381 were 5.2m by 3.5m in size, with documentary evidence indicating that they were inhabited by one labourer (Dyer 1998, 203; Schofield and Vince 2003, 117).

At ground level, most floors were constructed of earth or mortar and covered with straw. Only the wealthy could afford to have paving or tiles. When houses were divided up into individual tenements, ladders and external stairs were employed to allow access to the upper floors (Hanawalt 1993, 25). This would have greatly increased injury risk from falling, especially in areas of the town where streets were commonly filled with traffic. Privies were also a danger to health: they were located near property boundaries, often at the rear of plots, but the stench from them would still have been very apparent (ibid, 29; Schofield and Vince 2003, 82) (Fig 186).

The density of occupation fell following the Black Death. This led to an improvement in living standards for some as labour shortages caused wages to increase, and possibly also to better standards of housing for the urban population (Schofield and Vince 2003, 252). Archaeological evidence points to an increase in the building of stone houses and of window glazing, and in the different types of objects and materials being used (Thomas 2002, 169).

Fig 186 A chalk cellar from a medieval house at St Mary Spital; its doorway is on the right-hand side (0.5m scale)

Fig 187 A large back garden cesspit from a medieval house at St Mary Spital

Health risks and exposure to pollutants

Health risks from physical, biological or socio-cultural sources may increase in certain environments, such as densely populated settlements. Socio-cultural sources of risk may be divided into habitat, economy and society. Habitat involves the air, land and water surrounding an area of occupation, and includes pollution of water sources and the atmosphere, as well as from trace elements and the home environment. Economic stimuli may include the effects of agricultural or industrial activities on the health of a population. Society-related stimuli relate to the stressful impact of the environment on individuals, which can lead to a reduction in fitness (Howe 1976, 21–6).

'Urban heat islands' are specifically linked to areas of dense occupation. This phenomenon was first recognised in the first half of the 19th century through seasonal recording of urban and rural temperatures, and has been linked to increased combustion and the heat produced by large populations. Although modern cities produce a higher order of heat than in the past, Brimblecombe (1982, 14–16) argues that in calm conditions the temperatures of late medieval towns may have reached *c* 2°C above that of contemporary rural areas. In such cases, background environmental conditions created as a by-product of human activity and population density may themselves influence the level and type of health risk. Studies have shown that heatwaves are associated with disproportionately higher mortality in urban centres. This effect is not random but rather is dependent upon housing, socio-economic conditions, age and health (Kovats and Hajat 2007).

The water supply to any urban community is a priority, and there is evidence of substantial structural investment in 13th-century London, with the construction of the Cheapside conduit in 1236–45, which was linked to the River Tyburn via lead pipes (Thomas 2002, 73–4). Public wells for drinking and washing were also provided (Schofield and Vince 2003, 62). Although water was a blessing, it could also spread disease, such as typhoid, if its supply and disposal were mismanaged, while the density of the urban population increased the disease burden, compounding the severity of outbreaks (Storey 1992, 33). Running watercourses such as the Walbrook were probably used as dumps for all types of waste. There is evidence to suggest that large and important foundations such as St Mary Spital may also have used the Walbrook to carry waste away from their main drain (Thomas 2002, 101) (Fig 188). If so, our studies should take account of the pollution of towns from beyond their walls, not just that originating from within.

Efficient drainage is required in order to prevent flooding from precipitation. The rural environment provides plenty of space and porous soil for this, but the more waterproof materials used in town houses and roads can result in larger volumes of run-off leading to flooding of ditches and drains (Brimblecombe 1982, 16). This flooding can cause pools of water to form in areas that were not designed for the storage or drainage of liquids, and each has the potential to stagnate. This process provides a home for water-borne pathogens including bacteria, parasites, protozoa, algae and viruses, and these can cause disease in humans especially if there is a failure to maintain hygienic standards (Howe 1973, 2; World Health Organization 2009a). The example of rainfall demonstrates how environmental stimuli may combine to increase risk to health, in this case with rainfall (physical) acting on a constructed urban landscape (socio-cultural) to produce a haven for micro-organisms (biological).

The risk to health from water pollution would have been compounded by inadequate sanitation and poor hygiene (Brimblecombe 1982, 21). Public latrines were often placed above running water where they could be flushed by tidal flow, but severe flooding or poor maintenance would have led to overflow into the streets and into other sources of water (Hanawalt 1993, 29). Indeed, sediment studies on the River Fleet suggest that local watercourses became polluted in the 14th century (Schofield and Vince 2003, 213). The Assize of Building (1200) regulated the construction of drains and disposal of human waste in an attempt to keep private cesspits from overflowing into gardens or their construction from undermining neighbouring houses (Keene 1982, 26; Schofield and Vince 2003, 108). As cesspits were usually sited on property boundaries and built of timber, this was a common legal complaint between neighbours. After the early 13th century, stone-lined cesspits, which were less likely to leak and could be cleaned more easily, became more common (Nicholas 1997b, 333; Schofield and Vince 2003, 82–3).

It was not only human waste that could cause ill health. The population lived in close proximity to animals, some of which were kept within the house, compromising levels of hygiene. Animal waste, carcasses and everyday rubbish could also quickly build up in unattended public areas. In the denser areas of London manure, market stalls and building materials often blocked thoroughfares. The recognition of such problems led to the employment of street rakers and the creation of the assize of nuisance, and by 1300 there was an increase in the transportation of rubbish beyond the walls (Hanawalt 1993, 29; Dyer 2002, 200). The presence of horses, cattle, sheep and pigs within medieval towns would have required the disposal of great quantities of dung if the streets were to be kept clean. Added to this was the risk to health of rotting animal corpses (Keene 1982, 27).

Faecal contamination of drinking water sources leads to the spread of bacteria from the human or animal colon. At certain concentrations these bacteria can lead to illnesses such as dysentery, salmonella or cholera. Diarrhoeal diseases can then help to spread infection if faecal waste disposal facilities are inadequate (World Health Organization 2009b). Other water-borne agents that can cause disease include protozoa, viruses, spirochaetes and worms. Spirochaetal organisms include the *Leptospira* genus, which can cause a number of disorders including the acute Weil's disease (Ffrench 1979). This can be carried in water polluted with rat or cattle urine, and can infect the body by contact with cuts or through entering the mouth or nose. Initial symptoms are flu-like, and in the absence of treatment jaundice and death may follow. Although Weil's disease may have been found in rural areas, the concentration of rats in towns may have led to increased urban risk of contraction. Even churches became infested with rats (Hanawalt 1993, 30).

Parasitic eggs recovered from waste deposits at St Mary Spital suggest widespread, if mild, worm contamination of individuals. The most commonly encountered species were *Trichuris trichiura* (human whipworm); probable *Ascaris lumbricoides* (human roundworm) were also found (Rouffignac 1997).

Another potential risk of living within the crowded urban environment was insufficient street lighting, which may have increased the likelihood of accidental injuries or assault from muggers. The majority of reported accidents and nearly all murders occurred in the evening or at night (Hanawalt 1993, 77).

As with water, contamination of the air can have serious implications for health. The high population density within urban centres, accompanied by the concentration of human activity, can lead to increased levels of air pollution. The relationship between the contamination of the air and disease was at least partially recognised in medieval times, by the association of foul smells with 'bad airs' (Brimblecombe 1982, 18–19). Foul-smelling air may have carried pollutants that damaged health.

Diseases that can result from air pollution include pneumonia, bronchitis, sinusitis, emphysema and lung cancer (Howe 1973, 5; Roberts 2007, 792). Past reports of foul-smelling rubbish tips

Fig 188 St Mary Spital infirmary latrines, which were flushed out via two drains beneath Bishopsgate to the River Walbrook (1.0m scales)

and sewers are commonplace, but the effects of smoke were often cited as the most objectionable form of air pollution (Brimblecombe 1982, 18–19). Documentary records reveal that town dwellers objected to smoke on the grounds of its effect on health, and this pollution is likely to have become more severe with increased burning of coal from the 13th century, particularly by the lime-burning industry. Legislation attempted to force industries back to burning wood (despite its escalating cost). In the 14th century regulations concerning chimney heights were also introduced (ibid, 14–21). The noxious smoke and smell of sulphur would have caused unpleasant living conditions and increased the risk of lung disease in urban centres, especially as the sulphur level of coal in medieval London is believed to have been higher that that used today (ibid, 21).

The low crude prevalence rate of rickets at the cemetery of St Mary Spital suggests that London was not shrouded in smoke to the extent that the supply of sunlight was affected. Only small amounts of vitamin D are present in most foods, so the great majority is synthesised in the skin when exposed to ultraviolet light (Resnick 2002, 1913; Mays 2003, 144). However, it has been suggested that sulphur dioxide levels in the city may have been 30 times the level of contemporary rural areas (Brimblecombe 1982, 24).

The study of respiratory infections in human skeletal remains has been neglected in the past, although there is evidence to suggest that infection increased through time, possibly in association with urban growth (Roberts and Lewis 2002, 189). Lesions on the visceral surfaces of ribs are a reaction to soft tissue inflammation in the lower respiratory tract brought on by a number of causes, including chronic bronchitis and tuberculosis. At St Mary Spital, examples of both proliferative (bone-forming) and destructive lesions were found on the ribs. Some individuals displayed both types of lesion. As environmental pollution is one factor that can cause inflammation of the respiratory tract, it is feasible that the prevalence of rib lesions may vary with lifestyle and habitat. At St Mary Spital, higher numbers of individuals within the attritional cemetery were affected by rib lesions than those in the mass burial sample (Chapter 3.9) (Fig 189). This difference was statistically significant. It may be that the increased prevalence of chronic lung disease was caused by the inclusion of a large number of hospital inmates within the attritional cemetery. Alternatively, this variation may be the result of differences in lifestyle and habitat, with increased environmental stress leading to the development of lung disease (Lambert 2002). In such cases, the problems of interpretation of skeletal data relating to the 'osteological paradox' must be considered. It is possible that the individuals with skeletal lesions were actually healthier than those without, as the latter may have had lower resistance to disease and died before bone changes had time to develop (Wood et al 1992, 344–5). If this were the case, it would be possible to argue that the attritional sample was healthier than that from the mass burials.

Fuel for domestic fires probably consisted of wood, coal and organic waste. Apart from the obvious fire risk to timber structures, the smoke and fumes produced could be detrimental to health (Schofield and Vince 2003, 135). The occupants of domestic structures without chimneys or with insufficient ventilation would have been vulnerable to respiratory diseases such as chronic bronchitis (Roberts and Lewis 2002, 186). These problems may have increased in winter if shutters were kept closed to keep in the warmth.

Sinusitis is a pathological condition in which there is inflammation of the paranasal sinuses, which can lead to blocked airways, facial pain and headaches. In modern times it has been linked with allergies, asthma, upper respiratory tract infection, head injury, maxillary dental abscesses and exposure to environmental pollutants such as smoke and dust (Roberts 2007, 792, 795). Poorly ventilated medieval houses that burnt wood or coal may have increased the risk of developing sinusitis, and industrial pollutants within the urban environment of London may have exacerbated this. However, some rural sites have also produced high frequencies of sinusitis, perhaps reflecting the multifactorial nature of the disease (Roberts and Lewis 2002, 188).

The study of sinusitis in skeletal remains from archaeological contexts has been hampered by the location and structure of the sinuses, and by past recording methods. The portions of maxillary bone that form the nasal sinuses are thin and delicate, and prone to poor preservation in the burial environment. For purposes of function, the sinuses are internal cavities set within the mid facial region. This hampers the inspection of the sinus walls in crania that have survived intact, and has led to the development of new recording techniques such as the use of endoscopy (Boocock et al 1995). In order to produce true prevalence rates that can be compared with other sites, the numbers of sinuses present (and visible) need to be recorded in future work. The crude prevalence rates quoted in the results section (Chapter 3.9) are undoubtedly a gross under-representation of the number of individuals affected, and this should be taken into account in the interpretation of the results.

A greater number of females were affected by sinusitis than males. This difference was statistically significant. Roberts and Cox suggest that variation in prevalence between the sexes might potentially be related to gender roles, specifically to the amount of time spent in the home (Roberts and Cox 2003, 233).

Fig 189 Rib lesions in 18–25-year-old male [31293] from the catastrophic cemetery, period 16, c 1250–c 1400 (scale c 1:2)

However, the pattern seen at St Mary Spital may well result from the thinner bones of female crania being more susceptible to breakage in the burial environment, allowing exposure and macroscopic inspection of the sinuses. No variation by period or by burial type was identified (Chapter 3.9).

The severe changes in the frontal bones of 12–17-year-old [3263] (Chapter 3.9) may have been caused by osteomyelitic reaction to chronic sinusitis in the frontal bones (Fig 190). Symptoms would probably have included headache and facial pain, with unpleasant nasal drainage. It was not possible to determine the extent of infection in the other sinuses, as inspection of the maxillary and ethmoid sinuses was prevented by the intact nature of the facial bones. There was no evidence of dental caries or periapical abscess in this individual to suggest infection had spread from the dentition. The chronic nature of the infection suggests that it was not due to a single incident but to a recurrence of blockage or irritation. The fact that the lesion was resolved at the time of death demonstrates that the individual's health was strong enough to survive the infection, even though he or she did not live into adulthood. It is possible that this 12–17-year-old was involved in activities, either in the domestic environment or as an apprentice, which increased the risk of sinus infection through exposure to pollutants. However, considering that the disease is multifactorial, other possibilities cannot be discounted (Roberts and Cox 2003, 233).

Tuberculosis is a chronic infectious disease spread by droplet infection from human to human (*Mycobacterium tuberculosis*), from animals such as cattle to humans (*Mycobacterium bovis*) and vice versa, or from the ingestion of infected meat or milk (Ortner 2003, 227). The pulmonary form of the disease commonly results in transmission of tuberculosis between humans, while the bovine type commonly infects the digestive system. The symptoms of the disease include weakness, lethargy, night sweats, chest pain, shortness of breath, and coughing associated with bloody sputum (Roberts and Buikstra 2003, 20). The chronic nature of tuberculosis can lead to changes in the skeleton, but only in 5–7% of affected individuals (Aufderheide and Rodríguez-Martín 1998, 133). Diagnostic changes often involve destructive lesions on the vertebral bodies and spinal collapse (Pott's disease) (Fig 191).

While the origins of tuberculosis are ancient, the growth in evidence of the disease in late medieval contexts is believed to be associated with the increasing density of population that accompanied urban growth (Roberts and Manchester 2005, 183–92). The increased amount of close contact within the increasingly crowded environment of 13th-century London provided ideal conditions for droplet infection. Any person within range of a sufferer's cough or sneeze could potentially be infected. Regular contact with animals, either within the domestic environment, or as part of a trade such as leather working or butchery, would have increased the risk of contracting the bovine form of the disease (Roberts and Cox 2003, 229).

The total crude prevalence rate of tuberculosis at St Mary Spital was 1.9% (Chapter 3.9). While this rate is similar to that recorded for other medieval urban assemblages in England, the rural site of Wharram Percy had a higher prevalence of tuberculosis (2.6%) and that of Llandough, a rural site in Wales, was lower (0.9%), as discussed below (4.5) (Mays 2007; Loe 2003). On the basis that only 6% of individuals with the infection displayed bony changes, it is possible that the actual crude rate of tuberculosis at St Mary Spital was nearer 30.9% (1667/5387) of the population.

Fig 190 Osteomyelitis in the frontal sinuses of 12–17-year-old [3263] from the catastrophic cemetery, period 15, c 1200–50 (scale c 1:2)

Fig 191 Example of Pott's disease in 36–45-year-old male [19599] from the catastrophic cemetery, period 16 (scale c 1:2)

The total prevalence rate of tuberculosis at St Mary Spital remained at approximately 2% for most of the period of use of the cemetery, with a slight drop (to 1.7%) in period 15. However, there was a statistically significant decrease from period 16 to period 17. A number of factors can affect the infectious disease levels within a population, some of which may have contributed to this decline. London was less crowded following the Black Death, and there is evidence to suggest that, as labour became scarcer, wages and standards of living rose for much of the population with a better diet and improved standards of housing. Further outbreaks of plague probably prevented a rise in population sufficient to reach the density of occupation seen before 1348 (Schofield and Vince 2003, 252). This rise in living standards and reduction in population density may have contributed to the fall in the prevalence of tuberculosis, as the disease would be spread less rapidly from person to person. It is also possible that tuberculosis became gradually less virulent over time in London, as more of the inhabitants were exposed to the disease. The prevalence may only have begun to rise again following the increase in migration in the late 15th and early 16th centuries.

Periostitis, or bony changes resulting from inflammation of the periosteum, may be associated with a specific infection, or may be non-specific in nature with an unknown aetiology. Its presence in the tibia may be associated with repeated minor trauma to the shin (Roberts and Manchester 2005, 72). It is possible that the high prevalence of non-specific infection at St Mary Spital may reflect environmental stress associated with crowded urban conditions. Similar crude prevalence rates of periostitis to those at St Mary Spital were found at the urban sites of St Andrew Fishergate and St Helen-on-the-Walls, both in York (Stroud and Kemp 1993; Grauer and Roberts 1996, 538). However, the high prevalence of infection at St Mary Spital may be related to its function as a hospital, with a greater likelihood that inmates would be suffering increased rates of non-specific disease. When the prevalence rates were divided into burial types, the frequency of non-specific periostitis was higher in the attritional than in the catastrophic cemetery, to a statistically significant extent. This variation was most evident in period 16 (Chapter 3.9). The attritional sample may have been less healthy, and may have consisted of a larger number of hospital inmates. The results from period 16 would be consistent with the commencement of the burial of inmates in the main (attritional) cemetery in the second half of the 14th century. However, if this was the case we would not expect to see the same pattern in period 15.

Other illnesses that can spread rapidly in densely populated areas include influenza, measles and plague. Although these are acute diseases that progress rapidly, leaving no pathological evidence on the skeleton, they could have contributed to the mass burial deaths (below, 4.3).

Health risks in the domestic environment

The discovery of artefacts providing evidence of craft activity, such as spindle whorls for spinning, in household waste deposits suggests that domestic and trade activities may have overlapped to a degree (Schofield and Vince 2003, 79). At St Mary Spital itself, inside the busy precinct area, activities included brewing, baking, food cultivation and storage, and possibly the manufacture of medicines (Thomas 2004, 36, 45, 63). For those who could afford two-storey housing, the upper floor was often used for sleeping while the ground floor served as a living and working area (Dyer 2002, 199). This combination of functions was typified in the appearance of integrated 'row' buildings at the beginning of the 14th century (Schofield and Vince 2003, 92). For many people in medieval London there may have been little distinction between home and work, and they would have spent a large proportion of their time in the domestic environment. While this may have reduced some risks to health, such as those encountered while travelling and those resulting from increased contact with people in the community, it is also possible that the performance of a trade within the home could have increased other risks brought about by prolonged hours spent within poorly ventilated structures. There may also have been an increased likelihood of accidental injury from close and regular contact with domesticated animals (Judd and Roberts 1999) and from strenuous chores such as fetching and carrying water.

As far as hygiene was concerned, the details of household waste are rarely mentioned in written sources, although the straw and rushes that were used to cover floors may have been periodically swept up and disposed of (Keene 1982, 27). There is little doubt that some households would have been more proficient in maintaining cleanliness than others.

The size of the average household, and therefore the level of crowding, is difficult to estimate, although records suggest that family groups became smaller after the Black Death (Fleming 2001, 66). It may be that those migrants who could not find work as servants lived together in densely packed and undesirable accommodation. In 1244, the royal household at Westminster fed 20,000 paupers (Dyer 2002, 201). This suggests that there were large numbers of poor living in and around London.

The presence of animals in and around domestic structures would have increased the risk of infections such as tuberculosis, as previously discussed, and would also have compromised hygiene. Both pigs and dogs were reported to have attacked children in the home, with swaddled infants being particularly vulnerable (Fleming 2001, 63). The risk of accidental injury may also have been increased by the mud spread underfoot by animals, or simply by their presence within a crowded environment.

In some areas of London, danger lay immediately beyond the frontage of domestic structures, with children and the elderly particularly vulnerable to traffic and the general bustle of the urban street. Evidence of accidental death in rural communities reflects a society where male toddlers would spend increased amounts of time with their fathers outside the house, while young girls would remain within. This may also have affected the relative injury risk in urban centres (Hanawalt 1993, 65): the majority of female accidental deaths happened in the home, whereas for males they took place in public spaces (ibid, 75). Archaeological evidence from London suggests that candles or oil lamps provided lighting within the home (Thomas 2002,

72). While careless use of these lamps would have heightened the risk of fire, adequate illumination within the home would have helped to reduce the potential for accidental injury. Risks relating to interpersonal violence within the home, such as spousal abuse, are discussed later in this chapter.

Industry and occupation

Occupation is often used as a measure of socio-economic status, and many types of work can be associated with risks to health (Howe 1973, 5). Risks were common to rural and urban occupations, but in towns there was less emphasis on agrarian work and more on the service sector. At the time of the cemetery's use, urban industry was not yet fully developed, and domestic production predominated in medieval towns (Holt and Rosser 1990, 1). However, there must have been an intensification of industrial activity within and around London, especially during the rapid population growth of the 13th century which saw the expansion of hospitals such as St Mary Spital (Thomas et al 1997, 42).

More than 180 different trades are listed in the medieval records of London, and by 1422 there were 111 organised crafts (Veale 1990, 127; Dyer 2002, 320). Most work was labour intensive, especially before the Black Death when labour was cheap and wages were low (Schofield and Vince 2003, 121, 145).

Almost one-third of York's population were servants, and it is probable that there was a similar proportion in London (Hanawalt 1993, 179). This was a suitable occupation for young migrants because they were often given rooms in family houses. The great variety of occupations undertaken in service suggests that there was no uniform risk to health. Some servants such as journeymen were highly skilled in crafts, while others worked in the victualling trade, supplying food. The less skilled would fetch and carry, and perform everyday chores (ibid, 178). Labourers probably had to rely on irregular, poorly paid and possibly dangerous work (Dyer 2002, 202). This would have increased their injury risk in comparison with those in less active occupations, but not necessarily to the same level as rural workers. At the same time, the flow of migration from the countryside would have meant that some of those who died and were buried in London had suffered agrarian-related injuries earlier in their lives.

Married women with dependants would have adapted their occupations to suit their family situations, and were better able to access credit and engage in business (particularly brewing), as the London market was supportive of wives and widows acting as traders (Leyser 1995, 138–41, 148; McIntosh 2005). Although some women were involved in metalworking and leather working, there is no evidence that they worked in particularly dangerous occupations, such as building construction (Jewell 1996, 92). This appears to be reflected in the data from St Mary Spital, where for most age categories men display an increased prevalence of injury, especially to the shoulder and spine. It may be that this reflects particular forms of gender-specific, casual or labour-intensive work. Men may have carried out work that was more likely to result in broken bones, but this does not mean that there was no risk of injury in the daily activities and work of women. In fact, female rates of forearm and lower leg fracture were higher than those of males. 'Women were expected to clothe their families, launder, prepare food and stock up for the winter months, bake, brew, garden, tend livestock, rear children, perhaps sell produce on the streets as vendors or hucksters, as well as assist in the work of their husbands!' (Stevenson 1996, 97).

At St Mary Spital the number of males with fractures was higher (to a statistically significant extent) than the number of affected females, both overall and for each adult age category. This implies that male injury risk was higher than female risk. The large variance in the 18–25-year age category strongly suggests that the male risk may also have been higher in the 12–17-year age category. The number of subadult-type injuries recorded in adult individuals supports this hypothesis and includes greenstick fractures and epiphyseal plate injuries (Fig 192; Fig 193). A higher number of males than females displayed

Fig 192 Healed greenstick fracture in the sternal end of the right clavicle of 18–25-year-old female [9626] from the attritional cemetery, period 17, c 1400–1539 (scale c 1:1)

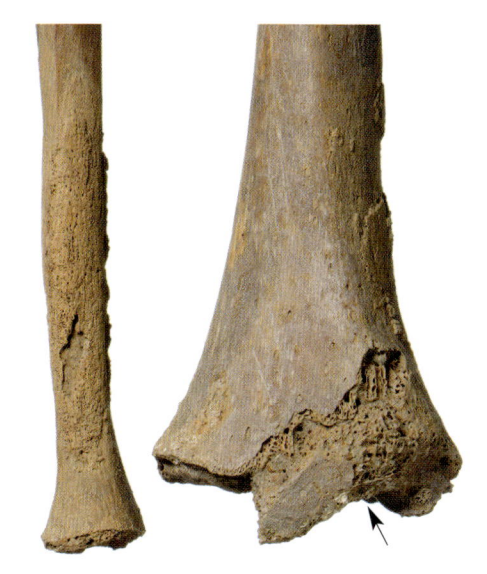

Fig 193 Epiphyseal plate injury in the right tibia of c 17-year-old [29075] from the catastrophic cemetery, period 16 (scale c 1:1)

evidence of such fractures (Chapter 3.8), and this difference was statistically significant. The evidence suggests that males had a higher risk of bone fracture than females from 12 years onwards.

There was also a difference in the age-related rates of increase of all fracture types between the sexes at St Mary Spital. From birth to the age of 25 years, the male crude fracture prevalence rate was higher than that of females (Chapter 3.8). This may well be a true reflection of the relative injury risk up to the age of 25, although it is possible that the strength of the result could have been affected by an increased chance of males who had suffered injuries earlier in life dying between the ages of 18 and 25. From the age of 25 onwards, though, the rate of increase in male fracture prevalence fell. However, the 18–25-year age category may include a large number of individuals who suffered injuries as subadults, and we might expect to find a higher number of injuries within this span of 25 years when compared to the shorter span (nine years) in each of the later age categories (26–35 years and 36–45 years). It may be reasonable to argue that we would expect to see a similarly large increase in the open-ended older adult category. However, this may be affected by the documented problems in ageing methods, causing the mixing of later middle-aged individuals with older adults (Cox 2000, 75).

For females, the peak increase in crude fracture prevalence occurs later than in males, at 26–35 years. The pattern suggests than women suffered low rates of fracture in subadulthood and early adulthood, but that there was a large increase in exposure to risk after this. It may not be possible to discover why there was such a difference, but it is possible that cultural factors determined the peak ages of exposure to injury for each sex. It may be that these factors partially reflect activity within the urban environment, although there is evidence that some women worked alongside men (Stevenson 1996, 98).

The difference in the prevalence rates of fractures between the sexes was not simply a function of increased risk frequency in males. The evidence suggests that the location and type of injury received were at least partially dependent upon the sex of the individual concerned, and this was not due to differential rates of osteoporosis-related fracture in the radius, femur and spine. It may therefore be that the fracture data reflect cultural differences in activity, in which the associated injury risk for men was higher (see following sections for discussion). However, there is evidence that widows inherited and ran their late husbands' businesses, including occupations that entailed hard labour and industry, such as tanning and heavy metalwork (Stevenson 1996, 98). The early death of a husband could have left a widow running such a business for a considerable length of time.

Both the husband and wife of a family may have worked, and not always in the same occupation. Within an urban environment it may have paid to diversify rather than to concentrate on a single trade. At some stage between 7 and 12 years of age, children began to contribute to the everyday work of the household, often through chores or by training in the family craft (Fleming 2001, 64). However, the exposure of children to risk from accidental injury or pollution may already have been high before they became directly involved, since many crafts were practised in the home.

Many people were involved in the processing and serving of food in order to meet the dietary demands of the growing population of London and its many visitors, and women commonly sold ale on the streets. Brewing was an activity that could pollute the air if not properly ventilated (Dyer 2002, 199–203). Women were particularly associated with the victualling trades, especially dairy and poultry products (Goldberg 1992, 104–5) (Fig 194).

Fig 194 A 15th-century illustration of a trader selling eggs (© The British Library Board, Bartholomaeus Anglicus IB 41688, Riiiv)

Another trade normally carried out by women was that of the huckster. Hucksters bought products in bulk from markets and sold them door-to-door in smaller portions to people who could not afford to buy in large quantities. For this service the huckster would take a slight profit (Dyer 2002, 203). The work probably entailed carrying heavy loads for some distance through muddy and slippery streets, which could have led to joint damage and a heightened risk of accidental injury. Records show that women were employed as wool-packers and porters, and the evidence suggests that they were not spared heavy loads (Goldberg 1992, 132). However, the osteological data revealed higher overall male crude prevalence rates of osteoarthritis and vertebral injury when compared to females. If these bone changes were caused by activity, they indicate that men were involved in heavy labour to a greater extent than women.

Manufacturing crafts in medieval towns included building, working with leather, furs and linen, and metalworking, but the chief source of employment was in the processing of wool, which was imported into towns for the weaving industry (Dyer 2002, 203; Schofield and Vince 2003, 133). Although the regulation of weaving and finishing cloth was controlled by the male-dominated guilds, women were commonly associated with the textile and clothing industry, especially in spinning and braidmaking, and they dominated the laundry trade (Goldberg 1992, 118–24, 135; Pritchard 1996, 111) (Fig 195).

Documentary records from the 14th and 15th centuries record the licensing of women to trade in a large number of textile crafts, including weaving, fulling and dyeing (Pritchard 1996, 113). The bases of large vats used for brewing or for dyeing cloths have been found in medieval strata one mile south of St Mary Spital, in Swan Lane (Schofield and Vince 2003, 142). The wool and linen crafts would not themselves have caused pollution of the urban environment, but clothmakers would have had to dispose of their waste dyestuffs while trying not to contaminate watercourses (Keene 1982, 27).

Those working with meat and other animal products were at risk of contracting zoonoses such as bovine tuberculosis and brucellosis (Roberts and Cox 2003, 229). Most animals were reared in suburban or rural areas and brought into town for slaughtering. There would have been livestock within the walls of London, but the relatively low rates of bone fracture in the human population in comparison with rural sites suggests either that fewer individuals living in London managed large live animals on a regular basis, or that fewer serious accidents resulted (Chapter 3.8). Specialist workers were involved in the slaughter of livestock once it reached the city. Cattle and sheep were driven to town for market and slaughter; there had been a longstanding tradition of cattle droving to London from areas such as the east Midlands and beyond, while pastoral farming in the manors surrounding the capital came to prominence in the 15th century (Keene 1989, 104–5).

A large number of animals would have been killed within the walls each day. Butchers were able to slaughter animals in the City of London, disposing of their waste nearby or in the suburbs. Butchery would have spilled blood, entrails and carcass off-cuts on to the streets, often close to crowded markets, with the potential to release micro-organisms into the water supply. The guilds issued rules governing waste disposal by butchers and scalding houses, and documents record how four female butchers were prosecuted for throwing waste on to the street. After 1361, the king and parliament issued a writ to the mayor and aldermen ordering all animals to be slaughtered outside the city walls (in Knightsbridge and Stratford), because their waste was considered to add to the ravages of the plague (Sabine 1933). This led to the provision of a more formalised disposal of entrails, which were chopped up and dumped in the middle of the Thames at ebb tide (Keene 1982, 27). Many butchers built piers into the Thames in order to do this but documentary evidence shows that butchers in the Stock Market continued to dispose of their waste into the Walbrook

Fig 195 Women spinning and carding wool, from an English text dating from c 1325–35 (© The British Library Board, Add MS 42130, fo 193)

stream through an open sewer (Sabine 1933; Thomas et al 1997, 128). It is not surprising that the stench of butchers' refuse led to this type of action, and it probably helped to reduce the number of people affected by the pollution of drinking water. Eventually the butchers were moved to their own market site at Smithfield, approximately 1.5km west of St Mary Spital (Hanawalt 1993, 32).

Following butchery, the hides of animals were taken for tanning. Leather workers and tanners often worked away from the centres of towns because of the putrid smell during treatment (Keene 1982, 27; Schofield and Vince 2003, 123). The drenching pits of the skinners also produced a foul smell, but the pollution of running water by the washing of hides was probably the greatest danger to health (Keene 1982, 27; Dyer 2002, 199).

As discussed above, the high price of firewood in London led to an increase in the burning of coal in the 13th century, causing complaints from travellers about the unclean air (Brimblecombe 1982, 19; Dyer 2002, 200). This change was probably most noticeable in industries that required constant supplies of heat (Schofield and Vince 2003, 135). Exposure to sulphur dioxide and coal smoke would have increased the risks of lung damage, especially in individuals with pre-existing respiratory problems. Burning coal could also lead to the build-up of fatal doses of carbon monoxide in poorly ventilated areas (Brimblecombe 1982, 20). As this gas is odourless, it is likely that most people were unaware of the risks. Lime kilns, which were used to make mortar from limestone, were frequently sited in towns and also burned a lot of coal (Schofield and Vince 2003, 126). Mortar was needed for the building of stone foundations and houses, and even if it was largely required only for higher status structures, the kilns must have been busy in times of rapid population expansion. Other industries that were sited in the centre of town include the rope walks, such as the one at the Steelyard in London. The rope processing industry was hazardous, as it required large amounts of tar for coating the rope (ibid, 139). The fumes from the burning of tar would have harmed the lungs if inhaled.

Although iron smelting was normally carried out in rural areas, much of the smithing would have taken place in towns, and formed what was probably a substantial industry in London (Schofield and Vince 2003, 126). The work of blacksmiths involved the manufacture of tools, fittings, weapons and armour; working conditions were hot and labour intensive. Smithing was not just a male preserve: a survey of documentary records from the 14th and 15th centuries found that approximately 10% of material concerning blacksmithing involved women (Geddes 1996, 102). While records of specific activities are rare, there is evidence to suggest that some of the women's work included breaking rock and working bellows (ibid, 103).

The location of such industry among the crowded wooden structures of London was a severe fire hazard (Schofield and Vince 2003, 123), and blacksmiths were often sited outside town gates and in suburban areas (Keene 1990, 116). It is not known to what extent such practices reduced the levels of pollution within the walls of medieval towns, but there was self-regulation by some London smiths, who agreed not to burn coal after dark (Brimblecombe 1982, 19).

Copper alloy workers produced cooking pots, buckles and other small items (Dyer 2002, 204). Bell casting was often carried out on the building sites of churches (Schofield and Vince 2003, 139), which not only spared the manufacturers the effort of transporting the bell, but may also have helped to reduce the risk of fire by keeping the works away from domestic structures. As with smithing, documentary records have revealed evidence of female involvement in bell casting, in both London and York (Geddes 1996, 104). Pictorial evidence from early 14th-century stained glass windows at York Minster suggests that women were working both with the molten metal and in the finishing process (ibid) (Fig 196).

Lead was present in water pipes and in products such as pottery vessels where lead glazes were applied, and studies have revealed relatively high levels in late medieval human remains

Fig 196 Detail from the early 14th-century bell founders' window in the north nave aisle of York Minster, depicting women casting a bell (© Crown copyright. EH)

(Thomas 2002, 73; Schofield and Vince 2003, 145; Budd et al 2004, 56). Lead poisoning is hazardous because it is cumulative and permanent, with women and children more sensitive to its effects than men (Howe 1976, 24). Symptoms associated with levels above 80 parts per million (ppm) include colic, extensor muscle weakness, vomiting and constipation (Keenleyside et al 1997, 41). Isotopic and trace element analysis on bone samples from 20 people from St Mary Spital, using an X-ray fluorescence spectrometer, produced an average lead concentration reading of 85 ± 37 ppm, suggestive of dangerously high levels. However, these results may be due to post-mortem changes in the ground leading to lead absorption in the dry bone, rather than a reflection of lead intake during life (Joseph and Black 2006, 4).

Health risks within London may have varied according to location, as artisans specialising in similar crafts tended to congregate in certain areas of town (Schofield and Vince 2003, 144). This may have had the effect of concentrating the levels of pollution within the air and water courses in their immediate vicinity. Land rents may have forced smaller industries to cluster in the outer areas of town or in the suburbs (ibid, 123). This would have polluted areas where the poorer inhabitants lived. As is the case today, the individual's level of exposure to pollutants depended on where he or she worked and lived. Some risks would have applied to urban populations in general, while others would have been more localised.

Diet and economy

Animal bones, plant remains (including seeds and pollen), artefacts employed in food cultivation and processing, structural remains related to food preparation and storage, and human remains can provide archaeological evidence of past diet. Dental disease and conditions associated with specific dietary components and deficiencies can be observed in skeletal material. Other evidence, often relating to food production, may be drawn from documentary and pictorial sources. For the medieval period, these tend to post-date the mid 13th century, a time when diet was dominated by cereals both in secular and religious houses (Schofield 2006, 246). The diet of Londoners only differed from other areas when the city became larger, as attested by the small number of wild animals in urban faunal assemblages (Schofield and Vince 2003, 216).

At St Mary Spital, animal bone evidence associated with the religious house suggested a dominance of beef in the diet, with some lamb and mutton, and a little pork (Thomas et al 1997, 113). The proportion of cattle bones to other animal bones by weight varied over the occupation of the priory, with a fall between the refoundation period (69%) and the second half of the 14th century (59%), together with a proportional rise in sheep and pig. This trend was reversed in the 15th century where cattle contributed 87%, sheep 11% and pig 1% (ibid). The overall rise in the proportion of cattle bone reflects a general increase following the Black Death, although the fall in the second half of the 14th century is unusual and may reflect husbandry or dietary practices peculiar to this site. The priory is known to have had estates in Essex in the 13th century, and possibly later. Primary butchery waste from the 12th and early 13th centuries found outside the priory precinct may represent the slaughtering of animals reared some distance from London (Thomas et al 1997, 127–8). There were buildings and enclosures within the southern precinct that may have been used for animal husbandry (Fig 197), and in the 13th and early 14th centuries the priory may have relied largely upon its own resources (Thomas 2002, 103). It is possible that this, together

Fig 197 Two men with clubs knocking down acorns for their pigs, depicted in the Queen Mary psalter, c 1310–20 (© The British Library Board, MS Royal 2 B VII, fo 81v)

with a shift in supply to more local markets in the 14th century, led to a change in the proportions of flesh meat consumed (the meat of beasts and birds, as opposed to fish). Zooarchaeological evidence from 13th-century features at 1 Poultry in London supports a varied diet: again beef predominated but it was supplemented with mutton, pork, chicken and goose, estuarine fish and shellfish. Cereal consumption was dominated by wheat, rye and oats. A range of vegetables and legumes such as lentils were also identified, together with domestic, wild and imported varieties of fruit (ibid, 73).

A large variety of marine and freshwater fish bone, especially herring and plaice or flounder, was recovered from St Mary Spital, and fish probably formed an important part of the diet, especially in the late 13th and 14th centuries (Thomas et al 1997, 113). Church impositions forbade the eating of meat during Lent, on Fridays and Saturdays, and in some households also on Wednesdays (Woolgar 2006a, 192). A greater proportion of fish may have been available in London at times of failed harvests and food shortages, although it is also possible that the increased availability of beef encouraged a fall in the consumption of fish in the 15th century.

Stable isotope evidence from the rural site of Wharram Percy indicates that even communities in inland areas had access to marine foods (Mays et al 2007, 95). Due to restrictions on river fishing rights, greater numbers of marine fish were available compared to freshwater fish, while the variety of species consumed was influenced by the availability of local resources (Mays 1997a).

The main component of the medieval diet was cereals, and evidence of their presence was found within the precinct of St Mary Spital in the form of charred grains and chaff, and the structural remains of a granary and brewery (Thomas et al 1997, 113; Davis in prep). Wheat was the cereal most frequently encountered, especially in period 17 (*c* 1400–1539), and would have been used to make bread. The next most common cereal was oats, possibly used to make pottage or as horse fodder (Davis in prep). Cereals were also malted for ale. Pottage was a basic food eaten by most status groups, consisting of a broth containing oats, vegetables, herbs and sometimes meat (ibid). The consumption of cereals may have inhibited the absorption of iron from the diet, although this deleterious effect can be solved by cooking (Wadsworth 1992, 72–85). Pulses probably formed a further significant part of the diet, especially for low-status groups, but these rarely survive in archaeological deposits (Thomas et al 1997, 113–14).

The grain harvest lasted from late July until September and was a time of plenty. Urban workers would sometimes participate in the harvest, indeed the rising numbers of urban poor may have relied on such seasonal work (Dyer 2006, 212) (Fig 198). The increases in population size from the 11th century onwards led to a reduction in the quantity of livestock per capita and a resultant fall in the productivity of animal husbandry (Woolgar et al 2006, 268).

Numerous varieties of other plants were also recovered from the environmental samples, including pulses (peas, *Pisum sativum*, and beans, *Vicia faba*), fruits (fig, *Ficus carica*, blackberry/raspberry, *Rubus fruticosus/idaeus*, grape, *Vitis vinifera*, and wild strawberry, *Fragaria vesca*), nuts, vegetables, herbs and spices (Davis in prep). Apples, plums and cherries may have come from the priory's orchards, and the priory had its own vineyards to supply it with wine (Thomas et al 1997, 114; Davis in prep). The evidence from areas within the inner precinct at St Mary Spital suggests that while the prior and other high-status occupants may have enjoyed a good variety of food and drink, the inmates relied on a more basic diet (ibid, 2).

The growth of London as a commercial centre in the medieval period exceeded that of other English towns and was part of a general expansion of the European economy. As in the Roman period it was the location of London, with its road and river systems and access to the trading ports of the North Sea and beyond, that provided the key to its commercial success (Keene 1989, 100). A good selection of food was available to

Fig 198 Harvesting a cereal crop, depicted in the Luttrell psalter, c 1325–35 (© The British Library Board, Add MS 42130, fo 172v)

London's wealthier inhabitants, including many varieties of meat, fish and bread, and beverages such as wine and ale (Schofield and Vince 2003, 232). Trade also encouraged the intensification of agriculture in surrounding rural areas, and resulted in increased provision of facilities for the storage of food, which aimed to avoid shortages caused by seasonal variations in supply (ibid, 225). Beyond the walls of the city, where the priory of St Mary Spital lay, there was probably a zone of mixed activity with pasture, meadows and areas for cereal production (Keene 1989, 104). Here grain could be grown, and dairy products, fodder and fattened livestock were within easy reach. At the same time, some aspects of food production, such as the rearing of domestic fowl and the growing of garden produce, remained outside the commercial networks (Woolgar et al 2006, 268). Fruit and vegetables were grown both in urban gardens and in suburban areas. The paucity of evidence for scurvy at St Mary Spital may reflect a wide availability of these foodstuffs in urban centres (Chapter 3.10) (Schofield and Vince 2003, 232).

The medieval period witnessed the rise of a market-based economy, in which the expansion of distribution networks allowed some sections of the population to enjoy a greater amount, variety and freshness of food (Müldner and Richards 2006, 236; Woolgar et al 2006, 268, 278). The regional markets encircling London probably played an important role in the system of provision that supplied the city (Keene 1989, 104). Local markets then sold food to consumers (Fig 199), with street vendors and hucksters providing further distribution (Hanawalt 1993, 37). Taverns would have served fast food to many working Londoners, often in the form of pies washed down with beer. Family meals would normally have consisted of food cooked in a single pot, with bread and beer (ibid, 77).

While the recorded presence of butchers in towns demonstrates that there was a ready supply of fresh meat, most animals were probably reared in rural areas. The keeping of pigs was popular in towns and they were often raised in yards, chiefly for their meat and lard (Schofield and Vince 2003, 226) (Fig 200). In many ways pigs were well suited to the urban environment, as they could be kept on poor quality land and could survive on scraps of food, while at the same time helping to keep yard and street areas clean of food waste (Albarella

Fig 199 Medieval market traders selling meat (© The British Library Board, Add MS 18852, fo 13)

Fig 200 Butchery of pigs, from the Queen Mary psalter, c 1310–20 (© The British Library Board, MS Royal 2 B VII, fo 82v)

2006, 72). Pig meat provided a source of fat in a period when other animals were leaner than in modern times, and was suitable for long-term preservation as bacon and ham, although high-status consumers were more likely to eat fresh pork (ibid, 72–3, 86). The preservation of meat was important in the maintenance of seasonal supplies of protein, and included smoking, salting and drying of the main cuts, and the preparation of brawn and puddings (Woolgar 2006b, 88). The value of year-round supplies of food would have been fully appreciated following the bad harvests of the late 13th and early 14th centuries. Most pigs may never have entered the market place, being consumed instead within the household that reared them (Albarella 2006, 84). Even so, it is likely that urban dwellers ate less pork and mutton than those in rural areas. Both historical and archaeological evidence confirms that beef was the most commonly eaten meat, and town inhabitants may well have consumed more than their rural counterparts (ibid, 73, 80). Animal bones recovered from archaeological sites indicate that there was a general increase in the proportion of sheep, and a reduction in the proportion of pig, throughout the medieval period (ibid, 74–7).

Before the Black Death most people had limited access to meat due to the small numbers of livestock relative to the size of the population. Government regulations attempted to provide a system where all could receive the provisions they required with reasonable ease, and no one could take advantage of others by selling poor quality or overpriced food (Hanawalt 1993, 37). Many of the lower status groups may have relied on dairy products for much needed protein and fat (Woolgar 2006b, 100). Compared to meat, dairy foods leave relatively few traces in the archaeological record, and historians often have to rely on records of consumption (ibid, 88). Milk from sheep became less popular after the 13th century as farmers concentrated more on selling wool, and in the 14th and 15th centuries most cream, together with preserved milk fat in the form of butter and cheese, was made from cow's milk (ibid, 88, 94–5).

The role of fish in the medieval period was both nutritional and spiritual (Fig 201). It was considered a penitential food and was an alternative to meat during Lent and on other fast days (Serjeantson and Woolgar 2006, 102). While some richer households and institutions had their own fishponds, the majority of fish in the medieval diet came from marine sources (Schofield and Vince 2003, 227; Serjeantson and Woolgar 2006, 102). Preserved fish, such as cod and herring, were widely traded and provided a ready food source in expanding urban areas, where archaeological deposits reveal extensive consumption of the larger marine species (Serjeantson and Woolgar 2006, 130; Woolgar et al 2006, 272). The eating of fish was considered to bring medical benefits and to aid recovery from illness. After the medieval period this belief appears to have faded, possibly as water courses became more polluted (Serjeantson and Woolgar 2006, 129).

The chief drink of the masses was ale, and later beer. Both formed an important part of the diet of the poor, while wine was a drink reserved for the wealthy (Woolgar et al 2006, 273–4).

The quality of food could vary considerably depending on wealth. At banquets, many courses of protein-rich food were consumed, washed down with ale and wine (Hanawalt 1993, 37). High-status groups were more likely to have access to alternative diets that allowed them to follow ordinances on the substitution of certain foods (especially meat) on religious days. In general, they were less vulnerable to food shortages and enjoyed a great variety of diet. For the poor, the options were far more limited. Grains and pulses provided up to 80% of their calories, leaving them particularly vulnerable to falls in harvest yields such as those recorded at the end of the 12th century, in the period 1290–1320 and at the end of the 1430s (Dyer 2006, 213). In the Great Famine of 1315–18, grain prices rose rapidly and perhaps 10% of the population died (Dyer 1989, 40, 116; Schofield 2006, 247). Any produce obtained from a poor household's garden or livestock would have to be maximised in order to replace the lost grain. Surplus plants or dairy produce could be sold to buy bread, and the fall in pig prices in times of shortage suggests that they were also sold for this purpose (Dyer 2006, 214). Those with no land or fixed property would have had limited options during periods of famine. It may be that even in times of relative plenty, many relied on the success of the commercial economy for their food, or perhaps on charity and leftovers from religious houses. In wealthier households, old bread was carved to form trenchers, edible plates on which food was served and consumed. When the meal was over, the trenchers, together with any sauce they had soaked up, were given to the poor (Hanawalt 1993, 76). We know that within religious hospitals, each inmate was provided with food as well as clothes and a bed (Orme and Webster 1995, 122). At St Giles

Fig 201 A medieval illustration of fish and imaginary aquatic creatures, c 1230–40 (© The British Library Board, MS Harley 4751, fo 68)

in Norwich, poor men received a daily allowance of bread and drink together with a dish of meat, fish, eggs or cheese (ibid).

Modern studies of famine have found that mortality rates are linked both to socio-economic status and to demographic characteristics (Choe and Razzaque 1990, 53). It is possible that harvest failure in the past triggered catastrophic mortality episodes, as malnutrition increased vulnerability to infectious disease. Historical famines have shown that individuals were far more likely to die from infections related to malnutrition than from actual starvation (Mokyr and Ó Gráda 1999, 1) (below, 4.3).

The strength of an individual's immune system depends to some extent on the amount and quality of food consumed (Roberts and Cox 2003, 6): our diet must provide sufficient protein, carbohydrate and fat, together with essential vitamins and minerals (Waldron 2006, 254). Chronic malnutrition predisposes populations to increased risk of infectious disease, and episodes of high mortality in the past may have been linked to poor nutritional status as much as to periods of famine (Schofield 2006, 240–1).

The onset of the Black Death may have led to deficiencies in the supply of food to large urban centres. For those unable to flee the town, a strict diet was encouraged in order to maintain 'complexional balance' through control of the four humours (Siraisi 1990, 129) (below, 4.2). However, general standards of living improved for all inhabitants of London during the course of the 14th and 15th centuries, in part due to the increased demand for labour following the Black Death. This was reflected in improved food provision (Hanawalt 1993, 34). There was a large increase in the number of livestock relative to the size of the human population, leading to an intensification of the meat trade and consequently to a rise in the numbers of butchers in towns (Woolgar 2006b, 90). Nonetheless, cereals remained the dominant element of the diet for most people, and the increase in pastoral farming and in the consumption of meat and dairy products in the second half of the 14th century may have had little impact on some of the poorest sections of the population, who probably continued to rely on a largely vegetarian diet (Albarella 2006, 73; Woolgar 2006b, 101).

The importance of grains after the Black Death may be reflected in the persistence of high levels of dental calculus at St Mary Spital. However, there is evidence that harvest workers received a more protein-rich diet than before, and the rise in supplies of meat would have increased the availability of relatively cheap offal from butchers (Woolgar 2006b, 94; Schofield 2006, 243). At the same time there was specific provision for the poor. At the end of the 14th century, the mayor ordered that farthing loaves of bread and measures of ale be sold. The prices of meat, eggs and fish were also controlled (Hanawalt 1993, 37). There is little osteological evidence, though, of a general enrichment of the diet: for example there was no significant increase in rates of diffuse idiopathic skeletal hyperostosis (DISH), a disease that may be associated with obesity (Rogers 2000, 171; Roberts and Cox 2003, 32) (below, 4.5).

As with butchery, there was an increase in dairying following the Black Death, due to the growth in numbers of livestock per capita (Woolgar 2006b, 90, 100). During the 13th and 14th centuries there was little dairy produce within high-status diets, with the exception of food for children (ibid, 99). The 15th-century expansion coincided with an increase in the popularity of desserts such as doucet (a custard), which was often followed by cheese at the end of the meal (ibid, 100). In the second half of the 14th century, there was a decline in the consumption of fish relative to meat (Serjeantson and Woolgar 2006, 127). At the same time, expanding markets created increased availability of a variety of imported luxury foods including spices, dried fruit, marine fish and wine (Woolgar et al 2006, 268). This was followed in the 15th century by a further expansion in the availability of animals such as rabbits and wild birds in urban centres (ibid, 269–70). By the 16th century, few high-status households ate pig meat, although the consumption of young animals such as calves, lambs, kids and piglets became increasingly popular (Albarella 2006, 80; Woolgar 2006b, 101). Evidence of dental caries from St Mary Spital suggests that the amount of sugar consumed increased over time for individuals in the attritional cemetery, especially in period 17 (Chapter 3.6).

Religious houses followed the Rule of St Benedict, who was the first to stipulate a monastic diet, requiring the provision of two cooked dishes (*pulmentaria*) at dinner with a further dish of seasonal vegetables or fruit (Harvey 2006, 215). This food probably consisted of a base of pottage supplemented with other ingredients according to availability, with loaves of bread and measures of drink for each monk (ibid). Records of the Augustinian canons at Bolton Abbey from the late 13th to the early 14th century show that their diet was dominated by cereals, with little meat and relatively small quantities of dairy produce (Woolgar 2006b, 99). The provision of additional plates, or pittances, served to highlight the distinction between normal days and feast days, and was a means of increasing the quality of food during periods of fasting, such as Lent (Harvey 2006, 218–19). Higher quality bread might be served, together with wine for those who normally drank ale (ibid, 220). By the end of the 13th century, the consumption of flesh meat was mentioned more often in monastic records, together with an increased emphasis on the provision of food and drink of a certain quality (ibid, 218–19; Woolgar et al 2006, 270). This suggests that in some groups the increase in the consumption of meat was not simply a post-Black Death phenomenon.

Isotopic investigation of medieval sites has discovered evidence of high nitrogen ratios at religious houses, indicative of greater fish consumption (Müldner and Richards 2006, 236; 2007a; 2007b). This would seem to confirm a diet where fish was eaten in order to comply with religious rules (Müldner and Richards 2006, 237). There is much potential in the study of stable isotope levels in human remains, although the reliability of results varies according to levels of diagenesis within a cemetery. The differing ‰^{13}C values of femoral samples taken from the attritional cemetery and the mass burial pits at St Mary Spital may reflect variations in group diet, but may also have resulted from the differing burial environments of the bones (Joseph and Black 2006, 16). Further work with carbon and nitrogen isotopes may provide evidence of dietary patterns, such as the relative amounts of fish consumed. Earliest indications are that there is little variation in isotope values between the cemetery at St Mary Spital and contemporary sites in other parts of England, perhaps reflecting a relatively standardised late medieval diet (Lakin 2008, 70). However, diets that are isotopically uniform can hide variations in the types of meat or grain consumed (ibid).

Dental evidence for diet at St Mary Spital

There are a number of methods of studying diet in skeletal remains. These include the analysis of dental disease and microwear, as well as the examination of food particles retained in calculus deposits. Other evidence of dietary deficiency can be found in signs of growth disturbance within the sample, through analysis of stature and dental hypoplasia (below, 4.5), and signs of vitamin deficiency such as rickets and scurvy.

Dental calculus is formed of mineralised plaque and is one of the most common diseases to affect the teeth. The supra-gingival form of calculus is often light brown in colour and is attached to the crown of a tooth. Sub-gingival calculus is attached to the root surface, and tends to be harder and smaller in size; it is often observed as thin bands on the root (Hillson 1996, 254–7). Poor standards of oral hygiene and a carbohydrate-rich diet can lead to the build-up of plaque which, if not removed, can mineralise to form dental calculus; supra-gingival calculus tends to increase with age and often produces heavier deposits in men (ibid, 259–60). However, Lieverse (1999, 224) cautions that the relationship between calculus formation and diet is difficult to quantify, and Hillson (2000, 260) has gone as far as to say that it is difficult to deduce much from the presence of calculus. This makes interpretation of any such data problematic.

At St Mary Spital, male teeth were affected more frequently by the supra-gingival form of calculus (21,430/36,471: 58.8%) than female teeth (18,033/32,227: 56.0%). This difference was statistically significant (χ^2 = 54.98, df = 1, p ≤ 0.001). When male and female rates were combined, there was found to be a statistically significant increase in true prevalence from period 14, c 1120–c 1200 (3434/6184: 55.5%) to period 15, c 1200–50 (9405/16,394: 57.4%) (χ^2 = 6.18, df = 1, p ≤ 0.025) (Chapter 3.6). This may reflect a slight change of diet in those buried within the cemetery after the 12th century, or possibly a variation in dental hygiene.

A larger proportion of female teeth were affected by sub-gingival calculus (8882/32,227: 27.6%) than male teeth (8668/36,471: 23.8%). Again, this difference was statistically significant (χ^2 = 129.47, df = 1, p ≤ 0.001). When male and female teeth were combined, the true prevalence fell from a high of 28.2% (1743/6184) in period 14 to 21.3% (1802/8460) in period 17. The fall from period 14 to 15 was statistically significant (χ^2 = 15.55, df = 1, p ≤ 0.001), as was that from period 16 (c 1250–c 1400) to period 17 (χ^2 = 82.60, df = 1, p ≤ 0.025) (Chapter 3.6).

Periodontal disease involves the inflammation of tissues surrounding the teeth (alveolar process, gingivae, mucosa and periodontal ligament) and can lead to horizontal and/or vertical bone loss in alveolar bone resulting in the exposure of tooth roots and eventual tooth loss (Hillson 1996, 260–5). As with sub-gingival calculus, the true prevalence rate (per tooth socket) of periodontal disease fell significantly from period 16 (25,737/50,649: 50.8%) to 17 (5464/11,887: 46.0% (χ^2 = 90.52, df = 1, p ≤ 0.001), possibly reflecting an improved diet through time (Chapter 3.6). This may have resulted from technological advances in flour refining or perhaps general advancements in living standards (and therefore diet).

Dental wear leads to destruction of tooth enamel and dentine exposure. It is commonly found in medieval samples, including that at St Mary Spital, and can be caused by abrasive inclusions within the diet (Freeth 2000, 232). An inverse relationship between dental attrition and caries has been found in some archaeological samples, but there is no evidence of a causal link between the two (Hillson 1996, 284). No study of attrition over time was carried out on this sample, but future work may prove of value, especially as the data could be compared with those from periodontal disease and sub-gingival calculus.

Populations with high dietary levels of carbohydrate are associated with increased rates of caries. Sugars are particularly damaging (especially sucrose), and can initiate fissure and approximal lesions from an early age (Hillson 1996, 278–83). A heavy, starchy diet, such as that of intensive cereal-based agricultural communities, leads to higher rates of caries than is found in communities with a more mixed subsistence base, such as fishing, pastoralism and agriculture (ibid, 283). Dietary proteins and fats produce low rates of caries. Dairy products may coat and protect the teeth to a certain extent, while calcium and phosphorus are beneficial to dental health (ibid, 279). The consumption of a high proportion of fish in the diet can also reduce caries rates (Freeth 2000, 230).

The true prevalence rates of caries at St Mary Spital were high when compared to burial samples from many other medieval sites in London (Chapter 3.6; below, 4.4). The adult prevalence increased over time, with a statistically significant jump from period 16 (4047/39,143: 10.3%) to 17 (1198/9029: 13.3%) (χ^2 = 64.89, df = 1, p ≤ 0.001). This rise in the number of carious teeth may reflect a wider availability of sugar over the course of the medieval period. There was also variation in the true prevalence rate of adult caries by burial type. Teeth in individuals from the attritional cemetery (4038/35,830: 11.3%) were more frequently affected by carious lesions than teeth in individuals from the catastrophic cemetery (3364/35,960: 9.4%). This difference was statistically significant (χ^2 = 71.18, df = 1, p ≤ 0.001) and was largely due to a rise in prevalence in both sexes within the attritional sample in periods 16 and 17. The second and third molars displayed the highest prevalence of caries, with the approximal surfaces of teeth the most commonly affected. This is in accordance with the general pattern of carious involvement in teeth from British archaeological sites, where initial demineralisation occurs most often at the cemento-enamel junction of the mesial or distal surfaces of the molar teeth (Hillson 1996, 282). The increase in caries seen over time at St Mary Spital (Chapter 3.6) is observed in medieval Britain generally; Roberts and Cox (2003, 259) point to caries rates (by tooth) increasing from 4.2% (1636/38,911) to 5.6% (1980/35,665) during the medieval period. This most likely reflects an increase in the availability of foodstuffs containing sugars, including fruits and honey. Honey was generally more widely available than sugar cane. Although sugar cane was imported from the 13th century onwards and became a larger component of the diet, it would only have been available to the better off (ibid, 243), and at St Mary Spital one would expect low sucrose consumption because the majority of the burial population are thought to have been poor.

The dental evidence suggests that there may have been dietary variation between the burials in the attritional cemetery and those in the mass burial pits in the 15th century, and possibly before. It appears that the diet of individuals in the attritional cemetery became richer in sugars over time, perhaps reflecting both increased availability and rising purchasing power in certain elements of the community.

Adult stature and nutritional status

Evidence of disease or growth retardation relating to nutritional stress may reflect dietary deficiency or imbalance. Nutritional status in childhood affects the probability of achieving full potential stature, although responses to short-term dietary changes are not detectable in bone (Roberts and Cox 2003, 366; Waldron 2006, 254). Mean male stature at St Mary Spital (168.2cm) was low when compared to other medieval sites, although female stature (161.4cm) was relatively high, an indication of low sexual dimorphism possibly related to poor nutritional status (below, 4.5). There was evidence of subadult growth retardation, especially for those aged 5–7 years and 9–12 years. It may be that the growth of males did not then catch up between 12 and 17 years. While the mean male stature of 173cm for the adult burials from the church, studied previously by Conheeney (1997, 223), was higher than that from the external, attritional or catastrophic cemeteries, it was based on a sample size of only six individuals, preventing definitive conclusions on the difference in height between the groups.

When male stature was compared by burial type, the individuals in the attritional cemetery displayed a higher mean than those in the mass pits. However, this difference was only evident in periods 14 and 17 (Chapter 3.3). It is possible that the mean stature of those in the attritional cemetery fell in response to nutritional stress. This may have been brought about by food shortages, environment, genetic variation or increased levels of childhood disease (Roberts and Manchester 2005, 39).

Skeletal evidence for nutritional status

The investigation of diet is of key importance to understanding past health status, as poor nutrition can lead to malnourishment and a compromised immune system, making individuals vulnerable to other diseases (Roberts and Manchester 2005, 223). An individual's health is directed correlated to diet, and nutritional status can be influenced by gender roles that might dictate portion size, food quality and meal frequency (McElroy and Townsend 1996, 224–5). Even when a family or household has sufficient food, it is possible that some members will not receive enough nourishment.

Cribra orbitalia is not pathognomonic of iron-deficiency anaemia (Lewis 2007, 114). However, it is possible that some of those individuals affected with this type of bone change were suffering from such deficiency, which can be brought on by insufficient iron in the diet as a result of gastrointestinal infection (including parasitical infection), blood loss or dietary deficiency (Ortner 2003, 369; Roberts and Cox 2003, 234). The prevalence of cribra orbitalia in females fell after period 15, suggesting that nutritional status improved, possibly reflecting reduced disease burden, or increased access to meat or fish and a resulting boost in protein consumption. There was far less variation in male rates throughout the use of the cemetery. However, as cribra orbitalia is a non-specific indicator of nutritional stress, these results could be due to differential rates of disease between the sexes, not simply to dietary differences (Chapter 3.10).

Rickets and osteomalacia are caused by inadequate mineralisation of bone, most often due to vitamin D deficiency (Resnick 2002, 1901; Ortner 2003, 393). While rickets, which affects subadults, is related to diet, it is believed to be chiefly associated with a lack of exposure to sunlight (Resnick 2002, 1913; Mays 2003, 144). Osteomalacia in adults is multifactorial but is more often linked to diet, and is often associated with deficiencies of protein, fat, calcium and phosphorus (Ortner 2003, 399). At St Mary Spital, very few individuals displayed evidence of rickets, and most of these died before they reached adulthood. Only one individual, a female, had osteomalacia. There was therefore little indication of dietary deficiency reflected in the prevalence of rickets or osteomalacia (Chapter 3.10).

Scurvy results from ascorbic acid (vitamin C) deficiency and has been linked to shortages of vitamin-rich foods such as fruits, vegetables and marine fish (Lewis 2007, 126; Brickley 2000, 185; Brickley and Ives 2006, 163). Its presence in skeletal remains may reflect populations that suffered periods of hardship or famine (Brickley 2000, 185; Brickley and Ives 2006, 163). The low rate of scurvy at St Mary Spital, regardless of burial type, suggests that there was a sufficient supply of vegetables and fruit to the population of London.

Although normally a disease of old age, osteoporosis in a child or young adult may result from dietary deficiency (Waldron 2006, 259). However, at St Mary Spital no individuals below later middle age displayed evidence of osteoporosis (Chapter 3.10).

Another disease commonly linked to age, diffuse idiopathic skeletal hyperostosis (DISH), which may result from a rich, high-calorie diet, is clinically associated with the elderly (particularly men), obesity and diabetes (Waldron 2006, 265;

Fig 202 Spine of individual [12498] from the attritional cemetery, period 15, with evidence of DISH shown by 'candlewax' osteophytes on the right anterior aspect of the vertebral bodies (scale c 1:2)

Resnick 2002, 1496–7; Roberts and Cox 2003, 32) (Fig 202) (Chapter 4.5). At St Mary Spital there was no evidence of variation in the crude prevalence of this disease by period (Chapter 3.7). If one of the chief causes of DISH within the sample was indeed dietary, there was no evidence that the majority of individuals were overindulging in rich foods such as meat and dairy products.

Conclusions

In the medieval period, diet was connected to spiritual and physical health, and varied according to both personal and group influence (Woolgar et al 2006, 270). Although different patterns of consumption must have existed between economically and/or environmentally differentiated groups (rich, poor, urban, rural, religious and secular), there must also have been some individual variation in diet within these groups (Schofield 2006, 244). Such variables may have included sex, age, marital status and occupation. In addition, cultural factors and personal choice may have been responsible for variation, even within low-status groups where there was less variety of diet (Woolgar et al 2006, 267).

Over time there is evidence from towns of an increased availability of meat, as a response to increased employment and income in the second half of the 14th century. There was also probably less fish in the diet and a reduction in the consumption of cereals, with increased consumption of beer and better living standards overall (Schofield and Vince 2003, 232). Religious houses appear to have responded to this rise in secular living standards outside their walls (Harvey 2006, 225).

As early as the 12th century, London was recognised as an important commercial centre which could command foodstuffs during times of low harvest yields. Coupled with storage resources and opportunities for employment, this would have provided ample incentive for migration to the city (Keene 1989, 104). The efficient organisation of food provision and storage was challenged by population growth, climatic deterioration and famine, possibly as early as the mid 13th century, but certainly by the time of the severe famine of the second decade of the 14th century. The commercial and trading networks that had emerged during the rapid population expansion of the previous century may have left some sections of the population particularly vulnerable to food shortages (Schofield 2006, 246). However, it is possible that the distribution networks continued to function in such a way that large towns and cities such as London were buffered, at least for a time, against the worst effects of food shortage and famine. The result may have been an increase in the rate of migration from rural areas.

The skeletal evidence from St Mary Spital suggests that carbohydrates (presumably from cereals) formed an important part of the diet. It also suggests that these became softer and perhaps more refined over time, especially in the 15th century. At the same time, rates of dental caries rose, perhaps reflecting the increased availability of sugar. The reduction in rates of cribra orbitalia in females after 1250 may reflect improvements in nutritional status relating to changes in diet. However, these are non-specific indicators and may be due to other variables, such as reduced disease burden.

A subadult perspective on medieval London

Rebecca Redfern

Our approaches to understanding the way of life of children in the past have been dominated by the Western perspective of childhood, which emphasises dependency and social marginalisation (Hockey and James 1995, 12). Such a perspective has been challenged within recent archaeological research (Gowland 2006; Lucy 2005; Sofaer 2006a), which has integrated anthropological data on the pluralities of ageing (Panter-Brick 1998a; 1998b).

In order to achieve a bioarchaeological perspective on the subadult way of life in medieval London, the subadult skeletal data are discussed here in their medieval and palaeopathological contexts. The data are divided according to the age categories employed at analysis (Chapter 2.2); it is recognised that these do not equate to stages of the medieval life course. For example, unmarried men were still considered to be adolescents until the age of 35 (Shahar 1990, 23–30). The emphasis of this chapter is upon 'growing up' in medieval London and an overview of the data is presented. Detailed temporal analysis and discussion of indicators of stress, growth, disease and subadult demography by burial type and with reference to catastrophic events are addressed in Chapter 4.3.

The social and cultural aspects of ageing

An individual's age identity is a composite created from their chronological, physiological and social ages (Sofaer Derevenski 1997, 486). The social aspect of ageing, defined by prescribed behaviours and gender, means that age identities are culturally specific and subject to change over time, often in response to wider economic and political events. In archaeology, age identity is investigated using a 'life-course' approach (Gowland 2006). The life course is the culturally determined manner in which a society is organised and includes rites of passage, particularly when individuals become 'adults'. It is related to, but separate from, the social structure of a society (Harlow and Laurence 2002, 3). Applying this analytical approach emphasises the interdependence of lives, the impact of early life events upon adulthood, and the effect of gender on the incidence, timing and duration of roles (Hareven 2001, 142–51).

Age theory has shown us that childhood is a social construct and as such is subject to cross-cultural variability. No universal childhood experience exists. It is influenced by status, age, gender, ethnicity, location, health and impairment, and as such often conflicts with our embedded concepts of how a child's life should be (Panter-Brick 1998b, 2–3; Panter-Brick 2000a, 9). This creates a tension in how past children's lives are understood, particularly when they strike against historical or archaeological stereotypes. For example, in the mid 19th century girls as young as nine were sent by their parents to sell flowers on the street, but many were actually sex workers (Panter-Brick 2000a, 8).

An overview of the archaeological discourse on children

Feminist and post-processual critiques of archaeological interpretations have shown that our 'traditional' assessments of past communities were biased towards men and male activities. Children were excluded from these assessments, and their participation and agency were poorly explored or accepted (Scott 1997). Baxter observes that 'archaeologists have always been excavating the remains of children. What is changing is our competence to interrogate the archaeological record' (2005, 115). This statement is supported by Lucy (2005, 46), who notes that before the presence of children is accepted, evidence and proof must be provided, as was previously thought necessary for women (see Conkey and Spector 1998). Many authors accord importance to the integration of anthropological data into the investigation of children from archaeological contexts, particularly when primary information is lacking. Such information provides new possibilities and suggests alternative ways of living that may not be identifiable from archaeological data alone (Lucy 2005, 47).

Bioarchaeological analysis provides an important data set with which to investigate the way of life of past children, primarily because it provides an estimation of an individual's biological age and supplies their 'osteobiography', although many of these studies regard the cultural and biological age of an individual as the same (Baxter 2005, 98). Sofaer's discussion of age emphasises that the body is key to the investigation of age but observes that skeletal data are often excluded from this (Sofaer 2006a).

The employment of osteological data in the discussion of age identities, particularly for subadults, should be undertaken with an awareness of methodological biases and limitations. For example, many biological developments such as the age of menarche (the start of menstruation) are culturally variable; populations will differ in the timings of dental development; and we must assume that the samples upon which methods of age estimation are generated were not affected by environmental and social stresses (Saunders and Barrans 1999, 200; Sofaer Derevenski 1997).

Medieval 'childhood'

Our knowledge of medieval children is derived from medical, religious, legal and social texts written by adults (Alexandre-Bidon and Lett 1999, 3), not directly from the experience and world view of children (James 1998). Childhood was regarded as the lowest, but separate, stage of life with its own qualities and characteristics (Shahar 1990, 15, 20). This perspective was related to the religious concept of original sin, influenced by the writings of St Augustine, and the perceived 'incompleteness' of children's bodies (ibid, 14–16). Religious and social texts divided 'childhood' into three seven-year phases, which were influenced by Classical Mediterranean beliefs. The attainment of maturity was not uniform, because it was influenced by socio-economic status. This is supported by the regional and temporal variations in criminal responsibilities (ibid, 23–30).

The first stage of life was *infantia* (0–7 years) which contained subdivisions based upon dental eruption, weaning and the acquisition of speech. This was followed by *pueritia* (7–12 years), the age at which they were able properly to express themselves and decide upon their career. *Adolescentia* (12–25 years) was the stage when they became more independent and took on greater responsibility. This stage was also influenced by gender: *adolescentia* ended at approximately 25 years old in females but for males it could last until the age of 35. After *adolescentia*, males would experience a period of *juventus* which only ended when they were married.

Medical texts specifically for the treatment of childhood illnesses were available; they included the *Liber de passionibus puerorum Galeni* (6th–9th century AD), a practical guide which made the connection between the health of the infant and that of the nurse. The 15th-century *Diseases of children still in the cradle* was a concise guide to common diseases which also directed treatment to the nurse, while Bartholomaeus Anglius's *De proprietatibus rerum* (1230) was the most widely disseminated medical text in Europe. In contrast, English texts such as John of Gaddesden's *Rosa Anglica* (1314) do not specifically focus upon childhood diseases and rarely mention them (Fildes 1986, 45–7). Medical practice, medical systems, and the understanding of illness have been shown to vary between ethnic groups and by socio-economic status, sex and age (Strathern and Stewart 1999, 16, 64, 114), and we should expect individuals to have taken a pragmatic approach to coping with and treating sickness in children.

Studies of age and childhood have shown that subadults would not have led homogeneous lives, particularly in light of the many political and catastrophic social and climatic events that took place in the medieval period. An individual's life course was dictated by socio-economic status and parental behaviour. Many children were abandoned due to poverty, donated to the Church, or sold as labourers (Boswell 1988, 402). Nevertheless, recent anthropological work has shown that abandoned children seek to promote their survival and do not regard themselves as victims (Panter-Brick 2000a, 20).

The osteological study of medieval subadults in Britain has been dominated by analysis of urban samples, particularly those from York (Lewis 2002; Grauer 1991), and by the rural sample from Wharram Percy (Mays 2007). More detailed analyses of subadult health during this period have been conducted on samples from Yorkshire and Northamptonshire (Lewis 2002). Palaeopathological studies of medieval subadults have focused on indicators of stress, specific infectious or metabolic diseases, growth and development (eg McEwan et al 2005; Ortner and Mays 1998; Ribot and Roberts 1996), and this research is supplemented by numerous case studies (eg Anderson 2002).

Biases affecting subadult samples

Archaeologically derived subadults represent those who did not reach biological and skeletal maturity. They are best understood within the paradigm of the osteological paradox (Wood et al 1992), which reminds us that those individuals able to produce a dental or osteological response to disease are the 'healthier' people. Conversely subadult skeletal samples, consisting of the non-survivors of their age cohort, may possess higher rates of disease than the source population (Saunders and Hoppa 1993). Subadults' responses to disease differ significantly from those of adults, because their skeletal and soft tissues are developing. For example, subadult long bones have a higher risk of infection because the vascular supply delivers the disease organisms to the rapidly growing ends (Lewis 2000; Scheuer and Black 2000, 27–30).

Preservation of subadult remains directly affects sample size, osteological evidence for a disease response, and the ability to record metric data. The review by Guy et al (1997) of infant taphonomy concluded that the bones of subadults under 2 years old were less dense than foetal skeletons, the tensile and compressive strengths and hardness of young children's bones were low, and their skeletons were highly susceptible to crushing. The comprehensive study of human taphonomy by Bello et al (2006) in three cemeteries dating from the 8th to the 19th centuries discovered that subadults aged 0–4 years were more poorly preserved than adults and that there were inter-sex differences that were also influenced by age at death. The influence of bone preservation upon demography, and therefore our interpretation of mortality risk (Chamberlain 2006, 89–92), has also been proven by Walker et al (1988), who analysed a historical cemetery with burial records, and demonstrated that the acidic soil resulted in two different demographic profiles. The osteological sample was dominated by young adults, but the burial record showed that the majority of the inhumed sample actually consisted of subadults and elderly adults.

In the medieval period, two important influences were the Church's restrictions on who was permitted to be buried in consecrated ground, and the spatial organisation of burial grounds. Newborns, stillborn infants and unbaptised infants were officially excluded from cemeteries, although excavation at a limited number of burial grounds has revealed a small number of infant or neonate prone burials, suggesting that the unbaptised were included (Orme 2001, 124; Gilchrist and Sloane 2005, 72). Additionally, women who died during pregnancy or delivery were not to be buried in consecrated ground unless the baby had been removed from their bodies; nevertheless, the burials of many pregnant women have been identified in medieval cemeteries (Gilchrist and Sloane 2005, 72).

Subadults were often buried in groups, as seen at St Helen-on-the-Walls, York, but such spatial organisation may not be identified unless an entire burial ground is excavated. Parish records have also shown that subadults could be buried in churchyards separate from the main burial ground, as at St Mary-at-Hill in the City of London (Gilchrist and Sloane 2005, 70). The spatial analysis of cemeteries associated with religious houses has also demonstrated the clustering of subadults, and at Greyfriars Franciscan friary in Norwich the concentration of subadult burials is believed to reflect that area of the cemetery being designated as the burial area of students (ibid, 68).

The biases outlined above demonstrate that taphonomic and excavation factors influence sample size, while the religious conventions governing burial may skew the age profile towards older individuals (see below, 4.3 and 4.4).

Growing up in medieval London

Inter-site analyses for London show that growing up in the city resulted in a unique pattern of disease and trauma (below, 4.5). To investigate why, the following discussion will examine subadult age at death, diet, dental health, growth, stress indicators, tuberculosis, treponematosis, and trauma.

INFANTIA: THE CARE AND TREATMENT OF SUBADULTS LESS THAN 1 YEAR OLD

The analysis of subadult age at death provides a unique insight into the well-being and general health of the population from which subadults were derived, because younger subadults are more dependent upon others for care and their morbidity risk is greater due to local environmental conditions (Bogin 1998, 21–2; Goodman and Armelagos 1989, 225; Saunders and Barrans 1999, 184). The demographic profile of the St Mary Spital subadults shows that the mortality rate of perinates was higher than those who reached one month of life. In order to determine whether genetic, maternal and parturition factors, or external hazards were the cause of death in these age groups, one can compare the percentage of neonatal and post-neonatal deaths (Lewis 2007, 84–6; Mays 2007, 89–90). Because of the ageing categories employed in recording, comparison was made between the number of inter-uterine or neonatal deaths and those aged 1–11 months at death. It is acknowledged that the use of linear regression age at death estimation may produce a peak in mortality at 38 weeks (Lewis and Gowland 2007). As individuals aged 1–6 months were not present in periods 14 (c 1120–c 1200) or 17 (c 1400–1539), possibly due to age-related burial exclusion (Gilchrist and Sloane 2005, 72), pooled data were employed to investigate morbidity risk. It was found that 6.6% (68/1027) of the total subadult sample were perinatal and 0.2% (2/1027) were aged 1–6 months. Further comparison between perinatal individuals and those aged 1–11 months confirms this result and indicates that genetic factors, such as birth defects causing individuals to be stillborn or die shortly after birth (see Barnes 1994, 5, 9–13), maternal disease such as influenza (Holzel 1993, 299–300) and traumatic parturition (Akpala 1993), presented a greater mortality risk than the general living environment. Despite the bias of medieval funerary rites, the influence on perinatal demography of environmental and social morbidity risks should not be discounted (Bogin 1998, 21–22), particularly since numerous catastrophic events affected this population (below, 4.3, for further discussion).

The mortality rate of those less than a year old was very low (4/1027: 0.4%). The extent to which this is a cultural trend or a result specific to St Mary Spital is not clear, particularly when the results are compared to other urban centres. For example, at St Helen-on-the-Walls in York, 22.5% (45/200) of subadults were aged 0.6–2.5 years at death and 5.0% (10/200) were 0–0.5 years old (Lewis 2002, 40). It should be noted that only part of the York cemetery was excavated so spatial biases may not have been fully understood, and infanticide may have been practised by the inhabitants of the local area which would explain the higher mortality rate in this group (Lewis and Gowland 2007, 120–1).

The hospital's mandate to care for confined mothers and orphans may have enabled a greater number of individuals to survive the risky post-partum stage. Many perinatal individuals may have been stillborn and, in the future, histological sectioning of the dentition may determine the presence of a neonatal line (an incremental striation in the tooth enamel formed at birth or soon afterwards), enabling this to be examined further (see Scheuer and Black 2000, 162; Smith et al 2006). In the medieval period, a successful delivery was often reliant upon the skill of the midwife and favourable local environmental conditions, particularly as the majority of births took place within the home (Orme and Webster 1995, 110; Orme 2001, 13–21). Today, the primary cause of death in newborns is infection, either due to maternal disease or intrapartum infection, usually acquired during the first three days of life as a result of direct contamination or cross-infection (Levene et al 2000).

Rousham and Humphrey (2002, 124–5) observe that the physical vulnerability of those less than a year old increases their susceptibility to disease, because they have an immature immune system and a high energy and nutrient requirement relative to body weight. The majority of deaths in this age group result from the interplay between infectious disease and nutrition. At St Mary Spital demonstrates the number of subadults who died between 7 and 11 months was the same as the number who died before the age of 6 months (2/1027: 0.2%). However, these numbers are unusually low, particularly in comparison to the urban cemetery of St Helen-on-the-Walls (0.6–2.5 years 45/200: 22.5%; 0–0.5 years 10/200: 5.0%), and the rural cemetery of Wharram Percy (Yorkshire), where 23% were aged 0.6–2.5 years (Lewis 2002, 40). This result is reinforced by palaeodemographic studies which compare the proportion of deaths by age (using computer modelling and Leslie matrices) and demonstrate that in a stable population, 0.4% of deaths will be those aged less than 1 year, compared to 0.08% in a plague year; similarly, 0.13% and 0.1% of population deaths will be those aged 1–5 years (Paine and Boldsen 2002, 176). It has also been found that neonatal death rates were higher in rural communities, so the data from Wharram Percy may not be applicable to all other British samples (see Vögele 1994). It is suggested in Chapter 4.3 that the result at St Mary Spital is influenced by temporal differences in demography (no individuals aged 7–11 months were recorded from periods 14 or 15) and by catastrophic events.

Today, individuals under a year old have a high morbidity risk from their surrounding environment: cracked skin can act as a portal for staphylococci organisms from dust, linen and their care givers, resulting in infection (Kelmar et al 1995, 96–187). Pneumonia is also common post-partum due to infection of the amniotic cavity, particularly in those whose mother experienced fever, a long labour, or ruptured membranes. Bathing within the first 24 hours also increases mortality and morbidity risks if water quality is poor (ibid).

In the medieval period, newborns were often abandoned (particularly in times of famine) at religious institutions and hospitals, including St Mary Spital (below, 4.2). Abandonment increased their risk of death, even though the receiving institution acted as a cultural buffer against poor nutrition and environmental conditions. For example, 14th-century documentary sources from the San Gallo hospital (Florence, Italy) show that 20% of infants died within one month of arrival (Boswell 1988, 421).

Medieval documentary sources, particularly those from coroners, provide a unique insight into additional socio-cultural causes of morbidity and mortality, though it should be remembered that these record a biased sample of events: crying infants who could not be consoled were placed in pits, those with fevers were put on roofs or in ovens, and many were accidentally smothered when sleeping in their parents' beds (Shahar 1990, 131).

A key socio-cultural practice to be considered in relation to health during *infantia* is the custom of swaddling. We cannot assume that this was universally employed but many primary social sources (child-rearing books, letters and diaries) suggest that most socio-economic status groups throughout Europe did swaddle babies. During the medieval period swaddling was thought to ensure proper physical development (following in the Classical medical tradition) and protect infants from the cold (Shahar 1990, 87). Despite the practice having many benefits if undertaken properly, such as keeping babies warm and secure and minimising restless sleep, it also presented a risk (van Sleuwen et al 2007). Medieval primary texts from Europe show that deaths due to swaddling occurred and were of concern to the community. In Barcelona, Spain, soiled swaddling bands were determined to be the cause of death for one infant. Other sources show that people understood that if swaddling clothes were unclean the infant would suffer from abscesses and sores, and that if swaddling was incorrectly practised, limbs would become deformed (Shahar 1990, 85).

Breastfeeding is an important aspect of biological development and also influences long-term health: it confers immunity from disease, particularly through the colostrum, and is associated with a decreased risk of asthma, obesity, diabetes and childhood leukaemia (Ip et al 2007). The mother and baby have reciprocal health benefits from its practice – lactation also reduces the risk of breast and ovarian cancers in the mother (ibid). However, breastfeeding can be discouraged because of cultural views on sexuality, fertility and status-related female behaviour (Stuart-Macadam 1995a, 6–9). Medieval breastfeeding practices were influenced by Classical medical and philosophical texts, and medical treatises recommended that wet-nurses should be used, although women's diaries show that they usually fed their babies for a few weeks before employing wet-nurses (Fildes 1986, 45–52). For high-status women wet-nursing was common practice, whereas urban working women typically nursed their own babies unless they themselves were employed as wet-nurses (Shahar 1990, 59). The low mortality rate for those less than a year old at St Mary Spital may confirm the widespread practice of breastfeeding, enabling the majority of babies to survive.

When wet-nurses were employed, babies were often fed by numerous women, usually upon request (Fildes 1986, 51–2). This practice would have increased their risk of morbidity as the nurse could have passed on diseases such as rubella or pneumonitis between babies (Hall and Peckham 1997, 19). Sickness associated with the inception of wet-nursing was frequently discussed in medical texts concerned with child health and death, and was recognised as being a morbidity risk (Shahar 1990, 68). Medical texts which connected the health of the nurse with that of the baby recommended that the nurse was treated before the nursling (Fildes 1986, 45–46). Newborns whose mothers could not breastfeed or had died during childbirth had a higher morbidity risk, as they would be wet-nursed or fed animal milk from a vessel. Animal milk, despite being considered to imbue the infant with animal properties, was often used, with the nursling taking milk directly from the udder or a vessel (ibid, 47, 52). Animal milk contains more calories, and the use of cow's milk may have led to bleeding in the gut and overloading of the kidneys (Stuart-Macadam 1995a, 20–2; Lewis 2007, 99). The risk of sickness was increased through the use of feeding vessels, which were made from pottery, glass, wood, pressed leather, metal and horn (Fildes 1986, 307–8). A horn feeding vessel is depicted in a 14th-century carving at Winchester Cathedral, and their use has been recorded in the Middle Saxon period (*c* AD 650–850) in the biography of St Liudgar of Frisia (Hooper 1996). The use of vessels requiring a teat makes it difficult for infants to suck thick liquids from them, while the feeding of thin liquids can result in stomach upsets and 'watery gripes' (Fildes 1986, 343). Medieval hospital records from Europe show that the use of wet-nurses and feeding vessels resulted in a high death rate among infants: in Florence, between 1300 and 1530, 17% of wet-nursed infants died (Boswell 1988, 421).

WEANING AND MORBIDITY RISK

European and British medieval medical sources advised that boys should be weaned 6–12 months later than girls, with weaning typically taking place at 1 to 2 years (Fildes 1986, 48, 54). The demographic data from St Mary Spital show a sharp increase in mortality between the ages of 1 and 5 years, which conforms to the expected increased morbidity risk associated with weaning and childhood diseases (Lewis 2007, 86). The cessation of breastfeeding removed protection from poor environmental conditions (Stuart-Macadam 1995b, 92–3) and would have presented what is now referred to as the 'weanling's dilemma': exclusive breastfeeding may result in faltering growth, but its removal may expose the infant to the health risks inherent in poor hygiene and contaminated food (Katzenberg et al 1996, 180).

Exclusive breastfeeding after the age of 6 months old makes breastfed babies less healthy compared to those who have a supplemented diet. Continuing the practice after one year of life ceases to have benefits for growth and development, as differences in socio-economic status then have a greater impact upon health (Maher 1992, 5; Rao and Rajpathak 1992). The process of weaning is open to numerous interpretations and is subject to considerable cultural variation (McElroy and Townsend 1996, 214–20); it is defined as 'the cessation of breastfeeding or the introduction of other foods while gradually reducing breastfeeding' and is therefore either an event or a process (Katzenberg et al 1996, 178–9). Medieval medical and instructional texts recommended rapid weaning, usually by painting the nipples with mustard and supplemental feeding with pap (flour or breadcrumbs cooked in water or milk) or panada (bread, broth, milk and/or eggs) (Fildes 1986, 48, 213). This type of food is necessary because of children's small gastrointestinal tracts and requires considerable time and effort to prepare (Bogin 1998, 34).

Stable isotope data can track the cessation of breastfeeding by identifying a change in the $\delta^{15}N$ trophic level (Katzenberg 2008, 429–30). At present we are solely reliant on the results from the rural site of Wharram Percy in Yorkshire (Fuller et al 2003; Richards et al 2002). Here, no differences were found between the weaning diet of survivors and non-survivors (Fuller et al 2003). However, rural–urban and spatial differences exist in the adult stable isotope data, which suggests that such differences could also be present in subadult samples (below, 4.5).

Enamel hypoplastic defects have been associated with the weaning period but do not represent direct evidence for the process, for both methodological and biological reasons (Blakey et al 1994; Hillson and Bond 1997; Goodman and Song 1999; Reid and Dean 2000). At Wharram Percy, Richards et al (2002, 209) determined that weaning took place before the age of 2 years with little to no sex difference. They also concluded that weaning took less than a year, indicating a prescribed cultural practice (ibid). This independent evidence for weaning taking place between the ages of 1 and 2 years suggests that the populations buried at Wharram Percy and at St Mary Spital followed the same practice, regardless of rural–urban differences.

Weaning in poor environmental conditions increases the risk of death. In all periods at St Mary Spital the pooled data from both burial types show an increase in mortality rate at the age of 1–5 years. However, only four individuals aged 1–11 months were recorded. This may reflect the widespread practice of breastfeeding, reducing mortality risk until weaning (Knodel and Kinter 1977) (below, 4.3). The proposed rapid weaning would have intensified morbidity risk, particularly from infectious diseases (Richards et al 2002; Rousham and Humphrey 2002, 124). Local environmental conditions in medieval London would have varied considerably. However, as discussed, the wider environment contained many sources of pollution. Many urban individuals would have been placed at a higher risk if they had been sent to be wet-nursed in a rural environment (Fildes 1986, 50), as disease resistance is transmitted through breastmilk, and is therefore adapted to the environment of the nurse (Hosea Blewett et al 2008; Kelly and Coutts 2000). There would also be an increased risk where a mother raised her own infant in the countryside and the family later moved to an urban area. The synergy between nutrition and infection begins during weaning, when the foods used may not contain sufficient quantities of the vitamins and minerals necessary for growth and development, making an individual more susceptible to infection (Rao and Rajpathak 1992).

The most frequent cause of death during weaning is diarrhoea, which is particularly prevalent where sanitation and personal hygiene are deficient. When the local environment is not kept clean, diarrhoea can be caused by animal rotaviruses, dirty surface water and flies contaminating food (Mata 1983). Chronic diarrhoea results in wasting, stunting, malnutrition and dehydration, and can be initiated by supplementing breastmilk with other liquids (Brown et al 1989, 38). The carer (who may be an older child) can place the weanling at a high risk of death by preparing poor quality food and/or giving him or her polluted water to drink (Panter-Brick 1998b, 87–8). The associations between diarrhoea, weaning and mortality risk were recognised in the medieval period, as medical and child-rearing texts advised beginning weaning in the spring or autumn to avoid the gastrointestinal diseases that commonly occurred in the summer (Fildes 1986, 366). Deaths from infectious diseases increase during the summer months, particularly in urban communities (Chamberlain 2006, 159; Fisman 2007).

If infants experienced compromised nutrition and were cared for in unsanitary conditions, they would have been at greater risk of acquiring an infectious disease. Clinical research has shown that individuals with diarrhoea frequently suffer from upper or lower respiratory tract infections and skin infections (Brown et al 1989). Particulate-laden atmospheres would have exacerbated the risk of respiratory tract infections, and infants would have been particularly vulnerable if their cradles were placed close to a hearth (Orme 2001, 62). Weaning was recognised as a critical period in the medieval life course and the survival of this process marked the ending of one subdivision of *infantia* (ibid, 66; Shahar 1990, 23).

POST-WEANING DIET AND DENTAL HEALTH

Infants who survived weaning would have consumed bread, fruit and eggs yolks in addition to milk and weak ale, and as they got older their diet would have been the same as adults. Medieval household accounts show us that children regularly consumed meat, ale, fish, fruit and bread (Orme 2001, 72). Those of a higher socio-economic status would have had this basic diet supplemented by (imported) fruit and sweets, often at times of religious festivals. A liking for sweet foods was often noted in personal documents and textual sources (ibid, 73). Children's diet would have changed in parallel with their erupting dentition. For a period of time after weaning their meals would still be specially prepared, but their care could be increasingly shared within the family and wider community (Bogin 1998, 21, 36).

Subadult dental health at St Mary Spital clearly displays temporal changes and variation between the burial types. Overall, deciduous and permanent dental health decreased with age, an expected and normal result. The presence of caries in the deciduous dentition indicates that subadults had regular access to fruit, honey or refined sugars. The large increase in the true prevalence rate of caries between early (1–5 years) and later childhood (6–11 years) suggests that the quantity of cariogenic foods consumed increased with age.

The true prevalence rate of calculus in the deciduous dentition also increased between early and later childhood. The development of calculus during the medieval period would have been influenced by a number of factors including the amount of protein consumed (high protein diets increase calculus production) and the unique mouth flora of an individual (Lieverse 1999, 224–5). The increase in prevalence between the ages of 1–5 and 6–11 years can be explained by a number of factors. From a biological perspective, the increase continues in parallel with growth and permanent dental eruption, allowing the child to process an adult-type diet (Bogin 1998, 22). This would increase both the variety and volume of food which could be consumed. By 5 years old the child would be mobile, have achieved adequate speech levels and be more independent. The increase in both calculus and caries may therefore relate to subadults taking greater control over their dental hygiene. The results also correlate with the ending of *infantia* at the age of 7 years, when children were no longer regarded as dependent upon others for care, and many were already working (Shahar 1990, 23).

As expected, with the exception of period 14 (*c* 1120–*c* 1200), the true prevalence rate of caries and calculus increased in the permanent dentition of those aged 6–11 years. The true prevalence rate of caries varied over time but the highest rate was in period 14 in the catastrophic cemetery, at 5.4% (7/130 permanent teeth in this age group). The highest rate of calculus was seen in period 17 (*c* 1400–1539), in the attritional cemetery (54.7%: 111/203 permanent teeth). The rates indicate that, for many individuals, the permanent dentition was at risk from dental disease from eruption onwards. This is supported by the data for 12–17-year-olds. The highest true prevalence rates for this age group were observed in period 15 (*c* 1200–50), with the attritional group showing a caries prevalence of 3.9% (48/1240 permanent teeth in this group) and the catastrophic group a true prevalence rate for calculus of 60.9% (1385/2275). The true prevalence rate of caries increased into adolescence (12–17 years). Further details of subadult dental health can be found in Chapter 3.6 (Table 26).

The results reflect the cumulative effects of poor dental hygiene and greater access to refined and natural sugars, the latter of which may have been related to occupation (eg bakers) and/or socio-economic status. Adolescent dental health corresponds to the patterns seen in the adults, where high rates of caries and calculus are thought to be a consequence of a diet rich in carbohydrates (above, 4.1).

Poor dental health was common in medieval children (James and Miller 1970). This may reflect the influence of famine and catastrophic events upon childhood during this period (see Antoine et al 2005). Clinical research has shown that children with mixed dentitions (aged 2–6 years) and suffering from malnutrition and iron deficiency have higher caries rates compared to their nourished peers (Clarke et al 2006). Carious lesions are more likely to occur in teeth affected by an enamel hypoplastic defect (Duray 1990; Johansson et al 1992; Psoter et al 2005). A longitudinal study of 209 Peruvian children under a year old who had experienced a period of malnutrition showed that dental eruption was delayed and that by 4 years old they had a significantly higher incidence of caries (Alvarez et al 1993). It is therefore possible that the dental health of the subadults from St Mary Spital reflects the longer-term outcomes of malnutrition, in addition to their age-related changes in diet.

SKELETAL EVIDENCE OF POST-WEANING DIET

Specific metabolic diseases present in the subadult sample demonstrate that for a small minority of individuals (nine), the diet was lacking in vitamins C or D. It is most probable that this occurred during episodes of famine. The role of the osteological paradox should be taken into consideration here: these diseases are only identified in those who were capable of surviving long enough to stimulate a diagnostic osseous response (Brickley 2000, 187; Wood et al 1992). It is therefore possible that more individuals experienced metabolic disease than can be recognised, including those who suffered short-term dietary insufficiencies. However, subadults are particularly vulnerable to developing a metabolic disease within a relatively short space of time, as they have a high bone turnover (Brickley and Ives 2006, 163–4).

Five subadults had evidence of rickets (vitamin D deficiency), three in early childhood and two in later childhood. All had been buried during periods 16–17 (*c* 1250–1539), during which episodes of famine occurred. These individuals may have experienced insufficient exposure to daylight or, less typically, suffered from disorders of the gut, liver or kidneys (Mays et al 2006, 362). The co-existence of disease and the development of rickets have been recognised. In the medieval period, sickly infants were kept indoors for long periods, thereby restricting the amount of sunlight they could effectively metabolise (ibid), especially if they were clothed in swaddling bands. Individuals developing rickets during early childhood could have done so during weaning, which could also have compromised the amount of vitamin D absorbed, as the weaning foods described in the primary sources did not include oily fish (Martin 2000, 703). The risk during weaning may have been heightened if infants had previously consumed breastmilk low in vitamin D (Lewis 2007, 120). If they were perceived as being ill they may have been kept indoors, increasing their risk yet further.

Socio-economic factors are important cultural buffers against disease and, as in later historical periods, high-status children may have had higher rates of metabolic diseases because they spent more time indoors (Lewis and Gowland 2007; Molleson and Cox 1993). Rickets was present in both rural and urban communities in medieval England (below, 4.5), which suggests that risk factors present in both environments, such as similarities in childcare, led to its development. However, urban subadults may have had greater risk compared to their rural counterparts due to poor local environmental conditions, greater population movement and reduced food quality (below, 4.3).

The presence of scurvy, rickets and also of porotic hyperostosis, which potentially also reflects a deficiency in vitamin D (Walker et al 2009), among those in adolescence (12–17 years) and later childhood (6–11 years), may be evidence that key stages in life may have increased the risk of developing metabolic diseases. At this time many may have changed households or migrated to London, either to begin an apprenticeship or because of economic stress in the countryside precipitated by environmental catastrophes. As a result, they could have been entirely self-reliant and independent of their families (see Panter-Brick 2000a), and may have suffered a downturn in their economic resources, preventing them from purchasing adequate food. However, affected individuals would have had to be nutritionally compromised for a long period of time before an osseous response was initiated (Brickley and Ives 2006) (below, 4.3), which may explain why such low rates of scurvy and rickets were observed: individuals may have died of other diseases before osseous changes were manifested.

Subadults can rapidly develop scurvy if a deficiency in ascorbic acid is sustained for 2–4 months, as their growing skeleton demands a high bone turnover (Brickley and Ives 2006, 163–4). Humans can only metabolise vitamin C through ingestion and young subadults are reliant upon others for feeding and food preparation (Lewis 2007, 126). Ortner (2003, 384) notes that populations who predominantly consume cooked food are at greater risk of developing scurvy and, unlike their rural counterparts, urban dwellers would have had greater opportunity to purchase cooked food from cookshops, pie bakers and taverns (Hammond 1998, 50–1). Males may have been at greater risk if, as some studies of modern populations have shown, their diets contained less fruit, fibre and vegetables than female diets (Courtenay 2003, 4). Their employment may have increased their chances of becoming ill, particularly if associated with other risk factors. Our ability to recognise rickets in these individuals may also be related to how active they were, as those who keep mobile often display the most severe deformities (Lewis 2007, 122).

THE IMPACT OF THE URBAN ENVIRONMENT ON GROWTH

The urban environment influences human biology in ways distinct from those of a rural way of life (Schell and Ulijaszek 1999, 3–6). Urban living affects growth, development, disease immunity and physiological adaptations, resulting in high mortality rates and rapid social change (Bogin 2001, 201).

Migration is the key to the survival and development of urban centres, and this process has been shown to have a direct influence upon health and well-being (Bogin 2001, 218). In the medieval period, migration was integral to urban demography as those in their late teens moved to towns and cities in large numbers in search of work (Goldberg 1997b, 12). Inter-site analysis of growth data supports the hypothesis for the migration to London of females aged 12–17 years, and the influence of the city environment on attained height (below, 4.5). Contemporary clinical research on the stature of male adults born to rural-to-urban migrants has shown that they are taller than their peers whose parents were born in urban centres (Kolodziej et al 2001).

Understanding the growth of the subadults buried at St Mary Spital is highly problematic, because the results are influenced by genetics, biological responses to catastrophic events, urban living conditions, migration and the heterogeneous medieval way of life (see Ulijaszek et al 2000). Research on Nepalese children has demonstrated that low-status groups, who are often perceived as being the most vulnerable, are not always the shortest (Panter-Brick 2000b). Street children, although having the highest number of health complaints, were taller than children who were squatters, lived in villages, or attended school (ibid). We therefore cannot assume that the shortest individuals were from the most vulnerable status groups.

Although demographic differences between burial types at St Mary Spital affected the number of individuals available for growth analysis (Chapter 3.2), the results showed that height was directly related to burial type. Overall, height-for-age increased over time, with period 17 adolescents being the tallest. This is in line with adult stature; similar patterns of growth were observed in periods 14 and 17, suggesting that period-specific social and environmental factors played a more significant role upon attained height than factors such as migration (below, 4.3).

INTERPRETING INDICATORS OF STRESS

Unfortunately, we cannot determine whether the individuals from the mass burial pits came solely from the city, or from a combination of suburban, rural and urban communities (below, 4.3). However, the osteological paradox suggests that the higher prevalence rates of indicators of stress show that those in the catastrophic cemetery were more able to adapt to disease or malnutrition than those buried in the attritional cemetery. The shorter stature of adults from the mass burial pits at St Mary Spital suggests that although many individuals were able to attain adulthood, their long-term health outcomes were poor (see Clark et al 1986; Kemkes-Grottenthaler 2005). This is supported by comparative data, which show that the male and subadult individuals from St Mary Spital were shorter than other samples from the UK (below, 4.5).

At St Mary Spital, those who died aged 1–5 years had high crude prevalence rates for indicators of stress (Chapter 3.10). This suggests that although these individuals were healthy enough to manifest a dental and/or osseous response to stress, they were ultimately unable to cope with the environmental and social stresses experienced from birth and were the most 'fragile' of their peers (see Wood et al 1992). Their inability to cope may have been exacerbated by diseases acquired during weaning or from breastfeeding. Individuals who died aged 6–11 years represent those who were able to survive early childhood but were not strong enough to achieve adolescence. Their morbidity and mortality risks increased from early childhood, as the primary sources show us that at this age they began employment, experienced dietary changes, and may have migrated to the city. Those who died aged 12–17 years appear to have been particularly vulnerable to the social and environmental stressors of medieval London, an interpretation which is underscored by the occurrence of trauma and infectious and metabolic disease in this group. Those with enamel hypoplastic defects, reflecting a 'weak constitution', were more likely to die in this age group (or during young adulthood) than those without defects, because they were unable to continue long-term adaptation to stressors (Goodman et al 1988; Humphrey and King 2000). In Lewis's study of medieval children, individuals who had an observable enamel hypoplastic defect or cribra orbitalia lived up to one year longer than those without (Lewis 2002, 46), highlighting the role of the osteological paradox in the interpretation of these lesions, ie those who developed a response were less 'frail' (see Wood et al 1992).

The crude prevalence of indicators of stress was directly linked to burial type and period (below, 4.3), which suggests that they also reflect responses to climatic and social catastrophes (see also Antoine et al 2005). Given this strong connection, it is possible that the subadult adaptations to large-scale events (eg plague or famine) mask indicators formed in response to stressors present in *infantia*, such as weaning.

TUBERCULOSIS: A DISEASE OF CHILDHOOD

Migrants are at risk from diseases present in both their place of origin and their new environment (Bogin 2001, 218). In medieval England tuberculosis, a disease of childhood, was present in both rural and urban environments, indicating that similar risk factors and modes of transmission were present in both (Lewis 2007, 146).

Sixteen subadults with tuberculosis were recorded from periods 14–16 (*c* 1120–*c* 1400). Only those aged 6–11 years and 12–17 years were affected, the majority of them (ten) from the older group. Both age groups showed differences between burial types, explored below (4.3). The changing crude prevalence rate in subadults follows the overall disease pattern within the cemetery. The high prevalence rate of tuberculosis within the sample demonstrates that the disease was firmly established within the London population, compromising the health of both sexes and all age groups, particularly during periods of famine. Historical and modern clinical data show that gender difference in the prevalence of tuberculosis varies over time, and it is not always possible fully to understand the extent to which changing gender roles and access to treatment create bias (Roberts and Buikstra 2003, 45–6). Unfortunately, we are unable to sex subadults reliably using macroscopic methods and it is not possible to establish which sex was at greater risk.

Subadults are particularly vulnerable to acquiring tuberculosis, either by inhalation of the bacteria or from the consumption of infected milk (human or animal). On rare occasions they may acquire the disease congenitally via the placenta or by the consumption of infected amniotic fluid (Roberts and Buikstra 2003, 49). As we are only able to observe the osteological responses to this disease, we must infer that many individuals became infected with tuberculosis in infancy or early childhood but were unable to survive long enough to develop a recognisable osseous response (Wood et al 1992). Indeed, for many individuals the disease may only have manifested itself during adulthood, possibly as a reactivation of primary tuberculosis (Lewis 2007, 146).

Subadults are usually infected with tuberculosis by adults (Roberts and Buikstra 2003, 49), and the results from St Mary Spital show that a proportion of the adult population of London were recovering from or suffering from active tuberculosis, which would have promoted the spread of the disease within the community. Infants are particularly vulnerable to infection as they are in close contact with adults (promoting droplet spread) and because they have no control over their diet. Housing conditions would have played a significant role in the spread of the disease, through levels of crowding, the degree of ventilation, the presence of animals, and the carer's occupation (ibid, 49–60). Weaning would have been a particularly vulnerable period. An infant who developed diarrhoea would be susceptible to other infectious diseases, further complicated by the consumption of contaminated weaning food. If the milk used to make the pap or panada was infected, they could have developed the gastrointestinal expression of tuberculosis, which would have resulted in diarrhoea and generalised infection (Lewis 2007, 148–9), and which may not have been distinguished from the side-effects of weaning.

Victorian clinical information concerning tuberculosis in children provides an insight into how this age group adapted to the disease before the introduction of antibiotics and vaccination. The affected subadults from St Mary Spital had evidence of joint destruction at the hip, sacroiliac and elbow, in addition to Pott's disease of the spine and lesions to the mandible, clavicles, humeri and ribs. Destruction of these bones and joints would have meant that many experienced a long-term decline in mobility and dexterity. Since many cases were healed, we know that they would have had to adapt to cope with the onset of paralysis, an abnormal gait and ankylosed joints. One clinical publication describes how children with bone and joint destruction physically adapted to such changes, encapsulated by the observation 'it is an attitude of expectation, produced by the constant fear of sustaining a sudden shock' (Fraser 1914, 129–30). This disease would have resulted in many of these subadults experiencing considerable impairment, which could have prevented them from gaining employment and placed them in a situation of dependence. Others may have adapted to their situation by using crutches and other mobility aids, and by seeking employment in non-physical occupations. The adult evidence suggests that many affected subadults at St Mary Spital survived into adulthood without experiencing nutritional and physical stress, indicating that they were able to adapt and shape their way of life in order to survive.

TREPONEMATOSIS

The living environment is shaped by among other factors social status and organisation, gender roles, religion and technology (McElroy and Townsend 1996, 25). An individual's life course determines his or her relationship to the living environment: the lives of children are shaped by adults but also by their peers through play, language and work (Baxter 2005, 32–7). An individual's 'osteobiography' provides an insight into the complex relationship between health and environment (see Roberts and Manchester 2005, 14–21). Treponemal disease can be used to explore behaviour, gender roles and the living environment, as it is considered a 'social disease'.

Treponematosis in medieval England is suggested to be venereal syphilis, and those aged 12–17 years and 6–11 years at St Mary Spital display osteological changes that are consistent with the tertiary stage of the disease (Mays et al 2003). Because of their age, these cases most probably reflect late onset congenital syphilis (Lewis 2007, 154). These individuals could have become infected by the ninth week of gestation and may not have displayed any symptoms at birth; their mothers may also have appeared symptomless. It is also possible that they became infected post-partum from lesions on the mother's or wet-nurse's breast (ibid, 152). The affected subadults would not have begun to display lesions until the age of 2 years. Such an early age of onset may account for the severe bony changes observed in 10–11-year-old [6974] (Chapter 3.9). We cannot know whether this child was an inmate of the hospital, an orphan for whom St Mary Spital took responsibility. In *infantia*, such severe facial changes would have resulted in a saddle nose and 'syphilitic snuffles', preventing the child from being able to suckle or breathe normally (ibid, 155–6). Associated changes (eg mental defects and spastic paralysis) would have made the individual dependent upon others for basic needs (ibid; see Dettwyler 1991).

The majority of affected subadults were adolescents, reflecting the onset of the congenital form of the disease during puberty. The majority of observed lesions were active at the time of death and treponemal infection may have suppressed immunity, making it more likely for these individuals to die from a less severe illness (Martin 2000, 328).

Most of those at St Mary Spital with treponematosis were young adults, suggesting that they had acquired the disease during late childhood or adolescence, or were showing the symptoms of late congenital syphilis (Lewis 2007, 152–7; Powell and Cook 2005, 46–9). The age group affected also reflects the demography of medieval urban centres, which was biased towards young people: most servants were migrants aged between their mid teens and early twenties, with the minority of individuals aged over 25 (Goldberg 1997b). The greatest levels of female rural-to-urban migration took place in the late 14th and early 15th centuries (Goldberg 1992, 297–8), which corresponds to the increase in treponemal disease observed at St Mary Spital. Apprenticeships enabled individuals between the ages of 7 and 12 years old to migrate to towns (Singman 1999, 26). Laws were issued, particularly after the Black Death, to prevent the loss of agricultural workers to apprenticeships unless their parents had land or rent valued at 20 shillings; but by 1429 London was exempt from this law, allowing individuals aged 14 years or older to be in service for seven years. Interestingly their indentures often included sections forbidding the apprentices to visit prostitutes or taverns (Orme 2001, 311–12).

The presence of congenital syphilis suggests that the disease affected multiple generations. The Church and common law allowed girls to marry at 12 years and boys at 14 (Orme 2001, 329), making it possible for congenitally infected individuals to die in their mid twenties leaving behind infected children. This possibility is supported by the 8–11-year treponemal disease cycle, the late onset of congenital syphilis, and the delay in the appearance of tertiary stage lesions after infection (between 2 and 10 years) (Grassly et al 2005; Ortner 2003, 279).

TRAUMA: AN INSIGHT INTO AGEING

The analysis of trauma sustained during childhood provides an insight into the risks encountered in the living environment (Jiménez-Brobeil et al 2007). Analysis of fracture patterns and mechanisms provides an insight into the physical aspects of ageing, and in combination with the adult data, allows us to examine the range of trauma sustained throughout life.

Today, male subadults are more likely than females to sustain an injury (Klauber et al 1986), which reflects underlying differences in the engendering of children and the risk-taking behaviour of males (Courtenay 2003, 4). However, our inability to estimate the sex of subadult remains prevents the examination of such patterns in the past.

Clinical reviews of accidental trauma demonstrate that fractures are the most common severe injury sustained by subadults, with the arm being particularly affected. Subadult fracture risk and patterns have been demonstrated to correlate with increasing development and the level of dependence. For example, pre-mobile infants are more likely to fall from furniture and sustain head injuries (Warrington and Wright 2001), whereas those who are able to walk are more likely to sustain an arm injury (Glencross and Stuart-Macadam 2000, 200); other limb fractures are common during adolescence (ibid, 200–1). Subadults usually sustain fractures when learning new skills and are also vulnerable to accidents and unsafe local environments (Gratz 1979). Such incidents are recorded in miracle stories and coroner's rolls, which document unfortunate events such as animal attacks, falls, being run over by carts and crushings (Orme 2001, 100). Skull injuries are most frequently sustained by falls, usually between the ages of 8 and 9 years, and by interactions with animals (Klonoff and Robinson 1967; Smith et al 2004).

The subadult trauma pattern at St Mary Spital has aspects which parallel both rural and other urban samples, suggesting that similar fracture mechanisms existed in both environments, but that the nature of urbanism in London created a higher risk of trauma (below, 4.5). The prevalence of trauma increased over time (Chapter 3.8), with a marked increase in period 17 (see Tables 68–70). The subadult fracture prevalence was low: 2.3% of 6–11-year-olds (8/348) and 4.6% of 12–17-year-olds (25/544). This result is typical of archaeological populations: subadult bones are less likely to fracture as they are elastic and able to absorb more energy than adult bone. If fractured, the injury causes plastic deformation of the bone, a 'greenstick' fracture, which can be rapidly remodelled during growth (Currey and Butler 1975; Lovell 1997, 143; Roberts and Manchester 2005, 94). Subadults are also more likely to sustain lacerations or abrasions, which are unobservable in skeletal material, rather than fractures (Gratz 1979, 551).

Temporal differences in the elements affected by trauma were also observed. Those aged 6–11 years had fractures in the ribs and legs in period 16 (c 1250–c 1400) and the skull and foot in period 17. Adolescents (12–17 years) in period 16, particularly those from the mass burials, were the only group to sustain fractures to all body areas (skull, dentition, spine, ribs, arm, hand, leg and foot), an increase from period 15 where the spine, ribs, arm and foot were affected.

No infants or individuals in early childhood had evidence for fracture, which may be due to the rapid skeletal remodelling in these age groups but also suggests that trauma associated with birth was a very low risk. Clinical data have shown that death by accidental trauma is a low risk in these age groups (Rivara 1982); falls in pre-mobile infants are unlikely to result in fracture and, because they usually involve falls from furniture at a height of less than 3m, the injuries sustained are not severe (Warrington and Wright 2001).

In later childhood (6–11 years), two individuals had blunt force injuries to the skull, a common clinical finding. Subadults often have a higher skull fracture rate than adults, because their neck muscles are weaker and the head is relatively larger (Gratz 1979, 551). Male children have a higher prevalence rate of head injuries, and the majority of head fractures are sustained during play or from falls (Klauber et al 1986, 146–7). The fractures to the limb bones are commonly associated with increasing mobility, an 'insatiable curiosity, over activity, and fatigue, and … clumsiness due to instability of newly acquired motor skills' (Zelazo 1974, 62). The crude prevalence rate of arm fractures in this age group also conforms to clinical data, which have found that the upper limb is more frequently involved in severe injuries (Gratz 1979, 551). Where upper limb fracture mechanisms could be identified in the skeletal sample, they showed that injuries were produced by a fall on to a flexed elbow (Chapter 3.8), an injury usually associated with falls from a height or accidents during play (Apley and Solomon 2000, 275; Galloway 1999, 120). Although falls are usually considered to be accidental, this injury may also result from interpersonal violence (Judd 2004, 47). Fractures to the arm appear to have been common in medieval London, as the majority of subadult-type fractures identified in adults also affected this area and predominantly affected males (Chapter 3.8). Individual [2967], aged 12–17 years at death, had a healed fracture to the left second rib. Subadult rib fracture has been suggested as a positive predictor of non-accidental trauma, as for a subadult to sustain such an injury considerable compressive force must have been employed (Barness et al 2004; Walker et al 1997; Galloway 1999, 107).

Fractures affected the tibiae of [9233] and [21723], both aged 6–11 years from period 16, and were produced by torsion and fatigue. Tibial fractures are common in children and today are most frequently sustained during sports activities (Galloway 1999, 193). Fracture as the result of torsion indicates that the limb has been subject to a low energy load and a twisting or rotational force, which may have been combined with axial loading. This fracture type is usually sustained when the individual is a toddler and results from a fall (Resnick 2002, 2712, 2884). Fatigue fractures are produced by repetitive stress (Apley and Solomon 2000, 334). Recent clinical literature suggests that this type of fracture was probably sustained when the individual was learning to walk (Moorthy and Swischuk 1997; Niemeyer et al 2006). One individual, [19441], aged 6–11 years, had a healed fracture to the left fourth metatarsal. This fracture would have been produced by a direct force and was most likely caused by a heavy object falling on to the foot (Apley and Solomon 2000, 343).

Adolescents (those aged 12–17 years), particularly those from the mass burials in period 16, had fractures to the same body areas as those aged 6–11 years, and many of the fractures in the older group were probably sustained earlier in life. However, only adolescents from periods 15 and 16 had spinal fractures, to the thoracic and lumbar vertebrae. Spinal fractures were also common in the adults from St Mary Spital and form a large proportion of the subadult-type fractures identified in older individuals. Compression or avulsion forces from either extreme movement of the spine, or the transmission of force from blows to other areas of the body, caused such injuries (Galloway 1999, 95). In a clinical setting, these fracture are often associated with child abuse (ibid, 96); however, they are most frequently caused by falls, sports or play, particularly in those aged 10–14 years (Stulik et al 2006). It should also be noted that Schmorl's nodes were identified in individuals aged 6–17 years, with an increase in prevalence after the age of 11 years, suggesting spinal stress, exacerbated by genetic factors (Faccia and Williams 2008; Williams et al 2008).

Adolescents (aged 12–17 years) were the only subadult group to have suffered dental fractures (in periods 14 and 16): two individuals were affected. In period 16, [26933] from the mass burials had one fractured tooth, whereas the second individual, [25081], from the attritional cemetery, period 14, had more severe injuries. The mandibular incisors had been lost during life and the surrounding alveolar bone had resorbed; as a result the anterior maxillary teeth were maloccluded. Although caries can result in the loss of multiple teeth, the absence of evidence for inter-proximal caries and the equal state of remodelling in this individual are highly suggestive of interpersonal violence. Such violence is common in males between 15 and 29 years old (Elverland and Voss 1997). Severe tooth loss can have a negative impact upon well-being and social interaction, and cause problems in mastication (Cortes et al 2002). Dental trauma is commonly observed in children today and, as found at St Mary Spital, the permanent teeth, especially the incisors, are most frequently injured. Clinical studies have found that the majority of those affected are males aged between 7 and 14 years, and that they acquire dental fractures at home or at school, while playing or by being involved in sports, road accidents or fighting (Gabris et al 2001).

Individual [21766], aged 12–17 years, had the only reported case of a subadult hand fracture (an intermediate phalanx) recorded in the comparative assemblages (see Table 162). This result is most probably biased by the excavation and recovery practices implemented at St Mary Spital (ie block-lifting and sieving) and by bone preservation (Bello et al 2006; Lewis 2007, 23–30). The individual was probably undertaking manual tasks, making the hands vulnerable to trauma (Galloway 1999, 152). Clinical studies have shown that trauma to the hand phalanges is the second most frequently occurring fracture in children (Landin 1983). Foot fractures had been sustained by 6–11-year-old [19441] and adolescents aged 12–17 years (eg [14129] and [28052], both from the period 16 mass burials). The clinical literature suggests that this type of injury was most probably sustained before the age of 5 years (Owen et al 1995). Most hand and foot fractures did not heal satisfactorily: this may be because such fractures are hard to reduce and splint, or because the adolescents themselves did not consider that the injuries warranted treatment (see Grauer and Roberts 1996, 533).

Most of the remaining fractures observed in adolescents were produced by injuries occurring in later childhood. These included several unique cases of trauma to arm and leg elements, examples of which are described below. The only example of a healed (humeral) fracture with secondary osteomyelitis was also found within this age group ([20370]). The long-term survival of infected fractures by subadults is attested in miracle narratives (Gordon 1991, 155–7).

Adolescent [14381] from period 15 had avulsion fractures of the right humeral epicondyles; the lateral margin of the humeral condyle was enlarged and rugose and the epicondyle was hyperplastic and located inferior to its normal position. The medial epicondyle was also hyperplastic, and barely discernible as a raised rugose area and on the anterior aspect of the diaphysis. The medial border extended to the superior margin of the trochlear. The left humerus of 18–25-year-old male [12190], also from period 15, had a healed avulsion fracture to the medial epicondyle (Fig 203). In modern populations, this form of injury can be caused by direct violence, forced elbow abduction and sudden flexor contraction (McRae 2003, 289). The medial epicondyle can be avulsed when the wrist is forced into extension, and the lateral epicondyle avulsed when an individual falls with the elbow twisted inwards (varus) (Apley and Solomon 2000, 278–9). In this case the injury does not appear to have damaged the growth plate. The observed changes conform to what is colloquially termed 'little leaguer's elbow': such fractures have a high frequency today in children who engage in repetitive and lengthy baseball throwing (Klingele and Kocher 2002). The presence of this injury in a medieval child may be related to the practice of archery or other strenuous repetitive activities (Knüsel 2000, 113).

In period 16, adolescent [19204] had fractures to both humeri. The left humerus was shorter than the right with a healed fracture to the proximal epiphysis, while the right humerus had a healed fracture separation of the trochlea and capitulum, with secondary deformation to the proximal radius and ulna. Fractures to the subadult proximal humerus (Salter-Harris type I) usually occur due to birth trauma and are probably not recognisable in the archaeological record. It is therefore more likely that this injury occurred after the age of 10 years when Salter-Harris type II fractures predominate. Trauma sustained by the metaphysis and epiphysis during development will prevent or reduce growth (Galloway 1999, 56, 120). Intercondylar fractures to the right humerus are often observed in children, despite it being an uncommon fracture, and result in elbow instability and compromised movement (Resnick 2002, 2824). Both of the humeral fractures in this individual could have resulted from accidents which appear to have occurred in early or later childhood (ibid, 2805, 2824; see also Leventhal et al 1993).

Arm fractures sustained during growth formed 46.7% (49/105) of all observed adult fractures received in subadulthood at St Mary Spital, indicating that subadults had a high risk of sustaining such trauma. The adolescent data suggest that the majority of these injuries were sustained during *adolescentia*.

In period 16, adolescent [27661] had evidence of a healed stress fracture to the anterior aspect of the left femoral neck. This had resulted in posterior displacement of the femoral head, which was angled posteriorly. Due to changes in the angle of the femoral head, the acetabulum was wider and longer than normal and had discontinuity of the superior lunate surface (Resnick 2002, 3486). Stress fractures to this location in individuals are rare, particularly in those with an open capital femoral epiphysis, and are usually caused by increased activity or strenuous exercise, rather than by violent trauma (St Pierre et al 1995). The observed varus deformity (towards the midline) is a common complication of this fracture, which is most frequently reported in male children (Azouz et al 1993).

Also in period 16, 12–17-year-old [29075] had sustained a triplane fracture to the distal right tibia (Salter-Harris type IV). This resulted in the distal third of the tibial shaft becoming enlarged and the epiphysis misshapen, with premature, partial fusion. Secondary changes were observed on the talus, where the superior surface was dense, irregular and pitted. Active new bone formation was also seen on the right tibia and fibula. This type of fracture is observed in subadults from the age of 3 years, but is also common in adolescents. It is produced by an avulsion mechanism, or where the foot is trapped and the leg twisted to one side (Apley and Solomon 2000, 339; Galloway 1999, 201–2). The secondary changes of abnormal growth and deformity at the ankle are commonly observed if the fracture is sustained during adolescence (Apley and Solomon 2000, 339).

The identification of individuals with multiple injuries has proved a useful tool in the examination of fracture risk in past populations (Judd 2002a; 2002b); however, it has not been examined in relation to subadults or fractures sustained during

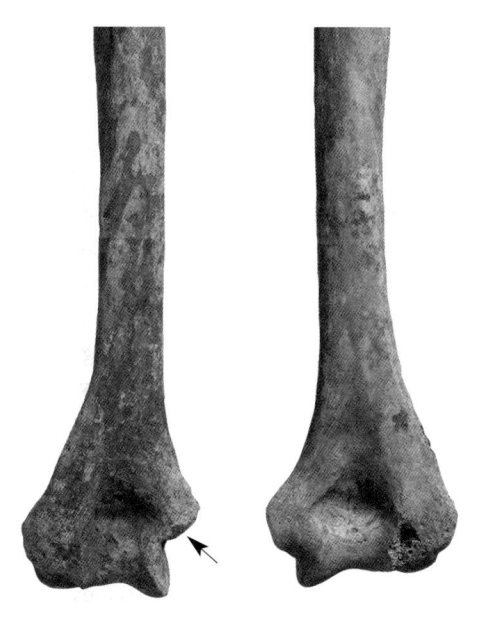

Fig 203 'Little leaguer's elbow' in 18–25-year-old male [12190] from the attritional cemetery, period 15 (scale c 1:2)

growth (see Glencross and Stuart-Macadam 2000, 198), except in the context of child abuse (Lewis 2007, 175–83). In the subadult sample from St Mary Spital, seven adolescents had more than one fracture present: [25081] had dental trauma; two adolescents had two [25312] or three [26962] vertebral fractures; and two individuals had multiple phalangeal [27166] or foot bone fractures [14129]. The context and mechanism of these fractures have been discussed above, and the majority appear to have been caused by accidents.

Two adolescents (12–17 years) had unique examples of multiple fractures. The first, [15647] from period 15, had a healing transverse fracture at the midshaft of one right rib and healed trauma to the margin of the nasal bones. Although infrequent, facial fractures in children usually affect the nasal bones and are common in males aged 16–18 years, who (excluding motor accidents) have been injured in falls and during play (Ferreira et al 2005; Anderson 1995); transverse rib fractures are produced by direct blows to the chest (Galloway 1999, 107). This adolescent has fractures caused by violent mechanisms, indicating that after the age of 12 some individuals had a higher risk of interpersonal violence. The second adolescent, [21971] from period 17, had a healed fracture to the mid third of the left humerus, which resulted in anterior angulation of the distal portion. The right tibia showed lateral bowing, and sclerotic bone formation was present to the postero-lateral margin of the proximal to mid third of the shaft. These features may represent a healing greenstick fracture, produced by repetitive stress; the new bone formation may indicate that the limb was not rested (Apley and Solomon 2000, 334). Humeral shaft fractures are usually produced by accident or direct violence, but in adolescents they can also be caused by torsional stress applied during muscular contraction (Galloway 1999, 125).

Due to the large body of primary textual information from the medieval period, we are able to investigate subadult trauma using miracle narratives. This has shown that the most frequently affected individuals were males under 13 years old; the minority of accidents resulted in fractures, sprains or dislocations; and the majority of accidents were sustained at home or nearby (Gordon 1991). It is interesting to note that these findings correlate to those reported in clinical data (eg Gratz 1979; Izant and Hubay 1966; Rivara 1982), allowing us to postulate that the majority of fractures observed in the St Mary Spital sample were sustained around the home and local environs, particularly for those classed as *infantia*. The majority of the individuals included in the miracle narratives had been involved in an accident before the age of four, usually because of poor care by their parents or siblings (Gordon 1991, 149–50, 158). The number of 'toddler's' fractures to the head, arms and legs observed in the sample reflects the risk from falls before the age of four. It is significant that in the miracle narratives adolescents, as defined by Gordon, have the lowest risk of accident. This may be because they were no longer at home or were deemed old enough to take care of themselves. In contrast, the osteological data suggest that they had a high risk of trauma.

The analysis of fracture location and mechanism in subadults from St Mary Spital has demonstrated that the majority of fractures were those commonly sustained during *infantia* (0–7 years) and associated with growth, greater mobility and play. The evidence from the miracle narratives and clinical data suggests that most injuries were sustained in the local environment, which contained many hazards, ranging from open hearths to animals (Gordon 1991, 152–5). Analysis of the adult data shows that many fractures, particularly those to the arm, were sustained during later childhood and adolescence. Many of the fractures observed in adults were sustained during *adolescentia* (12–25 years). Significantly, the evidence shows that subadults were engaging in repetitive and strenuous activity that resulted in stress fractures. The clinical data suggest that these individuals were more likely to be male, reflecting the sex bias commonly observed in modern and archaeological trauma data (Walker 1997). The fracture evidence supports the hypothesis for subadults migrating to urban centres in search of work but also their earlier participation in the agricultural economy, as their fracture distribution is unique within Britain (below, 4.5).

The most significant observation is the increase of indicators of interpersonal violence and risk of fracture during adolescence. *Adolescentia* was the point at which many would have taken up occupations which relied on manual labour. Many of the injuries recorded may have been sustained before these individuals migrated from a rural environment to London. The evidence for interpersonal trauma may be explained by the aggressive behaviour of male servants attested to in the court rolls of London, the beating of servants and the increased risk of violence in urban communities (Hanawalt 1993, 183–5) (above, 4.1 and below, 4.5). The greater fracture risk for males throughout life also reflects the engendering of children and the concepts of masculinity present in medieval society, which emphasised male association with employment and the 'natural' superiority of the male body (Smith 1997).

Conclusions

The evidence for subadult health at St Mary Spital indicates that the urban environment presented a risk to all age groups but particularly to *adolescentia* and those being weaned. The environmental and cultural aspects of the city produced a number of stressors to which some were not able to respond or adapt, and which promoted the transmission of diseases (eg tuberculosis) and affected attained height. The data show that for some, the dependent period of their lives was very hazardous, with the risk of compromised nutrition and injury. The trauma and growth data indicate that *adolescentia* was a key period in the life course, with health directly influenced by cultural change. The most important finding is the relationship between the defined stages of medieval childhood and the changing patterns of health with age, supporting the interpretation of the migration of young workers who were vulnerable to the hazards of city life.

Violence and the risk of injury or death

Don Walker

The World Health Organization defines violence as 'the intentional use of physical force or power, threatened or actual, against oneself, another person, or against a group or community, that either results in or has a high likelihood of resulting in injury, death, psychological harm, maldevelopment or deprivation' (World Health Organization 2002b, 5). The material remains of archaeology allow us to study the experience of individuals involved in violent conflict in the past, and to view such evidence within its social context (Carman 1997, 12, 19). However, many types of injury can result either from accident or from interpersonal violence, so categorisation by injury mechanism can prove to be a rather blunt tool. For example, falls resulting from violent attack may produce apparently accidental injuries, and direct 'parry' fractures to the mid or distal shaft of the ulna may be caused by accidental falls on to the forearm rather than defending violent blows. Although injuries to the face and cranium, as well as to the ribs and hands, may reflect episodes of interpersonal violence, fractures due to high-risk everyday activities and occupations may result in similar lesions. All skeletal evidence must therefore be considered in its socio-cultural context (Lovell 1997, 165–7). At St Mary Spital, evidence of bone fracture was found in 20.9% (1125/5387) of individuals. Males were affected more frequently than females, to a statistically significant extent.

The results on which this section is based can be found in Chapter 3.8.

Skull fractures

In clinical contexts, injuries to the skull and face are commonly associated with interpersonal violence, although they frequently result only in soft tissue injury (Judd 2002b, 49).

Just 2.9% (157/5387) of individuals at St Mary Spital exhibited evidence of fractures to the skull, with a significantly higher prevalence in males than females. Only 0.7% (7/1027) of subadults were affected. Most injuries involved blunt force trauma to the cranium, represented by depressed crush fractures (Fig 204). This type of injury can be produced by small blunt weapons such as small clubs or sling-shots striking a small, round area, or by an individual falling on to a sharp edge. There were few isolated examples of linear fractures caused by elongated weapons or falls on to flat surfaces (Lovell 1997, 156; Wakely 1997, 29) (see Fig 101).

Only 0.5% (27/5387) of individuals displayed evidence of sharp force trauma to the cranium. It is possible that this form of injury was more frequently associated with interpersonal violence than blunt force lesions (Wakely 1997, 30). However, this may also reflect a society where the more typical form of violent assault resulted in blunt force rather than sharp force injury. Male individuals were affected more frequently with sharp force injuries than females, to a statistically significant extent. Most lesions were found on the left side of the cranium (though not to a statistically significant level), indicating that if the injuries were received during face-to-face combat, the majority of assaults were carried out by right-handed individuals.

The male true prevalence rate of cranial vault injury rose significantly in period 16, and this increase was confined to individuals in the attritional cemetery (burial type ABC). To some extent, the rise in injuries to male crania may reflect the series of social and economic crises that affected England from the end of the 13th century. A growing population, combined with famine and a resultant rise in the price of food staples, would have increased competition for reduced resources and may have provoked conflict at various levels of society. There may also have been increased levels of violence during the outbreaks of plague in the second half of the 14th century. This was certainly the case in the 17th century, when there was violence as townspeople fled to the country in response to plague (Wear 1999, 339).

It is possible that some of the individuals with healed sharp force injuries were war veterans, although there was at least one example of non-military violence leading to the admission of an injured man to the hospital. Philip de Ashendon was admitted in 1321, following an argument in which he was attacked with a pole-axe. He died three weeks later (Thomas et al 1997, 104).

Although female skull fracture was rare, those with multiple injuries had a similar frequency to that of males with multiple injuries. This suggests that in individuals with multiple injuries, females and males were equally affected by skull fracture. It appears that, while in general females were less likely to suffer cranial and post-cranial trauma, those that were at greatest risk of injury were affected in a similar way to males, and may have been subject to comparable forms of accidental injury or

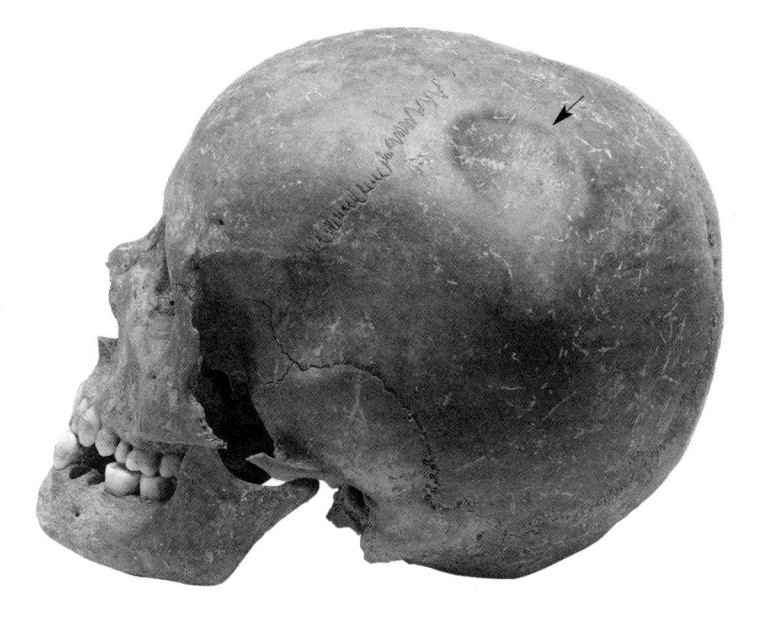

Fig 204 Left lateral view of healed blunt force injury to the skull of 12–17-year-old [21037] from the catastrophic cemetery, period 16 (scale c 1:2)

interpersonal violence.

In contrast to males, the prevalence of blunt force cranial vault injury in females fell over the period of the cemetery's use (Chapter 3.8). This may reflect a variation over time in the types of risk specifically associated with female trauma, whether the result of accidental injury of interpersonal violence.

Long bone fractures

The true prevalence rate of long bone fracture at St Mary Spital was 1.1% (550/48,749). This was slightly higher than that encountered at most other urban medieval sites, but far lower than the rate at the leprosy hospital of St James and St Mary Magdalene at Chichester (White 1988; Mays 1991b; Grauer and Roberts 1996; Judd and Roberts 1998). The inmates at Chichester may have suffered increased rates of accidental fracture due to loss of sensory function as the leprosy took its course (Judd and Roberts 1998). When the true prevalence rates from St Mary Spital were examined by side, a greater number of left bones were fractured, although only ulnae were affected to a statistically significant extent. Distal shafts were most frequently affected. Where characterisation was possible, the most common type of fracture was oblique, indicating that most injuries were due to indirect force. Oblique fractures are caused by rotational and angular stress on the long axis of a bone (Lovell 1997, 141). The force tends to travel along a limb until it reaches an area susceptible to fracture. For example, ribs experiencing antero-posterior compression tend to suffer oblique fractures at their lateral angles (Galloway 1999, 107).

Undisplaced transverse fractures of the mid or distal shaft of the ulna may result from the defensive action of parrying a blow (Judd 2002b, 51). They can also be caused by falls in which the forearm strikes a sharp object, or possibly by fatigue fracture brought on by repetitive strain (Lovell 1997, 165). No specific relationship was found between the prevalence of skull fracture and that of transverse mid or distal ulna shaft fracture at St Mary Spital. This suggests that individuals with ulna fractures were no more likely to be affected by skull fracture than those without, and that the majority of 'parry' fractures were caused by a mechanism unrelated to that which led to skull injuries. There is insufficient evidence from St Mary Spital to determine whether the mechanism of transverse mid or distal ulna shaft fractures was accidental or related to interpersonal violence.

Grauer and Roberts suggested that indirect fractures in the lower arm of individuals from St Helen-on-the-Walls in York may have resulted from involvement in light craft industries, where much of the work involved the use of the upper limb (1996, 539). Such fractures can also result from falls from a standing height on to an outstretched hand (Judd 2002b, 51). At St Mary Spital, 18.0% (132/732) of all female fractures were located in the radius or ulna, compared to 9.1% of male fractures. Unlike at York, the true prevalence rate of male ulna fracture at St Mary Spital was slightly lower than that of females, though not to a statistically significant extent (Fig 205). The same was true of tibiae and fibulae (Fig 206). Males displayed significantly higher true prevalence rates of fractures to the clavicle, humerus, spine and ribs. This variation in the distribution of fracture risk probably reveals divisions in habitual activities between the sexes. To some extent, it may also be related to differences in forms of interpersonal violence, but this is difficult to demonstrate when there are relatively few clearly definable examples of assault within the sample.

Ulna shaft fractures in males and in females were found to have occurred statistically more often on the left side. Transverse fractures were more common in female ulna shafts than in male, and when male and female transverse ulna fractures were combined, the left side was more frequently affected than the right. The evidence reveals that individuals were more likely to injure the forearm in their non-dominant upper limb. This might be due to parrying a blow while holding an object, perhaps a weapon, in the right hand.

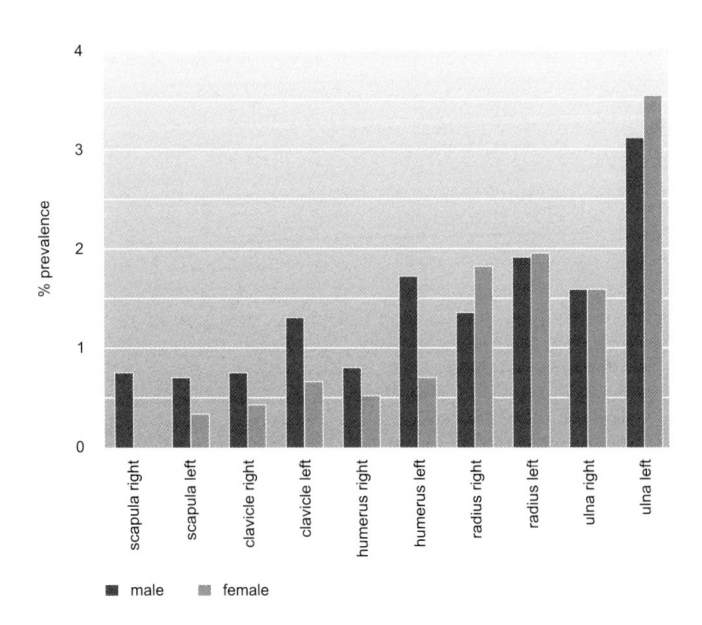

Fig 205 True prevalence rates of upper limb fractures

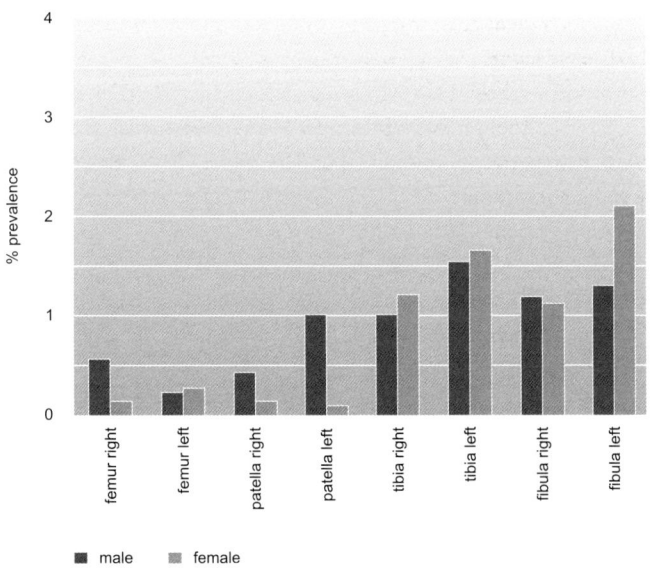

Fig 206 True prevalence rates of lower limb fractures

Alternatively, it could be caused by a fall while carrying a load in the stronger arm. The higher frequency of transverse fractures, representative of direct injuries, in females may reflect a greater risk of assault.

Some fractures were tentatively assigned to specific mechanisms on the basis of the macroscopic analysis of their type and location. Of these, 38.2% (332/870) may have involved falls on to the forearm, elbow or outstretched hand, while 14.7% (128/870) may have resulted from torsion of the lower limb through twisting or falling on to a foot; 31.8% may have been caused by direct blows (see Fig 131).

Knife injuries and rib fractures

A further factor that must be considered in the analysis of interpersonal violence is that of knife use. Evidence of attack with a sharp blade will not be visible unless a bone has been pierced or nicked. Even then, the lesion might leave only a shallow scratch which may be invisible to macroscopic inspection in archaeological material. In medieval London, both men and women carried knives as a matter of course for the purpose of slicing their food at meals (Hanawalt 1993, 75). There may be a number of individuals in the cemetery sample who suffered knife attack, though we have no proof of such. It is likely that there were many who died from soft tissue injuries that left no mark on the bone.

Of those individuals who displayed evidence of unhealed wounds that may have been related to the cause of death, 40.6% (26/64) had healing rib fractures. These can be caused by accidents, falls, direct blows or even coughing (Judd 2002b, 50). In some circumstances, these types of fractures would have been life-threatening, as inward displacement of rib fragments may have caused irreparable damage to the pleura and lungs (Lovell 1997, 159).

Multiple injuries and recividism

Today, clinical studies have focused on the need to reduce the level of accident and emergency admissions to urban hospitals. Part of this work has involved the identification of 'injury recidivists' – those individuals and groups most likely to suffer repeated episodes of assault-related injury. In many of these studies, the groups most at risk include young adult males from socially and economically disadvantaged backgrounds with a history of unemployment and drug or alcohol abuse. In some urban centres such groups have been identified as chronic sufferers with a high probability of re-admission to accident and emergency departments, together with an elevated risk of death (Judd 2002a, 90–1).

It is this relationship between socio-cultural variables and trauma that has led to increased interest in the study of multiple injuries in cemetery samples, with attempts to relate individual status and local environment to the skeletal evidence of injuries accumulated throughout life. Most modern studies have concentrated on evidence of male trauma, as clinical data reveal a low percentage of female involvement in repeated injury. In the analysis of trauma at St Mary Spital, we wanted to see if this held true for medieval urban centres and whether there were any socio-cultural factors that may have influenced injury risk throughout life.

The large sample allowed the study of patterns of injury by age and sex, as well as an investigation of the possible causes, such as accidents or violence. 'Injuries' were defined as all fractures to the axial and appendicular skeleton and to the dentition, as well as dislocations and other evidence of soft tissue trauma such as myositis ossificans. Blunt and sharp force lesions were included. All individuals were divided into three groups: those without injuries, those with a single injury, and those with two or more injuries. Those with single injuries were defined as individuals with a single traumatic lesion, or with two or more lesions that probably resulted from a single incident. Those with two or more injuries that may have resulted from more than a single incident were classified as having multiple injuries. These groups were then analysed by age category in order to investigate the accumulation of injury throughout life.

A total of 364 individuals (364/5387: 6.8%) exhibited evidence of multiple injuries. This equated to 30.0% (364/1214) of those individuals affected by trauma. Males were found to be more frequently involved than females (Table 143).

A significant increase in the frequency of adults with multiple injuries was identified in period 17 (c 1400–1539), in both the attritional cemetery (burial type ABC) and the mass burial cemetery (burial type D). This mirrored the increase in fracture crude prevalence rate in the same period. The evidence suggests that an increasing number of individuals were suffering both fractures and multiple injuries in period 17. When divided into age ranges, males displayed a greater prevalence of multiple injuries throughout adulthood than females (Fig 207).

The increase in the percentage of individuals with multiple

Table 143 Multiple injuries in adults of known age and sex

	Female			Male		
Age (years)	No. individuals	No. affected	%	No. individuals	No. affected	%
18–25	428	5	1.2	481	20	4.2
26–35	716	38	5.3	752	64	8.5
36–45	467	39	8.4	700	116	16.6
≥46	211	20	9.5	222	37	16.7

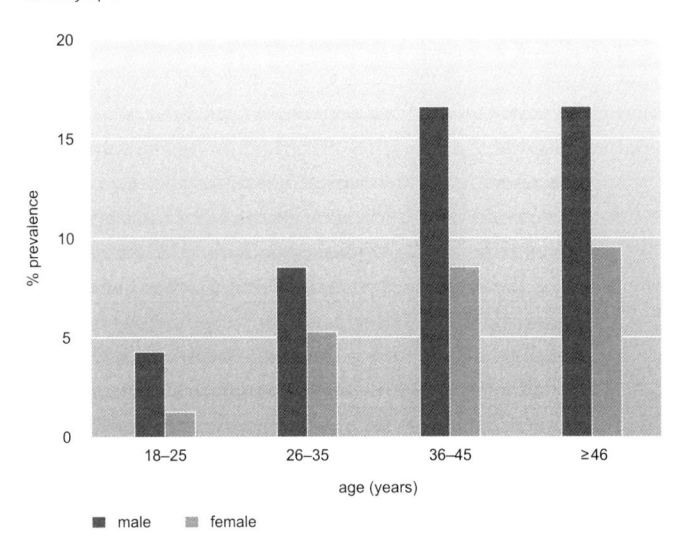

Fig 207 Crude prevalence rate of adults with multiple injuries by age and sex

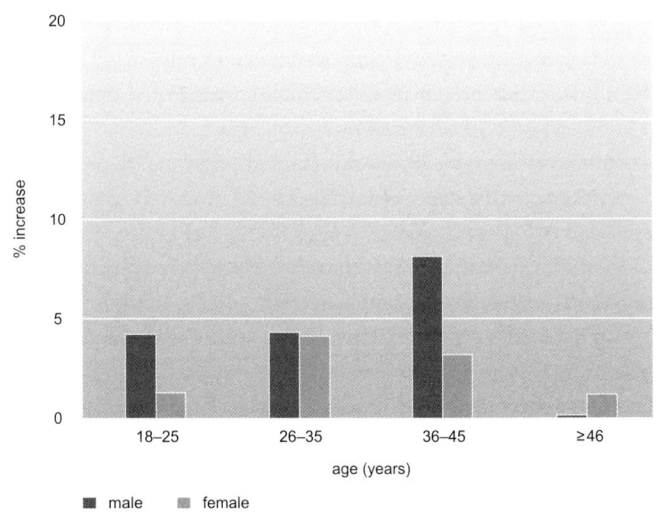

Fig 208 Age-related percentage increase in number of individuals with multiple injuries

injuries in each succeeding age category revealed differing trends in the levels of risk throughout life (Fig 208). This was calculated by subtracting the percentage of recidivists in a particular age group from the percentage in the age group above (eg 8.4% [females 36–45] – 5.3% [females 26–35] = 3.1%). There was no increase in the male rate over 46 years of age, suggesting that injury risk fell. The slightly higher increase in older adult females may have been due to bone mineral loss caused by the onset of osteoporosis (Lovell 1997, 166), although there is little direct skeletal evidence of this disease within the sample. Perhaps the most interesting trend involved the similarity in the rate of increase in multiple injuries in both males and females between early adulthood (18–25 years) and early middle age (26–35 years). This appears in stark contrast to the increase up to 18–25 years of age as well as that up to 36–45 years, where males experienced a far greater rate of multiple injury.

Although individuals with multiple injuries represented only 6.8% of the study sample, these results may reflect gender-related trends in injury risk. They also support evidence of a similar pattern in fracture rates, where 26–35-year-old females exhibited a large increase relative to other age ranges. The results suggest that this group was particularly vulnerable to injury and suffered high mortality rates when compared to other age categories (Fig 209). Although the rate of increase in male fractures fell in each succeeding age range, male multiple injury increased dramatically between 36 and 45 years, suggesting an enhanced injury risk in this age range in males compared to females.

A feature of females with multiple injuries was a significantly higher involvement of long bone fracture than in males. In contrast, males with multiple injuries were more likely to have fractures of the spine (spines with two or more fractures from a single episode of trauma were counted only once). Evidence from periods 15 and 16 (c 1200–c 1400) suggests that there may have been some variation in fracture risk according to burial type. Males were found to have higher rates of ulna

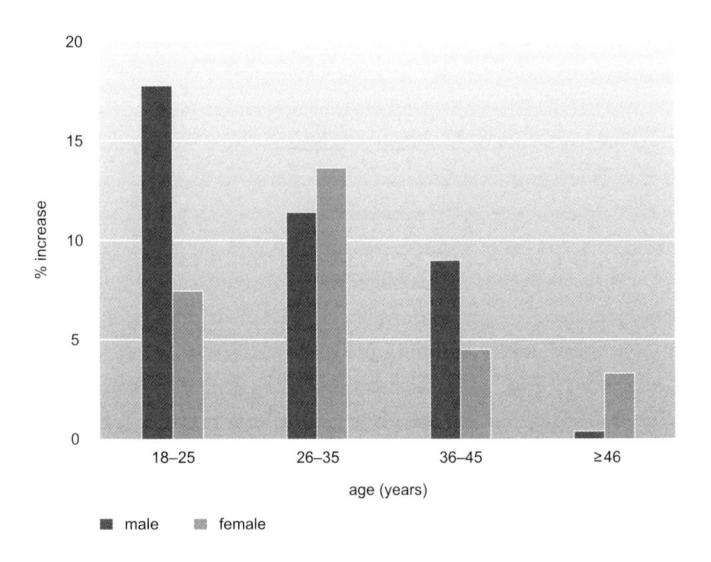

Fig 209 Age-related percentage increase in number of individuals with fractures

fracture than females in the attritional cemetery, while in the mass burial cemetery the rates were similar. However, there was no evidence that the rise in the male rate of ulna fracture was related to the increase of sharp force injuries in the attritional cemetery.

Multiple injuries can of course result from single incidents, and it cannot be assumed that all these individuals gradually accumulated markers of physical insult on the skeleton throughout life. Absolute proof of repeat trauma is difficult to establish in skeletal remains in the absence of two or more lesions at different stages of healing. As Judd points out, there are problems in determining the number of episodes of injury suffered by each individual (Judd 2002a, 93).

Medieval urban injury risk

The majority of the inhabitants of medieval towns were poor. They included journeymen, labourers, servants, beggars and vagrants (Dyer 1989, 196). Women are rarely mentioned in medieval documentary records, which has been interpreted as demonstrating a lack of power and control over their own lives (Skinner 1997); but the records that do exist indicate that urban women were far more involved in trading and retail than their rural counterparts, although they generally carried out more basic tasks than men (Goldberg 1992, 104; Jewell 1996, 89, 92).

The division between domestic and public spheres is often associated with a reduced social role for women in modern Western society, but the cultural conceptions of gender in medieval London would have been influenced by the social and economic conditions of the time (Moore 1988, 40). Married women had domestic duties but could supplement the family income by brewing or spinning yarn (Dyer 1998, 229). While wives or widows may have worked at their husbands' trades, single women were often objects of charity (Leyser 1995, 161). At the lower end of the scale were spinsters and other 'pieceworkers', who earned such low wages that they were barely able to support themselves (Jewell 1996, 108). Even if the capital outlay required to break out of poverty could be found, there may have been little point in doing so, as guilds were run for the benefit of men and would have reduced female job security, especially in times of hardship (Goldberg 1992). This was reflected in low rates of pay for women workers, which would have left some particularly vulnerable to poverty (Skinner 1997, 214). This may have encouraged spinsters and other low paid workers to seek out other menial and temporary jobs in order to supplement their incomes. Such jobs, some of which may have required manual labour or the lifting and carrying of loads, could have carried an increased risk of injury. Without the option of remaining in the same occupation for long periods of time, women may have required more flexibility in order to earn a living in times of economic hardship (Goldberg 1992).

Some activities, such as child-rearing, are today more often linked to women than men, and this can affect both mobility and roles within the community, leading to divisions of labour (Sørensen 2000, 68). These forms of pre-existing social practice could have determined that some women were at less risk of injury, and this may be reflected in the overall low prevalence of injury recidivism within the older adult females at St Mary Spital. Alternatively, it is possible that injured females died younger than the uninjured.

The law provided reasonably well for widows. If they did not remarry, they could remain in their deceased husband's home. They could often continue their husband's craft or trade, and even take on apprentices (Leyser 1995, 177). Although widows of poor men were perhaps reliant on charity and casual trading for survival, as a whole they may have been less vulnerable to destitution than young female migrants, who may have had fewer contacts in London. Female migrants who lacked family connections in London would have had less chance of securing a job in service, with its advantages of food and accommodation. The foundation and growth of charitable institutions was partly the result of increased impoverishment and migration, and a subsequent demand for both spiritual and medical care, during the 12th- and 13th-century expansion of London. If employment in service could not be found, women often moved into cheap shared accommodation in poor and insecure suburban areas of towns (Jewell 1996, 101).

Research by Hanawalt identified the leisure hours following the evening meal as the time of greatest risk for the occupants of medieval London (1993, 77). Drunken brawling among groups of young men was common and led to a curfew in which the city gates and taverns were closed. This and other lawlessness may have contributed to the higher rate of bone fracture and increased frequency of cranial and multiple injuries in males than in females. Wards patrolled the streets to enforce the curfew, but this did not prevent the inhabitants from enforcing justice for themselves: in one incident, a shopkeeper attacked a group of late night revellers when they refused to keep quiet, killing one with his staff (ibid, 10).

Violent incidents during the day may have been less frequent, but there were apprentice riots, servant revolts (part of the 1381 Peasants' Revolt) and trade fights between different guilds, often involving guild members, their apprentices and their servants (Hanawalt 1993, 125). Live-in servants, who made up 20–30% of an urban population, were drawn from both locals and migrants. Girls could begin in service from about the age of 12, often leaving to marry in their mid twenties (Goldberg 1986, 21–3). In a tradesman's house, female servants were often involved in both production and domestic work. However, their wages were only about half those of men, and they often worked just for food and lodging (Goldberg 1992, 186). Although some women were apprenticed to the silk trade in London, apprenticeships in general were dominated by men, leaving women on shorter contracts and more vulnerable to unemployment and impoverishment, especially if they were migrants who had no family contacts in town (Leyser 1995, 156–7).

In medieval society, violence without acceptable justification was considered a lesser crime when carried out on those of lower social rank than the perpetrator (Maddern 1992, 98). This would have left unmarried women and servants vulnerable to physical attack. The chastisement of servants may often have been considered justifiable, though deliberately to cripple them would have been counter-productive. The threat of severe punishment may have led to increased workload and fatigue, which itself could increase the risk of accidental injury.

For women, a period in service was commonly followed by marriage, but not necessarily by reduced risk of injury. Threats of physical attack towards wives are found in court records, and violence may have been used as a tool to reinforce an assumed hierarchy and to enable the husband to maintain respect among his peers (Maddern 1992, 94). It was considered the duty of the head of the household to control the women, by force if necessary (Weisl 1998, 115).

Some poor and unmarried women (including migrants) carried out tasks that involved different types of risks from those experienced by men. The growth of towns and the commercial economy encouraged prostitution. Spinsters and other poorly paid women may have supplemented their incomes with such work when times were hard (Jewell 1996,

109; Karras 1996, 15). In these circumstances, the numbers of working prostitutes may have been influenced by the economic conditions of the time. Many of the identified prostitutes in York were migrants, and some servants may have been sold into the profession (Leyser 1995, 159; Jewell 1996, 110).

While there was some regulation of prostitution in areas such as Southwark, laws banned sex workers from living within the city walls (Karras 1996, 14). Such work must have been dangerous as workers would have been vulnerable to attack from clients (Leyser 1995, 159). While most attacks may have led to soft tissue injury, some may have caused bone fracture. Women prostitutes probably had a low average life expectancy, compounded by the risks of childbirth.

Fractures to the cranium and face, ribs, hands and feet may result from interpersonal violence, as they can result from common forms of assault such as kicking and punching (Lovell 1997, 166). However, modes of interpersonal violence may vary according to socio-cultural context. The growth of kicking and punching as methods of attack has been associated with the rise in the popularity of boxing at the beginning of the 18th century. Before this, clubs may have been the favoured tool for assaults and beatings, both for street and domestic violence (Walker 1997, 167). Spousal abuse in the medieval period may therefore have affected different areas of the body from those seen in modern clinical studies. At St Mary Spital males were found to have a higher prevalence of fracture overall, although the greater number of females affected by direct force ulna fractures may represent defensive action in response to violent attack.

Drinking could also lead to accidents or violence in the home. Women perhaps suffered to a greater extent than men in the medieval domestic environment, with 92% of reported female accidental deaths and all murders of women occurring in the evening or at night (Hanawalt 1993, 77).

At St Mary Spital, although female rates of multiple injuries were lower than male, there was a similar rate of increase in both sexes between early adulthood (18–25 years) and early middle age (26–35 years). It would be too simplistic to assume that females were becoming involved in traditionally male occupations, as there was a higher prevalence of long bone injury in women and a higher prevalence of spinal injury in men. Initial indications are that females who suffered multiple injuries were more at risk of accidental falls on to outstretched arms and possibly to direct forearm injuries due to interpersonal violence. Men with multiple traumas were more often affected by spinal injury, specifically compression fractures of the vertebral bodies, perhaps due to falls or jumping from a height (Lovell 1997, 159). When all individuals with fractures were considered, males were more likely to suffer clavicle and humerus fractures than females, again possibly due to falls. These differences may reflect gender-related variations in injury risk relating to activity or interpersonal violence.

One example of a ≥46-year-old adult male with a large number of injuries was individual [19735]. He had a healed sharp force weapon injury to the left parietal which penetrated both tables of the cranium, a healed blunt force injury to the nose, and six fractures in the ribs, some of which were healed while others were still healing at the time of death (all rib fractures may have been from the same episode of trauma). Where fracture type was apparent the breaks were transverse, reflecting direct blunt force. There was a healed burst fracture and anterior wedging in the vertebral bodies of the lower thoracic spine, the results of axial compression and flexion (Resnick 2002, 2985–6, 2991–2). The distal diaphysis of the right ulna had a healed short oblique fracture, possibly the result of parrying a blow or of a fall (Lovell 1997, 165; Judd 2002b, 51). The evidence of trauma from this individual may reflect the types of injury associated with interpersonal violence. Although healed fractures usually prevent the identification of the age of a wound, the healing fractures in the ribs demonstrate that he was vulnerable to injury in mature adulthood.

An example of a female who may have suffered injuries due to assault was young adult female [9916] (aged 18–25 years), who had a double fracture of the mandible (to the right body and the left angle), probably due to direct force. Both fractures had failed to unify and were still remodelling at the time of death. A dental fracture and ante-mortem molar loss may have resulted from this injury. There was a healed fracture to the fourth sacral vertebra, which had caused displacement of the fifth vertebra and coccyx upwards, forming an L-shape. This may have been caused by a direct blow or a fall on to a hard surface (Resnick 2002, 2914); perhaps she was hit in the face and then fell backwards on to the coccyx. There was also a healed but non-united fracture of the left acromion. This type of fracture tends to be caused by direct force and is commonly associated with fractures to the skull, ribs and clavicle (ibid, 2814–16). The left ulna had a probable short oblique healed fracture with minimal displacement on the distal third of the diaphysis. This may have been caused by indirect trauma, but may also have been the result of parrying a blow (ibid, 2831–2; McRae 2003, 308). This young woman suffered at least two episodes of trauma during her short life. Although her injuries may have been due to accidental trauma, it is possible that she was the victim of interpersonal violence (Walker 1997; Judd 2002a, 90–1).

There was a far less severe rise in multiple injuries in women who lived beyond their mid thirties, with an apparently low rate of exposure to injury, when compared to those who died aged 26–35 years. Perhaps these were individuals of higher status, or they were involved in low-risk activities. Married women may have been less exposed to certain injury risks, and this may be reflected in the low rate of injury in those above the age of 35 in the sample.

Clinical studies indicate that there is often a higher mortality risk in outside employment than in the home (Miles 1991). However, there were many potential risks of accidental injury in the domestic environment, including crowded living conditions, poor standards of building construction, dim lighting and loose animals (see 'Health risks', above). Some animal husbandry would have taken place in towns, and involved both men and women, especially where livestock were kept close to the home, allowing domestic duties to be combined with animal care (Jewell 1996, 95). Clinical research has shown that working with farm animals carries a high risk of physical injury (Judd and Roberts 1999, 238). An archaeological study of rural fracture patterns identified a high proportion of oblique fractures to the distal forearms of women (ibid). These types of injury are commonly associated with extension of the arms during attempts to break falls. Activities such as carrying loads over poorly prepared ground surfaces could predispose a person to stumble or trip, and it is possible that some of the forearm injuries at St Mary Spital were the result of similar mechanisms.

Men appeared to have accumulated injuries at a fairly even rate until later middle age when there was a peak in multiple injuries. This was not due to increased risk of accident as they grew older, as the increase in older adult injuries was minimal. Instead, it may represent a period of increased risk of death in those with multiple injuries, whether obtained through accident or violence. In contrast, the highest overall rates in women were between the ages of 18 and 35, suggesting more vulnerability to injury at this age. These patterns of multiple injuries perhaps represent gender-related variation, and are reflected in differences in fracture distribution between the sexes. It is possible that there was an influx of migrant women from rural areas who carried pre-existing injuries. Their previous lack of exposure to pathogens common to the urban environment would have increased their risk of developing certain infections, such as tuberculosis (Roberts and Buikstra 2003, 64). However, there may have been similar numbers of male migrants, in which case the same pattern might have been expected. Women in medieval London may have suffered different forms of injury from men through spending increased time within the domestic environment. This was unlikely to have led to a higher mortality rate than for males, although injuries due to spousal abuse may have increased female mortality, and may be reflected in the prevalence of direct fractures to the left ulna and an increased rate of cranial trauma in female injury recidivists.

The risk of female injury within our sample was generally low throughout life. However, the evidence from the analysis of multiple injuries suggests that while females showed most overall injuries in those aged 18–25 and 26–35 years, there was a peak in the 26–35-year range. For those who survived until their late thirties or older, the risk of injury fell, while the rate of male injury remained comparatively high. Age and social class are important in the level of risk that people are exposed to, and young migrants living in high-density pockets may well have been vulnerable to stress through increased competition for resources (Carman 1997, 18). Such circumstances may have encouraged increased levels of interpersonal violence. Many women had to be prepared to carry out more menial work than men, for less reward. They were also more vulnerable to economic change, with reduced security of employment and a requirement to be more adaptable in the work they chose.

Impairment and disability

Rebecca Redfern

In recent years, with the increased application of theories about the body to archaeological discussion, there has been a greater appreciation of how individuals engage with society and culture (eg Finlay 1999; Hamilakis et al 2002). 'The body represents the particular site of interface between several different irreducible domains: the biological and social' (Meskell 1999, 21). A recognition of the extent to which impairment affects an individual's social interactions and status has highlighted the significance of any impairment (Shilling 1996, 23, 109, 199; Hamilakis et al 2002, 4). This has allowed us to challenge perceptions of the 'natural' body in past societies (Woodward 1997). A universal definition of impairment and disability does not exist (Metzler 2006, 3–4; Roberts 2000a, 46–7) but two models, the social and medical, are most frequently used to define these terms.

The medical model defines impairment as 'a loss, loss of use, or derangement of any body part, organ system, or organ function' and disability as 'an alteration of an individual's capacity to meet personal, social, or occupational demands because of an impairment' (Cocchiarella and Andersson 2000, 3). In contrast, the social model emphasises the limitations placed on disabled people by the society they live in, and the adaptations that can be used to reduce the effects of disability: 'the social model locates disability not in the individual's impairment but in the environment – in social attitudes, institutional structures, and physical or communicational barriers' (Davidson 2006, 119). Using this model, impairment is described as a 'the subsequent effects of an illness, accident or medical condition upon the way a person functions' and disability may be understood as a 'functional limitation that has been caused by an illness, accident or medical condition' (Disabled Living Foundation 2006, 5). Importantly, the social model divides impairment into visible and invisible conditions (such as epilepsy). Individuals can suffer from both visible and invisible impairments resulting from one condition or inter-related illness; for example, those with advanced diabetes may have visual impairment and mobility difficulties (ibid). Both models show that a range of inherited and acquired conditions may lead to impairment and that the disability may be temporary, such as a fractured limb, or permanent. Impairment may also be accommodated through the use of aids such as prosthetic limbs (ibid).

As recent work suggests that the medieval concept of impairment differed considerably from our own (Metzler 2006), the clinical model has been employed here.

Impairment, disability and health

Impairment is not synonymous with poor health, as health is defined as 'a state of complete physical, mental and social well-being and not merely the absence of disease or infirmity' (World Health Organization 2006). Good health and impairment can co-exist and the distinction between well-being and health is important. Concepts of well-being are subjective, based upon symptoms or feelings but determined in part by physical health, and many clinical tests exist to determine the individual's perception (eg Broadbent et al 2006). A clinical study of well-being in men with spinal cord injuries found that those with a lesser degree of paralysis experienced more intense pain and consequently assessed their own health as poorer than that of those with more severe injuries (Rintala et al 1998). Social well-being can also be influenced by physical limitations (Stewart 1992, 12–15).

Numerous clinical and medical anthropology studies have demonstrated that individual psychology or outlook will directly influence the outcome of illness or impairment (Jenkins 1996, 71). Clinical research into physical disabilities has shown that quality of life is not always directly related to well-being: the greatest risk to quality of life is the duration of the disability and an individual's ability to accept his or her physical appearance, and the longer individuals are impaired, the more likely they are to accept their disabilities (Taleporos and McCabe 2002). Where individuals had supportive social networks and an occupation or involvement in meaningful activities, they reported a high level of satisfaction regardless of their impairment. This is often termed the disability paradox (Viemero and Krause 1998; Albrecht and Devlieger 1999).

A high satisfaction with life has been found to correlate with greater self-perceived health (Zullig et al 2006), and should not be underestimated as a determining factor in well-being and coping with impairment; nor should religious or spiritual faith, which would have been more prevalent in medieval society (Jantos and Kiat 2007; Rossiter-Thorton 2002). This is emphasised by Finucane's (1995) assessment of miracles and faith-healing. A modern study of the Christian faith held by disabled adults and families caring for children with developmental disabilities demonstrated that religion provided a model for care and that their faith strengthened their well-being (Treloar 2002). The psychological adaptations that individuals make to their impairment, and individual concepts of well-being, frequently influence biological adaptations.

Clinical and medical anthropology research has also demonstrated that the cultural frameworks in which an individual operates, the 'abilities, notions and forms of behaviour persons have acquired as members of society' (Hylland Eriksen 2001, 3), dictate their understanding and experience of well-being. For example, Chinese-Americans died significantly earlier than European-Americans if their birth year and the disease suffered were considered ill-fated (Moerman 2002, 78). Culture also determines the extent to which an individual is able to adapt to physical or mental impairments. McElroy and Townsend (1996, 106) emphasise the ability of culture to define the meaning of impairment and thereby influence adaptation strategies, through differences in medical systems and the expression of pain (Idler 1993; Strathern and Stewart 1999, 176), while 'Through the pain and suffering that foreshadow its own mortality, the body drives us to seek meaning' (Kirmayer 1992, 325). Community and cultural responses to impairment and disability are also subject to temporal and spatial variation, which will directly influence aspects of daily life such as social inclusion and access to food (both in quality and quantity) (see Roberts 1999, 82). The World Health Organization employs 'disability adjusted life years' to measure the time lived with a disability and the time lost due to premature mortality, enabling differences between countries to be assessed on a global scale. In the year 2000, the European region lost over 5 million disability-adjusted life years to musculoskeletal diseases, and clear east–west divisions in the burden of disease were found (World Health Organization 2002a, 19). Considering these factors, disability may be regarded as 'that which exceeds a culture's predictive capacities and effective interventions' (Mitchell and Snyder 2000, 3). Above all, responses to impairment and disability are heterogeneous (community or culture specific).

A medieval perspective on impairment

Although diseases and congenital or developmental anomalies that resulted in impairment (such as deafness, blindness and crippling conditions) were recognised in the medieval period, and physical ailments were described by medical texts, 'we can only speak of impairment, but not of disability, during the Middle Ages' as our understanding of the past is compromised by the language used in the description of such conditions (Metzler 2006, 4–5, 190). For example, the Middle English term *disese* was used to describe both discomfort and impairment, uniting psychological and physical symptoms. A number of Latin terms such as *defectus* were also employed to refer to disability. However, we cannot reliably establish that our understanding of these terms corresponds to their medieval usage (ibid, 4–5). Written evidence for impairment and disability is predominantly found within medical and philosophical texts. Miracle texts provide interesting insight into the range of impairments present within a medieval population, from injuries acquired in warfare or assault to congenital or developmental anomalies (particularly those deemed incurable). They also tell us of the adaptations that people made. For example:

> a poor woman from Bury St Edmunds, who had been bent double for many years … walked to Norwich with trestles which she held in her hands … she came as near to the tomb of the saint [St William of Norwich] … Scarce had she ended her prayer when she was seized with a sudden and acute pain … and herself stretched to her full length. (Jessop and James 1896, cited in Metzler 2006, 210, W V.xiv)

Pictorial evidence provides further proof of the adaptations made by impaired people, for example the use of wheelbarrows to transport immobile people and the use of hand blocks or crutches (Covey 1998, 46–7) (Fig 210).

Our perception of medieval life has in many respects been influenced by Thomas Hobbes's observation in *Leviathan* (published in 1661) that it was 'nasty, brutish, and short' (Hobbes 1985), and the assumption that the life of impaired people was even more so. This view has been challenged by

Fig 210 Miniature of a crippled man using wooden blocks to move himself around (© The British Library Board, from the lower margin of fo 30v of Royal MS 13 B VIII, Gerald of Wales, Topographia Hiberniae, *c 1196–c 1223)*

research on impairment and disability, which has shown that those affected were not always marginalised (Finlay 1999; Metzler 2006). As Stiker (1999, 65) observed, 'normality was a hodge-podge … it was only natural that there should be malformations'. Kinship ties and participation in wider social networks protected many people whose families, carers and friends were accepting and supportive (Covey 1998, 18, 25). However, others lay on the margins of society and were associated with poverty and charity (ibid, 16; Sriker 1999, 68–9).

The emphasis on charity within Church teaching enabled impaired people to be classed as the 'deserving poor', and to receive donations (Covey 1998, 11). The Church's influence on the well-being of the impaired during the medieval period was crucial. The Gospels enabled their spiritual integration into society, because it accorded them a right to participate fully in religious and social life; however, this did not always lead to inclusion (Stiker 1999, 35, 89). The Church also identified 'changelings' (usually infants with severe developmental anomalies) and maintained centres of pilgrimage and healing (Covey 1998, 239). In the words of the 11th-century reformer Ulrich of Cluny, 'hump-backed, deformed, dull or unpromising children' were often given into the care of monasteries (cited in Safford and Safford 1996, 13), and such children were often accepted in return for money and land (ibid, 14). However, the Church did restrict the burial rights of impaired people, and in 1234 a *titulus* (decree) was issued that included a section on the exclusion of people with physical deformities from higher orders (Covey 1998, 31; Metzler 2006, 40–1). The Church, medical writers and wider society recognised that impairments could be the result of congenital or developmental factors or environmental and social forces, although each group interpreted the causes within a different knowledge framework (Metzler 2006, 32, 40–95). Congenital malformations were frequently regarded as being monstrous, 'an exhibit, demonstrative of something other than itself' (Cohen 1999, xiv), and helped demarcate what was human, affirming the natural world's diversity and divine power (Olsen and Olsen 2001, 6–12; Bovey 2002, 10).

The religious background is important to understanding impairment in a medieval context, particularly with regard to the role of St Mary Spital. St Augustine believed that 'monsters' marked the boundaries of what was human, establishing the variety and diversity in creation (Olsen and Olsen 2001, 6–10). The Augustinian rule required canons to empathise with the afflicted, and to minister to the sick (Lorentzon 1992, 106). The medieval concept of charity enabled many impaired people who could not support themselves to receive alms, and the Augustinian order itself saw charity as an important aspect of its function. Endowments and bequests to hospitals (including St Mary Spital) provided surgical and medical care, and enabled food to be distributed to the poor and inmates (Covey 1998, 11; Dyer 1998, 234–57). Nevertheless, charity was not equally distributed within the community and some authors suggest that the poor sought to provide relief for their peers (Bennett 1992). Stiker (1999, 87) suggests that 'medieval Christianity never found an entirely stable position, nor an effective praxis to address disability'. From 1100 to 1400, religious views on impairment remained constant with the exception of those expressed in healing miracles. Here the emphasis shifted from healing towards spirituality, and accorded importance to physical suffering experienced in religious fervour rather than that endured because of acquired or congenital impairments (Metzler 2006, 188–9).

It is evident that impairments arising from disease, accident or warfare would have been common in the medieval period, and perhaps regarded as 'part of the great human lot of misery' (Stiker 1999, 79).

Impairment from a bioarchaeological perspective

Within archaeology, the interpretation of past communities has been dominated by socially active male behaviours, and this has directly affected our perception of their societal composition, although these preconceptions are challenged by the inclusion of feminist theory in post-processualism (Sørensen 2000, 24–40; Conkey 2005). Our views of past communities are now becoming less homogeneous, allowing greater 'visibility' of impaired and disabled individuals, although they are predominantly discussed in specialist publications (eg Hubert 2000; Mitchell and Snyder 2000). Our assumptions that most archaeological populations were productive and self-sufficient may be incorrect (Dettwyler 1991, 379). This view is supported by the World Health Organization's (2005) estimate that 10% of the world's current population (roughly 600 million people) are impaired or disabled due to malnutrition, poverty, violence, or chronic conditions, all variables which existed in the medieval period. Identifying disability is a social process: the disabled can only be defined by their physical characteristics if those of non-disabled people have also been defined (Shakespeare 1996, 100).

Such clinical and sociological research underlines the requirement for more inclusive and wide-ranging archaeological interpretations.

Within palaeopathology, impairment and disability have usually been explored through case studies, particularly those focusing on severe congenital or developmental anomalies (eg Phillips and Sivilich 2006). This reflects both the rarity of these conditions and the perpetuation of implicit assumptions that include the belief that survival is indicative of compassion (Dettwyler 1991, 379–82). The skeletal analysis of impairment is problematic. The body will attempt to adapt to a condition, particularly if that condition was acquired early in life when it may have generated a larger osseous response (Knüsel 1999, 36; Roberts 1999, 84). In order to investigate what abnormalities can be defined as 'impairing', skeletal changes must be interpreted with care (to avoid over-interpretation) and with reference to clinical data and to the society in which an individual lived (Roberts 1999, 81; 2000a, 47, 52). However, the correlation of clinical and palaeopathological data can be challenging: for example, osteoarthritis can lead to impairment, but reliably establishing this is highly problematic. Jurmain and Kilgore (1995, 446) suggest that moderate and severe osteoarthritic changes to the peripheral joints would cause a degree of impairment, but that the method used to score osteoarthritic changes (and what are recorded as such) will directly influence the interpretation of this degenerative disease (Bridges 1993, 293). Further, the comparison of macroscopic and radiographic examinations of knee joints in skeletal material has demonstrated that osteoarthritic changes such as large osteophytes and eburnation were not always visible on radiographs and consequently would not be reported in the clinical literature, preventing like-with-like comparisons (Rogers et al 1990). Clinical research has also demonstrated that there may be little or no correlation between radiographic findings, symptoms and disability; and studies of osteoarthritis in the knee joint have found that a number of patients whose symptoms improved actually experienced a reduction in mobility and an increase in the severity of their osteoarthritis visible on radiographs (Claessens et al 1990; Massardo et al 1989). The outcome of osteoarthritis between 'good bone formers' and 'poor bone formers' is a further complication to interpretation, as 'good bone formers' may be better able to adapt to diseases and musculoskeletal stresses (Rogers et al 1997, 89). Any interpretation must therefore account for variations in well-being and perceptions of impairment, the role of individual adaptation, and psychological and physical coping strategies.

The combination of a bioarchaeological and clinical approach avoids the assumption that an individual's survival is due to the community acting morally, or that his or her impairment is disabling or permanent (Dettwyler 1991, 382–3; Roberts 2000a, 57). The analysis of a young adult male from New Mexico who had suffered from juvenile chronic arthritis typifies this approach: musculoskeletal stress markers were used to construct an 'osteobiography', enabling the range of movement and disease progression to be reconstructed (Hawkey 1998).

The interpretation of past communities from skeletal samples is also governed by the osteological paradox. Selective mortality, hidden heterogeneity in risks, and demographic factors all affect the osseous lesions observed; the frequency of disease will be greater among non-survivors; and individuals with healed lesions will appear to have a reduced morbidity risk compared to those with active lesions (Wood et al 1992, 344–5, 353). Consequently many diseases, such as tuberculosis, which can result in impairment and/or disability, will only be identified in those who lived long enough to create a diagnostic osseous response, and a fraction of those impaired by such conditions will be recognised (Roberts and Buikstra 2003, 88–9).

Evidence for impairment at St Mary Spital

To investigate impairment at St Mary Spital, selected conditions which have been clinically proven to affect mobility and physical function are discussed; as outlined above, we may only infer impairment from skeletal remains with reference to clinical data (Roberts 1999, 86–92). Here, emphasis has been placed on the major joints and long bones, except where specific conditions were identified, and examples such as ankylosis of hand phalanges, although known to impede function and affect well-being, were therefore excluded. Due to the interpretative problems outlined above, osteoarthritic conditions are not presented. Congenital or developmental anomalies (eg oxycephaly) and trauma that may have resulted in mental retardation are also excluded, as there is a paucity of literature placing such conditions in their medieval context.

The following skeletal conditions were selected for further examination: cleft palate, scoliosis, kyphosis, kyphoscoliosis, radioulnar synostosis, hip dislocation, pes planus (flat foot), talipes equinovarus (clubfoot), Pott's disease and tubercular destruction of the large joints, fractures resulting in abnormal joint formation or ankylosis, and dislocation or subluxation caused by trauma or joint instability. The study focused on adults of known sex and on subadults. Crude prevalence rates were calculated using sex and age data pooled from all periods (c 1120–1539).

Impairment resulting from tuberculosis was present in both the adult and subadult populations. The highest crude prevalence of Pott's disease was 0.7% for females aged 26–35 years old (5/716). In the adult population a range of joints were affected, including unilateral tubercular destruction of the hip and elbow among females and unilateral changes to the wrist and bilateral destruction of the hip in males. Subadults aged 6–11 and 12–17 years had evidence for Pott's spine. Of the three impaired subadults aged 12–17 years who had suffered from tuberculosis, one had both a Pott's spine and destruction to one hip joint, 0.2% of this age group (1/544) (Table 144).

The majority of traumatic changes that would have caused impairment resulted from dislocations. All cases were unilateral and males were predominantly affected. One case of unilateral subluxation of the shoulder was recorded in male [5018] from period 14 (c 1120–c 1200), from the attritional

Medieval London

Table 144 Crude prevalence rate of conditions indicative of impairment

Sex or age	Age (years)	No. individuals	Osteonecrosis No. affected	%	Osteoarthritis (selected forms) No. affected	%	Perthes' disease No. affected	%	Congenital disease and developmental anomalies (selected cases) No. affected	%	Leprosy No. affected	%	Trauma (selected cases) No. affected	%	Tuberculosis (selected cases) No. affected	%	Burden of impairment (total of all selected conditions) No. affected	%
Subadult	6–11	348	0	-	0	-	0	-	0	-	0	-	0	-	2	0.6	2	0.6
	12–17	544	0	-	0	-	1	0.2	1	0.2	0	-	0	-	3	0.6	2	0.4
Male	18–25	481	1	0.2	1	0.2	2	0.4	5	1.0	0	-	1	0.2	2	0.4	12	2.5
	26–35	752	0	-	0	-	2	0.3	7	0.9	0	-	1	0.1	5	0.7	15	2.0
	36–45	700	0	-	12	1.7	0	-	7	1.0	0	-	4	0.6	7	1.0	30	4.3
	≥46	222	0	-	10	4.5	1	0.5	3	1.4	0	-	0	-	2	0.9	16	7.2
	Adult	82	0	-	1	1.2	0	-	0	-	0	-	1	1.2	2	2.4	4	4.9
Female	18–25	428	0	-	1	0.2	1	0.2	6	1.4	0	-	0	-	7	1.6	15	3.5
	26–35	716	0	-	2	0.3	0	-	8	1.1	1	0.1	3	0.4	5	0.7	19	2.6
	36–45	467	1	0.2	2	0.4	0	-	3	0.6	0	-	1	0.2	2	0.4	9	1.9
	≥46	211	0	-	4	1.9	0	-	1	0.5	1	0.5	0	-	1	0.5	7	3.3
	Adult	61	0	-	0	-	0	-	0	-	0	-	1	1.6	0	-	1	1.6

cemetery (1/2237: <0.1%). The sternoclavicular and radioulnar joints were also affected in men (2/2237: 0.1%), while in females only the shoulder and hip joints were affected (5/1883: 0.3%). The only evidence for ankylosis of a large joint was in the knee of 26–35-year-old female [21769] (1/1883: 0.1%) (Fig 211).

One craniofacial anomaly with a clinically established impairment was identified in 12–17-year-old subadult [2480] and consisted of a cleft palate (1/544 subadults of this age: 0.2%). Foot anomalies affected two males (2/2237: 0.1%), while bilateral hip dislocation (2/1883: 0.1%) and radioulnar synostosis (1/1883: 0.1%) were seen in females. Both sexes were affected by spinal anomalies, consisting of kyphosis, kyphoscoliosis and scoliosis.

The skeletal evidence shows that the population of medieval London sustained a range of impairments, resulting from their local environment and genetic heritage. Many individuals were able to survive, and often developed a skeletal adaptation to long-term disease or trauma.

IMPAIRMENT DURING CHILDHOOD

The patterning of impairment in subadults is particularly interesting; we are able to track the occurrence over 'known' time intervals as we can age subadults more accurately than adults (Lewis 2007, 38–47). At St Mary Spital, the first examples of impairing conditions occur at 6–11 years and 12–17 years of age. These age groups also contain the largest numbers of subadults, indicating an elevated mortality risk at this stage of growth and development (ibid, 86–7). The ability of these subadults to form a healed osseous response to impairing conditions such as tuberculosis demonstrates that they were 'healthy' individuals (Wood et al 1992, 345). The acquisition of these conditions at this stage of the life course provides an important insight into ageing in medieval society. Though it must be remembered that those with congenital conditions would have been affected since birth, the occurrence of impairment in subadults from the age of six reflects biological

Fig 211 Ankylosis of the left knee of 26–35-year-old female [21769] from the catastrophic cemetery, period 16 (scale c 1:4)

growth and development which enables them to become independent of their carers (Bogin 1998, 21–3; Rousham and Humphrey 2002, 124). The age of onset also highlights socio-cultural changes which occur at specific ages, primarily the greater involvement in employment and wider and more varied interaction with the urban environment (Rousham and Humphrey 2002, 125–37).

Childhood impairment could have been sustained through the increased risks of trauma and exposure to infectious diseases associated with employment, particularly the commencement of an apprenticeship. Those migrating from rural areas would have been exposed to new agents of disease and new modes of disease transmission, and therefore increased their risk of acquiring an impairing condition. Subadults with Pott's disease may have been unable to walk, have experienced convulsions and fevers, and would have required care and assistance (Odey et al 2007). The cumulative impact of city life is visible in the comparison of impairment between age groups, which indicates that between the ages of 6 and 25 years individuals sustained numerous assaults from disease and trauma, and were exposed to many life-threatening infections.

THE INFLUENCE OF SEX AND GENDER

Differences between the sexes for the prevalence of impairing conditions show that while some were the result of underlying developmental and congenital conditions present in the population, many, such as tuberculosis, resulted from living in an urban environment. Recent studies of medieval populations have shown that biological differences between the sexes, particularly with respect to immune responses, can influence the conditions suffered and risk of mortality (DeWitte and Bekvalac 2010; DeWitte 2010). However, trauma is independent of immune response as it is caused by accidental or intentional mechanisms (Lovell 1997). The higher male prevalence of traumatic impairments can be explained by the fact that male health cannot be separated from roles dictated by social concepts of masculinity (World Health Organization 2001, 12; see also Halberstam 1998). Many of these concepts have negative impacts upon health-promoting behaviour and increase the likelihood that an individual will become a victim of violence, or be involved in an accident (Stillion 1995, 51, 56, 59), though individual differences in the expression of masculinity, and therefore risky behaviour, exist (Courtenay 2002, 298). Males are also more likely to be employed in occupations that are physically demanding and have greater risk of injury compared to females (see above) (Waldron 1995, 24). Analysis of medieval masculinity has shown that men learned how to be 'unlike' women, and sought to find ways to demonstrate their manliness (Karras 2002, 151, 167).

The lower trauma burden experienced by females suggests that adult gender roles differed. Many women did not marry, but remained in service, and this greater diversity in female roles created a variety of impairment risks. Those who continued in service or in occupations related to domestic roles may have maintained a level of risk similar to that experienced during their youth. Anthropological studies have shown that marriage, if socio-economic resources allow, removes women from the labour force and increases gender inequalities (Moore 1988, 107–8; Kimmel 2004, 127–8). In medieval urban centres females married in their mid twenties, whereas their rural counterparts were married from their mid teens to early twenties (Goldberg 1997b, 7–8). Women's occupations were multi-skilled and changed throughout life, particularly when they married and upon leaving service (ibid, 99), and this would have directly affected their risk of impairment.

ORTHOPAEDIC TRAUMA AND IMPAIRMENT

In human populations, acquired impairment is more common than developmental or congenital conditions (Covey 1998, 4), and may have greater consequences, with significant implications for occupation, family relations and loss of income, in addition to the effects upon well-being and self-perception (Li and Moore 1998; Verbrugge 1994). Trauma is a leading cause of impairment. This was recognised during the medieval period, and the outcome of orthopaedic trauma was often worsened by the medical profession not wishing to intervene in terminal or complicated cases. Many interventions were carried out by 'itinerant specialists [or] empirics' (Rawcliffe 1997, 70–1).

Dislocation and subluxation are painful conditions that restrict or inhibit movement and, if the limb is not reduced, can result in compromised mobility (Apley and Solomon 2000, 268). At St Mary Spital, dislocation or subluxation affected the shoulder, elbow and hip (Chapter 3.8) and the individuals involved had frequently developed osseous reactions, particularly false joints. This indicated that the joint had failed to be successfully reduced or that reduction had not been attempted. Although traction was not commonly used and salves or physiotherapy were employed instead, some medical texts (such as Roger of Salerno's *Chirurgia*) did include instructions on how to reduce such injuries (Metzler 2006, 106, 109). The lack of reduction does not necessarily equate to a want of intervention, as attempts at reduction may not be successful. For example, in the shoulder, the glenohumeral joint can spontaneously sublux or dislocate due to the nature of the underlying joint morphology (Apley and Solomon 2000, 121–2).

Fractures that limited or denied movement were recognised by formal medical treatise and their poor outcome may not have resulted in stigma or have been regarded as a failure (Metzler 2006, 109; Knüsel et al 1995, 46). Many miracle narratives contain references to the curing of individuals with an orthopaedic impairment, for example a monastic lay brother whose hand had been crushed by a millstone (Metzler 2006, 191–258), but the treatment of fractures may itself have led to impairment. Some texts recommended that the leg should be splinted by tying the lower leg against the back of the upper leg, and many orthopaedically impaired people in medieval art are shown with a leg bent at the knee at a 90° angle (ibid, 113). The example of ankylosis following a knee fracture mentioned above (in female [21769], aged 26–35 years) had resulted in the left leg becoming fixed in just such a position, with no evidence of disuse atrophy (Fig 211). The presence of an osseous adaptation to a damaged limb or joint observed in many individuals from St Mary Spital suggests that they may have accepted this as a 'normal' or 'expected' outcome following trauma(s), particularly if they had to continue working. Direct evidence of treatment of orthopaedic injuries has been most frequently reported from religious cemeteries in England. For example, at the Gilbertine monastery in York (St Andrew Fishergate), an older adult male had evidence of a healed knee twist-fracture and septic osteoarthritis, which had been treated with a copper-alloy knee brace (Knüsel et al 1995; Knüsel 1999) (below, 4.2).

JOINT DISEASE AND THE IMPLICATIONS FOR MOBILITY

Clinical studies have shown that joint impairment can significantly inhibit movement, which may be made worse by osteoarthritis, particularly when multiple joints are involved (eg Keenan et al 2006). The range of conditions seen at St Mary Spital, such as developmental hip dislocation and the effects of tuberculosis, would have resulted in joint impairment. The individuals suffering from pes planus (flat foot) and talipes equinovarus (clubfoot) may also have had compromised mobility (Resnick 2002, 4614–16). As with impairment resulting from trauma, the consequences of these diseases may have been within the range of 'expected' consequences of daily life. Illness and pain have been shown to vary according to socio-economic status, gender and age (Miles 1991, 58–62), and as already discussed clinical studies have shown that physical symptoms, limited movement, pain and impairment do not always correlate to radiographic evidence, but although skeletal evidence does not provide a complete view of impairment it can often show the physical adaptations made to the condition (Hawkey 1998).

Analysis of the miracle narratives demonstrates that mobility was of key concern to people (Metzler 2006, 130–3). We know that individuals with compromised mobility used crutches, staffs or wheelbarrows; many were carried on litters, and people employed trestles or hand blocks to move about (Covey 1998, 46–7; Metzler 2006, 169–71). The skeletal evidence from St Mary Spital shows that compromised mobility was a common phenomenon, and (osteological paradox not withstanding) was often directly caused by the urban way of life. As systems of medicine and the meaning of illness and disease vary temporally and spatially, impairment identified in the miracle narratives may not correspond to the conditions used for our study (Fábrega 1999, 189–99; Good 2003, 5; Miles 1991, 42–6).

CONGENITAL AND DEVELOPMENTAL IMPAIRMENT

Congenital and developmental anomalies have been the focus of research in both disability and palaeopathological studies. However, the correlation between social exclusion and severity of impairment is poorly understood. Few of the developmental defects observed in the skeletal sample (such as supernumerary vertebrae) would have affected mobility or function, or changed an individual's physical appearance (Sture 2002). Additionally, many conditions that are considered by modern communities to be socially excluding (eg deafness: see McElroy and Townsend 1996, 303) appear not to have been so in the medieval period (Stiker 1999, 65, 79). It has been suggested that, during the medieval period, developmental anomalies apparent at birth such as cleft palate would have caused parents to abandon their baby or give it into the care of others (Safford and Safford 1996, 2). However, Covey (1998, 8, 25) proposes that affected individuals were protected by the ties of kinship despite being regarded as subhuman or inhuman. Nevertheless, many medieval primary sources indicate that some individuals were given to monasteries, or cared for in hospitals or within the wider community (ibid, 25, 251; Safford and Safford 1996, 13–14). Medieval medicine may have attempted to 'correct' the impairment through surgery, as attested by the procedure to rectify a harelip (Metzler 2006, 103), although many conditions, such as scoliosis, were not treatable.

Many of the congenital and developmental anomalies identified at St Mary Spital have an inherited component (eg radioulnar synostosis) and may have been understood within a vernacular framework of 'normal variation', particularly as humoral imbalances were widely believed to be transmissible between mother and foetus (Metzler 2006, 82). Analysis of medieval pilgrimage has shown that feelings of indignity were of most concern to high-status individuals, whereas the lower classes freely recognised poor health (Finucane 1995, cited in Metzler 2006, 163).

Many of the spinal anomalies observed had resulted in severe deformity. Some individuals had skeletal evidence highly suggestive of paralysis; severe atrophy was seen in the lower limbs of 18–25-year-old male [6571] and 18–25-year-old female [20488]. The majority of spinal anomalies identified at St Mary Spital would not have compromised mobility and/or motor function until skeletal maturity had been reached, as paralysis and extreme spinal curvature follow the adolescent growth spurt (Apley and Solomon 2000, 160–3; McMaster and Singh 1999). Clinical studies of untreated adults with kyphosis and kyphoscoliosis have demonstrated that severe deformity and neurological problems can develop, and those with scoliosis have been shown to have more physical impairment than the population norm (McMaster and Singh 1999; Freidal et al 2002); 18–25-year-old male [6571], for example (Fig 212), also exhibited associated limb atrophy. The greater number of adults than subadults with congenital and developmental anomalies is to be expected, as many conditions do not manifest themselves until adulthood (Barnes 1994; see also Sture 2002, 334). Medieval texts have numerous references to paralysed individuals (many of them children), and demonstrate that such people were not dependent, passive social agents (see Dettwyler 1991, 379–82), as they were often described as using crutches and other equipment to remain mobile, and were assisted by their family or other support networks. The texts also demonstrate that paralysed individuals came from a range of status groups, and many were employed or were able to work (Metzler 2006, 159, 164–5).

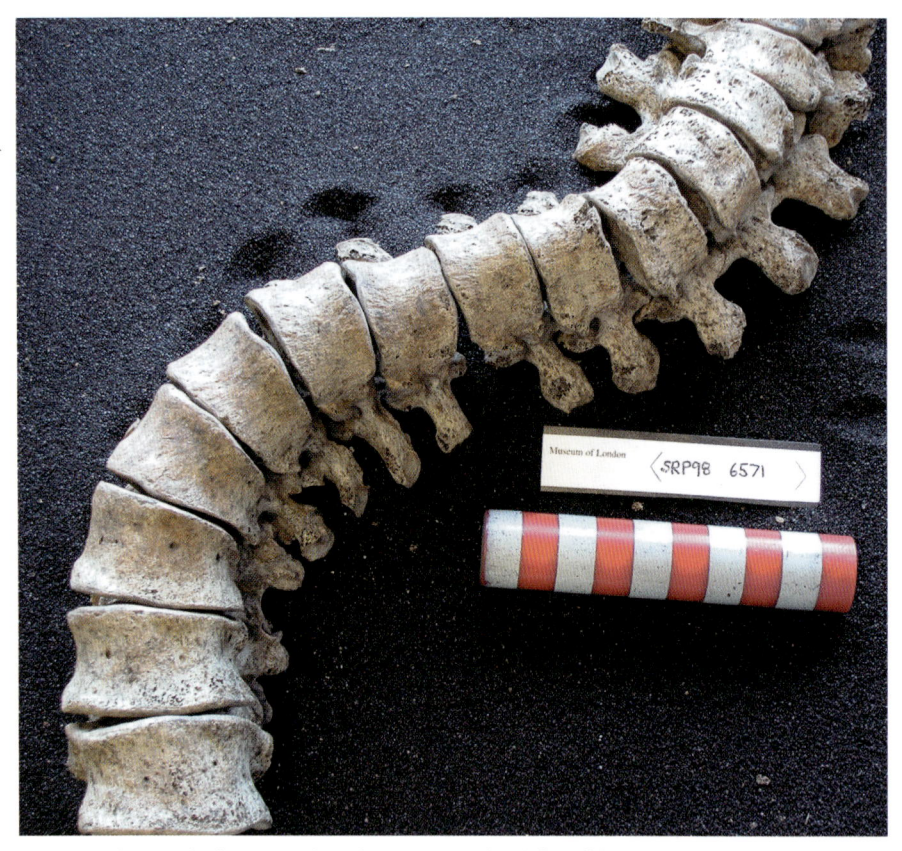

Fig 212 Scoliosis in the thoracic vertebrae of 18–25-year-old male [6571] from the attritional cemetery, period 14 (scale c 1:2)

Conclusions

Using a bioarchaeological approach to work from a clinical base to determine those conditions that could have resulted in impairment in medieval London (Roberts 2000a, 47) a range of conditions were identified, most of which affected adults over the age of 35 years. The results indicate that most of these conditions were acquired, and as such may have been understood differently by the medieval community than those of a developmental or congenital origin. In conjunction with the results of the inter-site analysis (below, 4.5) this shows that while impairing conditions existed in both rural and urban communities, urban living was more hazardous. The large sample analysed from St Mary Spital has demonstrated that many congenital and developmental conditions, often considered 'rare' within palaeopathology, were present in the medieval period and many of these individuals survived into adulthood. By examining social factors, the 'lived-experience' of these conditions can be understood in context. The osteological evidence demonstrates that many people successfully adapted to their impairment, and clinical research supports such findings. This enables us to achieve a more nuanced perspective on the medieval way of life and provides an independent assessment of communities, emphasising their heterogeneity, by providing an 'osteobiographical' insight into medieval life.

4.2 Hospitals, well-being and treatment

Don Walker

The foundation of charitable hospitals reflected the attitudes of the wealthy to the poor, who made up as much as 25% of a town's population in medieval England (Schofield and Vince 2003, 255). Donations may have come about as a result of what was regarded as both a civic and a religious duty to supply the needy with free care (Thomas 2002, 168).

While leprosy hospitals had been built away from the main areas of habitation, the charitable hospitals were frequently sited in suburban areas, often close to the town walls (Keene 1990, 118) (Fig 213). This allowed some relief from the smells and noise of the urban centres, while remaining within easy reach of the population. Hospitals were frequently located on main roads. St Mary Spital, which became one of the largest hospitals in the country, was sited on one of the most important roads in London, which led directly north out of the city, where it could offer lodging to pilgrims (Thomas et al 1997, 125).

The priory of St Mary Spital was founded to care for pilgrims and for the sick and poor of medieval London. It also catered for poor priests and retired rich people in good health, and housed orphans, widows, royal servants, canons, lay sisters and brothers, and servants, all of whom could have been buried in the cemetery, which also accepted citizens and burials from St Botolph's (Thomas et al 1997, 104–6). As in the case of other Augustinian foundations, it was primarily a religious house and as such concentrated on the spiritual well-being of inmates. It

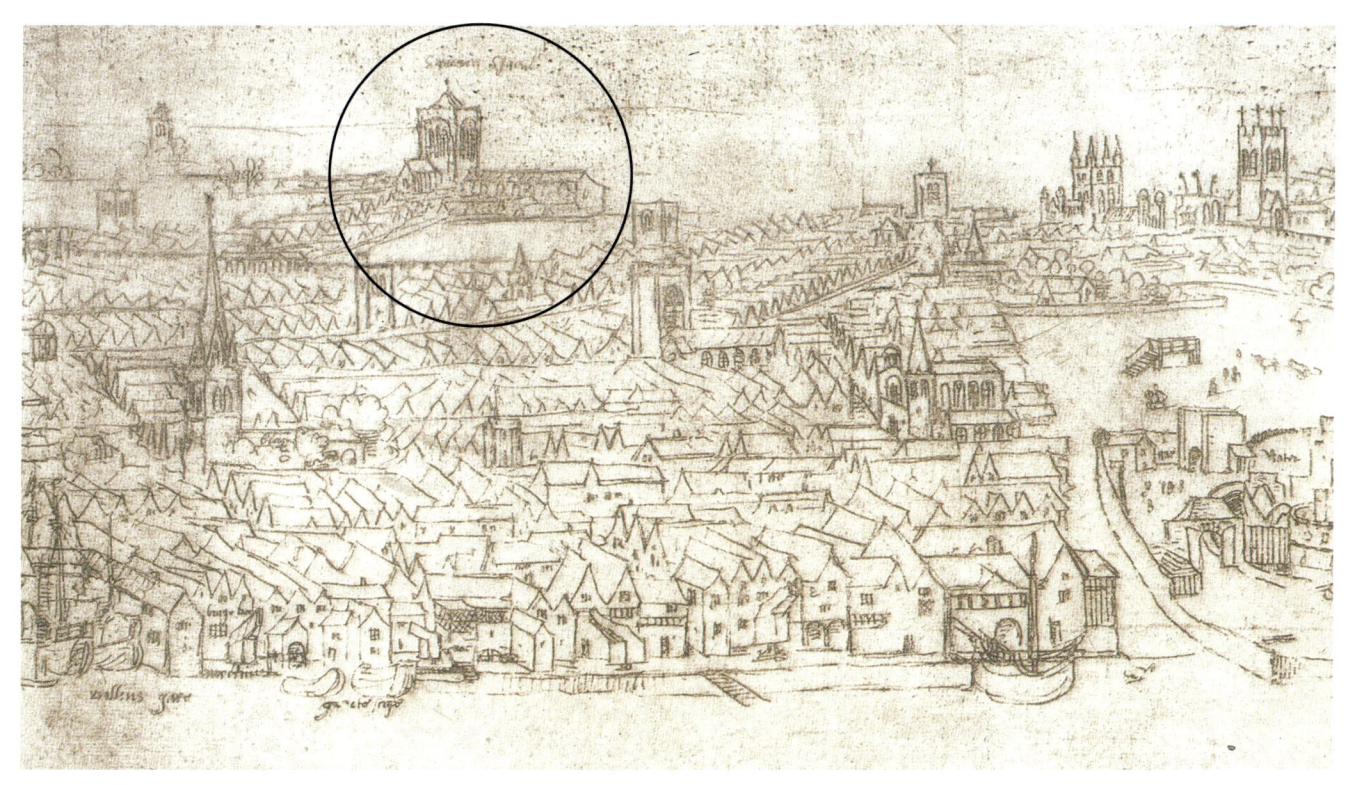

Fig 213 Detail from Wyngaerde's panorama of the city c 1540, showing St Mary Spital on the skyline (circled) (© Ashmolean Museum, University of Oxford)

also took in pregnant women, as well as the children of any mothers who did not survive, who were cared for up to the age of seven. The development of schools at similar establishments to St Mary Spital suggests that some form of education may have been provided for these children. Records from the second half of the 13th century imply that the hospital was taking in the poor overnight, and caring for the sick poor. It appears that St Mary Spital acted not only as a place to cure the sick but also as a sanctuary from the dark streets of the city (ibid, 104; Thomas 2002, 68, 98). While the poor may have been cleansed, rested and fed before being shown the gate, there is evidence from the 14th century that wealthy or well-connected elderly and disabled people were sometimes permanently retired to the priory (Orme and Webster 1995, 58, 62).

The original foundation may have been a simple rectangular hall, which could hold 12 or 13 beds. Medieval hospitals commonly assigned two or three people to each bed, so the number of actual inmates may have been far higher. The refoundation of 1235 increased the number of beds to 60, equally divided between the sexes within a 60m infirmary block. This hall formed part of a T-shaped structure that incorporated a church at its centre, splitting the infirmary into male and female sections (Figs 214–16). Beds were placed against the walls and a large central aisle allowed access for the lay sisters. The bedding was of straw covered by sheets, and the floor was constructed of clay and mortar. A door from the infirmary led out to the infirmary cemetery, a convenient exit for the recently departed (Thomas et al 1997, 103; Thomas 2002, 98–9). The proximity of the inmates to the chapel reflected the belief that without a healthy soul, the body could not recover (Horden 2007, 141).

The low rate of burial in the 1235 infirmary cemetery (A–H, OA5) – 180 burials over approximately 45 years – suggests that there may have been a slow turnover of inmates, or that care within the infirmary proved relatively successful. Alternatively, hopeless cases may have been refused admission, or those who were clearly dying may have been expelled. Medieval hospitals were not concerned with palliative care but with treatment of the soul (Rawcliffe 1999, 316). The high proportion of older subadults and young adults within this cemetery has been interpreted as reflecting a large intake of migrants and pilgrims, many of whom may have lacked immediate family support (Conheeney 1997, 223; Thomas et al 1997, 103). The recovery of a set of keys within the infirmary has led to the suggestion that the sick had their own lockers (Thomas et al 1997, 34–5, 109–10, 202–3) (Fig 217). Did this mean that the hospital expected to be looking after at least some of the inmates for long periods of time, or that the sick within were often destitute and alone with nowhere else to keep their possessions?

A new two-storey infirmary built at the end of the 13th century (about 1280) took over from the hall, which was turned into a chapel. Archaeological evidence suggests that the infirmary at St Mary Merton, an Augustinian priory in Surrey, also had a second floor, added perhaps during the 15th century, and other examples have been found at the Cistercian abbeys of Furness in Lancashire and Fountains in the West Riding of Yorkshire (Miller and Saxby 2007, 126). At St Mary Spital, each floor was probably designated as male or female, with approximately 30 beds on each level (Thomas et al 1997, 103). The north-east corner of the ground floor contained a hearth, possibly used for cooking or for the heating of herbal remedies.

St Mary Spital in context

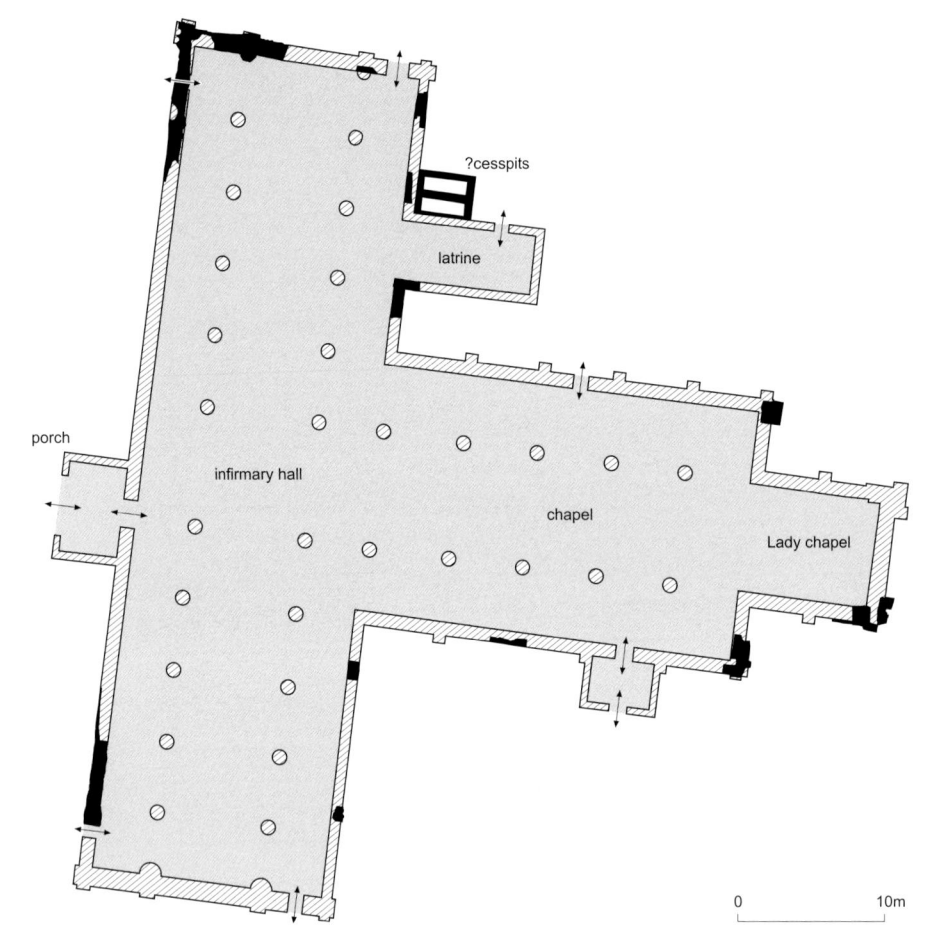

Fig 214 Plan of the infirmary block after the refoundation of St Mary Spital in 1235 (scale 1:500)

Fig 215 Suggested appearance of the infirmary and chapel at St Mary Spital c 1250, seen from the north-west

Fig 216 The 15th-century infirmary hall at the hospital at Beaune, France (Hospices de Beaune)

Fig 217 Group of small keys discarded c 1280 and thought to open infirmary lockers at St Mary Spital

No other hearths were found, although it is possible that some were constructed in order to heat the rooms and were later truncated (ibid, 48). In 1278 a new water supply was built for the hospital. The main drain served the hospital latrines and kitchen, carrying waste water westwards away from the precinct, possibly ending up at the Walbrook. Before this the latrines probably emptied into cesspits. Lighting was normally provided in infirmaries, although it appears to have been lacking in 1303 when the hospital was ordered to restore it to the building (Orme and Webster 1995, 121). Outside the infirmary a large amount of animal and fish bone was found, with plaice and herring the most numerous species of fish; the meat consisted of beef with some mutton (Thomas 2002, 99–101). Documentary records imply that the lay sisters were permitted to eat from the same kitchen that fed the sick within the hospital (Orme and Webster 1995, 121).

In the second quarter of the 14th century (c 1320–50) a two-storey extension was added on to the west side of the building, presumably to cater for increased demand (Fig 218) (Thomas 2002, 100). The hospital now had 180 beds (Thomas et al 1997, 103–5). We know that there were seven lay sisters caring for the sick in 1303, and six in 1379. They were provided with a stone house, incorporating a dormitory and refectory, which was located next to the infirmary. Even so, they were the last to be supplied with a stone building, which accords with documentary evidence implying their low rank (Thomas 2002, 150–1). Their duties included care of the poor and sick, together with domestic chores (Thomas et al 1997, 105).

By 1400 the canons' infirmary had been built. This was separate from the main hospital and had its own kitchen. It is plausible that there would have been different standards of treatment compared to the main infirmary, but osteological investigation of this is hampered by the homogeneous nature of the majority of the cemetery.

The building of the new two-storey infirmary at the end of the 13th century perhaps demonstrates that immediate contact with the church and its altar was not considered as important as before (Fig 219). This could be interpreted as a decline in the emphasis on spiritual care within the hospital (Thomas et al 1997, 115). Perhaps it was also a reflection of a rise in the importance of medical treatment in hospitals following the Black Death (Gottfried 1986, 260). Patronage was becoming ever more important to religious houses, and it may be that the inmates were removed in order to allow the dedication of family chapels. Regular confession by the chronically ill was not only for curative purposes; it was also deemed important by patrons who believed that it increased the effectiveness of intercessionary prayers for the souls of the dead (Rawcliffe 1999, 320, 327, 331–2).

In the medieval world, treatment was based on the balance of the humours and on general experience of what had or had not worked in past cases, together with magical remedies (Amulree 1964, 13). In many ways, medieval medicine in Western Europe was founded on Classical teaching: 'Christian ideas about medical science and about spiritual and physical healing were formed in late antiquity' (Siraisi 1990, 7).

The birth of rational medicine was seen in the Hippocratic treatises from around the turn of the 5th century BC. These concentrated on accurate prognosis as well as control of diet to maintain health and avoid disease. Aristotle's physical theory, employing scientific exploration and technical methodology, further influenced the development of medical models, and encouraged scientific observation in the study of illness. The anatomical observations of Galen (died c AD 200) built on the earlier studies of Herophilus and Erasistratus to produce the most important pre-Vesalian work on the subject. Galen was

Fig 218 Excavation of the north arm of the church with the infirmary hall and its extension

Hospitals, well-being and treatment

Fig 219 Plan of the church, infirmary and adjacent buildings at St Mary Spital at the time of the Dissolution (scale 1:1250)

also able to bring together all the disparate fields of Greek medicine to form a single field of study (Siraisi 1990, 1–4). The theories of Galen were studied by Islamic scholars and led to the production of works such as the *Isagoge* of Johannitus (Humayn ibn Ishaq, died *c* AD 877), which became widely available in Europe in a partly translated (Latin) form. This work included the concepts of the 'naturals' (the four elements) and the 'contra-naturals' (the causes and consequences of disease). There were also the 'non-naturals', the factors that determined health, and included everyday functions and actions such as exercise and rest, food and drink, and evacuation and repletion. Also included in the non-naturals were 'accidents of the soul', which were the emotions that emerged from within the body. Strong feelings such as anxiety or anger were to be avoided, while joy was believed to be beneficial to health. Importance was therefore attached to both the physical and emotional well-being of an individual (Horden 2007, 134–7).

The four humours, consisting of blood, phlegm, yellow bile and black bile, were a very early Greek concept involving the balancing of bodily fluids to maintain correct physical function. They were believed to play a vital role in nutrition: ingested food would be carried to the liver where it would metabolise all four humours, and the blood would then nourish the body. The complexional balance relied on the relative quantities of each fluid and determined psychological and physical well-being (Siraisi 1990, 104–6). The body was perhaps regarded as a medium through which the symptoms of different illnesses of the soul might be observed. The humoral theory of medicine remains prominent in some areas of the modern world (Rubel and Hass 1996, 118).

Horden offered three main conclusions on the role of medieval healers based on his studies of European medicine. The first was the importance of the verbal interview in which the patient would be asked a series of questions, with medical judgements made on the basis of the answers given. The second involved prognosis, where a judgement was made on what was going to happen to the patient with, or without, treatment. The third was that the importance of regimen within medieval hospitals led to a focus on preventative medicine (Horden 2007, 138). This regimen extended to the fastidious observance of religious ritual within priory hospitals. As the body was merely a housing for the soul, it was the soul that primarily required treatment. The cure was achieved through Christ the healer (*Christus medicus*), although practical methods, such as the treatment of broken bones, could be used to prevent the onset of permanent impairment (Metzler 2006, 123). Conditions that could not be successfully treated by practical medicine were considered to require miraculous intervention: 'earthly medicine and divine medicine interplayed and complemented each other' (ibid, 184).

Medicine in England was the preserve of a hierarchy of practitioners. The most important were the physicians, who were literate, of high status and used the ancient method of balancing the humours to affect cures. They worked with apothecaries to determine a healthy lifestyle and diet for wealthy patients who could afford their fees, and are unlikely to have attended free hospitals. Then there were the master-surgeons, who formed their fraternity in 1369, and their rivals the barber-surgeons, whose treatment of soldiers during the Hundred Years War led to an improvement in surgical skills and techniques. Finally there were the apothecaries, who practised pharmacology, preparing medicines based on Arabic and Greek texts (Thomas et al 1997, 106–7). Gottfried noted that London would have been relatively well served by medical practitioners compared with other towns or rural communities, and up to 50–60% of these may have been relatively inexpensive barber-surgeons, who would have carried out routine medical practices such as letting blood by leeching and cupping, cautery, the application of ointments and perhaps some bone-setting (Gottfried 1984, 169–72).

Some doctors had religious backgrounds, but surgeons and barber-surgeons came from the laity. In 1163, the Pope forbade the shedding of blood by the clergy, and the Fourth Lateran Council of 1215 ruled that those belonging to the major orders could not perform surgery or cautery (Siraisi 1990, 26; Egan 2007, 66). This suggests that blood-letting was carried out by medical practitioners. Within religious hospitals, a regular pattern of prayers, chants and masses, from matins to compline, provided a full 24-hour cycle of treatment for the soul. This devotional atmosphere was amplified by surrounding religious iconography, such as wall paintings, hangings and crosses (Rawcliffe 1999, 316–17, 322).

Rawcliffe notes that, in contrast with the practices of the great urban hospitals of France and Italy, English physicians and surgeons did not attend the poor. This was partly due to the greater organisational power of the civic authorities in these countries, when compared to the less utilitarian practices of ecclesiastical organisations such as priory hospitals (Rawcliffe 1999, 159–60). At St Mary Spital, the lay sisters were probably responsible for most of the care of inmates. However, some doctors were assigned to hospitals in London and documentary evidence implies that the surgeon Thomas Thorneton supplied free treatment at St Mary Spital between 1480 and 1525, suggesting that care of the sick poor may not always have been confined to spiritual needs alone. Dr Smyth, a prominent physician, was recorded as residing next to the priory gatehouse, and may also have attended the inmates (Gottfried 1984, 178; Thomas et al 1997, 107).

From the 13th century, nearly all surgery was carried out by surgeons and barber-surgeons, although physicians continued to practise cautery and phlebotomy (blood-letting by opening a vein) to balance the humours. The surgeon's work was more akin to a craft, in which the chief skills were the suturing and bandaging of cuts, bites, burns and swellings, and the correction of fractures and dislocations through bone-setting and manipulation. The splinting of broken bones would have required a degree of anatomical knowledge. In the 14th century strong links between France and England encouraged the flow of anatomical and surgical learning from mainland Europe, which included the works of Guy de Chauliac and Lanfranc, and by the end of the century English surgeons such as Mirfield and Arderne were writing medical treatises in Latin and English (Beck 1974, 24). The growth in technical literature in the late 14th and early 15th centuries suggests that many practitioners may have been literate, but no doubt there remained a tradition of learning by practical experience, perhaps through apprenticeship (Siraisi 1990, 20, 154–5).

Guy de Chauliac listed the essential equipment required by surgeons. This included knives, razors, lancets, cautery irons, grasping tools, probes, needles, cannulae and a tool for trepanation (Siraisi 1990, 155). No surgical instruments were found within the limited stratified deposits of the later medieval infirmary at St Mary Spital, but it is probable that medieval surgeons were not resident at hospitals (Thomas et al 1997, 111). Indeed, no examples have been found in any medieval hospital contexts from England (Egan 2007, 65).

Two 'urinals' were recovered from St Mary Spital. These vessels are used in the science of uroscopy, which involves the visual examination of the urine as a diagnostic tool (Thomas et al 1997, 111). By 1400 uroscopy played an important role at the heart of English medicine (Gottfried 1986, 178). Each variation in colour, often compared to detailed colour charts, led to a certain prognosis. In many cases, the practitioner may have used observation of the urine in preference to inspection of the patients' symptoms (Siraisi 1990, 125).

Healing and treatment

Healing is the process by which an individual is restored to health or 'made sound' (Pearsall 2002, 656). Caring for the sick and injured is a frequently encountered facet of human behaviour (Wakely 1997, 41). Technically, healing is the physiological mending of a disorder or lesion at a microscopic and macroscopic level but, as previously discussed, it is also dependent upon the subjective judgement of the affected individuals and those around them. A person may not be fully recovered and yet may feel and appear to be in good health. Alternatively, they may be fully fit but yet to display all the required culturally accepted signs of recovery (Rubel and Hass 1996, 127). The accuracy of assessments of recovery, or stage of recovery, is important because it can determine whether future treatment is deemed necessary and at what level. In other words, it was not only the original insult that may have had consequences for the life of an individual, but also the success, or otherwise, of the care administered.

Medieval treatment

Medieval treatment was based on spiritual well-being, and evidence of spiritual life was found in the cemetery at St Mary Spital in the form of eight burials containing chalices (some with patens) (Fig 220). These grave goods are believed to have accompanied members of the clergy, and perhaps carried symbolic significance in the form of protection for the dead (Gilchrist and Sloane 2005, 160). There were four burials associated with lead seals from papal *bullae*. These appear to have been clenched in the hands of the diseased, perhaps in the belief that they would ease the passage through purgatory (Thomas et al 1997, 123). Increased ownership of *bullae* and their associated documents may have been driven by a demand for charms following the onset of the Black Death (Gilchrist and Sloane 2005, 96). Seven gold coins from the reign of Henry VIII, known as 'angels', may also have had a remedial function. These coins were often donated by the king to sufferers of scrofula, or the 'king's evil' – swelling of the glands thought to have been tuberculosis of the lymph nodes. These types of finds reflect the spiritual function of religious houses rather than physical healing within hospitals (Egan 2007, 69–70, 76).

Where physical methods of treatment are concerned, the study of the methods employed, together with their level of success, allows us to examine the technological capabilities of medieval practitioners. The way in which a society treats its sick can help us to understand attitudes towards different groups of people. We need to explore the variables that may have determined the type, standard and success of treatment in medieval London, especially as individuals would have had varying levels of access to care. These variables may have included age, sex, gender and social status.

The detailed recording of skeletal samples should allow the determination of variations in treatment and care between economically and socially diverse populations. There is potential in this regard in the study of the treatment of trauma, involving both cranial injuries and post-cranial fractures. One area of interest for medieval scholars is the study of the lives of people living in the contrasting environments of the town and the country. In theory, the large number of hospitals and concentration of medical practitioners in London would have ensured that treatment was easier to come by for urban residents. However, the migration of rural peasants to the town, some with pre-existing injuries, may obscure such evidence, especially in cemeteries such as St Mary Spital, which may have contained large proportions of poor individuals (Chapter 1.2).

In terms of what we today would consider to be practical

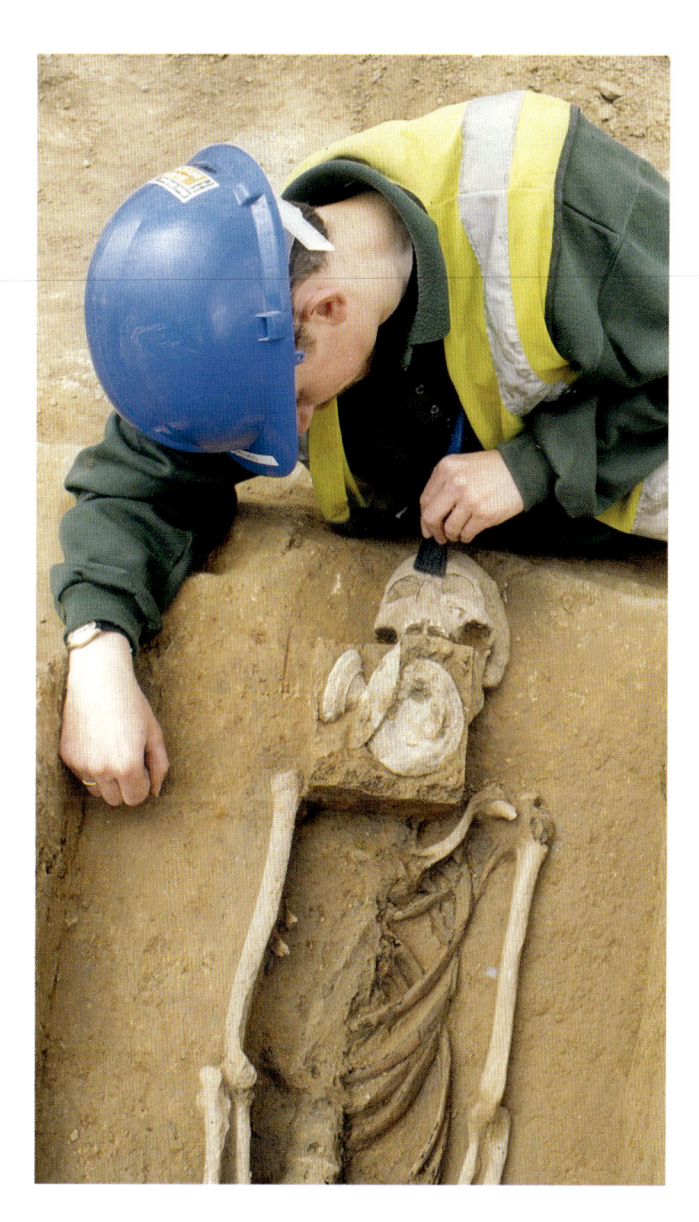

Fig 220 Individual [7652], found with chalice and paten, as excavated

medicine, most medieval therapeutic texts concentrated on surgical treatment of orthopaedic impairment, often involving the 'mending' of broken bones (Metzler 2006, 124). Fractures are subject to a number of possible complications. These include delayed union, non-union, mal-union, secondary infection, avascular necrosis, nerve injury, post-traumatic haematoma ossification and secondary osteoarthritis (Lovell 1997, 146–7). One method of examining the success of attempted treatment is through the measurement of the extent of healing in fractures at the time of death. Physical manipulation (reduction) is the method employed to set broken bones and to realign dislocations in modern medicine, and was also practised in the medieval period (Hunt 1999). Where fractured bones were well aligned, this may have resulted from splinting of the affected limb following reduction, together with the allowance of satisfactory periods of time for rest. The broken ends of the bone would then be given the chance to knit together. If the success of fracture healing can be measured in skeletal remains, it may be possible to say something about the level of treatment in the population under study, as well as any intra- or inter-population variation. In contrast, the level of pain and suffering endured by those with healing and healed fractures cannot be accurately assessed through the archaeological record (Judd and Roberts 1998, 49) (see also above, 4.1).

Long bone fracture management and healing

The attritional cemetery sample (burial type ABC) contained a higher rate of female long bone deformity (67/111: 60.4%) than male (69/156: 44.2%), a statistically significant result (Fig 221). There were no such differences in the mass burial pits (burial type D) (Fig 222). The results suggest that females in the attritional cemetery sample were more vulnerable than males to an increased frequency of deformity following long bone fracture. As the attritional sample showed no evidence of increased diversity between the sexes with regard to fracture

Table 145 Long bone deformity type (n = 550)

Deformity	No.	% of all fractures
Linear angulation	186	33.8
Rotation	20	3.6
Overlap	101	18.4
Apposition	73	13.3

location and type, the higher rate of female long bone deformity may have resulted from differential treatment. The most commonly recorded type of deformity was linear angulation. Rotational deformity was rare (Table 145).

Deformity was recorded in half of all fractured long bones (279/550: 50.7%). The femur (17/23: 73.9%) and radius (82/119: 68.9%) displayed the highest rates of deformity. Of these, unsuccessful healing (as defined by Grauer and Roberts 1996, 535) was found in 8.5% (47/550) of long bone fractures. The tibia (17/81: 21.0%) and femur (4/23: 17.4%) were most commonly affected, while the ulna (6/172: 3.5%) was found to be the bone that healed most successfully (Fig 223).

There could be a number of reasons why the tibia and femur were most likely to heal unsuccessfully. Shortening and displacement of the femur could be caused by the strong pulling action of the surrounding quadriceps and hamstring muscles, which may contract following fracture. This can result in difficulties in reduction of the bone. In modern clinical treatment such problems are normally remedied by traction of the leg (McRae 2003, 410). Although Guy de Chauliac recorded a method of femur extension through traction, using a pulley system with a cord attached to a lead weight, these facilities may not have been available to many of those buried at St Mary Spital, leaving them with crippling deformity for the remainder of their lives (Beck 1974, 25). However, there are two examples of well-aligned complete fractures of the femoral

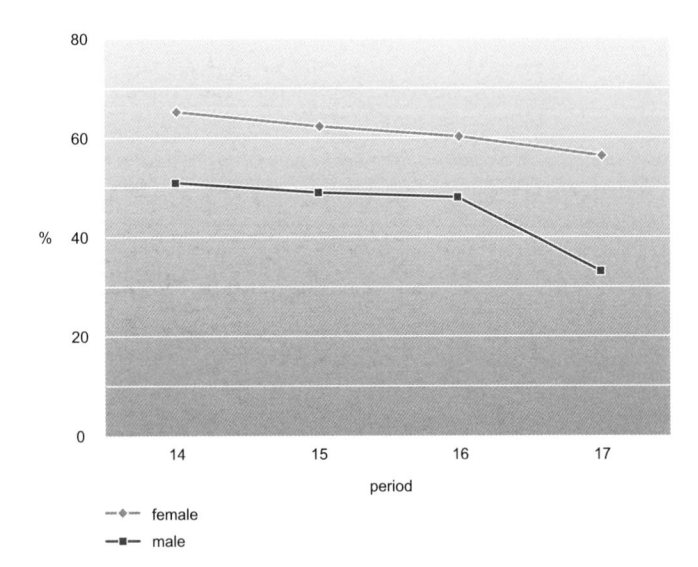

Fig 221 Proportion of long bone fractures with deformities in the attritional cemetery by period

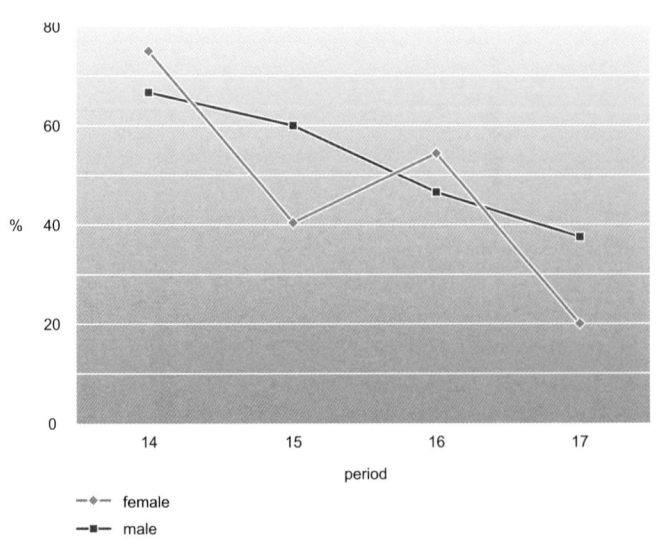

Fig 222 Proportion of long bone fractures with deformities in the catastrophic cemetery by period

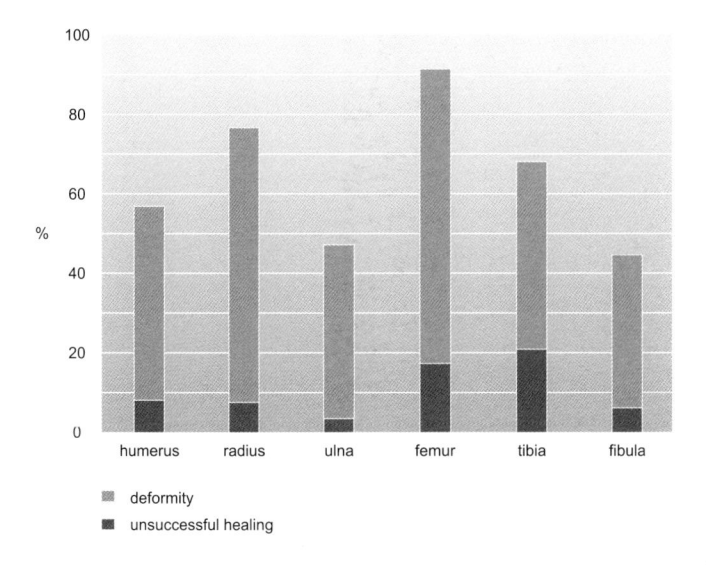

Fig 223 Rates of unsuccessful healing of united fractures in long bones

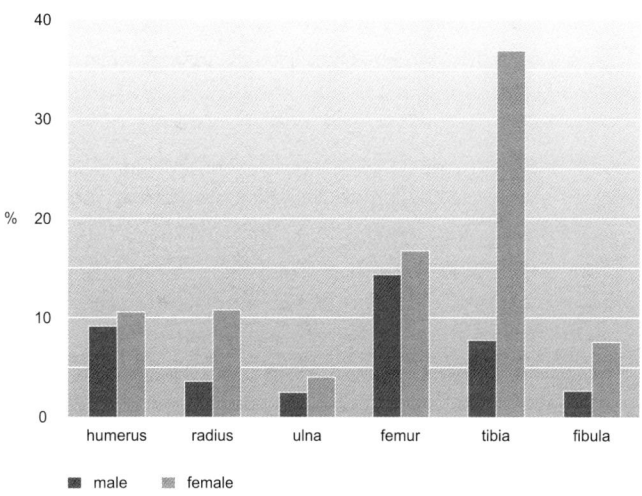

Fig 224 Rates of unsuccessful healing of united long bone fractures by sex

shaft in early middle-aged males [20325] and [31483] from the period 15 (*c* 1200–50) mass burial pits.

The healing of tibial fractures may have suffered in comparison to other bones due to the function of the bone and to a lack of immobilisation of sufferers. An individual could walk without causing serious damage to a healing arm bone. However, weight placed on a tibia through walking before full healing could lead to permanent displacement. The Italian surgeon Theoderic (1205–98) stated that the healing of tibial fractures was problematical (Metzler 2006, 112). As modern tibial fractures take an average of 16 weeks simply to unite, one might expect to find well-healed fractures only in those who could afford to spend so long off their feet. The least affected bones, the ulna (6/172: 3.5%) and the fibula (5/81: 6.2%), are both paired, and it is possible that they were anatomically splinted by the radius and tibia respectively.

Of the long bone fractures affecting females, 12.3% (29/235) were unsuccessfully healed. This compared with 5.1% (14/276) of male fractures, a statistically significant difference by sex. As with deformity, the attritional cemetery revealed a higher rate of unsuccessful healing in females (17/111: 15.3%) than males (7/156: 4.5%), a statistically significant result. The distribution by bone suggests that females were especially affected in the tibia, fibula and radius. The femur was equally affected in males and females, possibly due to the inherent problems in fracture reduction in this bone (Fig 224).

When the relative proportions of the types of deformity leading to unsuccessful healing in each long bone were examined, it was clear that there was variation between the bones. Rotational deformity was found only in the forearm and femur, while the humerus and tibia suffered equally from overlap and linear angulation. The fibula was affected only by overlap. It is probable that these results were a product of a number of variables. These include the variation in biomechanical stresses applicable to different areas of the skeleton, and specifically to each bone. For example, the location and musculature of a bone may make it less vulnerable to severe rotation. It is also possible that the specific types of fracture to which people were most vulnerable in medieval towns were most likely to cause certain forms of deformation in certain bones. Another factor might be the ease with which different bones could be manipulated back into normal alignment and apposition, without access to modern surgical procedures such as internal fixation (Fig 225).

While there was little overall difference between males and females in the rates of deformity of healed fractures, female fractures were more likely to heal unsuccessfully. Females were therefore at increased risk of loss of function, or loss of correct function, in damaged limbs. This suggests that, for whatever reason, women were less able to recuperate fully from fractures. It is possible that men had increased access to treatment and care, or that they were able to take more time away from activities that risked compromising the healing process. In the latter case, this would have implications for the study of culturally defined gender roles, either in the domestic or work environment.

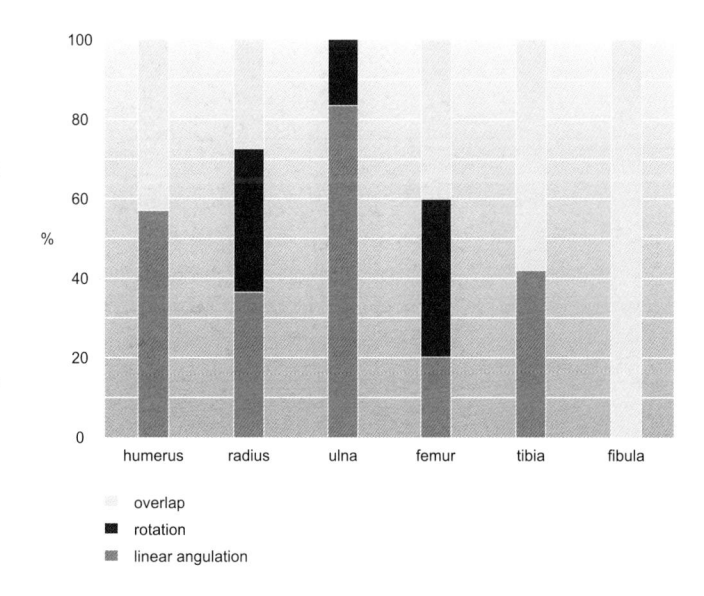

Fig 225 Types of deformity resulting from unsuccessful healing

The overall pattern exhibited a low rate of unsuccessful healing in fractured long bones (8.5%), although 50.7% displayed some sign of deformity. This suggests that fracture treatment was available to the majority of individuals within the burial sample, whether through immobilisation of the affected limb, or through more proactive care such as manipulation and splinting. Most people who suffered long bone fracture regained good function.

Medieval hospitals were expected to bury those who died while in their care and it is likely that some areas of the cemetery at St Mary Spital contained individuals who were inmates at the hospital, either at the time of their death or at some other period in their lives (Gilchrist and Sloane 2005, 63). We do not know where they were buried so we cannot distinguish them from other inhumations. However, there was evidence of variation by sex in the rates of long bone fracture deformity and healing success between the attritional and mass burial samples. Such differences may reflect more egalitarian access to treatment for individuals buried in the mass pits, but this does not preclude the possibility that admission and treatment policies at the hospital resulted in increased female fracture deformity within the attritional cemetery.

The majority of individuals buried in the much earlier infirmary cemetery in Open Area 5 may have been hospital inmates, but the sample size was too small (n = 101) for any meaningful comparison with the main cemetery (Thomas et al 1997, 222).

When examined over time, the rate of bone fracture deformity fell from period 14 (*c* 1120–*c* 1200) (27/45: 60%) to period 17 (*c* 1400–1539) (32/83: 38.5%), and the rate of unsuccessful healing fell from 15.6% (7/45) of long bone fractures in period 14 to 4.8% (4/83) in period 17 (Chapter 3.8). This suggests that there may have been a gradual improvement in standards of fracture treatment and care over time. The archaeological evidence suggests that none of the burials in the main cemetery from period 14 were hospital inmates, and in this case we might expect to find a lower level of successful treatment. However, there would also have been a lack of inmate burials in the cemetery before the building of the second infirmary at St Mary Spital *c* 1280, when the 1235 infirmary cemetery in Open Area 5 was closed (Thomas et al 1997, 47). As period 15 ended *c* 1250, we might therefore have expected to find similar levels of unsuccessful treatment in the first two periods, and then an improvement in period 16 (*c* 1250–*c* 1400) when hospital inmates began to be buried within the cemetery. As there is no apparent evidence of a direct association between hospital inmates and improved fracture treatment, and there is no reason to believe that St Mary Spital was specifically involved in fracture care, it appears that there was a general improvement in fracture treatment over time in those buried within the cemetery (Fig 226).

The frequency of unsuccessful healing by sex suggested that there were similar standards of care for males and females in period 14, and that these improved over time for men but not for women. However, these results were based on sample sizes that were too small to test statistically (Fig 227).

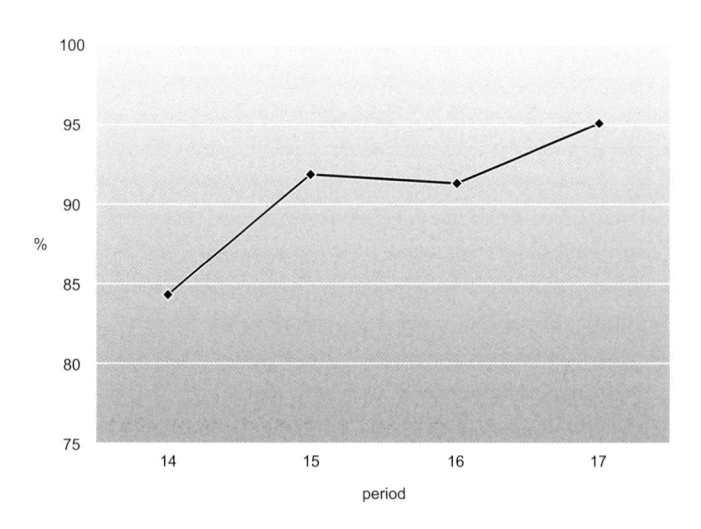

Fig 226 Successful healing of united long bone fractures by period

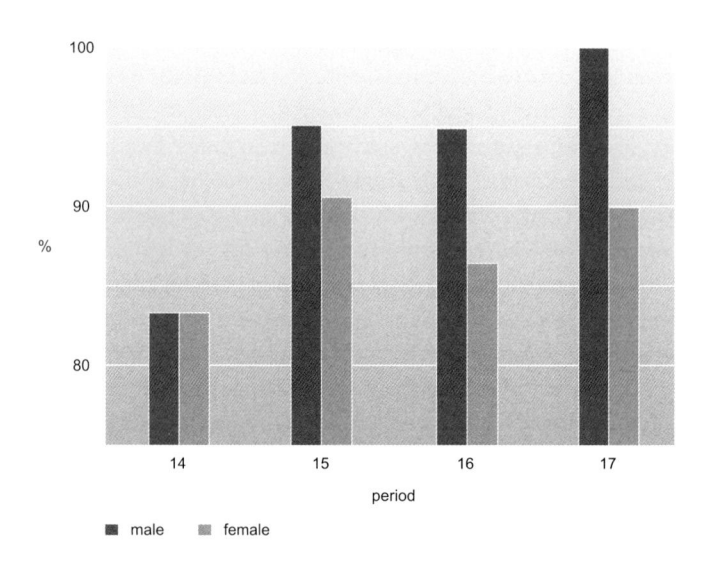

Fig 227 Successful healing of united long bone fractures by sex and period

The hospital cared for pilgrims and the sick and poor of London and, while there is no evidence that it refused admittance to individuals who suffered acute traumatic injury, the latter may not have been part of the typical intake. The level of orthopaedic provision within the hospital is unknown, and individuals who suffered fracture may often have been treated elsewhere. Records from medieval Europe reveal the existence of specialist bone-setters and barber-surgeons who practised fracture reduction (Grauer and Roberts 1996, 539). However, the lay sisters themselves may have been skilled at this form of treatment. When similar data become available for other sites in London, it should be possible to measure the relative success of fracture treatment between different types of urban cemetery samples, and between urban and rural samples. This may tell us how widespread effective treatment had become by the medieval period.

Grauer and Roberts note that several factors might complicate the study of healing in fractures, especially when comparison is made with modern clinical data. There might be variation in healing times between different populations due to varying levels of nourishment and health. For example, a poor diet may result in a reduced capacity to heal successfully. In addition, simple fractures that were not deformed at the time of injury may be mistaken for fractures that had been efficiently set (Grauer and Roberts 1996, 535).

It is clear that the results of this analysis give only an approximation of the amount of deformity and standards of treatment within the St Mary Spital sample. Caution must be exercised in the interpretation of the data, as the correct degree of deformity could not be accurately determined in the absence of radiographs. However, the data do suggest that male long bone fractures healed with more success than female fractures. This was not the result of variation in fracture type or location: statistically significant differences in overall long bone fracture rates between the sexes were found only in the humerus, where male bones were more frequently affected, and there was no significant variation in long bone fracture type. When fracture mechanism was analysed, a greater number of female ulnae were found with direct injuries to the mid and distal shafts. This result was statistically significant. However, the ulna was the least deformed long bone, so the high female prevalence would not have increased the rate of unsuccessful healing. This suggests that males may have had better access to treatment than females.

In general, the management of fractures appears to have improved over the period of use of the cemetery. The paucity of evidence of peri-mortem fracture (5/5387: 0.1%) suggests that death rarely resulted from bone fracture alone, or from related infection of open fractures. In the absence of antibiotic remedies, the risk of death from open fracture would have been higher than today and perhaps this indicates that there were treatments that increased the chances of survival, such as the removal of bone splinters and the suturing of open wounds (Clark 1937, 51). Only 1.2% (28/2394) of all fractures at St Mary Spital were found to be associated with infectious change, a surprisingly low frequency which may indicate that compound fractures were rare. The tibia was the long bone most commonly affected by infection secondary to fracture, both for periostitis and osteomyelitis, which suggests that it was the most vulnerable bone for compound fracture and the resultant invasion of bacteria beneath the skin (Fig 228).

Fracture complications

Approximately half of all long bone fractures at St Mary Spital were subject to at least minimal deformity, with linear deformity the most commonly identified type (186/550: 33.8%). Overlap of broken ends was identified in 18.4% (101/550) of long bone fractures (Table 145). At St Mary Merton, Surrey, 41.9% (36/86) of individuals with bone fractures were left with malalignment (Miller and Saxby 2007, 270). The low level of unsuccessful healing due to deformity at St Mary Spital (47/550: 8.5%) when compared to the cemetery at St Helen-on-the-Walls in York (16/41: 39.0%) was reflected in the prevalence of secondary osteoarthritis at each site (St Mary Spital 31/550:

Fig 228 Medial view of the fractured tibia of ≥46-year-old male [22429] with secondary osteomyelitis from the catastrophic cemetery, period 16 (scale c 1:1)

5.6%; St Helen-on-the-Walls 16/41: 39.0%) (Grauer and Roberts 1996, 537). While no extreme examples of shortening of affected limbs due to overlap of fractured ends were found at St Helen-on-the-Walls, 26.8% (11/41) of long bones there exhibited unsuccessful healing due to linear deformity, a far higher rate than that found at St Mary Spital (22/550: 4.0%).

At the leprosy hospital of St James and St Mary Magdalene in Chichester, Sussex, linear deformity leading to unsuccessful healing was found in 16.7% (5/30) of fractured long bones, with 30.0% (9/30) suffering secondary osteoarthritis (Judd and Roberts 1998, 48). This evidence, together with that from St Mary Spital, suggests that individuals buried in hospital cemeteries had received higher standards of fracture treatment. However, it may also reflect an admissions policy that largely excluded purely traumatic injuries. Whatever the case, the study of fracture healing suggests that basic immobilisation of limbs was practised within even the poor communities of London.

Evidence of localised periosteal reaction was far more common on the fractured long bones of individuals from St Helen-on-the-Walls (13/41: 31.7%) and St James and St Mary Magdalene (10/30: 33.3%) than at St Mary Spital (17/550: 3.1%), though one might expect to find more evidence of infection in a sample of inmates from a leprosy hospital (Grauer and Roberts 1996, 537; Judd and Roberts 1998, 48). A low rate of infection secondary to fracture suggests that the majority of fractures were closed or that treatment may have helped to reduce the chances of bacterial infection. At St Mary Merton, 7.0% (6/86) of individuals with fractured bones were recorded as suffering secondary infection (Miller and Saxby 2007, 270).

Severely fractured or poorly aligned bones are vulnerable to non-union, especially when a limb is not immobilised for sufficient time to allow the broken bones to knit together. Union may also be prevented or delayed by the intrusion of soft tissue between the fractured bone ends (Lovell 1997, 147). Within the cemetery, 3.3% (79/2394) of all fractures were non-united. The ulna was the most commonly involved long bone.

It is vulnerable to failed union, even if the fracture is not displaced, due to rotational stresses within the forearm which can lead to late slippage if movement is not adequately restricted for a sufficient period of time (Lovell 1997, 161; Dandy and Edwards 1998, 204; McRae 2003, 308). Theoderic emphasised the problems of effective reduction of ulna fractures (Metzler 2006, 111). At St Mary Spital, the evidence is somewhat contradictory, in that united ulna fractures were most likely to heal successfully when compared with the other long bones, yet they were also most vulnerable to non-union. In patients today, full arm casts are required in order to hold the arm immobilised and in flexion until the broken ends fuse (Dandy and Edwards 1998, 204). The high prevalence may have resulted from insufficient knowledge of this risk, especially as non-union may not have been evident in non-displaced fractures. It may also have been due to inadequate periods of immobilisation. There was no evidence of change in the rate of non-union in ulnae or any other bones throughout the use of the cemetery, and there were no discernible differences between the attritional sample and that from the mass burial pits (Fig 229).

Some fractures can cause temporary or permanent failure in the supply of blood to a section of bone, where cellular death can lead to bony collapse. This is known as avascular necrosis, and is most often found in the epiphyses where there is limited blood supply to the subchondral bone. This causes breakdown in the bone's trabecular structure, and death of the articular cartilage due to nutrient deficiency (Lovell 1997, 146). At St Mary Spital, only four examples of avascular necrosis secondary to fracture were identified (4/2394: 0.2% of all fractured bones). Three of these were located in the humeral head and may have caused pain and dysfunction in the shoulder joint. In the absence of modern surgical techniques such as joint replacement, the treatment of necrosis would probably have been restricted to attempts to tackle the symptoms. However, no evidence of this survived with the affected individuals.

Possible evidence of nerve damage secondary to fracture was found in five individuals (5/2394: 0.2% of all fractures). Three of these were identified through the presence of Charcot joints in the hand bones. There was also a severe fracture of the fourth sacral vertebra that may have affected the sacral nerves, possibly leading to incontinence. A long oblique fracture to the distal shaft of the right humerus of 26–35-year-old [29384] displayed evidence of radial nerve damage. This took the form of a sharp-edged notch in the proximity of the fracture, which may have resulted in compromised nerve function. Associated hypervascularity suggested that the fracture may have been open, and the long oblique fracture line would have extended the length of time required for union. However, the bone was well healed and aligned (with approximately 10° posterior angulation) with full apposition. This may be evidence of successful treatment of a fracture.

It is probable that some of the individuals who displayed multiple and severe trauma would have suffered associated soft tissue injuries that included neural damage. However, in the absence of evidence of muscle atrophy directly associated with bone fracture it is difficult to prove. As in the case of avascular necrosis, nerve damage would not have been directly treatable, although sufficient immobilisation would have assisted in the repair of temporary damage.

In medieval London, survival for some depended on the charity and care of others. Many of the charitable hospitals were founded to care for those who did not have the means or ability to house or feed themselves, so those who were not cared for within the family may have sought help at institutions such as St Mary Spital. These may have included individuals with congenital diseases that caused crippling changes to the body. Injuries could also lead to loss of bodily function, which could sometimes affect the ability to live by independent means (above, 4.1).

A 26–35-year-old probable female [14250] from the period 16 attritional cemetery had sustained possible sharp force injury to the right frontal bone that may have resulted from interpersonal violence (Walker 2001). The injury showed extensive healing, although sequestrum was present on the inner cranial table posterior to the right orbit and nasal bone. Above the right orbit there was an oblique line that ran from the orbital margin to the mid portion of the frontal bone. This fracture was associated with two lacunae that penetrated the

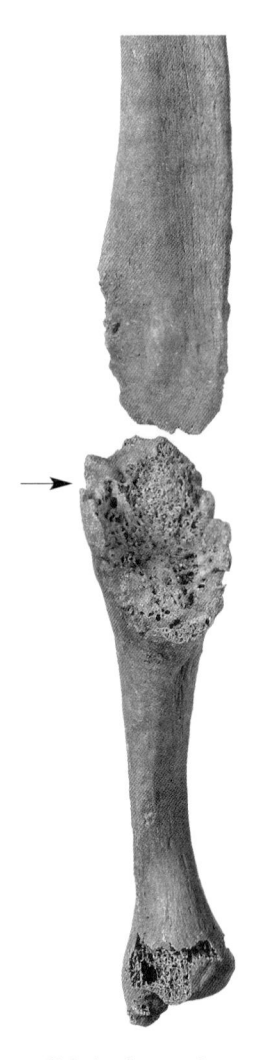

Fig 229 Non-union of left ulna fracture of 36–45-year-old male [23722] from the catastrophic cemetery, period 14 (scale c 1:1)

cranial tables. The orbital roof had a distinct plaque-like layer of remodelling smooth lamellar bone located on its medial aspect, adjacent to the nasal area. This injury may have been caused by sharp force trauma from a weapon such as a sword, which penetrated both tables of the cranium. The blow had sufficient strength to open up the frontal bone and prevent it from uniting during a lengthy healing period that may have taken many months. Treatment of this type of injury would have been required to prevent death from infection of the bone or soft tissue. This may have included the removal of bone splinters from the endocranium. Although the fracture was healed, evidence of remaining infection up to the time of death suggests that serious complications remained. If full healing of the soft tissue were compromised, the wound would have remained vulnerable to new infections. This individual would have been severely scarred and possibly blind in the right eye, but the fact that she survived long enough for the fracture to heal suggests that she may have received treatment and care.

A 26–35-year-old male [29693] from the period 16 mass burial pits exhibited a long curvilinear healed fracture on the ectocranial surface of the left frontal bone. For the majority of its length the lesion was sagittally orientated, and towards its posterior end there was a long sub-oval area where both tables of the cranium had been fully penetrated. The anterior end of the fracture cut the left orbit as far down as the junction of the frontal bone with the orbital plate of the ethmoid. Throughout the length of the lesion, the part of the frontal bone on the lateral side of the wound had been depressed in comparison with that on the medial side. This suggests that before healing the original lesion may have penetrated both cranial tables, in effect splitting open the frontal bone. The amount of force required to inflict such a wound may also have been responsible for the fracture of six teeth, one of which had been broken off level with the top of the alveolar process (Fig 230).

Fig 230 Sharp force injury to the cranial vault of 26–35-year-old male [29693] from the catastrophic cemetery, period 16 (scale c 1:2)

The shape and size of the cleft in the cranium suggest that sharp force trauma was applied with considerable downward force, from an anterior direction. Such a wound might be produced by a thick-bladed sword or an axe, and would carry a high risk of haemorrhage, infection, brain damage and shock. It would have left the individual with a very large and obvious scar on the forehead, with probable blindness in the left eye. This type of impairment was recognised as a possible consequence of accidental trauma or of battle injury, but the medical texts did not proffer treatments, as it was clear that none would have restored sight to the individual (Metzler 2006, 101). Frontal brain injury may have led to permanent psychological damage, with serious implications for the continuing care of someone who may have suffered a loss in communication and organisational skills, or even have become totally unresponsive. Damage to the frontal lobe of the brain may also have caused retrograde amnesia and behavioural difficulties. Modern treatment of traumatic brain injury normally involves stabilisation, sometimes followed by surgery to repair blood vessels and brain tissue (NINDS 2002). While individual [29693] would not have had access to this level of reparative care, he managed to survive the original injury together with any infections that may have followed. The evidence suggests that treatment was required in the case of this individual, and that it was successful, although continuing care may have been necessary for the remainder of his life.

We have already discussed how long bone fractures may provide us with evidence of treatment in medieval London. At St Mary Spital there were also examples of severe fracture in other areas of the post-cranial skeleton. Traumatic changes in a ≥46-year-old probable male [12388] from the period 16 attritional cemetery consisted of a well-healed transverse fracture of the left ilium, with clear cortical disruption on the ventral surface. There was good apposition and no evidence of infection, angulation or rotation. This type of injury, known as a Duverney fracture, can be produced by high-energy trauma such as a fall from height, and can take up to 5 months to heal successfully. This individual must therefore have been immobile for a prolonged period, during which he would have required care (Resnick 2002, 2908–17). There was also a well-healed fracture of the left tibia that may or may not have been contemporary with the iliac injury.

It is possible for individuals to recover naturally from severe injuries, as long as they are allowed sufficient time to rest and none of the possible associated complications prove fatal (Wakely 1997, 35). The survival of an injury is not itself proof of treatment, and this makes the recovery of evidence of care from archaeological remains especially significant.

The therapeutic use of metal plates

Occasionally, non-skeletal signs of treatment accompanied evidence of injury. A 36–45-year-old male [2570] from the period 15 attritional cemetery was found to have bony fusion between the distal ends of the tibia and fibula at the left ankle. The articular surfaces of the talocrural joint were dense and eburnated, and had undergone severe contour change. There was also a large vertical groove on the posterior surface of the medial malleolus, at the location of the inferior transverse ligament. The secondary osteoarthritis and ligament strain probably resulted from continued use of a damaged ankle. The distal shaft of the fibula had suffered an oblique fracture, probably associated with rupture of the tibio-fibular and medial ligaments, leading to tibio-fibular diastasis (separation). This type of injury could have been caused by a fall on to the foot, and would have required the individual to be immobilised for sufficient time to allow all the elements to heal. The diastasis and resulting secondary joint disease demonstrate that the injury was either not correctly reduced or that the individual used his left ankle before full healing. Green staining was evident on the anterior surface of the medial malleolus, possibly a remnant of a copper-alloy plate that was employed to stabilise the joint. If so, this was perhaps an example of therapeutic action taken to compensate for the effects of a lack of success in the original treatment. Evidence suggests that medieval medical practitioners were aware of the remedial properties of copper (Roberts and Manchester 2005, 130). The plate would have supported the ankle and allowed the individual to use his left leg, but it did not prevent the onset of severe secondary osteoarthritis.

A ≥46-year-old adult female [1961] from the period 16 attritional cemetery also had a healed oblique fracture of the distal shaft of the left fibula. The medial aspect of the distal shaft of the left tibia exhibited a green stain, just above the level of the fracture. This may also represent an attempt to stabilise a weakened ankle. However, the presence of green staining on bone is not a rarity at St Mary Spital, and stray copper-alloy objects in the burial soil must also be considered as a possible cause.

Three examples of metal objects that may have been used for remedial purposes were found within the cemetery (3/5387: 0.1% of individuals). The first was a copper-alloy oval plate (90 × 57mm) (<2678>) with a series of holes along the edges (Fig 231). It was arched in section, and contained textile fibres and possibly leather within the corrosion products of its outer surface. The inner surface contained traces of what may have been leaves, and it is possible that it was applied as a dressing treatment, which was held in place by a leather thong (G Egan, pers comm). The sheet was found between the knees of 36–45-year-old male [12441] from the period 14 attritional cemetery. Although there were no pathological changes in the lower limb bones of this individual, it is possible that this copper-alloy plate was used for purposes of treatment. It may have been employed to support a medicinal dressing, on a limb that had suffered soft tissue injury or infection. There is a possibility that the plate was replaceable and therefore capable of long-term use (Egan 2007, 71). Alternatively, it may have functioned as a brace to support the knee following ligament or cartilage damage. At the Gilbertine monastery of St Andrew Fishergate in York, an older adult male was found with septic arthritis secondary to severe trauma in the right knee; damage to the anterior cruciate ligament had led to joint laxity and would have left the individual with a limp. The copper-alloy plates may have been applied to support the knee while walking. As with individual [12441], eyelets were cut around the margins of the plates and leather was noted within the corrosion products (Knüsel et al 1995, 380–1). Hallbäck reported the discovery of an almost pure copper plate from Varnhem Abbey in Sweden that was used to stabilise a possible sword or axe wound on a humerus. Copper has antibacterial properties, but it may have been used in this case for its combined strength and flexibility (Hallbäck 1976–7, 80).

Individual [7186], a 26–35-year-old probable female from the period 16 attritional cemetery, was found with lead sheeting (<1312>) around her right shin (Fig 232). Originally a large, rolled rectangular sheet, with the edges folded inward to form an approximate oval (c 216 × 125mm), this large plate contained brownish hairs, possibly from an animal, on its inner surface. It may have been employed as a means of retaining medication close to a diseased limb (G Egan, pers comm). However, the possible use of animal hair within a poultice suggests either that there was a lack of awareness of the risk of infection or that some other form of medicine, possibly involving magic, was at play. Pathological changes in the skeleton included active periostitis on the long bones of both legs. This may simply be coincidental, or it may be evidence of treatment of a chronic non-specific infection that was unresolved at death. Lead was associated with cooling and drying properties, and was used to treat inflammation and to dry up the humours (Culpeper 1653). The size of the sheet suggests that a large area of the shin required treatment, possibly for infection of the soft tissue surrounding the inflamed periosteum. Examples of treatment of the shins of monks are commonly described in the infirmarers' rolls from the Benedictine monastery at Westminster Abbey (Amulree 1964, 19). Tibial periostitis was frequently encountered at St Mary Spital (1507/7453: 20.2% true prevalence rate), although we do not know to what extent these lesions resulted in clinical symptoms.

Fig 231 Copper-alloy plate <2678>, with a possible therapeutic use, found between the knees of 36–45-year-old male [12441] from the attritional cemetery, period 14 (scale 1:1)

Fig 232 Lead sheeting <1312> around the right shin of 26–35-year-old female [7186] from the attritional cemetery, period 16 (0.5m scale)

A further sub-oval convex sheet (60 × 53mm) of copper alloy (<2973>) was discovered within the period 17 burial soil. The corrosion products on both sides contained plain-woven fabric (G Egan, pers comm). It is possible that this was originally used for the application of medical treatment, and would be the first post-Black Death example of its type to be found in a medieval cemetery in Britain (Gilchrist and Sloane 2005, 104). However, this sheet is not securely dated.

Similar examples of the use of copper-alloy plates in the apparent treatment of disorders of the upper and lower limbs have been found in other medieval cemeteries (Wells 1964; Janssens 1987; Knüsel et al 1995; Gilchrist and Sloane 2005, 103–4). At St Mary Spital the burial ground was not always exclusively reserved for the bodies of those who resided within the priory, and one of the treated individuals [12441] (a 36–45-year-old male) from period 14 had died before the founding of the hospital. At least four of the five individuals with evidence of treatment with metal fittings were found in the attritional cemetery; none has been attributed to the mass burial pits. This might suggest that a higher standard of care was available to certain groups of people in London, although there may have been other forms of poultice or brace that employed less durable materials, which were less likely to survive. At St Mary Merton a copper-alloy object, which may have been used as a medical support plate to treat osteochondritis dissecans of the knee, was found with an older adult male [2595], while a possible hernia belt was discovered with individual [2105] (Miller and Saxby 2007, 102, 128).

Other evidence of treatment

Important epidemiological evidence for an increase in the prevalence of treponematosis in the 15th century was recovered from the skeletal analysis of St Mary Spital. Although there were earlier cases, they may have been quite rare and were possibly confused with better-known diseases such as leprosy. During the course of period 17, syphilis emerged as a recognised disease, and along with this recognition came attempts to affect a cure. Skin diseases such as scabies were often treated with mercury combined with heat treatment to aid absorption (Arrizabalaga et al 1997, 30, 138). It is possible that this type of treatment was attempted on skin lesions associated with syphilis. There is evidence that ointment 'laced' with mercury was prescribed as a remedy by the end of the 16th century (Boehrer 1990, 201).

It is possible that a number of individuals with treponemal disease were cared for at St Mary Spital, but we cannot determine whether they received different forms of treatment from the other inmates. Blood-letting and cauterisation were employed to treat syphilis sufferers in the 16th century, but these methods were also used for just about every other ailment (Arrizabalaga et al 1997, 29; Porter 1997, 75).

Past studies of medieval medicine have emphasised the importance of superstition and magic, but Van Arsdall (2007) challenged the emphasis by citing the evidence of surviving texts, which revealed a strong botanical background based on Classical learning. Roger of Parma's *Surgery* (*c* 1180), which described and illustrated the use of plants for medicinal purposes, was one example (Hunt 1999, 59). Phytotherapy, involving the application of herbal or botanical remedies, is now a long-established complementary medical treatment. There is sufficient evidence to believe that many of the medieval remedies would have proved physiologically beneficial; and any accompanying charms or prayers would not have diminished their effect and indeed may have been of psychological benefit. In fact, the folklore associated with plants may have aided the recollection of recommended applications that helped to ensure a favourable outcome (Van Arsdall 2007, 195–8). Other remedies would not have proved successful, such as the strong-smelling spices carried on the person or in the

St Mary Spital in context

clothes as one of the precautions against the 'bad airs' that were thought to spread plague (Siraisi 1990, 129).

By 1293, London apothecaries had their own distinct trade and were recognised in city records (Matthews 1967, 26). Medieval botanical texts rarely contained detailed descriptions of the uses of medicinal plants, but these texts were probably for reference only, and most practical information would have been passed on by teaching and apprenticeship (Van Arsdall 2007, 200). Two apothecaries were tenants at St Mary Spital: Richard Hakedy in 1455 and John Matthew in 1515. It is possible that they were using the hospital gardens, and perhaps other land to the east of the priory and in the outer precinct, to prepare medicine to treat the inmates (Thomas et al 1997, 107, 178). Plants and herbs could be employed in a wide range of treatments for the sick, such as in the preparation of ointments, laxatives, diuretic purges and soporific sponges. A large number of plants used in medieval remedies, together with many of their seeds, were found at St Mary Spital. These included henbane (*Hyoscyamus niger*), a powerful sedative, and wild cabbage (*Brassica oleracea*), which was used for illnesses such as gout and rheumatism. Common mallow (*Malva sylvestris*), often employed in poultices, was also found, along with many other plants that could potentially have been used in medicine. However, the cultivation of particular species for medicinal purposes is difficult to prove if they could also occur naturally or be grown for dietary consumption (Thomas et al 1997, 114). Davis suggests that a number of plants recovered from the area of the prior's garden may have been grown specifically for medicinal use (Davis in prep). These include borage (*Borago officinalis*), which was used to treat melancholy, madness and hypochondria, and catmint (*Nepeta cataria*), which was employed in obstetrics and gynaecological medicine. Borage flowers may also have been added to a cordial for the treatment of heart and lung conditions in the chronically sick (Culpeper 1653). Hyssop (*Hyssopus officinale*), which was used as a treatment for bruising and throat disorders, was also identified, together with alexanders (*Smyrnium olusatrum*), parsley (*Petroselinum crispum*), feverfew (*Tanacetum parthenium*), pot marigold (*Calendula officinalis*), hop (*Humulus lupulus*) and opium poppy (*Papaver somniferum*) (Fig 233) (Davis in prep). The petals of marigolds when added to vinegar were believed to cure smallpox, measles, scrofula and toothache, while opium poppy in syrup or boiled in water could be used for pain relief (ibid). Evidence of a number of plants that could potentially have been used for medicinal purposes was also found at St Mary Merton in Surrey. These included black mustard seeds, used for treatment of skin lesions, toothache and coughs, and greater celandine seeds (*Chelidonium majus*), a remedy for warts and eye problems (Miller and Saxby 2007, 128–9).

At one end of the canons' infirmary was a small building that had half of its floor covered in peat-burning hearths. This was an industrial method commonly employed in distilling. Residual evidence of arsenic, lead, copper and iron was found in this building, and an unusual assemblage of glass and ceramic vessels, which may have been used for distilling purposes, was discovered in a pit outside (Fig 234). Tests on residues within

Fig 233 A white (opium) poppy from Culpeper's Herbal *(1653)*

Fig 234 14th-century distillation vessel from St Mary Spital: alembic in Kingston-type ware from [5516] (height 290mm)

the vessels revealed the presence of mercury, lead, iron, arsenic and copper; one deposit also contained calcium and phosphorus, possibly originating from crushed bone. It is possible that this building was used for the production of remedies for inmates. In medieval England, mercury was used in a large number of medicines, while preparations containing lead carbonate were employed in the treatment of conjunctivitis (Thomas et al 1997, 178; Thomas 2004, 63; Ponting 2004). There is evidence that apothecaries practised distilling, and this led them into conflict with the distillers of beverages (Matthews 1962, 44). The preparation of 'electuaries, oxymels, cholagogues, plasters and ointments' was recorded at Westminster Abbey (Amulree 1964, 19). Although St Mary Spital was primarily concerned with treating the poor, it is possible that there was provision for similar work to be carried out in some form of chemist's workshop. We cannot say whether such a facility would have benefited all, or only those within the canons' infirmary. Ceramic evidence from St Mary Merton, which includes a possible albarello (drug jar) of Spanish tin-glazed ware, suggests that medicines may have been kept in its infirmary (Miller and Saxby 2007, 128).

Maternity care and childbirth

Contemporary texts on women's health provide an insight into the medieval understanding and practice of childbirth. The *Trotula*, an Italian text probably dating from the 11th century, focused on gynaecological medicine and obstetrics. Although much of it was based on the inaccurate assumptions of astrology and humoral theory, it was far more competent in its sections on childbirth. These included instructions on delivery and Caesarean section, as well as a number of practical treatments for different types of birth (Gottfried 1986, 193–4). An English physician, Gilbertus Anglicus (died *c* 1250), later combined some of his own ideas with those of the *Trotula* in a section of text entitled *De passionibus mulierum*. Although no further advances in this field were seen in clinical texts until the 16th century, the restriction of obstetric medicine to midwives appears to have led to relatively high standards of practice (ibid, 194). The nurses or midwives who delivered a baby were responsible for inspecting its body for defects or marks. They were also expected to straighten, stretch and bind the limbs, a practice which was thought to ensure correct growth of the child (Metzler 2006, 94). Certain objects and materials were believed to benefit the expectant mother. Jet was thought to have medicinal properties, and a piece placed in water for three days was believed to ease childbirth. Although none was recovered from St Mary Spital, a large jet bowl from the Thames waterfront may have served a similar purpose (Egan 2007, 69).

Botanical remains from the prior's garden at St Mary Spital included catmint (*Nepeta cataria*), which was believed to have obstetric benefits (Davis in prep). The seeds and leaves of the plant were thought to increase a mother's lactation (Culpeper 1653). Feverfew (*Tanacetum parthenium*) could be boiled in white wine to produce a concoction that would clean and strengthen the womb following childbirth, and repair any damage done by a careless midwife (ibid). However, we have no evidence that the plants were put to these specific uses.

A number of medieval cemeteries have been found to contain females associated with possible stillborn neonates buried within the same grave (Gilchrist and Sloane 2005, 72). One such example was discovered in the infirmary cemetery from the refoundation of St Mary Spital in 1235 (Thomas et al 1997, 39). However, in the absence of DNA analysis the relationship between the two cannot be proven (Roberts and Cox 2003, 253). Unlike most religious infirmary hospitals, St Mary Spital had a duty to admit pregnant women, although we do not know how many were accommodated (Thomas et al 1997, 104). The law forbade the burial of women with *in utero* foetuses, so many who died within the walls of the infirmary may have been buried elsewhere. However, the analysis of 13 female burials with perinatal remains found in positions indicating that they were *in utero* at the time of burial demonstrates that this rule was not always applied at St Mary Spital. Ten of these burials were found in the attritional cemetery, and the remainder in the mass burial pits.

Intrauterine death can occur due to haemorrhage, puerperal sepsis, breach birth and other difficulties in delivery such as an oversized foetus or a pelvic defect in the mother (Lewis 2007, 34). In the absence of signs of deformity in the child or mother, it is rarely possible to determine the specific cause of death. Of the three *in utero* foetuses within the current study sample, two could be precisely aged (37 weeks and 40 weeks) and were found to be full term. The ages of the women who died with their unborn children may throw light on the circumstances of their admission to the hospital. While it is not certain that these were all inmates, the nature of the hospital charter suggests that many if not all may have been cared for at St Mary Spital. By the mid 14th century, the hospitals of both St Mary Spital and St Bartholomew were admitting pregnant women, and both continued this practice into the 15th century (Orme and Webster 1995, 110). Of the 13 women with intrauterine foetuses, ten were included in the study sample and three were recorded to assessment level only. Seven (70.0%) were aged 18–25 years, two (20.0%) were 26–35 years and one (10.0%) was aged 36–45 years. Such a distribution may reflect a general vulnerability of young servants, migrant workers and the destitute in medieval urban centres, or perhaps risky first pregnancies of women marrying in their early twenties. Orme and Webster noted that childbirth normally happened at home and that those women who went to the hospital probably had nowhere else to go (ibid, 109). There may have been a greater proportional need for such facilities in London, where increased levels of migration, poverty, prostitution and female servitude may have contributed to a relatively high number of destitute unmarried mothers (ibid, 109–10). Evidence of disease was found in some of these females. Three displayed signs of cribra orbitalia and two of porotic hyperostosis. One was suffering from tuberculosis.

The data suggest that, of those buried within the cemetery, both 26–35-year-old and adolescent females were less vulnerable than young adult females to death with foetuses *in utero*. Higher relative female mortality in the third and fourth decade of life within archaeological samples has often been linked to death in pregnancy or childbirth. The evidence from St Mary Spital suggests that in some groups in medieval London this may have applied more frequently to young adult females than to those aged 26–35 years. It is possible that female mortality between the ages of 18 and 25 was inflated to a greater extent by this cause of death than that in other age categories.

Gilchrist and Sloane observed that the excavated cemetery samples of religious houses and hospitals contained lower proportions of infants and young children than parish cemeteries (2005, 204–5). This is certainly true of perinatal and infant individuals at St Mary Spital, where only 1.5% (83/5454) of the fully analysed sample from the entire medieval cemetery were under 1 year old. However, the East Smithfield cemetery in London, which was founded in order to bury victims of the Black Death, also contained a low number (15/1031: 1.4%). Most of the youngest individuals at St Mary Spital were perinatal (78/5454: 1.3%), with only five individuals between 1 month and 1 year old at death (5/5454: 0.1%). Perhaps there was a far greater risk of perinatal mortality when compared to infant mortality, although the combined data from the East Smithfield Black Death cemetery and the St Mary Graces cemetery, where 0.6% (6/1012) of burials were perinatal and 0.9% (9/1012) were infants, suggest that there was a difference in burial practice (Grainger et al 2008; Grainger and Phillpotts 2011). Similar results from the mass burial pits, where differential burial practices may well have been absent, support this evidence. There was a large increase in perinatal burials in period 17 (26/650: 4.0%) compared to the previous period (period 16 22/2835: 0.8%). When the burial types are separated, it is apparent that this increase takes place in the attritional cemetery (24/526: 4.5%) but not in the mass burial cemetery (2/124: 1.6%). This variation is statistically significant and may have been caused by differential burial practices or by an increase in perinatal mortality risk in the 15th century. However, it may also have resulted from an increase in admissions of pregnant women in this period: St Mary Spital was known to admit pregnant women, and the increase could be interpreted as an indication that the attritional cemetery contained a greater number of inmates from the hospital, at least in period 17 (Fig 235).

A survey of the taphonomic literature by Lewis revealed that the preservation of subadult bone should not be disproportionately poor in conditions where survival of adult bone is good (Lewis 2007, 185). Skeletal preservation was generally good at St Mary Spital, which indicates that it was burial practice rather than skeletal preservation that was responsible for the low number of infants. In fact, infant bones contain a lower proportion of delicate cancellous bone relative to stronger cortical bone when compared to older individuals. The mineral content of subadult bones varies with age, being at its lowest point in the post-neonatal period (ibid, 25).

Unbaptised infants could not be buried in consecrated ground as they were considered to be unclean (Gilchrist and Sloane 2005, 72). The prone burial of neonate B[355] in the western cemetery at St Mary Spital may represent an individual who died before baptism and yet was permitted inclusion within the cemetery (Thomas et al 1997, 38). Prone burial was normally reserved for criminals or the unclean.

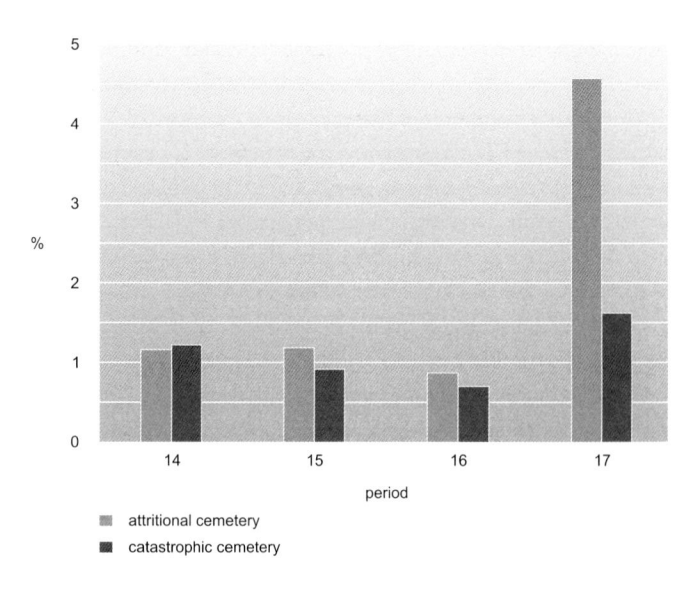

Fig 235 Proportion of perinatal individuals by period and burial type

Surgery

Surgery was regarded as one of the major methods of preventing the onset of permanent impairment in injured individuals (Metzler 2006, 187). Although documentary evidence of specific surgical procedures is rare, there are indications of injuries and illnesses for which treatment was administered in the infirmarers' rolls of Westminster Abbey, which mention 89 surgical procedures between the end of the 13th century and the Dissolution. These include an injury to a foot due to an axe blow, and more immediately life-threatening conditions such as punctured stomachs (Amulree 1964, 19). Soporific sponges, ointments and alcohol may have helped to partially dull the pain of a procedure, but there were few anaesthetics that could fully relieve suffering (Gottfried 1986, 237). Having said this, the identification of opium poppy (*Papaver somniferum*) at St Mary Spital suggests that effective pain relief was available at some hospitals (Davis in prep). The high risk of infection probably determined that most of the surgery performed in medieval England was associated with emergencies when individuals were close to death (Siraisi 1990, 154; Van Arsdall 2007, 199). Both patient and surgeon confessed before an operation (Rawcliffe 1999, 318). In this respect emergency treatment was very different from the care of the chronically sick in medieval hospitals.

Trepanation

There were six individuals who exhibited evidence of surgical procedures within the skeletal remains from St Mary Spital, three of whom had evidence of trepanation. This was a procedure in which a piece of the cranium was cut and removed, exposing the soft tissue within. It followed careful inspection of the wound by the medical practitioner, who may have shaved the head of the patient before using his fingers to gauge the extent of the damage to the cranium (Hunt 1999, 9, 15, 27). The soft tissue wound in the scalp may have been enlarged before the drilling of perforations in the cranium on either side of the lesion using a *trepanum*. A surgical chisel (*spatumen*) would then be employed with the aid of a mallet to enlarge the hole in the skull in order to remove bone splinters, possibly with the aid of forceps (ibid, 10, 15) (Fig 236). The disruption of the dura mater was correctly recognised as a great risk to the survival of the patient (Metzler 2006, 100). English surgeons such as Mirfield were aware of the potentially fatal consequences of this form of surgery, and in the medieval period its use was probably restricted to emergency treatment (Gottfried 1986, 223).

A 36–45-year-old male [1934] from the period 15 mass burial pits exhibited two healed trepanations (Fig 237). On the left parietal, there was an oval lesion (36.1 × 16.3mm) with smooth, slightly scooped, rounded margins. The floor of the lesion was also smooth, but was slightly porous. The walls were 6.8mm deep, suggesting that the original wound penetrated both cranial tables. This is supported by the presence of an island of smooth lamellar bone on the endocranium. The proximity to the sagittal sinus increased the risk of the procedure, as damage to the sinus would result in a fatal haemorrhage. Extending forwards from this lesion was a linear defect that penetrated the outer table and diploë to a depth of 2.2mm. This lesion may have resulted from sharp force weapon trauma, or may have formed part of the surgical procedure itself. The linear defect may have resulted from the use of a *spatumen* during the connection of holes inserted on either side of the fissure in order to expand the wound (Hunt 1999, 15). The methods of treating head wounds described in Roger of Salerno's *Chirurgia* (c 1180) include the exploration of lesions in which a cross-incision was made in preparation for opening and probing the wound (Gottfried 1986, fig 4). The linear defect immediately anterior to the trepanation on individual [1934] may have formed part of a similar procedure.

A further oval trepanation (20.2 × 23.6mm) was located on the right parietal. On both the superior and posterior sides of the lesion, 7.6mm from its margins, was a fine semicircular line visible only in oblique light. There is a possibility that this line represented an early phase of treatment, where a scalpel-like tool was employed to cut the soft tissue of the scalp and allow fuller access to the bone. There was no evidence of injury to this individual, although it is conceivable that any lesions may have been obliterated by treatment.

Individual [19893], a 36–45-year-old male from the period 16 attritional cemetery, displayed a number of pathological changes to the skeleton – bilateral fusion of the sacroiliac joints, early stage fusion of some apophyseal facets, and ossification of supporting ligaments in the thoracic and lumbar spine – characteristic of ankylosing spondylitis. New bone growth on

Fig 236 A surgeon treating a head wound, depicted in an early 14th-century copy of the Chirurgia *(© The British Library Board, Sloane MS 1977, fo 2)*

Fig 237 Superior view of the cranium of 36–45-year-old male [1934] from the mass burial pits, period 15 (scale c 1:2)

the rib heads may have been part of an inflammatory response to these changes, but it is also possible that the ribs were reacting to chronic pulmonary infection. This man also displayed a number of traumatic lesions: soft tissue injuries to the muscle attachments of the right (lateral head of triceps) and left (brachioradialis) humeri, a double fracture of the sixth left rib, and a number of injuries to the skull.

The right nasal bone had a healed crush fracture as a result of direct blunt force. The right frontal bone displayed a well-defined but healed vertical sharp force injury which was probably due to a receiving a blow from slightly left of centre from an edged weapon. The force of the blow resulted in the displacement of bone away from the impact area, leading to the formation of a raised area immediately to the right of the lesion. The frontal injury was aligned with the nasal fracture and both may have occurred in the same assault, possibly due to the blade, the butt of the implement or even the striking hand of the assailant (Fig 238). These injuries would have caused severe soft tissue damage to the forehead, nose and perhaps the right eye. In addition to scarring, the man's facial expression would have been affected by muscle damage (Powers 2005, 10).

A sub-oval lesion was located on the right side of the supraoccipital bone and penetrated both cranial tables. The inferior half of the lesion consisted of a protruding sub-rectangular 'flap' of bone that appeared to have been forced in an inferior direction. This may have resulted from the strong downward pull of the trapezius muscle (Powers 2005, 10), which may have opened the wound yet further. Although healed new bone covered the area, the original shape and size of the injury were evident. This lesion probably resulted from a slicing wound inflicted by a sharp-edged weapon such as a sword or axe. It was administered from a supero-posterior direction at an approximate angle of 45° to vertical. The person who inflicted the wound would almost certainly have been to one side (left or right) of the victim, either at the same height or above. If the victim was on the ground, the assailant may have been attempting to sever the head. Such a severe injury would have carried a high risk of brain injury, haemorrhage and infection. Survival would have depended upon the depth of the wound and the avoidance of dural sinuses (Weber and Czarnetzki 2001, 354–5).

A sub-triangular hole with smooth margins penetrated both cranial tables, and was situated in the centre of the posterior half of the right parietal. The form of this lesion suggests that a bladed instrument or weapon was again used with extreme force. Enlargement of the right mastoid is thought to result from soft tissue injury as the result of the force of this blow and a subsequent 'whiplash' effect (Powers 2005, 8). The assailant may have been at the same level as the victim or possibly above him. This injury was also healed, although the hole in the parietal remained large. The anterior corners of the lesion were rounded, enlarged and externally bevelled. They appeared to have been deliberately enlarged, possibly by scraping, in an attempt to open up the area of the wound for inspection and/or cleaning (ibid, 11). The ectocranial opening of the hole was partially covered by a thin sheet of smooth and slightly polished necrotic bone, which may have resulted from the detachment of this fragment from the blood supply following the injury (Fig 239).

Trepanation was a means of removing bone splinters from wounds, and could also relieve the build-up of pressure following injury. The apparent surgical modification of the parietal wound in [19893] suggests that treatment was available to this individual, and that it was of a sufficiently high standard to allow survival (Powers 2005, 11). It is also possible that some form of surgery was attempted on the occipital wound. If so, all evidence was obliterated by bone remodelling. Unfortunately, it

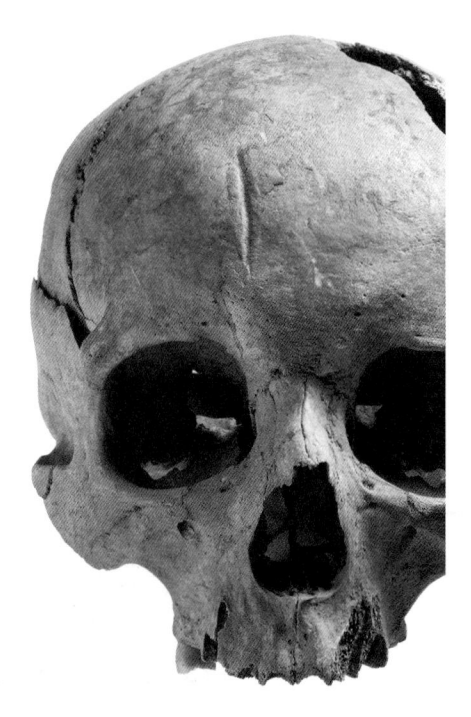

Fig 238 Anterior view of the cranium of 36–45-year-old male [19893] from the attritional cemetery, period 16, showing the alignment of a nasal fracture and sharp force (weapon) injury to the frontal bone (scale c 1:2)

Fig 239 Right postero-lateral view of the cranium of 36–45-year-old male [19893] (scale c 1:2)

was not possible to establish whether these wounds were all inflicted and therefore treated at the same time; nor was it possible to estimate the age(s) at which this individual received his wounds, as all were well healed. The severity of these cranial insults may have led to bacterial invasion and resultant infection, but there is no evidence of this in the healed lesions.

Male [26580], aged 36–45 years, from the period 16 attritional cemetery displayed four healed injuries to the cranium and fractures of the right forearm. A smooth ectocranial crack extended vertically from the inferior margin of the left squamous temporo-sphenoid suture to the centre of the left parietal. This injury would have resulted from sharp force trauma to the left side of the cranium, possibly caused by a sword, a pole-axe or an axe. It was well healed at the time of death, and bone remodelling hindered the reconstruction of the angle of the strike, although the shape of the lesion suggests that it may have originated from an antero-lateral direction. It appears to have cut through a pre-existing depressed sub-oval lesion with gradually sloping sides, which was caused by a weapon or projectile with a rounded or oval profile striking the head with considerable force from a lateral direction.

On the squamous part of the left temporal bone was an oval depression with gradually sloping sides and a flat base. This displayed the typical form of a pond fracture and probably resulted from a weapon or projectile with a rounded or oval profile striking the left temporal bone with moderate force. However, the squamous temporal is relatively thin and the injury could have been caused by a punch, a sword pommel or possibly the follow-through of the butt of a weapon.

An oval injury that penetrated both cranial tables was located on the top of the left parietal. The lesion was well defined with smooth edges, and although it was well healed no new bone had grown across the wound, so the angle of entry was preserved. The parietal bone had been perforated at an angle of c 45°, from an antero-superior direction. It was this angle of entry that gave the lesion its oval form. When viewed along its true axis, it appeared to be circular, with a diameter of c 15mm, and this more accurately reflected the true shape of the object that punctured the cranium. It may have been caused either by a weapon used at close quarters or by a projectile with a rounded profile fired into the air from longer range and hitting its target from the front and above at an angle of c 45° to horizontal. It must have been delivered with great force or at a relatively high velocity to puncture the cranium (Gurdjian and Webster 1958). Circular projectile injuries can result from the rounded profile of arrow skirts, and the diameter of c 15mm would come within the expected size range of an arrow (Novak 2000, 98). However, the large size and regular outline of the lesion may have been due to treatment, in which a wound caused by non-specific blunt force injury was enlarged by use of a trephine (Hunt 1999, 27). While this lesion was well healed, there was evidence of associated endocranial bone change, which took the form of areas of nodular and spicular mature bone throughout the left parietal and temporal bones. These changes were especially prevalent in the area of the skull perforation, and they reflected hypervascularisation in an attempt to heal the insult. They may also have resulted from bony reaction to soft tissue injury to the brain. Both the bone and soft tissue injuries appear to have resolved before death.

At a distance of 8.8mm anterior to the lesion were two very thin but sharply defined semicircular grooves which mirrored the shape of the anterior outline of the wound (Fig 240). These may have been the result of incisions with a very sharp scalpel-like instrument, part of a process in which the skin and periosteum were lifted around the area of the wound in order to provide fuller access for cleaning and the removal of bone fragments. These incisions may also have served to cut away loose skin in order to tidy up the area of the wound (Hunt 1999, 10–11, 21). Roger of Salerno recommended that initial work after cranial injury should involve the removal of any loose or partly detached skin, and that the wound should then be cleaned and medicated before trepanation. Narrow wounds were to be enlarged and pus removed by the introduction of a silk or fine linen cloth into the space between the cranium and the cerebrum (Gottfried 1986, 209).

The fractures of the right forearm (radius and ulna midshafts) probably occurred in a single incident, and were of the type which is today associated with motor vehicle accidents, falls on to the forearm or outstretched hand, or fights (Resnick 2002, 2831; McRae 2003, 302). This injury could have been sustained while parrying a blow, falling as the result of a blow to another part of the body, or falling as the result of an accident. When the individual's other injuries are taken into consideration, it would seem more likely that the forearm fracture was the result of interpersonal violence, and was possibly contemporary with one or more of the cranial injuries. Although the distal right ulna did not survive, both bones had unusually large calluses, a sign of problematic healing. In addition, beyond the fracture site on its distal shaft, the radius was angled 25° medial to its normal position. This suggests that the forearm was not well reduced or immobilised, and provides an interesting contrast to the evidence

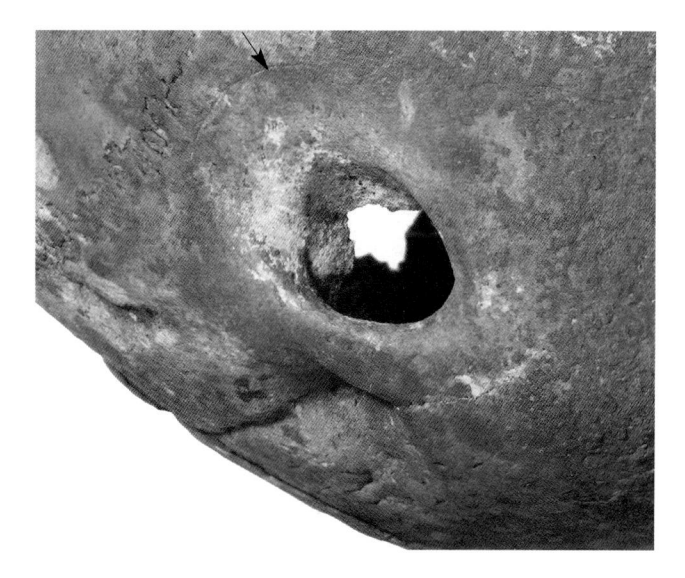

Fig 240 Left parietal of the cranium of 36–45-year-old male [26580], showing an oval lesion perforating the skull and surrounded by two semicircular grooves (arrow) (scale c 2:1)

of cranial treatment. The severity of the injuries to the cranium together with the possible treatment of the puncture wound would support the hypothesis that this individual received both emergency surgery and sufficient care to survive his wounds. This evidence provides an interesting contrast with the failure properly to treat the forearm fracture: it may be that the forearm fractures were received contemporaneously with one of the more life-threatening cranial injuries, which was given priority treatment, or it may reflect changes in the quality of care that this individual received during his life. If he had seen military service, he may well have received treatment from skilled surgeons who were more interested or concerned with battlefield injuries to the head.

Five cases of trepanation have been identified from other medieval cemeteries in Britain and Ireland. In three of these, signs of healing were visible, indicating at least partial success of the treatment in so far as immediate death was avoided. Only one individual with trepanation was found to have suffered cranial trauma (Roberts and Cox 2003, 252; Roberts and McKinley 2003). It is likely that techniques varied between surgeons, and some, such as Thomas Morstede (died 1450), a prominent London surgeon, developed their own tools, such as the 'separatory' for dividing the periosteum from the cranium (Gottfried 1986, 234).

Amputation

Two examples of amputation were found at St Mary Spital. One of these involved, young adult male [20508] from the period 15 mass burial pits, had damage to an unsided distal hand phalanx, possibly reflecting the accidental loss of a fingertip. The second example was in 26–35-year-old male [32152] from the period 16 mass burial pits, who had a healed amputation of the right lower leg. The right tibia and fibula terminated at the same level, at the distal end of the midshafts, in healed, rounded calluses. Comparison with the right leg suggested that c 170mm had been removed from the length of the right fibula. The bones had been cut approximately perpendicular to their long axes. The medullary cavities had healed over, a process which would have taken a number of weeks, and were covered by smooth, dense bone (Aufderheide and Rodríguez-Martín 1998, 30). Irregular spicules of dense lamellar bone extended from the posterior aspect, and osteophytes projected from the anterior aspect. A horizontal bony bridge ankylosed the tibia and fibula (Fig 241).

Areas of both bones, as well the distal femur, were covered in porotic and striated lamellar bone and this suggests that infection may have spread up the leg. The form of the stump indicated that healing was either complete or near completion. The associated periostitis was not active, but in the process of remodelling. However, there was no evidence of atrophy in the affected limb, implying that not enough time had passed for the disuse of the associated muscles to be evident in the bone. In such a case, it would seem unlikely that the amputation was performed many years before death. There was also evidence of joint deterioration in the talo-calcaneal, navicular-cuneiform and first metatarso-phalangeal joints of the left foot, possibly indicative of increased musculoskeletal stress brought about by compensating for the loss of the right foot.

Mays suggests three broad categories of amputation in archaeological remains: surgical amputation, judicial punishment and sharp force trauma (Mays 1996, 107). Amputation as a form of punishment was rare during the 13th and 14th centuries, and although definitive determination of the cause is not possible, the evidence is more indicative of a surgical procedure. The shin was amputated at the thinnest part of the tibial shaft and, if the foot was damaged or infected, this would have allowed enough distance from the compromised area to permit healing, as well as the retention of sufficient remaining skin to effectively close the wound. If this was the result of surgery, the healed stump together with the resolving infection suggests that the operation was successful. Surgery in the form that we know today was only carried out in emergencies, and amputation was probably a rarity before the 16th century due to the risks of bleeding and infection (Siraisi 1990, 157). Only three examples of amputation have been found in skeletal remains from the late medieval period (Roberts and Cox 203, 251). Guy de Chauliac knew the risks of haemorrhage and advised that amputation be used only when the limb had already been partially severed (Beck 1974, 25). Although the right knee of this individual was flexed in the grave, there was no evidence for the use of a prosthesis or crutches (Fig 242).

Periosteal new bone covered the entire lengths of the visceral surfaces of the right ribs, indicating that this individual was suffering from a chronic pulmonary infection. This may or may not have been related to changes in lifestyle following the leg

Fig 241 Remodelling following amputation of the right leg of 26–35-year-old male [32152] from the mass burial pits, period 16 (scale c 1:1)

it may simply be due to a lower risk of cranial injury, as reflected in the skull fracture crude prevalence rates (female 51/1883: 2.7%; male 98/2237: 4.4%). Surgeons had to weigh the risks of treatment against the severity of the injury. This would have required skill and knowledge that could only have been achieved through training. In the case of cranial fractures, most textbooks advised that the sharp edges of the lesion be smoothed, and any opening enlarged to allow the removal of bone splinters and the elevation of depressed fragments (Siraisi 1990, 158–9). Documentary records suggest that the surgeon Thomas Thorneton attended the poor and sick at St Mary Spital from 1480 to 1525, and may have provided some form of surgical treatment within the hospital (Thomas et al 1997, 107). In theory, individuals who suffered cranial injuries could have been successfully treated at the hospital and then buried in the cemetery many years later. However, surgeons and barbers were frequently taken on military campaigns during the Hundred Years War (Beck 1974, 32). There would certainly have been a number of veteran soldiers living in London, and while those who suffered permanent mental or physical damage may have been cared for by the hospital, there is no evidence that this care included the emergency surgical treatment of wounds.

4.3 Defining catastrophe: mass burial at St Mary Spital

Amy Gray Jones

During excavations of the cemetery at St Mary Spital, 175 large burial pits containing multiple interments were encountered. These were predominantly located on the edges of the cemetery within the southern and eastern boundaries. The largest pit contained 43 individuals and more than 100 pits contained 15 or more burials. The bodies were laid out with relative care, usually supine and extended, in multiple layers, separated by a thin layer of soil (Fig 243). The burials included men, women and children; the majority were orientated roughly east–west but some north–south, apparently to fill up gaps. These mass burials were similar to those seen in catastrophic cemeteries and specifically those relating to the Black Death of 1348–9 (see Gilchrist and Sloane 2005). However, at St Mary Spital, dating revealed that the majority of these mass burials pre-date the known episodes of the Black Death in London.

The mass burial pits were found in each of the four phases of the cemetery but there was considerable variation in their size and the numbers of individuals buried in them. In period 14 (*c* 1120–*c* 1200) quarry pits were reused for the multiple or mass burials. These made up 32.2% (165/512) of the burials of the period and have been radiocarbon dated to *c* 1155–65 (Chapter 3.2). The first major phase of what could be considered as 'purpose-dug' pits occurred in period 15 (*c* 1200–50): these were medium-sized, tightly packed rectangular pits, on a WNW–ESE alignment, containing an average of 8–20 individuals. These were followed in period 16 (*c* 1250–*c* 1400)

Fig 242 Individual [32152] with amputated right lower leg, as excavated

amputation. It is possible that the surgery or some related illness compromised the health or immune status of this individual.

Evidence of surgical treatment at the priory hospital

Although we know that Philip de Ashendon was admitted to the hospital with a mortal wound (above, 4.1), the relatively low number of individuals with possible surgical treatment (6/5387: 0.1%), together with the paucity of peri-mortem injury (5/5387: 0.1%), indicates that the hospital did not typically admit people with life-threatening wounds. Those with evidence of surgical treatment following severe blunt force, sharp force or penetrating injuries may have been involved in military campaigns in which their wounds were successfully treated by surgeons.

There was certainly no shortage of conflict in the 15th century, with the Scottish campaigns, the disputes over claims to the English throne and the continuing wars with France (Beck 1974, 55). No evidence of surgery was found in females, and while this might suggest gender-related differences in treatment,

St Mary Spital in context

Fig 243 The top layer of a mid 13th-century mass burial pit under excavation in the hospital cemetery

by a phase of larger (*c* 20–40 individuals), squarer pits which were dug on a slightly different alignment and were located in between and cutting the earlier pits. These two phases of pits are very close in date, and probably fall either side of the boundary between the periods (radiocarbon dated to *c* 1235–55) (Chapter 1.1). In fact where the burials intercut one another, articulated limbs were found in the fill of the later pits, suggesting that they were dug only shortly after the first phase. Interment in mass burial pits dominates burial practice in periods 15 and 16, accounting for 63.3% (880/1390) and 50.9% (1443/2835) of those burials analysed in each respectively. A few mass burial pits were also recorded in period 17 (*c* 1400–1539), containing 19.1% (124/650) of all burials in this period.

Possible explanations for the mass burials fall into two broad groups: first, that the cemetery ran out of space, due to either a rise in population or the expansion of the cemetery's catchment, resulting in the need for multiple burial; and second, that there was a sudden rise in mortality to a level that the normal functioning of the cemetery was unable to cope with, which necessitated the use of mass burials.

London's population certainly did rise throughout the life of the cemetery, which may have placed a strain on the existing burial grounds and resulted in a change of burial practices. In this case the mass burial pits would simply be an enhancement of the 'normal' cemetery population and would be attritional in character, sharing common demographic and other patterns. The alternative is that they represent a sudden rise in mortality. Radiocarbon dating shows that the major phases of mass burial pre-date the recorded outbreaks of bubonic plague (the Black Death of 1348–9, and subsequent epidemics of 1361–2, 1369, 1375 and 1391) but outbreaks of infectious disease are well documented throughout the medieval period, as are famines. Warfare may also account for a rise in the rate of death, although this is a less likely cause as there is no evidence for interpersonal violence existing exclusively within the mass burials and no documented accounts of conflict close to London. In this case the mass burials would represent the victims of some sort of catastrophic event such as an epidemic and would be different from the normal, attritional, cemetery.

This section explores these issues in more detail through an examination and comparison of the individuals in each burial type. Based on the assumption that burial type ABC represents an attritional cemetery, a comparison with burial type D, the mass burials, should explain the relationship between the burial types. In particular the age-at-death profile of each group will be compared and specific health indicators will be examined to elucidate differences in health status. These include the so-called 'stress indicators': dental enamel hypoplasia, cribra orbitalia and porotic hyperostosis (Chapter 3.10), growth profiles (femoral length for (dental) age), stature, and rates of infectious disease, such as periostitis and tuberculosis. Particular attention is paid to subadult health, which is a more sensitive indicator of conditions over the short term: within the mass burials, which appear to have taken place over a short period of time, subadult health indicators may provide a more detailed record of the prevailing conditions of the time (see also the discussion of subadult health and the osteological paradox in Chapter 4.2).

Comparison of burial types *c* 1120–*c* 1200 (period 14)

Demography

In period 14 both the attritional and mass burials had a very similar age-at-death profile: there were low proportions of children under 5 years old and the number of burials increased with age, reaching a peak in middle age, followed by a decrease in older adults (Chapter 3.2). The only striking difference between the two burial types was that there were significantly more subadults in the mass burials than in the attritional burials: specifically, significantly more subadults in later childhood and adolescence. There was also a greater proportion of young adults in the mass burials, but this difference was not statistically significant. Consequently the individuals in the mass burials were, in general, younger.

Another significant difference between the two types of burial in this period was found in the proportion of males and females. There were statistically significantly more males than females in the attritional burials, a male to female ratio of 1.4:1.

Monastic cemeteries frequently contain a higher proportion of males, and urban populations have also been shown to contain more males, possibly due to the migration of male labour (Thomas et al 1997, 39–40). In the mass burials, however, the ratio of males to females was more equal, 1.15:1, with no statistically significant difference between the proportions of the two sexes. This would either imply that males and females were equally as likely to be buried in the mass burial pits, and therefore equally likely to be affected by whatever the cause of the mass burials was; or that fewer males from the population were affected by what caused mass burial.

Female age at death peaked in early middle age, whereas for males it peaked in later middle age, and this did not differ between burial types. In the attritional burials there was a significantly higher proportion of early middle-aged females than males but the difference was not significant in the mass burials.

Health status

GROWTH

A comparison of subadult growth suggests that it was those children and adolescents whose health had already been compromised in some way (resulting in a lower height-for-age) who were buried in the mass burial pits (see also Chapter 3.4). Growth profiles of those aged between 6 and 17 years showed that subadults in the mass burials were, apart from at 6 years of age, smaller than those in the attritional burials (Fig 244). The growth trend also showed that those in the mass burials were less likely to achieve their height potential.

STATURE

Adult stature did not vary significantly between the burial types (Chapter 3.3). Average female stature in this period was c 162cm in both the mass and attritional burials. Males were slightly taller than females, at 169.4cm in the attritional cemetery, and only slightly shorter, 167.0cm, in the mass burials.

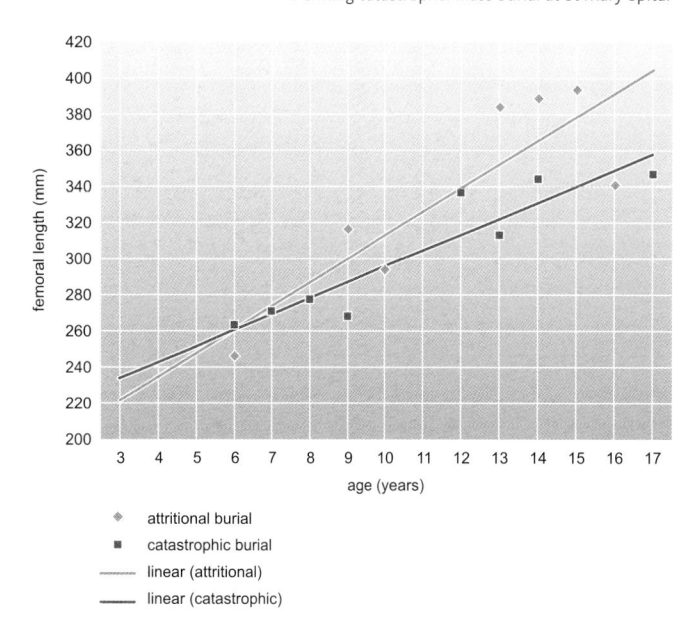

Fig 244 Comparison of subadult growth between the attritional and catastrophic burials, c 1120–c 1200 (period 14)

DENTAL ENAMEL HYPOPLASIA

Rates of enamel hypoplasia suggest that those subadults who were buried in mass burial pits experienced a greater amount of childhood stress.

Those who died in later childhood and adolescence and were buried in mass burial pits had a higher prevalence of enamel hypoplastic defects (crude prevalence 6/13: 46.2% and 20/27: 74.1% respectively) compared to those of the same ages buried in the attritional cemetery (37.5%: 3/8 and 44.1%: 15/34) (Table 146) (Chapter 3.10). In both burial types, those who survived later childhood only to die in adolescence had a higher prevalence of hypoplastic defects. The increase in prevalence was greater in the mass burials.

Table 146 Crude prevalence rate of dental enamel hypoplasia in subadults by period and burial type

Period	Age (years)	Attritional No. individuals	No. affected	%	Catastrophic No. individuals	No. affected	%
14	1–5	5	0	–	0	0	–
	6–11	8	3	37.5	13	6	46.2
	12–17	34	15	44.1	27	20	74.1
15	1–5	3	2	66.7	8	1	12.5
	6–11	28	9	32.1	75	42	56.0
	12–17	60	31	51.7	109	65	59.6
16	1–5	17	0	–	14	1	7.1
	6–11	87	41	47.1	100	41	41.0
	12–17	91	45	49.5	174	97	55.7
17	1–5	10	0	–	1	0	–
	6–11	24	13	54.2	13	9	69.2
	12–17	36	23	63.9	13	9	69.2

Among adults in this period males experienced slightly higher true prevalence rates than females. Males in the mass burials had a prevalence (16.1%: 193/1198 of teeth affected) both higher than that for females in the mass burials (11.3%: 115/1018) and higher than that for males (14.1%: 316/2234) and females (13.4%: 231/1723) in the attritional burials (Chapter 3.6).

CRIBRA ORBITALIA

Analysis has shown that subadults and males in the mass burials had a much higher prevalence of cribra orbitalia than those in the attritional burials. This suggests that in this period people buried in mass burial pits had experienced biological stress, for example, nutritional deficiency or a higher pathogen load, to a greater degree than those who died and were buried in the attritional cemetery.

Only five individuals in early childhood (1–5 years) were recovered, all from attritional burials, and one of them had cribra orbitalia (see Table 119, Chapter 3.10). Where a comparison could be made between the two burial types, rates were highest in the mass burials. In later childhood (6–11 years) 69.2% (9/13) of those in the mass burials were affected, compared to none of the attritional burials (0/8), and 51.9% (14/27) of adolescents (12–17 years) in mass burials had cribra orbitalia compared to 35.3% (12/34) of those in the attritional cemetery.

Of the cribra orbitalia observed in adults, females had similar proportions in both the attritional and mass burials (c 30–35%). The males in the attritional burials had a lower prevalence, c 26–28%, but the males in the mass burials had a significantly higher rate of c 40% (χ^2 = 5.48, df = 1, p ≤ 0.025).

POROTIC HYPEROSTOSIS

In addition to the high rates of cribra orbitalia among subadults in the mass burials, there were also high prevalence rates of porotic hyperostosis.

Of subadults, only those in later childhood and adolescence were affected and those in the mass burials had a higher prevalence: for example, 15.4% (2/13) of 6–11-year-olds in the mass burials were affected compared to none in the attritional burials (Chapter 3.14) (Table 147). In adolescents porotic hyperostosis was found in both types of burial: 25.9% (7/27) of those in the mass burials were affected compared to 14.7% (5/34) of those in the attritional, though this difference was not statistically significant. Adolescents in the mass burials also had the highest true prevalence rates of porotic hyperostosis among subadults: for example, 29.2% (21/72) of all parietal and occipital bones were affected.

Porotic hyperostosis, healed or healing, was also observed in the adults. Again prevalence rates were higher in mass than attritional burials for both males (attritional 20.6%: 33/160; mass 31.7%: (20/63) and females (attritional 6.1%: 7/115; mass 14.5%: 8/55), but the difference was not statistically significant. However, it could be shown that the prevalence in males was significantly higher than in females, both for the attritional burials (χ^2 = 11.77, df = 1, p ≤ 0.001) and the mass burials (χ^2 = 4.80, df = 1, p ≤ 0.05).

Although the higher prevalence rates among both adults and subadults in the mass burials could not be shown to be statistically significant, it does reinforce the findings for cribra orbitalia.

SPECIFIC DISEASES OF MALNUTRITION

No examples of specific metabolic disease were observed in this period. It is worth noting that a relatively low number of subadults were recovered (n = 94), only 32 of which were below the age of 12 years.

Table 147 Crude prevalence rate of porotic hyperostosis by period and burial type

Period	Sex or age (years)	Attritional No. individuals	No. affected	%	Catastrophic No. individuals	No. affected	%
14	6–11	8	0	-	13	2	15.4
	12–17	34	5	14.7	27	7	25.9
	male	160	33	20.6	63	20	31.7
	female	115	7	6.1	55	8	14.5
15	6–11	28	2	7.1	75	3	4.0
	12–17	60	6	10.0	109	6	5.5
	male	219	55	25.1	313	80	25.6
	female	167	26	15.6	334	41	12.3
16	1–5	17	0	-	14	1	7.1
	6–11	87	6	6.9	100	9	9.0
	12–17	91	11	12.1	174	30	17.2
	male	628	143	22.8	564	162	28.7
	female	474	62	13.1	535	71	13.3
17	6–11	24	1	4.2	13	0	-
	12–17	36	8	22.2	13	1	7.7
	male	239	58	24.3	51	5	9.8
	female	164	16	9.8	39	2	5.1

INFECTIOUS DISEASE: TUBERCULOSIS

Of the specific infections tuberculosis was the most prevalent in the cemetery (Chapter 3.9). In period 14 2.1% (11/512) of burials showed the osseous changes associated with tuberculosis. There was a slightly higher prevalence in the mass burials (2.4%: 4/165) than in the attritional burials (2.0%: 7/347) but the numbers involved were too small to be tested for statistical significance (Table 148).

Although there was a higher proportion of subadults in the mass burials, tuberculosis was only found in those in the attritional burials. Of these, only adolescents were affected, 2.9% (1/34) of this age group. This suggests either that those subadults who were buried in the mass burials did not suffer from tuberculosis at all or that they died before the osseous changes of the disease could develop.

In this period the overall prevalence of tuberculosis in adults was 2.0% (6/295) of attritional burials and 3.2% (4/123) of mass burials. The proportions of males and females affected were very similar, but there was some variation between the burial types. In the attritional burials, where demographically there were significantly more males than females, there was a higher prevalence of tuberculosis in males, 2.5% (4/160) compared to 1.7% (2/115) of females. In the mass burials, however, where males and females were more equal in number, this situation was reversed: more females had tuberculosis, 3.6% (2/55) compared to 1.6% (1/63) of males. In this period prevalence appeared to increase with advancing age, with the highest prevalence found in adults ≥46 years.

NON-SPECIFIC INFECTION: PERIOSTITIS

Rates of periostitis varied with sex, age and burial type. Adolescents and young males experienced high rates in the mass burials, whereas young females were affected in higher proportions in the attritional burials.

In the attritional burials those in later childhood and adolescence experienced similar rates of periostitis, 12.5% (1/8) and 11.8% (4/34) respectively. In the mass burials those in later childhood were not affected and a higher proportion of adolescents (18.5%: 5/27) had periostitis. The frequencies were too low to test for statistical significance.

In adults, males generally had a higher prevalence than females in both burial types (Chapter 3.9). Prevalence in young females was higher in the attritional burials, where 23.5% (4/17) were affected compared to 7.1% (1/14) in the mass burials,

whereas for young males the opposite was true – those in the mass burials were predominantly affected (41.7%: 5/12) compared to 12.0% (3/25) of attritional burials. At all other ages there was little difference in prevalence between the burial types. With increasing age prevalence in males decreased and rates were always slightly lower in the mass burials.

Summary

The principal difference between the mass and attritional burials in this period was the health of the subadult population. Demographically there were significantly younger individuals, particularly those in later childhood and adolescence, in the mass burials pits. Health indicators suggest that this element of the population had also suffered from more periods of childhood stress. These children had a shorter height-for-age than their peers buried in the attritional cemetery, and had a higher prevalence of dental enamel hypoplasia, cribra orbitalia and porotic hyperostosis. There were also indications that adolescents buried in the mass burial pits had a higher prevalence of non-specific infection. However, there was no evidence for higher rates of specific infectious diseases, as tuberculosis was only present in subadults in the attritional burials.

A similar history of poor childhood health among those in the mass burials could be seen in the adult population. Adult males in the mass burials had higher rates of cribra orbitalia and slightly higher rates of enamel hypoplasia, while both sexes had a higher prevalence of porotic hyperostosis. Interestingly, while the overall prevalence of porotic hyperostosis was higher in the mass burial pits, its distribution between the sexes remained the same, with significantly higher rates in males than females.

Rates of tuberculosis were also slightly higher in the mass burials, which showed a different distribution between the sexes from that seen in the attritional burials. Males had less tuberculosis than females in the mass burials. However, the 'osteological paradox' must be considered in the interpretation of these data: individuals who suffer poor health have lower resistance to disease when compared to the healthy, and this means that they may develop and die from a disease before there is time for skeletal changes to develop. In contrast, healthy individuals more able to fight the illness can survive longer and are more likely to recover, thus allowing more time for bony

Table 148 Crude prevalence rate of tuberculosis by period and burial type

	Attritional			Catastrophic			Total		
Period	No. individuals	No. affected	%	No. individuals	No. affected	%	No. individuals	No affected	%
14	347	7	2.0	165	4	2.4	512	11	2.1
15	510	8	1.6	880	15	1.7	1390	23	1.7
16	1392	31	2.2	1443	29	2.0	2835	60	2.1
17	526	5	1.0	124	1	0.8	650	6	0.9

lesions to appear. In a burial sample containing tuberculosis sufferers, those individuals with skeletal changes may therefore represent a relatively healthy group compared to those without lesions (Wood et al 1992, 344–5).

As well as differences in health, there were significantly more males among the attritional burials whereas the ratio of males to females was more equal in the mass burials.

Comparison of burial types c 1200–50 (period 15)

Demography

During this period, 63.3% (880/1390) of the skeletons analysed were interred in mass burial pits. Again the attritional and mass burials had a similar age-at-death profile: there were few perinates among those individuals for whom age could be assigned (attritional 6/496: 1.2%; mass burial 8/860: 0.9%), no infants (1–11 months) and few individuals aged 1–5 years (attritional 3/496: 0.6%; mass burial 8/860: 0.9%), before rising to peak at 26–35 years and 36–45 years, with a lower proportion of older adult burials (Chapter 3.2). There was no significant difference between the proportion of subadults in the attritional (100/510: 19.6%) and mass burials (201/880: 22.8%) overall, but there was a significantly higher proportion of 6–11-year-olds in the mass burials.

As in the preceding period, there were significantly more males than females in the attritional cemetery. The ratio of males to females was 1.3:1 in the attritional cemetery but 1:1 in the mass burials. This difference was due to the fact that there were significantly fewer males in the mass burials than in the attritional burials.

Once again, there was little difference between male and female age at death in the two burial types. Young adult males and females (18–25 years) were found in similar proportions (c 25%) in the mass and attritional burials. Male age at death did appear to peak slightly later than for females, with a female peak at 26–35 years and a more prolonged peak for males, and with most burials spread over 26–35 years and 36–45 years. In the mass burials there were significantly more 36–45-year-old males than females.

Health status

GROWTH

Once again, subadult growth profiles showed that those in the mass burials had a comparatively lower height-for-age than those in the attritional burials, evidence for interruptions in growth in this group (Fig 245) (see also Chapter 3.4).

STATURE

There was very little difference in adult stature between the burial types (Chapter 3.3). Average female stature in this period was 159.7cm and 161.4cm in the attritional and mass burials respectively. Males were slightly taller than females, at 168.5cm in the attritional cemetery, and only slightly shorter, 167.7cm, in the mass burials.

DENTAL ENAMEL HYPOPLASIA

Rates of enamel hypoplasia suggest that those who died aged 6–17 years old and were buried in the mass burial pits had experienced a greater amount of childhood stress, but rates among adults did not differ.

Those who died aged 6–11 years or 12–17 years and were buried in mass burial pits had a higher prevalence of enamel hypoplastic defects (crude prevalence 42/75: 56.0% and 65/109: 59.6% respectively) than those of the same ages buried in the attritional cemetery (9/28: 32.1% and 31/60: 51.7%) (Chapter 3.10). The rates for those aged 6–11 years were significantly different (χ^2 = 4.64, df = 1, p ≤ 0.05). In both burial types rates increased with age: those who survived later childhood (6–11 years) only to die in adolescence (12–17 years) had a slightly higher prevalence of hypoplastic defects, and the relative increase was similar in each burial type (Table 146).

Of those who died in early childhood (1–5 years), however, the opposite was true: those buried in the attritional cemetery had a higher prevalence at 66.7% (2/3) than those in the mass burials (12.5%: 1/8). However, only low numbers of individuals in this age group were recovered (11), including only three from attritional burials, so the prevalence rates are somewhat inflated.

Among adults in this period there was little difference in the true prevalence rates of enamel hypoplasia between the sexes or between burial types. Male prevalence was c 15% in both the attritional (459/3149: 14.6%) and mass burials (744/4897:15.2%) and female prevalence was 12.7% (356/2814) in the attritional and 14.0% (771/5507) in the mass burials (Chapter 3.6).

CRIBRA ORBITALIA

In this period there was no significant difference in the prevalence of cribra orbitalia between the burial types. There was a relatively high prevalence in all subadults (higher than the attritional rate in the preceding period), with between a third to a half of subadults

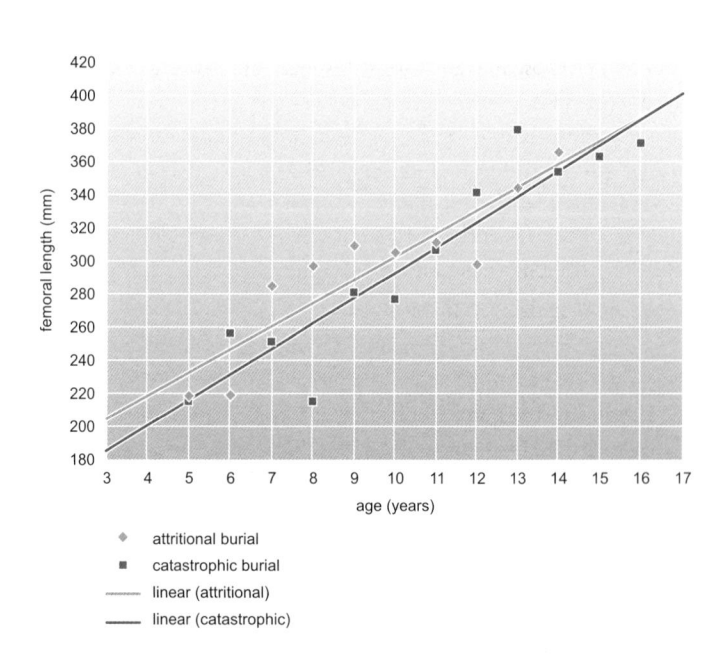

Fig 245 Comparison of subadult growth between the attritional and catastrophic burials, c 1200–50 (period 15)

affected. Females had a higher prevalence than males and both sexes had slightly higher rates in the attritional cemetery.

Rates for those aged 6–11 years were 43–47% and 12–17-year-olds rates were lower (though not significantly), at 38–40% (see Table 119, Chapter 3.10). As in period 14, adolescents (12–17 years old) had slightly lower rates than those aged 6–11 years. It was difficult to compare those in early childhood (1–5 years) as so few individuals of this age were recovered in this period (11), but crude prevalence was higher in the attritional burials (66.7%: 2/3) than the mass burials (37.5%: 3/8).

Of the healed or healing cribra orbitalia observed in adults, females from the attritional group had higher prevalence rates (42–44%) than the mass burials (37–38%). This pattern was the same for males but they had a lower overall prevalence than females: 30–35% of males in the attritional and 28–33% in the mass burials. There was no statistically significant difference between males and females.

POROTIC HYPEROSTOSIS

No significant difference in the prevalence of porotic hyperostosis was found between burial types. However, as in the preceding period, there were significantly more males than females affected in both burial types.

Of the subadults only those aged 6–11 years and 12–17 years were affected by porotic hyperostosis (Chapter 3.14; Table 147). In both age groups those in the attritional burials had a slightly higher prevalence: 7.1% (2/28) of 6–11-year-olds in the attritional burials were affected, compared to 4.0% (3/75) in the mass burials, and 10.0% (6/60) compared to 5.5% (6/109) of 12–17-year-olds. Prevalence also increased with age, with adolescents (12–17 years) having a slightly higher prevalence rate. However, neither the difference between burial types nor that between age groups was found to be statistically significant.

Healed or healing lesions were also observed in adults. Prevalence rates were similar for males in both mass and attritional burials, at c 25%, and lower in females, at 15.6% (26/167) of those in the attritional burials and slightly less, at 12.3% (41/334), in the mass burials. The prevalence in males was significantly higher than in females, both in the attritional burials ($\chi^2 = 5.21$, df = 1, $p \leq 0.025$) and the mass burials ($\chi^2 = 18.75$, df = 1, $p \leq 0.001$).

SPECIFIC DISEASES OF MALNUTRITION

Diseases of malnutrition occurred at the same low frequency in both burial types. In this period only one individual, [26421], was identified as suffering from scurvy. This child was aged 6–11 years at death and was buried in a mass pit, giving a prevalence rate for scurvy of 1.3% (1/75) in this age group.

Another individual, male [15599] aged 36–45 years, was identified as having the bowing deformities of resolved rickets. He was buried in the attritional cemetery, representing 1.5% (1/68) of his age group.

TUBERCULOSIS

Of the burials in period 15, a total of 1.7% (23/1390) showed the osseous changes associated with tuberculosis (Chapter 3.9).

Overall, there was no difference between prevalence rates in the attritional and mass burials (Table 148).

Among subadults, those in the mass burials had a higher prevalence (2.0%: 4/201) with tuberculosis, compared to 1% (1/100) of those in attritional burials. In both burial types 6–11-year-olds were affected, 3.6% (1/28) of attritional and 1.3% (1/75) of mass burials, but adolescents with tuberculosis were only found in the mass burials (2.8%: 3/109).

In this period the overall proportion of females showing the skeletal changes of tuberculosis (2.0%: 10/501) was slightly higher than the proportion of males (1.3%: 7/532) (though this was not statistically significant); this difference between the sexes appeared to originate in the mass burials. In the attritional burials males and females had similar prevalence rates of 1.8% (males 4/219; females 3/167) affected, but in the mass burials 2.1% (7/334) of females were affected compared to 1.0% (3/313) of males. Males in the mass burials appeared to have lower rates of tuberculosis and this was also observed in period 14. For both sexes tuberculosis was highest among young adults and prevalence decreased with increasing age.

NON-SPECIFIC INFECTION: PERIOSTITIS

There were predominantly higher rates of periostitis in subadults, males and females in the attritional burials than in the mass burials. There was a significantly higher prevalence among subadults who died aged 6–11 years in the attritional burials (25.0%) than in the mass burials (8.0%) ($\chi^2 = 5.34$, df = 1, $p \leq 0.025$) (Chapter 3.9).

In adults, males had a higher prevalence of periostitis than females, as was also observed in period 14. In each adult age group prevalence was either higher among those in the attritional burials (eg 22/53: 41.5% of 18–25-year-old males in the attritional and 21/76: 27.6% in the mass burials) or similar in both burial types (eg 24/68: 35.3% (attritional) and 33/97: 34% (mass burial) in 36–45-year-old males).

Summary

Unlike period 14, there was less of a clear distinction between the two burial types. While demographically there were significantly more 6–11-year-olds in the mass burials, both subadult populations exhibited signs of poor childhood health. As in period 14, 6–11-year-olds in the mass burials had a shorter height-for-age and, along with 12–17-year-olds, had a higher prevalence of dental enamel hypoplasia. However, rates of porotic hyperostosis were higher in the attritional burials rather than the mass burials, and there was no significant difference in the rate of cribra orbitalia between burial types. Subadults as a group also had a slightly higher prevalence of tuberculosis in the mass burials but rates of non-specific infection were higher in the attritional burials.

Among the adult population most of the evidence for childhood stress occurred within the attritional burials. Rates of cribra orbitalia were higher in the attritional burials than the mass burials, as were rates of porotic hyperostosis among females. There was no significant difference in the prevalence of enamel hypoplasia.

Patterns of adult infection followed a similar pattern: rates of periostitis were higher in the attritional burials and the prevalence of tuberculosis was roughly the same between burial types. The distribution of tuberculosis between the sexes did differ between burial types, and interestingly this was the same as that observed in period 14. In the catastrophic sample, the female prevalence of tuberculosis was higher than the male.

There were distinct differences in the proportions of males and females in the burial types. The attritional burials contained more males than females whereas the mass burials contained males and females in equal proportions. This pattern was due to the fact that there were significant fewer males in the mass burials than in the attritional burials.

Comparison of burial types c 1250–c 1400 (period 16)

Demography

During this period 50.9% (1443/2835) of the skeletons analysed were interred in mass burial pits. Again the attritional and mass burials had a similar age-at-death profile, with low numbers (as a proportion of individuals with assigned ages) of perinates (22/2718: 0.8%), infants (2/2718: 0.1%) and 1–5-year-olds (31/2718: 1.1%) (Chapter 3.2). Burials increased with advancing age up to a peak at 26–35 years (attritional 414/1327: 31.2%; catastrophic 400/1391: 28.8%) and 36–45 years (344/1327: 25.9%; 301/1391: 21.6%) and then decreased again to lower proportions of those ≥46 years (117/1327: 8.8%; 127/1391: 9.1%). There was a significantly higher proportion of subadults in the mass burials (299/1443: 20.7%) than the attritional burials (209/1392: 15.0%) and in particular there were significantly higher proportions of 12–17-year-olds in the mass burials.

As in the preceding periods, there were significantly more males than females in the attritional cemetery: the ratio of males to females was 1.3:1 in the attritional cemetery and 1.1:1 in the mass burials. This difference was due to the fact that there were significantly more males in the attritional burials than the mass burials (χ^2 = 10.57, df = 1, p ≤ 0.001).

Female age at death followed the same trend regardless of burial type: 22.8% (220/964) of females for whom age could be assigned were 18–25 years old; age at death peaked with 39.2% (378/964) of females dying aged 26–35 years; and proportions then decreased with advancing age, with 26.0% (251/964) aged 36–45 years and only 11.9% (115/964) aged ≥46 years.

Male age at death was also broadly comparable between the burial types. However, among males for whom age could be assigned, there were significantly more 18–25-year-old males in the mass burials (135/543: 24.9%) than in the attritional burials (118/599: 19.7%). Compared to females, male age at death had a more prolonged peak, spread over both the 26–35-year and 36–45-year age groups in both burial types, 34.8% (397/1142) and 32.2% (368/1142) of males in these age categories respectively; there were thus significantly more 36–45-year-old males than females in the attritional burials. Older adult males (≥46 years) were buried in similar proportions in both mass and attritional burials, c 11%, and in similar proportions to older females.

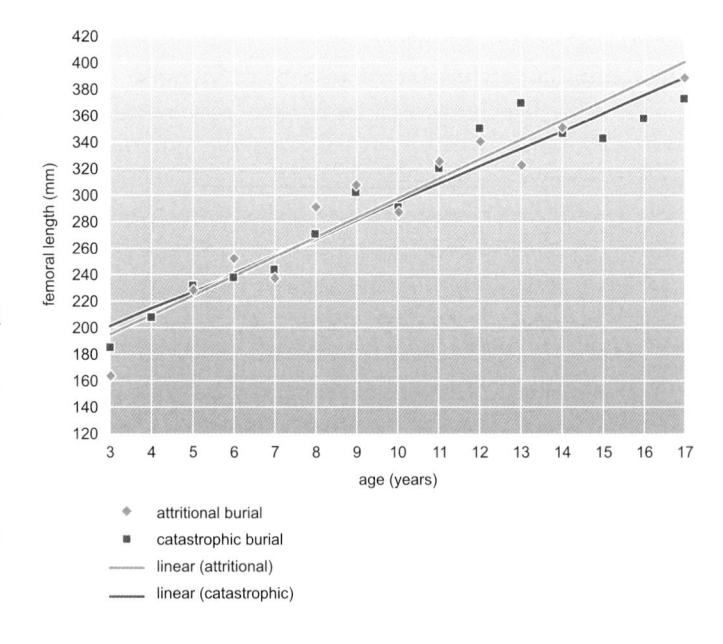

Fig 246 Comparison of subadult growth between the attritional and catastrophic burials, c 1250–c 1400 (period 16)

Health status

GROWTH

In this period there was little difference in height-for-age between the two burial types (Fig 246).

STATURE

Once again, there was little difference in adult stature between the burial types. Average female stature in this period was c 161cm in both the mass and attritional burials. Males were taller than females, at 168.4cm in the attritional cemetery, and only slightly shorter, 167.2cm, in the mass burials.

DENTAL ENAMEL HYPOPLASIA

Rates of enamel hypoplasia among subadults did not vary between burial types, and affected up to half of those buried (Table 146). Prevalence in adults was also similar in both burial types.

In early childhood (1–5 years) crude prevalence of enamel hypoplasia was relatively low and only those in the mass burials (1/14: 7.1%) were affected (Chapter 3.10). Those aged 6–11 years had much higher rates, 47.1% (41/87) in the attritional burials and 41.0% (41/100) in the mass burials, but there was no significant difference between the burial types. Rates among adolescents (12–17 years) were higher still, 49.5% (45/91) in the attritional burials and 55.7% (97/174) in the mass burials, and again there was no significant difference between the burial types.

In adults, males and females had similar true prevalence rates of enamel hypoplasia. In the attritional burials prevalence for males was 11.8% (1120/9519) and 13.2% (1030/7812) of females were affected (Chapter 3.6). Rates among those in the mass burials were only slightly higher, at 13.8% (1436/10,409) for males and 14.3% (1413/9865) for females.

CRIBRA ORBITALIA

In this period, individuals aged 1–11 years had similar crude prevalence rates of cribra in the attritional burials, where 29.8% (31/104) of both age groups were affected, and lower rates in the mass burials, 14.3% (2/14) and 2.0% (2/100) of each age group respectively (see Table 119, Chapter 3.10). Those who died in adolescence (12–17 years) had higher rates: 37.4% (34/91) of those in the attritional burials and 41.4% (72/174) of those in the mass burials were affected.

Adult males were affected in similar proportions in both the attritional burials, where the true prevalence rate was c 37–38% (right orbit 133/363: 36.6%; left orbit 141/368: 38.3%), and mass burials, where the rate was c 36–37% (right orbit 137/385: 35.6%; left orbit 144/388: 37.1%). Overall prevalence among females was slightly lower than for males, with c 33–36% (right orbit 100/307: 32.6%; left orbit 110/305: 36.1%) affected in the attritional burials and fewer, c 29–32% (right orbit 116/401: 28.9%; left orbit 122/387: 31.5%), affected in the mass burials.

POROTIC HYPEROSTOSIS

Males in the mass burials had higher rates of porotic hyperostosis and there were no other differences between the burial types.

Rates of porotic hyperostosis in subadults appeared to increase with advancing age and there was no significant difference between the two burial types (Chapter 3.14; Table 147). Only one individual aged 1–5 years (1/31: 3.2%) was affected, from a mass burial pit (1/14: 7.1%). In the older age groups, c 7–9% (attritional 6/87: 6.9%; catastrophic 9/100: 9.0%) of those aged 6–11 years and c 12–17% (attritional 11/91: 12.1%; catastrophic 30/174: 17.2%) of 12–17-year-olds were affected.

Among adults, males always had a significantly higher prevalence than females and a significantly higher proportion of males in the mass burials (162/564: 28.7%) were affected than in the attritional burials (143/628: 22.8%). Females had the same, significantly lower, rate regardless of burial type (attritional 62/474: 13.1%; catastrophic 71/535: 13.3%).

SPECIFIC DISEASES OF MALNUTRITION

Rates of these diseases were again very low in this period. There was some indication that there was a greater prevalence of dietary deficiencies during childhood among those who were buried in the mass burial pits.

Two adolescents ([21042] and [32355]) were identified as suffering from scurvy. They were both buried in mass pits, a prevalence of 1.1% (2/174). Four subadults and two adults were identified as having suffered from rickets. Of these, two 1–5-year-old children ([8464] and [18339]) were buried in the attritional cemetery. The remaining individuals, two 6–11-year-olds ([29118] and [31688]), a female aged ≥46 years ([31639]) and 26–35-year-old male [31257], were all buried in mass burials and had probably suffered from rickets during infancy or early childhood.

TUBERCULOSIS

Of the burials in period 16, a total of 2.1% (60/2835) showed the osseous changes associated with tuberculosis and these were found in equal proportions in the attritional and mass burials (Chapter 3.9; Table 148). Among subadults, 2.1% (4/187) of 6–11-year-olds and 2.3% (4/174) of adolescents (12–17 years) were affected, and there was no difference in prevalence between the burial types.

The overall proportion of females showing the skeletal changes of tuberculosis was higher than the proportion of males, 2.6% (26/1009) compared to 1.8% (21/1192), and this difference between the sexes was seen in both the attritional and mass burials. Higher rates in females were observed in both the preceding periods, but usually in the mass burials only.

In this period the prevalence of tuberculosis remained at the same level with increasing age, until it finally fell in older adults.

NON-SPECIFIC INFECTION: PERIOSTITIS

Overall, rates of periostitis in subadults and males did not differ significantly between the burial types. However, adolescents and females both experienced higher rates in the attritional burials.

In this period, subadults from the ages of 1–5 years were affected by periostitis, with a prevalence rate ranging between 10.2% and 14.7%, and with little difference between the burial types (Chapter 3.9). Adolescents (12–17 years) in the attritional burials, however, experienced a relatively higher prevalence (20/91: 22.0%), a similar rate to the preceding period.

Again in this period there was a higher prevalence among males than females. Male periostitis peaked at 36–45 years and did not vary between the burial types. Females had a lower prevalence than males and those aged 26–35 years and 36–45 years were most affected. Females in the mass burials always had a significantly lower prevalence than those in the attritional burials ($\chi^2 = 11.89$, df = 1, $p \leq 0.001$).

Summary

As with the previous period, although a greater proportion of subadults were buried in the mass burial pits, there were no consistent differences in health between the burial types. Specifically, while there were significantly more 12–17-year-olds in the mass burials, there was no difference in their growth or the prevalence of enamel hypoplasia, cribra orbitalia and porotic hyperostosis between burial types. Conversely, rates of periostitis among this age group were significantly higher in the attritional burials than the mass burials.

More generally, in younger subadults there was no clear trend for indicators of childhood stress between the burial types. There was no difference in subadult growth between the attritional and mass burials or in the incidence of enamel hypoplasia (with the exception of 1–5-year-olds, where it was absent in the attritional burials). Cribra orbitalia was lower in those in the mass burials and yet specific diseases of malnutrition, although in very low frequencies, were found mainly in those in the mass burials. Furthermore there was no difference in the prevalence of tuberculosis in subadults, or of periostitis other than for 12–17-year-olds.

A similar pattern can be observed in the adult population, where no one burial type had a clear correlation with the prevalence of stress indicators. The prevalence of enamel hypoplasia was the same, while rates of porotic hyperostosis in the mass burials were higher in men, and rates of cribra orbitalia in the attritional burials were higher in women. This is not to say that these differences are not important, but in general prevalence was not confined to a single burial type.

Clear differences between the burial types were observed in the demography of the adult population. While a higher proportion of males was found in the attritional burials the ratio of males to females in the mass burials was equal. The mass burials also contained significantly more 18–25-year-old males than the attritional burials.

There was no clear trend in the prevalence of infectious disease in adults. The prevalence of tuberculosis was similar in both burial types as was the rate of periostitis in males. Females, however, had a higher rate of periostitis in the attritional burials.

Comparison of burial types c 1400–1539 (period 17)

Demography

During this period mass burial was less common; nevertheless, 19.1% (124/650) of individuals were interred in mass burial pits. Unlike the preceding periods there were some differences in the age-at-death profile of each burial type. There were still few infants and those in early childhood but there was a higher proportion of perinatal burials than had been observed before, particularly among the attritional burials, where 4.7% (24/514 aged skeletons) died at this age, significantly more than in the preceding period. In the mass burials the proportion of perinates was more like that previously observed, at 1.6% (2/122) of burials.

In keeping with previous periods, there was a higher proportion of subadults in the mass burials when compared to the attritional cemetery, though this difference was not significant. Of those individuals for whom age could be assigned, there was a higher proportion of those aged 6–11 years (13/122) and 12–17 years (13/122) in the mass burials, both age groups comprising 10.7% each of mass burials, compared to 4.7% (24/514) and 7.0% (36/514) of the attritional burials.

As in the preceding periods there was also a significant difference in the ratio of males to females between the burial types: there were significantly more males than females in the attritional burials, a ratio of 1.5:1, but there was no significant difference between males and females in the mass burials, where there was a ratio of 1.3:1.

Female age at death differed between the burial types, with greater proportions of 36–45-year-old and ≥46-year-old females in the mass burials, both statistically significant results. Male age at death also differed between burial types. There were similar proportions of 18–25-year-old males in both burial types but, as for females, there were more 26–35-year-old males among the attritional burials, although this difference was not significant. There was a greater proportion of 36–45-year-old males in the mass burials but similar proportions of ≥46-year-old males in each burial type.

Overall, therefore, the attritional burials contained greater proportions of 18–25-year-old and 26–35-year-old adults, while the mass burials, as well as containing high proportions of 6–17-year-olds, contained more 36–45-year-olds and older adults.

Health status

GROWTH

There was little difference between the trends for the attritional and mass burials (Chapter 3.4; Fig 247). Subadults in this period achieved the highest final growth compared to the earlier periods.

STATURE

There was little difference in adult stature between the burial types (Chapter 3.3). Average female stature in this period was c 161cm in both the mass and attritional burials. Males were generally taller than females, at 169.6cm in the attritional cemetery, and slightly shorter, 165.7cm, in the mass burials. Overall there was little difference in attained height between the periods.

DENTAL ENAMEL HYPOPLASIA

Rates of enamel hypoplasia in subadults and adults did not vary significantly between the burial types. Among subadults, only individuals aged 6–11 years and 12–17 years were affected (Chapter 3.10; Table 146). Those aged 6–11 years had relatively

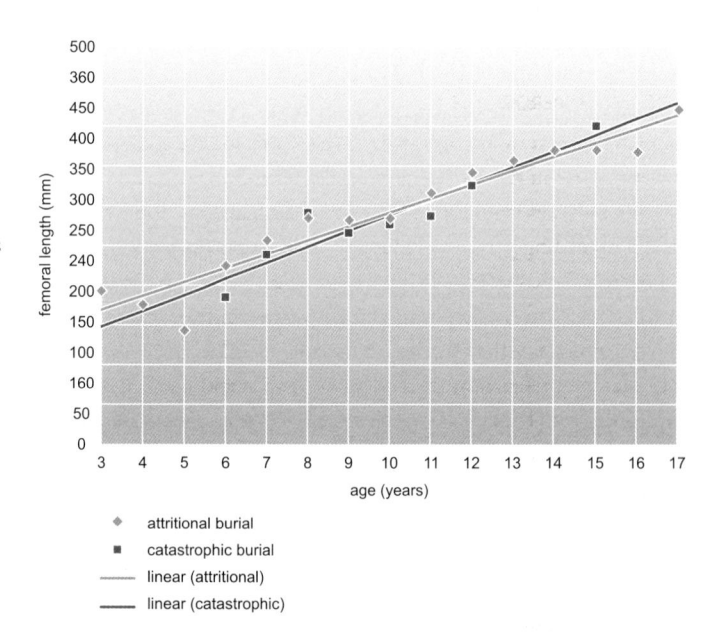

Fig 247 Comparison of subadult growth between the attritional and catastrophic burials, c 1400–1539 (period 17)

high prevalence rates: 54.2% (13/24) of those in the attritional burials and 69.2% (9/13) of those in the mass burials were affected. Although the rate was higher in the mass burials there was no significant difference between the burial types. Rates increased in the attritional burials for adolescents (12–17 years) to 63.9% (23/36) and stayed the same, 69.2% (9/13), in the mass burials, and again there was no significant difference between the burial types.

In adults, males and females experienced very similar overall true prevalence rates of enamel hypoplasia. In the attritional burials prevalence for males and females was c 12%, and in the mass burials it was c 13% for both sexes (Chapter 3.6).

CRIBRA ORBITALIA

In this period there was little difference in the prevalence of cribra orbitalia in subadults between the burial types, and prevalence rates were high, with between a third and a half of subadults affected. Overall about a third of adults were also affected but females had significantly lower rates in the mass burials.

Crude prevalence rates for cribra orbitalia were slightly higher among subadults in the mass burials but there was no statistically significant difference between the burial types (see Table 119, Chapter 3.10). The exception was those aged 1–5 years, where only those in the attritional burials were affected (40.0%: 4/10); however, only one individual of this age was buried in the mass burials so comparative data are lacking. Rates for 6–11-year-olds were c 50–54% and in 12–17-year-olds they were slightly, but not significantly, lower at c 33–46%.

Males and females in the attritional burials had similar true prevalence rates of cribra; c 30% of each sex were affected. In the mass burials, however, females experienced significantly lower rates of cribra, at c 11–19%, than in the attritional burials ($\chi^2 = 4.89$, df = 1, $p \leq 0.05$), and lower than the male prevalence in the mass burials. Males in the mass burials had slightly higher rates overall: 35.6% (26/73) were affected.

POROTIC HYPEROSTOSIS

In general there was a higher prevalence of porotic hyperostosis among those in the attritional burials. This difference between the burial types was particularly significant among males and, as in the preceding periods, males generally experienced higher rates of porotic hyperostosis than females.

Relatively few subadults, and only those in later childhood or adolescence, were affected in this period (Chapter 3.14; Table 147). Among 6–11-year-olds only those in attritional burials were affected (1/24: 4.2%). Among 12–17-year-olds there was a greater prevalence in the attritional burials, where 22.2% (8/36) were affected, compared to 7.7% (1/13) of those in the mass burials.

In adults, porotic hyperostosis affected males more than females. In the attritional burials males had a significantly higher prevalence than females, 24.3% (58/239) compared to 9.8% (16/164). The prevalence in males in the attritional burials was also significantly higher than that among males in the mass burials (5/51: 9.8%). In females there also appeared to be a higher prevalence in the attritional burials, but the numbers were too small for statistical testing.

SPECIFIC DISEASES OF MALNUTRITION

Rates of diseases of malnutrition were again very low in this period. In contrast to previous periods all the cases were observed in individuals buried in the attritional cemetery. However, their occurrence was not frequent enough to observe any significant differences between the burial types.

One individual aged 6–11 years ([3933]), 4.2% (1/24) of this age group, was identified as having suffered from vitamin C deficiency. This represents the only case buried in an individual grave and this period therefore had the highest crude prevalence rate for scurvy.

Another subadult, [10373], aged 1–5 years old, buried in the attritional cemetery, was identified as having suffered from rickets (1/10: 10.0% of this age group). As well as extensive widening of all long bone metaphyses, bowing deformities of the lower limbs suggested that this child was walking while suffering from rickets.

A ≥46-year-old female, [3699], buried in the attritional cemetery, was the only case of osteomalacia (1/19: 5.3%) identified in the whole cemetery (see Fig 156). Multiple fractures of the ribs and bodies of the scapulae, and thinning of the bones of the pelvis, were consistent with the criteria suggested by Brickley et al (2007).

TUBERCULOSIS

In this period frequencies were too low to show significant variations in the occurrence of tuberculosis between the sexes or burial types (Chapter 3.9). This period had the lowest overall prevalence of tuberculosis, with only 0.9% (6/650) of burials displayed the osseous changes associated with tuberculosis, a significantly lower rate than in the preceding period (Table 148). No subadults were affected; the majority of affected individuals, three males and two females, were buried in the attritional cemetery; and one ≥46-year-old female with tuberculosis was buried in a mass burial. The females in the attritional burials were both 18–25 years old, and of the three males one was 18–25 years old and two were 36–45 years old. Overall there was a slightly higher prevalence among females, 1.5% (3/203), than males, 1.0% (3/290), although in the attritional burials alone prevalence rates were similar (1.2–1.3%).

NON-SPECIFIC INFECTION: PERIOSTITIS

In this period the prevalence of periostitis was relatively low among subadults and only those aged 6–11 years and 12–17 years were affected (Chapter 3.9). Of individuals aged 6–11 years only those in mass burials were affected (1/13: 7.7%). Adolescents (12–17 years) in the mass burials experienced a similar rate, but those in the attritional cemetery had a slightly higher prevalence of 11.1% (4/36) affected.

Again, in this period males generally experienced higher rates of periostitis than females. Prevalence in males peaked at

36–45 years (27/67: 40.3%) in the attritional burials but earlier, at 26–35 years (9/14: 64.3%), in the mass burials. The 26–35-year-old male prevalence in the mass burials was more than double that in the attritional burials.

For females, all ages in the attritional burials were affected, with the highest prevalence between 26 and 35 years, at 27.1% (16/59). In the mass burials only 36–45-year-olds (4/11: 36.4%) and ≥46-year-olds (1/10: 10.0%) were affected.

Summary

Once again in this period a significantly higher proportion of subadults were buried in mass burials but there was no clear association of stress indicators with one particular burial type.

For the first time the proportion of perinatal burials increased above very low levels, particularly in the attritional burials. The increase in burials of perinates in this period could be due to a number of factors. It may represent a real increase in infant mortality, and subsequently burial, in this period; or it may simply be the case that more of these burials survived and were recovered because they were subject to less truncation than those of earlier periods. Alternatively perhaps there was a change in burial practice, whereby more perinates were buried within the cemetery.

While once again there were significantly higher proportions of those in later childhood and adolescence in the mass burials, patterns of health and disease in these groups were less clear cut. There was no significant difference in subadult growth, dental enamel hypoplasia or cribra orbitalia between the burial types, but the prevalence of porotic hyperostosis was higher in the attritional burials. Non-specific infection also varied between the burial types: only 6–11-year-olds in the mass burials were affected but 12–17-year-olds had higher rates in the attritional burials. There were no cases of tuberculosis in subadults observed in this period.

A similar pattern can be observed in the adult population, where the correlation of burial type and the prevalence of stress indicators were mixed. The rates of enamel hypoplasia in adults were the same in each burial type (as they were for subadults), but rates of cribra orbitalia in females, and porotic hyperostosis in males, were higher in the attritional burials. The prevalence of specific diseases of malnutrition and tuberculosis, although low, also predominated in the attritional burials. Prevalence of periostitis was also mixed: males in the mass burials generally had higher rates and females in the attritional burials were affected most.

Although the pattern of health indicators in adults was mixed there were clear differences in adult demography between the burial types. Again, as in the earlier periods, while there was a significantly higher proportion of males in the attritional burials there was no significant difference in the ratio of males to females in the mass burials. In general there were also greater proportions of 18–25-year-old and 26–35-year-old adults in the attritional cemetery, and, in contrast, greater proportions of 36–45-year-old and ≥46-year-old adults in the mass burials.

Volcanoes and vicissitudes

The fact that there were two distinct burial practices in each period of the cemetery's use – individual burials, considered to be attritional, and mass burials – prompted questions regarding the circumstances surrounding these dual burial practices. Was there an increase in population and/or a shortage of burial space, or were the mass burials a response to a sudden, short-lived rise in mortality and if so, what was the cause? The fact that mass burials occur within each phase of the cemetery would suggest that they were not simply the result of a lack of burial space: if this were the case, we might expect the mass burials to be restricted to the later phases of the site. Instead, the mass burials occur within each phase, suggesting a number of separate incidences of increased mortality. Furthermore, differences in the demographic profiles of the two burial groups outlined above suggest that the mass burials were the result of something other than the normal, attritional, causes of death.

Stress indicators were more prevalent within the mass burials in period 14 (c 1120–c 1200) and the demographic profile of each phase of mass burial shows a higher proportion of subadults than the corresponding phase of the attritional cemetery. The dating of the first three phases of mass burials closely tallies with documented occurrences of famine, suggesting that this was at least partly responsible for the differences in burial practice.

While the main phases of mass burial pre-date the Great Famine or Agrarian Crisis of the early 14th century, documentary sources show that this was just one of a long series of poor harvests and subsequent famines that occurred periodically throughout the 12th and 13th centuries. Grain prices are good evidence for the frequency and severity of harvest failures: the demand for grain was inflexible and therefore prices would rise considerably in response to any shortage (Goldberg 2004, 157). By the later 13th century prices were fluctuating markedly (ibid) and there is evidence that this fluctuation began with a series of bad harvests from at least the 12th century. Farr (1846, 160) collated numerous episodes of bad harvests, grain shortages, high prices and famines documented in the 12th and 13th centuries by contemporary chroniclers and historians:

1111   long, heavy and severe winter; cattle murrain (disease)
1124   famine
1125   spoiled harvests, famine and pestilence
1126   incessant summer rains; wheat scarcity
1162   'a great famine all over the world'
1175   pestilential distemper and dearth
1176   'a great famine and mortality'
1183   severe famine in both England and Wales
1189   'famine and great mortality'
1196   famine, 'through untimely rains', 'for some years' in England and Wales, followed by 'the fiercest pestilence'
1203   great mortality and famine
1224   dry winter, 'bad seed-time' and great famine
1252   lack of rain, severe famine, and 'great mortality of men

1257 'the inundations of autumn destroyed the fruit and grain'; poverty and fatal fevers

1258 harvest failure the previous year, resulting in 'innumerable multitudes of poor people' dead; 'in London alone 15,000 of the poor perished; in England and elsewhere thousands died'

1271 (Canterbury area): 'a violent tempest and inundation, followed by a severe famine'

1289 'a tempest destroyed the seed'; high wheat prices in London

1294 severe famine in England; many thousands of poor people perished

1295 no grain or fruits; the poor died of hunger

1315 high prices for provisions; grain spoiled by rains

1316 'universal dearth prevailed' affecting both cattle and people.

This last entry refers to the start of the Great Famine, which lasted intermittently at least until 1322.

While there may be some exaggeration in these rather dramatic descriptions of events (the last example goes on to say that people ate horses, fat dogs and even children), and political or religious bias, evidently there were recurrent bad harvests and episodes of famine during this period.

Specific years of famine do correspond with the dates of the mass burial pits at St Mary Spital, suggesting that those interred in them were the victims of famine. Dating places the mass burials in the first period of the cemetery's use to about the middle of the 12th century, perhaps corresponding with the 'great famine all over the world' (Farr 1846) in 1162. The two major phases of mass burial, containing c 2300 of the skeletons that were analysed, occurred close together and over the boundary between periods 15 and 16, dated to c 1235–55. The famines of 1252 and 1257–8 are close to these dates and occur in quick succession. In fact sources suggest that in 1258 'in London alone 15,000 of the poor perished' (Farr 1846, 161) and that these years of famine were second only to the crisis of the early 14th century (Jordan 1996). This certainly suggests that they caused a significant increase in mortality, killing a substantial proportion of the population, more than enough to necessitate a change in burial practice.

The last, much smaller phase of mass burials dates to between the 15th and early 16th centuries when at least nine famine years are known (1401, 1416, 1434, 1439, 1440, 1486, 1491, 1497 and 1521) (Farr 1846). There are, however, a number of other possibilities. Although these burials post-date the major plague epidemics, endemic plague is thought to have remained a killer during the first two-thirds of the 15th century. Furthermore, while plague may have waned, mortality levels are thought to have remained high in the last third of the 15th and first third of the 16th century due to major outbreaks of tuberculosis and 'sweating sickness' (possibly a viral pulmonary disease; Taviner et al 1998) recorded in 1485, 1508, 1517 and 1528 (Goldberg 2004, 85–6).

The cumulative effect of successive years of famine on London's population would have been devastating. For the rural population strategies for coping with isolated years of harvest shortfalls, such as savings or credit, would have been exhausted; peasant smallholders would have been forced to sell their land, thereby becoming landless and relying on their labour to make a living (Goldberg 2004, 158). To these 'dispossessed', migration into towns may have been an increasingly attractive proposition. Not only did towns offer alternative sources of employment, but they had formalised institutions for the care of the poor, such as St Mary Spital, and the distribution of alms.

The urban population of Britain was already increasing during the 12th and 13th centuries; the proportion of people living in towns rose from 10% to 20% (Dyer 2002, 187). By about the mid 12th century London had become the leading town in Britain and one of the largest and most important in north-west Europe. By 1200 its population is considered to have been c 40,000, and by 1300 it is thought that this had swelled to at least double this, c 80–100,000 (Keene 1984, 11–12), three or four times larger than other large towns in England, such as Bristol, Norwich or York. Towns both served and depended on a hinterland, usually of c 10–12km, from which the rural population could habitually and easily travel to market, but London's extended the farthest, for example, drawing grain from ten counties up to 80km away (Dyer 2002, 192).

Urban growth in this period was fuelled by migration and London's large hinterland drew people from considerable distances, frequently from the surrounding counties and from as far as the east Midlands and East Anglia (Dyer 2002, 193). To many people towns were attractive because they were permanently established concentrations of people pursuing a variety of non-agricultural occupations (ibid, 187). The larger the population the more complex and varied its life became, supporting over a hundred different occupations: crafts and trades predominated but they also included 'administrators, clergy, doctors, lawyers, schoolteachers, prostitutes and other specialists' (ibid, 188). Towns pulled in newcomers because they offered positive advantages – in particular, opportunities to make a living from different skills and talents (ibid). The largest towns like London supported groups of wealthy merchants, trading in luxury goods such as wine, or in bulk for distant markets. Towns were also familiar as centres of local administration: London benefited particularly from the centralisation of royal government there, and contained other institutions such as hospitals and friaries. The attraction of towns was coupled with difficulties in the countryside brought about by a general rise in population. Dyer (ibid, 187) suggests that the rural economy could no longer give everyone an adequate living and that young people and those with smallholdings faced impoverishment in villages which were already well supplied with labour and where land was scarce. Occasional food shortages in already overpopulated villages as well as the positive opportunities provided in towns pushed people to leave.

The increase in urban population at a time of rural economic stress could hardly have been sustainable when the inhabitants of the town were dependent on the countryside for food. In fact documentary sources describe in some detail the effects of famine and poverty in London. Heavy summer rains and very cold winters in 1257 and 1258, possibly caused by climate change resulting from a massive volcanic eruption in the tropics, ruined crops throughout Europe (Stothers 2000). Palaeoclimate data (tree rings and climate reconstructions) also show that the summers of 1257 to 1259 were unusually cold (Oppenheimer 2003, 422). A correlation between this and a massive sulphate anomaly identified in the ice core records at the same date (eg Hammer et al 1980) has led some researchers to suggest that a massive volcanic eruption, potentially the largest of the historic period and possibly located somewhere in the tropics, was responsible for climatic fluctuation during these years (Oppenheimer 2003; Stothers 2000). Such eruptions in modern times have obvious meteorological consequences: not only do they release large quantities of ash and dust into the atmosphere, but the large volumes of sulphur volatiles released create an aerosol veil which blocks incoming sunlight and alters atmospheric circulation patterns, causing cooling of the Earth's surface and increased precipitation, and adversely affecting agriculture (Lowe and Walker 1997, 368; Stothers 2000, 362).

Records suggest that England suffered particularly during these years, and famine in the countryside drove thousands of villagers into London, where many of them died from hunger (Anon 1890; Fitz-Thedmar 1274). Matthew Paris, writing in 1259, records outbreaks of various famine diseases, especially among the 'numerous urban paupers' (cited in Stothers 2000, 365), and a further source states that in 1257 over 20,000 people died of starvation and its attendant diseases in London alone (Keys et al 1950). This was followed by 'the great pestilence' of April 1259, possibly influenza, which is known to have affected London, Paris, other areas of France, Italy and probably Austria (Stothers 2000, 366). During the period of the Great Famine, the chronicler Trokelowe describes the deaths of 55 poor men and women who were crushed to death while waiting for a distribution of alms at the Dominican friary in London in 1322, and he also describes seeing bodies lying in the streets (Goldberg 2004, 158). At the height of the Great Famine it is likely that food was both scarce and expensive; there is anecdotal evidence for an increase in thefts of foodstuffs, despite the punishment being hanging, and London authorities had to prosecute bakers for selling bread that was underweight or made from adulterated or rotten grain (ibid, 159).

While it is relatively easy to relate historically documented incidences of famine to the dates of the mass burial pits, observing evidence for famine osteologically is far more problematic. Several individuals with specific diseases of malnutrition (scurvy and rickets) were found in period 16 (c 1250–c 1400) and, although they were few, the majority were buried in the mass pits. However, malnutrition would not have been the sole cause of death during famine. Although coroners' rolls for Bedfordshire in the 1270s describe the deaths of indigent women from exposure and hunger (Goldberg 2004, 158), those affected by famine would not necessarily have died from starvation. Studies of the demography of past famines reveal that the 'main cause of excess mortality was not literal starvation but infectious disease' (Dyson and Ó Gráda 2002, 2). Modern studies have also shown that excess deaths result rather from a combination of hunger-induced diseases, such as dysentery, and other diseases which are more a product of the social disruption caused by famine, such as typhoid fever (ibid). They also suggest that where infectious diseases are endemic in a population they will figure prominently during times of crisis (ibid). We could certainly suggest that tuberculosis was endemic in medieval London; c 2% (100/5387) of the St Mary Spital burials showed skeletal changes relating to tuberculosis, and given that these changes are only seen in 5–7% of cases, an estimated 37% (c 2000/5387) may have had tuberculosis; we would expect that it would have been responsible for many deaths during episodes of famine.

Comparison between a 'typical' famine profile and the demography of St Mary Spital shows some areas of similarity. First, famine usually amplifies the 'normal' distribution of deaths, though this may be complicated, and overlain, by outbreaks of infectious disease (Dyson and Ó Gráda 2002, 2). With the exception of subadults (see below) there is little difference at St Mary Spital between the age-at-death profiles of the mass and attritional burials in each period. If the attritional cemetery represents a 'normal' attritional distribution then the mass burials are largely an amplification of this: the population is dying in the same relative proportions but over a much shorter period of time. Second, during a famine young children and the elderly experience the greatest increase in mortality, although the greatest proportional increase usually occurs among those where death rates are normally low (eg 10–45 years) (ibid). The age-at-death profiles at St Mary Spital do show a greater proportion of subadults in the mass burials than in the attritional cemetery within each period, suggesting periodic increases in mortality among the younger members of the population. While the mortality of very young and very old individuals is also expected to increase, their absence from the mass burials at St Mary Spital is likely to be the result of cultural factors and difficulties with ageing older individuals. Third, male mortality increases more than that of females and this is most pronounced when starvation, rather than infectious disease, has a greater role in mortality (ibid). At St Mary Spital, however, equal numbers of males and females were buried in the mass burial pits, in contrast to a higher proportion of males to females in the attritional cemetery. Yet male mortality is only expected to increase when the principal cause of death is starvation, suggesting that, at St Mary Spital, infectious diseases accompanying periods of famine were significant causes of death. Comparison with profiles from other known catastrophic events shows a different pattern from that observed at St Mary Spital. In general these show higher proportions of deaths of younger individuals, with mortality decreasing with age (eg Chamberlain 2006, 125, fig 4.11). In contrast, at St Mary Spital, although there is an increase in subadult deaths in the mass burials, mortality still increases with age.

We can also demonstrate osteologically that the population underwent a period of prolonged stress that may reflect the repeated incidences of famine and associated infectious disease.

In the first period of burial there was a clear distinction between the health of those buried in the pits and those in the attritional cemetery. There were significantly more children aged 6–11 and 12–17 years in the mass burial pits and these children were shorter for their age. Furthermore, both children and adults had a higher prevalence of stress indicators than those buried in the attritional cemetery. This suggests that a higher proportion of those who were buried in the mass pits were those whose health had already been compromised in some way, had suffered childhood stresses, such as illness or poor nutrition, and did not achieve their growth potential. In period 15 (c 1200–50) the evidence suggests that the population as a whole had experienced similar rates of malnutrition and stress. While the number of 6–11-year-olds was higher in the mass burials and these children were shorter than those in the attritional cemetery, high rates of stress indicators were found in both burial groups. In fact for some stress indicators there was no difference in the prevalence rates between the burial types. Similarly, in period 16 the majority of stress indicators occurred at the same rates in both burial types, indicating that both burial groups had experienced similar levels of these biological 'stresses'. This pattern is repeated in the final phase of the cemetery, period 17 (c 1400–1539), where evidence of malnutrition and stress was seen in similar proportions in both burial groups. This change, from a clear relationship between the mass burials and evidence for poor health in the first period of burials to a more even distribution of stress indicators between the burial groups in the later periods, supports the occurrence of repeated episodes of famine throughout the period of use of the cemetery. In period 14 a higher proportion of those buried in the mass burials had already experienced previous malnutrition or stress and may have been more susceptible to infection. In the subsequent periods this distinction is less clear, suggesting that the population as a whole was experiencing stresses early in life. Some of those buried in the attritional cemetery in period 15 would have been the survivors of earlier, perhaps less severe famine years, and would therefore show evidence of childhood stress. Similarly those buried in the attritional cemetery in period 16 had survived the major famine events that caused the increased levels of mortality resulting in the two phases of mass burials. This relationship between incidences of famine can also be seen in the demographic profile for period 16. Here, the higher proportion of older subadults in the mass burials, related to the famine of 1257–8, may be a product of their increased susceptibility to famine and related diseases due to stresses suffered during the previous period of elevated mortality, the famine of 1252, when they would have been young children.

The archaeological evidence also supports the idea of a period of prolonged stress and shows an evolving response to increased mortality over time. In the first period the reaction to greater numbers of people dying and needing burial appears to have been an opportunistic use of some disused quarry pits on the site. The response to a second, presumably larger, increase in mortality (perhaps some 90 years later) is more organised, with the excavation of rows of purpose-dug rectangular pits (containing an average of 8–20 people). A third increase in deaths followed very shortly afterwards (perhaps as little as five years later) and required yet more, larger, pits to be excavated; these were located in between those from the previous phase and designed to hold more people (an average of 20–40 individuals). Interestingly, though there are two subsequent periods of increased mortality, the Great Famine of 1315–18 and the Black Death of 1348–9, there are no corresponding mass burials. Perhaps the experience of the previous famines made the authorities aware of what they could deal with. When faced with deaths on an even larger scale, such as those during the Great Famine or Black Death, the earlier events may have provided an awareness that altogether different coping strategies were required. We know that whole cemeteries were created to deal with those who died during the Black Death: the elongated trenches for multiple burial at East Smithfield, for example, could even be seen as a natural extension of the methods employed (or even learned) at St Mary Spital. Although circumstances required mass burial pits again in the last period of the cemetery (c 1400–1539), when about ten pits were excavated, the relatively small numbers suggest a response to a localised or short-lived rise in mortality.

The mass burials at Spital reflect highly elevated levels of mortality occurring over relatively short periods and at intervals throughout the whole period of the cemetery's use. Most dramatically, over 2300 individuals from the osteologically studied sample were buried during periods 15 and 16 in two closely spaced phases, perhaps only a few years apart, when by comparison only 1900 individuals were interred in the attritional cemetery over the course of both periods (c 1200–c 1400). Historical sources reveal a series of recurrent famines and epidemics during this period, a number of which correspond closely with the dates of mass burial at Spital. While some individuals may be under-represented, namely infants (who may be buried elsewhere) and older adults (where osteological method limitations mean distinction is difficult), the mass burials did not demonstrate a 'classic' catastrophic demographic profile. A relatively larger proportion of 6–17-year-olds within the mass burials was the main difference in age-at-death data when compared to that from the attritional burials. This does share some similarity with the known demographic effects of famines, whereby the 'normal' distribution of deaths is amplified with the greatest proportional increases in those where death rates are normally low. There was also evidence that the population as a whole became more biologically 'stressed' over time. While those in the mass burials clearly experienced higher levels of 'stress' and reduced growth in the earliest phase of burial, increasingly as time progressed those in the attritional burials showed similar or higher levels of 'stress', consistent with a prolonged period of recurrent food shortages and epidemics. St Mary Spital evidently managed the frequent and episodic increases in mortality caused by these periodic years of famine, but when it came to events on a much greater scale, such as the 'swift and cataclysmic' Black Death (Goldberg 2004, 164), they used this experience to evolve new ways of coping.

4.4 Comparison between St Mary Spital and other London cemeteries

Brian Connell

The large size of the St Mary Spital medieval cemetery allows it to be used as a baseline for comparison with other medieval cemetery sites from across London. Indeed, we are perhaps fortunate in this respect, because a series of published human skeletal assemblages from London provides a broad base of data for comparative purposes and allows us to examine possible differences between groups from different socio-economic backgrounds from one urban centre.

Throughout the period that this cemetery was in use (*c* 1120–1539), London underwent a series of complex social, environmental and political changes; commercialisation increased and an ever more complex network of trade links developed, reaching across the globe. The skeletal remains from St Mary Spital allow us to assess the impact of these changes on human populations by providing cross-sectional data for the disease load of a medieval population. The need to clarify the role disease has played in the process of adaptation between human groups and their environment has already been stressed by Ortner (1991, 10).

This section examines the general prevalence of disease in medieval London and considers a wider view of health by comparing some of the more commonly encountered skeletal pathology. The tabulated data reflect those provided in the published references and thus the number of affected individuals could not always be provided.

Prevalence of specific infectious diseases

Leprosy, tuberculosis and treponematosis were found at St Mary Spital in addition to a wide array of non-specific osseous changes. In some respects, the high prevalence of infectious disease in this cemetery is to be expected: in an expanding urban population overcrowding and poor levels of sanitation would have increased potential for the transmission of communicable disease.

Leprosy

The charter at St Mary Spital stated that the hospital and priory were to exclude leprosy sufferers (Thomas et al 1997, 104), so the presence of two adult females, [2487] and [19821], dated to period 16 (*c* 1250–*c* 1400) and period 17 (*c* 1400–1539) respectively, with osseous changes suggestive of leprosy comes as a surprise. It is possible that these individuals showed no external signs of leprosy, or that it was misdiagnosed. Although the pathognomonic rhinomaxillary changes were not observed in either case, characteristic changes were detected in the hands and feet, pointing towards the tuberculoid form of the infection. These are among the first cases of leprosy found in medieval London. Comparative prevalence rates from sites elsewhere in London are shown in Table 149.

Up to 270 leprosaria were founded during the medieval period, mostly between the 11th and 13th centuries. In London, leprosy hospitals were founded well away from settlements in areas of open land (Thomas et al 1997, 125) and as yet no leprosaria have been excavated in the capital. Leprosy began to decline after the 14th century and the case from period 17 ([19821]) is therefore quite late. The absence of (bony) facial changes in these individuals may reflect a lack of overlying soft tissue lesions which might have meant that they were not considered leprous at the time. Skeleton [2487] was interred in a pit containing 22 individuals, and it is possible that the leprosy was missed because the circumstances may have required the burial of a large number of people at one time.

Bekvalac and Kausmally (2011, 184–5) describe two putative leprosy cases, in an unsexed adult and a 36–45-year-old male, from the east cloister and nave of the church of St Mary Graces, dated to 1350–1539. These may represent further cases of the disease, but the diagnosis is not firm. More secure cases have been identified in later (post-medieval) cemeteries, pointing to the continued presence of leprosy in London: for example an 18–25-year-old male (dating from 1750–1850) from St Marylebone, Westminster (Walker 2009). Given the scant evidence for leprosy in medieval London, further cases are required to fully evaluate patterns in this disease over time.

Table 149 Comparison of crude prevalence of specific infectious disease in London medieval cemetery samples

Cemetery sample	Tuberculosis No. affected	Tuberculosis %	Leprosy No. affected	Leprosy %	Treponematosis No. affected	Treponematosis %
St Mary Spital	100	1.9	2	<0.1	25	0.5
St Mary Merton	4	0.6	0	-	0	-
Holy Trinity Aldgate	3	11.1	0	-	0	-
St Mary Graces	3*	0.8	2	0.5	1	0.3
East Smithfield, Black Death cemetery	4	0.6	0	-	1	0.2
St Mary Stratford Langthorne	present	-	0	-	0	-
St Saviour Bermondsey	1	0.5	0	-	0	-
St Nicholas Shambles	0	-	0	-	0	-

* Two further cases were previously identified by examination of aDNA but are not included here.

Tuberculosis

A large sample of 100 cases of tuberculosis was recorded from St Mary Spital (36 males, 43 females, 16 subadults and 5 adults of indeterminate sex) (Chapter 3.9). The majority had died between c 1200 and c 1400 (periods 15 and 16).

Tuberculosis has been identified in several other London monastic sites (Table 149): for example, a single case of tuberculosis was seen in a young adult from the Cluniac burial ground at Bermondsey Priory/Abbey (Connell and White 2011, 269). White (2004, 177) also identified several cases of tuberculosis in the Cistercian cemetery at St Mary Stratford Langthorne, where both bones and joints were affected. A high frequency of tuberculosis was reported at Holy Trinity Aldgate in the City of London, where Conheeney (2005, 262) describes three cases (11.1% of the total number of individuals). The Cistercian burial ground at St Mary Graces contained two children aged 6–11 years with tuberculosis (2/199: 1.0%), providing a crude prevalence rate of 2.0% for the total sample (Bekvalac and Kausmally 2011, 171). At the adjacent East Smithfield site containing mass burials from the Black Death, a further four cases of tuberculosis (two children and two adult males) were noted (Cowal et al 2008, 51). At the priory of St Mary Merton, which like St Mary Spital was part of the Augustinian order, four cases were identified based on characteristic spinal changes. These burials mostly came from an area of the cemetery likely to contain lay personnel other than the upper classes (Conheeney 2007, 275). Previous excavations at St Mary Spital produced a single case of possible tuberculosis, where Conheeney (1997, 229) reports a juvenile (C[1302]) with erosions in the thoracic and lumbar vertebrae.

Clearly, tuberculosis was widespread in London. As previously discussed (Chapter 4.1), increased levels of residential overcrowding, combined with poor sanitation, would have meant that the risk of exposure to tuberculosis was all too great.

Treponematosis

In Britain there has been an enormous amount of debate surrounding the question of the timing and emergence of treponematosis. Multiple theories about the origins of treponemal disease abound in the literature. Roberts (2000b, 154) points out that 'the accurate identification of cases is one of the highest priorities because of the numerous hypotheses and questions which have been raised over the years about the treponematoses'. The first indication that the analysis of the skeletal assemblage associated with St Mary Spital could contribute to this debate came in 1926 with the discovery of a skull with the pathognomonic changes of treponemal disease. Found during the westward extension of the Spitalfields Market building in 1926, this skull originates from the truncated upper levels of the cemetery complex. The skull was described by Wells (1964) and is now archived in the Duckworth Collection, Cambridge.

As already noted, 25 individuals have been diagnosed with treponemal disease at St Mary Spital, forming 0.5% (25/5387) of the recorded sample (Chapter 3.9). Given the huge number of skeletons excavated from medieval London it is perhaps surprising that just one other cemetery has produced evidence for treponematosis (Table 149). The cemeteries of St Mary Graces and East Smithfield together produced two individuals with probable treponemal changes (2/1012: 0.2%). The first was a male aged 26–35 years from the abbey churchyard at St Mary Graces, dating from 1350–c 1400. Diagnosis was based on the characteristic post-cranial changes, 'snail tracking' within inflammatory new bone deposition, but the skull was absent (Bekvalac and Kausmally 2011, 177). A second case, from the Black Death mass burial trenches at East Smithfield, dated 1348–50, was a subadult, although a more precise age is not provided. The diagnosis is based on the presence of Hutchinson's incisors and mulberry molars in an incomplete skeleton (Cowal et al 2008, 52).

The total number of treponematosis cases from medieval London is 28: the 25 individuals from St Mary Spital described here, the case found in 1926 (Wells 1964) and the two cases from St Mary Graces and East Smithfield. These form the largest sample of archaeologically derived cases of treponematosis in Europe. The dating suggests that treponematosis, both congenital and acquired syphilis, was present in the population of medieval London as early as the 13th century. In patients infected with treponematosis it is estimated that only 5–20% will show bony lesions (Roberts and Manchester 2005, 208), so the actual number of sufferers in the living population would have been higher. The high prevalence of non-specific infection in the sample from St Mary Spital (ie diffuse periostitis, which typically affects the lower limbs, and osteitis) may represent further cases of treponemal disease in the early stages of osseous involvement and therefore not yet showing any changes that enable differentiation from non-specific infection. The identification of treponemal disease in 13th-century London clearly points to a pre-Columbian origin, and suggests that in any evaluation of the evolutionary dynamics of treponematosis and its origins in Britain, the exploratory voyages of Christopher Columbus and his crew should not be considered as the principal contributing factor.

Prevalence of non-specific infection

Osteomyelitis and osteitis

Evidence for osteomyelitis at St Mary Spital consisted of only 30 cases, which made it difficult to ascertain whether there was any meaningful pattern over time. A low frequency of these conditions was also observed in other sites across London (Table 150). Osteomyelitis was seen at St Mary Stratford Langthorne, where White (2004, 177) describes individuals with large sinus drains affecting lower limb bones, and unusually, a sacrum. In the abbey churchyard at St Mary Graces, osteomyelitis affected the right proximal femur of a young female, the left tibia of another female, and the right acromion and clavicle (an unusual location) of a further individual (Bekvalac and Kausmally 2011, 171).

Table 150 Comparison of non-specific infectious disease rates in London medieval cemetery samples (* = true prevalence rate)

Cemetery sample	Osteomyelitis		Periostitis	
	No. affected	%	No. affected	%
St Mary Spital	30	0.6	1204	22.4
St Mary Merton	0	-	158	32.6*
Holy Trinity Aldgate	0	-	0	-
East Smithfield, Black Death cemetery	0	-	32	5.1
St Mary Graces	5	1.3	53	14.0
St Mary Stratford Langthorne	present	-	0	31.2*
St Saviour Bermondsey	0	-	27	13.9
St Nicholas Shambles	0	-	0	-

In total there were 50 cases of osteitis across periods 14–17, with males and females equally affected. As with osteomyelitis, it is rarely reported in other monastic sites; Bekvalac and Kausmally (2011, 177) found osteitis in a 36–45-year-old male from the abbey churchyard at St Mary Graces in the right tibia and left fibula.

Periostitis

It has already been noted that periostitis is frequently seen in archaeological populations and is usually described as a non-specific stress indicator. Periostitis was particularly prevalent in the lower limbs: two-thirds (67.7%) of all cases were in the tibiae and/or fibulae. Overall, at St Mary Spital, just under a quarter of the total population were affected (Chapter 3.9). This does not come as much of a surprise as the majority of all other cases across London also occur in the lower limb bones. For example, at Bermondsey Priory/Abbey 27.6% (27/98) of the right tibiae and 34.6% (26/75) of the left tibiae were affected (Connell and White 2011, 270). Similarly, at St Mary Stratford Langthorne, White (2004, 177) reports a high prevalence rate of periosteal lesions in 31.2% of all tibiae. Periostitis was also fairly common at Holy Trinity Aldgate, with most changes being restricted to the lower leg bones (Conheeney 2005, 262).

At St Mary Graces churchyard, 10.6% (24/226) of tibiae were affected (Bekvalac and Kausmally 2011, 170). Cowal et al (2008, 46) state that non-specific infection was present, presumably in the form of periosteal lesions, in 29 individuals from the Black Death graves, but no further details were given. They also point to three subadults with periosteal growth on long bones, including one in the early post-neonatal age group. A much higher frequency of periostitis was noted at St Mary Merton, where 32.6% (158/484) of individuals with tibiae showed periosteal lesions (Conheeney 2007, 273). This demonstrates that the frequencies of the condition can be highly variable.

Harvey (1993, 109, cited in Gilchrist and Sloane 2005, 212) found that infirmarers' accounts from Benedictine Westminster Abbey contained descriptions of a condition known as *morbus in tibia*. It is not too difficult to imagine a link between this description and the numbers of tibiae with inflammatory changes seen at many sites.

Sinusitis

Sinusitis has been found in other London sites, but none of the assemblages has been subject to a systematic study, making direct comparisons of frequency data difficult. Connell and White (2011, 270) report four adult males at Bermondsey Priory/Abbey with bone formation in the maxillary sinuses, and White (2004, 177) describes five affected adults from Stratford Langthorne. Bekvalac and Kausmally (2011, 170) describe four affected males and one female, or 8% of the individuals with broken skulls which allowed inspection. Frontal sinusitis is also reported in two males from the central nave area, and attributed to exposure to a smoky environment (ibid).

Dental disease

Caries

In the St Mary Spital population tooth decay was very common (Chapter 3.6; Table 27). The frequencies ranged from 8.6% (period 14) to 13.3% (period 17), with an overall total of 10.3%. In general the caries frequencies across medieval London are highly variable, with an average value of 6.3%; this is little different from a British average of 5.6% given by Roberts and Cox (2003, 259). However, the rate at St Mary Spital is considerably higher than this. Several other researchers have reported low caries frequencies, such as 5.5% at the parish cemetery of St Nicholas Shambles (White 1988, 39), 4.5% and 6.5% from the monastic cemeteries at Stratford Langthorne and Bermondsey (White 2004, 179; Connell and White 2011, 274), 5.9% at St Lawrence Jewry churchyard (White 2007, 501) and dropping as low as 2% at Holy Trinity Aldgate (Conheeney 2005, 260).

Caries frequency has also been shown to vary between men and women. There is a paucity of meaningful data for comparing male and female caries frequencies, as not all researchers have dealt with male and female dentitions separately (see also Roberts and Cox 2003, 265). At St Mary Spital, the overall total frequency of caries in the sexes was very similar, 10.0% (3663/36,471) in men and 10.5% (3399/32,227) in women. At Merton Priory, Conheeney (2007, 274) gives a frequency of 10.1% for males and 10.9% for females, and at St Mary Graces Bekvalac and Kausmally (2011, 173) report a higher prevalence in men (8.7%) than women (5.4%), with a combined adult tooth frequency of 8.9%. Cowal et al (2008, 48) also report a higher frequency in men (8.5%) than women (5.2%) from the Black Death mass burial trenches at East Smithfield.

Finding comparative data for subadult dental pathology from London is even more difficult. Even when data have been recorded, sometimes authors exclude deciduous or mixed transitional dentitions from the calculations of disease prevalence on the basis of small sample sizes. In the case of trivial data sets clearly this is justified, as at Holy Trinity

Aldgate or St Lawrence Jewry churchyard, Guildhall, for example. The only site for which data from the children's teeth have been presented is St Mary Graces. Here, caries prevalence in subadults was low: in most cases only a few children showed caries. In the later ?epidemic sample, only 0.8% (3/354) of children's teeth showed caries, and in the churchyard sample 18 subadults from the 6–11 and 12–17-year-old age groups had caries. In the ?epidemic samples caries was seen in 15.0% (12/80) of subadults, and only three cavities were seen in deciduous teeth; in the mass burial trenches 19.5% (26/133) of subadults exhibited carious lesions. A total of 11.4% of all children's teeth at Merton Priory were carious.

Enamel hypoplasia

In total, some 13.4% of all teeth at St Mary Spital showed defects of enamel formation (see also Chapter 3.6). It is well known from the clinical literature that canine teeth in particular are most sensitive to disruptions in enamel formation and this is also seen here: maxillary canines showed hypoplastic defects ranging from 21.6% to 29.8% and even higher frequencies were seen in mandibular canines, ranging from 27.1% to 32.9%. This was also observed in the Black Death burials from East Smithfield, where Cowal et al (2008) report higher frequencies in mandibular canines (45.6%) compared to maxillary (38.3%). At St Mary Stratford Langthorne one-third of all individuals with intact dentition showed these enamel defects (White 2004, 176). At Holy Trinity Aldgate, Conheeney (2005, 260) gives a crude prevalence rate of 15.4%. Bekvalac and Kausmally (2011, 173–4) report that in the western ?epidemic cemetery at St Mary Graces men were more commonly affected (62.2%) than women (46.2%). They also note that when the adult canine tooth was considered in isolation the frequency was 53.9% (41/76).

The crowns of canine teeth are usually completely developed by the age of 7 years (Van Beek 1983) and the presence of hypoplasia therefore suggests that the majority of the stress periods occurred in early childhood. It has been suggested that events such as harvest failures would have led to deprivation, particularly for the poor (Chapter 4.3). It is possible that a high frequency of dental hypoplastic defects in the later medieval period could be related to famine, seasonal variations in food supply or waves of an endemic disease.

The Great Famine of 1315–18 has been well documented, and many argue that this might be responsible for the high frequencies of enamel defects in medieval London. Cowal et al (2008, 53) consider the Great Famine as a factor in the high frequency of hypoplastic defects in the Black Death cemetery. This is further supported by the work of Bekvalac and Kausmally (2011) with the St Mary Graces samples. Here the highest frequencies of defects were observed at either end of the age spectrum, with the lowest prevalence in the 26–35 and 36–45 age groups. Cowal et al (2008, 53) argue that some of the oldest adults who had been subjected to periods of malnutrition or other environmental stress during early childhood development would have lived through the Great Famine of 1315–18. At St Mary Spital, enamel defects were distributed evenly through periods 14–17 (see Fig 38; Fig 39) and there was no peak in period 16 (c 1250–c 1400), when we might have expected children exposed to stress such as malnutrition to have shown hypoplastic defects.

Finding comparative data for enamel hypoplasia in deciduous dentition is extremely difficult as it is rarely reported. At St Mary Spital, out of a total of 2327 deciduous teeth only seven (0.3%) showed any evidence of enamel hypoplastic defects. This is much lower than the 2.9% of deciduous teeth from Merton Priory with hypoplasia (Conheeney 2007, 275).

Periapical lesions

The frequencies of periapical lesions at St Mary Spital varied from 2.5% to 3.3% of observable tooth positions; overall the frequency was 2.7% (2466/92,259 tooth positions) (Chapter 3.6). Comparable frequencies were seen at Bermondsey Priory/Abbey, where Connell and White (2011, 273) report frequencies of 3.3% in the maxilla and 2.6% in the mandible. At other sites, such as Holy Trinity Aldgate, the frequency is also highly variable, with prevalence rates of 3.0–11.1% (Conheeney 2005, 260). Across London in general frequencies for periapical lesions are on the whole much lower than for St Mary Spital. Very few lesions were seen in the Black Death burials from East Smithfield where Cowal et al (2008) also report a low frequency of 1.6%. A low frequency (<1%) was reported at St Lawrence Jewry churchyard (White 2007, 501). However, the prevalence at St Mary Spital does not appear exceptional when compared to data from beyond London (Chapter 4.5) (Holst and Coughlan 2000, 83).

Although periapical lesions are principally an end stage of either a cariogenic process or (to a lesser extent) pulpal exposure due to heavy dental wear, it might be expected that the proportions of periapical lesions will closely mirror the caries frequency. This is not always true; Bekvalac and Kausmally (2011, 173) found a low frequency of 0.6% from St Mary Graces, which is much lower than the 2.7% from St Mary Spital, even though the caries frequencies are roughly the same. This serves to reinforce the notion that periapical lesions are cumulative features and that many factors contribute to the frequency of dental abscesses in archaeological populations.

Calculus

There were considerable numbers of individuals with calculus deposits in the St Mary Spital population through all periods, with between 81.5% and 83.9% of teeth showing at least some mineralised plaque (Chapter 3.6). Roberts and Cox (2003, 262) also provide overall frequencies pointing to high calculus rates during the medieval period, with up to 71% of teeth affected. However, data are scant and direct comparisons are difficult because calculus is a cumulative process and is therefore seen more frequently in groups with higher numbers of older individuals. The high frequency of sub-gingival calculus seen at St Mary Spital correlates with the evidence of periodontal disease and the high frequency of root caries. In clinical contexts the distribution and extent of sub-gingival calculus deposits correlate well with the presence and severity of inflammatory periodontal disease (Hillson 1996, 260).

Most other skeletal reports from the London region do not give detailed breakdowns of the position of a calculus deposit relative to the cemento-enamel junction so it is difficult to compare frequencies. The high frequency at St Mary Spital might argue against any regular dental hygiene practices or suggest that any tooth-brushing was not sufficiently routine or rigorous to prevent the build-up of calculus over time. Many reports on skeletal assemblages from London suggest that high rates of calculus are evidence of poor oral hygiene: indeed Roberts and Cox (2003, 262) propose that high calculus rates during the medieval period are more likely to reflect a lack of effective oral hygiene than dietary influences. However, as previously discussed, the interpretation of these data in relation to diet and oral hygiene is somewhat difficult (4.1, above).

Across London monastic sites the proportion of teeth showing calculus deposits is very high. Three-quarters of teeth (75%) in adult jaws at St Nicholas Shambles had mineralised plaque (White 1988, 38); Conheeney (2005, 260) describes a frequency of 84.5% at Holy Trinity Aldgate as 'a moderate to severe problem' and again at Merton Priory (2007, 274) describes calculus as a widespread and severe problem. In the population from St Mary Graces, 56% of male and female teeth showed calculus accumulation, while in the abbey churchyard sample from the same site frequencies of 60% in men and 80% in women in the 26–35-year-old age group were seen (Bekvalac and Kausmally 2011, 178). Cowal et al (2008) also point to high frequencies of 79.8% in females and 58.6% in males from East Smithfield. Compared to these data the number of teeth with calculus deposits at St Mary Spital is within the range seen at other sites.

Periodontal disease

The epidemiology of periodontitis is problematic: it involves genetic, environmental, dietary and oral hygiene factors (Hillson 1996, 269; Hildebolt and Molnar 1991, 237). Accurate diagnosis is hampered by the effects of continuing eruption and by other factors such as hypercementosis, which can lead to methodological problems (Glass 1991; Hillson 2000; Lavigne and Molto 1995, 271). Indeed, Freeth (2000, 228) has suggested that these factors result in the over-reporting of periodontitis in archaeological publications. Clinical studies demonstrate that there is a clear relationship between periodontitis and age: a skeletal sample with an older average age is likely to show more periodontitis than a younger one (Hillson 1996, 266; Hildebolt and Molnar 1991, 236). Attempts to compare these data to other medieval sites in London are also marred by the problem of data being presented either as detailed frequency by tooth position, or as crude prevalence by individual (Roberts and Cox 2003, 261).

A multifactorial epidemiology and lack of comparative data make it difficult to draw meaningful conclusions from the periodontitis data for St Mary Spital; however, the condition was present in the population in varying degrees of severity. For St Mary Spital periodontitis is best considered as a contributing factor in other oral pathology and the high frequency goes some way towards explaining why 9.9% of caries cavities are on the roots of teeth and why there is such a high level of sub-gingival calculus.

The methodological problems mentioned above make direct comparisons between populations extremely difficult, especially in view of differing mortality profiles. Nevertheless, other researchers who have looked at skeletal material from London have systematically recorded periodontal disease and this does at least give the impression of how commonly it is diagnosed. At St Nicholas Shambles, 56% of adult jaws showed periodontitis, and in the later ?epidemic sample at St Mary Graces there was an overall prevalence of 23.1% (White 1988, 39; Bekvalac and Kausmally 2011, 173). At the adjacent East Smithfield Black Death site, Cowal et al (2008, 48) report a frequency of 64.9% in females aged 36–45 years old and 50.9% for males aged over 46 years. At Merton Priory, 34.5% of men and 40.2% of women were affected (Conheeney 2007, 274).

Ante-mortem tooth loss

Severely diseased teeth, principally those that have been partially destroyed by caries or loosened by periodontitis, will result in the disruption of the tooth socket and loss of the tooth. The tooth socket (alveolus) will then remodel and fill with new bone. Loss of the tooth represents an end stage in a sequential process of tooth decay, loss and alveolar remodelling. Severe attrition, calculus and periodontitis are known to complicate ante-mortem loss, and as seen above, the latter two conditions are very common in this population.

The overall frequency of ante-mortem tooth loss at St Mary Spital was 11.9% (10,985 teeth lost out of an available total of 92,259 tooth positions). Across London ante-mortem tooth loss is widely reported, although not always in the same format. A frequency of 7.6% of available tooth positions was seen at St Nicholas Shambles (White 1988, 40), and Connell and White (2011, 273 table 25) report a frequency of 8.1% among males at Bermondsey Priory/Abbey. Similar figures emerge at other sites, such as an overall rate of 9.3% for the later ?epidemic sample from St Mary Graces (Bekvalac and Kausmally 2011, 172). This suggests that the frequency of 11.9% at St Mary Spital is not unusual when compared to the rest of London.

Joint disease

Osteoarthritis is a commonly observed pathological feature in human skeletal remains and is one of the most common forms of joint disease in both modern and ancient populations (Rogers 2000, 165). At St Mary Spital, there was roughly the same crude prevalence rate in each period (Chapter 3.7). Generally speaking males had a higher prevalence of osteoarthritis than females. The minor variations in the prevalence of osteoarthritis within different sub-samples can be attributed to the fact that there is a

Table 151 *Comparison of crude prevalence of osteoarthritis and DISH in London medieval cemetery samples*

Cemetery sample	DISH		Osteoarthritis	
	No. affected	%	No. affected	%
St Mary Spital	34	0.6	349	6.5
St Mary Merton	57	8.6	-	-
Holy Trinity Aldgate	0	-	-	11.1–36.7
East Smithfield, Black Death cemetery	0	-	4	1.6
St Mary Graces	7	1.9	-	2.3–10.9
St Mary Stratford Langthorne	22	8.7	-	-
St Saviour Bermondsey	15	7.8	-	8.8–9.8
St Nicholas Shambles	0	-	-	-

higher prevalence among older individuals.

There is an abundance of comparative evidence for osteoarthritis from across London (Table 151). At St Mary Stratford Langthorne, White (2004, 176) reported an infrequent occurrence of osteoarthritis, although this may be because only 23% of the population were over 45 years of age. The shoulder and knee joint were most frequently involved, with little osteoarthritis in the wrist, ankle and elbow, although the distribution in the hands and feet was comparable to modern populations (ibid). Conheeney (2005, 261) reported a high prevalence of osteoarthritis of between 11.1% and 36.7% at Holy Trinity, even where the age profiles of each sub-sample were similar. Here, the parts of the body most frequently affected were the ankles, wrists and hands, with the common involvement of the smaller hand and foot joints.

At East Smithfield the crude prevalence rate for osteoarthritis was as low as 1.6% (Cowal et al 2008, 45). At St Mary Graces, the burials from within the church displayed a crude prevalence of 10.9%; however, the rates for those interred within the associated churchyard (2.6%) and later ?epidemic burials (2.3%) were extremely low (Bekvalac and Kausmally 2011, 180, 175, 170). The distribution of osteoarthritis in the skeleton was also variable. Typically, the small joints of the hands and feet were affected but also the larger peripheral joints such as the wrist, knee and hip. A similar distribution of osteoarthritic joints was also described by White (2007, 500) when he examined the skeletons from St Lawrence Jewry churchyard, namely the shoulder, elbow, wrist, knee and ankle.

At Merton Priory the distribution of osteoarthritic changes suggested frequent weight bearing and an apparent difference in males and females was attributed to differing work roles (Conheeney 2007, 271), although it was acknowledged that the relationship between osteoarthritis and activity-related patterns is tenuous (Jurmain 1999). The distribution of joints involved included (in decreasing frequency) the shoulder, ankle, hip, wrist, knee and elbow joints. At Bermondsey Priory/Abbey, a high prevalence of osteoarthritis in acromioclavicular (shoulder) joints was reported, giving a crude prevalence rate of 9.8% (Connell and White 2011, 269); this joint is acknowledged to be one of the most frequently affected by osteoarthritis (Rogers 2000, 168). A similarly high frequency of osteoarthritis was noted in the knee (a crude prevalence rate of 8.8%); again most of the affected individuals were over 45 years old (Connell and White 2011, 269 table 23).

Diffuse idiopathic skeletal hyperostosis (DISH)

DISH occurs in older individuals, usually over 50 years, is far more common in males than in females (Resnick 2002), and is commonly seen in medieval monastic communities in London (Table 151). It has been suggested that the high prevalence at monastic sites may be related to a calorie-rich diet and obesity (with attendant late onset diabetes) (Julkunen et al 1971; Waldron 1985): the relationship between a monastic and/or high-status way of life and DISH was initially proposed by Waldron (1985) (see also Patrick 2007). More recently, however, Rogers and Waldron (2001) have described DISH as a multi-system hormonal disorder and work by Mays (2006a) has questioned this association. Mays failed to find statistically valid differences in frequency between a poor rural community from Wharram Percy and high-status individuals from a series of monastic sites, and demonstrated that the link between monasticism and DISH lacked published statistically valid evidence (ibid, 185, 188). Taking account of differing diagnostic criteria and recording methods, Mays concluded that there is 'no evidence of a higher DISH rate in monastic collections' (ibid, 186). It is also possible that the reported rate of DISH at monastic sites is related to the higher number of older males within high-status sites (Rogers 2000, 171). The relationship between DISH and monastic diet in a national perspective is discussed further in Chapter 4.5.

At St Mary Spital, 34 individuals, predominantly males (23/34: 67.6%), were affected. The most frequently affected age group was 36–45 years. In period 14 (*c* 1120–*c* 1200), only five males were affected, with no pattern between the burial types. In period 15 (*c* 1200–50), 15 individuals had DISH (eight males and seven females). Later, during period 16 (*c* 1250–*c* 1400), only nine individuals were affected; again the majority of affected individuals were ≥46-year-old adults. In period 17 (*c* 1400–1539) only five males were affected.

Overall some 1.0% (23/2237) of males and 0.6% (11/1883) of females were affected, which is a very low frequency compared to other sites in London. For example, at Bermondsey Priory/Abbey the crude prevalence rate was 7.8% and at St Mary Stratford Langthorne it was 8.7%; as expected most affected individuals were men aged over 45 years (Connell and White 2011, 271; White 2004, 176). In the St Mary Graces churchyard, seven individuals (6.9%) had DISH (Bekvalac and Kausmally 2011, 182). At Merton Priory, Conheeney (2007, 273) gives an overall crude prevalence of 8.6%. Here, there was a lower prevalence in an area of the cemetery for mixed lay and clerical burials, and a higher rate in the possible canons' cemetery and among burials from within the chapter house and church, the most likely location for the burial of privileged individuals. Previous excavations at St Mary Spital produced three cases of DISH from the church (B1) (3/15: 20%), again the area most likely to contain wealthy or clerical burials. However, the pattern is most likely to be age related as discussed above.

In London, the crude prevalence rate of DISH at monastic sites ranges from 6.9% to 8.7%. This is high compared with a modern clinical prevalence of 3–5% (Rogers 2000, 171). Not all sites contain people with DISH: no cases were reported at Holy Trinity Aldgate, which was the earliest established Augustinian house in the London area (Conheeney 2005), or at the St Lawrence Jewry churchyard (White 2007, 500). In these sites, however, the absence of DISH might be attributed to small sample sizes. The crude prevalence at St Mary Spital of 0.8% (34/4120 sexed adults) is very low. Gilchrist and Sloane (2005, 212) note that there are apparent distinctions between different monastic orders, pointing to low frequencies (2%) at vegetarian Carthusian houses and similarly low frequencies at Carmelite houses. They also note that greater consistency is needed in the diagnosis of DISH before broad comparisons are made (ibid).

Trauma: evidence of injury or violence

There is an abundance of evidence for trauma across London during the medieval period (Table 152), with all the other comparative sites containing traumatic lesions of varying types and severity. At St Mary Spital a larger proportion of trauma was found in men than women (see Table 64). A wide variety of traumatic lesions were present including dislocations, amputations, cranial trauma and a variety of minor injuries. Fracture frequencies increased with age, although the rate of increase had slowed down by older adulthood.

Healed fractures of limb bones were the most commonly seen injuries, and ranged from single fractures of one limb bone, such as a clavicle or radius, to more serious injuries involving several major limb bones. At Stratford Langthorne, frequencies of fractures varied between 0.5% and 3.2%. Most of the fractures had healed badly, and White (2007, 178) argued that they had not been reduced or treated. The types of trauma included dislocation of a right shoulder joint (glenohumeral). Conheeney (2005) also encountered a wide variety of traumatic lesions at Holy Trinity Aldgate but there was no particular pattern within the data. Depressed cranial fractures and a possible greenstick fracture in a femur were notable cases from this site. The general appearance of all the fractures seen suggested that no treatment had been given to those injured (ibid, 261).

A detailed view of traumatic lesions with frequency data emerged during the analysis of the adjacent St Mary Graces and East Smithfield sites. In the later ?epidemic rows from St Mary Graces there was a low trauma frequency of 4.7%, with only males affected. In the abbey churchyard a further three individuals (3.8%) showed evidence of trauma. Seven individuals with fractures at differing stages of healing were found interred within the church itself, a crude prevalence for this subgroup of 6.9% (Bekvalac and Kausmally 2011, 183). In the Black Death mass burial trenches from East Smithfield, 16 individuals (6.5%) showed signs of trauma in long bones from both the upper and lower limbs, including unhealed hypertrophic non-union of a midshaft right radius (Cowal et al 2008, 46).

Most of the trauma noted at comparative sites was healed but there were several cases where fractures were not united, mostly due to hypertrophic non-union of forearm fractures. At St Mary Spital, 1.2% of individuals had fractures that were unhealed at the time of death (64/5387). The prevalence rises to 5.7% (64/1125) when it is considered as a proportion of the individuals with fractures: 3.3% of all fractured bones (79/2394) were not united. Complications from trauma are well documented at St Mary Spital but rarely reported elsewhere in London. In contrast to the conclusions regarding non-treatment of fractures drawn by both Conheeney (2005) and White (2004), Bekvalac and Kausmally (2011, 170, 176–7, 183) point to all fractures at St Mary Graces being well healed, and argue that the reduction of fractures suggests that injured individuals there had received some form of treatment, probably splinting. The disparity between these three sites is probably due to differences in interpretation of the data by the authors rather than any substantive evidence for treatment or otherwise.

At Merton Priory there was also evidence of a wide variety of traumatic lesions. Here, the majority of fractures occurred in ribs and clavicles, along with Colles fractures. Conheeney (2007, 269) gives a crude prevalence rate for individuals with at least one fracture as 13.0%, much lower than the 22.5% seen at St Mary Spital, and argues that a major contributory factor to this high frequency is the larger proportion of elderly individuals in the sample.

At St Mary Spital fractures were much more common in the upper limb (16.7–24.6%) than in the lower limb (7.8–12.6%). This is also generally observed elsewhere in London: at St Nicholas Shambles, for example, trauma was found to be more common in the upper limbs, particularly the forearm (White 1988, 44). However, at Stratford Langthorne the lower limbs were affected more frequently (0.8–3.2%) than the upper limbs (0.6–0.8%). The latter injuries consisted mostly of 'parry' fractures (White 2004, 178). At St Lawrence Jewry churchyard, fractures occurred chiefly in the rib cage, though other cases were noted in two ankles, one hand and one ulna (White 2007, 500).

Table 152 Comparison of crude prevalence of trauma in London medieval cemetery samples

Cemetery sample	Fractures		Cranial trauma	
	No. affected	%	No. affected	%
St Mary Spital	1125	20.9	157	2.9
St Mary Merton	-	13.0	7	1.1
Holy Trinity Aldgate	present	-	0	-
East Smithfield, Black Death cemetery	18	2.8	3	0.5
St Mary Graces	-	3.8–6.9	2	0.5
St Mary Stratford Langthorne	-	0.5–3.2	1	0.2
St Saviour Bermondsey	13	6.7	0	-
St Nicholas Shambles	0	-	3	1.3

Cranial trauma

At St Mary Spital there were a total of 157 cranial vault fractures, and males were affected more often than females (see Table 73). Cranial trauma was also commonly observed in medieval London, with most of the other monastic sites producing evidence for head injuries. Seven cases of cranial trauma were reported at Merton Priory, including 'slice, puncture and depression type wounds', all of which were healed, indicating that the individuals had survived the incident (Conheeney 2007, 270). All but one of the affected individuals were male, which is consistent with the pattern seen at St Mary Spital. Injury recidivism is an issue which has become of interest only recently and while multiple (two or more) injuries are reported by other authors, there are no comparative data by sex.

In terms of evidence for interpersonal violence at St Mary Spital there was a true prevalence of 0.1% sharp force trauma, with more sharp force injuries occurring in males (Chapter 3.8). Unfortunately there are no comparative frequencies of sharp force trauma from sites in London, although it is frequently reported. For example, at St Nicholas Shambles, White (1988, 44–8) describes three cases of cranial trauma including one sharp force injury and one penetrating skull injury. Later work by White (2007, 500) at St Lawrence Jewry churchyard also describes two males with cranial trauma, one with a depressed fracture and one with a well-healed injury from an edged weapon. At Stratford Langthorne, a young male with a sharp force injury to the head from an edged weapon was identified (White 2004, 178). St Mary Graces produced evidence of a projectile injury in a fifth thoracic vertebra together with sharp force trauma in the cranium of a young man; both injuries were healed (Bekvalac and Kausmally 2011, 170, 184). Cowal et al (2008, 46) report that interpersonal violence accounted for 12.5% of all observed trauma at East Smithfield, including two men with sharp force cranial injuries and one female with a blunt force facial injury.

Examples of trepanation from medieval assemblages are something of a rarity in Britain as a whole and in London specifically where, despite relative large cemetery samples, little evidence exists. Of particular importance therefore is a ≥46-year-old female with a healed trepanation from St Lawrence Jewry churchyard, who pre-dates the examples from St Mary Spital (White 2007, 500–1). At St Mary Spital two cases of trepanation were seen in adult males [1934] and [26580]. The latter case is of particular interest because this individual had also suffered a fractured right radius and ulna and had suffered blunt force cranial trauma. It was considered that the trepanation followed the cranial trauma as indicated by an inflammatory response on the endocranial surface of the skull.

Metabolic disease

Scurvy

Four cases of scurvy were identified at St Mary Spital, a crude prevalence of 0.1% (4/5387). The crude prevalence rate for subadults was 0.4% (4/1027). Scurvy is rarely reported in medieval London (Table 153); the only other cases are two instances in subadults from St Mary Graces church, one in a 12-month-old child and one in a child of 6 years (2/378: 0.5%; Bekvalac and Kausmally 2011, 166). Two further possible cases of scurvy were found at Merton Priory, where the diagnosis was based on the Ortner and Eriksen (1997) criteria (Conheeney 2007, 273).

Table 153 Comparison of crude prevalence of vitamin deficiency diseases in London medieval cemetery samples

Cemetery sample	Rickets No. affected	%	Scurvy No. affected	%
St Mary Spital	8	0.1	4	0.1
St Mary Merton	0	-	2	0.3
Holy Trinity Aldgate	0	-	0	-
East Smithfield, Black Death cemetery	1	0.2	0	-
St Mary Graces	0	-	2	0.5
St Mary Stratford Langthorne	2	0.3	0	-
St Saviour Bermondsey	0	-	0	-
St Nicholas Shambles	0	-	0	-

Rickets

Evidence for rickets at St Mary Spital was seen in eight individuals, an overall crude prevalence rate of 0.1% (8/5387) (Chapter 3.10). All five affected subadults had died c 1250–1539 (periods 16 and 17) and there were no cases in the earliest phase of cemetery use (period 14). This low prevalence is in common with other sites in London during this period (Table 153). A single case of rickets (healed) was identified in the lower limb bones of an individual from Stratford Langthorne, together with a severely distorted sacrum which was attributed to rickets in childhood (White 2004, 175). A single case of rickets was also found at East Smithfield, in a 5-year-old child with bowed lower limb bones (Cowal et al 2008, 47). A further case is reported from St John Clerkenwell (Conheeney 2004, 399).

At St Mary Spital a single case of osteomalacia was identified in a ≥46-year-old adult female from period 17 ([3699]). The crude prevalence rate for osteomalacia in females from period 17 is 0.5% (1/203).

Indicators of stress

The interpretation of osteological indicators of stress has been discussed in Chapter 3.10, and cribra orbitalia has been selected for comparative purposes.

Cribra orbitalia is considered to be suggestive of iron-deficiency anaemia; however, it is now more frequently seen as representing an adaptive response to increased pathogen loads (Stuart-Macadam 1992), as a potential synergism with infection has been suggested (Goodman et al 1988). Steckel et al (2009) also note that not all examples of cribra orbitalia are indicators of iron-deficiency anaemia.

Table 154 *Comparison of crude prevalence of cribra orbitalia in London medieval cemetery samples*

Cemetery sample	Cribra orbitalia	
	No. affected	%
St Mary Spital	-	17.2–27.8
St Mary Merton	41	6.1
Holy Trinity Aldgate	2	3.4
East Smithfield, Black Death cemetery	-	2.4–34.9
St Mary Graces	42	11.1
St Mary Stratford Langthorne	22	18.8
St Saviour Bermondsey	5	5.2
St Nicholas Shambles	-	17.0

Cribra orbitalia is a commonly observed lesion and St Mary Spital was no exception (Chapter 3.10). Overall, the frequencies observed at St Mary Spital ranged from 17.2% to 27.8%, which is generally higher than other London sites (Table 154). At Bermondsey Priory/Abbey for example, Connell and White (2011, 271) found an overall crude prevalence rate of 5.2%, and White (2004, 176) reports a frequency of 18.8% (22/117) at Stratford Langthorne. Only two individuals showed evidence of cribra orbitalia at Holy Trinity Aldgate (Conheeney 2005, 262) and it was also seen in several children from the St Lawrence Jewry churchyard, although no figures are given (White 2007, 501). At Merton Priory, Conheeney (2007, 273) discovered an overall prevalence of 6.1%. Bekvalac and Kausmally (2011, 184) report an unusually high frequency of 34.1% at St Mary Graces; here subadults were most commonly affected (43.3%), but in the abbey churchyard the frequency was much lower at 7.1%. Cowal et al (2008, 47) report a prevalence of 34.9% (37/106) in the East Smithfield Black Death cemetery, but only 6.6% in subadults; in the mass burial trenches from the same site frequencies of 4.3% (14/328) in males and 2.7% (9/328) in females were seen, with the highest prevalence of 7.9% (26/328) seen in subadults. Cribra orbitalia was present in 17% of skulls from St Nicholas Shambles (White 1988, 41).

Porotic hyperostosis was not often reported at other monastic cemeteries. No cases were reported at Bermondsey Priory/Abbey, the abbey of St Mary Stratford Langthorne, Holy Trinity Aldgate, St Lawrence Jewry churchyard, the East Smithfield and St Mary Graces sites, or Merton Priory. This absence may be in part due to the fact that some of the skeletal analysis was undertaken before the introduction of systematic recording protocols which stipulated its inclusion. Nevertheless, it is difficult to compare detailed frequency data from this site to other sites in London, where frequencies are usually quoted as a crude prevalence in an individual (regardless of survival of all cranial bones) rather than as true prevalence (bones affected as a percentage of bones observed).

Neoplastic disease

There were relatively few cases of neoplastic disease at St Mary Spital (Chapter 3.11). This might be expected, as neoplastic disease is rare in archaeological populations. One possible reason for its palaeopathological rarity is that in modern populations neoplastic disease tends to affect older age groups, and in antiquity survival into old age may have been less common than it is today (Manchester 1987, 173; Anderson 2000, 217). In addition, factors in today's environment which were not present in the past (eg chemicals, dietary additives, pollution) may induce neoplasms.

Primary malignant tumours are extremely rare in archaeological material (Anderson 2000, 205) and London is no exception; even with the large sample sizes available, there is little evidence for malignant disease. An interesting case is reported by Conheeney (2007, 277), who describes a metastatic carcinoma in an adult female from Merton Priory.

The preponderance of neoplastic disease is benign. At St Mary Spital a total of 132 skeletons showed evidence of neoplastic disease (132/5387: 2.5%; see Table 120). There was no evidence of neoplastic disease in individuals under 6 years old, but 0.7% (7/1027) of subadults were affected together with 2.9% of adults (125/4360). These lesions consisted predominantly of bone tissue neoplasms (77/132: 58.3%; see Table 122), and over half of the neoplastic disease seen was in the form of button osteomas (70/132: 53.0%). The majority of these osteomas were situated on the cranium (64/70: 91.4%). A smaller proportion of cartilage tissue neoplasms was found (39/132: 29.5%); 84.6% (33/39) of these were osteochondromas, which were more common in males than females (Chapter 3.11).

All the other medieval sites in London contain little evidence for neoplastic disease, and as at St Mary Spital, the most commonly seen neoplasms were button osteomas and solitary osteochondromas. At St Lawrence Jewry churchyard, a button osteoma was noted on a parietal bone (White 2007, 501), and at Stratford Langthorne three osteomas were found on the parietal of one individual (White 2004, 178). Two males with solitary button osteomas, together with another male with nine distributed all over the skull, were observed at Bermondsey Priory/Abbey (Connell and White 2011, 272). The same pattern was also seen at St Nicholas Shambles, where White (1988, 44) noted that neoplastic disease consisted of either single or multiple osteomas.

Osteochondromas are infrequently reported, though Bekvalac and Kausmally (2011, 185) describe a 17-year-old individual from the north cloister of St Mary Graces church with an osteochondroma in the distal right femur. At the East Smithfield site, Cowal et al (2008, 46) also report several osteochondromas, one in an adolescent (scapula) and one in an adult male (humerus), together with two further cases from the Black Death trenches, also on humeri (ibid, 52). At Merton Priory Conheeney (2007, 277) reports a crude prevalence rate for neoplasms of 5.1%, mostly comprised of osteomas, but with two possible meningiomas. Connell and White (2011, 272) also report an osteochondroma in a fibula at Bermondsey Priory/Abbey.

In looking at the prevalence of neoplastic disease across medieval London it can be seen that benign neoplasms are most common and typically consist of button osteomas or osteochondromas.

Other pathological conditions

Hyperostosis frontalis interna (HFI)

The only evidence of endocrine (hormonal) disorders consisted of bony changes suggestive of hyperostosis frontalis interna (HFI). These new bone growths are very distinctive and differential diagnosis does not represent a problem (Aufderheide and Rodríguez-Martín 1998, 419). HFI was identified in 0.4% of the St Mary Spital population (22/5387) (Chapter 3.14). Barber et al (1997, 163) suggest that when recording HFI the number of skulls internally examined or radiographed should be stated; however, in this study the endocranial surface of the frontal bone could only be thoroughly examined in skulls that were broken post mortem. The prevalence rate will therefore be an under-representation of the true frequency of the condition.

Of the 22 cases, 18 (81.8%) were adult females. The highest prevalence rate was observed among ≥46-year-old adult females, from period 16 (c 1250–1400) (Chapter 3.14). This is to be expected because HFI is a condition found almost exclusively in females (Aufderheide and Rodríguez-Martín 1998). The modern prevalence for HFI in women aged over 40 years is up to 70%, compared to archaeological frequencies of 1–4% (Barber et al 1997, 157).

Given that the condition is distinctive and easy to identify it is perhaps surprising that it is rarely reported at other sites in London (Table 155). Conheeney (2005, 262) describes a case in an adult female from Holy Trinity Aldgate, and one ≥46-year-old female showed HFI at St Mary Graces (Bekvalac and Kausmally (2011, 185). A low crude prevalence rate of 0.8% was also seen at Merton Priory (Conheeney 2007, 277).

Paget's disease of bone

Paget's disease of bone is a chronic disorder resulting from defective bone turnover; its exact cause is not known but a viral aetiology has been suggested (McRae and Kinninmonth 1997, 16). This disease is most prevalent in individuals over the age of 40; it is more common in males than in females and most often seen in white populations. The modern incidence in the UK is high but it is uncommon in other parts of the world. The defective bone turnover usually involves a single bone or small groups of bones and rarely affects all the bones in the body. At St Mary Spital, 17 cases of Paget's disease were diagnosed; these were found in all periods but the highest frequency was seen in period 16. In contrast to the modern clinical tendency for Paget's disease to be more common in males, at St Mary Spital it was seen in both sexes equally.

Reported cases of Paget's disease of bone in the palaeopathological record are rare (Roberts and Manchester 2005; Stirland 1991a) and one reason for this might be the fact that Paget's disease of bone can only be recognised (macroscopically) in its later stages, so many earlier stage cases will be missed. In London only a handful of cases have been identified at other medieval sites (Table 156). At Bermondsey Priory/Abbey, Connell and White (2011, 274) describe a single

Table 155 Comparison of crude prevalence of HFI in London medieval cemetery samples (* = true prevalence rate)

Cemetery sample	HFI No. affected	%
St Mary Spital	22	0.4
St Mary Merton	-	0.8*
Holy Trinity Aldgate	1	1.7
East Smithfield, Black Death cemetery	0	-
St Mary Graces	1	0.3
St Mary Stratford Langthorne	0	-
St Saviour Bermondsey	0	-
St Nicholas Shambles	0	-

Table 156 Comparison of crude prevalence of Paget's disease of bone in London medieval cemetery samples

Cemetery sample	Paget's disease No. affected	%
St Mary Spital	17	0.3
St Mary Merton	13	2.0
Holy Trinity Aldgate	0	-
East Smithfield, Black Death cemetery	0	-
St Mary Graces	1	0.3
St Mary Stratford Langthorne	0	-
St Saviour Bermondsey	1	0.5
St Nicholas Shambles	0	-

case in an adult male. At Merton Priory there were 13 possible cases, giving an overall crude prevalence rate of 2.0% (Conheeney 2007, 277). Bekvalac and Kausmally (2011, 172) report a single case of Paget's disease of bone in an unsexed individual aged 36–45 years old from the St Mary Graces sites.

Patterns and trends in population structure

It comes as no surprise that a skeletal sample as large as that from St Mary Spital contains individuals in all age ranges, from neonates to elderly adults. The cemetery contains thousands of burials made over a broad timescale, and the contributing population included the general community and those from the infirmary, as well as high-status burials of monks, lay sisters and wealthy benefactors.

General trends in mortality profiles: children

The charter at St Mary Spital states that the hospital catered for the sick poor, pregnant women and children, so a relatively high proportion of subadults might be expected. A total of 1027 individuals from the studied sample were subadult, 19.1% of the total recorded population. In the early part of the cemetery's use (period 14, c 1120–c 1200) both the attritional burial ground and mass burials showed a similar age-at-death profile and there were few subadults below 6–11 years old.

Overall, 18.4% of the burials in this period were of subadults (94/512). The most striking difference is in the proportions of children when the two burial types are compared: there is a significantly higher proportion of subadults in the mass burials (42/165: 25.5%) than in the attritional burials (52/347: 15.0%). There were very few perinatal individuals in either burial type and neither contained individuals who died in the first year of life. Only the attritional burials contained any subadults who died aged 1–5 years (Chapter 3.2).

During the second period of the cemetery's use (period 15, c 1200–50) the age-at-death profile did not change significantly and the attritional and mass burials again followed the same trend. The proportion of subadults in period 15 was 21.7% (301/1390), 19.6% of the attritional group (100/510) and 22.8% of the mass burial group (201/880). Again there were few subadults below the age of 6–11 years.

Period 16 (c 1250–c 1400) is characterised by a continuation of this pattern and a much higher proportion of subadults in the mass burial group (299/1443: 20.7%) than in the attritional cemetery (209/1392: 15.0%), with subadults accounting for 17.9% of the population overall (508/2835).

In period 17 (c 1400–1539) subadults accounted for 19.1% of the recorded population (124/650). This suggests that there is little, if any, temporal change in the proportion of children being buried in the cemetery. There was a lower proportion of subadults in the attritional burial group (95/526: 18.1%) than in the mass burial group (29/124: 23.4%), and this difference was most marked in the 6–11-year age group (Chapter 3.2).

The proportion of subadults in other London cemeteries is highly variable (Fig 248). Proportions even higher than those at St Mary Spital were seen in the East Smithfield Black Death cemetery (214/634: 33.8% of the population; Cowal et al 2008; see also Sloane 2011) and at St Mary Graces (104/378: 27.5%; Bekvalac and Kausmally 2011). To compare the relative proportions of subadults between two complex cemetery sites, data from the adjacent St Mary Graces and East Smithfield groups were pooled, resulting in a figure of 31.3% subadults (317/1012), still higher than the 19.1% seen at St Mary Spital. At St Lawrence Jewry churchyard, White (2007, 499) describes a relatively high proportion of subadults (32.8%) but reports that there were no neonates and about half the children had lived into adolescence. At the other extreme, surprisingly low numbers were seen at Merton Priory, where out of an assemblage of 664 skeletons only 4.1% were below 17 years of age (Conheeney 2007, 266); however, this is principally a monastic site. Similarly low numbers were seen at Stratford Langthorne, where 'children were in the minority' at 4.3% (28/647; White 2004, 160).

Saunders et al (1995a) note that infant mortality is generally considered to be an important public health index for assessing the sanitary and social conditions that surrounded an infant in life. Infant mortality, defined here as those who die before reaching their first birthday, is relatively low at St Mary Spital, although the influence of archaeological factors and differential burial rites cannot be completely excluded (above, 4.2 and 4.3). During period 14, infants account for 1.2% of the population (6/512) and this hardly changes in period 15 (15/1390: 1.1%). In period 16 the proportion is still fairly constant at 0.8% (24/2835) but this rises to 4.2% in period 17 (27/650). Overall the total number of perinatal deaths was 1.3% (72/5387).

This is surprising as it would be reasonable to expect that in the areas of the cemetery serving the poor there should be a higher proportion of infant deaths, caused by infection and malnutrition. The under-representation of this age group is often reported in archaeological samples: for example, when Grauer (1991) examined the (low socio-economic status) sample from St Helen-on-the-Walls, York, subadult mortality appeared to be low and the life expectancy rate for the population was high. Grauer suggested that some of these results could be explained by the exclusion of unbaptised infants from the cemetery and adult over-enumeration due to immigration. In addition, the whole cemetery was not excavated. Unfortunately, with the exception of East Smithfield and St Mary Graces (see below and above, 4.2), few London sites provide comparative figures for infant mortality, mostly because of the low numbers of children present, while at others infants are grouped as 0–5 years old.

In addition to the low numbers of perinatal deaths at St Mary Spital, two individuals died aged 1–6 months, and two aged 7–11 months. Equally low infant deaths were reported by Bekvalac and Kausmally (2011, 168) at St Mary Graces, where there were only two perinatal individuals (2.8%) from the later ?epidemic cemetery and none in the abbey churchyard or church; only three individuals were aged 1–12 months. When St Mary Graces and East Smithfield are considered together, only 1.4% (14/1012) of individuals died in infancy, a figure which is more or less identical to that seen at St Mary Spital.

General trends in mortality profiles: adults

During period 14 the adult age at death at St Mary Spital peaks in the 26–35-year-old age group. In the attritional cemetery,

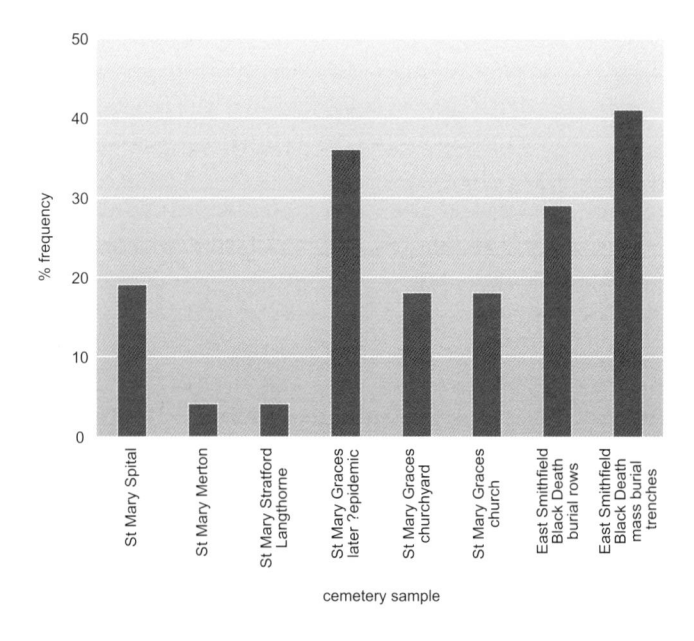

Fig 248 Frequency distribution of subadults in larger medieval cemetery samples

adult female age at death peaks at 26–35 years, but in males the peak is later, at 36–45 years. The majority of men and women in period 14 died between the ages of 26 and 45 years. Low numbers of older adults were also seen at the St Lawrence Jewry churchyard site, where only 10% were over 45 years old when they died (White 2007, 499). In the mass burials at St Mary Spital a similar pattern emerges: female age at death peaks at 26–35 years whereas for males the proportions aged 26–35 years and 36–45 years are similar. Compared to the attritional cemetery there is a higher proportion of young males and females in the mass burials. In the attritional cemetery, 46.1% (160/347) were male and 33.1% (115/347) were female, a male to female ratio of 1.4:1. A similar picture emerges in the mass burial group, with 33.3% (55/165) females and 38.2% males (63/165).

The adult age-at-death profile during period 15 again peaks at 26–35 years, with few individuals in the ≥46-year-old adult category. In the attritional cemetery, there are similar proportions of males and females in the 18–25-year-old age group. The age at death for males peaks at 26–35 years and this is also seen in females (as in period 14). In the mass burial group there is a similar proportion of younger adults. Again in period 15 both male and female age at death shows the highest frequency at 26–35 years old. In general during this period, little difference is seen in age-at-death profiles for both men and women in both types of burial. During period 15 in the attritional group of burials the adults consisted of 42.9% males (219/510) and 32.7% females (167/510), a sex ratio of 1.3:1. In the mass burials 35.6% were male (313/880) but there was a slightly larger proportion of females (334/880: 38.0%), giving a sex ratio of 1:1.1.

During period 16, the adult age-at-death distribution shows the highest numbers of deaths occurring in the 26–35-year-old age group, as for both periods 14 and 15. The overall proportion of people dying at this age is roughly the same in both the attritional (414/1392: 29.7%) and catastrophic (400/1443: 27.7%) cemetery samples. The attritional cemetery contained a larger proportion of males (628/1392: 45.1%) than females (474/1392: 34.1%), giving a male to female ratio of 1.3:1. However, this difference was much less marked in the mass burials where males accounted for 39.1% of burials (564/1443) and females 37.1% (535/1443), giving a sex ratio of 1.1:1. Roughly equal numbers of men and women were also observed at the St Lawrence Jewry churchyard site (White 2007, 499), although the sample of 64 individuals is much smaller than that at St Mary Spital.

In period 17 both attritional and mass burial cemetery samples show similar overall patterns in age at death to the earlier periods, with more 26–35-year-olds in the attritional cemetery group. The cemetery contained a higher proportion of males: 44.6% skeletons (290/650) compared to 31.2% females (203/650). This pattern is seen in both of the burial types: in the attritional burials males comprised 45.4% of the population (239/526) compared to 31.2% females (164/526), giving a sex ratio of 1.5:1, and in the mass burials females accounted for 31.5% of burials (39/124), compared to 41.1% males (51/124), a male to female ratio of 1.3:1.

The average male to female ratio throughout the cemetery at St Mary Spital was 1.2:1. Direct comparisons with some of the other cemeteries in London are difficult: monastic cemeteries tend to be biased towards male burials as most clerics were men. Gilchrist and Sloane (2005, 205), in their assessment of the demographic character of all hospital cemeteries (both monastic and non-monastic), note that they contained a significant proportion of younger males. At Merton Priory, for example, Conheeney (2007, 267) reports 78.1% of the population as male, with a male to female ratio of 11.2:1, and acknowledges that the sample is not drawn from a normal population where we might expect approximately equal proportions of males and females. The excavation of the earlier part of the St Mary Spital cemetery also showed a strong male bias: of the 101 individuals from A–H, Open Area 5 (see Fig 214) the male to female sex ratio was 2.39:1 (Conheeney 1997, 223). Even higher sex ratios were seen at other London religious establishments: at Stratford Langthorne it was 19:1 (White 2004, 160) and at Bermondsey Priory/Abbey 17:1 (Connell and White 2011). The Cistercian burial ground at Stratford Langthorne is fairly typical of a chiefly monastic cemetery with 90.5% males, as would be expected at a monastic house (White 2004, 160).

The male to female ratio of 1.2:1 for St Mary Spital is almost identical to that seen at the urban parochial cemetery of St Nicholas Shambles, where White (1988, 29) reported a ratio of 1.27:1. At Holy Trinity Aldgate most groups were of mixed sex, although there was some evidence of spatial patterning in sex bias (Conheeney 2005, 257–8). At St Mary Graces, the male to female ratio for the later ?epidemic cemetery was 1.54:1, and a stronger bias emerged in the abbey churchyard and burials from the church of 2.77:1 and 2.60:1 respectively (the average was 1.85:1) (Bekvalac and Kausmally 2011, 167). It is not surprising that there were more males in all areas of the church. In the East Smithfield Black Death burial rows there was a male to female ratio of 1.66:1; the overall figure for the Black Death mass burial trenches was 1.98:1, which is only slightly higher than at St Mary Spital (Cowal et al 2008, 43).

Comparison of the mass burials with a catastrophe cemetery from London

An important feature of the St Mary Spital cemetery sample is that it contains both single and multiple burials, the latter occurring in such large numbers that it can be described as a separate and distinct catastrophe sample. Catastrophic cemetery samples reflect interment within a narrow timescale, and Waldron (1994, 22) has pointed out the importance of timescales in the interpretation of prevalence rates of disease; differences in disease frequencies over time are often obscured by broad timescales. The importance of catastrophe samples in bioarchaeological studies is widely recognised (Conheeney 1999; Waldron 2001; Margerison and Knüsel 2002; Chamberlain 2006; Gilchrist and Sloane 2005). In the living contributing population of medieval London during periods 14 to 17 (*c* 1120–

1539) it is clear that a very large number of people died within a very short space of time; the possible reasons for the catastrophic event that caused St Mary Spital to bury so many people have been discussed in Chapter 4.4. This type of cemetery sample is very rare: the only other catastrophic samples from the UK come from the Black Death assemblage from East Smithfield (Cowal et al 2008), Towton, Yorkshire (Fiorato et al 2000) and the *Mary Rose* (Stirland 2000) (below, 4.5).

At East Smithfield, four separate subgroups, all closely dated to 1348–50, were identified. During their analysis Cowal et al (2008, 49) reported that no significant differences were seen between different Black Death burial trenches, and therefore argued that data should be pooled. This allows us to compare the demographic characteristics with the mass burials at St Mary Spital. To make the comparison more accurate, only burials from period 16 (*c* 1250–*c* 1400) are compared as this is contemporaneous with the East Smithfield catastrophe sample.

In terms of the age distributions one of the most significant findings at East Smithfield was the high proportion of subadults, comprising 40.5% of the catastrophe sample. This is double the proportion of children seen in the St Mary Spital catastrophe sample (299/1443: 20.7%; see Table 15). However, even that figure is higher than the 15.0% of subadults seen in the attritional cemetery from the same site during the same period (209/1392; see Table 14). The East Smithfield sample showed an almost complete absence of neonates and young infants, which was also seen at St Mary Spital, where neonates comprised less than 1% of individuals. Cowal et al (2008, 50) report that the subadult population at East Smithfield consisted mostly of older children, which was a feature also observed at St Mary Spital: in the mass burials the largest proportion of subadults (174/1443: 12.1%) fell in the 12–17-year age category, compared to 6.5% (91/1392) of the attritional burials. Gilchrist and Sloane (2005) note that the East Smithfield Black Death mass burial graves had higher numbers of children, which are within the range of 21% and 47% observed in parish cemeteries, and also suggest that children may not have been affected disproportionately by the first outbreak of plague in an urban population. Examination of the East Smithfield cemetery plan and phasing has suggested that initially the plague killed greater numbers of adults but that at its peak a higher number of subadults died (ibid, 209).

The adult sample from the East Smithfield catastrophe group consisted of 48.7% males (95/195), 24.6% females (48/195) and a further 52 skeletons that could not be sexed, giving an overall male to female sex ratio of 1.98:1. In contrast, at St Mary Spital the mass burial group showed a more or less equal sex distribution (see above), with a sex ratio of 1.1:1, although the attritional burial group during the same period shows a more male bias at 1.3:1 (see above). The reason for the disparity in the sex composition in London catastrophic samples is not clear. Although the East Smithfield data point to significantly larger numbers of males in catastrophic samples, an increase in men is also seen in the St Mary Spital attritional group. An influx of migrants into London might account for this – migrant labour from regions outside London would have played an important role in sustaining the economic development of the city. Sloane (1999) suggests that during the medieval period large numbers of young men migrated to London seeking work. If the population was undergoing extrinsic expansion then migrants, whose disease load experience might be partially or wholly derived from a rural environment, might influence patterns of pathology, diluting the character of an urban group. The blurring of distinctions between urban and rural groups is a problem that has been highlighted by Mays (1998, 200).

Whatever the actual size of London's population during the medieval period, the population structure would have changed drastically when the Black Death epidemic arrived during the autumn of 1348 (during period 16 at St Mary Spital). The demographic disturbance caused by the plague has implications for this cemetery population as it is possible that burials made in the cemetery before the epidemic, ie in periods 14–15 (*c* 1120–*c* 1250), will differ greatly in demographic character from those buried afterwards, in period 17 (*c* 1400–1539). Following the Black Death most parts of the country experienced further plague outbreaks and London was particularly hard hit: between 1442 and 1459, for example, London suffered on at least six separate occasions (Gottfried 1983). Gilchrist and Sloane (2005) evaluated the proportions of children among the various burial types and have suggested that repeat visitations of the plague are responsible for the differing numbers. It is therefore possible that during period 16 the cemetery might contain some pits for plague deaths. The St Mary Spital cemetery population thus contains the residue of a variety of demographic disturbances, including the probable famine responsible for the late 13th-century mass deaths.

Work by Margerison and Knüsel (2002) on the demographic characteristics of catastrophe samples in pre-industrial populations has shown that while mortality profiles are indeed different from attritional ones, it is not possible to identify the specific type of catastrophic event from demography alone. However, they suggest that demographic features that are the hallmark of an indiscriminate catastrophic event include a low proportion of infants, a low proportion of 15–25-year-olds and a peak in the adult age group. This is further supported by the work of Paine (2000), who noted that catastrophic events leave a clear signature on the palaeodemographic record. Detecting a catastrophic death assemblage in the archaeological record is also possible using Bayesian statistical techniques (Gowland and Chamberlain 2005).

At St Mary Spital, burials made during periods 14 and 15 should be largely unaffected by the major demographic disturbance brought about by the plague, but the attritional cemetery will be more extensively affected by the shifts in population structure that followed it. Assessing the impact of the Black Death on large urban populations by comparing samples that pre-date and post-date this event might shed light on the role of migration in sustaining population growth. However, as Mays (1998, 196) points out, due to the problems of dating cemetery samples, little has been done in this direction.

4.5 St Mary Spital in a national and European perspective

Rebecca Redfern

Inter-site analysis enables the health status of a cemetery population to be understood within its temporal and geographical context. This is of particular importance for understanding the health of Londoners, because the medieval city was unique in its degree of urbanisation and environment due to population migration, settlement density, trade and government (Thomas 2002). The sample from St Mary Spital provides a unique insight into the health of urban, rural and suburban dwellers, in addition to groups who had a high morbidity risk during the medieval period, such as the poor, migrants and pregnant women. This section compares the osteological evidence for health outside London but within the UK and, where data were available or accessible, from other countries on the Continent. Unfortunately, international comparison is restricted by the limited dissemination of non-UK data in quickly usable format (population-based analyses rather than case studies) (Chapter 1.2).

Inter-site analysis of disease is reliant on adequate description and documentation (Lovell 2000) in addition to the identification and classification of osseous change. Miller et al's (1996) test of inter-observer differences in disease classification has shown that the majority of observers assign lesions to a general disease category rather than to a specific disease. It is understood that the use of such classifications is also determined by taphonomic processes (ie poor preservation), the limitations of an osseous response and individual variation in disease expression. A number of studies examining inter-observer differences in recording pathology have demonstrated that good concordance is frequently found at the presence/absence level, but concordance decreases when recording includes scoring variation in severity of disease expression (eg Jacobi and Danforth 2002). Miller et al (1996, 222) suggest that the use of general disease categories increases comparability between samples. However, despite Miller et al's recommendations, it has been noted in the course of the present study that many site reports do not adequately state the methods or literature used to record and/or diagnose osseous changes, and due to taphonomic processes (among other factors) some pathological changes can only be assigned to a general disease category. Furthermore, it is not always possible to assign a disease category to many conditions due to insufficient description or references, and it is notable that observers also differ as to how they classify diseases (eg whether osteochondritis dissecans should be classed as a circulatory disease or as a type of trauma). Consequently, the focus of comparison in this inter-site analysis is on specific diseases where there is less ambiguity in recording and diagnosis.

Data from over 30 sites were collected, and divided into the following categories: urban, rural, monastic (including urban and rural religious houses), catastrophic, hospital (ie urban) and international (Table 157). Wherever possible the data from articulated inhumations were used; however, for many sites it was impossible to separate disarticulated/articulated data due to the lack of burial catalogues or sufficient information. Data were only included if diagnosis was unambiguous or of sufficient detail to permit comparison; the data in this section will therefore vary from those cited in the published reports. As

Table 157 Summary of sites used for comparative purposes, by category, with additional sites listed separately if used for specific disease categories

Site type	Location	Site name	Sample size (where known)	Date (c = century)	Data source
Rural	Glamorgan, Wales	Llandough	643	4th–12th c	Loe 2003
	Yorkshire	Wharram Percy	687	10th–16th c	Mays 2007; 2006b
	Essex	Rivenhall	109	10th–17th c	O'Connor 1993
	Scotland	Isle of Ensay	>450	16th–19th c	Miles 1989
Monastic	Essex	St Mary Stratford Langthorne	601	1135–1538/9	White 2004
	Cleveland	Gisborough Priory	47	12th–16th c	Anderson 1994
	Canterbury, Kent	St Gregory's Priory	90	1084–1537	Anderson 2005
	Bristol	St James's Priory	278	13th–15th c	Loe 2006
	Suffolk	Whitefriars Ipswich	13	12th–16th c	Mays 1991a
		Blackfriars Ipswich	111	1239–1538	Mays 1991b
	Lincolnshire	Whitefriars Lincoln (St Mark's railway station)	10	13th–15th c	Boylston and Roberts 1997
	Leicestershire	Austin Friars Leicester	26	12th–16th c	Stirland 1981
	Wales	Greyfriars Carmarthen	34	13th–16th c	Wilkinson 2001
	Scotland	Jedburgh Abbey	4	11th–16th c	Lewis 1995
Catastrophic	Yorkshire	Towton	37	1461	Fiorato et al 2000
	Solent	*Mary Rose*	110	1545	Stirland 2000
Urban	York, Yorkshire	Fishergate House	402	11th–16th c	Holst 2005
		Jewbury	455	late 12th–13th c	Lilley et al 1994
		St Andrew Fishergate	223	mid 14th–15th c	Stroud and Kemp 1993
		St Helen-on-the-Walls	1037	1140–1550	Dawes and Magilton 1980
	Lincoln, Lincolnshire	Silver Street	12	–	Boylston and Roberts 1997
		Lawn Hospital	36	–	Boylston and Roberts 1997
	Barton-on-Humber, Lincolnshire	St Peter's (periods C, C/D, D)	632	11th–16th c	Waldron 2007

Table 157 (cont)

Site type	Location	Site name	Sample size (where known)	Date (c = century)	Data source
Hospital	Bristol	St Bartholomew's	45	13th–16th c	Stroud 1998
	Chichester, West Sussex	St James and St Mary Magdalene (leprosarium)	198	12th–16th c	Ortner et al 1991; Roberts 1987; Roberts et al 2002
	Lutterworth, Leicestershire	St John the Baptist	20	13th–15th c	Priest and Chapman 2002
	Buckinghamshire, High Wycombe	St Margaret	5	11th–16th c	Farley and Manchester 1989
International samples	Ireland	Waterford (urban)	251	mid 11th–early 17th c	Hurley et al 1997
	Netherlands	Breda (Beguines, nunnery)	102	1267–1530	Rijpma and Maat 2005
		Saint Servaas; Oude en Nieuwe Gasthuis; Franciscan friary (monastic)	-	medieval	Hanson 1992; Maat 2005
	France	Rouen (urban)	375	10th–12th c	Tatham 2004
		Cherbourg (urban)	81	10th–11th c	Tatham 2004
		Arras (urban)	51	11th–12th c	Tatham 2004
Trauma	Czech Republic	Prague and Melnik (urban)	-	15th–18th c	Prokopec and Halman 1999
	Sweden	Wisby (catastrophic)	1185	1361	Thordeman 2001
	Denmark	Æbelholt Kloster (urban)	-	medieval	Møller-Christensen 1958
	York, Yorkshire	St Helen-on-the-Walls	-	1140–1550	Dawes and Magilton 1980; Grauer and Roberts 1996
Infectious disease	Hull, England	Augustinian priory (magistrates court site)	-	14th–16th	Roberts 1994
	Norwich, England	-	-	medieval	Stirland 1991b
	Sweden	Lund (urban)	3305	medieval	Arcini 1999; Crane-Kramer 2000
	Netherlands	Maastricht (urban)	-	medieval	Maat 2005
	Russia	Rostov Velikiy (urban)	32	mid 16th c	Buzhilova 1999
	northern Europe	-	-	medieval	Anderson et al 1986; Crane-Kramer 2000; Mays et al 2003
	Denmark	Naestved (leprosarium)	-	medieval	Møller-Christensen 1953, 1969
		Æbelholt Kloster (urban)	-	medieval	Møller-Christensen 1958
Congenital and developmental anomalies	York, Yorkshire	St Helen-on-the-Walls	-	1140–1550	Sture 2002
	Hull, Yorkshire	Augustinian priory (magistrates court site)	-	14th–16th c	Sture 2002
	Yorkshire	Raunds Furnells	-	10th–12th c	Sture 2002
		Wharram Percy	289	10th–16th c	Sture 2002
Stature	Trondheim, Norway	St Gregory's church (urban)	-	1150–1350	Hanson 1992
	Netherlands	Maastricht	-	medieval	Maat 2005
	Denmark	Æbelholt Kloster (urban)	-	medieval	Møller-Christensen 1958
Growth	Yorkshire	Raunds Furnells	-	10th–12th c	
	York, Yorkshire	St Helen-on-the-Walls	-	1140–1550	
Paget's disease	Cheshire	Norton Priory	-	medieval	Boylston and Ogden 2005
Endocranial lesions	Yorkshire	Raunds Furnells	-	10th–12th c	
		Wharram Percy	-	10th–16th c	
Pathological and stature data	United Kingdom	-	-	medieval	Roberts and Buikstra 2003; Roberts and Cox 2003

total sample sizes selected varied depending on the disease under study (eg males or female, adults, teeth present) and in some instances only prevalence rates were cited in the original text, total sample size has been omitted from the tabulated data in this section, but may be found in the accompanying text.

Data for males, females and subadults were employed; because there were considerable disparities in subadult age ranges between reports, all individuals from 40 weeks to 18 years old were included in this group. Sexed adults were used, where possible, in order to investigate the relationship between site type and location, gender and health. Data collated by Roberts and Cox (2003) and Roberts and Buikstra (2003) were only included when cited by sex.

Because the quantity and detail of data available from St Mary Spital were vast, it was frequently impossible to find comparable data sets in terms of numbers of individuals and the systematic use of true prevalence rates. Consequently, in order to provide a more focused perspective on inter-site differences in health, a limited number of palaeopathological categories were examined, concentrating on specific disease types.

Disparities in data quality and quantity also directly influenced the level of inter-site analysis. The fundamental issue was the inability to compare true prevalence rates between sites. To provide consistency the crude prevalence rate was therefore calculated by sex or age group for all disease groups, except trauma (see below). Additionally, where the total number of males and females or age group could not be obtained and only the site total was available, crude prevalence rates were calculated using the site total. This was specifically done in order to increase the number of samples available for the inter-site comparison of tuberculosis.

It should be noted that because of the large sample size from

St Mary Spital, the crude prevalence rates are low: for example, although St Mary Spital has the greatest number of individuals with tuberculosis seen in a medieval cemetery, the crude prevalence rate is lower than that for a smaller cemetery with fewer tubercular individuals (see Waldron 1994).

Dental health

The comparison of dental health was constrained by the way in which the data were presented, and due to the large sample at St Mary Spital the crude prevalence rates do not provide a true picture. Not all sites or data could be included in the analysis because of differences in the presentation of information. For subadults, the comparable data were limited to caries and enamel hypoplastic defects, and carious lesions were reported from both urban and monastic cemeteries (Table 158; Table 159).

St Mary Spital had the highest adult prevalence rates of enamel hypoplastic defects in the incisors, canines, premolars and molars seen in those from monastic sites. Enamel hypoplastic defects were absent in the populations from Lincoln, making St Mary Spital the only urban site examined where such defects were present (Table 158). Interestingly, the crude prevalence rate of subadult enamel hypoplastic defects is lower at St Mary Spital than at the rural site of Wharram Percy (Table 159). Examination of the crude prevalence rates between groups shows that monastic cemeteries have the highest crude prevalence of caries, ante-mortem tooth loss and abscesses, and urban cemeteries have the lowest crude prevalence of these diseases. The levels of caries and enamel hypoplastic defects in the incisors and canines were most similar between St Mary Spital and the catastrophic site of Towton (Table 158).

Holst and Coughlan (2000, 83) compared the frequency of

Table 158 Inter-site comparison of adult dental health

Site type	Site name	Sex	Tooth	Caries No. affected	%	Enamel hypoplasia No. affected	%	Ante-mortem loss No. affected	%	Periapical lesions No. affected	%
Monastic	Whitefriars Ipswich	male	incisor	0	-	1	1.8	7	12.5	2	3.6
		female		0	-	0	-	3	18.7	0	-
		male	canine	4	12.5	0	-	2	6.2	2	6.2
		male	premolar	14	23.1	0	-	6	9.8	4	6.5
		female		1	7.7	0	-	5	38.5	2	15.4
		male	molar	15	23.1	0	-	33	50.8	8	12.3
		female		4	33.3	0	-	9	75	2	15.4
	Whitefriars Lincoln (St Mark's railway station)	male	incisor	0	-	0	-	1	2.6	0	-
			canine	0	-	0	-	1	4.3	0	-
			molar	1	1.3	0	-	3	4	4	5.3
	Jedburgh Abbey	male	premolar	1	3.8	0	-	1	3.8	1	3.8
			molar	5	29.4	0	-	2	11.8	2	11.8
Rural	Llandough	male	-	0	-	7	3.1	0	-	0	-
		female	-	0	-	6	3.1	0	-	0	-
Urban	Silver Street	male	incisor	2	8.7	0	-	0	-	0	-
		male	premolar	0	-	0	-	1	5.9	0	-
		female		0	-	0	-	1	4.2	0	-
		male	molar	4	14.8	0	-	7	25.9	0	-
		female		0	-	0	-	5	16.1	1	3.2
	Lawn Hospital	female	canine	0	-	0	-	1	20	0	-
		male	premolar	0	-	0	-	1	3.1	0	-
		female		0	-	0	-	1	11.1	0	-
		male	molar	4	11.4	0	-	6	17.1	1	2.8
		female		3	27.3	0	-	4	36.4	0	-
Catastrophic	Towton	male	incisor	7	3.9	23	12.7	0	-	0	-
			canine	2	2	9	9	0	-	0	-
			premolar	15	7.9	3	1.6	0	-	0	-
			molar	38	16.7	0	-	0	-	0	-
			all teeth	0	-	0	-	0	10.2	0	-
Hospital	St Mary Spital	male	incisor	9	2.7	1341	14.1	-	-	-	-
		female		13	2.6	1293	15.5	-	-	-	-
		both sexes		-	-	-	-	1182	5.1	298	1.3
		male	canine	276	5.3	1443	27.3	-	-	-	-
		female		216	4.2	1322	27.6	-	-	-	-
		both sexes		-	-	-	-	382	3.2	175	1.5
		male	premolar	1016	10.2	1353	13.4	-	-	-	-
		female		892	9.2	1178	13.1	-	-	-	-
		both sexes		-	-	-	-	2053	8.6	598	2.5
		male	molar	2143	18.6	746	6.2	-	-	-	-
		female		2032	18.9	536	5.1	-	-	-	-
		both sexes		-	-	-	-	7368	21.8	1395	3.8

Table 159 Inter-site comparison of subadult dental health

Type	Site	Published dental data	Caries No. affected	%	Enamel hypoplasia No. affected	%	Calculus No. affected	%	Periapical lesions No. affected	%
Rural	Wharram Percy	permanent dentition	-	-	-	30.6	-	-	-	-
Hospital	St James and St Mary Magdalene	no. of subadults in sample	3	7.5	1	2.5	-	-	-	-
Urban	St Helen-on-the-Walls	decidous dentition	-	-	2	3.8	-	-	-	-
	St Andrew Fishergate	decidous dentition	12	3.4	8	2.2	-	-	3	0.8
	Jewbury	no. of subadults in sample	-	-	6	3.9	-	-	-	-
Monastic	Gisborough Priory	no. of deciduous teeth	-	8.1	-	-	-	-	-	-
	St Gregory's Priory	total no. of deciduous teeth	9	3.4	-	-	8	4.6	-	-
		no. of permanent teeth	-	-	7	10.9	7	10.9	-	-
Hospital	St Mary Spital	no. of deciduous teeth	259	11.1	16	0.6	-	-	-	-
		no. of permanent teeth	376	2.8	-	-	-	-	-	-

periapical lesions in ten medieval cemeteries and noted that it varied widely, from as little as 0.7% at rural sites to 4.5% in urban ones, with an average of 1.9%. Roberts and Cox (2003, 259) give similar frequencies of 0.3–4.4% for late medieval cemeteries. Compared to these data, the St Mary Spital prevalence (2.7%: 2466 lesions/92,259 tooth positions) is not exceptionally high. However, the age-at-death profile and presence of other dental pathology such as ante-mortem tooth loss might affect the frequencies of lesions observed and it should be remembered that to provide true frequencies radiography is needed to identify all abscess cavities (Hillson 2008, 322).

Joint disease

Diffuse idiopathic skeletal hyperostosis (DISH)

DISH was reported from monastic, hospital, rural and urban cemeteries. The majority of affected individuals were males. The highest male crude prevalence was reported from St Peter's, Barton-on-Humber (12/150: 8.0%), followed by St James's, Bristol (7/112: 6.3%), Fishergate House, York (3/57: 5.3%) and St Mary Stratford Langthorne (22/542: 4.1%) (Table 160). Women were only affected at St Andrew

Table 160 Inter-site crude prevalence rate of joint disease

Type	Site	Age or sex	DISH No. affected	%	Septic arthropathy No. affected	%	Ankylosing spondylitis No. affected	%
Rural	Llandough	male	0	-	1	0.4	0	-
	Wharram Percy (phases 2–2/3)	all adults	13	1.1	0	-	-	0.3
Monastic	St Mary Stratford Langthorne	male	22	4.1	1	0.2	1	0.2
	Norton Priory	male	1	1.2	0	-	0	-
	St James's Priory, Bristol	male	7	6.3	0	-	0	-
		female	1	2.7	0	-	0	-
	Whitefriars Ipswich	male	0	-	0	-	0	-
Urban	Lawn Hospital	male	0	-	0	-	0	-
		female	0	-	0	-	0	-
	Silver Street	male	0	-	0	-	0	-
		female	0	-	0	-	0	-
	St Helen-on-the-Walls	male	4	1.8	0	-	0	-
		female	0	-	0	-	0	-
	St Andrew Fishergate	male	6	2.7	0	-	0	-
		female	1	1.1	0	-	0	-
	Jewbury	male	3	1.8	0	-	0	-
	Fishergate House	males	3	5.3	0	-	0	-
		female	1	1.9	0	-	0	-
	St Peter's (periods C, C–D, D or early period)	male	12	8.0	0	-	0	-
		female	0	-	1	0.7	0	-
		subadult	0	-	1	0.8	0	-
Hospital	St Bartholomew's	male	0	-	0	-	0	-
	St John's	male	2	1.2	0	-	0	-
	St Mary Spital	male	23	1.0	5	0.2	4	0.2
		female	11	0.6	8	0.4	0	-
		subadult	0	-	1	0.1	0	-
International	Breda, Netherlands	female	20	22.2	0	-	0	-

Fishergate, Fishergate House, St James's, St Mary Spital and the Beguine cemetery from Breda, which had the highest reported crude prevalence rate (20/90: 22.2%). St Mary Spital had the lowest crude prevalence rates for both sexes seen at any site.

Septic osteoarthritis

Septic osteoarthritis was reported at four sites and only at St Mary Spital were subadults and adults of both sexes affected. The male crude prevalence rate observed at Llandough (1/223: 0.4%) was identical to that seen in females from St Mary Spital (8/1883: 0.4%). Males from Stratford Langthorne (1/542: 0.2%) and St Mary Spital (5/2237: 0.2%) were equally affected (Table 160).

Seronegative osteoarthritis

St Mary Spital was the only site with more than one type of seronegative osteoarthropathy present. This result may be due to authors assigning osteological changes to disease category rather than to a specific disease (see Miller et al 1996). Fishergate House had the highest crude prevalence for both sexes (1/57: 1.8% males and 1/53: 1.9% females). Only St Mary Spital and St Peter's had evidence for psoriatic arthropathy. Beguine females had the highest rates for Reiter's disease (2/90: 2.2%) (Table 160).

Erosive arthropathy

As with the reported evidence for seronegative osteoarthritis, the majority of reported data assigned osseous changes to disease category, and again the lack of accessible data from rural samples biases the data. Erosive arthropathy was reported in adults from monastic, urban and hospital sites. Gout was most frequently reported in males, with the highest male crude prevalence rate observed at the Lawn Hospital site, Lincoln (1/14: 7.1%), and the lowest at St Mary Spital (1/2237: <0.1%) and Stratford Langthorne (1/542: 0.2%). Only at St Peter's (2/151: 1.3%) and St Mary Spital (1/1883: 0.1%) were females present with the disease. Rheumatoid arthritis was reported in both sexes at St Helen-on-the-Walls, St Peter's and St Mary Spital (Table 160).

Trauma

Distribution of ante-mortem fractures

In order to undertake inter-site comparison, data on long bone fractures (humerus, radius, ulna, femur, tibia and fibula) were collected. Frequency of fracture per element was calculated in order to produce true prevalence rates for each long bone as well as total long bones (Chapter 3.8). Element grouping followed that described in Chapter 2.2, and was employed to investigate differences between sites and by demographic group. In order to investigate variations in injuries by sex, male and female long

Gout		Rheumatoid arthritis		Seronegative spondyloarthropathy		Erosive arthropathy		Reiter's disease		Psoriatic arthropathy	
No. affected	%	No. affected	%	No. affected	%	No. affected	%	No. affected	%	No. affected	%
0	-	0	-	0	-	0	-	0	-	0	-
0	-	0	-	0	-	0	-	0	-	0	-
1	0.2	0	-	0	-	0	-	0	-	0	-
0	-	0	-	0	-	0	-	0	-	0	-
0	-	0	-	0	-	0	-	0	-	0	-
0	-	0	-	0	-	0	-	0	-	0	-
0	-	0	-	1	9.1	2	18.2	0	-	0	-
1	7.1	0	-	0	-	0	-	0	-	0	-
0	-	0	-	0	-	1	9.1	0	-	0	-
0	-	0	-	0	-	1	25.0	0	-	0	-
0	-	0	-	0	-	1	16.7	0	-	0	-
0	-	9	4.1	0	-	0	-	0	-	0	-
0	-	2	0.8	0	-	0	-	0	-	0	-
0	-	0	-	1	0.4	0	-	0	-	0	-
0	-	0	-	0	-	1	1.1	0	-	0	-
0	-	0	-	0	-	0	-	0	-	0	-
0	-	0	-	1	1.8	0	-	0	-	0	-
0	-	0	-	1	1.9	0	-	0	-	0	-
0	-	2	1.3	0	-	1	0.7	0	-	1	0.7
2	1.3	1	0.7	0	-	1	0.7	0	-	1	0.7
0	-	0	-	0	-	0	-	0	-	0	-
0	-	0	-	0	-	1	8.3	0	-	0	-
0	-	0	-	0	-	0	-	0	-	0	-
1	<0.1	3	0.1	3	0.1	18	0.8	1	<0.1	1	<0.1
1	0.1	1	0.1	0	-	12	0.6	0	-	1	0.1
0	-	0	-	0	-	0	-	0	-	0	-
0	-	0	-	0	-	0	-	2	2.2	0	-

bone fractures were calculated as a percentage of the number of individuals present. This method allowed for inter-site comparison.

The results from St Mary Spital were compared with the data collated from medieval skeletal populations in Britain by Grauer and Roberts (1996, 538) (including St Helen-on-the-Walls and St Andrew Fishergate in York, Blackfriars Friary in Ipswich, St Nicholas Shambles in London, and the hospital of St James and St Mary Magdalene, Chichester) (Table 161). Data from the Cistercian abbey of St Mary Stratford Langthorne, Essex, the War of the Roses mass grave at Towton, and the churchyard at Wharram Percy were also employed (Fiorato et al 2000; White 2004; Mays et al 2007). The data exclude any sharp and blunt force peri-mortem injuries, of which there were a considerable number from Towton. Where long bone fracture data were not available, crude prevalence rates (numbers of individuals with fractures) were used.

When long bone fractures were combined, there was a particularly high frequency of injury in the sample from St Nicholas Shambles (18/296: 6.1%), but Grauer and Roberts suggest that this was the result of the low numbers and poor preservation of long bones within the burials (1996, 538, 542). Of the other sites, the hospital of St James and St Mary Magdalene, Chichester, had the highest rate of long bone fracture (30/1293: 2.3%), perhaps a reflection of the atypical nature of the sample from what was originally a leprosarium (ibid, 538). Judd attributed these injuries to accidental trauma, possibly because those suffering from leprosy had an increased risk of tripping and falling (Judd 2008, 229–38). The policy of St Mary Spital was not to accept known leprosy sufferers as inmates, and this may account for the lower rate of injury here and at most other sites in the study.

Towton, where no female individuals were identified, had the next highest rate of long bone fracture (6/356: 1.7%). This might be expected, both as males from medieval samples tended to suffer greater numbers of fractures than females, and because the individuals in the mass grave may have been involved in previous combat and have suffered more long bone fractures than non-combatants. However, the frequency of long bone fracture at Towton was not higher to a statistically significant extent than that at St Mary Spital (550/48,749: 1.1%), which had similar rates to the York sites and St Mary Stratford Langthorne in Essex.

Judd and Roberts (1999) found a greater frequency of long bone fracture in rural sites than urban. However, the low prevalence of long bone fracture at Wharram Percy (16/3338: 0.5%) demonstrates that this was not always the case (Mays et al 2007, 150). There may well have been a general trend of increased risk of injury in agricultural workers, but one might expect to see anomalies in such a pattern according to variations in geographical position, farming practices and social structure. As with the findings of Judd and Roberts (1999), there was no significant variation in the frequency of long bone fracture between the sexes at Wharram Percy (Mays et al 2007, 143). In the urban samples, males were affected more frequently than females, but at St Mary Spital (male 215/2237: 9.6%; female 161/1883: 8.6%) and Fishergate (male 15/220: 6.8%; female 5/89: 5.6%), the differences were relatively small. At St Mary Spital the evidence of the distribution of bone fractures implied that there was variation in male and female injury patterns (Chapter 3.8).

Overall, with the exception of Towton, St James and St Mary Magdalene, Chichester, and St Nicholas Shambles, the frequency and distribution of long bone fracture varied little between the samples under study. In all cases, the long bones of males suffered greater number of fractures than those of females. However, females at St Mary Spital suffered comparatively high rates of long bone fracture (161/1883: 8.6%) than those at the other sites under study, and higher to a statistically significant extent than that from St Helen-on-the-Walls in York (11/285: 3.9%) (χ^2 = 7.46, df = 1, p ≤ 0.01).

For further comparison the proportion of fractures in each body area was calculated as a percentage of the total number of fractures by sex. Discussion here focuses on those samples where the total number of fractures was 20 or more, with all comparative sites displayed (Table 162).

In rural samples, the highest proportion of rib fractures observed in males was seen in the Isle of Ensay (14/20: 70.0%). Fractures to the arm were observed most frequently in males from Llandough (19/61: 31.1%), followed by St Mary Spital (245/1486: 16.5%); the lowest proportions were found in males

Table 161 Inter-site true prevalence rates of fracture by site and long bone

Site	Site type	Humerus No.	No. affected	%	Radius No.	No. affected	%	Ulna No.	No. affected	%	Femur No.	No. affected	%	Tibia No.	No. affected	%	Fibula No.	No. affected	%	Total No.	No. affected	%
St Mary Spital	hospital	8739	74	0.8	8476	119	1.4	8537	172	2.0	8471	23	0.3	7453	81	1.1	7073	81	1.1	48,749	550	1.1
St James and St Mary Magdalene	hospital	243	2	0.8	218	7	3.2	217	6	2.8	228	1	0.4	276	6	2.3	111	8	7.2	1293	30	2.3
St Helen-on-the-Walls	urban	891	7	0.8	770	10	1.3	752	11	1.5	937	1	0.1	864	6	0.7	725	6	0.8	4939	41	0.8
St Nicholas Shambles	urban	38	2	5.3	57	5	8.8	49	4	8.2	53	2	3.8	50	3	6.0	49	2	4.1	296	18	6.1
St Andrew Fishergate	urban	528	2	0.4	523	4	0.8	518	7	0.8	577	1	0.2	558	3	0.5	531	9	1.7	3235	26	0.8
St Mary Stratford Langthorne	monastic	502	3	0.6	508	4	0.8	471	4	0.8	501	4	0.8	462	14	3.0	377	12	3.2	2821	41	1.5
Blackfriars Ipswich	monastic	369	1	0.3	370	5	1.4	371	2	0.5	393	2	0.5	393	2	0.5	358	1	0.3	2254	13	0.6
Towton	catastrophic	59	1	1.7	60	1	1.7	54	0	-	64	0	-	71	1	1.4	48	3	6.3	356	6	1.7

Table 162 Fracture distribution in the comparative sample

Type	Site	Age or sex	Skull No.	Skull % affected	Ribs No.	Ribs % affected	Spine No.	Spine % affected	Arm No.	Arm % affected	Hand No.	Hand % affected	Leg No.	Leg % affected	Foot No.	Foot % affected	Total No. affected
Catastrophic	Towton	male	8	38.1	0	-	2	9.5	3	14.3	2	9.5	4	19.0	2	9.5	21
	Mary Rose	male	18	26.1	9	13.0	0	-	4	5.8	0	-	23	33.3	15	21.7	69
Hospital	St Bartholomew's	male	1	50.0	0	-	0	-	0	-	1	50	0	-		-	2
		female	1	50.0	0	-	0	-	0	-	0	-	0	-	1	50.0	2
	St James and	male	0	-	0	-	0	-	22	62.8	0	-	13	37.1	0	-	35
	St Mary Magdalene	female	0	-	0	-	0	-	2	50.0	0	-	2	50.0	0	-	4
	St Mary Spital	male	110	7.4	439	29.5	373	25.1	245	16.5	109	7.3	117	7.9	92	6.2	1486
		female	42	6.0	162	23.2	157	22.5	172	24.6	48	6.9	88	12.6	29	4.2	698
		subadult	5	12.8	7	17.9	8	20.5	7	17.9	1	2.6	3	7.7	8	20.5	39
Monastic	St Mary Stratford Langthorne	male	2	3.4	2	3.4	0	-	11	19.0	12	20.7	30	51.7	1	1.7	58
	Norton Priory	male	0	-	0	-	0	-	1	100.0	0	-	0	-	0	-	1
	Jedburgh Abbey	male	0	-	0	-	0	-	-	-	1	100.0	0	-	0	-	1
	Gisborough Priory	male		22.2		11.1		11.1		11.1	0	-	0	44.4	0	-	
		female	0	-	0	-	0	-		100.0	0	-	0	-	0	-	0
	St Gregory's Priory	male	1	10.0	4	40.0	2	20.0	1	10.0	1	10.0	0	-	1	10.0	10
	Whitefriars Ipswich	male	0	-		50.0	0	-		50.0	0	-	0	-	0	-	
		female	0	-	0	-	0	-	-	-	1	100.0	0	-	0	-	1
Rural	Llandough	male	11	18.0	15	24.6	4	6.5	19	31.1	7	11.5	4	6.6	1	1.6	61
		female	0	-	1	8.3	1	8.3	6	50.0	1	8.3	2	16.7	1	8.3	12
	Wharram Percy	male	10	9.3	51	47.7	17	15.9	8	7.5	7	6.5	7	6.5	7	6.5	107
	(phases 2/2–3)	female	1	2.0	30	61.2	6	12.2	1	2.0	6	12.2	3	6.1	2	4.1	49
		subadult	0	-	0	-	0	-	1	100.0	0	-	0	-	0	-	1
Urban	Lawn Hospital	male	0	-	1	20.0	1	20.0	1	20.0	1	20.0	1	20.0	0	-	5
		female	0	-	0	-	1	100.0	-	-	0	-	0	-	0	-	1
	St Helen-on-the-Walls	male	4	11.4	5	14.3	1	2.8	17	48.6	1	2.8	7	20.0	0	-	35
		female	0	-	3	11.5	0	-	10	38.5	9	34.6	4	23.5	0	-	26
		subadult	2	50.0	0	-	0	-	-	-	0	-	2	50.0	0	-	4
	St Andrew Fishergate	male	1	1.5	20	29.4	10	14.7	10	14.7	5	7.3	13	19.1	9	13.2	68
		female	0	-	7	29.2	1	4.2	8	33.3	3	12.5	4	16.7	1	4.2	24
	Jewbury	male	2	28.6	0	-	0	-	3	42.8	0	-	2	28.6	0	-	7
		female	3	21.4	0	-	2	14.3	5	35.7	0	-	4	28.6	0	-	14
		subadult	1	100.0	0	-	0	-	-	-	0	-	0	-	0	-	1
	Fishergate House	male	3	5.6	38	67.8	5	8.9	4	7.1	3	5.4	3	5.3	0	-	56
		female	2	6.7	17	56.7	3	10.0	6	20.0	1	3.3	1	3.3	0	-	30
	Silver Street	female	0	-	0	-	0	-	1	100.0	0	-	0	-	0	-	1
International	Prague and Melnik,	male	0	-	0	-	0	-	-	-	0	-	5	100.0	0	-	5
	Czech Republic (urban)	female	0	-	0	-	0	-	1	20.0	0	-	4	80.0	0	-	5
	Æbelholt Kloster,	male	-	-	-	24.4	-	14.6	-	51.2	-	9.8	-	-	-	-	0
	Denmark (urban)	female	-	25.0	-	50.0	-	-	-	12.5	-	12.5	-	-	-	-	0
	Breda, Netherlands (Beguines, nunnery)	female	1	3.6	0	-	13	46.4	9	32.1	0	-	2	7.1	3	10.7	28
	Isle of Ensay, Scotland	male	0	-	14	70.0	1	5.0	2	10.0	0	-	3	15.0	0	-	20
	(rural)	female	0	-	0	-	2	28.6	-	-	5	71.4	0	-	0	-	7
	Waterford, Ireland	male	1	4.0	2	8.0	0	-	6	24.0	10	40.0	3	12.0	3	12.0	25
	(urban)	female	2	15.4	1	7.7	0	-	3	23.1	1	7.7	3	23.1	3	23.1	13
		subadult	0	-	0	-	1	33.3	1	33.3	0	-	0	-	1	33.3	3

at Wharram Percy (8/107: 7.5%) and on the Isle of Ensay (2/20: 10.0%). The majority of hand fractures were observed in males from Llandough (7/61: 11.5%). No hand fractures were reported among males from the Isle of Ensay. After the Isle of Ensay (3/20: 15.0%), St Mary Spital had the highest proportion of leg fractures (117/1486: 7.9%); Llandough (4/61: 6.6%) and Wharram Percy (7/107: 6.5%) were similarly affected. The *Mary Rose* had the highest proportion of foot fractures and Llandough had the lowest (Table 162). A high proportion of spinal fractures (373/1486: 25.1%) was seen at St Mary Spital.

Rural females had different fracture patterns, with rib and hand fractures dominating the Wharram Percy sample, hand and spine fractures in the Isle of Ensay material, and arm fractures in the Llandough sample. The females from St Mary Spital had the highest proportion of skull fractures (42/698: 6.0%) (Table 162). The highest proportion of rib fractures among females was observed at Wharram Percy and St Mary Spital. A high proportion of spinal fractures was observed at St Mary Spital (157/698: 22.5%). The Isle of Ensay sample had the highest proportion of hand fractures, though this was due to the small sample size (Table 162). The highest rate of foot fractures was observed at Llandough, though again this was influenced by the small number of fractures present. No foot fractures were present in the females from the Isle of Ensay.

The examination of urban samples revealed that subadults were only affected at St Mary Spital, St Helen-on-the-Walls and Jewbury, and that only at St Mary Spital did subadults present with fractures to two or more body areas. Skull fractures were observed in subadults at all three cemeteries, but St Mary Spital was the only cemetery where all areas of the body were affected by injuries (Table 162).

At all urban cemeteries, males had evidence of fractures. Healed skull fractures were observed at all sites apart from Lawn Hospital, Lincoln. Rib fractures were recorded at all sites, with males at Fishergate House having the highest proportion at 67.8% (38/56). The proportion of rib fractures at St Mary Spital (439/1486: 29.5%) was comparable to that of St Andrew Fishergate (20/68: 29.4%). St Mary Spital had the highest proportion of spinal fractures (373/1486: 25.1%). The majority of arm fractures were observed at St Helen-on-the-Walls (17/35: 48.6%). The lowest proportion of hand fractures was recorded at Fishergate House (3/56: 5.4%). Foot fractures were only recorded at St Mary Spital (92/1486: 6.2%), Jewbury (9/68: 13.2%) and St Gregory's Priory (1/10: 10.0%) (Table 162).

Inter-cemetery differences for females were most noticeable between urban cemeteries. At the Lawn Hospital and Silver Street cemeteries, Lincoln, females only had fractures to one area of the body (spine and arm respectively). Only the cemeteries from York (Fishergate House and St Andrew Fishergate) and St Mary Spital have six or more body areas affected, and St Mary Spital is the only site to have all seven body areas affected. Skull fractures were observed at St Mary Spital, Jewbury and Fishergate House. Fishergate House (17/30: 56.7%), St Andrew Fishergate (7/24: 29.2%) and St Mary Spital (162/698: 23.2%) have the highest proportion of rib fractures, and the lowest was observed at St Helen-on-the-Walls (3/26: 11.5%). Again only St Mary Spital and York cemeteries had evidence for this injury type. A high proportion of arm fractures was seen at St Helen-on-the-Walls (10/26: 38.5%) and the lowest proportion (of those sites where arm fractures were present) was observed at St Mary Spital (172/698: 24.6%). Hand fractures were observed in all cemeteries apart from Silver Street and Lawn Hospital; the highest proportion was recorded at St Helen-on-the-Walls (9/26: 34.6%). Foot fractures were only reported at St Andrew Fishergate (1/24: 4.2%) and St Mary Spital (29/698: 4.2%).

Comparison between monastic sites demonstrates that each has a unique trauma profile. The pattern of trauma at St Mary Spital is most similar to that seen in males from St Mary Stratford Langthorne (Essex), with healed fractures affecting five to six areas of the body. Only at St Mary Stratford Langthorne and Gisborough Priory were skull fractures recorded. Spinal fractures were only recorded at Gisborough Priory and St Mary Spital. Arm fractures were recorded in all males, with St Mary Spital having the lowest proportion (245/1486: 16.5%). Leg and foot fractures together were only recorded in males from St Mary Stratford Langthorne (30/58: 51.7% and 1/58:1.7% respectively) and St Mary Spital (117/1486: 7.9% and 92/1486: 6.2% respectively), though leg fractures were also seen at Gisborough Priory. Females at Gisborough Priory and Whitefriars Ipswich had only one body area affected (the arm and hand respectively), whereas St Mary Spital females had fractures to seven body areas, predominantly to the arms (Table 162).

There are clear disparities between St Mary Spital and other English hospitals. At St James and St Mary Magdalene, Chichester, males and females only had two body areas affected by fractures (arms and legs), whereas at St Mary Spital seven body areas were affected. Outside St Mary Spital, skull fractures and hand fractures were only reported at St Bartholomew's, Bristol, although sample sizes were too small for valid comparison. St James and St Mary Magdalene was the only other hospital cemetery that had evidence for fractures to the leg and St Bartholomew's was the only other site with foot fractures (Table 162).

The data available from catastrophic sites consisted of samples of males only, although it should be noted that females from St Mary Spital had a similar fracture distribution to both of these samples, in that more than five body areas were affected by trauma. It should also be remembered that the catastrophic sites examined (Towton and the *Mary Rose*) related to episodes of warfare, so the people involved would have experienced greater risks than the general population. Nonetheless, although the St Mary Spital male sample has a different trauma pattern from these two sites, the distribution of fractures is similar. All samples had skull fractures but St Mary Spital had the lowest proportion (110/1486: 7.4%); only Towton and St Mary Spital had spinal fractures (2/21: 9.5% and 373/1486: 25.1% respectively) and hand fractures (2/21: 9.5% and 109/1486: 7.3% respectively). St Mary Spital had a higher proportion of arm fractures (245/1486: 16.5%) than the *Mary Rose* (4/69: 5.8%) and Towton (3/21: 14.3%) samples. All male samples had fractures to the leg and foot, although St Mary Spital had the lowest proportions (Table 162).

Data were only available from a small number of medieval samples from outside the UK. They were often restricted to long bones only and comparison therefore is limited.

St Mary Spital has a similar fracture distribution to Waterford (Ireland): at both sites all body areas were affected, although Waterford had no evidence of spinal fractures. Males at St Mary Spital had a higher proportion of skull (110/1486: 7.4%) and rib (439/1486: 29.5%) fractures, and males at Waterford had a higher proportion of hand (10/25: 40.0%), leg (3/25: 12.0%) and foot (3/25: 12.0%) fractures.

The data from the Beguinage cemetery from the city of Breda (Netherlands) are restricted to females, who entered the monastic compound but were able to buy or build their own houses and support themselves (Rijpma and Maat 2005, 1). Unlike the females from St Mary Spital, the Beguinage females did not have fractures to the hands or ribs. The Beguinage females also had a higher proportion of spinal (13/28: 46.4%), arm (9/28: 32.1%) and foot (3/28: 10.7%) fractures, although St Mary Spital had a higher proportion of skull fractures among females (42/698: 6.0%).

The data from urban cemeteries from the Czech Republic were confined to long bones and small sample sizes prevented valid comparison of the proportion of injury locations with St

Mary Spital. The Danish fracture data (for Æbelholt Kloster) are similarly limited due to the small sample, the presentation of data and the amount of information available in English (Møller-Christensen 1958, 272–4).

The catastrophic sample from Wisby (Sweden), dating from 1361, and the result of a battle, consisted of a minimum of 1185 individuals, including at least 63 females (Thordeman 2001, 150–2). The ante-mortem fracture data were not presented by sex or age, but in comparison to St Mary Spital the site had no evidence of spinal fractures, healed skull fractures or rib fractures, and a higher proportion of leg fractures (60.5%; ibid).

ANTE-MORTEM SHARP FORCE WEAPON TRAUMA

The body distribution of ante-mortem sharp force weapon trauma was focused at the skull and predominantly recorded in urban cemeteries. Only males from St Andrew Fishergate had evidence for healed injuries to the arm, hand and leg. The only monastic cemetery with evidence for healed injuries was St Mary Stratford Langthorne. Wisby (Sweden) was also dominated by cranial injuries consisting of penetrating and depressed traumas (Thordeman 2001, 196). In females, the distribution of injuries focused upon the skull, with healed injuries observed at St Mary Spital and Jewbury. Only at Fishergate House did females have healed injuries to the arm.

Infectious disease

Leprosy

The crude prevalence of leprosy was, as expected, highest in leprosaria cemeteries. High prevalence rates were observed at Naestved leprosarium in Denmark, where 268 subadult and

Table 163 Inter-site crude prevalence rate of infectious disease

Type	Site	Age or sex	Treponemal disease No. affected	%	Leprosy No. affected	%	Tuberculosis No. affected	%	Osteomyelitis No. affected	%
Urban	Lawn Hospital	female	0	-	0	-	0	-	1	9.1
	Fishergate House	subadult	0	-	0	-	2	1.8	1	0.9
		male	0	-	0	-	0	-	1	1.7
		female	0	-	0	-	0	-	0	-
	Jewbury	male	0	-	0	-	2	1.2	0	-
		female	0	-	0	-	4	2.5	0	-
	St Andrew Fishergate	subadult	0	-	0	-	2	2.2	0	-
		male	0	-	0	-	4	1.8	1	0.4
	St Helen-on-the-Walls	male	0	-	0	-	0	-	2	0.9
		subadult	0	-	0	-	0	-	0	-
	St Peter's	female	0	-	0	-	1	0.7	0	-
Rural	Llandough	male	0	-	0	-	2	0.9	0	-
		female	0	-	0	-	1	0.9	0	-
	Rivenhall	female	0	-	1	2.4	0	-	0	-
	Wharram Percy (phases 2/2–3)	male	0	-	1	0.5	6	2.8	2	0.9
		female	0	-	0	-	3	2.1	0	-
Hospital	St James and St Mary Magdalene	male	0	-	0	-	2	1.6	0	-
		adults	0	-	0	-	0	-	0	-
	St Margaret's	male	0	-	2	100.0	0	-	0	-
		female	0	-	3	100.0	0	-	0	-
	St Mary Spital	male	11	0.5	0	-	36	1.6	18	0.8
		female	8	0.4	2	0.1	43	2.3	8	0.4
		subadult	3	0.3	0	-	16	1.6	4	0.4
Monastic	Whitefriars Ipswich	male	1	9.1	1	9.1	0	-	1	9.1
	Blackfriars Ipswich	female	1	3.7	0	-	0	-	0	-
	Gisborough Priory	female	0	-	0	-	0	-	2	10.5
	St Gregory's Priory	subadult	1	4.8	0	-	0	-	0	-
	St James's Priory, Bristol	male	0	-	0	-	0	-	3	2.7
	Jedburgh Abbey	male	0	-	0	-	0	-	1	25.0
	St Mary Stratford Langthorne	male	0	-	0	-	0	-	5	0.9
International	Waterford, Ireland (urban)	subadult	1	1.2	0	-	0	-	0	-
	Breda, Netherlands (Beguines, nunnery)	female	0	-	0	-	2	2.2	0	-
	Rouen, France (urban)	male	0	-	0	-	3	3.2	0	-
		female	0	-	0	-	2	3.5	0	-
	Arras, France (urban)	male	0	-	0	-	2	18.2	0	-
		female	0	-	0	-	3	25.0	0	-
	Lund, Sweden (urban)	total sample	10	0.3	42	1.3	1	<0.1	34	1.0
	Naestved, Denmark	male	0	-	-	71.1	0	-	0	-
		female	0	-	-	76.6	0	-	0	-
		subadult	0	-	-	36.0	0	-	0	-
	Æbelholt Kloster, Denmark	male	0	-	-	0.6	0	-	0	-
		total sample	0	-	-	0.9	0	-	0	-

adult individuals had facies leprosa, 115 had leprous changes to the hands, 147 to the feet, and 329 had 'definite' leprosy (Møller-Christensen 1953; 1969). St Mary Spital had the lowest reported rate (2/1883 females: 0.1%) (Table 163), supporting Crane-Kramer's (2000, 382) assertion that it is 'no longer tenable to accept the assertion that a medieval diagnostic confusion existed' between leprosy and treponematosis.

Medieval examples of leprosy, aDNA studies and primary documents attesting its presence have been identified in the Czech Republic, Hungary, Germany and Finland (Roberts et al 2002; Dixon and Roberts 2001). Boldsen and Mollerup (2006, 350) suggest that in the city of Odense (Denmark) the vast majority of the population were infected with leprosy during the early medieval period, but this pattern declined during the late medieval period, which may be related to cross-immunity obtained by tuberculosis (Roberts and Buikstra 2003).

Treponematosis

In Britain, individuals with diagnostic evidence for treponematosis have been identified at monastic, rural and urban sites, such as medieval material from Gloucester (Roberts 1994) or Rivenhall, Essex (Mays et al 2003). Many of these cases, including some individuals from St Mary Spital, are pre-Columbian in date (ibid). At the time of writing, the majority of cases involved adults (eg von Hunnius et al 2007) but subadult evidence has been recorded at two sites: three subadults were identified at St Mary Spital and one at St Gregory's Priory in Canterbury (Anderson 2005). In this study, the majority of affected individuals were females, but it is more typical for males to have a higher prevalence of venereal syphilis (Powell and Cook 2005, 43).

Stirland (1991b) recorded treponematosis in an adult male from Norwich and a disarticulated cranium from St Helen-on-the-Walls, York, had evidence for ulceration of the ectocranial surfaces of the frontal and parietal bones (Dawes and Magilton 1980, 98). The latter case has been radiocarbon dated to c 1197–1419.

Outside the UK, two syphilitic individuals have been identified from Rostov Velikiy (Russia), dating from the mid 16th century (Buzhilova 1999), four individuals from medieval Trondheim (Sweden), dating from the 16th century, with suspected endemic syphilis (Anderson et al 1986), one congenital case of syphilis in a 14–15-year-old individual from 13th-century Nicaea (Anatolia) (Erdal 2006), and a subadult example of congenital syphilis (14th–15th centuries) has been reported from medieval Waterford in Ireland (Hurley et al 1997). Lewis (2007, 157–8) notes one reported Old World case of congenital syphilis in a 12–15-year-old from Poland, which may date to the medieval period (14th–19th centuries). Ten treponemal cases were reported from Lund, Sweden (Table 163).

Tuberculosis

Skeletal evidence for tuberculosis was recorded at rural, urban, hospital and international sites. The male crude prevalence rate observed at St Mary Spital of 1.6% (36/2237) is most comparable to males from the urban cemetery of St Andrew Fishergate (4/220: 1.8%), and lower than the rates for males (6/211: 2.8%) and females (3/140: 2.1%) at the rural site of Wharram Percy, the Beguines of Breda (females 2/90: 2.2%); and males (3/93: 3.2%) and females (2/57: 3.5%) from Rouen (France). Subadults with tuberculosis were reported from three urban sites (cf Roberts and Cox 2003, 231–2), with the lowest rates at St Mary Spital (16/1027: 1.6%) (Table 163).

The prevalence of tuberculosis in males was highest at the French site of Arras (2/11: 18.2%) and the rural sample from Wharram Percy (6/211: 2.8%). St Mary Spital and the leprosy hospital of St James and St Mary Magdalene both had a male crude prevalence of 1.6%. In females, the highest crude prevalence rate was observed in the sample from Arras (25.0%), whereas none of the English sites exceeded 2.5% (Table 163).

Osteomyelitis

Osteomyelitis data were predominantly obtained from urban and monastic sites, which in part reflects the availability of rural data sets (see Roberts and Cox 2003, 240), and in this case has resulted in the data set being predominantly made up of males. The highest male crude prevalence was recorded from monastic samples, particularly Jedburgh Abbey (1/4 males: 25.0%) and the highest female prevalence rate at Gisborough Priory (10.5%). The majority of urban sites have crude prevalence rates of less than 2.7%, and St Mary Spital has the lowest rate (Table 163).

Nutritional and metabolic disease

Metabolic disease was frequently reported and rickets was observed in the majority of samples (Table 164). St Mary Spital had a low crude prevalence rate, particularly for subadults, and was the only site apart from Fishergate House where subadults had both rickets and scurvy. The highest subadult crude prevalence of rickets was observed in the urban cemeteries from York (Fishergate House 4/115: 3.5%; St Helen-on-the-Walls 7/200: 3.5%) and the rural cemetery of Wharram Percy (8/327: 2.4%). The rural site of Llandough had the highest crude prevalence of subadult scurvy (3/226: 1.3%); the condition was only observed at two other sites. St Mary Spital was the only site where females were affected with rickets (1/1883: 0.1%), osteomalacia (1/1883: 0.1%) and osteoporosis (2/1883: 0.1%). In the Beguine sample from Breda, rickets (6/90: 6.7%) and osteoporosis (2/90: 2.2%) were reported in the female assemblage; they were also present at Gisborough. Males were also reported with metabolic disease, predominantly rickets, and with osteoporosis at St Mary Spital (2/2237: 0.1%), osteomalacia on the *Mary Rose* (2/92: 2.2%) and osteoporosis at Gisborough Priory (1/21: 4.8%), the only monastic site where males presented with this disease.

Neoplastic disease

The majority of the published data relate to benign neoplasms, which were reported at monastic, urban and hospital sites. Malignant neoplasms were also reported from monastic, urban

Table 164 Inter-site crude prevalence rate of metabolic disease

Type	Site	Age or sex	Scurvy No. affected	%	Rickets No. affected	%	Osteomalacia No. affected	%	Osteoporosis No. affected	%
Rural	Llandough	subadult	3	1.3	0	-	0	-	0	-
	Wharram Percy	subadult	0	-	8	2.4	0	-	0	-
	Wharram Percy (phases 2/2–3)	adult	0	-	0	-	0	-	-	2.5
Catastrophic	Mary Rose	male	0	-	2	3.3	2	2.2	0	-
Urban	St Helen-on-the-Walls	male	0	-	6	2.7	0	-	0	-
		female	0	-	6	2.5	0	-	0	-
		subadult	0	-	7	3.5	0	-	0	-
	Jewbury	female	0	-	1	0.7	0	-	0	-
		subadult	0	-	2	1.3	0	-	0	-
	Fishergate House	male	0	-	2	3.5	0	-	0	-
		female	1	1.9	0	-	0	-	6	11.3
		subadult	1	0.9	4	3.5	0	-	0	-
	Silver Street	female	0	-	0	-	0	-	2	33.3
	St Peter's	male	0	-	1	0.7	0	-	-	3.2
	(periods C, C/D, D or early period)	female	0	-	1	0.7	0	-	-	9.0
		subadult	0	-	1	0.8	0	-	0	-
Monastic	Gisborough Priory	male	0	-	0	-	0	-	1	4.8
		female	0	-	1	5.3	0	-	3	15.8
Hospital	St Bartholomew's	female	0	-	0	-	0	-	1	8.3
	St John's	male	0	-	1	5.5	0	-	0	-
	St Mary Spital	male	0	-	2	0.1	0	-	2	0.1
		female	0	-	1	0.1	1	0.1	2	0.1
		subadult	3	0.3	4	0.4	0	-	0	-
International	Breda, Netherlands (Beguines, nunnery)	female	0	-	6	6.7	0	-	2	2.2
	Waterford, Ireland (urban)	male	0	-	2	2.1	0	-	0	-
		subadult	0	-	1	1.2	0	-	0	-

Table 165 Inter-site crude prevalence rate of neoplastic disease

Type	Site	Age or sex	Malignant neoplasm No. affected	%	Osteosarcoma No. affected	%	Osteochondroma No. affected	%	Osteoid osteoma No. affected	%	Metastatic carcinoma No. affected	%
Monastic	Norton Priory	male	0	-	1	1.2	0	-	0	-	0	-
	Gisborough Priory	male	0	-	0	-	1	4.8	0	-	0	-
	St Gregory's Priory	male	0	-	0	-	1	2.0	2	4.0	1	2.0
	Whitefriars Ipswich	male	2	18.2	0	-	0	-	0	-	0	-
Urban	St James's	male	1	0.6	0	-	0	-	0	-	0	-
	St Andrew Fishergate	male	0	-	1	0.4	1	0.4	2	0.9	0	-
	St Peter's	male	-	0.5	0	-	0	-	0	-	0	-
Hospital	St James and St Mary Magdalene	male	0	-	0	-	0	-	0	-	1	0.8
	St Mary Spital	male	0	-	0	-	2	0.1	1	<0.1	0	-
		female	0	-	0	-	1	<0.1	0	0.1	0	-
		subadult	0	-	0	-	1	0.1	1	0.1	0	-

and hospital cemeteries. Only St Gregory's Priory, St Andrew Fishergate and St Mary Spital had two or more types of neoplastic disease present. The highest crude prevalence rate was reported in males at Whitefriars Ipswich, for a malignant neoplasm (2/11: 18.2%). Females and subadults were only affected at St Mary Spital (Table 165).

Circulatory disease

The highest prevalence rates of circulatory disease were observed in males from Towton, Fishergate House and Wharram Percy (Table 166). Subadults were only affected at Fishergate House (1/113: 0.9%) and St Mary Spital (1/1027: 0.1%) and only had evidence for Perthes' disease. Slipped femoral epiphysis was observed in males at St Mary Stratford Langthorne (1/542: 0.2%) and Fishergate House (1/57: 1.8%). Scheuermann's disease was observed in females from Wharram Percy (1/140: 0.7%) and in both sexes at St Mary Spital (males 7/2237: 0.3%; females 3/1883: 0.2%). Hypertrophic osteoarthropathy was observed in males from Llandough (1/223: 0.4%) and Wharram Percy (5/211: 2.4%) and both sexes at St Mary Spital (males 2/2237: 0.1%; females 3/1883: 0.2%).

Table 166 Inter-site crude prevalence rate of circulatory disease

Type	Site	Age or sex	Perthes' disease No. affected	%	Scheuermann's disease No. affected	%	Slipped femoral epiphysis No. affected	%	Necrosis No. affected	%	Hypertrophic osteoarthropathy No. affected	%
Rural	Llandough	male	0	-	0	-	0	-	0	-	1	0.4
	Wharram Percy	male	1	0.5	0	-	0	-	1	0.5	5	2.4
		female	0	-	1	0.7	0	-	0	-	0	-
Monastic	St Mary Stratford Langthorne	male	0	-	0	-	1	0.2	0	-	0	-
Catastrophic	Towton	male	0	-	0	-	0	-	1	4.3	0	-
	Mary Rose	male	1	1.1	0	-	0	-	0	-	0	-
Urban	Fishergate House	male	1	1.7	0	-	1	1.8	0	-	0	-
		subadult	1	0.9	0	-	0	-	0	-	0	-
Hospital	St Mary Spital	male	11	0.5	7	0.3	0	-	1	<0.1	2	0.1
		female	1	<0.1	3	0.2	0	-	1	<0.1	3	0.2
		subadult	1	0.1	0	-	0	-	0	-	0	-

Overall, St Mary Spital was most similar to the rural site of Wharram Percy, in that a wide variety of diseases were observed.

Congenital and developmental anomalies

In the comparative material, a wide range of congenital and developmental anomalies were only observed in monastic and urban cemeteries (Table 167). The highest crude prevalence rates for developmental skull anomalies were observed at St Helen-on-the-Walls, the only cemetery apart from St Mary Spital at which four types of skull anomaly were found in females. Overall, more females were affected and typically males only presented with one anomaly. The population from St Mary Spital had the widest range of anomalies recorded, perhaps unsurprisingly given the large sample size. However, conditions such as hydrocephalus, which occurs in three in 1000 live births, were anticipated but were not found to be present. St Mary Spital also provided the only observed evidence for a range of mandibular defects and cephalocele. Subadults with congenital and developmental anomalies were only observed at Fishergate House (hydrocephalus) (1/113: 0.9%), St Andrew Fishergate (suture agenesis) (1/90: 1.1%) and St Mary Spital (hemifacial microsomia, mandibular defects, hypoplasia of the nasal bones and cleft palate). Maxillary clefts were seen at St Mary Spital and St Helen-on-the-Walls.

There were few comparative data for developmental spinal anomalies as these were limited to two cases of scoliosis observed at Wharram Percy (one female, 1/140: 0.7%) and Gisborough Priory (one male, 1/21: 4.8%) (Table 168). Only at St Mary Spital were subadults with spinal anomalies observed.

Developmental and congenital defects of the limbs and joints were observed in few sites and predominantly in urban cemeteries (Table 169). At the comparative sites, developmental hip dislocation was the most frequently observed defect, which may in part be due to its more obvious appearance (Mitchell and Redfern 2008), and more females than males were affected. Subadults with recorded anomalies (developmental hip dysplasia) were observed at Fishergate House and Wharram Percy, in addition to St Mary Spital.

Table 167 Inter-site crude prevalence rate of congenital skull anomalies

Type	Site	Age or sex	Suture agenesis No. affected	%	Hydrocephalus No. affected	%	Cephalocele No. affected	%
Monastic	St Mary Stratford Langthorne	male	0	-	0	-	0	-
Urban	Fishergate House	subadult	0	-	1	0.9	0	-
	Jewbury	male	1	0.6	0	-	0	-
		female	1	0.6	0	-	0	-
	St Andrew Fishergate	subadult	1	1.1	0	-	0	-
	St Helen-on-the-Walls	male	0	-	0	-	0	-
		female	0	-	0	-	0	-
		subadult	0	-	0	-	0	-
Hospital	St Mary Spital	male	1	<0.1	0	-	0	-
		female	0	-	0	-	1	0.1
		subadult	0	-	0	-	0	-

Table 168 *Inter-site crude prevalence rate of congenital spinal anomalies*

Type	Site	Age or sex	Kyphosis No. affected	%	Kyphoscoliosis No. affected	%	Scoliosis No. affected	%
Rural	Wharram Percy	female	0	-	0	-	1	0.7
Monastic	Gisborough Priory	male	0	-	0	-	1	4.8
Hospital	St Mary Spital	male	1	0.1	5	0.2	11	0.5
		female	2	0.4	2	0.1	8	0.4
		subadult	1	0.1	0	-	0	-

Table 169 *Inter-site crude prevalence rate of congenital and developmental joint anomalies*

Type	Site	Age or sex	Congenital limb/joint anomaly No. affected	%	Developmental hip dysplasia No. affected	%	Developmental hip dislocation No. affected	%
Rural	Wharram Percy (phases 2/2–3)	adult	0	-	-	1.1	0	.
Monastic	St Gregory's Priory	female	0	-	0	-	1	5.3
Urban	Fishergate House	subadult	0	-	1	0.9	0	-
	Jewbury	female	0	-	0	-	1	0.6
	St Andrew Fishergate	male	0	-	0	-	1	0.4
	St Peter's (period C/D)	female	0	-	1	0.7	0	-
Hospital	St Mary Spital	male	4	0.2	17	0.7	4	0.2
		female	4	0.2	7	0.4	5	0.3
		subadult	0	-	2	0.2	0	-

Miscellaneous pathological conditions

Paget's disease of bone

Paget's disease of bone was only reported from monastic and urban sites. The males from Norton Priory had the highest crude prevalence (6/81: 7.4%), followed by those from St Peter's (5/150: 3.3%). Jewbury (1/147: 0.7%) and St Peter's (1/151: 0.7%) showed the highest female prevalence. The lowest prevalence was observed in females from St Mary Spital (4/1883: 0.2%) (Table 170).

Endocranial lesions

Endocranial lesions were most frequently observed in subadults, and the highest crude prevalence was reported at Fishergate House (30/90: 33.3%). St Mary Spital subadults had the lowest prevalence rate for those sites where cases were reported (34/1027: 3.3%). Adult males were affected at St James's (1/172: 0.6%) and at St Mary Spital (22/2237: 1.0%). Affected females were also reported from two sites, Jewbury (7/147: 4.8%) and St Mary Spital (13/1883: 0.7%) (Table 171).

Cleft palate No. affected	%	Hypoplasia of the nasal bones No. affected	%	Mandibular defects No. affected	%	Atresia No. affected	%	Hemifacial microsomia (cranium and/or mandible) No. affected	%	Orbital asymmetry No. affected	%
0	-	0	-	0	-	1	0.2	0	-	0	-
0	-	0	-	0	-	0	-	0	-	0	-
0	-	0	-	0	-	0	-	0	-	0	-
0	-	0	-	0	-	0	-	0	-	0	-
0	-	0	-	0	-	0	-	0	-	0	-
1	0.4	0	-	0	-	0	-	0	-	0	-
3	1.2	1	0.4	0	-	0	-	0	-	1	0.4
2	1.0	0	-	0	-	0	-	0	-	0	-
0	-	3	0.1	1	0.2	0	-	5	0.2	0	-
0	-	2	0.1	6	0.1	0	-	2	0.1	0	-
1	0.1	0	-	1	0.1	0	-	1	0.1	0	-

Table 170 Inter-site crude prevalence rate of Paget's disease of bone

Type	Site	Age or sex	Paget's disease No. affected	%
Monastic	Norton Priory	male	6	7.4
Urban	St Helen-on-the-Walls	male	1	0.4
	Jewbury	female	1	0.7
	St Peter's (periods C, C/D, D)	male	5	3.3
		female	1	0.7
Hospital	St Mary Spital	male	13	0.6
		female	4	0.2

Table 171 Inter-site crude prevalence rate of endocranial lesions

Type	Site	Age or sex	Endocranial lesions No. affected	%
Rural	Llandough	subadult	-	5.1
	Wharram Percy	subadult	-	15.0
Monastic	St James's Priory, Bristol	male	1	0.6
Urban	Jewbury	female	7	4.8
		subadult	8	5.2
	Fishergate House	subadult	30	33.3
Hospital	St Mary Spital	male	22	1.0
		female	13	0.7
		subadult	34	3.3

Stature

The results of the stature analysis show that the British medieval population exhibited sexual dimorphism (Table 172; Fig 249). The difference between the sexes is smallest at St Mary Spital (6.8cm), and the largest differences (>11.0cm) are most often observed in urban groups (in Britain and Norway), with Llandough and two monastic sites, St Mary Stratford Langthorne and Whitefriars Ipswich, showing a similar level of dimorphism. Interestingly, average male stature in rural and urban cemeteries is almost the same (170.4cm and 170.3cm respectively), whereas the average male stature at St Mary Spital (168.2cm) is slightly shorter; this is also shorter than the average male stature at the comparative hospital sites. Average female stature in the comparative urban sites varies very little, with St Mary Spital being among the tallest groups (161.4cm). Overall, female stature shows less variation (10.0cm) than male, which is a typical result (Overfield 1995, 166).

In comparison to populations from the rest of Europe, males from St Mary Spital are the second shortest, the shortest being those from Breda (161.2cm); the tallest males were reported from Saint Servaas basilica, Maastricht (173.9cm) (Hanson 1992;

Table 172 Summary of inter-site stature data

Type	Site	Male stature (cm)	Female stature (cm)
Rural	Wharram Percy (Yorkshire)	168.8	159.5
	Llandough (Wales)	169.6	156.8
	Rivenhall (Essex)	172.7	163.6
Urban	St Helen-on-the-Walls (York)	169.3	157.4
	St Andrew Fishergate (York)	171.0	159.0
	Jewbury (York)	170.0	160.0
	Fishergate House (York)	170.1	159.1
	Silver Street (Lincoln)	167.2	159.5
	Lawn Hospital (Lincoln)	172.3	159.3
	St Peter's (Lincolnshire)	170.5	158.5
Monastic	St Mary Stratford Langthorne (Essex)	173.0	159.7
	St Gregory's Priory (Canterbury)	172.8	161.8
	St James's Priory (Bristol)	172.0	159.0
	Gisborough Priory (Cleveland)	170.6	162.7
	Greyfriars Carmarthen (Wales)	172.0	164.5
	Whitefriars Ipswich (Suffolk)	171.9	157.4
	Austin Friars Leicester (Leicestershire)	176.8	-
	Whitefriars Lincoln (St Mark's railway station)	174.8	-
	Jedburgh Abbey (Scotland)	171.5	-
Catastrophic	Towton (Yorkshire)	171.6	-
	Mary Rose (Solent)	171.0	-
Hospital	St Bartholomew's (Bristol)	171.0	156.0
	St John the Baptist (Lutterworth, Leicestershire)	170.0	166.0
	St Mary Spital (all periods and burial types)	168.2	161.4
International	St Gregory's church (Norway, urban)	170.2	158.1
	Waterford (Ireland, urban)	170.1	160.3
	Breda (Netherlands, Beguines, nunnery)	161.2	159.9
	Saint Servaas (Maastricht, urban)	173.9	-
	Oude en Nieuwe Gasthuis (Netherlands, urban)	168.9	-
	Franciscan friary (Netherlands, monastic)	170.6	-
	Æbelholt Kloster (Denmark)	170.9	160.6

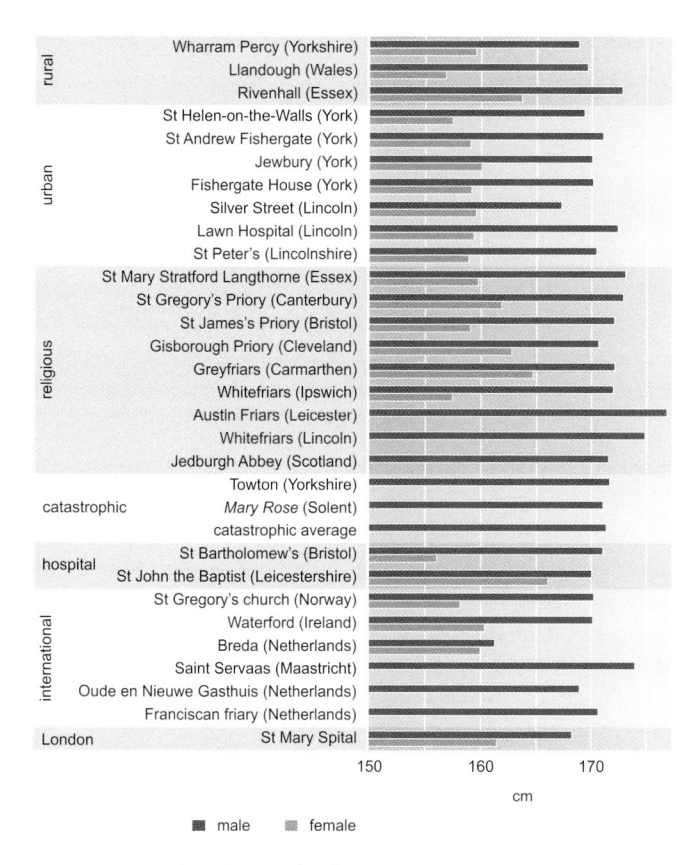

Fig 249 Average (mean) stature for all comparative sites

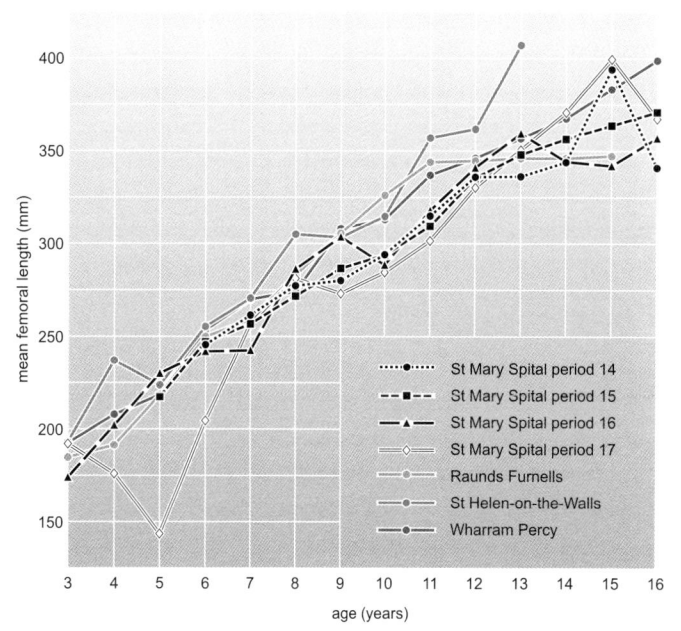

Fig 250 Inter-site analysis of growth profiles

Maat 2005). Conversely, the females from St Mary Spital are the tallest (161.4cm). The majority of the European communities show greater sexual dimorphism in stature than St Mary Spital with the exception of the small number of males recorded at the Beguine cemetery at Breda, who were only 1.3 cm taller than the females (159.9 cm).

Growth

The average growth pattern at St Mary Spital was compared to two rural and one urban sample from medieval England (Fig 250) (Lewis 2002). The pattern in rural samples shows that subadults in these environments have different growth trajectories, although there is little difference until the age of 9 years. Rural–urban differences have been shown to be greatest during adolescence (Schell 2000b, 408), and this was observed here, particularly at the age of 13 years when there was a difference of 61mm in femoral length between individuals from Raunds Furnells and St Helen-on-the-Walls. The subadults from St Helen-on-the-Walls were found to be taller throughout development than those at St Mary Spital. This may result from the sample being drawn from a smaller urban centre and by the pooling of data from St Mary Spital, because during period 16 individuals aged 5 years are taller (femoral length 230.0mm) than their peers at St Helen-on-the-Walls (femoral length 223.7mm). Lewis (2002, 66) notes that the individuals from urban York were considerably taller than their rural counterparts from the age of 12 years. This could reflect the greater number of females in the York sample, because females start their puberty growth spurt earlier than males. Overall, the subadults from St Mary Spital are shorter throughout the majority of their development, particularly between the ages of 5–7 and 9–12 years. Although the role of underlying genetics is accepted as a bias in this result, the outcome could mean that the individuals included in the sample were unable to achieve 'catch-up' growth because of the nature of London's living environment. However, the influence of the numerous catastrophic events that affected the city's population should not be underestimated (above, 4.3).

Living environment and health

Comparing the distribution of injuries to interpret risk

The analysis of trauma provides an insight into past communities. Because violence is present in every society, the patterning of lesions within a skeleton can provide data on past way of life and socio-cultural frameworks (Goodman and Martin 2002, 40), highlighting risk of injury, how injuries were created and who were victims of violence. These data cannot be simply and easily interpreted, as many fractures can be caused by violent or accidental mechanisms. The evidence should be interpreted with comparison to clinical data sets and socio-cultural context (Jurmain 1999, 230; Judd 2004).

Grimm's (1980, 348) temporal analysis of fractures in European populations showed that the highest male prevalence rates were observed in late medieval populations, while Grauer and Roberts's (1996) analysis of urban fractures demonstrated that the prevalence of long bone fractures was low in urban centres. The arm is the most commonly fractured limb in both rural and urban samples; urban males typically sustain more fractures to more body areas than their rural counterparts; and rural and urban females have similar fracture locations, but urban female fracture frequency was significantly lower than that of rural females.

At St Mary Spital, the femur, tibia and fibula had the lowest prevalence rates; the highest were observed in the forearm and no association was found between skull and 'parry' fractures (Judd 2008) (Chapter 3.8 and above, 4.1). In many urban cemeteries, long bone fractures had low prevalence rates, and the arm was the most frequently fractured limb. Urban and rural females also had similar fracture locations but each rural sample used in the study had a different fracture pattern. In contrast to Grauer and Roberts's (1996) research, both urban and rural males sustained fractures to all body areas, although differences in distribution were noted.

In females, the patterns of trauma differ by site but at most urban sites they sustained fractures to all body areas. The exceptions are females at Lawn Hospital and Jewbury, and females at hospital sites. In manual occupations, fractures to the extremities are common (Rowe and Cliff 1982, 123). A higher crude prevalence of hand fractures would be expected in urban females because greater numbers of females were employed as servants and formed a large part of the urban community, and this is particularly true for York females. The remainder of sites had prevalence rates between 2.4% and 7.0%, apart from the females from the Isle of Ensay (Table 162). This disparity may indicate that females buried at St Helen-on-the-Walls were engaged in gender-specific tasks that were limited to that area of the city. The crude prevalence of rib fractures also varied: the highest crude prevalence rate was observed at the rural site of Wharram Percy and the urban site of Fishergate House, and no rib fractures were observed at hospital sites. Rib fractures are typically produced by blunt force trauma (Brickley 2006) and can be caused by agricultural accidents (Brison and Pickett 1992). Their higher prevalence at urban sites may relate to the greater risk of trauma experienced by females. Arm fractures also varied by site, with the highest crude prevalence observed at the rural site of Llandough and at the hospital site of St James and St Mary Magdalene. No clear patterns between the sexes existed at each site type or overall. Arm fractures may have been sustained by injuries sustained in an occupation, in falls, or due to defensive behaviour (Apley and Solomon 2000, 274–88).

The male fracture pattern was similar at all site types, apart from hospital and monastic sites. The low hospital fracture prevalence may reflect the low fracture risk of patients (see also Judd and Roberts 1998), or the fact that injuries sustained by individuals in these contexts were more likely to be to the soft tissues. The fracture distribution is comparable to rural samples, which may reflect the agrarian nature of the monastic regime. It is also considered that the inclusion of founders, patrons and benefactors in the cemetery, many of who would have military backgrounds, would have also influenced the trauma patterns found at monasteries (Gilchrist and Sloane 2005, 61–2).

The similarities between rural and urban cemeteries not only provide evidence for the migration of rural workers to urban centres (Gilchrist and Sloane 2005, 224), but also, at St Mary Spital, reflect the agricultural aspects of the London suburbs and work undertaken at the monastery. The fracture pattern between the sexes observed at St Mary Spital was similar to that found at St Andrew Fishergate and Fishergate House in York. This may indicate that both sexes engaged in similar activities, or in activities that exposed them to comparable fracture risks, in addition to the greater risks presented by urban life (Larsen 1999, 112–13). The majority of males from the sites examined had higher crude prevalence rates of skull and rib fractures, suggesting that they were at greater risk of interpersonal violence, as rib fractures are typically produced by blunt force mechanisms (Apley and Solomon 2000, 309), and skull fractures are 'highly suggestive' of interpersonal violence (Jurmain 1999, 199). Courtenay's analysis of male behaviour has shown that if men carry weapons they are more likely to increase their risk of injury, and they have a higher incidence of fighting compared to females (2002, 303–4). These data support the textual evidence for frequent episodes of violence in medieval London and other urban centres (eg Hanawalt 1993, 116). This is supported by data from Towton and the *Mary Rose*, where males sustained fractures to all body areas. However, these are unusual samples as they include individuals who died in a military context and males from the *Mary Rose* have high proportions of leg and foot fractures, which Stirland (2000) believes to be occupationally related.

The trauma pattern of subadults provides the most interesting insight into rural–urban differences. As with London adults, St Mary Spital subadults have fractures to all body parts and two injury recidivists were identified, whereas only a single arm fracture was seen at the rural site of Wharram Percy. This also contrasts to the distribution observed at York, where skull and leg fractures were reported. The London and York data suggest that subadults had a higher risk of fracture in medieval urban centres, which most probably reflects their engagement in a wider range of tasks and occupations than their rural counterparts (eg Panter-Brick 1998a, 85–6). It is also worth noting that documentary evidence for medieval London refers to the playing of games, which included wrestling, mock battles and football, outside the city walls and particularly at Moorfields (Hanawalt 1993, 117), all of which could result in injury. The evidence for violence among apprentices is considerable in London (ibid, 116) and may also have been a cause of trauma (above, 4.1). Orme also notes that children were the victims of assaults, and physical abuse from employers, and cites an example of kidnapped children being taken to London where they were mutilated and had bones broken so that they could be used to earn money as beggars (2001, 91, 101).

There is a paucity of fracture studies relating to medieval subadults in Britain, including the identification of subadult fractures in adult remains (see Lewis 2007, 169–75; Glencross and Stuart-Macadam 2000) (Chapter 3.8). Many of the fractures sustained by London subadults would have been as part of their daily life, influenced by their growth and physical development (above, 4.1).

Comparison to international samples was limited by small sample sizes, though St Mary Spital appears similar to Waterford, Ireland (with the exception of spinal fractures) and Æbelholt, Denmark. This may be because these sites include rural migrants exposed to the risks of urban living. The females from Breda were similar to those from St Mary Spital, reflecting both their urban way of life and the mixture of status groups at both sites.

Walker notes that 'direct evidence of interpersonal violence … is immune to the interpretative difficulties posed by literary sources' (2001, 574), and sharp force weapon injuries are among the clearest indicators of such acts (Byers 2002, 312–22; Symes et al 2002, 404). The context of such injuries is discussed in Chapter 4.1. Roberts and Cox's review identified weapon injuries in 154 individuals from Britain, the majority of whom were male (2003, 275); they were reported from all site types, with the city of York having the most individuals affected. In the present study, injured females were only identified at urban cemeteries. At St Mary Spital, females had healed skull injuries and at Fishergate House they had healed arm injuries. Women are usually portrayed as victims and active female engagement with violence during the medieval period remains under-explored, despite primary textual evidence demonstrating that women participated as combatants in the Third Crusade (1189) (Nicholson 1997). Anthropological data also support the female capacity for violence (Kimmel 2004, 272). However, the court rolls of London record numerous assaults upon women involving bladed weapons (Ackroyd 2001, 64).

The presence of individuals who had survived serious episodes of cranial trauma and continued to engage in warfare is shown in the Towton sample (Fiorato et al 2000) and supported by textual evidence. Knüsel and Boylston (2000, 172–3) cite the example of Thomas Hestelle, who was blinded in one eye at Harfleur, France, in 1415 but fought again at the Battle of Agincourt in the same year, where he sustained crushing injuries to his hand and body. Later, Thomas petitioned King Henry VI to help relieve his poverty-stricken old age. Healed cranial injuries have also been identified in early medieval European contexts (Weber and Czarnetzki 2001). The survival of such individuals may indicate their occupation as professional soldiers or their high social status; 'no quarter' fighting usually killed injured retainers (Knüsel and Boylston 2000, 175; see also Mays 2006b). Those of high status may have had access to medical treatment immediately after the battle from a barber-surgeon (Knüsel and Boylston 2000, 175). It is highly likely that many of these individuals would have experienced neurological and sensory impairment. Healers may have provided the medical treatment of lower status individuals (Mays 2006b), and the presence of competing systems of medicine is common in all societies, because 'people are pragmatic and will use anything that seems to work' (Strathern and Stewart 1999, 64). The survival of these individuals demonstrates the interplay of socio-economic and immune status, medical treatment and care (above, 4.2).

The majority of weapon injuries seen were sustained to the skull. Knüsel and Boylston's analysis of wound patterning observed that the majority of injuries were directed to the head, which they propose may be related to men removing their helmets or head protection before engaging in close quarter combat in order to see better (2000, 172–4; see also Mitchell et al 2006). Targeting of the head is common in all societies, as blows will result in highly prominent injuries (Walker 1997, 160).

The finding that more individuals from urban centres displayed signs of interpersonal violence suggests that the risk of injury was higher in towns and cities, particularly for women. Many individuals' dress included weaponry, and acts of violence appear to have been regular occurrences, as attested in the court rolls (Ackroyd 2001, 62–3). The bioarchaeological evidence from St Mary Spital of medieval Londoners with injuries to the skull corroborates the documentary record, and provides an insight into martial activities during the medieval period.

Leprosy, treponematosis and tuberculosis as indicators of population health

The study of infectious diseases shows that for diseases to persist in a community, a large population is required (Mitchell 2003a, 172). The population of England during the medieval period was subject to considerable fluctuation due to epidemics and agricultural crises, and estimates of population based upon primary texts may exclude some groups, for example vagrants (Dyer 1998, 25). One estimate, however, based on Domesday (1086), poll tax records (1377), the subsidies of 1524–5, the military survey of 1522 and manorial records, puts the English population at about 2 million in 1100, rising to over 5 million in the 1330s, declining after a series of famines (1315–22) and plagues (1348–50) to about 2 million in 1350–1400, and only returning to about 3 million between 1450 and 1500. In London, plague epidemics may have reduced the population from an estimated 80,000 in the early 14th century to about 50,000 in 1377; this rose to over 60,000 by the 1520s (Dyer 2002, 235, 304).

Leprosy is most likely to be caught by people who 'are living close to the soil' in an area where the disease is endemic (Stanford and Stanford 2002, 30–1). Roberts's research on British samples has shown that the majority of individuals with leprosy during the medieval period have been identified in the south and east of England, and greater numbers of leprous skeletons have been reported from non-leprosy funerary contexts (2002, 214–15). The sites used in this study are predominantly from leprosaria, and as such have a higher crude prevalence than St Mary Spital (particularly Naestved, Denmark). The apparent lack of leprosy in urban centres, particularly London, is misleading, as many urban dwellers who contracted the disease in the towns or cities would have been taken to leprosaria located away from urban centres (Roberts and Cox 2003, 272; Boldsen and Mollerup 2006). The presence of individuals in non-leprosaria monastic cemeteries with leprous changes supports Roberts's (2002) observation that greater numbers of leprosy skeletons are known from non-leprosaria contexts. In contrast, Crane-Kramer's (2000) palaeoepidemiological examination of leprosy and treponematosis in cemeteries from northern Europe concluded that in the medieval period a diagnostic confusion did not exist between these two diseases.

Leprous individuals would therefore have been recognised and removed from the community.

The evidence for leprosy at St Mary Spital is limited to two females, one ([2487]) buried in period 16 (*c* 1250–*c* 1400) and the other ([19821]) in period 17 (*c* 1400–1539). In each case the osseous changes are diagnostic of the tuberculoid form, which is highly immune-resistant (Roberts and Cox 2003, 267). Because tuberculoid leprosy initially presents with skin lesions (Aufderheide and Rodríguez-Martín 1998, 146–7), these changes may not have been recognised as leprosy by these women or medical practitioners (if they sought medical treatment) and, after death, by those washing and shrouding the body. Female [19821] was from a catastrophic burial context and the urgency of corpse disposal may have overridden any suspicion of leprosy.

Individuals with treponemal and syphilitic skeletal changes have been identified at monastic, rural and urban centres; however, the majority of individuals are from cemeteries located in urban areas. This pattern may reflect the limited number of excavated medieval rural cemeteries rather than a 'true' distribution of treponematosis in medieval Britain. Roberts and Cox (2003, 272) suggest that the limited data set may in part be due to people dying before they are able to develop the tertiary stage lesions. Unfortunately, aDNA cannot be reliably used to identify venereal syphilis in past populations, as treponemal DNA does not appear to survive in human bone, particularly in individuals who died during the later stages of the disease process (Bouwman and Brown 2005; von Hunnius et al 2007; see also Harper et al 2008). Mays et al (2003, 141) propose that treponemal disease in Britain is the venereal not the endemic form of syphilis, because this form is particularly associated with urbanism. Armelagos (2004, 14) states that urbanism promotes greater promiscuity and changes in sexual practice compared to rural environments, and it is therefore more likely that infected individuals will be identified in urban cemeteries.

The presence of individuals with tertiary stage gummatous lesions in individuals from the attritional cemetery at St Mary Spital is at odds with the primary textual evidence which states that affected people were to be refused admittance to hospitals, and evicted from cities (Allen 2000, 43). The inter-site comparative data demonstrate that the majority of affected individuals were female, which may reflect their immunological advantage but also the fact that it was common for poor women and girls to become prostitutes in urban areas, and there was little protection for unmarried servants against rape (ibid, 46; Wiesner 2000, 60). It may also reflect the demographic bias in urban centres caused by greater female migration, particularly in the late 14th and early 15th centuries (Goldberg 1992, 297–8; 1997b). The majority of individuals at St Mary Spital appear to have acquired the infection during adolescence or were showing the symptoms of late congenital syphilis (Lewis 2007, 152–7; Powell and Cook 2005, 46–9). Orme's review of children in the medieval period found that from the age of 7 years, with the termination of the period of *infantia*, they could be sexually active, and London was renowned as a place of child abuse (Orme 2001, 68, 103).

Epidemiological research into the incidence of venereal syphilis in the United States from 1941 to 2002 found that the temporal oscillations in incidence observed every decade could be in part explained by the natural dynamics of the disease, whereby the incidence decreases because the syphilitic infection offers a degree of immunity for 8–11 years, after which the number of non-immune people increases (Grassly et al 2005, 417–21). With this result in mind, it is interesting to note that two individuals with treponematosis were recorded at St Mary Spital dating to period 15 (*c* 1200–50), and it is therefore possible that they were infected with the disease before the 13th century.

The dating of treponemal and syphilitic cases in the UK by radiocarbon methods has been very limited, and only the cases from St Mary Spital, and possibly the disarticulated cranium from St Helen-on-the-Walls, are definitively pre-Columbian (see also Powell and Cook 2005), dating from before 1265 (Roberts 1994; Mays et al 2003). The time range of archaeologically dated skeletons shows that the disease may have been present in England from 1100: a skeleton from a well-sealed context with lesions supporting a diagnosis of treponemal disease was found at St Margaret's, Norwich, which was in use from 1100 to 1468 (Roberts 1994, 107; Stirland 1991b). The presence of congenital syphilis in 4th-century France (Pálfi et al 1992) should also be noted here. The link between the Crusades (1096–1270) and the presence of treponematosis in Europe was made by Hudson (1963), who suggested that the Crusader armies would have come into contact with populations who lived in areas affected by treponematosis (cited in Mays et al 2003, 141). Recently a cranium with evidence for treponematosis radiocarbon dated to the 14th century has been identified in Israel (Mitchell 2003b), supporting this theory. The medieval court rolls from London show that soldiers often stayed in the city, and militia were also raised from there (Thomas 1926, roll A1b ii). Hudson (1964) also suggested that Europeans might have been exposed to treponematosis from the migration of African populations with the establishment of the Moorish empire in Spain from the 8th century, and because of the Portuguese slave trade from 1442 with west Africa (cited in Mays et al 2003, 142; see also Harper et al 2008). The slave industry was banned in Italian cities by 1299 (Heer 1993, 55). International trade and migration were also important factors in the transmission of disease. Individuals travelled across Europe and many towns and cities had permanent enclaves of traders: for example, Flemish towns hosted English, German, Italian and French merchants, and the Hanse organisation connected London to Russia, Germany and Scandinavia (ibid, 62, 64).

It is not clear whether the increase in the evidence for treponematosis and syphilis in London (and Britain) from the 15th century reflects the greater availability of skeletal samples from this date, or the cumulative impact of socio-economic events. In Britain, for example, war with France, Ireland, Wales and Scotland during the late 13th and 14th centuries, the growth in population from 1500, an increase in trade with Europe and the east, and the increasing colonisation of the Americas would have enabled the disease to spread quickly between communities because of the movement of large numbers of individuals (Griffths 1988; Guy 1988; Powell and Cook 2005). Medical writings about syphilis are known from 1493 (Spain) and 1496 (Germany), and the disease has been identified in primary texts from Shrewsbury, where in 1493–4 the presence of the 'French pox' was recorded. Further possible evidence has been proposed by some authors, such as Bernard André's reference in 1508 in his *Annals of Henry VII* to 'a wasting pox' in England *c* 1484, following an episode of sweating sickness (cited in Waugh 1973, 193; Boehrer 1990, 201).

From 1493 to 1530 Europe experienced a syphilis epidemic, which has been blamed in part on the disbanding of armies after the French invasion of Italy (1493–4), and was considered by the Pope to be the result of the godlessness of humanity; however, by 1520 it was acknowledged as a venereal disease (Kiple 1997, 111–13). The spread of venereal diseases in urban centres may have been more widespread, as cities maintained public brothels (Nicholas 1997b, 275). In London, the Bishop of Winchester controlled a number of brothels in Southwark and in places such as Cheapside; primary evidence shows that they were frequented by prostitutes (ibid, 276; Allen 2000, 47). Court rolls from 1373 recorded that one Zenobius Martyn, who had been indicted in Langbourne ward as a 'common bawd and associate of prostitutes', admitted his offence and put himself at the mercy of the court. He also admitted that 'though he was not a freeman of the City, he kept a lodging-house for aliens and had acted as a broker against the ordinances of the City', and 'had admitted to his house men of ill-fame, evildoers, thieves and prostitutes' (Thomas 1929, roll A18). Prostitution was also associated with the suburbs because many travellers stayed in hostels or hospitals on their way into the city (Rossiaud 1988, 10).

The highest crude prevalence of tuberculosis was observed in urban cemeteries and in monastic sites based in, or serving, urban centres. The high prevalence of infectious disease in urban centres reflects the ability of a larger population to support a wider range of diseases and greater ease in their transmission in those environments (Harrison et al 1988, 520; Roberts and Manchester 2005, 17). Cohen and Crane-Kramer (2003, 90) note that the transmission of many infectious diseases can be attributed to large-scale population movement caused by migration and organised warfare. Migration to urban centres during the medieval period was particularly common for adolescents and young adults, especially women, as it offered them greater economic opportunities (Dyer 2002, 155, 194; Goldberg 1997b, 5). Grauer's (1991) palaeopathological analysis of St Helen-on-the-Walls found that a greater number of women were recorded but had a lower prevalence of chronic infection than males. At St Mary Spital, females had a higher crude prevalence of tuberculosis and tuberculoid leprosy than males. This can be understood in the light of Ortner's assertion that the immune system of females is enhanced because of their childbearing role, and that this allows them to stave off infection successfully or sustain an infection long enough for an osseous response to be generated (Ortner 1998, 86; 2003, 115–18; see also DeWitte 2010).

The high prevalence of tuberculosis in urban centres should not be taken at face value. The limited data available from rural centres show that the disease was present throughout Britain, and many rural-to-urban migrants could have been infected during their childhood in the countryside. Bogin (2001, 219) observes that these migrants have a greater risk of acquiring or becoming re-infected with tuberculosis after they have initially settled in an urban area. This is because their immune systems then have to deal with new pathogens and environments, for example overcrowding and worsening levels of sanitation. Roberts and Buikstra (2003, 21) identify risk factors that can be used to discuss inter-site differences. The results for tuberculosis at St Mary Spital indicate that a large proportion of the sample show skeletal evidence for this disease, demonstrating that an even greater number of the source population(s) were infected, as skeletal changes are only typically present in 3–5% of those affected (ibid, 89; see also Donoghue et al 2009; Wilbur et al 2009; Zink et al 2004; 2005; 2007).

The link between poverty and tuberculosis is well established, and it is highly likely that for some of those buried at St Mary Spital, poverty was a significant risk factor. During the medieval period, London was three times larger than other important British centres such as Bristol, Norwich and York, and was one of the largest cities in north-west Europe (Dyer 2002, 190). Urban centres attracted poor people because they contained institutions that regularly gave out food and shared food surpluses with the 'deserving poor' (Dyer 2000, 312). The urban poor had high death rates and were more vulnerable to infection due to a poor diet which contained only small quantities of fish or meat (ibid, 102). Their exposure to disease in the local and wider environment from a young age would have placed them at increased risk of disease transmission compared to other status groups, and their inadequate and crowded housing conditions would have exacerbated their plight (Singman 1999, 172–88). The high rate of tuberculosis among women could be related to the 'feminisation of poverty' (Goldberg 1991, cited in Leyser 1995). A significant proportion of women trod a fine line between poverty and destitution (Leyser 1995, 155). St Mary Spital was established to help such people, providing a hostel for migrants and a safe place for childbirth; other hospitals often left women to die in childbirth outside their doors rather than allow them admittance (Orme and Webster 1995, 110–11). The tuberculosis results from St Mary Spital demonstrate that there is a higher prevalence rate in females, particularly those between the ages of 18 and 35. This reflects the observed clinical pattern in which, during subadulthood, more females are affected. In women of reproductive age the progression from infection to disease and risk of fatality are also higher than in males (World Health Organization 2003, 2). The identification of tuberculosis in all age groups implies that risk of infection was present throughout life, with risk increasing due to socio-economic factors, at a time when many individuals could have become trapped in poverty due to the recurrence of agricultural crises and epidemics.

Animals are important vectors of disease transmission and tuberculosis affects (among others) cattle, pig, horse, dog, cat, horse, fox, hare, goat, deer and sheep (Roberts and Buikstra

2003, 81). Tuberculosis can be transmitted to humans from animals through the consumption of infected milk, dairy products and butchery waste, in addition to exposure to animal dung and urine (ibid, 77, 81). Provisioning and waste disposal in London were discussed in Chapter 4.1 and we know that resources were imported from up to 80km away, while markets regulated the selling of meat according to quality, condition and price (Dyer 2002, 192; Hammond 1998, 44–5).

Little difference would have existed in the slaughtering, butchery, processing of secondary products and disposal of waste between rural and urban centres; individuals in both would therefore have experienced similar modes of transmission. However, the degree and environmental impact would have differed: the scale of infection in London must have been unique in England due to the population size and environment. As discussed in Chapter 4.1, butchers and individuals who specialised in crafts dependent on animal products (eg tanning or hornworking) would have been exposed to increased risk (Cohen and Crane-Kramer 2003, 90). The high proportion of servants in urban centres may also have experienced greater risk, due to their involvement in food preparation and the care of domestic animals (Dyer 2002, 202, 204). Women may have been at greater risk than men, because servants in urban centres undertook sex-specific tasks associated with food, and women were more likely than men to be servants in towns (Smith 1997, 37; Goldberg 1997a, 110). Patients in the hospital could have been exposed to infected meat and dairy products through the consumption of milk, beef, mutton and pork (Rawcliffe 1999, 178). Medical treatment may also have played a part in re-infection or exposure to the disease, as horse saliva was thought to be a successful remedy for tuberculosis (Roberts 1987, 170).

Poor local environmental conditions, particularly overcrowding and poor hygiene, are key factors in tuberculosis. As St Mary Spital provided a burial ground for many status groups, we cannot assume that all individuals experienced equal risk from their local environment or that if they were migrants they only became infected with tuberculosis once they had settled in London (Wood et al 1992). In both rural and urban housing, the role of ventilation would have influenced the transmission of disease. Roberts and Lewis's temporal analysis of maxillary sinusitis observed that urban cemeteries had the highest crude prevalence rates compared to rural and hospital sites, which they considered to reflect the increase in industrial pollution, particularly the burning of fuel (2002, 184, 187). They noted that the rate of maxillary sinusitis and tuberculosis increased in the later medieval period (Roberts 2007). Lewis et al's study of rural and urban medieval populations found that only urban males had significantly more sinusitis than rural males (1995, 502). This demonstrates that atmospheric pollution would have increased people's risk of becoming infected with tuberculosis by airborne transmission and pathogens (see above, 4.1). Clinical studies of tuberculosis have shown that prolonged contact with an infected individual (who may be symptomless) is necessary for transmission. If medieval atmospheric conditions were such as to promote coughing, each cough could have infected 1% of contacts (Roberts and Buikstra 2003, 7).

Hygiene practices have been shown to be culturally defined and subject to considerable variation (Curtis 2001), and we cannot assume that attitudes to sanitation and cleanliness were homogeneous in medieval London. Singman's overview of daily life (1999, 43–9) suggests that hands and faces, the only parts of the body usually visible in public, were washed regularly (religious institutions regularised this), hair was frequently deloused, and only the very poor went without shoes or stockings. If individuals had low levels of hygiene that exposed them to a range of illnesses and diseases, then they would be at greater risk of developing tuberculosis, because they would not be strong enough to provide a sufficient immune response to a new exposure or dormant infection.

Bogin (2001, 192) suggests that rural living 'set up conditions for infectious disease' but that urban life amplified the possibility of spreading epidemic diseases. Rural–urban mobility took various forms Dyer (2002, 155–94): the rural population frequently travelled to urban markets to sell produce, and primary sources show that London attracted migrants from the east Midlands, East Anglia and within an 80km radius. Young women and older men were most likely to migrate, particularly during the 12th and 13th centuries, entering the hired labour market or establishing businesses in trade or manufacturing. Hospitals played a significant role in stimulating migration during the medieval period, as religious houses had the responsibility to care for travellers and the poor (above, 4.2). Their location meant that they could be used by those who had not entered the city before the gates opened or shut (Orme and Webster 1995, 35, 43, 45–8, 118). Warfare also increased mobility: in 1347, for example, Edward III ordered the sheriffs of London to issue a proclamation demanding that those who had left the army in France before it reached Calais and returned to England should go back to Calais via Sandwich or Dover (Sharpe 1904, fo cxli).

The presence of tuberculosis in medieval London demonstrates that urban living conditions promoted the spread of the disease by airborne transmission or through the consumption of infected animal products. These modes of transmission were also present in rural communities, but the density of population and frequent migration to the capital meant that infection operated on a scale not seen in other urban centres.

Diet

The diet of most medieval people was dictated by the Church, which prescribed how often fish should be consumed and, for those in holy orders, the timing of meals and the quantity of meat included in the diet (Woolgar 2006a, 194–5; Harvey 1992, 60–6). Diet was also influenced by agricultural crises (1315–22) and the Black Death (1348–9); the north of Britain was more affected than the south and these catastrophic events predominantly affected cereals but also salt prices, which in turn influenced the preservation of meat and the production of butter and cheese (Dyer 2000, 228–9). The average medieval diet consisted of carbohydrates from cereals, protein from meat and eggs, and vitamins, mineral salts and fibre from fruits and vegetables. Unlike today, it would have been governed by the seasons and what produce could be preserved or stored – milk and cream, for example, were usually only purchased by the rich in the summer (Hammond 1998, 7–25, 68). Dyer's analysis of food consumption has shown that the average diet did not improve until the 15th century due to long-term changes in demography (Dyer 2000, 85–102). The diet of the lower classes consisted of cereals and small quantities of meat and fish, while the very poor ate a similar diet but with smaller and more infrequent portions of meat and fish. The most inadequate diets were probably eaten by rural and urban people who did not own or have access to gardens or land (Woolgar et al 2006, 271). Rural communities living near the coast ate shellfish but the majority of their diet consisted of pottage, broths and soup, supplemented by meat, eggs, fruit and vegetables. Urban dwellers relied on imported foods, or foods grown in the suburbs or town gardens; they regularly consumed beef, mutton, poultry and pork, with wild species restricted to the luxury market. Socio-economic factors would have influenced access to types of food, but many foods had fixed prices (Hammond 1998, 40–3). High-status individuals would have had a basic diet similar to urban and rural communities, but they ate more meat, a wider variety of fish and shellfish and greater quantities of vegetables and fruit; these foods were enhanced with spices and rare imported foods such as nuts (ibid, 63–5). Because the capital was a centre of European trade, Londoners had more opportunities to purchase nuts, rice, spices and fruits such as oranges (ibid, 11–12).

There would also have been age-related differences in diet, as well as physical factors such as ante-mortem tooth loss (McElroy and Townsend 1996, 233). Children require appropriate weaning foods, because they are unable to digest enough of the adult diet to meet their nutritional requirements. Their erupting and changing dentition allows them to progress to an adult diet and because these changes occur over many years, they are able to develop the physical and cognitive capacity to obtain their own food and protect themselves from disease (Bogin 1998, 22, 34). Orme (2001, 71–3) notes that household accounts include the purchase of milk for children, and their food was predominantly porridge or gruel, supplemented as for adults with meat, fish and vegetables; as they grew older they would have drunk ale.

Stable isotope analysis of human remains demonstrates the average protein consumed for the last 10–30 years of life, with carbon and nitrogen isotope values indicating the proportion of marine and terrestrial foods consumed (Katzenberg 2000, 314–15; Müldner and Richards 2006, 229). Analysis of medieval diet by Müldner and Richards (2005), using five sites from northern England, showed that little dietary difference existed between them. The individual sites show slight inter-status differences that reflect their social status or settlement location. Overall, the results show that aquatic resources formed a large portion of daily food consumption and that diets consisted of a mixture of terrestrial and freshwater/marine protein, with little evidence for significant amounts of plant protein, which may be a result of the isotopes used in the study. Mays's carbon stable isotope study of diet in north-east England compared lay and monastic diets with those from inland and coastal communities, and found that the majority of the diet consisted of terrestrial foods; monastic diets contained more marine resources, probably reflecting their observance of fasting and abstinence, as did the diets of people who lived on the coast (Mays 1997a). Data from the poor rural village of Wharram Percy suggested that marine food formed only a minor part of the diet there (ibid). Urban dwellers from Hereford had higher nitrogen ratios that those at Wharram Percy, indicating that they consumed more meat, together with some aquatic protein, though in smaller quantities than those buried in the Augustinian friary in Warrington (Müldner and Richards 2006, 231–8; 2007a). Such analyses have demonstrated that dietary differences between classes may have been slight, and that urban populations ate a greater variety of foods than those at rural sites (Müldner and Richards 2006, 235, 236).

The presence of scurvy in rural and urban populations and the small number of subadults affected at St Mary Spital (eight) suggest that the disease was not common, but that factors present in both environments led to the development of the disease. The role of the osteological paradox (Wood et al 1992) may mean that some individuals died before the condition created an osseous response, and the dearth of examples may, as Brickley suggests (2000, 187), be because diagnosis requires relatively complete and well-preserved skeletal material. The food that these subadults were given must have been inadequate: the diet of young children who could not access food by themselves mainly consisted of porridge and gruel (Orme 2001, 71–3), and it is possible that their carers were not able to afford sufficient quantities of fresh fruit and vegetables. The inability of some adults to access sufficient amounts of vitamin C is evidenced by a female with scurvy at Fishergate House, York (Holst 2005).

The existence of osteoporosis in men and women from urban, monastic and hospital cemeteries supports the primary textual evidence indicating that monastic and hospital institutions cared for the elderly, and suggests that in addition to age and post-menopausal hormonal changes, diet may have played a role in the development of this disease (Brickley 2000, 191; Brickley and Ives 2008, 158). Dyer's analysis of diet shows that the elderly may have had reduced access to adequate nutrition, due to poor arrangements with their family or land tenants, and that many urban dwellers may have had a compromised diet (Dyer 1998, 152, 197). The elderly were more vulnerable to deprivation, and it was likely that many individuals spent all their lives in poverty, which increased their chances of developing osteoporosis due to insufficient consumption of dairy products. The poor of London may have been unable to afford dairy products, whereas the diet of elite individuals could have placed them at risk too, because it typically contained low quantities of cheese and milk (ibid, 63).

Dental health represents the outcome of the inter-related diseases and biomechanical forces acting on the jaws and teeth, which can provide information on diet (Hillson 2000, 249).

Understanding differences in dental disease between sites is problematic due to the presentation of the data (see Freeth 2000, 232–3). Roberts and Cox's review of medieval dental health (2003, 258–65) has shown that it increases from the early medieval period, and that rates of carious lesions were high but varied from 6% to 94%; abscesses had a mean of 26%; mean periodontal disease rates varied from 6% to 100%; mean calculus rates varied from 38% to 71%; and mean ante-mortem tooth loss ranged from 5% to 75%. The results of this present study are comparable to these findings, supporting the evidence for broad similarities in basic dietary staples between status groups and site types. The higher prevalence of carious lesions in monastic and rural sites is interesting, as the greater consumption of dairy products in those locations (Dyer 1998, 63) should have protected their teeth, because casein (milk protein) provides a protective covering, reducing the risk of developing a carious lesion (Hillson 1996, 279).

The inter-site analysis of diffuse idiopathic skeletal hyperostosis (DISH) was highly problematic due to differences in the criteria used to diagnose the disease (eg Mays 2006a, 185), and the results are therefore tentative. A total of 113 individuals with DISH were reported from urban, rural, hospital and monastic sites; DISH was not observed in the catastrophic samples. More males than females were affected but it is considered that this finding reflects the samples included in the study rather than representing a real trend, as more males were present overall. This is supported by the highest female crude prevalence reported from Breda, which was a female monastic cemetery.

In contrast to other studies (Waldron 1995), more affected individuals (46 cases) were observed in urban cemeteries rather than monastic ones (23 cases). This finding may support Roberts and Cox's analysis of late medieval DISH, which found a statistical significance between the number of monastic and non-monastic cemetery sites (2003, 246). The role of diet in this disease process has been suggested by many authors, again linking the development of the disease to the amount of food consumed by high-status individuals or those in monastic orders (Mays 2006a, 183; Roberts and Manchester 2005, 161). However, the disease has also been identified at rural and poor urban cemeteries, and in monastic orders which kept strict vegetarian diets (White 2004, 176; Mays 2006a, 183). The role of diet in this disease process during the medieval period deserves greater attention (Mays 2006a, 187; Spencer 2007), particularly as a recent study of modern bodies found a relationship between obesity and DISH (Moore 1988). At many cemeteries, including St Mary Spital, the individuals with DISH may be high-status men and women, who due to social and environmental buffers were able to live long enough to develop an osseous response (Roberts and Manchester 2005, 161).

Local environmental conditions

Rickets was observed at all site types but, although the sample from St Mary Spital contained a greater number of subadults than any other, it had the fewest individuals affected (eight) compared to 13 individuals from the York cemeteries. As rickets has been identified at rural (eight cases) and urban sites in the medieval period, the role of urbanisation cannot be regarded as a primary factor in its development. Factors inhibiting the production of vitamin D in the medieval period would have included swaddling which would have restricted the amount of sunlight babies were exposed to, especially if they were kept indoors. Parenting advice also warned that babies should not be kept in the light when they were awake (Orme 2001, 63). The identification of rickets at the rural site of Wharram Percy led Ortner and Mays (1998) to suggest that the individuals with rickets were already suffering from another disease and were kept indoors, increasing the likelihood of developing rickets.

Osteomalacia was identified at both St Mary Spital and in the *Mary Rose* catastrophic sample; however, the skeletal changes described at the latter are not as diagnostic as previously thought (see Brickley et al 2005; Brickley et al 2007; Brickley and Ives 2008, 125). A regular consumption of fish and dairy products may have helped to maintain adequate levels of vitamin D; nevertheless, the result is thought to be biased by the low survival rates of poorly mineralised bone in the burial environment, and the need for samples to be re-analysed in light of new methodologies. Recent clinical research highlighted by Brickley et al (2007, 75) has demonstrated that osteomalacia may be more common in older adults due to a reduction in vitamin D absorption by the intestine. Other factors identified include co-morbidity with diseases such as hypertension, poorly lit houses and inadequate diets (ibid, 76; Brickley and Ives 2008, 113). Because osteomalacia causes muscle weakness, it may have prevented individuals from spending time outdoors, thereby reducing the amount of vitamin D they could metabolise. Older individuals may have been more vulnerable to developing this disease during the medieval period due to frequent episodes of famine, and also because they would have been more reliant on others for housing and food, and on charitable institutions for care (Rosenthal 1996; Shahar 2004).

Medieval populations experienced a range of neoplastic disease: for example, Grupe (1988) observed metastasising carcinoma in an older adult male in Germany, while Anderson et al (1992) and Wakely et al (1995) identified an example of prostatic carcinoma from Canterbury. In addition to the influence of the demographic pattern of archaeologically derived populations (above, 4.4), the identification of neoplasms is hindered by the lack of routine radiography, bone preservation and skeletal completeness, all of which are important factors in achieving a diagnosis (Roberts and Manchester 2005, 252–3). Similarities in bone response between the different types of malignant neoplasm, in addition to infectious disease, also make diagnosis difficult (Ortner 2003, 503, 537). In the present study, the majority of reported data concerned benign neoplasms and often those associated with growth, such as osteochondroma. This study and the data collected by Roberts and Cox (2003, 280–1) demonstrate that benign and malignant neoplasms have been identified at all site types in medieval Britain. The reasons behind the development of neoplasms are multifactorial and include genetic mutations, but a number of risk factors also increase the likelihood of developing secondary neoplasms, such as chemical and physical agents (Aufderheide and Rodríguez-Martín 1998, 373).

The greater number of males identified with neoplasms in this study conforms to clinical epidemiological data (Aufderheide and Rodríguez-Martín 1998, 372), and the cultural buffering experienced by religious orders may have increased their likelihood of living into old age, increasing their potential to develop a neoplasm later in life. The engendered nature of urban employment during the medieval period made it more likely for males to work in more hazardous occupations such as metalwork or the production of leather (Smith 1997, 37), which would have exposed them to chemical and physical agents. Within urban centres, these occupations were often concentrated in certain areas (Fitzpatrick and LaGory 2000, 48), thereby raising the risk to all involved. As rural and religious communities also engaged in metalworking and other hazardous occupations, such risks were also present in these communities. However, the scale and density of industries in London would have increased the number of people vulnerable to pollutants, particularly if they were exposed from a young age (above, 4.1).

Individuals with skeletal evidence for osteomyelitis represent those who were able to sustain an immune response long enough to recover from the infection, reflecting its chronic and long-term nature (Ortner 1998, 80). The higher male crude prevalence of osteomyelitis observed in this study has been reported clinically, and even when both sexes have comparable exposure to sources of infection, males still have higher rates of disease, which is considered to reflect the enhanced immune response of females (ibid, 80, 86). However, Larsen (1999, 92) suggests that higher male prevalence may be related to 'factors that are unique to specific circumstances', for example greater involvement in agriculture and risky activities such as warfare in the medieval period.

Causes of infection in medieval London exposing people to infection included poor hygiene, sanitation and waste disposal practices and housing conditions (above, 4.1). As these conditions would have varied throughout the city and suburbs, the introduction of bacteria would have occurred by many different pathways. For example, social status would have influenced how people were shod: poor people often went barefoot or in stockings, whereas monks received new shoes every year (Singman 1999, 42–3). Shoes found at St Mary Spital reveal that they were often perforated or thinned by wear (Thomas et al 1997, 61) and would not have prevented penetrating injuries. Shoes, as a socio-cultural buffer of disease, have been shown by other palaeopathological studies to be associated with the prevalence of osteomyelitis (Larsen 1999, 92–3). Higher levels of non-specific and specific infections in urban environments also reflect increased population size and density (ibid, 90). The high crude prevalence in religious communities, even though monks regularly received new shoes, could have resulted from the agricultural aspect of their way of life and their pastoral role with the poor, which highlights the multifactorial nature of disease and risk (Wilkinson 2001).

Endocranial lesions are predominantly reported in subadults and can have many origins, including metabolic and infectious diseases, trauma, neoplasms, venous drain disorders and chronic meningitis (Lewis 2004, 82–3). The observation of these lesions is governed by the diagnostic criteria employed, skeletal completeness and preservation, and whether the endocranium is observable; the results of any inter-site comparison will therefore be biased by such differences. The presence of adults with endocranial lesions at St Mary Spital conforms to the limited evidence from other medieval urban centres, suggesting that the factors in their formation continued for both sexes. At sites where adult and subadult data were available, the highest crude prevalence was always observed in subadults, which may be explained by their greater vulnerability to disease at key life stages, such as during weaning (see Katzenberg et al 1996), the remodelling of childhood lesions in adults and the osteological paradox (Wood et al 1992). Lewis's analysis of endocranial lesions (2004, 91) observed that medieval rural populations had the highest prevalence rates, but it should be noted that this study did not include individuals who did not have an occipital bone present. In contrast, the present study found that the highest prevalence rate was observed at the urban cemetery of Fishergate House, and the greatest numbers of individuals affected were derived from urban centres: 30 subadult cases were recorded at Fishergate House and 34 subadult cases at St Mary Spital (Table 171). This data set suggests that urban living conditions and way of life placed individuals at a greater risk of developing endocranial lesions, due to a higher exposure to pollutants and diseases in the local environment and the larger population aiding disease transmission and carrying capacity. The influence of urbanism on the prevalence of these lesions is supported by Schultz's temporal analysis of endocranial lesions in Central Europe and Anatolia, which found they increased in conjunction with population growth and socio-political changes (Schultz 2001).

The cause of Paget's disease of bone is unknown, but this slow and often debilitating condition is most frequently observed in males (Roberts and Manchester 2005, 250). A small number of individuals have been identified with this disease in the UK, although as Roberts and Cox caution, histological analysis is needed to confirm the diagnosis (2003, 284). Individuals affected with the disease have been identified in monastic, urban and hospital sites (ibid). In this study, the majority of individuals affected were males, conforming to the clinical data (Roberts and Manchester 2005, 250); the highest crude prevalence rate is from Norton Priory, where all status groups were affected (Boylston and Ogden 2005). From the sites included in this study, Paget's disease of bone does not appear to be associated with particular site types or status groups during the medieval period.

Circulatory disease was observed at all site types, emphasising the presence of similar risk factors in all living environments. The dominance of the data by males also conforms to clinical evidence (Apley and Solomon 2000). The presence of many different types of circulatory disease reflects the sample size analysed, with the scale of urbanism in London increasing the probability of encountering risk factors. The limited number of specific cases of this disease type reported in the literature may also reflect the finding that researchers are more likely to assign osteological changes to a disease group (ie circulatory) rather than diagnose a specific form of disease (eg Perthes' disease) (Miller et al 1996).

Inter-site analysis shows that St Mary Spital is the only site to contain a wide range of specific osteoarthritic conditions, again reflecting the large number of individuals analysed. The limited number of people affected by these conditions elsewhere not only reflects the disease process and aetiology, but conforms to the observed low clinical prevalence (Roberts and Manchester 2005, 154). Additional factors biasing this result include taphonomic factors and those identified by Miller et al (1996).

The high crude prevalence of septic osteoarthritis recorded in all age groups at St Mary Spital correlates to the presence of other infectious diseases such as tuberculosis and conforms to the results reported by Roberts and Cox (2003).

Gout was only identified at monastic, hospital and urban cemeteries. This may reflect not only the hereditary nature of the primary form of the disease, but also the acquisition of the secondary form due to factors such as being overweight and consuming excessive amounts of alcohol (Apley and Solomon 2000, 33). Elite individuals were more likely to be buried in these contexts (Gilchrist and Sloane 2005, 60–4), and their diet would have contained richer foods that increased their risk of developing gout (Hammond 1998). It is interesting to note that at St Mary Spital females have a higher crude prevalence rate than males, a result not observed in the other sites.

The influence of the environment on the human body can also be seen in the presence of congenital and developmental anomalies. As the majority of these anomalies affect the soft tissue, the osteological evidence may only focus on those that affect the skeleton and are compatible with life (Roberts and Manchester 2005, 44–5). The presence of these anomalies within a population reflects underlying genetic risk factors, the 'open-ended' nature of our genetic microstructure that allows for biological change to occur, their interaction with environmental factors which include chemicals, and the presence of infectious and/or metabolic diseases in the mother (Barnes 1994, xx–xxx; Levene et al 2000, 147–53). Most individuals with skull, spine, limb and joint anomalies were reported from urban areas, which supports Sture's (2002) findings. The link between urban living conditions, greater disease exposure and higher levels of pollution has been proven in the clinical literature (eg Dolk and Vrijheid 2003). Roberts and Cox (2003, 277) also found that many affected individuals were buried in monastic and rural cemeteries. Anderson (2000, 217) noted that the majority of reported examples of congenital and developmental anomalies within the palaeopathological literature were from the Anglo-Saxon and medieval periods, which he cautions may reflect greater numbers of individuals excavated and analysed, rather than factors specific to those populations.

The majority of reported anomalies affected the axial skeleton, indicating that environmental (and/or genetic) factors had affected the foetus during the first eight weeks after conception (Barnes 1994, 3). The foetus can be affected by maternal lifestyle and because diseases can cross the placental barrier. As outlined earlier (above, 4.1), the medieval urban environment, particularly London, placed individuals at a greater risk of developing a congenital or developmental anomaly. Clinical studies have shown that air pollution can result in low birthweight, growth retardation and congenital malformations, predominantly of the soft tissues (Vrijheid et al 2003, 138–40). Many females may have been exposed to air pollution through their employment and poor ventilation in their dwellings, which would have been exacerbated if they worked in or lived close to industries which caused smoke or other particulates, such as metalworking. Exposure to heavy metals would also have increased the risk of anomalies. High quantities of lead have been recovered from European archaeological sites, indicating that smelting and manufacturing processes had a significant impact in the medieval period (Marshall 2003). Contact with lead would also have occurred in the pottery, glass and metalwork industries, through make-up, paints and tableware, and in the construction and decoration of buildings (Pulsifer 1888). The exposure to lead, particularly in drinking water, could have resulted in the foetus developing neural tube defects. Clinical studies have also linked males born with cleft lip or palate to paternal lead exposure (Vrijheid et al 2003, 109–11).

Medieval urban centres in England, particularly London, contained organic and inorganic pollutants created by the human and animal population, industry, food production and waste disposal. Mothers would have been at risk of toxoplasmosis from undercooked food or animal faeces, which if spread to the foetus would have resulted in microcephaly or hydrocephalus (Holzel 1993, 302–4). Studies of neural tube defects have also demonstrated that diet, seasonality and migration all influence the development of these anomalies (Jorde et al 1983; Dickel and Doran 1989).

The finding in the present study that a greater number of females were affected by congenital and developmental anomalies does not correspond to Sture's results (2002) or those reported in the clinical literature (eg Lary and Paulozzi 2001). This result may be biased by the sample from St Mary Spital which had more females affected (36) than at all other sites (a total of 17). Other factors responsible for this result may include greater male environmental sensitivity resulting in a higher number of male pre-term deaths and stillbirths (Stinson 1985, 125–6), and female migration increasing the risk of anomalies (Dickel and Doran 1989). Urban populations today are not static (Schell and Ulijaszek 1999, 9–11), and in the past, greater population variation, in conjunction with environmental factors, may have created 'a population (with) its own genetic pattern of developmental tendencies' (Barnes 1994, xxx).

Growth and stature

In subadults, height-for-dental-age reflects the interplay of nutrition, living environment, socio-economic status and disease with underlying genetic influences on the tempo of growth (Hauspie and Susanne 2000, 128; Humphrey 2000, 193), and adult stature indicates the outcome of development, in addition to physical activity and whether catch-up growth was achieved if a person had been 'stressed' (Bogin 1998, 269, 303, 311; Ulijaszek and Strickland 1993, 136–7; Komlos 1993, 240; Clark et al 1986, 148). In subadults, urban–rural differences in growth may exist throughout development but the sum effect can result in the attainment of similar statures, because comparison of growth patterns between people in the two environments is rarely able to isolate the specific factors responsible for differences in these patterns (Schell 2000b, 408–9). The growth profile from St Mary Spital shows that throughout the majority of their development, the subadults are most comparable to rural populations. It should be remembered that these pooled data do not represent temporal changes in growth or account for the impact of catastrophic events such as famines (see Antoine et al 2005). The similarities between rural and urban cemeteries may stem from both communities having a broadly similar diet throughout the medieval period, and comparable child-rearing practices (Lewis 2002, 9–10; see Panter-Brick 1998a, 73–4).

Our inability to sex subadults accurately (Lewis 2007, 187–8) hinders a true understanding of these growth profiles; Lewis argues that differences in the number of male and female subadults included in the samples used for comparison results in disparities to the observed growth spurts (2002, 54).

Lewis's suggestion that the urban data from York may be biased by the presence of more female adolescents (2002, 66) could provide an explanation for the sharp rise in height observed at St Mary Spital between the ages of 14 and 15 years, reflecting the migration to the capital of adolescent females who were in or at the start of their growth spurt, two years ahead of their male counterparts, due to menarche (ibid, 54). The influence of migration on the results is highlighted by the fact that height disparities between rural and urban populations are greatest during early adolescence due to differences in who had their growth spurt first (Schell 2000b, 408).

The adult data show that average rural and urban male statures are equal (170.3cm) and the average female stature shows little difference between the two site types (Table 172), suggesting that the role of genetics and the long-term consequences of environmental and social factors outweighed the deleterious effects of migration and living in an urban centre. This correlates with Steckel's observation (1995, 1922) that urban stature has exceeded rural only recently. It should be noted that variations in the methods used to calculate stature between the cemeteries will also have influenced the results, compounded by differences in limb lengths between rural and monastic populations (Schweich and Knüsel 2003). Nevertheless, other studies have shown that there is limited or no difference in contemporary rural–urban child growth (Schell 2000b, 408–9). The ability of female migrants or existing urban dwellers in the St Mary Spital sample to achieve catch-up growth after the age of 16 years (after delayed skeletal maturation), perhaps because they obtained greater socio-economic security through employment or marriage, enabled them to be taller than their average rural counterparts. Physical anthropology studies confirm that with better nutrition, medical care and parents who have achieved their growth potential, urban children will grow larger than their rural counterparts. However, if urban conditions are unhealthy, childhood growth may be poor (ibid, 408), and this could explain the short height of 5–12-year-old subadults at St Mary Spital compared to their York and rural counterparts, if we accept the historical evidence for limited child migration before the age of 12 years (Orme 2001, 308–9). The data also reflect the variety of social status within the cemetery, because of the role played by the hospital in the local and wider community (ie as a home for orphans), and provide further support for the suggestion that industrialisation rather than urbanism had a deleterious effect upon growth (Lewis 2002, 54). The inability to associate subadults directly with indicators of social status prevents us from investigating intra-urban differences in growth.

In contrast to average female stature, average male stature shows greater variability, due to men's greater environmental sensitivity (Stinson 1985). Long-term trends in male stature show variation in attained height (eg Maat 2005), reflecting the plasticity which allows them to adapt to environmental stressors and conditions such as episodes of famine (Bogin 1998, 267). The height of males from monastic cemeteries is greater than rural or urban samples, which most probably results from many having entered these establishments as children (oblates), in friaries which accepted boys in their early teens (Orme 2001, 225). A religious life would have provided them with good quality regular meals, medical treatment, care and security, enabling them to fulfil their growth potential. The dietary similarities between rural and urban centres are most probably one of the significant factors in males attaining the same average height.

The average male stature from St Mary Spital (168.2cm) is biased by males from mass burial contexts (type D), who were found to be 0.5–5.0cm shorter than their attritional counterparts over time, reflecting the catastrophic factors influencing mortality in these samples, but also perhaps canalisation of the growth process. Male stature has been shown to be a good indicator of social status, with high social status resulting in greater attained height (Larsen 1999, 18–19). As the results from St Mary Spital cannot be married to indicators of status, we must look to wider social factors and environmental conditions. The number of servants in medieval households was particularly high in urban centres: Smith (1997, 35–6) estimated that between 1377 and 1379 one-fifth to one-third of all urban households contained servants, who were most likely to be in their mid teens (Goldberg 1997b, 5). Although the majority of migrants may have been women, men also migrated in their teens to become servants or, if they were rich enough, to take up apprenticeships in the city, living in their master's house for up to ten years (Hanawalt 1993, 131). It is possible that the growth data contain a greater number of females who had reached menarche, biasing the hypothesised growth evidence for migration in the sample. Physical anthropology studies using historic data from Italian populations found that those who migrated to Belgium before the age of 25 years were taller than those who migrated after this age (Susanne et al 2000, 406), so it is striking that the average male at St Mary Spital is shorter than both his rural and urban counterparts.

Environment, influenced by socio-economic status, food availability and health status, is the most significant factor in biological change after migration (ibid, 407). As the male growth spurt has been proposed to be subject to greater environmental sensitivity (Bogin et al 1992), the shorter stature of the London males suggests that the living conditions experienced by many individuals in the sample were inadequate, and that these conditions were compounded by deficient nutrition and poor health status, hindering them from reaching their full potential height or slowing down their growth and skeletal maturation. The men's occupations would also have influenced their stature: men in manual occupations have been found to be shorter than those who moved from manual occupations to non-manual work by becoming more socially mobile (Power et al 2002). Many apprentices and servants were engaged in activities associated with polluting industries, such as in the manufacturing of cloth, metals and leather (Dyer 1998, 189), exposing them to toxins and harmful waste products that may have resulted in compromised growth. The role of poverty on attained stature would also have been significant, because it would have denied the poor access to good diets and forced them to live in crowded and insanitary conditions. It has been estimated that one-fifth of Coventry's medieval population were poor (ibid, 196), and we can only assume that the number was far greater in London, which contained more and larger institutions that were obligated to help them through charity and alms (ibid, 240–8); however, 'the survival of the medieval poor still remains something of a mystery' (ibid, 257).

The long-term consequences of climatic changes, famines and epidemics during the medieval period would also have affected growth and attained height. Clinical studies of the long-term consequences of the 'Hunger Winter' experienced in the western Netherlands (1944–5) have shown that individuals born at this time had low birthweights, females continued to experience reproductive problems and individuals affected during early gestation had long-term health problems (Lumey and Van Poppel 1994; Rosebloom et al 2006), all factors affecting development, growth and stature. Low birthweight babies are more likely to experience developmental delay and are less likely to grow more during childhood. At 7 years old, height is positively correlated with birth size, but low birthweight does not always result in short adult stature (Schell 2000a, 291–4). Schweich and Knüsel's (2003) analysis of body proportions in medieval males concluded that environmental factors did not have a statistically significant effect.

As the sample from St Mary Spital covers a substantial period (c 1120–1539), the results indicate the long-term consequences of the medieval economy, society and environment, rather than shorter-term consequences observed in the comparative data, which derive from smaller cemeteries that were not in use for the same period of time. This is supported by Schweich and Knüsel's findings (2003) that stature changed throughout the period. The difference between St Mary Spital and the comparative sites indicates that the nature and scale of urbanism in London, together with greater migration and population variation, greater variability in living conditions and local environmental quality, affected growth and adult stature.

Summary

The cemetery of St Mary Spital has similarities to sites of all types from the UK, in addition to those elsewhere (eg Breda in the Netherlands), highlighting the many roles that the site fulfilled within London and the suburbs. St Mary Spital is a unique cemetery within Britain in terms of sample size, disease type and prevalence, emphasising the development of London throughout the medieval period and the impact of this on the local environment and population. The scale of urbanism, in combination with population movement, established a living environment within London that created suitable conditions for diseases to develop and be transmitted; established cultural and environmental buffers and stressors that altered throughout the life course; and, as today, increased mortality risk.

5 Conclusions

5.1 An overview of the data set

Amy Gray Jones

The cemetery at St Mary Spital was dominated by recurrent episodes of mass burial. Pits containing up to 40 people were created intermittently throughout the cemetery's use. They began to be used in the first period of burial, around the middle of the 12th century, with the opportunistic use of disused quarry pits for mass burials, containing about one-third of those buried in the whole of period 14, *c* 1120–*c* 1200 (165/512 individuals). A century later, in the middle of the 13th century, and most conspicuously, 2323 individuals – over half of those in periods 15 and 16, *c* 1200–*c* 1400 (a total of 1390 in period 15 and 2835 in period 16) – were buried in intentionally excavated burial pits, in two phases that occurred in quick succession. During the last period of the cemetery's use (*c* 1400–1539), about one-fifth of burials were interred in several more multiple burial pits (124/650 individuals).

It is important to note that substantial areas of truncation occurred in some parts of the cemetery, particularly on the eastern side, and it is likely that as much as 40% of the original cemetery population has been destroyed by later activity.

These mass burial practices suggested that a number of periods of increased mortality had occurred. High-precision radiocarbon dating within a well-defined stratigraphic framework provided an unparalleled level of confidence in the phasing of the burials. The majority of mass burials pre-date the known plague epidemics, or Black Death, and analysis found that episodes of war or violence, or practicalities such as a shortage of space, were unlikely reasons for these mass burials. Historical sources revealed a series of recurrent famines and epidemics during this period, a number of which closely correspond with the dating of the mass burial phases. The largest phases of mass burials, in the mid 13th century, correspond with major outbreaks of famine which are thought to have been caused by climatic fluctuations as a result of a massive volcanic eruption in the tropics.

Demographically the individuals in mass burial pits did not display a straightforward catastrophic profile. The demographic profile of those interred in pits was similar to that of the individual burials in the cemetery, although there were higher proportions of older subadults (6–17 years) in the mass burials, and whereas there were more males than females in the attritional cemetery, the sexes were buried in equal proportions in the mass burial pits. This pattern shares some similarity with the known demographic effects of famine, whereby the 'normal' distribution of deaths is amplified with the greatest proportional increases in those where death rates are normally low. This is complicated by the fact that the main cause of excess mortality during periods of famine is usually infectious disease rather than starvation. We would expect that infectious diseases would be a major problem in medieval London, considering the conditions of urban life.

Osteological analysis also revealed that the population interred in the cemetery underwent a period of prolonged stress, probably reflecting these repeated incidences of famine and associated infectious disease. In the first episodes of increased mortality and mass burial there was a clear distinction between the health of those buried in the pits and those in the attritional cemetery: there were significantly more children aged between 6 and 17 years in the mass burials and these children were shorter for their age; and both children and adults in the mass burials had a higher prevalence of stress indicators than those in the attritional cemetery. Although there were always greater proportions of 6–17-year-olds in the mass burials, over time the distinction between their health and that of those in the attritional cemetery began to blur: in the later periods high rates of stress indicators could be found in both burial groups, suggesting that the population as a whole was experiencing biological stresses early in life. This change, from a clear relationship between the mass burials and evidence for poor health in the first period of burials to a more even distribution of stress indicators between the burial groups, is thought to reflect the impact of repeated incidences of famine throughout the cemetery's use.

5.2 Relationship between St Mary Spital and London

Brian Connell

Undoubtedly the hospital and priory of St Mary Spital served an important function in terms of the health and well-being of medieval Londoners, providing a lifeline for many of the poor and sick. St Mary Spital would also have catered for medieval migrants, many of whom may have travelled to London from all parts of England to settle or find work. The evolution, growth and development of this monastic institution would have been affected by major social upheavals, including the Great Famine and the Black Death. The services provided by the hospital and priory, both religious and medical, would have had to adapt in the face of these crises. The general social function of St Mary Spital may also have changed over the course of its development. Gilchrist and Sloane (2005, 207) point to a greater intolerance for the general sick poor in the later Middle Ages, suggesting that there could have been a shift in focus to target groups of more 'deserving' poor and that charitable efforts could have been directed towards them (ibid).

The role of St Mary Spital in relation to the rest of medieval London is difficult to quantify. Thomas et al (1997, 126) state that there is not much evidence for the relationship between St Mary Spital and other religious houses in London and what does exist seems to be confined to affairs of property. Hospitals in general have received little attention from historians documenting English medieval religious houses (ibid, 2). St Mary Spital does seem to have enjoyed a close relationship with the other major monastic hospital in the north of the city, St Bartholomew's (ibid, 127), and each could possibly have acted as an overflow cemetery for the other. More pertinent may be St Mary Spital's relationships with the City authorities and St Paul's, for example the ceremonies held at the pulpit cross. It is these relationships that perhaps might explain the high number of burials at St Mary Spital.

5.3 Health status of medieval Londoners

Rebecca Redfern

The health perspective provided by the analysis of the skeletal material from St Mary Spital indicates that the scale and nature of urbanisation in London created a living environment that promoted the transmission of communicable diseases and increased the risk of injury. Overall, it demonstrates that the city environment in its broadest sense, rather than just the impact of industrialisation, affected well-being. The impact on health was mediated by the medieval life course, which influenced when individuals would begin employment, become apprentices and change their living environments, all of which affected the cultural and environmental buffers and stressors they experienced. The similarities between data from the cemetery and other British rural, urban and monastic sites reflect the environmental catastrophes which these communities experienced, but also the social, political and economic relationships between them, supporting the primary evidence for migration and economic activity.

The city depended on migrants to sustain its population and contribute to the economy. At this time the majority of migrants were females between 13 and 20 years old (Goldberg 1997a; Hanawalt 1993). Their presence could be detected within the data resulting from growth and trauma; the St Mary Spital growth profile was similar to rural sites until the age of 14 to 15 years when it increased, perhaps indicating the presence of migrant adolescent females.

The subadult fracture pattern is (as yet) unparalleled within Britain but it is comparable to the adult pattern, suggesting that occupation and city environment were influences. Adult fracture patterns bore parallels to rural and other urban sites, indicating that many individuals could have sustained injuries before moving to the city. The results also support the findings of Grauer and Roberts's (1996) analysis of fracture frequency in long bones at St Helen-on-the-Walls (York), but the St Mary Spital data differed in skeletal distribution. Unlike other sites, there was no obvious difference between the sexes, suggesting that they experienced the same degree of risk or were (for the most part) engaged in the same employment.

The stature data provide an interesting insight into male adaptation to the urban environment and into the make-up of the London population. Males at St Mary Spital were shorter than their rural, urban and monastic counterparts, which implies that many were unable to rally successfully after migrating to the city, a finding emphasised by the minor variation in female stature between site types.

The living environment of the city encouraged the spread

of infectious diseases to all age groups, particularly tuberculosis, as a result of poor quality living conditions, the consumption of infected meat, and airborne transmission exacerbated by air pollution. The identification of treponemal disease indicates that factors specific to urban environments – particularly a non-static population, trade and established brothels – were important in its transmission during the medieval period. Its presence within an urban hospital population is interesting as documentary evidence tells us that cities evicted sufferers, who were also excluded from hospitals (Allen 2000, 43). The presence of venereal syphilis and lack of lepromatous leprosy sufferers at St Mary Spital support Crane-Kramer's (2000) assertion that a diagnostic confusion did not exist between the diseases. Despite the many hazards within the medieval city, human behaviour also played a role in the development of disease. The small number of subadults with changes conforming to the diagnosis of scurvy indicates that its causative factors existed in both rural and urban settings, and demonstrates that the care of children was more important in its development than the urban environment itself. This was also true of subadults with rickets, supporting Ortner and Mays's (1998) hypothesis that these individuals were already suffering from another disease that meant they were kept indoors. This is supported by the low prevalence of osteomalacia in both this and other medieval samples (Brickley et al 2007).

The health status of medieval Londoners represented by the sample from St Mary Spital indicates that the local environment presented many hazards. It posed most risks for subadults because of their developing immune systems and dependence on older individuals for care. This view of city life is supported by primary source material. Nevertheless, it appears that London maintained a strong draw for migrants and traders.

5.4 Value of a bioarchaeological approach

Rebecca Redfern

The medieval population of Britain lived through some of the most tumultuous episodes of social and environmental stresses known in British history (Fagan 2000). This period also saw a growth in urbanism and industry, and increased population mobility (Dyer 1998; 2000). These changes were accompanied by an increase in infectious diseases (eg tuberculosis) and the introduction of treponematosis, whose distribution (on current evidence) appears to be associated with trade and migration (Hudson 1963; Mays et al 2003).

We are fortunate to have a wealth of primary texts relating to the family, medicine, diet, travel and urban living (Roberts and Cox 2003, 390–6; Metzler 2006). The archaeological and historical evidence available for this period therefore makes it highly suited to bioarchaeological investigation, an approach which relies upon the integration of social, cultural and environmental data. Importantly, because this approach has been developed by those working with human remains and other environmental data, it is a system attuned to the primary goal of archaeology: to reconstruct and understand past communities (Buikstra and Beck 2006).

By employing a bioarchaeological approach, it has been demonstrated that archaeology does not have to be 'left behind in the quest for past social life' (Sofaer 2006a, 30). Analysis has shown that the health status of those buried at St Mary Spital reflects intimately the complexities of urban living. Clear age and sex patterns of disease show how the medieval life course and gender roles directly influenced injury and impairment risk, exposure to disease and age at death. The health of younger subadults was governed by socially determined age transitions, particularly the onset of weaning and the beginning of employment. We have also highlighted the range of violence experienced by females, thought to be related to their social class, the nature of their employment and their migrant status.

Migration has been a key theme of this study. By connecting skeletal data to primary source information concerning economic and social factors (such as famine and the search for employment), independent biological evidence has been provided to support data which suggest that most migrants were in their late teens and female (Goldberg 1997b). The role of the hospital in rural-to-urban migration is supported by the similarities in trauma patterns and the presence of metabolic diseases, such as rickets, between St Mary Spital and British medieval rural cemeteries. An insight into urban working lives and the health of some of the poorest members of society is suggested by the young age at death of many in the sample, and the possible osteological evidence for manual labour, including fractures and osteoarthritis (see Weiss and Jurmain 2007). The impact of the urban living environment is also attested by the prevalence of tuberculosis, sinusitis and rib periostitis, indicating that many people lived and worked in poorly ventilated buildings and in locations with inadequate sanitation and water supplies.

The function of hospitals within medieval society has also been explored, particularly through the evidence for surgical and medical care, with examples of trepanation and amputation. The enormous number of individuals buried at St Mary Spital reinforces its unique status within the city of London. It was the preferred burial ground for deaths from famines, highlighting the advantages of its suburban location and experience in coping with such calamities. Interestingly, however, it does not seem to have been used for mass burial during the Black Death.

In 1341 the responsibilities of St Mary Spital were described as being 'to receive and entertain pilgrims and the infirm who resorted hither until they were healed, and pregnant women … and also to maintain the children of women who died there in childbirth until the age of seven' (*Calendar of Close Rolls* 1339–41, 600, cited in Sheppard 1957). A bioarchaeological approach, applied to the interpretation of individuals who had relied upon the help of the hospital and had been given burial in its precincts, has demonstrated that the founders, the Augustinian order and the lay sisters and brothers fulfilled their responsibilities to the people of London.

Conclusions

5.5   Achievement of the project aims

Brian Connell and Christopher Thomas

After the lengthy process of excavation, processing and assessment, the painstaking task of osteological data recording began in 2003. Four osteologists set out to understand the skeletal population in two basic ways: in terms of its demographic characteristics and in terms of the general prevalence of disease. Once this had been grasped, attention could turn to interpreting any patterns that emerged in relation to the socio-cultural and environmental conditions of the time. The aim of this monograph was to investigate the medieval way of life in the city of London, recognising the strong relationship between urbanism and health (Schell and Ulijaszek 1999). In tandem, the skeletons were ascribed to land uses and chronological periods by a team of stratigraphic specialists.

All these remains have been subject to many complex biological and non-biological processes and to set about understanding what the data meant represented a formidable challenge. A complicating factor was that the skeletons were recovered from four different periods and those periods were further subdivided into different burial types. These archaeological and stratigraphic subdivisions had to be applied to any data sets even before any attempt could be made to apply biological ones such as age and sex.

The analysis can be set against a backdrop of changes that have taken place in British human osteology, the study of which has advanced significantly in recent years. Studies on human remains have become increasingly more integrated with mainstream archaeological research and the results from the St Mary Spital osteological analysis have been integrated with the accompanying data on the medieval archaeology, allowing a cross fertilisation of ideas. One of the keystones in this process has been the gradual shift away from singular case study approaches towards viewing biological data in a wider cultural context, something that this project took on board from the outset. In describing something of the character of current human bone research in Britain in general, not just in London, Mays (1997b; 1998) highlighted the shift towards more population-based approaches to human bone studies. We hope that this shift of emphasis in human bone work has been underpinned by the St Mary Spital project by offering a glimpse of what life was actually like for the 'average' medieval Londoner.

A rare feature of the St Mary Spital cemetery was the large number of mass burial pits, and an important achievement for the project was developing an understanding of the nature of the catastrophic assemblage. The presence of the mass burial pits gave rise to one of the more pressing questions for the project: to determine the cause of death in these pits, or at least to attempt to identify the nature of the catastrophic event. Many, if not all, of the mass burials pre-dated the Black Death, so alternative theories had to be explored (Chapter 4.3). The first three phases of mass burials could be correlated with documented occurrences of famine but hard evidence was needed to link the burials with these events. It was revealed that the clear change in the relationship between the mass burials and evidence of poor health during the first period of burials (period 14, *c* 1120–*c* 1200), to a more even distribution of stress indicators between burial groups from the second period of burials (period 15, *c* 1200–50) onwards, supported the likelihood of repeated incidences of famine throughout the duration of the cemetery's use. The archaeology of the mass burials also supported the theory that this was a period of prolonged stress and demonstrated a gradually changing response to increased mortality.

It was understood from an early stage that, due to the size of the skeletal assemblage and association with a hospital, we could expect to encounter a wide range of diseases. Naturally, it followed that another major research theme was to examine the prevalence of skeletal pathology within the cemetery and to understand this in terms of the health status of medieval Londoners (Chapter 4.4). Of particular importance within this broad theme were questions relating to how the cases of treponematosis fitted in with the often debated ideas about the introduction and emergence of the disease in Britain (Chapters 4.4 and 4.5).

The results pointed to venereal syphilis, and the presence of three subadults (including a 10–11-year-old child) with pathological changes consistent with the tertiary stage of the disease also pointed towards the presence of congenital syphilis. This suggested that syphilis affected multiple generations. St Mary Spital has the highest number of subadults (three) with evidence for treponematosis recorded from one site and it was crucial to understand the dating of the treponemal material. The dating of treponemal, and specifically syphilitic, cases by radiocarbon methods is very limited, and the individuals from St Mary Spital represent the only complete burials from Britain with this disease dated to before 1265 (period 15, *c* 1200–50), the earliest cases of this disease yet discovered in this country. This adds to a growing body of evidence of the presence of pre-Columbian treponematosis in Britain and represents an important achievement for the project.

Syphilitic skeletal changes have been identified in monastic and urban locations. This finding might reflect the limited number of medieval rural cemeteries excavated in Britain. It is not clear from this study whether the increase in the evidence for syphilis in London (and Britain as a whole) from the 15th century reflects the greater availability of skeletal samples from this date or an increasing prevalence of syphilis itself, resulting from the cumulative impact of socio-economic events: the large-scale movement of people, increasing trade, population growth and the colonisation of the Americas would have enabled the disease to spread quickly between communities.

The results of this extensive osteological project have been many, but the fundamental aims and objectives set out at the start have been largely achieved and the project has been entirely successful in achieving its goals.

5.6 Future research potential of the St Mary Spital skeletal sample

Don Walker

Only 51.7% of the assessed individuals from the medieval cemetery (5387/10,417; 51.2% of the 10,516 excavated) underwent full skeletal study (although *c* 25% were so poorly represented that skeletons could be neither sexed nor aged). While there is already a large data set, there is future potential for collecting even more information on the burial population. In addition to work that could not be undertaken within the remit of this project, and that which was not selected for detailed analysis, several areas of interest came to light as a result of the analysis. All recorded data are available to researchers through the Centre for Human Bioarchaeology.

Demography

The demographic analysis of the cemetery was based on the compilation of age and biological sex data from the skeletal remains. Although some interesting variation was evident in the proportion of females and males between certain sub-samples such as the attritional cemetery and mass pits, the elucidation of details of population structure from archaeological data is generally problematic (Chamberlain 2000, 101). One of the major factors affecting the success of such work is the difficulty of accurately establishing age at death from skeletal evidence, especially in middle-aged and older adults. Further investigation of the demographic structure could be attempted utilising a Bayesian statistical approach, especially with regard to the comparison of the attritional and mass burial samples. Previous work has shown that these methods may produce age structures that can more accurately reflect living populations from the past (Gowland and Chamberlain 2005, 155). This may prove particularly effective on large samples such as that from St Mary Spital, and will aid the investigation of population shifts due to migration, famine and the spread of infectious disease. It would also be possible to compare results from the mass pits with those from other catastrophic burial grounds, such as the East Smithfield Black Death cemetery in London.

The St Mary Spital cemetery was divided into four periods. One of these, period 16 (*c* 1250–*c* 1400), covered at least two episodes of severe mortality, the Great Famine and the Black Death. Following further analysis of dating evidence, it may be possible to distinguish between burials occurring before and after these catastrophic events, allowing comparison of demography and the health of populations living with different levels of stress. Further analysis of the mass pits, by pit, pit phase and between periods, should allow the generation of hypotheses regarding burial rates and the numbers of individuals who were dying each day and each week. This may aid the investigation of the motives behind the digging of different forms and sizes of pit within the cemetery.

Skeletal methodology allows relatively accurate ageing of subadults, and particularly of those below the age of 1 year. The detailed recording of age at death of perinatal individuals will allow further study of mortality around the time of birth. It is possible to compare the numbers dying between 38 and 40 weeks' gestation with neonates with a gestational age of 41–48 weeks in order to estimate the rates of *in utero* and post-partum mortality (Lewis 2007, 85–6). This will help to refine the evidence of mortality prevalence and risk in the early stages of life in medieval London.

Non-metric traits

Although data for skeletal non-metric traits are not presented in this volume, these data were collected for a sample of skeletons (*c* 2000 individuals) and the opportunity therefore remains for them to be analysed (see Chapter 2.2). The very size of the burial sample from St Mary Spital may also be of value for future research into methods of analysing such data. This would not necessarily apply primarily to fundamental questions of genetics and heritability, but as Tyrrell points out, to the methodological problems concerning bias in correlating trait frequency with age and sex, and with other traits (2000, 298).

Tuberculosis

A total of 100 individuals with skeletal evidence of tuberculosis were recorded from the cemetery of St Mary Spital. This large sample provides potential for significant microbiological study of the pathogen. Ongoing work by Jane Buikstra of the School of Human Evolution and Social Change, Arizona State University, in the investigation of tuberculosis phylogenies is attempting to map the co-evolution of humans and strains of tuberculosis. Samples have been taken from a number of St Mary Spital skeletons in order to identify the strains and subspecies involved, and to compare pre-contact pathogens with those recovered from American examples. As St Mary Spital contained skeletons dated to a largely pre-Columbian sequence from the Old World, the analysis of these samples may provide evidence relating to the possible contribution of Old World pathogens to those found in the New World. This work will also contribute to work on predicting future evolutionary trends in tuberculosis by expanding our knowledge from the past into the present. Sequences are to be obtained through the study of aDNA, and involve the search for IS*6110*, which is found in most forms of *M tuberculosis*, the species of bacteria which causes tuberculosis (Salo et al 1994). The analysis will also attempt to identify the species *M tuberculosis* complex. Future work involving larger sample sizes may help to provide a more accurate reflection of tuberculosis prevalence rates in medieval London. If methods are further developed, it may also be possible to conduct microbiological investigations into treponematoses, both to check diagnoses and to study the evolution of the diseases.

Trauma

A systematic radiographic study of all long bone fractures would allow the accurate measurement of apposition, alignment and deformity in each bone, together with the identification of fracture type in many cases (Roberts 2000c, 349). These data could then be compared with radiographic records of modern clinical cases to determine the possible mechanisms of fracture and the success of healing. This would have implications for the further analysis of gender-related fracture risk and access to treatment in medieval London.

Combining evidence from the radiographs with the cemetery phasing data at St Mary Spital would allow us to investigate variations in the availability and success of treatment over time. It might also contribute to the study of specific fracture types in the past, such as 'parry' fractures, where the mechanism is often disputed. Radiographic investigation could accurately assess fracture type in the large number of mid and distal shaft ulna injuries within the cemetery sample, helping us to refine the interpretation of these fractures in the medieval urban context. The large sample would also enable detailed study of fractures in other areas of the body, such as the dentition, hands and feet, in order to search for patterns of injury. Left side elbow injuries to male adolescents, often involving the medial epicondyle of the humerus, merit further research, possibly alongside a study of the handedness of the affected individuals. This form of evidence, together with other signs of biomechanical and repetitive stress such as os acromiale, may offer insights into forms of subadult gender-related activity. There is also scope for a more detailed analysis of vertebral body and rib fractures, both of which feature prominently in the male sample.

Furthermore, there is potential for further study of individuals with skeletal evidence of severe debilitating diseases, often the result of congenital or developmental defects. This would include the analysis of the level of impairment and the consequences for the individuals concerned. A study of relative robusticity might provide clues as to the ways in which bodies responded to impairment within their socio-cultural context, and how people lived and coped with daily life in the urban environment of medieval London.

Markers of stress

Systematic radiographic examination of long bones, and especially the distal tibiae, would allow the study of the prevalence of Harris lines (Suter et al 2008). These radio-dense transverse lines represent growth interruption in subadulthood, possibly due to non-specific stress (Resnick 2002, 3465). Comparison of the data with other indicators of childhood stress, such as enamel hypoplasia and cribra orbitalia, could provide pertinent information on the relationship between these skeletal changes.

Many perinatal individuals from the cemetery may have been stillborn and future histological sectioning of the dentition could determine the presence of neonatal lines, enabling further exploration of *in utero* stress (Scheuer and Black 2000, 162; Smith et al 2006).

Unfortunately, because the growth of individuals under 3 years old could not be determined, it was not possible to investigate growth faltering as an outcome of weaning (King and Ulijaszek 1999, 176–7).

Diet

There is much potential for the further study of dental remains from St Mary Spital. The destruction of enamel and dentine through dental attrition is a common finding in medieval assemblages. The evidence from calculus deposits and periodontal disease suggests that diet improved over time, especially after the 14th century. A study of variation in rates of dental attrition by period would allow us to examine whether this apparent softening of the diet was reflected on the occlusal surfaces of the teeth. Other evidence of diet may be gained through the study of food particles preserved in dental calculus. The large number of periapical lesions, which number over 2000, will allow for a detailed study within this medieval population, enabling the aetiology and prevalence of each type of lesion and the consequences for the individuals concerned to be analysed.

Stable isotopes

There is potential for the investigation of intra-cemetery stable isotope variation. The diet of those in different burial locations, such as within the church, can be compared with the open cemetery in order to detect any evidence of status-related change. If similar food element proportions were encountered in different status groups, this might result from subtle variations in diet, such as the consumption of different cuts from the same animals (Müldner and Richards 2006, 235). It may also be possible to identify changing tastes, such as preferences for fish and the relative importance of riverine, estuarine and marine resources over time in a large urban centre such as London. The relatively well-phased open cemetery at St Mary Spital offers the potential of observing changes and trends in diet throughout the medieval period. The mass burial pits may produce evidence of variation in diet in times of stress, whether through infectious disease, famine or natural disaster. The inclusion of nitrogen isotope work, together with the use of animal bone in an attempt to provide a control for diagenesis within the differing burial environments, may permit the comparison of different areas and phases of the cemetery. The study of nitrogen isotopes may also provide data on weaning stress in young subadults (Mays et al 2002c).

Other work

While the osteological database used for the recording of the skeletal assemblage from Spitalfields contained several features that aided the accurate systematic recording of individuals, there are areas in which amendments should produce more detailed data collection in future. One example of this is the recording of sinusitis, where the methodology would be enhanced by allowing the presence or absence of sinuses to be noted. This would produce more accurate prevalence rates for the infection, and would also allow comparison with other evidence of respiratory disease, such as rib periostitis (Roberts 2007, 804).

Finally, the data gathered from St Mary Spital can be used to compare the health of medieval Londoners with those who lived in the city at other times, such as the Roman and post-medieval periods and the periods immediately preceding and following the use of the cemetery, placing the sample from St Mary Spital within the temporal framework of London's past.

FRENCH AND GERMAN SUMMARIES

Résumé

Charlette Sheil-Small

Le prieuré augustinien et hôpital de Notre-Dame hors Bishopsgate (connu par la suite sous le nom de Notre-Dame de Spital) dans les quartiers est de Londres, était l'un d'environ 200 hôpitaux fondés en Angleterre au XIIe siècle. Il devint l'un des plus grands hôpitaux du pays à l'époque médiévale, servant de refuge aux malades, aux pauvres, aux vieux et aux sans-abris. En avance d'un projet de réaménagement du quartier de l'ancien marché de Spitalfields, une série de fouilles archéologiques avait été exécutée entre 1992 et 2007. Durant la principale phase de fouilles de 1999 à 2002, les restes de plus de 10 500 personnes furent récupérés. Ce cimetière médiéval se trouvait à l'intérieur d'un site archéologique complexe, mais une précision sans précédent au niveau de la datation et des phases fut obtenue au moyen d'un programme ciblé qui alliait des techniques de datation relatives (stratigraphiques) à des techniques absolues (radiocarbone). Les inhumations étaient divisées en quatrepériodes chronologiques : la période 14, entre vers 1120 et vers 1200 ; la période 15, entre vers 1200 et vers 1250 ; la période 16, entre vers 1250 et vers 1400 ; et la période 17, entre vers 1400 et 1539.

En 2003, quatre ostéologues débutèrent la tâche colossale de l'étude des inhumations de Notre-Dame de Spital. Ce volume présente les résultats, l'interprétation et la discussion de l'analyse ostéologique d'un échantillon de 5387 sujets provenant du cimetière. Parmi les découvertes significatives, se trouvent quelques-uns des cas de syphilis les plus anciens d'Europe. Les résultats nous donnent un unique aperçu de la vie des londoniens médiévaux entre le XIIe siècle et le début du XVIe siècle et ont favorisé la discussion des effets de la vie urbaine sur la santé des enfants, le rôle et l'influence de l'hôpital, ainsi que les raisons derrière l'enterrement collectif de près de 4000 personnes.

La majorité des inhumations collectives datent d'avant l'épidémie de peste connue sous le nom de « Mort Noire » (1348 et 1349), mais les sources historiques révèlent une série de fréquentes famines et épidémies avec des dates qui correspondent de près. Les plus importantes phases d'inhumations collectives, au milieu du XIIIe siècle, correspondent à une période de famine, dont on pense qu'elle a été causée par des variations climatiques dues à une énorme éruption volcanique aux tropiques. L'analyse ostéologique a également révélé que la population enterrée au cimetière avait subi une période de stress suivi, ce qui reflétait probablement des incidences répétées de famine.

L'analyse de ce groupe indique que la vie à Londres favorisait la transmission de maladies infectieuses et augmentait le risque de blessures, par comparaison avec la vie dans d'autre villes et cités ou à la campagne.

Zusammenfassung

Iris Rodenbüsch

Das Augustinerkloster und Krankenhaus St. Mary ohne Bishopsgate (später bekannt als St. Mary Spital) in Ost London, war eines von rund 200 Krankenhäusern die im 12. Jh. in England gegründet wurden. Im Mittelalter wurde es zu einem der größten Krankenhäuser des Landes und bot Schutz für die Kranken, Armen, Alten und Obdachlosen.

Im Vorfeld eines Sanierungsantrages für das Gebiet des ehemaligen Spitalfield Marktes wurden in den Jahren von 1992 bis 2007 eine Reihe archäologischer Evaluierungen durchgeführt. Während der Hauptphase der Ausgrabungen, von 1999 bis 2002, wurden die menschlichen Überreste von mehr als 10.500 Individuen geborgen. Dieser mittelalterliche Friedhof befand sich innerhalb einer komplexen archäologischen Fundstätte, doch mit Hilfe eines gezielten Programms das relative (stratigraphische) und absolute (Radiokarbonmethode) Datierungsmethoden kombinierte, wurde eine bis dahin noch nie dagewesene Genauigkeit in der Datierung und Phaseneinteilung erzielt. Die Bestattungen wurden in vier chronologische Perioden unterteilt: Periode 14, ca. 1120–ca. 1200; Periode 15, ca. 1200–50; Periode 16, ca. 1250–ca. 1400 und Periode 17, ca. 1400–1539.

Im Jahr 2003 begannen vier Osteologen mit der enormen Aufgabe, die Bestattungen von St. Mary Spital zu untersuchen. Der vorliegende Band präsentiert die Ergebnisse, Auswertungen und Besprechungen osteologischer Analysen einer Skelettserie von 5387 Individuen aus dem Friedhof. Zu den bedeutenden Entdeckungen gehören auch einige der frühesten Fälle von Syphilis in Europa. Die Ergebnisse liefern einen einzigartigen Einblick in das Leben mittelalterlicher Londoner des 12. bis frühen 16. Jhs und haben Diskussionen über die Auswirkungen städtischen Lebens auf die Gesundheit von Kindern, die Rolle und den Einfluss des Krankenhauses, sowie die Gründe für die Massenbestattung von fast 4000 Menschen ermöglicht.

Die Massengräber datieren zum Grossteil noch in die Zeit vor der Pestepidemie, auch bekannt als der Schwarze Tod (1348–9), aber historische Quellen zeigen eine Reihe von wiederkehrenden und zeitlich nahe zusammenliegenden Hungersnöten und Epidemien. Die umfangreichsten Phasen der Massenbestattungen, in der Mitte des 13. Jhs, decken sich mit einer Periode der Hungersnot die vermutlich eng mit klimatischen Veränderungen verbunden ist, die durch eine Vulkaneruption in den Tropen verursacht wurde. Auch die osteologischen Analysen zeigten, dass die auf dem Friedhof beigesetzte Bevölkerung eine längere Stressphase durchlief die wahrscheinlich auf wiederholte Fälle von Hungersnot zurückzuführen ist.

Die Analyse dieser Skelettgruppe lässt erkennen, dass das Leben in London im Vergleich zu anderen Städten oder auf dem Land, die Übertragung ansteckender Krankheiten förderte und das Verletzungsrisiko erhöhte.

BIBLIOGRAPHY

Ackroyd, P, 2001 *London: the biography*, London

Albarella, U, 2006 Pig husbandry and pork consumption in medieval England, in *Food in medieval England: diet and nutrition* (eds C M Woolgar, D Serjeantson and T Waldron), 72–87, Oxford

Akpala, C O, 1993 Perinatal mortality in a northern Nigerian rural community, *J Roy Soc Health* 113(3), 124–7

Albrecht, G L, and Devlieger, P J, 1999 The disability paradox: high quality of life against all odds, *Social Science and Medicine* 48(8), 977–88

Alexandre-Bidon, D, and Lett, D, 1999 *Children in the Middle Ages, 5th–15th centuries*, Notre Dame, IN

Allen, P L, 2000 *The wages of sin: sex, disease, past and present*, London

Alvarez, J O, Caceda, J, Woolley, T W, Carley, K W, Baiocchi, N, Caravedo, L, and Navia, J M, 1993 A longitudinal study of dental caries in the primary teeth of children who suffered from infant malnutrition, *J Dental Res* 72(12), 1573–6

Amulree, Lord, 1964 Monastic infirmaries, in *The evolution of hospitals in Britain* (ed F N L Poynter), 11–26, London

Anderson, J, Wakely, J, and Carter, A, 1992 Medieval example of metastatic carcinoma: a dry bone, radiological, and SEM study, *Amer J Phys Anthropol* 89, 309–23

Anderson, P J, 1995 Fractures of the facial skeleton in children, *Injury* 26(1), 47–50

Anderson, S, 1994 The human remains from Gisborough Priory, Cleveland 1985–6, unpub Engl Heritage Ancient Monuments Lab rep 47/94

Anderson, T, 2000 Congenital conditions and neoplastic disease in British palaeopathology, in *Human osteology in archaeology and forensic science* (eds M Cox and S Mays), 199–226, London

Anderson, T, 2002 A bipartite patella in a juvenile from a medieval context, *Int J Osteoarchaeol* 12, 297–302

Anderson, T, 2005 The human bone, in *St Gregory's Priory, Northgate, Canterbury: excavations 1988–91* (eds M Hicks and A Hicks), The Archaeology of Canterbury ns 2, Canterbury

Anderson, T, Arcini, C, Anda, S, Tangerud, A, and Robertsen, G, 1986 Suspected endemic syphilis (treponarid) in 16th-century Norway, *Med Hist* 30, 341–50

Anon, 1265 (1890) *Flores historiarum* (ed H R Luard), Rolls Ser 95(2), 419–61, London

Antoine, D M, Hillson, S W, Keene, D, Dean, M C, and Milne, C, 2005 Using growth structures in teeth from victims of the Black Death to investigate the effects of the Great Famine (AD 1315–1317), *Amer J Phys Anthropol* 126, 65

Apley, A G, and Solomon, L, 2000 *Concise system of orthopaedics and fractures*, London

Arber, S, and Ginn J (eds), 1995 *Connecting gender and ageing: a sociological approach*, Buckingham

Arcini, C, 1999 Health and disease in early Lund: Osteopathologic studies of 3305 individuals buried in the first cemetery area of Lund 990–1536, unpub PhD thesis, Lund Univ

Armelagos, G J, 2004 Emerging disease in the third epidemiological transition, in *The changing face of disease: implications for society* (eds N Mascie-Taylor, J Peters and

S T McGarvey), 1–22, London

Arrizabalaga, J, Henderson, J, and French, R, 1997 *The great pox*, New Haven and London

Aufderheide, A C, and Rodríguez-Martín, C, 1998 *The Cambridge encyclopedia of human paleopathology*, Cambridge

Azouz, E M, Karamitsos, C, Reed, M H, Baker, L, Kozlowski, K, and Hoeffel, J C, 1993 Types and complications of femoral neck fractures in children, *Pediatric Radiology* 23(6), 415–40

Bailey, M, 1996 Demographic decline in late medieval England: some thoughts on recent research, *Econ Hist Rev* 2 ser 49, 1–19

Barber, G, Watt, I, and Rogers, J, 1997 A comparison of radiological and palaeopathological diagnostic criteria for hyperostosis frontalis interna, *Int J Osteoarchaeol* 7, 157–64

Barnes, E, 1994 *Developmental defects of the axial skeleton in paleopathology*, Niwot, CO

Barness, K A, Cha, E S, Bensard, D D, Calkins, C M, Partrick, D A, Karrer, F M, and Strain, J D, 2004 The positive predictive value of rib fractures as an indicator of nonaccidental trauma in children, *J Trauma, Infection and Critical Care* 54(6), 1107–10

Barrett, J H, Locker, A M, and Roberts, C M, 2004 'Dark Age economics' revisited: the English fish bone evidence AD 600–1600, *Antiquity* 78, 618–36

Barrett, J H, Johnstone, C, Harland, J, Van Neer, W, Ervynck, A, Makowiecki, D, Heinrich, D, Hufthammer, A K, Enghoff, I B, Amundsen, C, Christiansen, J S, Jones, A K G, Locker, A, Hamilton-Dyer, S, Jonsson, L, Lõugas, L, Roberts, C, and Richards, M, 2008 Detecting the medieval cod trade: a new method and first results, *J Archaeol Sci* 35, 850–61

Barron, C M, 2004 *London in the later Middle Ages: government and people, 1200–1500*, Oxford

Baxter, J E, 2005 *The archaeology of childhood: children, gender, and material culture* Oxford

Beck, L A, 2006 Kidder, Hooton, Pecos, and the birth of bioarchaeology, in Buikstra and Beck 2006, 83–94

Beck, R T, 1974 *The cutting edge: early history of the Surgeons of London*, London

Bekvalac, J, and Kausmally, T, 2011 The human bone, in Grainger and Phillpotts 2011, 166–88

Bello, S M, Thomann, A, Signoli, M, Dutour, O, and Andrews, P, 2006 Age and sex bias in the reconstruction of past population structures, *Amer J Phys Anthropol* 129, 24–38

Bennett, J M, 1992 Conviviality and charity in medieval and early modern England, *Past and Present* 134, 19–41

Berry, A C, and Berry, R J, 1967 Epigenetic variation in the human cranium, *J Anat* 101, 361–79

Binstock, R H, and George, L K (eds), 2001 *Handbook of aging and the social sciences*, 5 edn, New York

Blakey, M L, Leslie, T E, and Reidy, J P, 1994 Frequency and chronological distribution of dental enamel hypoplasia in enslaved African Americans: a test of the weaning hypothesis, *Amer J Phys Anthropol* 95, 371–83

Boddington, A, 1987 From bones to population: the problem of numbers, in *Death, decay and reconstruction: approaches to archaeology and forensic science* (eds A Boddington, A N Garland and R C Janaway), 180–97, Manchester

Boehrer, B T, 1990 Early modern syphilis, *J Hist Sexuality* 1(2), 197–214

Bogin, B, 1998 Evolutionary and biological aspects of childhood, in *Biosocial perspectives on children* (ed C Panter-Brick), 10–44, Cambridge

Bogin, B, 2001 *The growth of humanity*, London

Bogin, B, Wall, M, and MacVean, R, 1992 Longitudinal analysis of adolescent growth of Ladino and Mayan school children in Guatemala: effects of environment and sex, *Amer J Phys Anthropol* 89, 447–57

Boldsen, J L, and Mollerup, L, 2006 Outside St Jørgen: leprosy in the medieval Danish city of Odense, *Amer J Phys Anthropol* 130, 344–51

Boocock, P, Roberts, C A, and Manchester, K, 1995 Maxillary sinusitis in medieval Chichester, *Amer J Phys Anthropol* 98, 483–95

Boswell, J, 1988 *The kindness of strangers: the abandonment of children in Western Europe from late antiquity to the Renaissance*, Harmondsworth

Bouwman, A S, and Brown, T A, 2005 The limits of biomolecular palaeopathology: ancient DNA cannot be used to study venereal syphilis, *J Archaeol Sci* 32, 703–13

Bovey, A, 2002 *Monsters and grotesques in medieval manuscripts*, London

Boylston, A, and Ogden, A R, 2005 A study of Paget's disease at Norton Priory, Cheshire, England: a medieval religious house, in *Proceedings of the fifth annual conference of the British Association for Biological Anthropology and Osteoarchaeology* (eds S R Zakrzewski and M Clegg), BAR Int Ser 1383, 69–76, Oxford

Boylston, A, and Roberts, C, 1997 Lincoln excavations 1972–87: report on the human skeletal remains, unpub Engl Heritage Ancient Monuments Lab rep 13/97

Brickley, M, 2000 The diagnosis of metabolic disease in archaeological bone, in *Human osteology in archaeology and forensic science* (eds M Cox and S Mays), 183–98, London

Brickley, M, 2006 Rib fractures in the archaeological record: a useful source of sociocultural information?, *Int J Osteoarchaeol* 16, 61–75

Brickley, M, and Ives, R, 2006 Skeletal manifestations of infantile scurvy, *Amer J Phys Anthropol* 129, 163–72

Brickley, M, and Ives, R 2008 *The bioarchaeology of metabolic bone disease*, London

Brickley, M, and McKinley, J 2004 *Guidelines to the standard for recording human remains*, IFA Pap 7, Southampton and Reading

Brickley, M, Mays, S, and Ives, R, 2005 Skeletal manifestations of vitamin D deficiency osteomalacia in documented historical collections, *Int J Osteoarchaeol* 15, 389–403

Brickley, M, Mays, S, and Ives, R, 2007 An investigation of skeletal indicators of vitamin D deficiency in adults: effective markers for interpreting past living conditions and pollution levels in 18th and 19th century Birmingham, England, *Amer J Phys Anthropol* 132, 67–79

Bridges, P A, 1993 The effect of variation in methodology on the outcome of osteoarthritic studies, *Int J Osteoarchaeol* 3, 289–95

Bibliography

Brimblecombe, P, 1982 Early urban climate and atmosphere, in *Environmental archaeology in the urban context* (eds A R Hall and H K Kenward), CBA Res Rep 43, 10–25, York

Brison, R J, and Pickett, C W, 1992 Non-fatal farm injuries on 117 eastern Ontario beef and dairy farms: a one year study, *Amer J Ind Medicine* 21, 623–36

Broadbent, E, Petrie, K J, Main, J, and Weinman, J, 2006 The brief illness perception questionnaire, *J Psychosomatic Res* 60, 631–7

Brooks, S T, and Suchey, J M, 1990 Skeletal age determination based on the os pubis: a comparison of the Ascádi-Nemeskéri and Suchey-Brooks methods, *J Hum Evol* 5, 227–38

Brothwell, D R, 1981 (1963) *Digging up bones: the excavation, treatment and study of human skeletal remains*, 3 edn, London

Brothwell, D, 1994 On the possibility of urban–rural contrasts in human population palaeobiology, in *Urban–rural connexions: perspectives from environmental archaeology* (eds A R Hall and H K Kenward), Symposia Ass Environ Archaeol 12, Oxbow Monograph 47, 129–36, Oxford

Brown, K H, Black, R E, Lopez de Romana, G, and Creed de Kanashiro, H, 1989 Infant-feeding practices and their relationship with diarrheal and other diseases in Huascar (Lima), Peru, *Pediatrics* 83(1), 31–40

Buckberry, J, and Hadley, D M, 2008 An Anglo-Saxon execution cemetery at Walkington Wold, Yorkshire, *Oxford Archaeol* 26(3), 309–29

Budd, P, Montgomery, J, Evans, J, and Trickett, M, 2004 Human lead exposure in England from approximately 5500 BP to the 16th century AD, *Science of the Total Environment* 318, 45–58

Buikstra, J E, and Beck, L A (eds), 2006 *Bioarchaeology: the contextual analysis of human remains*, London

Buikstra, J E, and Ubelaker, D H (eds), 1994 *Standards for data collection from human skeletal remains*, Arkansas Archaeol Survey Res Ser 44, Fayetteville, AR

Bush, H, and Zvelebil, M, 1991 Pathology and health in past societies: an introduction, in *Health in past societies: biocultural interpretations of human skeletal remains in archaeological contexts* (eds H Bush and M Zvelebil), BAR Brit Ser 567, 3–10, Oxford

Buzhilova, A, 1999 Medieval examples of syphilis from European Russia, *Int J Osteoarchaeol* 9, 271–6

Byers, S, 2002 *Introduction to forensic anthropology: a textbook*, Boston, MA

Carman, J, 1997 Approaches to violence, in *Material harm* (ed J Carman), 1–23, Glasgow

Carrott, J, 1999 An assessment of intestinal parasitic nematode egg remains from excavations at Common Parts Basement, Spital Square, London E1 (site code: SRP98), Environmental Archaeol Unit, York, unpub rep 99/20, www.york.ac.uk/inst/chumpal/EAU-reps/eau99-28.pdf (accessed 3 October 2011)

Chamberlain, A, 2000 Problems and prospects in palaeodemography, in *Human osteology in archaeology and forensic science* (eds M Cox and S Mays), 101–15, London

Chamberlain, A, 2006 *Demography in archaeology*, Cambridge

Choe, M K, and Razzaque, A, 1990 Effect of famine on child survival in Matlab, Bangladesh, *Asia-Pacific Population J*, 5(2), 53–72

Claassen, C (ed), 1992 Workshop 3: teaching and seeing gender, in *Exploring gender through archaeology: selected papers from the 1991 Boone Conference* (ed C Claassen), Monographs in World Archaeol 11, 137–54, Madison, WI

Claessens, A A, Schouten, J S, van den Ouweland, F A, and Valkenburg, H A, 1990 Do clinical findings associate with radiographic osteoarthritis of the knee?, *Ann Rheumatic Diseases* 49, 771–4

Clark, G A, Hall, N R, Armelagos, G J, Borkan, G A, Panjabi, M M, and Wetzel, T F, 1986 Poor growth prior to early childhood: decreased health and life-span in the adult, *Amer J Phys Anthropol* 70, 145–60

Clark, W A, 1937 History of fracture treatment up to the 16th century, *J Bone and Joint Surgery* 19, 47–63

Clarke, M, Locker, D, Berall, G, Pencharz, P, Kenny, D J, and Judd, P, 2006 Malnourishment in a population of young children with severe early childhood caries, *Pediatric Dentistry* 28(3), 254–9

Cocchiarella, L, and Andersson, G B J (eds), 2000 *Guide to the evaluation of permanent impairment*, San Francisco, CA

Cohen, J J, 1999 *Of giants: sex, monsters and the Middle Ages*, London

Cohen, M N, and Crane-Kramer, G, 2003 The state and future of paleoepidemiology, in *Emerging pathogens: the archaeology, ecology, and evolution of infectious disease* (eds C L Greenblatt and M Spigelman), 79–91, Oxford

Coleman, D, 1999 Human migration: effects on people, effects on populations, in *Patterns of human growth* (ed B Bogin), 115–45, Cambridge

Conheeney, J, 1997 The human bone, in Thomas, C, Sloane, B, and Phillpotts, C, *Excavations at the priory and hospital of St Mary Spital, London*, MoLAS Monogr Ser 1, 218–31, London

Conheeney, J, 1999 Reconstructing the demography of medieval London from studies on human skeletal material: problems and potential, *Trans London Middlesex Archaeol Soc* 50, 78–86

Conheeney, J, 2004 The human bone, in Sloane, B, and Malcolm, G, *Excavations at the priory of the Order of the Hospital of St John of Jerusalem, Clerkenwell, London*, MoLAS Monogr Ser 20, 394–405, London

Conheeney, J, 2005 The human skeletal remains, in Schofield and Lea 2005, 255–62

Conheeney, J, 2007 The human bone, in Miller and Saxby 2007, 255–77

Conkey, M W, 2005 The archaeology of gender today: new vistas, new challenges, in *Gender in cross-cultural perspective*, 4 edn (eds C B Brettell and C F Sargent), 53–62, Upper Saddle River, NJ

Conkey, M, and Spector, J D, 1998 Archaeology and the study of gender, in *Reader in gender archaeology* (eds K Hays-Gilpin and D S Whitley), 11–46, London

Connell, B, 2002 The cemetery population from Spitalfields Market, London: an osteological pilot study and post-excavation assessment, unpub MOL rep

Connell, B, and Rauxloh, P, 2003 A rapid method for recording human skeletal data, unpub MOL rep

Connell, B, and White, W, 2011 Human remains, in Dyson, T, Samuel, M, Steele, A, and Wright, S M, *The Cluniac priory and abbey of St Saviour Bermondsey, Surrey: excavations 1984–95*, MOLA Monogr Ser 50, 263–74, London

Cortes, M I, Marcenes, W, and Sheiham, A, 2002 Impact of traumatic injuries to the permanent teeth on the oral health-related quality of life in 12–14 year old children, *Community Dentistry and Oral Epidemiology* 30(3), 193–8

Courtenay, W H, 2002 Behavioral factors associated with disease, injury, and death among men: evidence and implications for prevention, *Int J Men's Health* 1(3), 281–342

Courtenay, W H, 2003 Key determinants of health and well-being of men and boys, *Int J Men's Health* 2(1), 1–30

Covey, H C, 1998 *Social perceptions of people with disabilities in history*, Springfield, IL

Cowal, L, Mikulski, R, and White, W, 2008 The human bone, in Grainger et al 2008, 42–55

Cox, M, 2000 Ageing adults from the skeleton, in *Human osteology in archaeology and forensic science* (eds M Cox and S Mays), 61–81, London

Crane-Kramer, G M, 2000 The paleoepidemiological examination of treponemal infection and leprosy in medieval populations from northern Europe, unpub PhD thesis, Univ Calgary

Crawford, S, 1999 *Children in Anglo-Saxon England*, Stroud

Culpeper, N 1653 *The complete herbal*, available online at www.completeherbal.com/culpepper/completeherbalindex.htm (accessed 6 October 2011)

Currey, J D, and Butler, G, 1975 The mechanical properties of bone tissue in children, *J Bone and Joint Disease* 57(6), 810–14

Curtis, V, 2001 Dirt, disgust, and disease: is hygiene in our genes?, *Perspectives in Biology and Medicine* 44(1), 17–31

Dandy, D J, and Edwards, D J, 1998 *Essential orthopaedics and trauma*, Edinburgh

Davidson, M, 2006 Universal design: the work of disability in an age of globalization, in *The disability studies reader* (ed L J Davis), 2 edn, 117–30, London

Davis, A, in prep Plant remains, in Harward et al in prep

Dawes, J D, and Magilton, J R, 1980 *The cemetery of St Helen-on-the-Walls, Aldwark*, Archaeology of York 12/1, London

Daykin, A 2005 St Botolph's Hall Building 2: an archaeological evaluation report, unpub MOL rep

Daykin, A, Holder, N, and Jeffries, N, with Harward, C, and Thomas, C, in prep *The Spitalfields suburb 1539–1860: excavations at Spitalfields Market, London E1, 1991–2007*, MOLA Monogr Ser, London

Derevenski, J S, 2000 *Children and material culture*, London

Dettwyler, K, 1991 Can paleopathology provide evidence for compassion?, *Amer J Phys Anthropol* 84, 375–84

DeWitte, S N, 2009 The effect of sex on risk of mortality during the Black Death in London AD 1349–50, *Amer J Phys Anthropol* 139, 222–34

DeWitte, S N, 2010 Sex differences in frailty in medieval England, *Amer J Phys Anthropol* 143, 285–97

DeWitte, S N, and Bekvalac, J, 2010 Oral health and frailty in the medieval cemetery of St Mary Graces, *Amer J Phys Anthropol* 142, 341–54

Díaz-Andreu, M, Lucy, S, Babic, S, and Edwards, D N, 2005 *The archaeology of identity: approaches to gender, age, status, ethnicity and religion*, London

Dickel, D N, and Doran, G H, 1989 Severe neural tube defect syndrome from the Early Archaic of Florida, *Amer J Phys Anthropol* 80, 325–34

Disabled Living Foundation, 2006 *Disability awareness*, DLF Factsheet, London

Dixon, R, and Roberts, C A, 2001 Modern and ancient scourges: the application of ancient DNA to the analysis of tuberculosis and leprosy from archaeologically derived human remains, *Ancient Biomolecules* 3(3), 181–93

Dolk, H, and Vrijheid, M, 2003 The impact of environmental pollution on congenital anomalies, *Brit Med Bull* 68(1), 25–45

Donoghue, H D, Hershkovitz, I, Minnikin, D E, Besra, G S, Lee, O Y-C, Galili, E, Greenblatt, C L, Lemma, E, Spigelman, M, and Bar-Gal, G K, 2009 Biomolecular archaeology of ancient tuberculosis: response to 'Deficiencies and challenges in the study of ancient tuberculosis DNA' by Wilbur et al (2009), *J Archaeol Sci* 36, 2797–804

Dunwoodie, L, 1995 250 Bishopsgate, an archaeological evaluation, unpub MOL rep

Duray, S M, 1990 Deciduous enamel defects and caries susceptibility in a prehistoric Ohio population, *Amer J Phys Anthropol* 81, 27–34

Dyer, C, 1989 *Standards of living in the later Middle Ages*, 1 edn, London

Dyer, C, 1998 *Standards of living in the later Middle Ages: social change in England c 1200–1500*, rev edn, Cambridge

Dyer, C, 2000 *Everyday life in medieval England*, London

Dyer, C, 2002 *Making a living in the Middle Ages*, London

Dyer, C C, 2006 Seasonal patterns in food consumption in the later Middle Ages, in *Food in medieval England: diet and nutrition* (eds C M Woolgar, D Serjeantson and T Waldron), 201–14, Oxford

Dyson, T, and Ó Gráda, C (eds), 2002 *Famine demography: perspectives from the past and present*, Oxford

Effros, R B, 2001 Immune system activity, in *Handbook of the biology of aging* (eds E J Masoro and S N Austad), 5 edn, 324–50, London

Egan, G, 2007 Material culture of care for the sick: some excavated evidence from English medieval hospitals and other sites, in *The medieval hospital and medical practice* (ed B S Bowers), 65–76, Aldershot

Elverland, H H, and Voss, R, 1997 Facial fractures: a life style disease among young men?, *Tidsskrift for den Norske laegeforening* 117(23), 3354–8

Erdal, Y S, 2006 A pre-Columbian case of congenital syphilis from Anatolia (Nicaea, 13th century AD), *Int J Osteoarchaeol* 16, 16–33

Fábrega, H, 1999 *Evolution of sickness and healing*, London

Faccia, K J, and Williams, R C, 2008 Schmorl's nodes: clinical significance and implications for the bioarchaeological record,

Int J Osteoarchaeol 18, 28–44

Fagan, B, M, 2000 *The little ice age: how climate made history 1300–1850*, New York

Farley, M and Manchester, K, 1989 The cemetery of the leper hospital of St Margaret, High Wycombe, Buckinghamshire, *Med Archaeol* 33, 82–9

Farmer, S, and Pasternak, C B, 2003 *Gender and difference in the Middle Ages*, Minneapolis, MN

Farr, W, 1846 The influence of scarcities and of the high prices of wheat on the mortality of the people of England, *J Stat Soc London* 9(2), 158–74

Fay, I, 2006 Text, space and the evidence of human remains in English late medieval and Tudor disease culture: some problems and possibilities, in *Social archaeology of funerary remains* (eds R Gowland and C Knüsel), 190–208, Oxford

Fédération Dentaire Internationale, 1971 Two-digit system of designating teeth, *Int Dental J* 21, 104–6

Ferembach, D, Schwidetzky, I, and Stoukal, M, 1980 Recommendations for age and sex diagnoses of skeletons, *J Hum Evol* 9, 517–49

Ferreira, P C, Amarante, J M, Silva, P N, Rodrigues, J M, Choupina, M P, Silva, A C, Barbosa, R F, Cardoso, M A, and Reis, J C, 2005 Retrospective study of 1251 maxillofacial fractures in children and adolescents, *Plastic and Reconstructive Surgery* 115(6), 1500–8

Ffrench, G, 1979 Water in relation to human disease, in *Environmental medicine* (eds G M Howe and J A Loraine), 46–69, London

Fildes, V, 1986 *Breasts, bottles and babies: a history of infant feeding*, Edinburgh

Finlay, N (ed), 1999 Disability and archaeology, *Archaeol Rev Cambridge* 15(2)

Finnegan, M, 1978 Non-metric variation in the infra-cranial skeleton, *J Anatomy* 125, 23–37

Finucane, R C, 1995 *Miracles and pilgrims: popular beliefs in medieval England*, London

Fiorato, V, Boylston, A, and Knüsel, C (eds), 2000 *Blood red roses: the archaeology of a mass grave from the battle of Towton AD 1461*, Oxford

Fisman, D N, 2007 Seasonality of infectious diseases, *Annual Review of Public Health* 28, 127–43

Fitzpatrick, K, and LaGory, M, 2000 *The ecology of risk in the urban landscape: unhealthy places*, London

Fitz-Thedmar, A, 1274 Cronica Londoniensis, in *Ex rerum Anglicarum scriptoribus saec XIII*, Monumenta Germaniae historica, Scriptores 28, 1888, 534, Hanover

Fleming, P, 2001 *Family and household in medieval England*, Basingstoke and New York

Fraser, J, 1914 *Tuberculosis of the bones and joints in children*, London

Freeth, C, 2000 Dental health in British antiquity, in *Human osteology in archaeology and forensic science* (eds M Cox and S Mays), 227–38, London

Freidal, K, Petermann, F, Reichel, D, Steiner, A, Warschburger, P, and Weiss, H R, 2002 Quality of life in women with idiopathic scoliosis, *Spine* 27(4), 87–91

Fuller, B T, Richards, M P, and Mays, S A, 2003 Stable carbon and nitrogen isotope variations in tooth dentine serial sections from Wharram Percy, *J Archaeol Sci* 30, 1673–84

Gabris, K, Tarjan, I, and Rozsa, N, 2001 Dental trauma in children presenting for treatment at the Department of Dentistry for Children and Orthodontics, Budapest, 1985–99, *Dental Traumatology* 17(3), 103–8

Galloway, A (ed), 1999 *Broken bones: anthropological analysis of blunt force trauma*, Springfield, IL

Galloway, J A, 2000 One market or many? London and the grain trade of England, in *Trade, urban hinterlands and market integration c 1300–1600* (ed J A Galloway), 23–43, London

Geddes, J, 1996 Medieval women in the heavy metal industries, in *Women in industry and technology* (ed A Devonshire and B Wood), 101–9, London

genome.gov, 2011 Chromosome abnormalities fact sheet, www.genome.gov/11508982#6 (accessed 2 June 2011)

Gilchrist, R, 2000 Archaeological biographies: realizing human lifecycles, course and histories, *World Archaeol* 31(3), 325–8

Gilchrist, R, 2002 Women's archaeology? Political feminism, gender theory and historical revision, in *Reader in gender archaeology* (eds K Hays-Gilpin and D S Whitley), 47–56, London

Gilchrist, R, and Sloane, B, 2005 *Requiem: the medieval monastic cemetery in Britain*, London

Glass, G B, 1991 Continuous eruption and periodontal status in pre-industrial dentitions, *Int J Osteoarchaeol* 1, 265–71

Glencross, B, and Stuart-Macadam, P, 2000 Childhood trauma in the archaeological record, *Int J Osteoarchaeol* 10, 198–209

Goldberg, P J P, 1986 Female labour, service and marriage in the late medieval urban north, *Northern Hist* 22, 18–38

Goldberg, P J P, 1991 The public and the private: women in the pre-plague economy, in *Thirteenth-century England III* (eds P R Coss and S D Lloyd), 75–89, Woodbridge

Goldberg, P J P, 1992 *Women, work and the life cycle in a medieval economy*, Oxford

Goldberg, P J P, 1997a 'For better, for worse': marriage and economic opportunity for women in town and country, in *Women in medieval English society* (ed P J P Goldberg), 108–25, Oxford

Goldberg, P J P, 1997b Marriage, migration, and servanthood: the York Cause paper evidence, in *Women in medieval English society* (ed P J P Goldberg), 1–15, Oxford

Goldberg, P J P, 2004 *Medieval England: a social history 1250–1550*, London

Good, B J, 2003 *Medicine, rationality and experience: an anthropological perspective*, Cambridge

Goodman, A H, and Armelagos, G J, 1989 Infant and childhood morbidity and mortality risks in archaeological populations, *World Archaeol* 21(2), 225–43

Goodman, A H, and Martin, D L, 2002 Reconstructing health profiles from skeletal remains, in *The backbone of history: health and nutrition in the western hemisphere* (eds R H Steckel and J C Rose), 11–60, Cambridge

Goodman, A H, and Song, R-J, 1999 Sources of variation in estimated ages at formation of linear enamel hypoplasias, in *Human growth in the past: studies from bones and teeth* (eds R D

Hoppa and C M Fitzgerald), 210–40, Cambridge

Goodman, A H, Thomas, R B, Swedlund, A C, and Armelagos, G J, 1988 Biocultural perspectives on stress in prehistoric, historical, and contemporary population research, *Yearbook Phys Anthropol* 31, 169–202

Gordon, E C, 1991 Accidents among medieval children as seen from the miracles of six English saints and martyrs, *Med Hist* 35, 145–63

Gottfried, R S, 1983 *The Black Death*, London

Gottfried, R S, 1984 English medical practitioners, 1340–1530, *Bull Hist Medicine* 58, 164–82

Gottfried, R S, 1986 *Doctors and medicine in medieval England 1340–1530*, Princeton, NJ

Gowland, R, 2006 Ageing the past: examining age identity from funerary evidence, in *Social archaeology of funerary remains* (eds R Gowland and C Knüsel), 143–54, Oxford

Gowland, R L, and Chamberlain, A T, 2005 Detecting plague: palaeodemographic characterisation of a catastrophic death assemblage, *Antiquity* 79, 146–57

Grainger, I, and Phillpotts, C, 2011 *The Cistercian abbey of St Mary Graces, East Smithfield, London*, MOLA Monogr Ser 44, London

Grainger, I, Hawkins, D, Cowal, L, and Mikulski, R, 2008 *The Black Death cemetery, East Smithfield, London*, MoLAS Monogr Ser 43, London

Grassly, N C, Fraser, C, and Garnett, G P, 2005 Host immunity and synchronized epidemics of syphilis across the United States, *Nature* 433, 417–21

Gratz, R R, 1979 Accidental injury in childhood: a literature review on pediatric trauma, *J Trauma* 19(8), 551–5

Grauer, A L, 1991 Patterns of life and death: the paleodemography of medieval York, in *Health in past societies: biocultural interpretations of human skeletal remains from archaeological contexts* (eds H Bush and M Zvelebil), BAR Int Ser 567, 67–80, Oxford

Grauer, A L, and Roberts, C A, 1996 Paleoepidemiology, healing and possible treatment of trauma in the medieval cemetery population of St Helen-on-the-Walls, York, England, *Amer J Phys Anthropol* 100, 531–44

Gregory, W, 1876 William Gregory's chronicle of London, 1189–1249, in *The historical collections of a citizen of London in the 15th century* (ed J Gairdner), Camden Soc, new ser 17, 57–67, London, available online at www.british-history.ac.uk/report.aspx?compid=45552

Grenville, J, 1997 *Medieval housing*, London

Griffiths, R A, 1988 The later Middle Ages (1290–1485), in *The Oxford illustrated history of Britain* (ed K O Morgan), 166–222, Oxford

Grimm, H, 1980 Sex differences in the frequency of bone fracture in prehistoric and historic times, in *Physical anthropology of European populations* (eds I Schwidetzky, A B Chiarelli and O Necrasov), 347–9, The Hague

Grupe, G, 1988 Metastasizing carcinoma in a medieval skeleton: differential diagnosis and etiology, *Amer J Phys Anthropol* 75, 369–74

Gurdjian, E S, and Webster, J E, 1958 *Head injuries, mechanisms, diagnosis and management*, London

Gustafson, G, and Koch, G, 1974 Age estimation up to 16 years of age based on dental development, *Odontologisk Revy* 25, 297–306

Guy, H, Masset, C, and Baud, C A, 1997 Infant taphonomy, *Int J Osteoarchaeol* 7, 221–9

Guy, J, 1988 The Tudor age (1485–1603), in *The Oxford illustrated history of Britain* (ed K O Morgan), 223–85, Oxford

Hagestad, G O, and Dannefer, D, 2001 Concepts and theories of aging: beyond microfication in social science approaches, in Binstock and George 2001, 3–21

Halberstam, J, 1998 *Female masculinity*, London

Hall, A J, and Peckham, C S, 1997 Infections in childhood and pregnancy as a cause of adult disease: methods and examples, *Brit Med Bull* 53, 10–23

Hall, A R, and Kenward, H K, 2006 Development-driven archaeology: bane or boon for bioarchaeology, *Oxford J Archaeol* 25(3), 213–24

Hallbäck, D-A, 1976–7 A medieval(?) bone with a copper plate support, indicating an open surgical treatment, *OSSA* 3(4), 63–82

Hamilakis, Y, Pluciennik, M, and Tarlow, S (eds), 2002 *Thinking through the body: archaeologies of corporeality*, New York

Hammer, C U, Clausen, H B, and Dansgaard, W, 1980 Greenland ice sheet evidence of post-glacial volcanism and its climatic impact, *Nature* 288, 230–5

Hammond, P W, 1998 *Food and feast in medieval England*, Stroud

Han, E-S, van Remmen, H, Steinhelper, M, Pahlavanai, M A, Strong, J R, and Richardson, A, 2001 Effect of age on gene expression, in Binstock and George 2001, 140–78

Hanawalt, B A, 1993 *Growing up in medieval London*, Oxford

Hanson, C L, 1992 Population-specific stature reconstruction for medieval Trondheim, Norway, *Int J Osteoarchaeol* 2, 289–95

Hareven, T K, 2001 Historical perspectives on aging and family relations, in Binstock and George 2001, 141–59

Harlow, M and Laurence, R, 2002 *Growing up and growing old in ancient Rome: a life course approach*, London

Harper, K N, Liu, H, Ocampo, P S, Steiner, B M, Martin, A, Levert, K, Wang, D, Sutton, M, and Armelagos, G J, 2008 The sequence of the acidic repeat protein (arp) gene differentiates venereal from nonvenereal *Treponema pallidum* subspecies, and the gene has evolved under strong positive selection in the subspecies that causes syphilis, *Immunology and Medical Microbiology* 53(3), 322–32

Harrison, G A, Tanner, J M, Pilbeam, D R, and Baker, P T, 1988 *Human biology: an introduction to human evolution, variation, growth, and adaptability*, 3 edn, Oxford

Harvey, B, 1993 *Living and dying in England 1100–1540: the monastic experience*, Oxford

Harvey, B F, 2006 Monastic pittances in the Middle Ages, in *Food in medieval England: diet and nutrition* (eds C M Woolgar, D Serjeantson and T Waldron), 215–22, Oxford

Harward, C, 2002 St Botolph's Hall and the Curate's House, 35 Spital Square, London, E1: a report on the evaluation, unpub MOL rep

Harward, C, Holder, N, and Thomas, C, with Bowsher, D, McKenzie, M, and Pitt, K, in prep *The medieval priory and hospital of St Mary Spital and the Bishopsgate suburb: excavations at Spitalfields Market, London E1, 1991–2007*, MOLA Monogr Ser, London

Hatcher, J, 1996 Plague, population and the English economy, 1348–1530, in *British population history from the Black Death to the present day* (ed M Anderson), Cambridge

Hauspie, R C, and Susanne, C, 2000 Genetics of child growth, in Ulijaszek et al 2000, 124–8

Hawkey, D E, 1998 Disability, compassion and the skeletal record: using musculoskeletal stress markers (MSM) to construct an osteobiography from early New Mexico, *Int J Osteoarchaeol* 8, 326–40

Hazzard, W R, 2001 Aging, health, longevity, and the promise of biomedical research: the perspective of a gerontologist and geriatrician, in Binstock and George 2001, 445–56

Heer, F, 1993 *The medieval world: Europe 1100–1350*, London

Hildebolt, C F, and Molnar, S, 1991 Measurement and description of periodontal disease in anthropological studies, in *Advances in dental anthropology* (eds M A Kelley and C S Larsen), 225–40, New York

Hillson, S, 1996 *Dental anthropology*, Cambridge

Hillson, S, 2000 Dental pathology, in *Biological anthropology of the human skeleton* (eds M A Katzenberg and S R Saunders), 249–86, New York

Hillson, S, 2008 Dental pathology, in *Biological anthropology of the human skeleton* (eds M A Katzenberg and S R Saunders), 2 edn, 301–40, New York

Hillson, S, and Bond, S, 1997 Relationship of enamel hypoplasia to the pattern of tooth crown growth: a discussion, *Amer J Phys Anthropol* 104, 89–103

Hobbes, T, 1985 (1651) *Leviathan*, London

Hockey, J, and James, A, 1995 *Social identities across the life course*, London

Holst, M, 2005 Artefacts and environmental evidence: the human bone, in *Blue Bridge Lane and Fishergate House, York, report on excavations: July 2000 to July 2002* (eds C A Spall and N J Toop), York, www.archaeologicalplanningconsultancy.co.uk/mono/001/rep_bone_hum1a.html

Holst, M, and Coughlan, J, 2000 Dental health and disease, in Fiorato et al 2000, 77–89

Holt, R, and Rosser, G, 1990 The English town in the Middle Ages, in *The medieval town 1200–1540* (eds R Holt and G Rosser), 1–18, London

Holzel, H, 1993 Infection in pregnancy and the neonatal period, in *Fetal and neonatal pathology* (ed J W Keeling), 2 edn, 295–321, London

Hooper, B, 1996 A medieval depiction of infant-feeding in Winchester Cathedral, *Med Archaeol* 40, 230–3

Hoppa, R D, and Vaupel, J W, 2002 *Paleodemography: age distributions from skeletal samples*, Cambridge

Horden, P, 2007 A non-natural environment: medicine without doctors and the medieval European hospital, in *The medieval hospital and medical practice* (ed B S Bowers), 133–45, Aldershot

Horrox, R, and Ormrod, W M, 2006 *A social history of England, 1220–1500*, Cambridge

Hosea Blewett, H J, Cicalo, M C, Holland, C D, and Field, C J, 2008 The immunological components of human milk, *Advances in Food and Nutritional Research* 54, 45–80

Howe, G M, 1973 The environment, its influences and hazards to health, in *Environmental medicine* (eds G M Howe and J A Lorraine), 2 edn, 1–8, London

Howe, G M, 1976 Environmental factors in disease, in *Health and the environment: Vol 3* (eds J Lenihan and W W Fletcher), 1–30, London

Howe, G M, 1997 *People, environment, disease and death: a medical geography of Britain throughout the ages*, Cardiff

Hubert, J (ed), 2000 *Madness, disability and social exclusion: the archaeology and anthropology of 'difference'*, London

Hudson, E H, 1963 Treponematosis and pilgrimage, *Amer J Med Sci* 246, 645–56

Hudson, E H, 1964 Treponematosis and African slavery, *Brit J Venereal Diseases* 40, 43–52

Humphrey, L, 2000 Interpretation of the growth of past populations, in *Children and material culture* (ed J Sofaer Derevenski), 193–205, Cambridge

Humphrey, L T, and King, T, 2000 Childhood stress: a lifetime legacy, *Anthropologie* 38(1), 33–49

Hunnius, T E von, Yang, D, Eng, B, Waye, J S, and Saunders, S R, 2007 Digging deeper into the limits of ancient DNA research on syphilis, *J Archaeol Sci* 34, 2091–100

Hunt, T, 1999 *The medieval surgery*, Woodbridge

Hurley, M F, Scully, O M B, and McCutcheon, S W J, 1997 *Late Viking age and medieval Waterford excavations 1986–1992*, Waterford

Hylland Eriksen, T, 2001 *Small places, large issues: an introduction to social and cultural anthropology*, 2 edn, London

Idler, E L, 1993 Perceptions of pain and perceptions of health, *Motivation and Emotion* 17(3), 205–24

Ip, S, Chung, M, Raman, G, Chew, P, Magula, N, DeVine, D, Trikalinos, T and Lau, J, 2007 Breastfeeding and maternal and infant health outcomes in developed countries, *Evidence Report Technology Assessment* 153, 1–186

Iscan, M Y, Loth, S R, and Wright, R K, 1984 Age estimation from the rib by phase analysis: white males, *J Forensic Sci* 29, 1094–104

Iscan, M Y, Loth, S R, and Wright, R K, 1985 Age estimation from the rib by phase analysis: white females, *J Forensic Sci* 30, 853–63

Izant, R J, and Hubay, C A, 1966 The annual injury of 15,000,000 children: a limited study of childhood accidental injury and death, *J Trauma* 6(1), 65–74

Jacobi, K P, and Danforth, M E, 2002 Analysis of interobserver scoring patterns in porotic hyperostosis and cribra orbitalia, *Int J Osteoarchaeol* 12, 248–58

Jakob, B, 2004 Prevalence and patterns of disease in early medieval populations: a comparison of skeletal samples from fifth to eighth century AD Britain and southwest Germany, unpub PhD thesis, Univ Durham

James, A, 1998 From the child's point of view: issues in the social construction of childhood, in *Biosocial perspectives on children* (ed C Panter-Brick), 45–65, Cambridge

James, P M C, and Miller, W A, 1970 Dental conditions in a group of mediaeval English children, *Brit Dental J* 128, 391–6

Janssens, P A, 1987 A copper plate on the upper arm in a burial at the church in Vrasene (Belgium), *J Paleopathology* 1, 15–8

Jantos, M, and Kiat, H, 2007 Prayer as medicine: how much have we learnt?, *Med J Aust* 186(10), S51–53

Jenkins, J H, 1996 Culture, emotion, and psychiatric disorder, in *Medical anthropology contemporary theory and method*, rev edn (eds C F Sargent and T M Johnson), 71–87, London

Jessop, A, and James, M R, 1896 *The life and miracles of St William of Norwich by Thomas of Monmouth*, Cambridge

Jewell, H, 1996 *Women in medieval England*, Manchester

Jiménez-Brobeil, S A, Al Oumaoui, I, and du Souich, Ph, 2007 Childhood trauma in several populations from the Iberian peninsula, *Int J Osteoarchaeol* 17, 189–98

Johansson, I, Sellstrom, A K, Rajan, B P, and Parameswaran, A, 1992 Salivary flow and dental caries in Indian children suffering from chronic malnutrition, *Caries Res* 26(1), 38–43

Jordan, W C, 1996 *The great famine: northern Europe in the early 14th century*, Princeton, NJ

Jorde, L B, Fineman, R M, and Martin, R A, 1983 Epidemiology and genetics of neural tube defects: an application of the Utah genealogical database, *Amer J Phys Anthropol* 62, 23–31

Joseph, K, and Black, S, 2006 Report on isotopic and trace element analysis on human skeletal remains from the Spitalfields archaeological site, Tower Hamlets, London, Univ Reading unpub rep

Judd, M A, 2002a One accident too many?, *Brit Mus Stud in Ancient Egypt and Sudan* 3, 42–54

Judd, M A, 2002b Ancient injury recidivism: an example from the Kerma period of ancient Nubia, *Int J Osteoarchaeol* 12, 89–106

Judd, M, 2004 Trauma in the city of Kerma: ancient versus modern injury patterns, *Int J Osteoarchaeol* 14, 34–51

Judd, M A, 2008 The parry problem, *J Archaeol Sci* 35, 1658–66

Judd, M A, and Roberts, C A, 1998 Fracture patterns at the medieval leper hospital in Chichester, *Amer J Phys Anthropol* 105, 43–55

Judd, M A, and Roberts, C A, 1999 Fracture trauma in a medieval British farming village, *Amer J Phys Anthropol* 109, 229–43

Julkunen, H, Heinonen, O P, and Pyörälä, K, 1971 Hyperostosis of the spine in an adult population, *Ann Rheumatic Diseases* 30, 605–12

Jurmain, R D, 1999 *Stories from the skeleton: behavioral reconstruction in human osteology*, Amsterdam

Jurmain, R D, and Kilgore, L, 1995 Skeletal evidence of osteoarthritis: a palaeopathological perspective, *Ann Rheumatic Diseases* 54, 443–50

Karras, R M, 1996 *Common women: prostitution and sexuality in medieval England*, Oxford

Karras, R M, 2002 *From boys to men: formation of masculinity in late medieval Europe*, London

Katzenberg, M A, 2000 Stable isotope analysis: a tool for studying past diet, demography, and life history, in *Biological anthropology of the human skeleton* (eds M A Katzenberg and S R Saunders), 1 edn, 305–28, New York

Katzenberg, M A, 2008 Stable isotope analysis: a tool for studying past diet, demography, and life history, in *Biological anthropology of the human skeleton* (eds M A Katzenberg and S R Saunders), 2 edn, 413–41, New York

Katzenberg, M A, Herring, D A, and Saunders, S R, 1996 Weaning and infant mortality: evaluating the skeletal evidence, *Yearbook Phys Anthropol* 39, 177–99

Keenan, A M, Tennant, A, Fear, J, Emery, P, and Conaghan, P G, 2006 Impact of multiple joint problems on daily living tasks in people in the community over age fifty-five, *Arthritis and Rheumatism* 55, 757–64

Keene, D J, 1982 Rubbish in medieval towns, in *Environmental archaeology in the urban context* (eds A R Hall and H K Kenward), CBA Res Rep 43, 26–30, London

Keene, D J, 1984 A new study of London before the Great Fire, *Urban History Yearbook 1984*, 11–21, London

Keene, D J, 1989 Medieval London and its region, *London J* 14(2), 99–111

Keene, D J, 1990 Suburban growth, in *The medieval town 1200–1540* (eds R Holt and G Rosser), 97–119, London

Keenleyside, A, Bertulli, M, and Fricke, H C, 1997 The final days of the Franklin expedition: new skeletal evidence, *Arctic* 50(1), 36–46

Kelley, M A, and Micozzi, M S, 1984 Rib lesions in chronic pulmonary tuberculosis, *Amer J Phys Anthropol* 65, 381–6

Kelly, D, and Coutts, A G, 2000 Early nutrition and the development of immune function in the neonate, *Proc Nutrition Soc* 59(2), 177–85

Kelmar, C J H, Harvey, D, and Simpson, C (eds), 1995 *The sick newborn baby*, London

Kemkes-Grottenthaler, A, 2005 The short die young: the interrelationship between stature and longevity – evidence from skeletal remains, *Amer J Phys Anthropol* 128, 340–7

Keys, A, Brozek, J, Henschel, A, Mickelsen, O, and Taylor, H L, 1950 *The biology of human starvation*, Minneapolis, MN

Kimmel, M S, 2004 *The gendered society*, 2 edn, Oxford

King, S E, and Ulijaszek, S J, 1999 Invisible insults during growth: contemporary theories and past populations, in *Human growth in the past: studies from bones and teeth* (eds R Hoppa and C Fitzgerald), 161–82, Cambridge

Kiple, K F, 1997 *Plague, pox and pestilence*, London

Kirmayer, L J, 1992 The body's insistence on meaning: metaphor as presentation and representation in illness experience, *Med Anthropol Quarterly* 6(4), 323–46

Klauber, M R, Barrett-Connor, E, Hofsetter, C R, and Micik, S H, 1986 A population-based study of nonfatal childhood injuries, *Preventative Medicine* 15, 139–49

Klingele, K E, and Kocher, M S, 2002 Little league elbow: valgus overload injury in the paediatric athlete, *Sports Medicine* 32(15), 1005–15

Klonoff, H, and Robinson, G C, 1967 Epidemiology of head injuries in children: a pilot study, *Canadian Med Assoc J* 96(19), 1308–11

Knodel, J, and Kinter, H, 1977 The impact of breast feeding patterns on the biometric analysis of infant mortality, *Demography* 14(4), 391–409

Knüsel, C J, 1999 Orthopaedic disability: some hard evidence, *Archaeol Rev Cambridge* 15(2), 31–53

Knüsel, C, 2000 Activity-related skeletal change, in Fiorato et al 2000, 103–18

Knüsel, C, and Boylston, A, 2000 How has the Towton project contributed to our knowledge of medieval and later warfare?, in Fiorato et al 2000, 169–88

Knüsel, C, Kemp, R L, and Budd, P, 1995 Evidence for remedial medical treatment of a severe knee injury from the Fishergate Gilbertine monastery in the city of York, *J Archaeol Sci* 22, 369–84

Kolodziej, H, Szklarska, A, and Malina, R M, 2001 Young adult height of offspring born to rural-to-urban migrant parents and urban born parents, *Amer J Hum Biol* 13(1), 30–4

Komlos, J, 1993 The decline of mortality in Europe, *J Econ Hist* 53(1), 165–6

Kovats, R S, and Hajat, S, 2007 Heat stress and public health: a critical review, *Annu Rev Public Health* 29, 9.1–9.15

Lakin, K, 2008 Medieval diet: evidence for a London signature?, in *Food and drink in archaeology 1* (eds S Baker, M Allen, S Middle and K Poole), 65–72, Totnes

Lamb, H, H, 1995 *Climate, history and the modern world*, London

Lambert, P M, 2002 Rib lesions in a prehistoric Puebloan sample from southwestern Colorado, *Amer J Phys Anthropol* 117, 281–92

Landin, L A, 1983 Fracture patterns in children: analysis of 8,682 fractures with special reference to incidence, etiology and secular changes in a Swedish urban population 1950–79, *Acta Orthopaedica Scandinavica*, Supplementum 202, 1–109

Larsen, C S, 1999 *Bioarchaeology: interpreting behavior from the human skeleton*, Cambridge

Lary, J M, and Paulozzi, L J, 2001 Sex differences in the prevalence of human birth defects: a population-based study, *Teratology* 64(5), 237–51

Lavigne, S E, and Molto, J E, 1995 System of measurement of the severity of periodontal disease in past populations, *Int J Osteoarchaeol* 5, 265–73

Levene, M I, Tudehope, D, and Thearle, J, 2000 *Essentials of neonatal medicine*, Oxford

Leventhal, J M, Thomas, S A, Rosenfield, N S, and Markowitz, R I, 1993 Fractures in young children: distinguishing child abuse from unintentional injuries, *Amer J Diseases of Children* 147(1), 87–92

Lewis, J H, 1995 *Jedburgh Abbey: the archaeology and architecture of a border abbey*, Soc Antiq Scotl Monogr Ser 10, Edinburgh

Lewis, M E, 2000 Non-adult palaeopathology: current status and future potential, in *Human osteology in archaeology and forensic science* (eds M Cox and S Mays), 39–57, London

Lewis, M E, 2002 *Urbanisation and child health in medieval and post-medieval England: an assessment of the morbidity and mortality of non-adult skeletons from the cemeteries of two urban and two rural sites in England (AD 850–1859)*, BAR Brit Ser 339, Oxford

Lewis, M E, 2003 A comparison of health in past rural, urban and industrial England, in *The environmental archaeology of industry* (eds P Murphy and P E J Wiltshire), Symposia Ass Environ Archaeol 20, 154–61, Oxford

Lewis, M E, 2004 Endocranial lesions in non-adult skeletons: understanding their aetiology, *Int J Osteoarchaeol* 14, 82–97

Lewis, M E, 2007 *The bioarchaeology of children*, Cambridge

Lewis, M E, and Gowland, R L, 2007 Brief and precarious lives: infant mortality in contrasting sites from medieval and post-medieval England (AD 850–1859), *Amer J Phys Anthropol* 134, 117–29

Lewis, M E, and Roberts, C A, 1997 Growing pains: the interpretation of stress markers, *Int J Osteoarchaeol* 7, 581–6

Lewis, M E, Roberts, C A, and Manchester, K, 1995 Comparative study of the prevalence of maxillary sinusitis in later medieval urban and rural populations in northern England, *Amer J Phys Anthropol* 98, 497–506

Leyser, H, 1995 *Medieval women: a social history of women in England 450–1500*, New York

Li, L, and Moore, D, 1998 Acceptance of disability and its correlates, *J Social Psychology* 138, 13–25

Lieverse, A R, 1999 Diet and the aetiology of dental calculus, *Int J Osteoarchaeol* 9, 219–32

Lilley, J M, Stroud, G, Brothwell, D R, and Williamson, M H, 1994 *The Jewish burial ground at Jewbury*, Archaeology of York 12/3, York

Loe, L K, 2003 Health and socio-economic status in early medieval Wales: an analysis of health indicators and their socio-economic implications in an early medieval skeletal population from the cemetery site at Llandough, Glamorgan, unpub PhD thesis, Univ Bristol

Loe, L K, 2006 Analysis of the human bone from sites 1 and 2, in *Excavations at St James's Priory, Bristol* (ed R Jackson), Bristol and Region Archaeol Services Monogr, 105–20, Oxford

Lorentzon, M, 1992 Medieval London: care of the sick: a selective view of the literature, *Hist Nursing J* 4, 100–10

Lovejoy, C O, Meindl, R S, Pryzbeck, T R, and Mensforth, R P, 1985 Chronological metamorphosis of the auricular surface of the ilium: a new method for the determination of adult skeletal age at death, *Amer J Phys Anthropol* 68, 15–28

Lovell, N C, 1997 Trauma analysis in paleopathology, *Yearbook Phys Anthropol* 40, 139–70

Lovell, N C, 2000 Paleopathological description and diagnosis, in *Biological anthropology of the human skeleton* (eds M A Katzenberg and S R Saunders), 217–48, New York

Lowe, J J, and Walker, M J C, 1997 *Reconstructing Quaternary environments*, London

Lucy, S, 2005 The archaeology of age, in Díaz-Andreu et al 2005, 43–66

Lumey, L H, and Van Poppel, F W, 1994 The Dutch famine of 1944–45: mortality and morbidity in past and present generations, *Social Hist Medicine* 7(2), 229–46

Maat, G J R, 2005 Two millennia of male stature development and population health and wealth in the Low Countries, *Int J Osteoarchaeol* 15, 276–90

Macchiarelli, R, Bondioli, L, Censi, L, Hernaez, M K, Salvadei, L, and Sperduti, A, 1994 Intra- and interobserver concordance in scoring Harris lines: a test on bone sections and radiographs, *Amer J Phys Anthropol* 95, 77–83

McDade, T W, 2003 Life history theory and the immune system: steps toward a human ecological immunology, *Yearbook Phys Anthropol* 46, 100–25

McDonnell, K G T, 1978 *Medieval London suburbs*, London

McElroy, A, and Townsend, P K, 1996 *Medical anthropology in ecological perspective*, 3 edn, Oxford

McEwan, J M, Mays, S, and Blake, G M, 2005 The relationship of bone mineral density and other growth parameters to stress indicators in a medieval juvenile population, *Int J Osteoarchaeol* 15, 155–63

McIntosh, M K, 2005 *Working women in English society, 1300–1620*, Cambridge

MacIntyre, S, Hunt, K, and Sweeting, H, 1996 Gender differences in health: are things really as simple as they seem?, *Social Science Medicine* 42(4), 617–24

McKenzie, M, and Thomas, C, in prep *The northern cemetery of Roman London: excavations at Spitalfields Market, London E1, 1991–2007*, MOLA Monogr Ser, London

McMaster, M J, and Singh, H, 1999 Natural history of congenital kyphosis and kyphoscolosis: a study of one hundred and twelve patients, *J Bone and Joint Surgery* 81(10), 1367–83

McRae, R, 2003 *Pocketbook of orthopaedics and fractures*, Edinburgh

McRae, R, and Kinninmonth, A W G, 1997 *Orthopaedics and trauma*, Edinburgh

Maddern, P C, 1992 *Violence and social order: East Anglia 1422–42*, Oxford

Maher, V, 1992 Breast-feeding in cross-cultural perspective: paradoxes and proposals, in *The anthropology of breast-feeding: natural law or social construct* (ed V Maher), 1–37, Oxford

Manchester, K, 1987 Skeletal evidence for health and disease, in *Death, decay and reconstruction: approaches to archaeology and forensic science* (eds A Boddington, A N Garland and R C Janaway), 163–79, Manchester

Maresh, M M, 1970 Measurements from roentgenograms, in *Human growth and development* (ed R W McCammon), Springfield, IL

Margerison, B J, and Knüsel, C J, 2002 Paleodemographic comparison of a catastrophic and an attritional death assemblage, *Amer J Phys Anthropol* 119, 134–43

Marshall, P D, 2003 Reconstructing the environmental impact of past metallurgical activities, in *The environmental archaeology of industry* (eds P Murphy and P E J Wiltshire), Symposia Ass Environ Archaeol 20, 10–18, Oxford

Martin, E (ed), 2000 *Oxford concise medical dictionary*, 5 edn, Oxford

Massardo, L, Watt, I, Cushnaghan, J, and Dieppe, P, 1989 Osteoarthritis of the knee joint: an eight year prospective study, *Ann Rheumatic Diseases* 48, 893–7

Mata, L, 1983 Epidemiology of acute diarrhea in childhood: an overview, in *Acute diarrhea: its nutritional consequences in children* (ed J A Bellanti), 3–22, New York

Matthews, L G, 1962 *History of pharmacy in Britain*, Edinburgh and London

Matthews, L G, 1967 *The royal apothecaries*, London

Mays, S, 1991a The burials from the Whitefriars friary site, Buttermarket, Ipswich, Suffolk (excavated 1986–8), unpub Engl Heritage Ancient Monuments Lab rep 17/91

Mays, S 1991b The mediaeval burials from the Blackfriars friary, School Street, Ipswich, Suffolk (excavated 1983–5), unpub Engl Heritage Ancient Monuments Lab rep 16/91, parts I and II

Mays, S, 1992 Taphonomic factors in a human skeletal assemblage, *Circaea* 9(2), 54–8

Mays, S A, 1996 Healed limb amputations in human osteoarchaeology and their causes: a case study from Ipswich, UK, *Int J Osteoarchaeol* 6, 101–13

Mays, S, 1997a Carbon stable isotope ratios in medieval and later human skeletons from northern England, *J Archaeol Sci* 24, 561–7

Mays, S, 1997b A perspective on human osteology in Britain, *Int J Osteoarchaeol* 7, 600–4

Mays, S, 1998 The archaeological study of medieval English human populations, AD 1066–1540, in *Science in archaeology: an agenda for the future* (ed J Bayley), 195–210, London

Mays, S A, 2003 The rise and fall of rickets in England, in *The environmental archaeology of industry* (eds P Murphy and P E J Wiltshire), Symposia Ass Environ Archaeol 20, 144–53, Oxford

Mays, S, 2006a The osteology of monasticism in medieval England, in *Social archaeology of funerary remains* (eds R Gowland and K Knüsel), 179–89, Oxford

Mays, S, 2006b A possible case of surgical treatment of cranial blunt force injury from medieval England, *Int J Osteoarchaeol* 16, 95–103

Mays, S, 2006c Spondylolysis, spondylolisthesis, and lumbo-sacral morphology in a medieval English skeletal population, *Amer J Phys Anthropol* 131, 352–62

Mays, S, 2007 The human remains, in *Wharram Percy: the churchyard* (ed E A Clark), York

Mays, S and Taylor, G M, 2002 Osteological and biomolecular study of two possible cases of hypertrophic osteoarthropathy from medieval England, *J Archaeol Sci* 29, 1267–76

Mays, S, Brickley, M, and Dodwell, N, 2002a *Human bones from archaeological sites*, Centre for Archaeology Guidelines, Engl Heritage, Swindon

Mays, S, Fysh, E, and Taylor, G M, 2002b Investigation of the link between visceral surface rib lesions and tuberculosis in a medieval skeletal series from England using ancient DNA, *J Archaeol Sci* 119, 27–36

Mays, S A, Richards, M P, and Fuller, B T, 2002c Bone stable isotope evidence for infant feeding in mediaeval England, *Antiquity* 76, 654–6

Mays, S, Crane-Kramer, G, and Bayliss, A, 2003 Two probable cases of treponemal disease of medieval date from England, *Amer J Phys Anthropol* 120, 133–43

Mays, S, Brickley, M, and Ives, R, 2006 Skeletal manifestations of rickets in infants and young children in a historic population from England, *Amer J Phys Anthropol* 129, 362–74

Mays, S, Harding, C, and Heighway, C, 2007 *Wharram: a study of settlement on the Yorkshire Wolds: Vol 11, The churchyard*, York

Merbs, C F, 2001 Degenerative spondylolisthesis in ancient and historic skeletons from New Mexico Pueblo sites, *Amer J Phys Anthropol* 116, 285–95

Meskell, L M, 1999 Writing the body in archaeology, in *Reading the body: representations and remains in the archaeological record* (ed A E Rautman), 13–21, Philadelphia, PA

Metzler, I, 2006 *Disability in medieval Europe: thinking about physical impairment during the high Middle Ages, c 1100–1400*, London

Miles, A, 1991 *Women, health and medicine*, Buckingham

Miles, A E W, 1989 *An early Christian chapel and burial ground on the Isle of Ensay, Outer Hebrides, Scotland, with a study of the skeletal remains*, BAR Brit Ser 212, Oxford

Miller, E, Ragsdale, B D, and Ortner, D J, 1996 Accuracy in dry bone diagnosis: a comment on palaeopathological methods, *Int J Osteoarchaeol* 6, 221–9

Miller, P, and Saxby, D, 2007 *The Augustinian priory of St Mary Merton, Surrey: excavations 1976–90*, MoLAS Monogr Ser 34, London

Milner, G R, Wood, J W, and Bolsden, J L, 2000 Palaeodemography, in *Biological anthropology of the human skeleton* (eds M A Katzenburg and S R Saunders), 467–96, New York

Mitchell, D T, and Snyder, S L, 2000 Introduction: disability studies and the double bind of representation, in *The body and physical difference: discourses of disability* (eds D T Mitchell and S L Snyder), 1–31, Ann Arbor, MI

Mitchell, P, 2003a The archaeological study of epidemic and infectious disease, *World Archaeol* 35(2), 171–9

Mitchell, P D, 2003b Pre-Columbian treponemal disease from 14th century AD Safed, Israel, and implications for the medieval eastern Mediterranean, *Amer J Phys Anthropol* 121, 117–24

Mitchell, P D, and Redfern, R C, 2008 Diagnostic criteria for developmental dislocation of the hip in human skeletal remains, *Int J Osteoarchaeol* 18, 61–71

Mitchell, P D, Nagar, Y, and Ellenblum, R, 2006 Weapon injuries in the 12th century crusader garrison of Vadum Iacob Castle, Galilee, *Int J Osteoarchaeol* 16, 145–55

Moerman, D, 2002 *Meaning, medicine and the 'placebo effect'*, Cambridge

Mokyr, J, and Ó Gráda, C, 1999 Famine disease and famine mortality: lessons from Ireland, 1845–50, Papers 99/12, College Dublin, Dept of Political Economy

Møller-Christensen, V, 1953 Location and excavation of the first Danish leper graveyard from the Middle Ages – St Jørgen's farm, Naestved, *Bulletin of the History of Medicine* 27(2), 112–23

Møller-Christensen, V, 1958 *Bogen om Æbelholt Kloster*, Copenhagen

Møller-Christensen, V, 1969 Provisional results of the examination of the whole Naestved leprosy hospital churchyard – ab 1250–1550 AD, *Nordisk Medicinhistorisk Aarsbok*, 29–36

Molleson, T, and Cox, M (eds), 1993 *The Spitalfields project: Vol 2, The anthropology: the middling sort*, CBA Res Rep 86, York, http://archaeologydataservice.ac.uk/archives/view/cba_rr/rr86.cfm

Moore, H L, 1988 *Feminism and anthropology*, Cambridge

Moore, J, and Scott, E, 1997 *Invisible people and processes: writing gender and childhood into European archaeology*, Leicester

Moore, M K, 2008 Body mass estimation from the human skeleton in terms of paleopathology of the vertebrae, proximal tibia and heel spurs, *Amer J Phys Anthropol* 135(S46), 157

Moorrees, C F A, Fanning, E A, and Hunt, E E Jr, 1963a Age variation of formation stages for ten permanent teeth, *J Dental Research* 42(6), 1490–502

Moorrees, C F A, Fanning, E A, and Hunt, E E Jr, 1963b Formation and resorption of three deciduous teeth in children, *Amer J Phys Anthropol* 21, 205–13

Moorthy, J S D, and Swischuk, L E, 1997 Expanding the concept of the toddler's fracture, *Radiographics* 17(2), 367–76

Morant, G M, 1931 A study of the recently excavated Spitalfields crania, *Biometrika* 23, 191–248

Müldner, G, and Richards, M P, 2005 Fast or feast: reconstructing diet in later medieval England by stable isotope analysis, *J Archaeol Sci* 32, 39–48

Müldner, G, and Richards, M P, 2006 Diet in medieval England: the evidence from stable isotopes, in *Food in medieval England: diet and nutrition* (eds C M Woolgar, D Serjeantson and T Waldron), 228–38, Oxford

Müldner, G, and Richards, M P, 2007a Diet and diversity at later medieval Fishergate: the isotopic evidence, *Amer J Phys Anthropol* 134, 162–74

Müldner, G, and Richards, M P, 2007b Stable isotope evidence for 1500 years of human diet at the city of York, UK, *Amer J Phys Anthropol* 133, 682–97

Munby, J, 1987 Medieval domestic buildings, in *Urban archaeology in Britain* (eds J Schofield and R Leech), CBA Res Rep 61, 155–66, London

Nicholas, D, 1997a *The growth of the medieval city: late antiquity to the early 14th century*, London

Nicholas, D, 1997b *The later medieval city, 1300–1500*, London

Nicholson, H, 1997 Women on the Third Crusade, *J Medieval Hist* 23(4), 335–49

Niemeyer, P, Weinberg, A, Schmitt, H, Kreuz, P C, Ewerbeck, V, and Kasten, P, 2006 Stress fractures in the juvenile skeletal system, *Int J Sports Medicine* 27(3), 242–9

NINDS 2002 Traumatic brain injury: hope through research, Nat Inst of Neurological Disorders and Stroke, NIH Publication 02-2478, www.ninds.nih.gov/disorders/tbi/detail_tbi.htm

Novak, S A, 2000 Battle-related trauma, in Fiorato et al 2000, 90–102

Nutton, V, 1983 The seeds of disease: an explanation of contagion and infection from the Greeks to the Renaissance, *Med Hist* 27(1), 1–34

Odey, F A, Umoh, U U, Meremikwu, M M, and Udosen, A M, 2007 Pott's disease in children and adolescents in Calabar, Nigeria, *Internet J Infectious Diseases* 6(1), available online at www.ispub.com/journal/the_internet_journal_of_infectious

_diseases/volume_6_number_1_14/article_printable/potts_disease_in_children_and_adolescents_in_calabar_nigeria.html

Olsen R, and Olsen, KE, 2001 Introduction: on the embodiment of monstrosity in northwest medieval Europe, in *Monsters and the monstrous in medieval northwest Europe* (eds K E Olsen and L A J R Houwen), 1–22, Belgium

Oppenheimer, C, 2003 Ice core and palaeoclimatic evidence for the timing and nature of the great mid-13th century volcanic eruption, *Int J Climatology* 23, 417–26

OMIM, 2011 Online Mendelian inheritance in man, www.ncbi.nlm.nih.gov/sites/entrez?db=OMIM&itool=toolbar (accessed 6 October 2011)

Orme, N, 2001 *Medieval children*, London/New Haven, CT

Orme, N, and Webster, M, 1995 *The English hospital 1070–1570*, London

Ortner, D J, 1991 Theoretical and methodological issues in paleopathology, in *Human paleopathology: current syntheses and future options* (eds D J Ortner and A C Aufderheide), 5–11, Washington, DC

Ortner, D J, 1998 Male-female immune reactivity and its implications for interpreting evidence in human skeletal paleopathology, in *Sex and gender in paleopathological perspective* (eds A L Grauer and P Stuart-Macadam), 79–92, Cambridge

Ortner, D J, 2003 *Identification of pathological conditions in human skeletal remains*, 2 edn, London

Ortner, D J, 2006 Foreword, in Buikstra and Beck 2006, xiii–xv

Ortner, D J, and Eriksen, M F, 1997 Bone changes in the human skull probably resulting from scurvy in infancy and childhood, *Int J Osteoarchaeol* 7, 212–20

Ortner, D J, and Mays, S, 1998 Dry-bone manifestation of rickets in infancy and early childhood, *Int J Osteoarchaeol* 8, 45–55

Ortner, D J, Manchester, K, and Lee, F, 1991 Metastatic carcinoma in a leper skeleton from a medieval cemetery in Chichester, England, *Int J Osteoarchaeol* 1, 91–8

Orton, C, 2000 *Sampling in archaeology*, Cambridge

Overfield, T, 1995 *Biological variation in health and illness: race, age, and sex differences*, 2 edn, New York

Owen, R J, Hickey, F G, and Finlay, D B, 1995 A study of metatarsal fractures in children, *Injury* 26(8), 537–8

Paine, R R, 2000 If a population crashes in prehistory, and there is no paleodemographer there to hear it, does it make a sound?, *Amer J Phys Anthropol* 112, 181–90

Paine, R R, and Boldsen, J L, 2002 Linking age-at-death distributions and ancient population dynamics: a case study, in Hoppa and Vaupel 2002, 169–80

Pálfi, G, Dutour, O, Borreani, M, Brun J-P, and Berato, J, 1992 Pre-Columbian congenital syphilis from the late antiquity in France, *Int J Osteoarchaeol* 2, 245–61

Panter-Brick, C, 1998a Biological anthropology and child health: context, process and outcome, in *Biosocial perspectives on children* (ed C Panter-Brick), 66–101, Cambridge

Panter-Brick, C, 1998b Introduction: biosocial research on children, in *Biosocial perspectives on children* (ed C Panter-Brick), 1–9, Cambridge

Panter-Brick, C, 2000a Nobody's children? A reconsideration of child abandonment, in *Abandoned children* (eds C Panter-Brick and M T Smith), Cambridge, 1–26

Panter-Brick, C, 2000b Urban–rural differences in growth patterns of Nepali children, in Ulijaszek et al 2000, 407

Patrick, P, 2007 Overweight and the human skeleton, in *Proceedings of the 7th annual conference of the British Association of Biological Anthropology and Osteoarchaeology* (eds S Zakrewski and W White), BAR Int Ser 1712, 62–71, Oxford

Payne, S, 1975 Partial recovery and sampling bias, in *Archaeozoological Stud* (ed A T Clason), 7–17, Amsterdam

Pearsall, J (ed), 2002 *The concise Oxford English dictionary*, 10 edn (rev), Oxford

Pfeiffer, S, 1991 Rib lesions and New World tuberculosis, *Int J Osteoarchaeol* 1, 191–8

Phenice, T W, 1969 A newly developed visual method of sexing the os pubis, *Amer J Phys Anthropol* 30, 297–302

Phillips, S M, and Sivilich, M, 2006 Cleft palate: a case study of disability and survival in prehistoric North America, *Int J Osteoarchaeol* 16, 528–35

Pietrusewsky, M, 2000 Metric analysis of skeletal remains: methods and approaches, in *Biological anthropology of the human skeleton* (eds M A Katzenburg and S R Saunders), 375–415, New York

Ponting, M, 2004 Preliminary report on the chemical analysis of residues on ceramic and glass sherds from the canons' infirmary, Spitalfields, London, unpub MOL rep

Porter, R, 1997 *The greatest benefit to mankind: a medical history of humanity from antiquity to the present*, London

Powell, M L, and Cook, D C, 2005 Treponematosis: inquiries into the nature of a protean disease, in *The myth of syphilis: the natural history of treponematosis in North America* (eds M L Powell and D C Cook), 9–62, Gainesville, FL

Power, C, Manor, O, and Li, L, 2002 Are inequalities in height underestimated by adult social position? Effects of changing social structure and height selection in a cohort study, *Brit Med J* 325(7356), 131–4

Powers, N, 2005 Cranial trauma and treatment: a case study from the medieval cemetery of St Mary Spital, London, *Int J Osteoarchaeol* 15, 1–14

Powers, N (ed) 2008 *Human osteology method statement*, available online at www.museumoflondon.org.uk/NR/rdonlyres/2D513AFA-EB45-43C2-AEAC-30B256245FD6/0/MicrosoftWordOsteologyMethodStatementMarch2008.pdf

Priest, V, and Chapman, S, 2002 An archaeological excavation at the site of St John the Baptist's Hospital, Mill Farm, Lutterworth, Leicestershire, unpub Univ Leicester Archaeol Services rep 2003-135

Pritchard, F, 1996 The textile industry AD 500–1500, in *Women in industry and technology* (eds A Devonshire and B Wood), 111–14, London

Prokopec, M, and Halman, L, 1999 Healed fractures of the long bones in 15th to 18th century city dwellers, *Int J Osteoarchaeol* 9, 349–56

Psoter, W J, Reid, B C, and Katz, R V, 2005 Malnutrition and dental caries: a review of the literature, *Caries Res* 39(6),

441–7

Pulsifer, W H, 1888 *Notes for a history of lead*, New York

Rao, S, and Rajpathak, V, 1992 Breastfeeding and weaning practices in relation to nutritional status of infants, *Indian Pediatrics* 29, 1533–9

Rawcliffe, C, 1997 *Medicine and society in later medieval England*, Stroud

Rawcliffe, C, 1999 Medicine for the soul: the medieval English hospital and the quest for spiritual health, in *Religion, health and suffering* (eds J R Hinnells and R Porter), 316–38, London

Reid, D J, and Dean, M C, 2000 Brief communication: the timing of linear hypoplasias on human anterior teeth, *Amer J Phys Anthropol* 113, 135–9

Reinhard, K J, Geib, P R, Callahan, M M, and Hevly, R H, 1992 Discovery of colon contents in a skeletonized burial: soil sampling for dietary remains, *J Archaeol Sci* 19, 697–705

Renier, D, Cinalli, G, Lajeunie, E, Arnaud, E, and Marchac, D, 1997 Oxycephaly, a severe craniosynostosis: apropos of a series of 129 cases, *Arch Pediatr* 4(8), 722–9

Resnick, D (ed), 2002 *Diagnosis of bone and joint disorders*, 4 edn in 5 vols, Philadelphia, PA

Ribot, I, and Roberts, C, 1996 A study of non-specific stress indicators and skeletal growth in two mediaeval subadult populations, *J Archaeol Sci* 23, 67–79

Richards, M P, Mays, S, and Fuller, B T, 2002 Stable carbon and nitrogen isotope values of bone and teeth reflect weaning age at the medieval Wharram Percy site, Yorkshire, UK, *Amer J Phys Anthropol* 119, 205–10

Rijpma, F E, and Maat, G J R, 2005 *A physical anthropological research of the Beguines of Breda 1267 to 1530 AD*, Barge's Anthropologica 11, Leiden

Rintala, D H, Loubser, P G, Castro, J, Hart, K A, and Fuhrer, M J, 1998 Chronic pain in a community-based sample of men with spinal cord injury: prevalence, severity, and relationship with impairment, disability, handicap, and subjective well-being, *Archives of Physical Medicine and Rehabilitation* 79(6), 604–14

Rivara, F P, 1982 Epidemiology of childhood injuries, *Amer J Diseases of Children* 136, 399–405

Robb, J, 2000 Analysing human skeletal data, in *Human osteology in archaeology and forensic science* (eds M Cox and S Mays), 475–90, London

Roberts, C, 1987 Leprosy and tuberculosis in Britain: diagnosis and treatment in antiquity, *MASCA J* 4(4), 166–71

Roberts, C, 1994 Treponematosis in Gloucester, England: a theoretical and practical approach to the pre-Columbian theory, in *The origins of syphilis in Europe, before or after 1493?* (eds O Dutour, G Pálfi, J Berato and J-P Brun), 101–8, Toulon–Paris

Roberts, C, 1999 Disability in the skeletal record: assumptions, problems and some examples, *Archaeol Rev Cambridge* 15(2), 79–97

Roberts, C A, 2000a Did they take sugar? The use of skeletal evidence in the study of disability, in Hubert 2000, 46–59

Roberts, C, 2000b Infectious disease in biocultural perspective: past, present and future work in Britain, in *Human osteology in archaeology and forensic science* (eds M Cox and S Mays), 145–62, London

Roberts, C A, 2000c Trauma in biocultural perspective: past, present and future work in Britain, in *Human osteology in archaeology and forensic science* (eds M Cox and S Mays), 337–56, London

Roberts, C A, 2002 The antiquity of leprosy in Britain: the skeletal evidence, in Roberts et al 2002, 213–22

Roberts, C, 2003 Reflections on biological anthropology in the UK, *Archaeol Rev Cambridge* 16, 97–116

Roberts, C A, 2006 A view from afar: bioarchaeology in Britain, in Buikstra and Beck 2006, 417–39

Roberts, C A, 2007 A bioarchaeological study of maxillary sinusitis, *Amer J Phys Anthropol* 133, 792–807

Roberts, C, and Buikstra, J E, 2003 *The bioarchaeology of tuberculosis: a global view on a reemerging disease*, Gainesville, FL

Roberts, C, and Connell, B, 2004 Guidance on recording palaeopathology, in Brickley and McKinley 2004, 34–9

Roberts, C, and Cox, M, 2003 *Health and disease in Britain: from prehistory to the present day*, Stroud

Roberts, C A, and Lewis, M, 2002 Ecology and infectious disease in Britain from prehistory to the present: the case of respiratory infections, in *Ecological aspects of past human settlements in Europe* (eds P Bennike, E B Bodzsár and C Susanne), 179–92, Budapest

Roberts, C A, and McKinley, J, 2003 Review of trepanations in British antiquity focusing on funerary context to explain their occurrence, in *Trepanation: history, discovery, theory* (eds R Arnott, S Finger and C U M Smith), 56–78, Birmingham

Roberts, C A, and Manchester, K, 2005 *The archaeology of disease*, 3 edn, Stroud

Roberts, C, Lucy, D, and Manchester, K, 1994 Inflammatory lesions of ribs: an analysis of the Terry collection, *Amer J Phys Anthropol* 95, 169–82

Roberts, C A, Boylston, A, Buckley, L, Chamberlain, A C, and Murphy, E M, 1998 Rib lesions and tuberculosis: the palaeopathological evidence, *Tubercle and Lung Diseases* 79(1), 55–60

Roberts, C A, Lewis, M E, and Manchester, K (eds), 2002 *The past and present of leprosy: archaeological, historical, palaeopathological and clinical approaches*, BAR Int Ser 1054, Oxford

Rogers, J, 2000 The palaeopathology of joint disease, in *Human osteology in archaeology and forensic science* (eds M Cox and S Mays), 163–82, London

Rogers, J, and Waldron, T, 1995 *A field guide to joint disease in archaeology*, Chichester

Rogers, J, and Waldron, T, 2001 DISH and the monastic way of life, *Int J Osteoarchaeol* 11, 357–65

Rogers, J, Watt, I, and Dieppe, P, 1990 Comparison of visual and radiographic detection of bony changes at the knee joint, *Brit Med J* 300(6721), 367–8

Rogers, J, Shepstone, L, and Dieppe, P, 1997 Bone formers: osteophyte and enthesophyte formation are positively associated, *Ann Rheumatic Diseases* 56, 85–90

Rosebloom, T, Rooij, D E, and Painter, R, 2006 The Dutch

famine and its long-term consequences for adult health, *Early Human Development* 82(8), 485–91

Rosenthal, J T, 1996 *Old age in late medieval England*, Philadelphia, PA

Rossiaud, J, 1988 *Medieval prostitution* (trans L G Cochrane), Oxford

Rossiter-Thorton, J F, 2002 Prayer in your practice, *Complementary Therapies in Nursing and Midwifery* 8(1), 21–8

Rouffignac, C de, 1997 Parasite remains, in Thomas et al 1997, 247–8

Rousham, E K, and Humphrey, L T, 2002 The dynamics of child survival, in *Human population dynamics: cross-disciplinary perspectives* (eds H Macbeth and P Collinson), 124–40, Cambridge

Rowe, R G, and Cliff, K S, 1982 Agricultural accidents in Dorset: review of a pilot study, *J Soc Occupational Medicine* 32, 119–23

Rubel, A J, and Hass, M R, 1996 Ethnomedicine, in *Medical anthropology* (eds C F Sargent and T M Johnson), Westport, CT

Sabine, E L, 1933 Butchering in mediaeval London, *Speculum* 8, 335–53

Safford, P L, and Safford, E J, 1996 *A history of childhood and disability*, London

St Pierre, P, Staheli, L T, Smith, J B, and Green, N E, 1995 Femoral neck stress fractures in children and adolescents, *J Pediatric Orthopaedics* 15(4), 470–3

Salo, W L, Aufderheide, A C, Buikstra, J, and Holcomb, T A, 1994 Identification of mycobacterium tuberculosis DNA in a pre-Columbian Peruvian mummy, *Proc Nat Acad Sci, USA* 91, 2091–4

Salter, R B, 1999 *Textbook of disorders and injuries of the musculoskeletal system*, 3 edn, Baltimore, MD

Saunders, A, and Schofield, J (eds), 2001 *Tudor London: a map and a view*, London Topogr Soc Pub 159, London

Saunders, S R, and Barrans, L, 1999 What can be done about the infant category in skeletal samples?, in *Human growth in the past: studies from bones and teeth* (eds R D Hoppa and C M Fitzgerald), 183–209, Cambridge

Saunders, S R, and Hoppa, R D, 1993 Growth deficit in survivors and non-survivors: biological mortality bias in subadult skeletal samples, *Yearbook Phys Anthropol* 36, 127–51

Saunders, S R, Herring, D A, and Boyce, G, 1995a Can skeletal samples accurately represent the living populations they come from? The St Thomas' cemetery site, Belleville, Ontario, in *Bodies of evidence: reconstructing history through skeletal analysis* (ed A L Grauer), 69–89, New York

Saunders, S R, Herring, A, Sawchuk, L A, and Boyce, G, 1995b The 19th-century cemetery at St Thomas' Anglican church, Belleville: skeletal remains, parish records and censuses, in *Grave reflections: portraying the past through cemetery studies* (eds S R Saunders and A Herring), 93–117, Toronto

Saunders, T, 2002 *The boiled frog syndrome: your health and the built environment*, Chichester

Schell, L M, 1992 Risk focusing: an example of biocultural interaction, in *Health and lifestyle change* (eds R Huss-Ashmore, J Schall and M Hediger), MASCA Res Pap in Science and Archaeology 9, 137–44, Philadelphia, PA

Schell, L M, 1997 Culture as a stressor: a revised model of biocultural interaction, *Yearbook Phys Anthropol* 102, 67–77

Schell, L M, 2000a Environmental factors influencing birth-weight, in Ulijaszek et al 2000, 291–6

Schell, L M, 2000b Urbanism and growth, in Ulijaszek et al 2000, 408–9

Schell, L M, and Ulijaszek, S J, 1999 Urbanism, urbanisation, health and human biology: an introduction, in *Urbanism, health and human biology in industrialised countries* (eds L M Schell and S J Ulijaszek), 3–20, Cambridge

Scheuer, J L, Musgrave, J H, and Evans, S P, 1980 The estimation of late foetal and perinatal age from limb bone length by linear and logarithmic regression, *Ann Hum Biol* 7(3), 257–65

Scheuer, L, and Black, S, 2000 *Developmental juvenile osteology*, London

Schofield, J, 1997 Excavations on the site of St Nicholas Shambles, Newgate Street, City of London, 1975–9, *Trans London Middlesex Archaeol Soc* 48, 77–135

Schofield, J, and Lea, R, 2005 *Holy Trinity Priory, Aldgate, City of London*, MoLAS Monogr Ser 24, London

Schofield, J, and Vince, A, 2003 *Medieval towns: the archaeology of British towns in their European setting*, London

Schofield, P R, 2006 Medieval diet and demography, in *Food in medieval England: diet and nutrition* (eds C M Woolgar, D Serjeantson and T Waldron), 239–53, Oxford

Schultz, M, 2001 Paleohistopathology of bone, *Yearbook Phys Anthropol* 44, 106–47

Schweich, M, and Knüsel, C, 2003 Bio-cultural effects in medieval populations, *Econ Hum Biol* 1(3), 367–77

Scott, E, 1997 Introduction: On the incompleteness of archaeological narratives, in Moore and Scott 1997, 1–14

Serjeantson, D, and Woolgar, C M, 2006 Fish consumption in medieval England, in *Food in medieval England: diet and nutrition* (eds C M Woolgar, D Serjeantson and T Waldron), 102–30, Oxford

Shahar, S, 1990 *Childhood in the Middle Ages*, London

Shahar, S, 2004 *Growing old in the Middle Ages*, London

Shakespeare, T, 1996 Disability, identity and difference, in *Exploring the divide* (eds C Barnes and G Mercer), 94–113, Leeds

Shapiro, F, 2002 *Pediatric orthopaedic deformities: basic science, diagnosis, and treatment*, London

Sharpe, R R (ed), 1904 Folios cxli–cl: Aug 1347, in *Calendar of letter-books of the City of London F: 1337–52*, 167–78, London, available online at www.british-history.ac.uk/report.aspx?compid=33542 (accessed 6 October 2011)

Shashidhar Pai, G, Lewandowski, R C, and Borgaonkar, D S, 2003 *Handbook of chromosomal disorders*, Hoboken, NJ

Sheppard, F, 1998 *London: a history*, Oxford

Sheppard, F H W, 1957 The priory of St Mary Spital, in *Survey of London: vol 27: Spitalfields and Mile End New Town*, 21–3, www.british-history.ac.uk/report.aspx?compid=50149& (accessed 6 October 2011)

Shilling, C, 1996 *The body and social theory*, London

Sidell, J, Thomas, C, and Bayliss, A, 2007 Validating and improving archaeological phasing at St Mary Spital, London, *Radiocarbon* 49(2), 593–610

Singman, J L, 1999 *Daily life in medieval Europe*, London

Siraisi, N G, 1990 *Medieval and early Renaissance medicine*, Chicago, IL

Skinner, P, 1997 Gender and poverty in the medieval community, in *Medieval women in their communities* (ed D Watt), Cardiff

Sloane, B, 1999 Reversing the Dissolution: reconstructing London's medieval monasteries, *Trans London Middlesex Archaeol Soc* 50, 67–77

Sloane, B, 2011 *The Black Death in London*, Stroud

Smith, B H, 1991 Standards of human tooth formation and dental age assessment, in *Advances in dental anthropology* (eds M A Kelley and C S Larsen), 143–68, New York

Smith, G A, Scherzer, D J, Buckley, J W, Haley, K J, and Shields, B J, 2004 Pediatric farm-related injuries: a series of 96 hospitalized patients, *Clinical Pediatrics* 43(4), 335–42

Smith, R M, 1997 Geographical diversity in the resort to marriage in late medieval Europe: work, reputation, and unmarried females in the household formation systems of northern and southern Europe, in *Women in medieval English society* (ed P J P Goldberg), 16–59, Oxford

Smith, T M, Reid, D J, and Sirianni, J E, 2006 The accuracy of histological assessment of dental development and age at death, *J Anat* 208, 125–38

Sofaer Derevenski, J, 1997 Linking age and gender as social variables, *Ethnographischarchogische Zeitschrift* 39, 485–93

Sofaer, J R, 2006a *The body as material culture: a theoretical osteoarchaeology*, Cambridge

Sofaer, J R, 2006b Gender, bioarchaeology and human ontogeny, in *Social archaeology of funerary remains* (eds R Gowland and C Knüsel), 155–67, Oxford

Sørensen, M L S, 2000 *Gender archaeology*, Cambridge

Spencer, R K, 2007 Dietary analysis of diffuse idiopathic skeletal hyperostosis: using stable isotope analysis to investigate disease, *Amer J Phys Anthropol* 132(S44), 223

Stafford, P, and Mulder-Bakker, A B, 2000 *Gendering the Middle Ages*, Bodmin

Stanford, J L, and Stanford, C A, 2002 Leprosy: a correctable model of immunological perturbation, in Roberts et al 2002, 25–38

Steckel, R H, 1995 Stature and the standard of living, *J Econ Lit* 33, 1903–40

Steckel, R H, and Rose, J C (eds), 2002 *The backbone of history: health and nutrition in the western hemisphere*, Cambridge

Steckel, R H, Spencer Larsen, C, Sciulli, P W, and Walker, P L, 2009 The history of European Health Project: a history of health in Europe from the late Paleolithic era to the present, *Acta Univ Carolinae Medica*, 156, 19–25

Steinbock, R T, 1976 *Paleopathological diagnosis and interpretation*, Springfield, IL

Stevenson, J, 1996 Working women in medieval London, in *Women in industry and technology* (ed A Devonshire and B Wood), 97–9, London

Stewart, A L, 1992 The medical outcomes study framework of health indicators, in *Measuring functioning and well-being: the medical outcomes study approach* (eds A L Stewart and J E Ware), 12–26, Durham, NC

Stiker, H-J, 1999 *A history of disability*, Ann Arbor, MI

Stillion, J M, 1995 Premature death among males: extending the bottom line of men's health, in *Men's health and illness: gender, power, and the body* (eds D Sabo and D F Gordon), 46–67, London

Stinson, S, 1985 Sex differences in environmental sensitivity during growth and development, *Yearbook Phys Anthropol* 28, 123–47

Stirland, A J, 1981 The human bones, in *The Austin Friars, Leicester* (eds J E Mellor and T Pearce), CBA Res Rep 35, 168–9, London

Stirland, A, 1991a Paget's disease (osteitis deformans): a classic case?, *Int J Osteoarchaeol* 1, 173–7

Stirland, A, 1991b Pre-Columbian treponematosis in medieval Britain, *Int J Osteoarchaeol* 1, 39–47

Stirland, A, J, 2000 *Raising the dead: the skeletal crew of King Henry VIII's great ship, the* Mary Rose, Chichester

Storey, R, 1992 Preindustrial urban lifestyle and health, in *Health and lifestyle change* (eds R Huss-Ashmore, J Schall and M Hediger), MASCA Res Pap in Science and Archaeology 9, 33–42, Philadelphia, PA

Stothers, R B, 2000 Climatic and demographic consequences of the massive volcanic eruption of 1258, *Climatic Change* 45, 361–74

Strathern, A, and Stewart, P J, 1999 *Curing and healing: medical anthropology in global perspective*, Durham, NC

Stroud, G, 1998 The human bones, in *St Bartholomew's Hospital, Bristol: the excavation of a medieval hospital* (eds R Price with M Ponsford), CBA Res Rep 110, 175–81, London

Stroud, G, and Kemp, R, L, 1993 *Cemeteries of the church and priory of St Andrew, Fishergate*, Archaeology of York 12/2, York

Stuart-Macadam, P L, 1991 Anaemia in Roman Britain: Poundbury Camp, in *Health in past societies: biocultural interpretations of human skeletal remains in archaeological contexts* (eds H Bush and M Zvelebil), BAR Brit Ser 567, 101–13, Oxford

Stuart-Macadam, P, 1992 Anemia revaluated: a look to the future, in *Diet, demography and disease: changing perspectives on anemia* (eds P Stuart-Macadam and S Kent), 261–8, New York

Stuart-Macadam, P, 1995a Biocultural perspectives on breastfeeding, in *Breastfeeding: biocultural perspectives* (eds P Stuart-Macadam and K A Dettwyler), 1–37, New York

Stuart-Macadam, P, 1995b Breastfeeding in prehistory, in *Breastfeeding: biocultural perspectives* (eds P Stuart-Macadam and K A Dettwyler), 75–99, New York

Stulik, J, Pesl, T, Kryl, J, Vyskocil, T, Sebesta, P, and Havranek, P, 2006 Spinal injuries in children and adolescents, *Acta chirurgiae orthopaedicae et traumatologiae Cechoslovaca* 73(5), 313–20

Sture, J F, 2002 Biocultural perspectives on birth defects in urban and rural English populations, unpub PhD thesis, Univ Durham

Susanne, C, Vercauteren, M, and Zavattaro, M, 2000 Migration and changing population characteristics, in Ulijaszek et al 2000, 404–7

Suter, S, Harders, M, Papageorgopoulou, C, Kuhn, G, Székely, G, and Rühli, F J, 2008 Technical note: standardized and semiautomated Harris lines detection, *Amer J Phys Anthropol* 137, 362–6

Symes, S A, Williams, J A, Murray, E A, Hoffman, J M, Holland, T D, Sau, J M, Saul, F P, and Pope, E J, 2002 Taphonomic context of sharp-force trauma in suspected cases of human mutilation and dismemberment, in *Advances in forensic taphonomy: method, theory, and archaeological perspectives* (eds W D Haglund and M H Song), 403–33, Boca Raton, FL

Taleporos, G, and McCabe, M P, 2002 Body image and physical disability – personal perspective, *Social Science and Medicine* 54(6), 971–80

Tatham, S P, 2004 Aspects of health and population studies in northern Europe between the 10th and 12th centuries, unpub PhD thesis, Univ Leicester

Taviner, M, Thwaites, G, and Gant, V, 1998 The English sweating sickness, 1485–1551: a viral pulmonary disease?, *Med Hist* 42(1), 96–8

Thomas, A H (ed), 1926 *Calendar of the plea and memoranda rolls of the City of London: Vol 1, 1323–64*, roll A4, www.british-history.ac.uk/report.aspx?compid=36657 (accessed 7 October 2011)

Thomas, A H (ed), 1929 *Calendar of the plea and memoranda rolls of the City of London: Vol 2, 1364–81*, roll A18, www.british-history.ac.uk/report.aspx?compid=36682 (accessed 7 October 2011)

Thomas, C, 1990 Spitalfields Market archaeological impact assessment, unpub MOL rep

Thomas, C, 1992 An archaeological evaluation of the scheduled ancient monument at Spitalfields Market, unpub MOL rep

Thomas, C, 1993 An evaluation of 35 Spital Square, unpub MOL rep

Thomas, C, 1994 An evaluation at Lamb Street, Spitalfields Market, unpub MOL rep

Thomas, C, 1996 An evaluation of Spitalfields Market, unpub MOL rep

Thomas, C, 2000 The priory and hospital of St Mary Spital, London, *Medieval Life* 14, 21–5

Thomas, C, 2001 Eden House: an archaeological watching brief, unpub MOL rep

Thomas, C, 2002 *The archaeology of medieval London*, Stroud

Thomas, C, 2004 *Life and death in London's East End*, London

Thomas, C, Sloane, B, and Phillpotts, C, 1997 *Excavations at the priory and hospital of St Mary Spital, London*, MoLAS Monogr Ser 1, London

Thordeman, B, 2001 (1939) *Armour from the battle of Wisby 1361*, repr, Union City, CA

Treloar, L L, 2002 Disability, spiritual beliefs and the church: the experiences of adults with disabilities and family members, *J Advanced Nursing* 40(5), 594–603

Trotter, M, 1970 Estimation of stature from intact limb bones, in *Personal identification in mass disasters* (ed T D Stewart), 71–83, Washington, DC

Tuan, Y-F, 1978 The city: its distance from nature, *Geogr Rev* 68(1), 1–12

Tyrrell, A, 2000 Skeletal non-metric traits and the assessment of inter- and intra-population diversity: past problems and future potential, in *Human osteology in archaeology and forensic science* (eds M Cox and S Mays), 289–306, London

Ulijaszek, S J, 1999 Physical activity, lifestyle and health of urban populations, in *Urbanism, health and human biology in industrialised countries* (eds L M Schell and S J Ulijaszek), 250–79, Cambridge

Ulijaszek, S J, and Strickland, S S, 1993 Nutritional studies in biological anthropology, in *Research strategies in human biology* (eds G Lasker and C G N Mascie-Taylor), 108–39, Cambridge

Ulijaszek, S J, Johnston, F E, and Preece, M A (eds), 2000 *The Cambridge encyclopedia of human growth and development*, Cambridge

Van Arsdall, A, 2007 Challenging the 'eye of newt' image of medieval medicine, in *The medieval hospital and medical practice* (ed B S Bowers), 195–205, Aldershot

Van Beek, G C, 1983 *Dental morphology: an illustrated guide*, 2 edn, Oxford

Van Sleuwen, B E, Engelberts, A C, Boere-Boonekamp, M M, Wietse, K, Schulpen, T W J, and L'Hoir, M P, 2007 Swaddling: a systematic review, *Pediatrics* 120, 1097–106

Veale, E M, 1990 Craftsmen and the economy of London in the 14th century, in *The medieval town 1200–1540* (eds R Holt and G Rosser), 120–40, London

Verbrugge, L, 1994 The disablement process, *Social Science and Medicine* 38, 1–14

Viemero, V, and Krause, C, 1998 Quality of life in individuals with physical disabilities, *Psychotherapy and Psychosomatics* 67(6), 317–22

Vögele, J P, 1994 Urban infant mortality in imperial Germany, *Social History of Medicine* 7, 401–26

Vrijheid, M, Loane, M, and Dolk, H, 2003 Chemical environmental and occupational exposures, www.eurocat-network.eu/content/Special-Report-Env-Risk-III.pdf

Wadsworth, G R, 1992 Physiological, pathological and dietary influences on the hemoglobin level, in *Diet, demography and disease: changing perspectives on anemia* (eds P Stuart-Macadam and S Kent), 63–104, New York

Wakely, J, 1997 Identification and analysis of violent and non-violent head injuries in osteo-archaeological material, in *Material harm* (ed J Carman), 24–46, Glasgow

Wakely, J, Anderson, T, and Carter, A, 1995 A multidisciplinarian case study of prostatic(?) carcinoma from mediaeval Canterbury, *J Archaeol Sci* 22, 469–77

Waldron, H, A, 2001 Are plague pits of particular use to palaeoepidemiologists?, *Int J Epidemiology* 30, 104–8

Waldron, I, 1995 Contributions of changing gender differences in behavior and social roles to changing gender differences in mortality, in *Men's health and illness: gender, power, and the body* (eds D Sabo and D F Gordon), 22–45, London

Waldron, T, 1985 DISH at Merton Priory: evidence for a 'new' occupational disease, *Brit Med J* 291, 1762–3

Waldron, T, 1987 The relative survival of the human skeleton: implications for palaeopathology, in *Death, decay and reconstruction: approaches to archaeology and forensic science* (eds A Boddington, A N Garland and R C Janaway), 55–64, Manchester

Waldron, T, 1994 *Counting the dead: the epidemiology of skeletal populations*, Chichester

Waldron, T, 1998 A note on the estimation of height from long-bone measurements, *Int J Osteoarchaeol* 8, 75–7

Waldron, T, 2006 Nutrition and the skeleton, in *Food in medieval England: diet and nutrition* (eds C M Woolgar, D Serjeantson and T Waldron), 254–66, Oxford

Waldron, T, 2007 *St Peter's, Barton-upon-Humber, Lincolnshire: a parish church and its community: Volume 2, The human remains*, Oxford

Waldron, T, and Rogers, J, 1991 Inter-observer variation in coding osteoarthritis in human skeletal remains, *Int J Osteoarchaeol* 1, 49–56

Walker, D, 2009 The treatment of leprosy in 19th-century London: a case study from St Marylebone cemetery, *Int J Osteoarchaeol* 19, 364–74

Walker, P L, 1997 Wife beating, boxing, and broken noses: skeletal evidence for the cultural patterning of violence, in *Troubled times: violence and warfare in the past* (eds D L Martin and D W Frayer), 145–80, Amsterdam

Walker, P L, 2001 A bioarchaeological perspective on the history of violence, *Annu Rev Anthropol* 30, 573–96

Walker, P L, Johnson, J R, and Lambert, P M, 1988 Age and sex biases in the preservation of human skeletal remains, *Amer J Phys Anthropol* 76, 183–8

Walker, P L, Cook, D C, and Lambert, P M, 1997 Skeletal evidence for child abuse: a physical anthropological perspective, *J Forensic Sci* 42(2), 196–207

Walker, P L, Bathurst, R R, Richman, R, Gjerdrum, T, and Andrushko, V A, 2009 The causes of porotic hyperostosis and cribra orbitalia: a reappraisal of the iron-deficiency-anemia hypothesis, *Amer J Phys Anthropol* 139, 109–25

Warrington, S A, and Wright, C M, 2001 Accidents and resulting injuries in premobile infants: data from the ALSPAC study, *Archives of Diseases in Childhood* 85, 104–7

Waugh, M, 1973 Venereal diseases in 16th-century England, *Med Hist* 17, 192–9

Wear, A, 1999 Fear, anxiety and the plague in early modern England, in *Religion, health and suffering* (eds J R Hinnells and R Porter), London, 339–63

Weber, J, and Czarnetzki, A, 2001 Brief communication: neurotraumatological aspects of head injuries resulting from sharp and blunt force in the early medieval period of southwestern Germany, *Amer J Phys Anthropol* 114, 352–6

Weisl, A J, 1998 'Quiting' Eve: violence against women in the Canterbury tales, in *Violence against women in medieval texts* (ed A Roberts), 115–36, Gainesville, FL

Weiss, E, and Jurmain, R, 2007 Osteoarthritis revisited: a contemporary review, *Int J Osteoarchaeol* 17, 437–50

Weis-Krejci, E, 2005 Excarnation, evisceration, and exhumation in medieval and post-medieval Europe, in *Interacting with the dead: perspectives on mortuary archaeology for the new millennium* (eds G F M Rakita, J E Buikstra, L A Beck and S R Williams), 155–72, Gainesville, FL

Wells, C A, 1964 The study of ancient disease, *Surgo* 32, 743–72

Weston, D A, 2004 Approaches to the investigation of periosteal new bone formation in palaeopathology, unpub PhD thesis, Univ College London

Weston, D A, 2008 Investigating the specificity of periosteal reactions in pathology museum specimens, *Amer J Phys Anthropol* 137, 48–59

White, B, 2006 The Museum of London's Wellcome Osteological Research Database, in *Human remains and museum practice* (eds J Lohman and K Goodnow), 106–10, Unesco, Paris

White, W, 1988 *Skeletal remains from the cemetery of St Nicholas Shambles, City of London*, London Middlesex Archaeol Soc Spec Pap 9, London

White, W, 2004 The human bone, in Barber, B, Chew, S, Dyson, T and White, B, *The Cistercian abbey of St Mary Stratford Langthorne, Essex*, MoLAS Monogr Ser 18, 158–79, London

White, W, 2007 The human bone, in Bowsher, D, Dyson, T, Holder, N, and Howell, I, *The London Guildhall: an archaeological history of a neighbourhood from early medieval to modern times*, 2 vols, MoLAS Monogr Ser 36, 498–501, London

Wiesner, M E, 2000 *Women and gender in early modern Europe*, 2 edn, Cambridge

Wilbur, A K, Bouwman, A S, Stone, A C, Roberts, C A, Pfister, L-P, Buikstra, J E, and Brown, T A, 2009 Deficiencies and challenges in the study of ancient tuberculosis DNA, *J Archaeol Sci* 36, 1990–7

Wilkinson, E, and Marmot, E (eds), 2006 *Social determinants of health: the solid facts*, 2 edn, Oxford

Wilkinson, J L, 2001 *Excavations at Carmarthen Greyfriars 1983–97: analysis of skeletal remains: Vol 1, Summary of findings and photographs*, Cambria Archaeology, available online at www.cambria.org.uk/projects/CGF/BoneReportVol1(discussion).pdf

Williams, F M K, Manek, N J, Sambrook, P N, Spector, T D, and Macgregor, A J, 2008 Schmorl's nodes: common, highly heritable, and related to lumbar disc disease, *Arthritis and Care Research* 57(5), 855–60

Wiltse, L L, Widell, E H, and Jackson, D W, 1975 Fatigue fracture: the basic lesion in isthmic spondylolisthesis, *J Bone Joint Surgery Am* 57(1), 17–22

Wood, J W, Milner, G R, Harpending, H C, and Weiss, K M, 1992 The osteological paradox: problems of inferring prehistoric health from skeletal samples, *Curr Anthropol* 33(4), 343–70

Woodward, K (ed), 1997 *Identity and difference*, London

Woolgar, C M, 2006a Group diets in late medieval England, in *Food in medieval England: diet and nutrition* (eds C M Woolgar, D Serjeantson and T Waldron), 191–200, Oxford

Woolgar, C M, 2006b Meat and dairy products in late medieval England, in *Food in medieval England: diet and nutrition* (eds C M Woolgar, D Serjeantson and T Waldron), 88–101, Oxford

Woolgar, C M, Serjeantson, D, and Waldron, T, 2006 Conclusion, in *Food in medieval England: diet and nutrition* (eds C M Woolgar, D Serjeantson and T Waldron), 267–80, Oxford

World Health Organization, 2001 *Men, ageing and health: achieving health across the lifespan*, Geneva

World Health Organization, 2002a *The European health report 2002: reducing risks, promoting healthy life*, Geneva, www.who.int/whr/2002/en/whr02_en.pdf (accessed 13 October 2011)

World Health Organization, 2002b *World report on violence and health: summary*, Geneva

World Health Organization, 2003 *Gender and tuberculosis*, Geneva

World Health Organization, 2005 *Disability, including prevention, management and rehabilitation*, www.who.int/disabilities/en/index.html or http://apps.who.int/gb/ebwha/pdf_files/WHA58/A58_17-en.pdf

World Health Organization, 2006 Constitution of the World Health Organization, www.who.int/governance/eb/who_constitution_en.pdf

World Health Organization, 2009a Water sanitation and health: introduction to fact sheets on sanitation, www.who.int/water_sanitation_health/hygiene/emergencies/envsanfactsheets/en/index2.html

World Health Organization, 2009b Water sanitation and health: questions and answers: South Asia earthquake and tsunami, www.who.int/water_sanitation_health/tsunami_qa/en/

Youngs, D, 2006 *The life-cycle in Western Europe, c 1300–1500*, Manchester

Zelazo, P R, 1974 Psychological development, in *Health* (ed J Mayer), 74–97, New York

Zink, A R, Sola, C, Reischl, U, Grabner, W, Rastogi, N, Wolf, H, and Nerlich, A G, 2004 Molecular identification and characterization of *Mycobacterium tuberculosis* complex in ancient Egyptian mummies, *Int J Osteoarchaeol* 14, 404–13

Zink, A R, Grabner, W and Nerlich, A G, 2005 Molecular identification of human tuberculosis in recent and historic bone tissue samples: the role of molecular techniques for the study of historic tuberculosis, *Amer J Phys Anthropol* 126, 32–47

Zink, A R, Molnár, E, Motamedi, N, Pálfy, G, Marcsik, A and Nerlich, A G, 2007 Molecular history of tuberculosis from ancient mummies and skeletons, *Int J Osteoarchaeol* 17, 380–91

Zullig, K J, Ward, R M, and Horn, T, 2006 The association between perceived spirituality, religiosity, and life satisfaction: the mediating role of self-rated health, *Social Indicators Research* 79(2), 255–74

INDEX

Compiled by Margaret Binns

Page numbers in **bold** indicate figures
All street names and locations are in London unless specified otherwise
County names within parentheses refer to historic counties

accidental injury
  domestic environment 156–7, 186
  inter-site comparison 259–61
  subadults 177–8, 180
  see also trauma
adolescents
  fractures 178–80, **179**
  see also subadults
adult stature *see* stature
adulthood, age identity 169
Æbelholt Kloster (Denmark), fractures 253, 260
age at death
  burial type comparison 218, 222, 224, 226, 230, 242–3
  determination of 20–1
  extra-spinal osteoarthritis 62–5, **63**, **64**, **65**
  fractures 88, **88**
  future research 275
  period 14 29–30, **29**, **30**, 218, 242–3
  period 15 30–2, **30**, **31**, 222, 243
  period 16 32–3, **32**, **33**, 224, 243
  period 17 33–5, **34**, **35**, 226, 243
  subadults 170–1, 222, 224, 226, 230, 241–2
age identity 169
agriculture, injury risks 260
air pollution, health risks 153–5
amputation 216–17, **216**, **217**
anaesthetics 212
André, Bernard 263
Anglicus, Gilbertus 211
animal bones, dietary evidence 161–2, 164
animals
  butchery 159–60, 163–4, **163**
  health risks 156, 263–4
  injury risks 186–7
  waste 153
ankylosing spondylitis 75, **75**, 213–14, 248
ankylosis 72, 191, **191**, 192–3
ante-mortem tooth loss 46, 58
  inter-site comparison 247–8
  London cemeteries comparison 236
apothecaries 200, 210–11
apprentices
  health risks 177, 192, 270
  injury risks 185, 260
arm fractures 95–8, **96**, **97**
  injury mechanism 103–5, 182–3
  inter-site comparison 252, 259–60
  subadults 178
  unhealed 205–6, **206**
Arras (France), tuberculosis 254
arthritis *see* osteoarthritis; rheumatoid arthritis
Ashendon, Philip de 181, 217
atresia 257
attritional cemetery *see* burial type ABC
Augustinian houses
  cemeteries 15
  charity 189
  diet 165
avascular necrosis 106, 145, 206

bathrocrania 132–3
battle injuries 181, 217, 252, 253, 260, 261

Beaune (France), infirmary **197**
bell casting 160, **160**
Bermondsey Priory/Abbey *see* St Saviour Bermondsey
bilateral hypoplasia 133
bioarchaeology
  children 169
  health status 15–16
  impairment 189–90
  research approach 16–18, 273
birth, risks 171
Black Death (1348–9)
  burials 231
  demographic profiles 244
  impacts 12–13, 156, 165
  perinates 212
Blackfriars Ipswich (Suffolk), long bone fractures 250
blacksmithing 160
blood-letting 200
blunt force injuries, skull fractures 94, **94**, **95**, 178, 181–2, **181**, 215–16
breastfeeding 172
Breda (Netherlands)
  DISH 249, 266
  fractures 252
  metabolic disease 254
  Reiter's disease 249
  stature 258, 259
  tuberculosis 155, 254
brucellosis 117–18, **117**
burial type ABC (attritional) 13, **13**
  adult stature 36–7, **37**, 167, 219, 222
  age at death 218, 222, 224, 226, 230, 242–3
  caries 46–8, **47**, 165, 166
  comparison with burial type D 218–28
  cribra orbitalia 220, 222–3, 225, 227
  DISH **73**, 168
  enamel hypoplasia 49, **54**, 219–20, 222, 224, 226–7
  extra-spinal osteoarthritis 61–2, **61**, **64**
  fractures 89–90, **90**, **91**
  long bone deformities 202, **202**
  long bone fractures 96
  metal plates for treatment 208, 209, **209**
  ochronotic osteoarthropathy **72**
  period 14 28, 29–30, 218–22
  period 15 30–2, 222–4
  period 16 32–3, 224–6
  period 17 33–5, 226–8
  periostitis 109, **110**, 221, 223, 225, 227–8
  porotic hyperostosis 220, 223, 225, 227
  rheumatoid osteoarthritis **73**
  rib lesions 154
  scoliosis 136, **136**, **194**
  seronegative spondyloarthropathy **75**
  sexed adults 35
  sinusitis 111
  skull fractures 92–3, **92**, **93**, **94**
  spinal joint disease 78, **78**, 80–1, **81**, **82**
  stress indicators 126–7, **127**, 221–2, 223–4, 225–6, 228, 230–1
  subadult burials 242
  subadult fractures **101**
  subadult growth 38, **38**, 219, **219**, 222,

222, 224, **224**, 226, **226**
  tuberculosis 114, 115, 221, 223, 225, 227
burial type D (catastrophic) 13, **13**
  adult stature 36–7, **37**, 167, 219, 222
  age at death 218, 222, 224, 226, 230, 242–3
  amputation 216–17, **216**, **217**
  ankylosis **191**
  caries 46–8, **47**, 166
  cleft palate 133, **133**
  comparison with burial type ABC 218–28
  comparison with other cemeteries 243–4
  cribra orbitalia 220, 222–3, 225, 227
  diaphyseal aclasia 148, **148**
  enamel hypoplasia 49, **55**, 219–20, 224, 226–7
  extra-spinal osteoarthritis **61**, 62, 65
  fractures 89–90, **90**, **91**
  gout **74**
  hypertrophic osteoarthropathy 132
  kyphoscoliosis **135**
  leprosy 112, **112**
  long bone deformities 202, **202**
  long bone fractures 96, **96**, 206
  mass burial reasons 228–31, 271, 274
  mortality profiles 243–4, 271–2
  period 14 29–30, 218–22
  period 15 30–2, 222–4
  period 16 32–3, 224–6, 244
  period 17 33–5, 226–8
  periostitis 109, **110**, 221, 223, 225, 227–8
  porotic hyperostosis 220, 223, 225, 227
  sexed adults 35
  sinusitis 111
  skull fractures 92–3, **92**, **93**, **94**, **181**, **207**
  spinal joint disease 78, **78**, 80–1, **81**, **82**
  stress indicators 126–7, **127**, 175, 221–2, 223–4, 225–6, 228, 230–1, 272, 274
  subadult burials 242
  subadult growth 38, **38**, 175, 219, **219**, 222, **222**, 224, **224**, 226, **226**
  tuberculosis 115, **155**, 221, 223, 225, 227
burials
  bone preservation 22–3
  bone recovery 23–4, **23**
  dating 3–4
  numbers 19–20
  period 14 **6**, 25–30
  period 15 5, **7**, 26–7, 30–2
  period 16 5, **7**, 26–7, 32–3
  period 17 **7**, 26–7, 33–5
  recording 20–2
  sampling 19–20
  source population 13–14
  types 13, **13**
butchery 159–60, 163–4, **163**

calculus 56–8, **58**, **59**
  dietary evidence 166
  London cemeteries comparison 235–6
  subadults 173–4
cancer *see* neoplastic disease
carbohydrates, dental evidence 166, 168, 174
caries 41, 46–50, **46**, **47**, **48**, **49**, 55
  dietary evidence 165, 166–7
  inter-site comparison 247–8
  London cemeteries comparison 234–5
  subadults 173–4, 234–5
carpal anomalies 146
catastrophic cemeteries
  fractures 252
  inter-site comparison 245–59
  London comparisons 243–4

  see also burial type D; mass burials
cemeteries
  comparisons 232–59
  medieval London 14–15
cemetery chapel 3, 5, **8**
cephalocele 133, 256
cereals, in diet 162, **162**
cesspits **152**, 153
chalices and patens 14, 201, **201**
Charcot joints 71, 206
Chauliac, Guy de 200, 202, 216
Cheapside conduit 152
childbirth 211–12
childhood, medieval 169–70
children *see* subadults
chromosomal disorders 133, 144
circulatory disorders
  hypertrophic osteoarthropathy 132
  inter-site comparison 255–6
  osteochondritis dissecans 131, 209, 245
  osteochondroses 130–1, **131**
  osteonecroses 130
  risk factors 267–8
Cistercian houses, cemeteries 15
clay shoveller's fractures 99–100
cleft palate 133, **133**, 191, 193, 257
climate, medieval London 11
clubfoot 193
Cluniac houses, cemeteries 15
coal smoke 154, 160
coins, with burials 201
congenital and developmental abnormalities
  bathrocrania 132–3
  cranial anomalies 132, 256–7
  craniofacial anomalies 133, **133**, 191
  impairment 193
  inter-site comparison 256–7
  limb and joint anomalies 143–6, **144**, **145**, **146**, 191, 256–7
  medieval views 189
  risk factors 268
  spinal anomalies 133–43, **135**, **136**, **138**, 191, **194**, 256–7
copper-alloy objects, therapeutic use 208, **208**, 209
copper alloy working 160
cranial anomalies 132, 256–7
cranial fractures *see* skull fractures
cranial hyperplasia 132
cranial indices 39
cranial vault, porotic hyperostosis 123–4, 125, 220, 223, 225, 227
craniofacial anomalies 133, **133**, 191
cribra orbitalia 120–2, **122**
  burial type comparison 220, 222–3, 225, 227
  London cemeteries comparison 240
  stress indicator 126–7, 167, 168, 239–40
Crusades 262
crutches 188, **189**
culture, and disability 187–8
curfew 185

dairy products 164, 165
deformity, long bone fractures 106–8, 202–3, **202**
demography
  future research 275
  period 14 25–30, 218–19
  period 15 26–7, 30–2, 222
  period 16 26–7, 32–3, 224
  period 17 **7**, 26–7, 33–5, 226
dental disease 40–60
  dietary evidence 166–7, 174–5, 265–6, 276
  inter-site comparison 247–8
  London cemeteries comparison 234–6
  subadults 44–5, 173–4, 248
  see also ante-mortem tooth loss; calculus;

Index

caries; enamel hypoplasia; periapical lesions; periodontal disease
dental fractures 95, 178
diaphyseal aclasia 148, **148**
diarrhoea
  water pollution 153
  weaning 173
diet
  dental evidence 166–7, 174–5, 265–6, 276
  future research 276
  medieval 12, 161–8, **162**, **164**, 264–6
  monastic 165, 237
  skeletal evidence 167–8, 174–5, 266
  subadults 173–5, 265
  see also food
diffuse idiopathic skeletal hyperostosis (DISH) 72–3, **73**, 168
  dietary links 165, 167–8, 266
  inter-site comparison 248–9
  London cemeteries comparison 237–8
  monastic sites 237, 238
disability 187–94
disease *see* circulatory disorders; congenital and developmental abnormalities; dental disease; infectious disease; joint disease; neoplastic disease; nutritional and metabolic disease; trauma
DISH *see* diffuse idiopathic skeletal hyperostosis
dislocation 108, 192
distillation, medicines 210–11, **210**
domestic environment
  health risks 156–7
  injury risks 186–7
drink 164
Duverney fracture 207

East Smithfield cemetery 14, 15
  Black Death burials 231, 244
  calculus 236
  caries 234
  cranial trauma 239
  cribra orbitalia 240
  enamel hypoplasia 235
  fractures 238
  gender ratio 243
  neoplastic disease 240
  osteoarthritis 237
  periapical lesions 235
  perinatal burials 212
  periodontal disease 236
  rickets 239
  subadults 242, 244
  treponematosis 233
  tuberculosis 233
economy, medieval London 12
enamel hypoplasia 49, **51**, 52–5, **54**, **55**
  burial type comparison 219–20, 222, 224, 226–7
  inter-site comparison 247–8
  London cemeteries comparison 235
  stress indicator 126–7, 175, 235
  subadults 173, 219, 222, 224, 226–7
endocranial lesions 147–8
  causes 267
  inter-site comparison 257, 258
environment *see* urban environment
epiphyseal plate injuries 157, **157**, 179
erosive osteoarthropathies 73–5, **73**, **74**, 249
extra-spinal osteoarthritis 60–71

facial injuries 95
famine 12, 164–5, 228–31, 271, 274
females
  age at death 29–30, **30**, 31–2, **31**, 33, **33**, 34–5, **35**, 218–19, 222, 224, 226
  ankylosis **191**
  arm fractures 96–7, **97**, 104, 105, **105**,

182, 205
calculus 58, **59**, 166
caries 46, 48–9, **48**, **49**
congenital and developmental anomalies 268
cribra orbitalia 121, **122**, 167, 168
enamel hypoplasia 49, **51**
extra-spinal osteoarthritis 61–2, **61**, **62**, **63**, 64–5, **64**, **65**
fracture distribution 103, **103**, **104**, 260
fracture healing 107, 108, **157**, 203, 205
fractures 88, **88**, **89**, 90, **90**, 105, **105**, 157, 158, 252
Freiberg's disease 130, **131**
gout **74**, 268
HFI 241
impairment risks 192
injury risks 185–7
leprosy 112, **112**, 232
long bone deformities 202, **202**
long bone fractures 96–8, **96**, **97**, **98**
maternity care 211–12
multiple injuries 101–2, **102**, 184, 186
occupations 157, 158–9, **158**, **159**, **160**, 260
ochronotic osteoarthropathy **72**
percentage of sexed adults 35, **35**
scoliosis 135–6, **136**
sinusitis 154–5
skull fractures 94, 102, 181–2
spinal joint disease 77–81, **78**, **80**, **81**
stature 36–7, **37**, 167, 219, 222, 224, 226, 258–9, 269
treponematosis 262
tuberculosis 114–15, **115**, 263
unhealed fractures 105–6
violence victims 185, 261
see also gender ratios
femoral length, subadult growth indicator 37–8, **37**
femur, fracture healing 202–3
fish
  in diet 162, 164, **164**, 165–6
  trade 12
Fishergate House, York (Yorks)
  circulatory disease 255
  congenital anomalies 256
  DISH 248–9
  endocranial lesions 257, 267
  fractures 252, 260
  metabolic disease 254
  seronegative osteoarthritis 249
  sharp force trauma 253
flat foot 193
food
  production 162–4
  storage and distribution 168
  trading 158, **158**, 162–3, **163**
  see also diet
foot anomalies 146, **146**, 191
fractures
  complications 106, 205–7, **205**, **206**, **207**
  distribution 102–3, **103**, **104**, 249–53, 259–60
  epiphyseal plate injuries 157, **157**, 179
  facial injuries 95
  future research 275–6
  healing 105–8, **157**, 179, **179**, 202–5, 238
  injury mechanism 103–5, **104**, **105**, 182–3
  inter-site comparison 249–53
  London cemeteries comparison 238
  occupation-related 157–8, 260
  'parry' fractures 182, 186, 238, 276
  prevalence 88–91, **88**, **89**, **90**, **91**
  risks 259–61
  rural–urban comparison 259–60
  subadults 100–1, **100**, **101**, 103, **104**,

157–8, 177–80, 260
treatment of 202–5
unhealed 105–6, 205–7, **205**, **206**, 238
see also arm fractures; dental fractures; hand and foot fractures; joint fractures; long bone fractures; rib fractures; skull fractures; vertebral fractures
Freiberg's disease 130, **131**

Galen 198–9
gender ratios
  age at death 242–3
  caries 234
  catastrophic cemeteries 244
  cribra orbitalia 220, 223, 225, 227
  enamel hypoplasia 220, 222, 224, 227
  fracture distribution 103, **103**, 260
  London cemeteries comparison 243
  long bone fractures 250
  period 14 218–19
  period 15 222
  period 16 224
  period 17 226
  periostitis 221, 223, 225, 227–8
  porotic hyperostosis 220, 223, 225, 227
  tuberculosis 114–15, **115**, 221, 223, 225, 227
  see also females; males
Gisborough Priory (Yorks)
  fractures 252
  metabolic disease 254
  osteomyelitis 254
  scoliosis 256
glenoid cavity dysplasia 144
gout 74, **74**, 75, 249, 268
grave goods 14, 201, **201**
Great Famine (1315–18) 12, 229, 230, 235
Greyfriars Franciscan friary, Norwich (Norfolk) 170
growth profiles
  inter-site comparison 259, **259**
  rural–urban comparison 268–9
  subadults 37–8, **37**, 38, 175, 219, **219**, 222, **222**, 224, **224**, 226, **226**

Hakedy, Richard 210
hand and foot anomalies 145–6, **146**
hand and foot fractures
  inter-site comparison 251–2
  subadults 178–9
Harris lines 10, 124, 276
healing
  fractures 105–8, **157**, 179, **179**, 202–5, 238
  medieval treatments 201–11
health
  bioarchaeological perspective 15–16
  medieval London 272–3
  urban environments 10
  see also circulatory disorders; congenital and developmental abnormalities; dental disease; infectious disease; joint disease; neoplastic disease; nutritional and metabolic disease; trauma
heat islands 11, 152
hemifacial microsomia 133, 256, 257
Hestelle, Thomas 261
HFI *see* hyperostosis frontalis interna
hip dislocation 145, **145**, 257
hip dysplasia 144–5, **145**, 256, 257
Holy Trinity Aldgate
  calculus 236
  caries 234
  cemetery 14, 15
  cribra orbitalia 240
  DISH 238
  enamel hypoplasia 235
  fractures 238

gender ratio 243
HFI 241
osteoarthritis 237
periapical lesions 235
periostitis 234
tuberculosis 233
hospital cemeteries
  fractures 252
  inter-site comparison 245–59
hospitals, medieval period 8, 194–201, 273
housing, medieval London 11–12, 149–51, **150**, **151**, **152**
hucksters 159
humours, medical theory 198, 200
hydrocephalus 256, 268
hyperostosis frontalis interna (HFI) 146, 241
hypertrophic osteoarthropathy 132, 255, 256

impairment
  adaptation to 193, 194
  bioarchaeology 189–90
  congenital and developmental 193, **194**
  definitions 187
  evidence for 190–4
  future research 276
  gender differences 192
  and health 187–8
  joint disease 193
  medieval perspective 188–9
  orthopaedic trauma 192–3
  subadults 191–2
industry, health risks 157–61
infants
  mortality 170–2, 242
  trauma 177–8, 180
  weaning 172–3
  see also subadults
infectious diseases
  famine mortality 230–1
  inter-site comparison 253–4
  London cemeteries comparison 232–4
  non-specific 109–12, 233–4
  specific 112–18, 232–3
  transmission 261–4, 272–3
  see also brucellosis; leprosy; osteitis; osteomyelitis; periostitis; septic arthropathy; sinusitis; treponematosis; tuberculosis
influenza 151, 156, 230
injuries *see* trauma
inter-site comparison
  circulatory disease 255–6
  congenital and developmental abnormalities 256–7
  dental health 247–8
  endocranial lesions 257, 258
  infectious diseases 253–4
  joint disease 248–9
  neoplastic disease 254–5
  nutritional and metabolic disease 254, 255
  Paget's disease of bone 257, 258
  sites analysed 245–7
  stature 258–9, 259
  subadult growth 259, **259**
  trauma 249–53
international cemeteries
  fractures 252–3, 260–1
  inter-site comparison 245–59
  leprosy 254
  stature 258–9, **259**
  treponematosis 254
  tuberculosis 253, 254
interpersonal violence 181–7
  dental fractures 178
  fractures 180, 238, 260
  skull fractures 92–3, 181–2, **181**, 239, 260, 261

299

Index

subadults 180, 260
intestinal parasites 23, 153
iron smelting 160
Isle of Ensay (Scotland), fractures 250, 251, 260
isotope analysis *see* stable isotope analysis

Jedburgh Abbey (Scotland), osteomyelitis 254
jet, use in childbirth 211
Jewbury, York (Yorks)
    endocranial lesions 257
    fractures 252, 260
    Paget's disease of bone 257
    sharp force trauma 253
joint disease
    ankylosis 72, 191, **191**, 192–3
    Charcot joint 71
    diffuse idiopathic skeletal hyperostosis (DISH) 72–3, **73**, 165, 167–8, **168**, 237–8
    erosive osteoarthropathies 73–5, **73**, **74**, 249
    extra-spinal osteoarthritis 60–71
    impairment 193
    inter-site comparison 248–9
    London cemeteries comparison 236–8
    ochronotic osteoarthropathy 71, **72**
    rotator cuff injuries 72
    seronegative osteoarthropathies 75–6, **75**, 249
    spinal joint disease 76–87
joint dislocation 108, 192
joint fractures 98, 192–3
joint hypermobility syndrome 144

knife injuries 183
kyphoscoliosis 134, **135**, 191, 193, 257
kyphosis 134, 191, 193, 257

latrines 153, **153**, 197
Lawn Hospital, Lincoln (Lincs)
    fractures 252, 260
    gout 249
lead exposure, health risks 268
lead poisoning 161
lead sheeting, therapeutic use 208, **209**
leather working 160
leprosy 112, **112**, 191
    fracture risks 250
    inter-site comparison 253–4, 261–2
    London cemeteries comparison 232
leprosy hospitals 182, 194, 232, 261–2
lighting, lack of 153
limb fractures *see* long bone fractures
limb hypoplasia 144
limb and joint anomalies 143–6, 191
    congenital absence of styloid process 144
    glenoid cavity dysplasia 144
    hand and foot anomalies 145–6, **146**
    hip dislocation 145, **145**
    hip dysplasia 144–5, **145**
    inter-site comparison 256–7
    joint hypermobility syndrome 144
    limb hypoplasia 144
    radioulnar synostosis 144, **144**
    undiagnosed chromosomal disorder 144
lime kilns 160
'little leaguer's elbow' 179, **179**
Llandough (Wales)
    circulatory disease 255
    fractures 250, 251, 260
    metabolic disease 254
    septic osteoarthritis 249
    stature 258
    tuberculosis 155
locker keys 195, **195**
London
    bioarchaeology 15–16

cemeteries 14–15
cemetery comparisons 232–44
diet and economy 161–8
economy and trade 12
health risks 152–7, 161
health status 272–3
housing 11–12, 149–51, **150**, **151**, **152**
industry and occupation 157–61
medieval environment 11–12, 149
plan **150**
population fluctuations 12–13, 229–30, 261
socio-cultural change 12–13, 273
subadults 168–80
long bone fractures 95–8, **96**, **97**, **98**, 182–3, **182**
    complications 106, 205–7, **205**, **206**
    deformity 106–8, 202–3, **202**
    healing 106–8, 202–5, **204**
    inter-site comparison 249–50, 259–60
    subadults 178–9, **179**
Lund (Sweden), treponematosis 254

males
    age at death 29–30, **30**, 31–2, **31**, 33, 33, 34–5, **35**, 218–19, 222, 224, 226
    amputation 216–17, **216**, **217**
    arm fractures 96–7, **97**, 104, 182, 184, **206**
    calculus 58, **59**, 166
    caries 46, **46**, 48–9, **48**, **49**, 55
    cribra orbitalia 121, **122**, 167
    DISH 73
    enamel hypoplasia 49
    extra-spinal osteoarthritis 61–2, **61**, **62**, **63**, 64–5, **64**, **65**
    fracture complications **205**, **206**
    fracture distribution 103, **103**, 260
    fracture healing 107, 108, 205
    fractures 88, **88**, **89**, 90, **90**, 157–8, 252
    impairment risks 192
    interpersonal violence 180, 260
    long bone deformities 202, **202**
    long bone fractures 96–8, **96**, **97**, **98**, 182–3, **182**
    multiple injuries 101–2, **102**, 183–4
    neoplasms 267
    occupations 157, 260
    percentage of sexed adults 35, **35**
    rheumatoid osteoarthritis 73
    scoliosis 135–6, **136**, **194**
    seronegative spondyloarthropathy 75
    skull fractures 91–3, **91**, **92**, **94**, 102, 181, **207**, 214–16, 239
    spinal joint disease 77–81, **78**, **79**, **81**
    stature 36–7, **37**, 167, 219, 222, 224, 226, 258–9, 269–70, 272
    subadult fractures **101**
    trepanation 213–15, **213**, **214**, **215**
    tuberculosis 114–15, **115**
    see also gender ratios
malnutrition 165, 167, 220, 223, 225, 227, 230
    see also nutritional and metabolic disease
Martyn, Zenobius 263
Mary Rose (Solent)
    fractures 251, 252, 260
    osteomalacia 254, 266
mass burials 13, **13**, 217–18, **218**
    mortality profiles 243–4, 271–2
    reasons for 228–31, 271, 274
    see also burial type D; catastrophic cemeteries
maternity care 211–12
Matthew, John 210
measles 151, 156
meat, butchery 159–60, 163–4, **163**
medical treatment
    fractures 201–7
    hospitals 194–8

maternity care 211–12
medicinal plants 209–10, **210**
metal plates 207–9
theories 198–201
medieval period
    cemeteries 14–15
    diet 12, 161–8, **162**, **164**, 264–6
    disease transmission 261–4, 272–3
    health 15–16, 272–3
    hospitals 8, 194–201
    housing 11–12, 149–51, **150**, **151**, **152**
    impairment 188–9
    industry and occupation 157–61
    injury risk 184–5
    medical theories 198–201
    medical treatment 201–11
    migration 10–11, 12, 175, 229, 272–3
    socio-cultural change 12–13, 273
    subadults 168–80
    urban environment 10–12, 149, 229–30
men *see* males
mercury, as treatment 209, 211
Merton Priory *see* St Mary Merton
metal plates, therapeutic use 207–9, **208**, **209**
methods, cemetery sampling 19–20
migration *see* rural–urban migration
military campaigns *see* battle injuries
miracle narratives 177, 180, 188, 192, 193
monastic houses
    diet 165, 237
    DISH 237, 238
    fractures 251, 252
    gender ratios 243
    inter-site comparison 245–59
    stature 269
mortality profiles
    adults 242–3
    subadults 241–2, **242**
multiple injuries 101–2, **102**, 179–80, 183–4, **184**, 186, 239

Naestved (Denmark), leprosy 253–4, 261
nasal bone hypoplasia 133, 257
necrosis 256
    see also avascular necrosis; osteonecroses
neoplastic disease 127, **128**, **129**
    causes 266–7
    inter-site comparison 254–5
    London cemeteries comparison 240
neural arch fractures 99–100
Nicaea (Anatolia), treponematosis 254
non-metric data 21, 275
Norton Priory (Cheshire), Paget's disease of bone 257, 267
nutritional and metabolic disease 118–27
    inter-site comparison 254, 255
    London cemeteries comparison 239–40
    osteomalacia 120, **120**, 167, 227
    osteoporosis 127, 167
    skeletal evidence 167–8
    and stature 167
    stress indicators 124–7, **127**, 239–40
    see also cribra orbitalia; osteomalacia; osteoporosis; porotic hyperostosis; rickets; scurvy

occupation, health risks 157–61, 260
ochronotic osteoarthropathy 71, **72**
Odense (Denmark), leprosy 254
Open Area 5 (infirmary cemetery), gender ratio 243
opium poppies, pain relief 210, **210**, 212
orthopaedic trauma, impairment from 192–3
osteitis 109, 234
osteoarthritis 60–71, 190
    inter-site comparison 249, 268
    London cemeteries comparison 236–7
    osteoarthropathies 71, **72**, 73–6, **73**, **74**,

75, 132, 249
osteochondritis dissecans 131, 209, 245
osteochondroma 127, **129**, 240
osteochondroses 130–1, **131**
osteological paradox 154, 170, 174, 175, 190, 221, 265
osteomalacia 120, **120**, 167, 227, 239
    causes 266
    inter-site comparison 254, 255
osteomas 127, 240
osteomyelitis 109, 155, **155**, **205**
    causes 267
    inter-site comparison 253, 254
    London cemeteries comparison 233–4
osteonecroses 130
osteoporosis 127, 167, 265
    inter-site comparison 254, 255

Paget's disease of bone 146–7, **147**, 267
    inter-site comparison 257, 258
    London cemeteries comparison 241
pain relief 210, 212
papal bullae 201
parasites, intestinal 23, 153
Paris, Matthew 230
'parry' fractures 182, 186, 238, 276
pathology, recording and diagnosing 21–2
periapical lesions 46, 55–6, **55**
    inter-site comparison 247–8
    London cemeteries comparison 235
perinates 171, 211, 212, **212**, 228, 242
period 14 (*c* 1120–*c* 1200)
    adult stature 36, 219
    age at death 29–30, **29**, **30**, 218, 242–3
    ante-mortem tooth loss 46
    burial type comparison 218–22
    burials **6**
    calculus 56, **59**, 174
    caries **46**, 47
    cribra orbitalia 121, 220
    dating 3–4
    demographic data 26–30, 218–19
    dental disease 40–1
    DISH 237
    enamel hypoplasia **51**, 53, **54**, 55, 219–20
    endocranial lesions 147
    extra-spinal osteoarthritis 65
    fracture distribution 103, **103**
    fractures 89–90, **89**, **90**
    gender ratio 218–19
    hip dislocation 145, **145**
    long bone fractures 96, **96**, **97**, 204, **204**, **206**
    malnutrition 220
    mass burials 217, 271
    periapical lesions 46
    periodontal disease 58, **60**
    periostitis 221
    porotic hyperostosis 123, 220
    Schmorl's nodes 87
    scoliosis 136, **136**, **194**
    stress indicators 126, **127**, 221–2, 228, 231
    subadult burials 241–2
    subadult fractures **101**
    subadult growth 37, 219, **219**
    tuberculosis 114, 221
    vertebral border shifts 141–2
    vertebral segmentation failure 139
period 15 (*c* 1200–50)
    adult stature 36, 222
    age at death 30–2, **30**, **31**, 222, 243
    ante-mortem tooth loss 46
    burial type comparison 222–4
    burials 5, **7**
    calculus 57, **59**, 174
    caries **46**, 47, 55
    cribra orbitalia 121, 222–3
    dating 3–4

Index

demographic data 26–7, 30–2, 222
dental disease 40–1
diaphyseal aclasia 148, **148**
DISH 73, **168**, 237
enamel hypoplasia **51**, 53, **54**, **55**, 222
endocranial lesions 147, 148
extra-spinal osteoarthritis 66
foot anomalies 146, **146**
fracture distribution 103, **103**, **104**
fractures 89–90, **89**, **90**, 179, **179**
gender ratio 222
gout **74**
hip dysplasia 144–5, **145**
hypertrophic osteoarthropathy 132
kyphoscoliosis **135**
long bone fractures 96, **97**, 204, **204**
malnutrition 223
mass burials 217–18, 271
osteochondroma **129**
Paget's disease of bone 147, **147**
periapical lesions **46**, **55**
periodontal disease 58, **60**
periostitis 223
porotic hyperostosis 123, 124, 220, 223
rheumatoid osteoarthritis **73**
Schmorl's nodes 87
septic arthropathy 111–12, **111**
sinusitis 110–11, **155**
skull fractures 94, **94**
stress indicators 126–7, **127**, 223–4, 231
subadult burials 242
subadult fractures 179, **179**
subadult growth 38, 222, **222**
trepanation 213, **213**
treponematosis 113
tuberculosis 114, **116**, 221, 223
vertebral border shifts 142
vertebral segmentation failure 139, 140
period 16 (c 1250–c 1400)
　adult stature 36, 224
　age at death 32–3, **32**, **33**, 224, 243
　amputation 216–17, **216**, **217**
　ankylosis **191**
　ante-mortem tooth loss 46
　brucellosis 117–18, **117**
　burial type comparison 224–6
　burials 5, **7**
　calculus 57, **59**, 174
　caries 46, **47**
　cribra orbitalia 121, 122, 225
　dating 3–4
　demographic data 26–7, 32–3, 224
　dental disease 42–3
　DISH 237
　enamel hypoplasia **51**, 53, **54**, **55**, 224
　endocranial lesions 147, 148
　extra-spinal osteoarthritis 67
　fracture complications 205
　fracture distribution 103, **103**, **104**
　fractures 89–90, **89**, **90**, **157**, 179
　gender ratio 224
　hypertrophic osteoarthropathy 132
　long bone fractures 96, **97**, 204, **204**
　malnutrition 225
　mass burials 217–18, 244, 271
　ochronotic osteoarthropathy **72**
　osteochondroma **129**
　osteoporosis 127
　periapical lesions 46
　periodontal disease 58, **60**
　periostitis 156, 225
　porotic hyperostosis 123–4, 125, 220, 225
　radioulnar synostosis 144, **144**
　rickets 119, **119**, 174, 225
　Schmorl's nodes 87
　scoliosis 136, **136**
　skull fractures 92–3, **93**, 94, **181**, 214–16
　spondylolisthesis 138–9, **138**
　stress indicators 127, **127**, 225–6, 231

　subadult burials 242
　subadult fractures 179
　subadult growth 38, 224, **224**
　trepanation 213–15, **214**
　treponematosis 113
　tuberculosis 114–15, **114**, **116**, **117**, 155, 156, 221, 225
　vertebral border shifts 142
　vertebral segmentation failure 139, 140
period 17 (c 1400–1539)
　adult stature 36, 226
　age at death 33–5, **34**, **35**, 226, 243
　ante-mortem tooth loss 46
　burial type comparison 226–8
　burials **7**
　calculus 57, **59**, 174
　caries 46, **47**, 165
　cleft palate 133, **133**
　cribra orbitalia 121, 122, 227
　dating 3–4
　demographic data 26–7, 33–5, 226
　dental disease 42–3
　DISH 237
　enamel hypoplasia **51**, **54**, **55**, 226–7
　endocranial lesions 147, 148
　extra-spinal osteoarthritis 68
　fracture distribution 103, **103**
　fractures 89–90, **89**, **90**, **157**
　Freiberg's disease 130, **131**
　gender ratio 226
　leprosy 112, **112**
　long bone fractures 96, **97**, 204, **204**
　malnutrition 227
　mass burials 218, 271
　multiple injuries 101–2, **102**
　osteomalacia 120, **120**, 227
　osteoporosis 127
　periapical lesions 46
　perinatal burials 228
　periodontal disease 58, **60**
　periostitis 227–8
　porotic hyperostosis 124, 125, 220, 227
　Schmorl's nodes 87
　scoliosis 136, **136**
　scurvy 119
　seronegative spondyloarthropathy **75**
　skull fractures 92–3, **94**
　spondylolisthesis 138–9
　stress indicators 127, **127**, 228, 231
　subadult burials 242
　subadult growth 38, 226, **226**
　treponematosis 113, **113**
　tuberculosis 115, 156, 221, 227
　vertebral border shifts 142–3
　vertebral segmentation failure 139, 141
periodontal disease 58, **60**
　dietary evidence 166
　London cemeteries comparison 236
　stress indicator 126–7
　treatment of 208, **209**
Perthes' disease 130, 131, 191, 255, 256
pes planus (flat foot) 193
phalangeal anomalies 145
physicians 200
pigs, for food 163–4, **163**
plague 229
　see also Black Death
plants
　childbirth use 211
　food plants 162
　medicinal use 209–10, **210**
pollutants, health risks 152–6, 161, 264, 268, 270
population, fluctuations 12–13, 229–30, 261
porotic hyperostosis 123–4, 125

burial type comparison 220, 223, 225, 227
London cemeteries comparison 240
post-cranial indices 39–40
pottage 162
pottery, distillation vessel 210, **210**
Pott's disease **116**, 155, **155**, 176, 190, 192
1 Poultry 162
poverty
　and stature 270
　and tuberculosis 263
　women 185
Prague and Melnik (Czech Republic), fractures 252–3
prostitution 186, 262, 263
psoriatic osteoarthritis **75**, 249
public services, medieval London 11
pulpit cross 5, **7**, 14
pulses, in diet 162

quarry pits, mass burials 4, 217, 271

radioulnar synostosis 144, **144**
Raunds Furnells (Yorks), growth profiles 259, **259**
recidivism, multiple injuries 101–2, **102**, 179–80, 183–4, 239
Reiter's disease **76**, 249
religion
　and impairment 189
　and medical treatment 195, 198, 200, 201, **201**
research project
　future research 275–7
　results 274
　study area 1–3, **2**, **4**
respiratory diseases 154
rheumatoid arthritis **73**, **73**, 249
rib fractures 183, 250–1, 252, 260
rib lesions 109, **116**, **116**, 154, **154**
rickets
　burial type comparison 223, 225, 227
　causes 167, 174–5, 266, 273
　inter-site comparison 254, 255
　London cemeteries comparison 239
　prevalence 118–19, **119**, 154
Rivenhall (Essex), treponematosis 254
Roger of Salerno 192, 213, 215
rope processing 160
Rostov Velikiy (Russia), treponematosis 254
rotator cuff injuries 72
Rouen (France), tuberculosis 254
rural cemeteries
　inter-site comparison 245–59
　long bone fractures 250
rural–urban comparison
　fractures 259–60
　growth profiles 268–9
　stature 269–70
rural–urban migration
　disease risks 263, 264, 272–3
　gender ratios 244
　medieval period 10–11, 12, 229
　stature impacts 269–70, 272
　subadult growth impacts 175

St Andrew Fishergate, York (Yorks)
　congenital anomalies 256
　copper-alloy plates 208
　DISH 248–9
　fractures 252, 260
　knee fracture 193
　long bone fractures 250
　periostitis 156
　sharp force trauma 253
　tuberculosis 254
St Bartholomew's Hospital, Bristol (Glos), fractures 252
St Gregory's Priory, Canterbury (Kent)

　fractures 252
　neoplastic disease 255
　treponematosis 254
St Helen-on-the-Walls, York (Yorks)
　congenital anomalies 256
　fracture complications 205
　fractures 182, 252, 260
　growth profiles 259, **259**
　long bone fractures 250
　metabolic disease 254
　periostitis 156
　rheumatoid arthritis 249
　skull anomalies 256
　subadult burials 170, 171, 242
　treponematosis 254, 262, 263
St James and St Mary Magdalene, Chichester (Sussex)
　fractures 252, 260
　long bone fractures 182, 205, 250
　tuberculosis 254
St James's Priory, Bristol (Glos)
　DISH 248–9
　endocranial lesions 257
St John Clerkenwell, rickets 239
St Lawrence Jewry
　caries 234
　cemetery 15
　cranial trauma 239
　cribra orbitalia 240
　DISH 238
　fractures 238
　gender ratio 243
　neoplastic disease 240
　osteoarthritis 237
　periapical lesions 235
　subadults 242
　trepanation 239
St Margaret's, Norwich (Norfolk) 262
St Mary Graces 14, 15
　ante-mortem tooth loss 236
　calculus 236
　caries 234, 235
　cranial trauma 239
　cribra orbitalia 240
　DISH 237
　enamel hypoplasia 235
　fractures 238
　gender ratio 243
　HFI 241
　leprosy 232
　neoplastic disease 240
　osteitis 234
　osteoarthritis 237
　osteomyelitis 233
　Paget's disease of bone 241
　periapical lesions 235
　perinatal burials 212
　periodontal disease 236
　periostitis 234
　scurvy 239
　subadults 242
　treponematosis 233
　tuberculosis 233
St Mary Merton (Surrey)
　calculus 236
　caries 234, 235
　cemetery 14, 15
　cranial trauma 239
　cribra orbitalia 240
　DISH 237
　fracture complications 205
　fractures 238
　gender ratio 243
　HFI 241
　infirmary 195
　medicinal plants 210
　metal objects for treatment 209
　neoplastic disease 240
　osteoarthritis 237
　Paget's disease of bone 241

Index

periodontal disease 236
periostitis 234
scurvy 239
subadults 242
tuberculosis 233
St Mary Spital (priory and hospital)
  animal bones 161–2
  cemetery
    burial practices 13, **13**
    inter-site comparison 245–59
    layout 13
    London cemetery comparisons 232–44
    sampling 19–20
    source population 13–14
    see also burial type ABC; burial type D
  history 4–5, 8, **9**, 194–5, **195**
  infirmary 195–201
    distillation of medicines 210–11, **210**
    inmate burials 204
    layout 195–7, **196**, **197**, 198, **198**, **199**
    locker keys 195, **197**
    maternity care 211–12
    role 272, 273
    surgery 217
    treatment methods 201–11
    water supply 197
St Mary Stratford Langthorne (Essex)
  caries 234
  cemetery 14, 15
  circulatory disease 255
  cranial trauma 239
  cribra orbitalia 240
  DISH 237, 248
  enamel hypoplasia 235
  fractures 238, 252
  gender ratio 243
  gout 249
  long bone fractures 250
  neoplastic disease 240
  osteoarthritis 237
  osteomyelitis 233
  periostitis 234
  rickets 239
  septic osteoarthritis 249
  sharp force trauma 253
  sinusitis 234
  stature 258
  subadults 242
  tuberculosis 233
St Mary-at-Hill 170
St Nicholas Shambles
  ante-mortem tooth loss 236
  calculus 236
  caries 234
  cemetery 14, 15
  cranial trauma 239
  cribra orbitalia 240
  fractures 238
  gender ratio 243
  long bone fractures 250
  neoplastic disease 240
  periodontal disease 236
St Peter's, Barton-on-Humber (Lincs)
  DISH 248
  Paget's disease of bone 257
  psoriatic osteoarthritis 249
  rheumatoid arthritis 249
St Saviour Bermondsey
  ante-mortem tooth loss 236
  caries 234
  cemetery 14, 15
  cribra orbitalia 240
  DISH 237
  gender ratio 243
  neoplastic disease 240
  osteoarthritis 237
  Paget's disease of bone 241
  periapical lesions 235
  periostitis 234

sinusitis 234
tuberculosis 233
Saint Servaas, Maastricht (Netherlands), stature 258
sampling
  methods 19–20
  subadults 170
Scheuermann's disease 130, **131**, 255, 256
Schmorl's nodes 81, 82–7
  subadults 76, 178
scoliosis 134–6, **136**, 191, **194**, 257
scurvy
  burial type comparison 223, 225, 227
  inter-site comparison 254, 255
  London cemeteries comparison 239
  prevalence 118, **119**, 265
  stress indicator 167
  subadults 174–5, 273
septic osteoarthritis 111–12, **111**, 249, 268
seronegative osteoarthropathies 75–6, **75**, 249
seronegative spondyloarthropathy 75, **75**, 249
servants, violence risks 185
sex
  determination of 21
  see also females; gender ratios; males
sharp force injuries, skull fractures 93, **94**, 181, 206–7, 214, **214**, 239, 253
shoes 267
Silver Street, Lincoln (Lincs), fractures 252
sinusitis 109–11, **111**, 154–5, **155**
  future research 276
  London cemeteries comparison 234
  urban areas 264
skeletal completeness 20
skull anomalies *see* cranial anomalies
skull fractures 91–5, **91**, **92**, **93**, **102**, 181–2
  blunt force injuries 94, **94**, **95**, 178, 181–2, **181**, 215–16
  complications 206–7, **207**, 214–15
  inter-personal violence 260, 261
  inter-site comparison 251, 252
  London cemeteries comparison 238, 239
  sharp force injuries 93, **94**, 181, 206–7, 214, **214**, 239, 253
  subadults 178
  see also trepanation
slipped femoral epiphysis 255, 256
smoke, health risks 154, 160
Smyth, Dr 200
socio-cultural change, medieval period 12–13, 273
soft tissue injuries 108, **108**, 183
spinal anomalies 133–43
  border shifts 139, 141–3
  impairment 193
  inter-site comparison 256–7
  kyphoscoliosis 134, **135**, 191, 193, 257
  kyphosis 134, 191, 193, 257
  scoliosis 134–6, **136**, 191, **194**, 257
  segmentation failure 139–41
  spondylolisthesis 138–9, **138**
  spondylolysis 137–8
spinal fractures *see* vertebral fractures
spinal joint disease 76–87
spiritual life 201, **201**
Spitalfields Market, study area 1–3, **2**
spondylolisthesis 138–9, **138**
spondylolysis 137–8
stable isotope analysis
  diet analysis 162, 165–6, 265
  future research 276
  lead poisoning 161
  subadult weaning 172–3
stature
  adult burials 36–7, **37**
  burial type comparison 219, 222
  determination of 21

environmental factors 269–70, 272
  inter-site comparison 258–9, **259**
  and nutritional status 167
  subadults 37–8, 167, 175
stress indicators
  burial types 218, 221–2, 223–4, 225–6, 228, 230–1
  cribra orbitalia 126–7, 167, 168, 239–40
  enamel hypoplasia 126–7, 175, 235
  future research 276
  subadults 124–7, **127**, 175–6, 231, 272
  urban environments 10
study area
  archaeological context 3–5
  location 1–3, **2**, **4**
styloid process, congenital absence 144
subadults
  age at death 170–1, 222, 224, 226, 230, 241–2
  age identity 169
  burial practices 170, 212
  calculus 173–4
  caries 173–4, 234–5
  cribra orbitalia 220, 222–3, 225, 227
  dental health 44–5, 173–4, 248
  diet 173–5, 265
  enamel hypoplasia 173, 219, 222, 224, 226–7
  fractures 100–1, **100**, **101**, 103, **104**, 157–8, 177–80, 260
  growth profiles 37–8, **37**, **38**, 175, 219, **219**, 222, **222**, 224, **224**, 226, **226**, 259, 268–9
  impairment 191–2
  infants 170–3
  interpersonal violence 260
  mass burials 244, 272
  medieval lifestyle 168–80
  mortality profiles 241–2, **242**
  perinates 171, 211, 212, **212**, 228, 242
  periostitis 221, 223, 225, 227–8
  porotic hyperostosis 220, 223, 225, 227
  rickets 118–19, **119**, 167, 174–5, 225, 227, 266
  sample biases 170
  scurvy 118, **119**, 174–5, 223, 227, 273
  spinal fractures 178
  spinal joint disease 76, **76**, 178
  stress indicators 124–7, **127**, 175–6, 231
  trauma 177–80
  treponematosis 113, **113**, 176–7, 254, 274
  tuberculosis 116–17, **116**, **117**, 176, 221, 223, 225
  urban environment impacts 175
  weaning 172–3
subluxation 144–5, 190, 192
sugar, dental evidence 166–7, 168
surgeons 200
surgery 212–17
  amputation 216–17, **216**, **217**
  trepanation 212–16, **213**, **214**, **215**, 239
sutural agenesis 132, 256
swaddling 172, 266
Swan Lane 159
syphilis *see* treponematosis

talipes equinovarus (clubfoot) 193
tanning 160
tarsal coalition 146
teeth *see* dental disease
textile industry 159, **159**
Thorneton, Thomas 200, 217
tibia
  fracture complications 205, **205**
  fracture healing 202–3
  periostitis 234
Towton (Yorks)
  circulatory disease 255
  dental health 247

fractures 252, 260
healed injuries 261
long bone fractures 250
trade, medieval London 12
traders 158–9, **158**, 163
trauma 88–108
  future research 275–6
  impairment from 192–3
  inter-site comparison 249–53, 259–61
  London cemeteries comparison 238–9
  multiple injuries 101–2, **102**, 179–80, 183–4, **184**, 186, 239
  occupational risks 157–8
  subadults 177–80
  see also dislocation; fractures; soft tissue injuries
treatment methods *see* medical treatment; surgery
trenchers 164
trepanation 212–16, **213**, **214**, **215**, 239
treponematosis (syphilis) 112–13, **113**, 176–7
  inter-site comparison 253, 254, 262–3
  London cemeteries comparison 232, 233
  origins 233, 262, 274
  transmission 262–3, 273
  treatment 209
Trondheim (Sweden), treponematosis 254
tuberculosis 114–17, 118
  burial type comparison 221, 223, 225, 227
  future research 275
  impairment from 190–1
  inter-site comparison 253, 254
  London cemeteries comparison 232, 233
  prevalence 114, **115**, 155–6
  rib lesions 116, **116**
  risks 155–6
  skeletal distribution **114**, 115, **116**
  subadults 116–17, **116**, **117**, 176, 221, 223, 225
  transmission 263–4

unhealed fractures 105–6, 205–7, **205**, **206**, 238
urban cemeteries
  fractures 252, 259–60
  inter-site comparison 245–59
urban environment
  health impacts 10, 270, 272–3
  housing 149–51
  infectious diseases 261–4
  injury risks 184–7
  medieval London 11–12, 149, 229–30
  stature impacts 270, 272
  subadult impacts 175
  treponematosis 262
uroscopy 200–1

vertebral border shifts 139, 141–3
vertebral fractures 98–100, **99**
  inter-site comparison 251, 252
  subadults 178
vertebral segmentation failure 139–41
violence *see* interpersonal violence
vitamin C deficiency *see* scurvy
vitamin D deficiency *see* rickets
volcanic eruptions, cause of famine 230, 271

Walbrook river/stream, waste disposal 152, **153**, 159–60, 197
warfare *see* battle injuries
waste disposal, medieval London 11, 152–3, **153**, 159–60
water supply, pollution 152–3
Waterford (Ireland)
  fractures 252, 260
  treponematosis 254

302

Index

weaning, health risks 172–3
weaving 159
Weil's disease 153
wet-nurses 172
Wharram Percy (Yorks)
  circulatory disease 255
  dental health 247, 248
  diet 265
  fish bones 162
  fractures 251, 260
  housing 12
  long bone fractures 250
  metabolic disease 254
  rickets 266
  scoliosis 256
  subadults 171, 173
  tuberculosis 155, 254
Whitefriars Ipswich (Suffolk)
  fractures 252
  neoplastic disease 255
  stature 258
Wisby (Sweden), fractures 253
women *see* females
wool, processing 159, **159**